The Gospel of
JOHN

ADDRESSES ON THE GOSPEL OF JOHN

JOHN

By H. A. IRONSIDE, Litt. D

AUTHOR OF
LECTURES ON ROMANS, ADDRESSES ON GALATIANS,
LECTURES ON FIRST & SECOND CORINTHIANS,
IN THE HEAVENLIES, ETC., ETC.

LOIZEAUX BROTHERS, Inc.

Neptune, New Jersey

FIRST EDITION, OCTOBER 1942
EIGHTEENTH PRINTING, JUNE 1984

ISBN 0-87213-373-7
PRINTED IN THE UNITED STATES OF AMERICA

PREFACE

Like many of my other books of recent years, this volume consists of addresses, stenographically reported, which were delivered in the Moody Memorial Church of Chicago. While somewhat carefully edited, occasional repetitions will be found, and a colloquial style be apparent, which are almost unavoidable in a series given on Lord's Days for a period of over a year's duration and intended for the instruction, not of theologians or scholars, but the masses who attended the meetings in large numbers, or listened by many thousands over the Radio. They were broadcast over WMBI, the station of the Moody Bible Institute, which is wholly dedicated to the service of our Lord Jesus Christ.

In spite of their many imperfections I trust they may be useful and blessed to many readers as now sent forth in this more permanent form.

The Gospel of John has been well-called, "The greatest book in the world." Its presentation of the Eternal Word who became flesh for our redemption has brought life and assurance to millions.

H. A. IRONSIDE.

CONTENTS

CONTENTS

8

THE ETERNAL WORD

⚡ ⚡ ⚡

"In the beginning was the Word, and the Word was with God, and the Word was God. The same was in the beginning with God. All things were made by Him; and without Him was not any thing made that was made. In Him was life; and the life was the light of men. And the light shineth in darkness; and the darkness comprehended it not" (John 1:1-5).

⚡ ⚡ ⚡

IN beginning a study of any of the Gospels it is a good thing to ask and try to answer the question, Why are there four Gospels and why do they seem to differ one from another? Our God surely could have inspired one of His servants to write a continuous record of what Jesus did and said. Men write books in that manner, but it did not please the Father to do this. Instead of that He has given us four distinct records, and men have tried, since the second century of the Christian era, to weave these into one, as in the so-called "Harmonies of the Gospels." But often they find it difficult to fit everything together, because of ignorance of chronology and many other things connected with the times and customs when Jesus was here. These records are each complete in themselves.

They are divinely inspired, and although at times there seems to be evidence of conflicting testimony, it is simply because of our lack of knowledge of the facts.

In Matthew's Gospel we have no difficulty in seeing that the one outstanding object of the Holy Spirit was to present our Lord Jesus as the promised King and Messiah. Therefore we sometimes call Matthew's Gospel the Jewish Gospel. I always like to guard that expression, however, because of the misuse to which it has been subjected. We do not mean that it has no message to Christians. We do not mean that we can afford to dispense with it, but we mean it is the Gospel that was specially designed of God to present the life of the Lord Jesus Christ in such a way as to appeal to the Jewish mind, particularly that of the Jew who is interested in his Old Testament. I wish our modern Jews were more familiar with their Bible. If they were, it would be much easier to preach Christ to them. Unfortunately, through the centuries the Jew has given so much more attention to the Talmud than to the Bible that it is difficult to find an approach to his mind. But Matthew pre-supposes a knowledge of the Old Testament on the part of his readers, so all the way through we meet such expressions as, "That it might be fulfilled," "As it was written," by so-and-so, and he gives us incident after incident in the life of Christ which was a direct fulfilment of Old Testament prophecy. Matthew presents Jesus as the Messiah of Israel, and his outstanding message is, "Behold your King."

Mark, on the other hand, seems to be written from a different standpoint. He presents Jesus as the great Servant-Prophet, while in this world, doing the will of God. That accounts for the fact that in this book there is no genealogy given. The genealogies are in Matthew and in Luke, but we do not get any kind of genealogy in Mark. Why? Because you know when you advertise for a servant to work for you, you do not say, "Now let me ask, What is your genealogy? Are you descended from some famous character?" Not, "Who was your father?" but, "What can you do?" So in Mark's Gospel we have our blessed Lord accredited thus from the very beginning. He says, "Behold My Servant."

When we turn to the Gospel of Luke we see the Lord Jesus presented as the Perfect Man— the only perfect Man who walked this earth. So you have the Lord Jesus entering into all kinds of circumstances. On several occasions you have Him seated at the dinner-table. I do not know of any place where a man can be drawn out better than at the dinner-table. If you want to draw a man out, just set him down to a good dinner and start him talking! I have read many biographies of Martin Luther, but I never really knew him until after I got hold of *Luther's Table Talks*. So a great deal of Luke's Gospel is made up of the "table talk" of our Lord Jesus Christ. He says, "Behold the Man"—the one Mediator between God and man, "the Man Christ Jesus."

Now when we turn to the Gospel of John, we see the open heavens and the Eternal Son descending from above, taking His place in the womb of the Virgin—God and Man in one blessed, glorious Person—the Eternal Son manifest in the flesh. John says, "Behold your God." His Gospel was written to establish the truth of the Divinity and Deity of our Lord Jesus Christ. In the first twelve chapters we have the divine Son presented to the world, and in the character in which He could appeal to a world of sinners. We shall note these various characteristics as we go on with our study.

Beginning with chapter 13 and going on to the end, we have the revelation of our Lord Jesus as the Son, to His own beloved people, as He who keeps their feet free from defilement. This is a marvelous unfolding of His advocacy and the glorious truth of His care for His people during this age. Then we have the promise of His coming again in glory at the end of the dispensation, and the coming of the Comforter, who will guide into all truth.

John's Gospel, then, is emphatically that of the Deity of our blessed Lord. It presents Him as the Eternal Word, who in grace became flesh for our redemption. There is no human genealogy as in Matthew and in Luke, but we are carried back immediately into the past eternity. "In the beginning" here antedates the same expression in Genesis 1:1. There it is the beginning of creation, but here long before creation began we see the Son in the bosom of the Father. When everything that ever had beginning began to be, the Word was. Notice seven things that are brought before us.

1. Our Lord's Eternity of Being: "In the beginning was the Word."
2. His Distinct Personality: "The Word was with God."
3. His True Deity: "The Word was God."
4. His Unchanging Relationship: "The same in the beginning."
5. His Full Creatorial Glory: "All things were made by Him."
6. His Life-giving Power: "In Him was life."
7. His Incarnation: "The Word became flesh."

Let us follow these seven points thoughtfully. First, we note His Eternity of Being. Unitarianism of every kind is ruled out here. The Word never had a beginning. The Son is as truly eternal as the Father. To teach otherwise is to deny the very foundations of our faith. He could not have beginning, for He Himself *is* the beginning and the end (Rev. 22:13).

But it is not merely that He was eternally in the Godhead. Scripture is equally insistent regarding His distinct Personality. This is implied in the expression "The Word was with God." We are told of Wisdom, in Prov. 8:27, "When He prepared the heavens I was there." And again in verse 30, "I was by Him as One brought up with Him." The Eternal Wisdom and the Eternal Word are one and the same. Throughout all the ages of the past Christ was a distinct Personality in the Godhead. There was communion between the Father and the Son.

But this does not imply the inferiority of the Son. Full Deity was His: "The Word was God." Just as truly as the Father was God and the Holy Spirit was God, so the Word was God. More than this could not be said.

The next sentence might seem to be almost a repetition: "The same was in the beginning with God." But it really adds to what has already been put before us. It tells us of His unchanging Personality. He was the same from all eternity; that is, He was the Eternal Son. He did not become the Son when He was born into the world, but "The Father sent the Son to be the Saviour." He did not become the Son after He was sent, He was the Son from the beginning.

Creation is attributed to each Person of the Godhead. Here particularly it is stated, "All things were made by Him." Elsewhere we read, "The Lord by wisdom hath made the heavens" (Ps. 136:5). Elohim, the triune God, created the heavens and the earth. The Father planned, the Word was the agent, and the Spirit the executor of the divine counsels, and just as it is the Word who produced the first creation, so it is He who is "the beginning of the creation of God" (Rev. 3:14). This does not mean that He was the first being God created, but rather it is He who produces the creation of God, that is, the new creation to which all believers belong.

Apart from Him there is no life. He is the fountain of life, and that includes both natural life and spiritual. All natural life comes from Him, and concerning spiritual life it is written, "He that hath the Son hath life, and he that hath not the Son of God hath not life" (1 John 5:12). That life was seen in all its perfection in Him as Man on earth. "The life was the light of men." As He moved about in this scene, He cast light on every man, showing things up as God Himself sees them.

This brings us to the seventh point—His incarnation. "The Word became flesh." "Became" here is better than "was made." Strictly speaking, He was never "made" anything, but in lowly grace He became flesh in order that He might reveal the Father to man and redeem man to God.

The Gospel of John is devoted to this double theme. As we peruse its sacred pages we see the Eternal Word, having become flesh, moving about among men, glorifying the Father in all His perfect ways, telling out the mind of God completely and at last giving Himself as a ransom on the cross in order that men may be redeemed to God and share His glory for all the eternity to come.

It is well-known that the "Word" translates the Greek word *Logos*. This was a term already well-known to thinking people when our Lord appeared on earth. Everywhere in the Greek-speaking world the writings of Plato were circulated. He had spoken of the insolubility of many mysteries, but had expressed the hope that some day there would come forth a "Word" (*Logos*) from God that would make everything clear. John might even have had this in mind when, directed by the Holy Spirit, he penned the wonderful sentences with which this Gospel begins. It is as though God is saying: The "Word" has now been spoken. In Christ the mind of God is fully revealed. He who hears Him hears God, for "in Him are hid all the treasures of wisdom and knowledge."

As we glance down the chapter we notice with adoring hearts the many and varied titles and expressions that are used concerning Him. He is "The Christ," the Anointed One, Israel's Messiah. John the Baptist points Him out as "The Lamb of God," the Sin-Bearer, and he also declares Him to be "The Son of God." The disciples own Him as "Master." Philip is certain that in Jesus of Nazareth, the son of Joseph, as he at that time understood Him to be, he has found the One "of whom Moses in the law and the prophets did write." Nathanael also recognizes Him as "the Son of God" and proclaims Him "The King of Israel." Jesus Himself uses the expression which in after days was so commonly on His lips, "The Son of Man," and He shows us that this Son of Man is like Jacob's ladder, the connecting link between earth and heaven, upon whom the angels of God ascend and descend.

As we go through this Gospel we see Him presented in every possible way that the Spirit of God could portray Him and that the human mind, enlightened by divine grace, could understand.

THE MINISTRY OF JOHN THE BAPTIST AND THE INCARNATION

✔ ✔ ✔

"There was a man sent from God, whose name was John. The same came for a witness, to bear witness of the Light, that all men through Him might believe. He was not that Light, but was sent to bear witness of that Light. That was the true Light, which lighteth every man that cometh into the world. He was in the world, and the world was made by Him, and the world knew Him not. He came unto His own, and His own received Him not. But as many as received Him, to them gave He power to become the sons of God, even to them that believe on His name: which were born, not of blood, nor of the will of the flesh, nor of the will of man, but of God. And the Word was made flesh and dwelt among us (and we beheld His glory, the glory as of the only begotten of the Father) full of grace and truth" (John 1: 6-14).

✔ ✔ ✔

WE have seen already that Jesus is the Eternal Word, one with the Father from all past ages; that, when everything that ever began to be came into existence, He was already there. He did not begin to be, He was. He was the Word. He was with God. He was God and He was the Son in the beginning with God. He never underwent any change in His personality. He was the Son from all eternity

18

even as He was the Son before all creation. "All things were made by Him, and without Him was not anything made that was made." Has that really gripped our hearts? Do we realize that the One who hung on the cross was the Creator of the earth? I think people often misunderstand the sacrifice He made because they do not apprehend who it was that made it. Dr. W. P. McKay, in his book "Grace and Truth," tells how, on one occasion, after preaching the Word and setting forth the truth, a lady came up to him and said, "I can't accept that." "You can't accept what?" asked Dr. McKay. "Well, what you were telling us, that God allowed an innocent man to die for guilty men. That wasn't right. It wasn't righteous that guilty men should be saved in that way." He said, "Madam, you have misunderstood the whole meaning of the gospel. The gospel is not that an innocent Man died for guilty men. The first declaration of the gospel is that God became Man. The One who had been sinned against, in divine grace became Man that He might die for His creatures' sin. On the cross we do not see an innocent Man dying for guilty men; we see the offended God giving Himself, taking our humanity, in order that the guilt of His creatures might be taken away." "But is that righteous?" "Madam," he replied, "it is love. It is infinite love that led Him to give Himself for us." That is the clear teaching of the Gospel of John. He who died upon the cross was the Creator of all things and He was the One who had been wronged, sinned against by the creature, and yet when man could find no way to put his record right or to escape judgment, He came in grace to deliver those who put their trust in Him.

Now in verse 6 we enter into the story of the incarnation. First, our attention is directed to His forerunner. "There was a man sent from God, whose name was John." How often that has been true throughout the centuries! When God has called out a man to carry the gospel to a lost people, how frequently He has taken a man named John! In the Bible we have John the Baptist, the apostle John, and John Mark. Since then there have been many Johns whom the Lord called out to proclaim His Word. When we come down to the days of the Reformation we have John Knox and John Calvin, and later on in the great revival of the eighteenth century, we have John Wesley sent from God to preach to those who knew nothing of the assurance of salvation. I think one reason there are so many Johns is because the name appeals to the people of God. You know what "John" means. It signifies "the grace of Jehovah," "the grace of the Lord." John came to prepare the way for the coming of the

Lord Jesus Christ. He occupied a very unique place in Scripture testimony. We read, "The law and the prophets were until John." From that time the kingdom of God was preached, a kingdom of grace and truth. John was the last of the prophets, and he was the first herald of the new dispensation. The Lord Jesus Christ says that of those born of women there was not a greater than John. In what sense was John the greatest born of women? Because it was given to him, not only to prophesy of, but actually to welcome the Christ—to baptize Him in token of His identification with those for whom He came to die. As the baptizer of the Lord Jesus and as the proclaimer of the Lamb of God that taketh away the sin of the world, John had the highest place among all the prophetic brotherhood. Not one of them had the privilege that was given to him. Notwithstanding, Jesus tells us, "He that is least in the kingdom of God is greater than he." What does He mean by that? Well, it was given to John to call men to repentance in order to set up the kingdom of God here on earth. He opened the door to others, but he was not permitted to enter in himself. Nevertheless, he had a very unique place in relation to the Lord Jesus Christ. "He that hath the bride is the Bridegroom: but the friend of the Bridegroom, which standeth and heareth Him, rejoic-

eth greatly because of the Bridegroom's voice."
John was the Bridegroom's friend and rejoiced
in the coming of the Lord Jesus Christ. He rejoiced in the glorious work that He was to accomplish and the greatness that is to be His. He
said, "I am not the Messiah, I am simply the
Bridegroom's friend." What a wonderful privilege that was! And there was never a humbler,
less exalted servant of God than John the Baptist. When they questioned him as to his identity
he never exalted himself. When any demanded
his credentials he said, "I am the voice of one
crying in the wilderness, Prepare ye the way of
the Lord." You cannot see a voice, you can only
hear it. John did not want them to become occupied with him. It was his delight simply to
exalt the One whose herald he was, and in this
John becomes the example for every servant of
God. We are all too prone to want people to be
occupied with us. We like to be thought well of,
and it hurts us a bit if people misunderstand us
and speak unkindly. But all that was out of
John's thoughts. He was not concerned about
himself if only Christ could be glorified. The
apostle Paul was one who entered into that spirit.
His only concern was that Christ might be magnified, either by life or by death; and that was
the special purpose of John the Baptist—"a man
sent from God."

It is a great thing when God lays hold of a man and says, "I want you to go on My errand." I am quite sure He put His hand upon me when I was fourteen years old. He said, "I have saved your soul; I want you to go forth to preach My gospel." What a joy it has been, for fifty years, through good and evil, to proclaim that glad message! Sometimes a man goes on for a number of years before God puts His hand on him. Saul of Tarsus was a mature man, beyond thirty years of age, when the blessed Lord appeared to him on the Damascus road and said, "I have appeared unto thee for this purpose, to make thee a minister and a witness . . . delivering thee from the people and from the Gentiles, unto whom I now send thee."

He came to Peter when he was a man in the fishing business. He said, "Peter, leave your fish behind, and I will make you a fisher of men." He came to Matthew when he sat at the publican's desk. Someone has said that Matthew was probably the man who taught Peter to swear. Matthew was the Roman tax-collector and he was a Jew, putting heavy taxes upon his own people, and every time Peter brought in a boat-load of fish it was Matthew's business to go down and say, "Give me twenty per cent of those fish." I can imagine Peter and Matthew wrangling over the selection the government was to have, and Peter cursing and swearing because of the tax-collector's exactions! But the Lord came to Matthew the publican, and said, "Follow Me," and Matthew left the tax-collector's desk for good and all, and was chosen to write the first Gospel.

I wonder if there is anyone reading these lines to whom God is speaking? Often in the still hours of the night you may have heard a voice saying, "I want you as My servant, as My missionary. I want you to work for Me in some special way." Are you saying, "Here am I, Lord; send me?" Do not be afraid to yield to Him. Some day people will say of you, "There was a man, or a woman, sent from God." It was true of John, and he is going to get his reward for heeding the call when he stands at the judgment-seat of Christ.

Now John came for a witness. That is what every minister should be—a witness. A witness does not tell the things he thinks, but the things he knows. He came for a witness—to bear witness of the Light. Does light need a witness? Yes, in a dark world like this, where men are blind. They cannot see, and they need a witness to the fact that light has come. John knew that the world was blind and he came to tell men of the Light, and the wonderful thing was this: when men received and believed the message, they lost their blindness and were able to see. They beheld Christ, the Light, "that all men through Him might believe."

Who was the Light? Our Lord Jesus Christ Himself. "That was the true Light." And while we are at this point, let me draw your attention to a slightly different rendering of this verse. Here we read, "That was the true Light." Oh, there are so many false lights. There are so many false, flickering lights that men follow to tneir ruin. "That was the true Light, which lighteth every man that cometh into the world." What does that mean? Does Christ give spiritual light to every man that cometh into the world? Well, partly. He does give light through our consciences, and yet, I think there is more than that involved in this text. I believe it is really this: "That was the true Light, which, coming into the world, casts light on every man." That is, it is not light *in* man, but light shining *on* man. I mean this, the Lord Jesus Christ came into a world made up of wickedness—made up of sinful men who rolled sin as a sweet morsel under their tongues. He came as the only holy Man that ever walked this earth, and as He walked in and out among men all other men were shown up in contrast. He cast light on every man.

I wonder if among my readers there is someone who has been saying to himself, "I don't need this gospel. I am not a great sinner. I haven't killed anybody. I haven't robbed. I don't curse and swear. I am not a sinner." Wait a minute, my friend! Will you come and stand alongside of the Lord Jesus Christ? There you have Man in perfection. How does your life compare with His? How does your spirit, your words, and your way of looking at things compare with His? Oh, when we stand alongside of Him, He casts light on us, and that light shows up all our spiritual and moral deficiencies. "That was the Light which, coming into the world, casts light on every man."

The law was given to one nation and one people. Amos calls it a plumbline, by which all crookedness could be detected. He has in mind the building of a wall. One looks at it and says, "That wall is not straight." The builder resents this, but when he takes a plumbline and drops it down by the wall, it manifests its imperfection.

Here is a man who claims to be perfect and God says, "Test him by My law and you will find that he is crooked." Scripture says that if a man will keep the whole law and yet offend in one point, he is guilty of all. But Jesus answered its every claim; He met its every demand. "In Him is no sin." "He knew no sin." "He did no sin." That is what man should be for God. When you take your place beside Him, at once all your imperfection is shown up. He casts light upon you.

"That is the true Light which, coming into the world, casts light on every man." Well, has He only come to show up my sin? Has He only come to make manifest my imperfection? No, indeed. He must make me first to see my need, but it is only that He may reveal Himself as my Saviour!

"He was in the world, and the world was made by Him, and the world knew Him not." Not one of His fellow-townsmen dreamed that God Himself had come down to dwell among them.

I remember, as my wife and I were walking down the streets of Nazareth, we were appalled by the dirt and filth—the unclean children, playing about the open sewers running down both sides of the street. As we were walking along, my wife began to weep. The tears were running down her cheeks. I said, "Why, my dear, what is the matter? Are you ill?" "Oh, no," she said; "but I was thinking of Mary and Jesus—Mary bringing up her holy Child in a place like this, for it must have been even worse then than it is now." You know how those Oriental cities are, vile and terrible. Some of you think you have smelled terrible things in America, but unless you have visited the Orient, you haven't smelled anything yet! But Jesus grew up amidst all the filth and vileness like a pure white lily coming up from the muddy contaminated water at the bottom of the lake. Jesus, the pure; Jesus, the holy One. He was in the world and the Creator of all things and they knew Him not. He made their tables and chairs and fitted in the doors and windows into their houses, and nobody realized that it was God Himself, walking among them, until by-and-by He went to the cross and died for our sins, and they laid him away in the tomb, and on the third morning He burst the bands of death and arose in triumph. He is never to be humiliated again. He is the Head of the new creation—of those who have trusted Him and are one with Him in resurrection life.

"He came unto His own, and His own received Him not." The first "His own" is in the neuter; the second is personal. We might read, "He came unto His own things, and His own people did not receive Him." Yes, He came into His own world. He created this world. He came into the world His hands had made. He came to His own country, His own city, the city of Jerusalem. He came to His own temple—"In Thy sanctuary, every whit of it uttereth His glory," said David. He came unto His own things, but His own people of the Jews, the people who had been waiting for Him presumably, for all those hundreds of years, did not recognize Him and they "received

Him **not.**" Have you received Him? There were those who heard Him speaking and they opened their hearts to Him. "As many as received Him, to them gave He power to become the sons of God, even to them that believe on His name." We have the whole truth of the way of salvation right here, so far as our part is concerned. God has set Him forth a Prince and a Saviour, and when we receive Him we become His. Do you say, "How may I avail myself of His saving grace?" Here you have it. "As many as received Him." To receive Him is to trust Him, to open your heart to Him. Have you received Him? "As many as received Him." Do not make a difficulty out of that which is so simple. God has used the plainest possible terms. Jesus says, "Come unto Me, and I will give you rest." Believe on Me, and you will have eternal life. Look to Me, and you will be saved. Receive Me, and I will make you My own. To receive Him, throw the heart's door wide and He will come in. "Behold, I stand at the door and knock: if any man hear My voice, and open the door, I will come in to him, and will sup with him, and he with Me."

There is a beautiful gospel song that says, "You must open the door." *You* must open the door. Jesus will not force His way in. Will you open the door? Will you let Him in? At this very moment you can bow your head, and open your heart and say, "I want Thee to come in and be Lord of my life." Won't you receive Him? "As many as received Him, to them gave He power to become the children of God." You see, men are not God's children by natural birth. Jesus said to a certain group of His day, "Ye are of your father, the devil," and of all who are saved the apostle says, "Who were at one time children of wrath." We are born of sinful flesh. In order to become children of God we need to be regenerated. "As many as received Him." To receive Him is to believe in His name, to take Him at His word. It is to trust Him. Do not try to make a great mystery of faith. Faith is simply putting your "Amen" to what God says. We receive the witness of men. Some man comes to us in whom we have confidence. We believe what he tells us. We receive the witness of men. Very well, God has given us His witness concerning His Son. Do you receive His testimony into your heart? Would you dare make God a liar by refusing to believe the testimony He has given concerning His Son?

Notice what is said of those who believe in His name: "To as many as received Him, to them gave He the power (or authority) to become the children of God." There are three ways by which you *cannot* become a child of God:

1st. "Which were born, not of blood." That

means that even if your parents were two of the best Christians that ever lived, they cannot give you divine life. They cannot communicate their new nature to you. It is only God who can do that. You are not a child of God by blood.

2nd. "Nor of the will of the flesh." You cannot simply *make* yourself a Christian by your own will: "It is not of him that willeth or of him that runneth, but of God that showeth mercy." Here is a man who says, "Well, I haven't any employment, so I will become a soldier." He finds that he must have a uniform, so he goes to an outfitting shop and buys the uniform and comes down the street wearing it, and imagines he is a soldier. We may inquire, "How did you become a soldier?" "Well, I put on a uniform and I am a soldier." Does that make him a soldier? Certainly not. He must be enlisted. No man can become a Christian by simply saying, "From now on, I am a Christian." That does not make you a Christian. You must come to God as a sinner and receive Christ. He will make you a Christian. He will give you new life. It is not just by trying to be better, but by letting God make of you a new creature.

3rd. "Nor of the will of man." No one on earth can make you a Christian. People imagine some minister or priest can make Christians of them by baptism or sacraments. But these can-

not save you. "You MUST be born again."
"Which were born, not of blood, nor of the flesh,
nor of the will of man, but of God." God alone
produces that new life in the soul of every believer in His blessed Son.

Now the last verse in this section: "And the
Word was made flesh." That is not the best translation. Actually, as we have remarked already,
the Word was never *made* anything. The Word
became flesh. Link that up with the first verse,
"In the beginning was the Word, and the Word
was with God, and the Word was God." "And
the Word became flesh." He who was one with
the Father from all eternity became Man. It
means He took upon Him our humanity, body
and soul and spirit. He became a Man, and yet
He was God, "and dwelt among us." The word
"dwelt" might be rendered "tabernacled" among
us. Of old God dwelt in the tabernacle in the
wilderness. Now He has been manifested in His
Son. "The Word became flesh and tabernacled
among us, and we beheld His glory," the divine
glory shining out. John lived with Him, walked
with Him, prayed with Him. He saw in His holy
life "the glory as of the only begotten of the
Father, full of grace and truth."

These words were written by one who knew
Jesus practically all His life. He was related to
Him by natural ties, and he must have known

Him when He was growing up there in Nazareth. One of the earliest Church historians tells us that John was an adolescent when Christ called him to be a fisher of men. He spent three-and-a-half years of most intimate fellowship with Jesus, and he was the one who leaned on Jesus' breast at the last supper. He was probably about ninety years of age when he wrote this book, and as he looked back over the years he says, "We beheld His glory, the glory as of the only begotten of the Father, full of grace and truth." That revelation he shares with us as he pens these wonderful chapters.

FULNESS OF GRACE

✦ ✦ ✦

"John bare witness of Him, and cried, saying, This was He of whom I spake, He that cometh after me is preferred before me: for He was before me. And of His fulness have all we received, and grace for grace. For the law was given by Moses, but grace and truth came by Jesus Christ. No man hath seen God at any time; the only begotten Son, which is in the bosom of the Father, He hath declared Him" (John 1: 15-18).

✦ ✦ ✦

THESE four verses will be sufficient, I am sure, for our meditation at this time; they are so rich and so full. We notice first the testimony of John the Baptist, at which we were looking last Lord's Day morning. We hear the great forerunner of the Messiah declare, "This was He of whom I spake, He that cometh after me is preferred before me: for He was before me." John had come to baptize with water, but he said, "There standeth One among you, whom ye know not; He it is, who coming after me is preferred before me, whose shoe's latchet I am not worthy to unloose" (vers. 26, 27). Elsewhere we are told He was to baptize in the Holy Spirit and in fire.

34

Remember that John was speaking to a mis-
cellaneous company at that time, and there were
those among that vast number who were to be
baptized with the Holy Spirit, and those who
because they rejected the message should be baptized with fire. The one is grace in all its fulness
—the other is judgment. "Whose fan is in His
hand, and He will thoroughly purge His floor,
and gather His wheat into the garner; but He
will burn up the chaff with unquenchable fire."
The finality of judgment in the lake of fire is
pronounced at the Great White Throne, but the
One who will sit upon the Great White Throne
will be the same marvelous Person who hung on
Calvary's cross and died for our sins. Let us
never forget that He has commanded, "That all
men should honor the Son, even as they honor
the Father. He that honoreth not the Son honoreth not the Father which hath sent Him."

May I say to any who may be reading this,
that if you are out of Christ now, if you live and
die out of Christ, you will be raised out of Christ
in the resurrection of the unjust, you must stand
as a Christless soul at the Great White Throne,
and there you will face the One who once died to
save you, who would have saved you if you had
trusted Him, who longed to save you, who sent
the Holy Spirit to plead with you, to urge you
to surrender to Him and know His grace; but in

that day it will be too late to know Him as Saviour. Yours will be the awful baptism of fire. Thank God, it need not be. He came in grace to save you, He wants to save.

John points Him out definitely and says, "This was He of whom I spake, He that cometh after me is preferred before me: for He was before me." John delights to give honor, as every real servant of Christ does, to the Lord Jesus Himself. He would retreat into the background that Christ might loom large before the vision of the people, that He might be the One who would occupy the attention of every soul. "He is preferred before me," says John, "for He was before me."

That is a very significant statement. That implies in itself the pre-existence of our Lord Jesus Christ. If you take these words literally and refer them only to Christ's life here on earth, then they are not true. He was not before John the Baptist in this respect. John the Baptist was born some three months before the Lord Jesus Christ was born of the blessed Virgin Mary.

But John says, "He was before me." What does he mean? He means this: John began to be when he was born on earth, but Christ Jesus did not begin to be when He was born on earth. He is the One prophesied of in Micah 5:2, 4: "Whose

goings forth have been from of old, from everlasting. . . . And He shall stand and feed in the
strength of the Lord, in the majesty of the name
of the Lord His God; and they shall abide: for
now shall He be great unto the ends of the earth."
So John rightly says, "He was before me."

Then you will remember our Lord's own words
on one occasion when He spoke very intimately
of Abraham. He said, "Abraham rejoiced to see
My day." But the Jews looked upon Him in
astonishment and indignation and said, "Why,
Thou art not yet fifty years old, and hast Thou
seen Abraham?" They understood Him to say
He had seen Abraham, but that was not what
He said. He said Abraham had seen Him, and
was glad.

But they said, "Thou art not yet fifty years
old," and there is something significant in the
age-period they mention. They were addressing
One who, according to earthly years, was in His
early thirties. Was it not a rather remarkable
thing that they should say, "Thou art not yet fifty
years old"? Might we not have expected them
to say, thirty-five years, or at the utmost, forty
years old? Why, then, did they say to Him,
"Thou art not yet fifty years old"? Does that
not in itself tell of the deep-marked lines of grief
and sorrow that had already furrowed His face?
He was "marred more than any man, and His

form more than the sons of men." And it may have been that as He passed through this scene, the bitter anguish that He bore then and the pain and suffering that the sins of men had already caused Him, had so seamed His face that He appeared to them rather like a man a little beyond middle age, than one simply entering upon the best of his days. "Why, you have not yet reached fifty—have you?—and yet you say you have seen Abraham." Jesus answered, "Before Abraham was, I am." Before Abraham was? That goes back two thousand years and more. "Before Abraham was, I am." He takes the incommunicable name of Deity, "I Am;" in other words, He is saying, "I am before Abraham." He not only lived before John the Baptist, but before Abraham.

In the first chapter of Colossians the Holy Ghost says of Him, "For by Him were all things created, that are in heaven, and that are in earth, visible and invisible, whether they be thrones, or dominions, or principalities, or powers: all things were created by Him, and for Him: and He is before all things, and by Him all things consist."

Now look at that. John says, "He was before me." Jesus says, "I am before Abraham." The Holy Ghost says, "He is before all things," the Eternal One.

The Apostle John goes on to tell us, "Of His fulness have all we received, and grace for grace." Elsewhere we read that "in Him dwelleth all the fulness of the Godhead bodily." All divine fulness dwelleth in Him, and out of that divine nature His very life has been poured into us.

John wrote many, many years after Christ had gone back to heaven, and all down through the centuries since then, whenever poor sinners have turned to Him in repentance, that fulness of blessing has been poured into their souls. "Of His fulness have all we received, and grace for grace." Here the word translated "for" means "against," or "in place of." Grace in place of grace, grace following upon grace. We are not called upon to live upon past experiences. Many of us remember when we were first saved, of the grace that was poured into our souls when that took place, and we look back and sing,

> "O happy day, that fixed my choice,
> On Thee, my Saviour, and my God!"

But that is not our experience today. That was grace indeed, wondrous grace! What we have now should be grace against grace, grace following upon grace, all down through the years. People ask me sometimes if I have ever received "the second blessing." Why, dear friends, it has

been nothing but blessing upon blessing now for
almost fifty years, as I have been learning more
and more of the wondrous fulness of Christ. So,
if you have never trusted Him you do not know
what you are missing. You remember the old
Scotch woman who was asked to tell what Jesus
meant to her, and she said, "Weel, ye ken; it's
better felt than telt." If you walk in fellowship
with Him you are receiving in its fulness grace
upon grace, blessing following blessing, all
through the years.

"For the law was given by Moses, but grace
and truth came by Jesus Christ." Here we have
two dispensations. The law was given by Moses,
and the law prevailed until Christ. Now grace
and truth have come by Jesus Christ. The law
was truth, but it was truth without grace. In
the Gospels we have the law maintained and yet
grace preached to all men everywhere who will
put their trust in this Saviour.

Now, in verse 18, we have a very remarkable
statement: "No man hath seen God at any time;
the only begotten Son, which is in the bosom of
the Father, He hath declared Him." We might
read this as it has been otherwise translated: "No
man hath seen God at any time; the only begotten Son, subsisting in the bosom of the Father,
He hath told Him out." That is, He has given
us to know God in all His fulness.

Have you ever said to yourself, "I wish I knew God better; I wish I understood the mind of God more fully; how God looks at things; how He considers certain matters that perplex me and trouble me?" Let me say this, dear friend, if you would know God better, all you have to do is to get better acquainted with Jesus Christ, for the Lord Jesus Christ has fully told or manifested God. God—let me say it thoughtfully—God is *exactly like Jesus*. There is no other God than the God who has been revealed in Christ. The holiness of God is the holiness seen in Jesus. The righteousness of God is the righteousness maintained by Jesus. The purity of God is the purity manifested in Jesus. The compassion of God is the compassion shown by Jesus. The love of God is the love of Jesus, and the hatred of God is the hatred seen in Jesus. Why, you say, does God hate anything? Did Jesus ever hate? Yes; with a perfect hatred God hates sin. He says, "Do not this abominable thing that I hate." He hates all hypocrisy, all uncleanness, all impurity, and Jesus hated all these things perfectly. You and I hate them in measure.

Then, the anger of God shows the indignation of Jesus. Was God ever angry? "God is angry with the wicked every day." Why, you say, I thought God loved all men. He does love all men, but that does not hinder the fact that He becomes angry. You may love your own children, and yet you may get very angry at some of the wrong things they do. And so God, while He has shown His love by sending His only begotten Son into the world to die for sinners, is angry with the wicked every day. When God deals with unrepentant sinners, men will know that, "It is a fearful thing to fall into the hands of the living God."

Was Jesus ever angry? He was. He was angry with the hypocrites; He was angry when He saw certain religious propagandists whose hearts were hard and cruel in their dealings with the poor and needy. Think of the words He used about the Scribes and Pharisees who devoured widows' houses, and think of His indignation when He saw people so concerned about rites and ceremonies that they had no time for the things of God. Think of that time when He was in the synagogue where there was a poor little crooked woman who for eighteen years had been bowed down by that awful bondage. Jesus saw her there, and He was moved with compassion. He turned to the people and said, "Is it lawful to heal on the sabbath day?" and they answered Him not a word. They were so jealous of their sabbath and so unconcerned about the needs of humanity, that Jesus turned to this poor woman and asked them, "Ought not this woman, whom Satan hath bound, lo, these eighteen years, be loosed from this bond on the sabbath day?" He gave the word and she was healed, and He looked round upon them in anger. The anger of Jesus is the anger of God.

"No man hath seen God at any time; the only begotten Son, which is in the bosom of the Father, He hath declared Him." He has fully manifested the character of God.

But now look at the first clause of this verse, "No man hath seen God at any time." What does that mean? Do we not read again and again in the Old Testament of people who saw God? Is it not taken for granted that when Adam and Eve lived in the garden in all their purity and heard His voice as they walked in the garden in the cool of the day, when He called unto Adam, that in some sense they saw God, and hid themselves among the trees of the garden, their guilty consciences condemning them?

Abraham saw that mystic One of the three who came to him as he sat in the tent-door, and he talked to Him as the Lord Jehovah. Moses said, "Show me Thy glory," and the Lord said, "Thou canst not see My face; for there shall no man see Me, and live. Behold, there is a place by Me, and thou shalt stand upon a rock; and it shall come to pass, while My glory passeth by, that I will put thee in a clift of the rock, and will cover thee with My hand while I pass by." And we read that Moses saw God.

Ezekiel had visions of God. Again and again in the Old Testament we have these marvelous scriptures that tell of men beholding God, and yet it says here, "No man hath seen God at any time." What does it mean? It means this: that all of these to which I referred were but theophanies. Men did not actually see God in His essential Being, but He manifested Himself to them — as a man to Abraham, as an angel to Daniel, as a marvelous appearance to Ezekiel. No man has seen Deity at any time. "God is a Spirit; and they that worship Him must worship Him in spirit and in truth," and a spirit is not visible to mortal eyes.

But what do these words mean, then: "No man hath seen God at any time?" If this was the only passage in which these words were found we should take it for granted that the meaning was that until Jesus Christ came into the world no man had seen God, but that when they saw Him they had seen God, because He was "the only begotten Son, which is in the bosom of the Father." But when we turn over to the First Epistle of John (4:12), we find exactly the same words again, and these words were written many years after the Lord Jesus Christ had gone back to heaven. Here we read, "No man hath seen

God at any time." Now observe, these words were written when John was an old man, and again he says, "No man hath seen God at any time." What, then, are we to gather from this? Simply that Deity as such is invisible.

When Jesus was here, men in seeing Him did not see Deity. What they did see was a man like themselves, as far as they could tell; but He was not a sinner as they were; He was the Holy One of God. But Deity was enshrined within that Man, for "God was in Christ, reconciling the world unto Himself." But men could only see His humanity. Now He is gone back to heaven and the word comes to us again, "No man hath seen God at any time." God is still making Himself known to man, but He makes Himself known through those who walk in fellowship with Him. If you are walking in love you are manifesting God.

It is a very solemn thing to realize that I as a believer am here in this world to make God known, both by life and testimony. Jesus did this fully and completely. The closer I walk with Him, the more God will be seen in me.

THE RECORD OF JOHN

✓ ✓ ✓

"And this is the record of John, when the Jews sent priests and Levites from Jerusalem to ask him, Who art thou? And he confessed, and denied not; but confessed, I am not the Christ. And they asked him, What then? Art thou Elias? And he saith, I am not. Art thou that prophet? And he answered, No. Then said they unto him, Who art thou? that we may give an answer to them that sent us. What sayest thou of thyself? He said, I am the voice of one crying in the wilderness, Make straight the way of the Lord, as said the prophet Esaias. And they which were sent were of the Pharisees. And they asked him, and said unto him, Why baptizest thou then, if thou be not that Christ, nor Elias, neither that prophet? John answered them, saying, I baptize with water: but there standeth one among you, whom ye know not; He it is, who coming after me is preferred before me, whose shoe's latchet I am not worthy to unloose. These things were done in Bethabara beyond Jordan, where John was baptizing. The next day John seeth Jesus coming unto him, and saith, Behold the Lamb of God, which taketh away the sin of the world. This is He of whom I said, After me cometh a Man which is preferred before me: for He was before me. And I knew Him not: but that He should be made manifest to Israel, therefore am I come baptizing with water. And John bare record, saying, I saw the Spirit descending from heaven like a dove, and it abode upon Him. And I knew Him not: but He that sent me to baptize with water, the same said unto me, Upon whom thou shalt see the Spirit descending, and remaining on Him, the same is He which baptizeth with the Holy Ghost. And I saw, and bare record that this is the Son of God" (John 1: 19-34).

IN the last two messages we have been dealing with the testimony of John the Baptist. I fear that many Christians fail to realize how much God, by the Holy Spirit, committed to His

servant John. Many of us think of him as one who
had very little gospel light or understanding of
the Person of our Lord Jesus Christ. But we have
already seen that he recognized in the Lord Jesus
the pre-existent One.   He says in verse 15, "He
was before me," and those words are repeated in
verse 30.   So John recognized in our Lord Jesus
One who did not begin to live when He was born
here on earth, but One who had life with the
Father before He deigned in grace to come down
to this world and link His Deity with our humanity, apart from its sin, and be born as Mary's
Child.

If we are to take verses 16 to 18 as uttered by
John, we would have a wonderful unfolding of
truth indeed; but it seems much more likely that
these words are the Spirit's commentary through
the Apostle.   They form a parenthesis, and then
the record of John begins again in verse 19,
"when the Jews sent priests and Levites from
Jerusalem to ask him, Who art thou?"

Let us consider more fully the parenthetical
portion.   Out of the fulness of grace manifested
in Jesus, we who believe have received abundant
supply for every need—even grace for grace, or,
as we might read, grace upon grace.   It is just
one evidence after another of God's rich grace,
as we go on to know and enjoy communion with
our blessed Lord, whose ministry was so different

from that of Moses, the mediator and messenger of the old covenant. Through him the law was given, and that law was the revelation of the mind of God, according to which men (in Israel) were responsible to walk, until Jesus came. "The law," says Paul, "was our child-trainer up to Christ." Now grace and truth have been told out in Jesus, so "we are no longer under the child-trainer." We see in Christ the full revelation of the Father: grace and truth manifested in a Man here on earth, and that Man the delight of the Father's heart. The law, as we have pointed out, was truth, but it was truth without grace. God is light and God is love; so both the holiness, which is according to truth, and the grace, which covers every sin and meets every need, are seen in Jesus. He, the only-begotten Son, ever dwelling in the bosom of the Father, has told out God in all His essential glory. People speak of Jesus leaving the bosom of the Father. But that is not the language of Scripture. The bosom is the place of affection. He never left that. He subsists in the Father's bosom. When here on earth He was as truly the Object of the Father's love as when He was in the glory from which He came to redeem us by His atoning death.

If John the Baptist saw all this and spoke these words, then his was a knowledge of Christ far beyond that with which he is generally credited.

But if, as seems evident, we have here the Holy Spirit's later comment, we would not forget that all was true of Jesus even in John's day.

Let us now follow the Baptist's further testimony.

He had aroused wonderful interest by his preaching and baptizing. Over all the land of Palestine people were speaking of this strange new prophet who had appeared in the wilderness and was drawing great throngs after him. He sternly rebuked sin and iniquity, called men to a baptism of repentance and proclaimed the near coming of the Kingdom of God on earth. Many believed his message and manifested their faith by taking their place in baptism as those who deserved to die. Everywhere the people were stirred.

The Jews sent some of their important leaders down to Jerusalem to ask him, "Who art thou? And he confessed and denied not; but confessed I am not the Christ." He knew that many were thinking that probably he was the long-promised Messiah who was to bring in the era of peace. But he said, "I am not the Messiah. I am not the Promised One." They said, "Who are you then? Are you Elias?" Elias, you know, is just the Greek form for the Hebrew word, Elijah. Why did they put that question to him? One who prophesied four hundred years before John came

into the world, uttered this prediction, "Behold,
I send you Elijah the prophet. He shall turn the
hearts of the fathers to the children" (Mal. 4:
5, 6). And so they said to him, "Are you Elijah?
Are you he who was to bring the solemn message
warning of judgment?" John says, "No, I am
not." And yet you remember that the Lord Jesus
Christ Himself, when the disciples put the question to Him as to whether Elijah must not first
come, answered and said, "Elias is indeed come,
and they have done unto him whatsoever they
would." And they understood He spoke of John.
He came in the power and spirit of Elijah.

But John denied that he was personally Elijah.
He would not direct attention to himself. He had
come to occupy people with Another. Then they
asked him, "Art thou that prophet?" What did
they mean? To whom were they referring? In
the book of Deuteronomy it is written that Moses
said, "The Lord thy God will raise up unto thee
a prophet . . . like unto me." God had said, "I
will raise them up a prophet from among their
brethren, like unto thee, and will put My words
in His mouth; and He shall speak unto them all
that I shall command Him. And it shall come to
pass that whosoever will not hearken unto My
words which He shall speak in My name shall be
destroyed." These words refer to Christ, not to
John. So again he disavowed any such claim.

They asked, "Well, then, who art thou? What sayest thou of thyself?" He had not been talking about himself at all. We like to talk about ourselves, but John was not as we. He was not talking about himself. He was not trying to draw people's attention to himself. He came to occupy them with the coming One. So when they asked, "What sayest thou of thyself?" He replied, "I am the voice of one crying in the wilderness, Make straight the way of the Lord." You cannot see a voice. You can hear it, but you cannot see it. "I am just here as a voice crying in the wilderness, Make straight the way of the Lord, as said the prophet Esaias."

The fortieth chapter of Isaiah begins with these words, "Comfort ye, comfort ye My people, saith your God. Speak ye comfortably to Jerusalem, and cry unto her that her warfare is accomplished, that her iniquity is pardoned: for she hath received of the Lord's hand double for all her sins." That is, her sins are paid for, referring to the atoning work of our Lord Jesus Christ. And so the prophet then proclaims the gospel to comfort the people of God. In verse 23 we read, "The voice of him that crieth in the wilderness, Prepare ye the way of the Lord, make straight in the desert a highway for our God!" Whose way was to be prepared? The way of the Lord. Who was the Lord? "A highway for our *God*."

So John spoke in the full recognition of the fact that the One who was coming was God, manifest in the flesh. For when he said, "I am the voice of one crying in the wilderness, Prepare ye the way of the Lord, make straight in the desert a highway for our God," he used the word that means "Jehovah." This lowly Man, Jesus of Nazareth, who appeared among the people, was none other than Jehovah Himself, who came to redeem poor sinners. But let us follow the declaration of Isaiah. "The voice said, Cry." He asked, "What shall I cry?" and the Lord replied, "All flesh is grass, and all the goodliness thereof is as the flower of the field: the grass withereth, the flower fadeth: because the Spirit of the Lord bloweth upon it: surely the people is grass. The grass withereth, the flower fadeth: but the word of our God shall stand forever."

"Why," you say, "there isn't very much comfort in that." No; apparently not. But that is always the way God begins to comfort people. Men are so proud and so forgetful of their own sinfulness. Their consciences are so inactive that if God is going to do something for men, He must make them realize their own littleness and their own sinfulness. That is why the Apostle Peter linked this passage with the gospel and the new birth. "For all flesh is as grass, and all the glory of man as the flower of grass. The grass withereth, and the flower thereof falleth away: but the word of the Lord endureth forever. And this is the word which by the gospel is preached unto you" (1 Pet. 1:24, 25). Why do we need to be born again? Because "that which is born of the flesh is flesh," and "all flesh is as grass." Why do we need a new life? Because we are under judgment and this life is soon going to pass away and we must meet God. "It is appointed unto man once to die, but after this the judgment." Let this word sink into the depths of our souls. Let it rebuke our pride and self-sufficiency. All the glory of man—the things that men are most delighted with—is just like the flower that is soon gone. How we need life from God! "He that hath the Son hath life."

And so, John sees in this fortieth chapter of Isaiah a prophecy referring to himself. He says, "This is who I am. Simply a voice crying in the wilderness." They which were sent were of the Pharisees and they continued questioning. They were not satisfied. They just went on from one question to the other and did not stop to consider the answers. They were not interested in learning the truth of God. They started questioning him along another line. "Why baptizest thou then if thou be not that Christ, nor Elias, neither that prophet?" John did not attempt to defend himself or explain to them, for he knew their unbelieving attitude. He simply said, "I baptize with water: but there standeth One among you, whom ye know not; He it is, who coming after me is preferred before me, whose shoe's latchet I am not worthy to unloose." Apparently with that, these Pharisees went their way. They had no real interest in this matter that was exercising the minds and consciences of others.

But now in the next statement of the passage we find John giving utterance to one of the greatest truths of the gospel. "The next day John seeth Jesus coming unto him." No doubt he had often looked out over that great throng and mused, "I wonder if He is here yet. I wonder if the time for Him to be manifested has come." But day after day there was no answering voice to his heart's question. But now he sees Jesus coming toward him and the Spirit of God says, "There He is, John," and John immediately exclaims, "Behold the Lamb of God which beareth away the sin of the world."

Have you ever thought what must have been involved in that? All down through the centuries Israel had known of the sacrificed lamb. They knew that long years ago when Abraham and Isaac were going up the mountain, Isaac turned to his father and said, "Father, here is the fire and the wood, but where is the lamb?" And Abraham said, "My son, God will provide Himself a lamb for a burnt offering." And then they knew that when Israel was about to come out of Egypt God said, "You are to take a lamb and kill it and sprinkle the blood. The death angel is going through Egypt at midnight, but when he sees the blood he will pass over you." And they knew that in the temple service, every morning and every evening a lamb was placed upon the altar for a burnt offering. Isaiah had prophesied of the One who would be led as a lamb to the slaughter, in order to become the sacrifice for sins. At last He had come of whom the prophets had spoken, and John exclaimed, "Behold the Lamb of God which beareth away the sin of the world!" He recognized in Jesus the object of all prophetic testimony and the fulfilment of all the types of the law. Notice how he dwells on the vicarious atonement: "Behold the Lamb of God which beareth away the sin of the world." He knew that in Isaiah 53 it was written of the Lamb of God, "He was wounded for our transgressions, He was bruised for our iniquities: the chastisement of our peace was upon Him; and with His stripes we are healed." At last He had come in accordance with the word of God!

And you will notice this. He does not say merely "sins." It is *sin,* in the singular. I think that you will find that when people attempt to quote this verse they generally say *sins.* Sins are only the effect of a cause, and the Lamb of God came, not only to take away the individual's sins, but to take away or deal with, the sin-question as a whole. The Apostle Paul said, "God hath made Him to be sin for us, who knew no sin." He is not only the bearer of our transgressions, He not only atoned for all our acts of sin, but He died for what we are as sinners by nature. And let me say something to you that may make you think you can never trust me again: "I have been guilty of many sins which I have had to go to God and confess, and I know those sins have all been forgiven. But I am a worse man than anything I have ever done!" Would you like to trust me now? I mean this. Within this heart of mine there are tendencies to sin that are worse than any act of sin I have ever committed. This is true of us all. We are sinners by nature. Sin dwelleth in us. Christ died to put away *sin,* not merely *sins,* by the sacrifice of Himself. We have in us that thing which God calls "sin in the flesh." God took all that into account when Christ hung on the cross. He died because of what we were. He took our place. He was made sin for us, and sin, as a barrier, was taken away, and now the vilest sinner can come into the presence of God and find forgiveness. Do you know this Lamb of God which taketh away the sin of the world?

Then John says, "This is He of whom I said,

After me cometh a Man which is preferred before me: for He was before me. And I knew Him not." Evidently he had been out in company where Jesus was, but he did not understand that this was the Messiah until now. He "knew Him not: but that He should be made manifest to Israel, therefore am I come baptizing with water. And John bare record, saying, I saw the Spirit descending from heaven like a dove" — you see this event takes place after the baptism, which is not referred to here, but is mentioned in other Gospels—"I saw the Spirit descending from heaven like a dove, and it abode upon Him. And I knew Him not: but He that sent me to baptize with water, the same said unto me, Upon whom thou shalt see the Spirit descending, and remaining upon Him, the same is He which baptizeth with the Holy Ghost." The great work which John was sent to do was nearing an end, and now here is the climax; "I saw and bare record that this is the Son of God." Did John really know that? Yes, he did--"I saw and bare record that this is the Son of God." Do you know that, dear friend? Have you trusted Him for yourself? Oh, if you have never trusted Him before, won't you come to God, owning your sin? "Behold the Lamb of God which taketh away the sin of the world."

BRINGING OTHERS TO JESUS

✐ ✐ ✐

"Again the next day after John stood, and two of his disciples; and looking upon Jesus as He walked, he saith, Behold the Lamb of God! And the two disciples heard him speak, and they followed Jesus. Then Jesus turned, and saw them following, and saith unto them, What seek ye? They said unto Him, Rabbi (which is to say, being interpreted, Master), where dwellest Thou? He saith unto them, Come and see. They came and saw where He dwelt, and abode with Him that day: for it was about the tenth hour. One of the two which heard John speak, and followed Him, was Andrew, Simon Peter's brother. He first findeth his own brother Simon, and saith unto him, We have found the Messias, which is, being interpreted, the Christ. And he brought him to Jesus. And when Jesus beheld him, He said, Thou art Simon the son of Jona: thou shalt be called Cephas, which is by interpretation, A stone. The day following Jesus would go forth into Galilee, and findeth Philip, and saith unto him, Follow Me. Now Philip was of Bethsaida, the city of Andrew and Peter. Philip findeth Nathanael, and saith unto him, We have found Him, of whom Moses in the law, and the prophets, did write, Jesus of Nazareth, the son of Joseph. And Nathanael said unto him, Can there any good thing come out of Nazareth? Philip saith unto him, Come and see. Jesus saw Nathanael coming to Him, and saith of him, Behold an Israelite indeed, in whom is no guile! Nathanael saith unto Him, Whence knowest Thou me? Jesus answered and said unto him, Before that Philip called thee, when thou wast under the fig tree, I saw thee. Nathanael answered and saith unto Him, Rabbi, Thou art the Son of God; Thou art the King of Israel. Jesus answered and said unto him, Because I said unto thee, I saw thee under the fig tree, believest thou? Thou shalt see greater things than these.

58

And He said unto him, Verily, verily, I say unto you, Hereafter ye shall see heaven open, and the angels of God ascending and descending upon the Son of Man" (John 1: 35-51).

✓   ✓   ✓

OUR attention has been directed already to John's testimony concerning our Saviour as the Lamb of God. We have considered verse 29 where we read: "The next day John seeth Jesus coming unto him, and saith, Behold the Lamb of God, which taketh away the sin of the world." This announcement had to do with our Lord as the great sin offering. All through the Old Testament dispensation the types and shadows and direct prophetic messages had pointed on to the time when God would send the true sacrificial Lamb, and now John declares, "He has come."

The next day after, he exclaims again, "Behold the Lamb of God." It is not now "the Lamb of God that taketh away the sin of the world"—that was yesterday—but now it is, "Look at the walk of the Lamb of God." Jesus came walking across the plains and John's attention was directed to Him in a new way. There was something about the walk of God's blessed Son that led His forerunner to exclaim, "Behold the Lamb of God!" How different His walk was to that of any other, and by "walk," of course, we mean *behavior*. As

we think of the holy behavior of the Son of God
we cannot but realize how it stands out in contrast to our own devious ways. The great difference is this: our behavior is dominated so much
by selfishness. We act as we do because we are
so self-centered. We are occupied with ourselves.
We are concerned about self-pleasing and about
that which ministers to self. But the Lord Jesus
could say, "I came not to do Mine own will, but
the will of Him that sent Me." The only Man
who has ever walked through this scene who
never had one selfish thought, but who found all
His joy in doing the will of the Father, was our
blessed, adorable Lord. We may well "Behold
the Lamb of God" in this sense. If, at times, we
are tempted to justify things in ourselves which
are contrary to the mind of God, we need only
to gaze, by faith, upon the Lamb of God as He
was down here, and behold His unselfish walk, in
order to realize at once how far short we come
of that perfection which was manifest in Him.
The result will be that we will seek to become increasingly like Him. "But we all, with open face
beholding as in a glass the glory of the Lord, are
changed into the same image from glory to glory
even as by the Spirit of the Lord."

As we read this word, as we see the holy Saviour moving undefiled through the vile scenes
that are depicted for us by the Holy Spirit, as we

see how gentle, careful and considerate of others He was, surely it should rebuke our own wickedness and selfishness and lead us to confess our own failures in the presence of God and to desire to become more like Him. "Behold the Lamb of God!" Contemplate His lovely ways and dwell upon His subject spirit. We are told that when John uttered this exclamation, "Behold the Lamb of God," it so appealed to two of the disciples who were standing with him that "the two disciples heard him speak, and they followed Jesus." After all, this was the real object of John's ministry. He did not come to occupy people with himself or with his service, but he came as "the voice of one crying in the wilderness." He said, "He must increase, but I must decrease." "This is He, who, coming after me, is preferred before me." So you can well understand how John's heart thrilled with gladness when they went after Jesus. This was the very purpose for which he came baptizing with water. This should be the purpose of every servant of Christ. He should ever point others to this Lamb of God—the Lamb of God, the Sinbearer; the Lamb of God, the perfect example. The two disciples heard John speak and they went after Jesus. Of these, we read, one was Andrew, Simon Peter's brother. The other one keeps his own name hidden all through this Gospel, but he was the disciple who leaned on Jesus' breast, the disciple whom Jesus loved; that is, of course, the Apostle John. So these two, Andrew and John, followed Jesus. "Then Jesus turned and saw them following, and saith unto them, What seek ye?" I think the Lord Jesus might well address that question to many today who presumably seek His face. Many people come to Jesus, I think, because they hope to be benefited by Him. Some come hoping for physical relief. What do you have in mind when you come to Him? "What seek ye?" What would you have Jesus do for you? I am often grieved when I invite people who want to know Christ as their Saviour to come to our prayer-room, that our friends there may pray with them and make clear the way of life, and some come ostensibly because they are exercised and anxious to know the Lord, but it is soon evident they are far more concerned about temporal need than about their spiritual condition. I would rather have a man come to me and say honestly, "I am not concerned about my soul, but I am greatly concerned about my body; I need a place to sleep, or I need food." I am glad to do what I can for a man who comes to me like that; but it really hurts to have people come professing an interest in spiritual things when they are only concerned about temporal relief.

Well, Jesus turned to these men and said, "Why seek ye Me?" and they seem just a bit embar-

rassed. "They said unto Him, Rabbi (which is
to say, being interpreted, Master), where dwellest Thou?" as much as to say, "We would like to
go with You to Your home." Where did He really
dwell? He had no home here on earth. He could
say, "The foxes have holes, and the birds of the
air have nests; but the Son of Man hath not
where to lay His head." He was a homeless wanderer as He began His ministry, after leaving the
carpenter's shop in Nazareth. But He had a home
in the bosom of the Father, for we read, "No man
hath seen God at any time; the only begotten Son,
which is in the bosom of the Father, He hath
declared Him." That was where Jesus dwelt.
He dwelt in the Father's love and that place He
never left. He was always the object of the
Father's delight and always enjoyed the fellowship of the Father except when, upon the cross,
God's face was hidden from Him when He became
the substitute for our sins. Then He cried in
the anguish of His soul, "My God, My God, why
hast Thou forsaken Me?" Yet He was never
dearer to the Father's heart than in those dark
hours when He was "made sin" for us.

But here He did have a temporary abiding-
place. Just where it was we are not told; but He
said to them, "Come and see." So they went with
Him, "and abode with Him that day: for it was
about the tenth hour." That would be about four

o'clock in the afternoon, and oh, what a sacred
season that must have been! Doubtless they
plied Him with questions, and He probably answered them and gave them the revelation of His
love and grace, and from that time on they were
never the same. They were never able to settle
down to the earth or give themselves entirely to
earthly occupations. Their hearts were won for
Himself, and they longed to share this blessing
with others. Has He won your heart? Do you
really know Him as the sent One of the Father?
Has His love and His grace and His holiness been
so revealed to your soul that He has won your
affection for Himself? Then surely you want
others to know Him. I think this is one of the
surest proofs of a genuine conversion. One of
the first evidences that people really know Christ
is that they turn to others and say, "Come; I want
you to know Him as I know Him." The rest of
this chapter is devoted to service in seeking to
win others to Christ.

One of the two was Andrew. "He first findeth
his own brother, Simon." It might seem, simply,
that the first thing Andrew did was to find his
brother. But, we are told by scholars, that what
is really implied here is that John made off to find
his brother James, but Andrew was the first one
to find his brother. It is characteristic of the
Apostle John to hide himself. Two of the New

Testament writers, John and Luke, two very self-effacing men, never mention themselves, and yet they have quite a close connection with Jesus. They are always hiding themselves. The Lord, however, would have us know that, having come in vital contact with Christ for themselves, John at once thought of his brother, and Andrew thought of *his* brother. Have you a brother still out of Christ? Are you saved yourself? Is there a brother, a sister, a friend, who does not yet know the Saviour? Have you tried to find them? Perhaps you wrote a letter. Perhaps you could only send some gospel tracts. Perhaps you could only have a word with them, but you have been concerned about them; have you not? I cannot understand how you could really know and love Christ yourself and be indifferent to the claims of those who are still strangers to Him. Let us seek to emulate these men.

Andrew was the first to find his own brother Simon. They had both been listening to John. In the first chapter of Acts, Peter speaks of those who were with them "beginning from the baptism of John" (ver. 22). Thus they were prepared to receive the Messiah when He was manifested. So Andrew hurried off to find Peter and said, "We have found the Messiah, which is, being interpreted, the Christ," and then in the verse which follows we read, "He brought him to Jesus." Did you ever do that for anyone? Notice that he did not go out to argue with his brother, but he simply went and told him of the One who satisfies the heart. He probably told Simon of his own experience and then said, "Now, Simon, I want you to know Him too. Won't you come to Him?" Oh, there is many a longing heart you might lead to Christ. Too many of us are content to leave this to the preacher, or perhaps to those who teach in the Sunday School, or in some other public place. But every believer is called to be a representative of Christ, to go to men and women with this message, "We have found Jesus, the Saviour of sinners, who meets every need of the lost and the undone."

When Jesus saw Peter coming He turned to him and said, "Thou art Simon, the son of Jona: thou shalt be called Cephas, which is by interpretation, A stone." Jesus loved to give men new names. He does it still. Whenever you put your trust in Him He gives you a new name. "Now, Peter, you are going to be a rock-like man, and you are going to stand firmly for the truth in later days. Your name is Cephas. Your name is a stone." You remember how in Matthew 16 we read this: "And I say also unto thee, that thou art Peter, and upon this rock I will build My Church; and the gates of hell shall not prevail against it." And in his own first epistle, Peter

speaks of all believers as living stones, built upon
the rock foundation, Christ. Oh, are you afraid
to confess Christ, afraid to trust Him lest you
should not be able to stand? Come to Him! Acquaint yourself with Him, and He will make you
a rock-like man or woman. But, you tell me, Peter
himself failed. Yes, at one time he was a pretty
shaky sort of a rock; was he not? But after he
received the Holy Spirit it was different. Oh,
how Peter stood for Christ in those early days
of the Church, and after years of testimony and
suffering Peter sealed his testimony with his
blood. He became truly the rock-like man, as
Jesus, by giving him this name, indicated he
would.

We have not only Andrew and John going after
their brothers, but we find Jesus calling another
man. "The day following, Jesus would go forth
into Galilee, and findeth Philip, and saith unto
him, Follow Me. Now Philip was of Bethsaida,
the city of Andrew and Peter." We do not hear
of any great profession he made, but he heard
the words, "Follow Me," and at once we find him
going after a friend. "Philip findeth Nathanael,
and saith unto him, We have found Him." He
did not preach a long sermon. He said,
"We have found Him, Nathanael." "We have
found Him of whom Moses in the law, and the
prophets, did write, Jesus of Nazareth, the son

of Joseph." You say, Why does he call Him the son of Joseph? He was actually the Son of God. But Joseph, you see, by marrying Mary, had become the legal father of Jesus, and it is this which Philip recognizes. He says, as it were, "Why He has been among us all these years, and we did not realize that that carpenter in the shop at Nazareth was the Messiah." Philip says, "I want you to know Him too, Nathanael." And Nathanael said to him, "Can there any good thing come out of Nazareth?" "Can any good thing come out of that city?" If the Nazareth of today with its filthy streets resembles the Nazareth of old, it is no wonder that Nathanael asked that. It was the time for Philip to begin an argument, but he was too wise to do that. He simply said to him, "Come and see. If you only get to know Him as I know Him, you will be convinced." And this is my message to you unsaved ones. I think of some of you, torn by doubt, anxious and perplexed. You say, "Can it be possible that Jesus is really the blessed Son of God, the Saviour of sinners?" I say to you earnestly, "Come and see." Come to His feet. Let Him speak to you words of peace and pardon. Won't you come? He says, "Come unto Me, all ye that labor and are heavy laden and I will give you rest." "Come and see."

Nathanael decided to go. Jesus saw him coming—no one ever came toward Him but that He saw him coming; He sees you today if you are moving toward Him—and Jesus said, "Behold an Israelite indeed, in whom is no guile!" He was saying, "I know that he is genuine, that he rings true." "Behold an Israelite indeed, in whom is no guile," and Nathanael catches the word and says, "Whence knowest Thou me?" and Jesus said, "Before that Philip called thee, when thou wast under the fig tree, I saw thee." What did He mean? Why, I suppose that Nathanael had a fig tree in his garden behind the wall and possibly he was under that fig tree studying the Word of God, or praying for light, and Jesus saw him there long before Philip called Him. Wherever you are today, friend, Jesus sees you, and if your heart yearns for light and peace, He waits to give them. "Before that Philip called thee, when thou wast under the fig tree." This so stirred the heart of Nathanael that he said, "This must be He." He cried out at once, I believe that "Thou art the Son of God; Thou art the King of Israel." You see, "Faith cometh by hearing and hearing by the Word of God," and so in faith Nathanael was added to the little company.

"Jesus answered and said unto him, Because I said unto thee, I saw thee under the fig tree, believest thou?" When you did not think I could see you I knew—does that make it clear to you that I am more than man? "Verily, verily, I say unto you, Hereafter ye shall see heaven open, and the angels of God ascending and descending upon the Son of Man." He was speaking of His second coming in power and glory. The mind of Nathanael went back to the book of Genesis, when Jacob lay down to sleep in Bethel, and there saw in his dream a ladder (an ascent, really) reaching up to heaven, and the angels going up and down. Jesus practically says to Nathanael, "I am the One by whom man ascends from earth to heaven, and some day when I come again in power and glory I will come accompanied by the angels of God." He is Himself the connecting link between earth and heaven, soon to be manifested in power and glory!

CHRIST'S FIRST MIRACLE

❧ ❧ ❧

"And the third day there was a marriage in Cana of Galilee; and the mother of Jesus was there: and both Jesus was called, and His disciples, to the marriage. And when they wanted wine, the mother of Jesus saith unto Him, They have no wine. Jesus saith unto her, Woman, what have I to do with thee? Mine hour is not yet come. His mother saith unto the servants, Whatsoever He saith unto you, do it. And there were set there six waterpots of stone, after the manner of the purifying of the Jews, containing two or three firkins apiece. Jesus saith unto them, Fill the waterpots with water. And they filled them up to the brim. And He saith unto them, Draw out now, and bear unto the governor of the feast. And they bare it. When the ruler of the feast had tasted the water that was made wine, and knew not whence it was (but the servants which drew the water knew): the governor of the feast called the bridegroom, and saith unto him, Every man at the beginning doth set forth good wine: and when men have well drunk, then that which is worse: but thou hast kept the good wine until now. This beginning of miracles did Jesus in Cana of Galilee, and manifested forth His glory; and His disciples believed on Him" (John 2: 1-11).

❧ ❧ ❧

THROUGHOUT John's Gospel the word translated "miracles" means *signs*. There are only eight mentioned in this Gospel. Each one is for a very specific purpose, as when, for instance, Jesus healed the palsied man by the pool of Bethesda. We see in Him the One who

has almighty strength, able to impart power to
those who have none of their own. And here in
this first sign recorded in the Gospel, the Lord
Jesus is seen in a very definite character. He
comes before us as the Creator of all things. John
has already told us that doctrinally, when he
said, "In the beginning was the Word, and the
Word was with God, and the Word was God.
The same was in the beginning with God. All
things were made by Him; and without Him was
not any thing made that was made." But now
in this sign, we have a visible manifestation of
this: the putting forth of His creatorial power
so that He does in one moment of time what
ordinarily is done in weeks and months. Notice
the occasion of the miracle. "The third day (after
the calling of Nathanael) there was a marriage
in Cana of Galilee, and both Jesus was called and
His disciples, to the marriage." In chapter 21: 2
we read that Nathanael was of Cana of Galilee;
so evidently, in the course of their journey up to
Judea, they stopped at Nathanael's home-town,
where this wedding took place. Some have supposed that it was the marriage of Nathanael himself, but there is no proof of this. The names of
the bride and groom are not given in the Word.
The important thing is that we have the blessed
Lord's approval of that intimate relationship
which is so often dishonored today. It carries

our minds back to the time when, at the dawn of history, God gave our first parents each to the other: "Therefore shall a man leave his father and his mother, and shall cleave unto his wife: and they twain shall be one flesh." It was God who instituted the marriage-relationship, and we have Christ blessing and sanctifying it. Alas, that in our day marriage should often be so degraded through the wilfulness and wickedness of men and women! How careful we as Christians should be to recognize its sanctity! Take the terrible evil of divorce, increasing on every hand these days. Surely it is something that a Christian ought to have a conscience about. Of course, there are cases where no self-respecting woman could continue to live with a certain type of man, but Scripture tells us that if people must be separated, they are not to be remarried to someone else, unless that divorce was because of infidelity on the part of the other party. In such a case our Lord Jesus Christ has said, "Whosoever shall put away his wife and marry another, except it be for fornication, committeth adultery against her." We recognize the exception which He has made, but outside of that we do not find any other ground for the re-marriage of divorced people. Things are in such a confused state today, and oh, the terrible effect of divorce upon children!

So I take it here that the Lord Jesus was put.

ting His approval upon marriage when He accepted the invitation to attend the wedding. The mother of Jesus was present. That would suggest that she was well acquainted with the family. In fact, she seems to have had a certain measure of responsibility. (Might I just go aside again to say that it is a delightful thing at any marriage if Jesus and His disciples are called to attend it. It is a pitiful thing if people cannot invite Jesus. How precious it is to have the fellowship of those who love Christ, as one enters upon this relationship!)

But now we consider the occasion of this miracle, and, first, we will notice the conversation between Jesus and His mother. We read, "When they wanted wine, the mother of Jesus saith unto Him, They have no wine. Jesus saith unto her, Woman, what have I to do with thee? Mine hour is not yet come. His mother saith unto the servants, Whatsoever He saith unto you, do it."

Wine is, in Scripture, where rightly and wisely used, the symbol of joy. We read of "wine that cheereth God and man." The fact that the wine was giving out at a marriage-feast suggests that Israel had so far departed from God that her joy had disappeared, in large measure. Nothing much remained but empty forms and ceremonies, as pictured by the empty waterpots. But the Christ of God was there, and His mother felt instinctively that He could do something to remedy the situation. Naturally the bride's mother would be put to confusion by the scant supply of refreshment, and the guests would wonder at the lack of proper preparation. Mary was, in all probability, an intimate acquaintance, if not actually a relative. She was a resourceful woman and, as such, felt that a word to her Son would be all that was necessary. How much maternal pride may have been mixed with this, we do not know, but she evidently longed to see Jesus give some manifestation of His power, and so give others to realize something of His mysterious divine-human personality.

So, we are told she turned to her Son and said, "They have no wine." She did not actually request Him to do something about it. She carried in her bosom a secret which other people never would have understood. She had been waiting for the time when this wonderful Being, whom she had carried beneath her heart as a babe, should manifest Himself as indeed the Son of God, and it is very likely that she saw here an opportunity for Him to do this. But Jesus turned to her and said, "Woman, what have I to do with thee? Mine hour is not yet come."

Some people have thought that the Lord spoke a little bit roughly, but we may be sure He never did that. We may be quite certain that He never

said one thing to her which the most dutiful son
might not have said. What He did say loses a
little by our translation. We distinguish between
"lady" and "woman." "Lady," at one time, was
simply the wife of a lord or knight. The word
"woman" in our day has come to seem a little
less respectful than the word "lady," and so we
think of the Lord saying, "Woman, what have I
to do with thee?" as though He were reproaching
His mother. The term He really used was one
that any woman might glory in. He said to her,
"My lady, what have I to do with thee?" or really,
"What is there between thee and Me?" That is,
"What is it that you would have of Me? What
is the thing that you have in your heart?" And
then He adds, "Mine hour is not yet come." All
through this Gospel He has before Him this
"hour." He had brothers after the flesh, and one
time His brothers wanted Him to go up to the
feast, but Jesus said to them, "Mine hour has
not yet come, but your time is always ready." And
we read in the eighth chapter of this Gospel,
"These words spake Jesus in the treasury as He
taught in the temple: and no man laid hands on
Him: for His hour was not yet come." And
again, "Then said Jesus unto them, When ye have
lifted up the Son of Man, then shall ye know
that I am He, and that I do nothing of Myself;
but as My Father hath taught Me I speak these

things." They were going to lift Him up, but the hour had not yet come. Then (in John 12:23) when the Greeks came, saying, "We would see Jesus," He answered saying, "The hour is come, that the Son of Man should be glorified." He recognized in their coming to Him the beginning of the hour when His glory was to be manifested following His crucifixion. In chapter 13, when He was about to wash His disciples' feet, we read, "Jesus knew that His hour was come, that He should depart out of this world unto the Father." And in chapter 17, where He spoke to the Father, we read, "These words spake Jesus, and lifted up His eyes to heaven and said, Father, the hour is come; glorify Thy Son, that Thy Son also may glorify Thee." It was the hour when He was to go to the cross; when He was to bear the sin of the world; the hour when He was to be raised up upon the tree, and following that God was to raise Him from the dead and glorify Him openly. This was not His hour, and when His own dear mother tried to press Him to act ahead of time, as it were, He says, "What is there between thee and Me? Mine hour is not yet come." It is very evident that His mother, knowing His heart, was not in the least disturbed over His answer to her. She turns to the servants and says to them, "Whatsoever He saith to you, do it." Here may I point out to those who pray to the blessed Vir-

gin and ask her to intercede for them, that her
own Son did not immediately answer the petition
she asked of Him.   Mary said to the servants,
"Whatsoever He saith unto you, do it." In other
words, the mother of Jesus turns us away from
herself to her blessed Son, Jesus Christ.

We read, "And there were set there six waterpots of stone, after the manner of the purifying
of the Jews, containing two or three firkins
apiece."   That is, they held about a barrel of
water each.   They had to do with Jewish cere-
monial cleansings.   They were connected with
outward purification.   They were all empty, like
the forms and ceremonies of the law.   But the
Lord Jesus turns to the servants and says, "Fill
the waterpots with water."   In obedience to His
word they fill them to the brim.   We can see a
picture here of the living water of the truth of
the gospel poured into the typical ceremonies of
old.   Everything is changed when the waterpots
were filled with water.   Jesus said unto them,
"Draw out now and bear unto the governor of
the feast."   And as they poured the water out,
lo, and behold, in the very act of pouring out, it
became wine!   It was a wonderful miracle, and
yet, after all, it was just a duplication of what
our Lord Jesus Christ has been doing for millenniums on ten thousand hillsides, changing
water into wine.   When this wine was brought to

the ruler of the feast, he tasted it and exclaimed, "Every man at the beginning doth set forth good wine; and when men have well drunk, then that which is worse: but thou hast kept the good wine until now." God always reserves the best for the end of the feast.

The only comment the Holy Ghost makes on this sign is in verse 11, "This beginning of miracles did Jesus in Cana of Galilee, and manifested forth His glory; and His disciples believed on Him." That might well be linked up with chap. 1:14. There we read that our Lord Jesus Himself "was made flesh and dwelt among us." The word "dwelt" is really "tabernacled" among us, "And we beheld His glory, the glory as of the only begotten of the Father, full of grace and truth." That verse gives us the key to all the wonderful symbolism of the tabernacle in the wilderness. It was a house of curtains, and inside, in the holiest of all, between the cherubim, a glorious Light was shining, which was the visible manifest presence of God. The people could not see the glory. But if you can imagine, for a moment, the curtains parting and the brilliant light revealed between those golden boards, it would be the glory shining out. Well, that is what we have here in the miracles of Jesus. It was like drawing back the curtains of the earthly tabernacle to expose the Shekinah, for "God was in Christ, reconciling the world unto Himself."

So this first miracle shows Him as the Creator, the One who upholds all things through His power, the One who provides for us everything that we need; and the wonderful thing is this, that this great Creator became our Saviour. He was always God from eternity. He, by whom all things came into existence, came down into this world to suffer for our sins, that we might be saved and have everlasting life.

One word could have filled those waterpots if it had been His will. It took more than a *word* to save our souls. It took the *work* of the cross. But because of that work, one word, *"believe,"* brings life and peace. "Today, if ye will hear His voice, harden not your heart." "If thou shalt confess with thy mouth the Lord Jesus, and shalt believe in thine heart that God hath raised Him from the dead, thou shalt be saved."

THE CLEANSING OF THE TEMPLE

✓ ✓ ✓

"After this He went down to Capernaum, He and His mother, and His brethren, and His disciples: and they continued there not many days. And the Jews' passover was at hand, and Jesus went up to Jerusalem, and found in the temple those that sold oxen and sheep and doves, and the changers of money sitting: and when He had made a scourge of small cords, He drove them all out of the temple, and the sheep, and the oxen; and poured out the changers' money, and overthrew the tables; and said unto them that sold doves, Take these things hence; make not My Father's house an house of merchandise. And His disciples remembered that it was written, The zeal of Thine house hath eaten Me up. Then answered the Jews and said unto Him, What sign shewest Thou unto us, seeing that Thou doest these things? Jesus answered and said unto them, Destroy this temple, and in three days I will raise it up. Then said the Jews, Forty and six years was this temple in building, and wilt Thou rear it up in three days? But He spake of the temple of His body. When therefore He was risen from the dead, His disciples remembered that He had said this unto them; and they believed the Scripture, and the word which Jesus had said" (John 2: 12-22).

✓ ✓ ✓

FOLLOWING the baptism of our Lord He went out into the wilderness, where, as we learn from the other Gospels, He was tempted of the devil. Then He returned to Judea and began a slow progress toward Galilee. We have already followed Him in the calling of His earliest disciples and considered His presence and His

action at the marriage in Cana of Galilee. Now
the Lord went on from Cana to Capernaum.
Capernaum is called elsewhere "His own city."
It was not His own birthplace, we know, neither
was it the city in which He had lived as a child
and young man, but it was the city which He
chose as a residence as He began His ministry.
Of course, He was not there very much, and He
could say, "The foxes have holes and the birds of
the air have nests, but the Son of Man hath not
where to lay His head." He was seldom at home,
but if He had a home at all, it was Capernaum.
Capernaum, therefore, was one of the most privileged of the Galilean cities. There He often appeared in the synagogue. I cannot express the
emotion that overwhelmed several of us as we
stood in the recently excavated synagogue in
Capernaum and realized we were standing, in all
probability, on the very stones where His feet
once stood; and as we looked down from that
raised platform, we could imagine the healing of
the withered arm and the deliverance of the poor
woman who had been so crippled that her body
was bent together for so many years. We remembered that it was there that He delivered His
great discourse—"I am the Bread of Life." We
could look down to the seashore and we knew
that there Matthew once had his office as collector
of customs, and we noticed the road going by

and thought of the Lord Jesus as He raised the daughter of Jairus, after healing the woman who pressed her way through the crowd, crying in faith, "If I may but touch the hem of His garment I shall be healed."

Capernaum, blessed above all places on earth, for Jesus chose it as His home, and there He taught and did His works of power, but, alas, it was of this very city that later on He said, "Thou, Capernaum, which art exalted unto heaven, shalt be brought down to hell," the city so privileged! Do you know, that very city was blotted out of existence? For centuries no one knew where it stood, until in recent years it was excavated from under a mound of sand. Surely Capernaum's fate should be a solemn warning for us today. The greater our privileges, the greater our responsibility. If God has, in loving-kindness, permitted us to live in a country where Bibles are found on every hand, and yet we turn a deaf ear to His proclamation and despise His Word, how dreadful it will be, some day, to face Him in the judgment whom we have rejected while on earth. God grant that the lesson of Capernaum may sink deeply into the heart!

He went down to Capernaum and with His mother and brethren and disciples continued there a short time, and then He started south again to manifest Himself at Jerusalem. The

Jews' passover was at hand. In the Old Testament the passover is called the passover of the Lord, but wherever you turn in the New Testament you find it called the Jews' passover, as we also read of the Jews' feast of the tabernacles. Why the change? Why are they not called "feasts of the Lord?" Why are they designated "feasts of the Jews?" Because the Jews had turned away from the Lord, and the keeping of these feasts had become mere formality, so that the Lord no longer owns them as His. Let us be warned by this of the danger to which we are all exposed, of putting outward observances in the place of spiritual realities.

The Jews' feast of the passover was at hand and Jesus went up to Jerusalem, and when He reached the temple He was shocked to see business going on in its courts as though it were a worldly market or counting-house. What had, perhaps, begun innocently enough, as an accommodation to supply lambs for visiting passover-guests, and the exchanging of money for those from distant lands, had degenerated into a feverish effort to make merchandise of what was needed in order to observe the sacrificial service connected with the passover. Covetousness and over-reaching prevailed to such an extent that God was dishonored and the temple scandalized. There was the bleating of sheep and the cooing of doves disturbing the worship of the Lord, and these who offered them for sale thought only of enriching themselves. They were commercializing the things of God, and that is always repugnant in His sight. So Jesus asserted Himself as the Lord of the Temple. We read in Malachi, "And the Lord, whom ye seek, shall suddenly come to His temple," and shall purify it.

He appeared suddenly before the people with a whip of small cords and began to drive out the sheep and the oxen. He said, "Make not My Father's house an house of merchandise." Since then, how much there has been of the commercializing of the things of the Church of God. Whatever the Lord gives, He gives freely, and what His servants have to offer in the way of ministry to needy souls should be offered just as freely. We bring our gifts out of the appreciation and gratitude of our hearts. What we do for the glory of our Lord Jesus Christ should be done because we want to do it.

It must have seemed strange to see Jesus with this whip of cords, crying aloud, "Take these things hence; make not My Father's house an house of merchandise." "My house shall be called a house of prayer; but ye have made it a den of thieves." Notice the tone of authority. It is, "My Father's house," and "My house." He was the Lord of the temple, because He was Lord over all. The disciples remembered that it was written, "The zeal of Thine house hath consumed Me." How well that applied to Him!

The Jews began to object, and asked, "What sign showest Thou?" They challenged Him to work some miracle in order to attest His authority; to do something marvelous in order to accredit Himself. But He said, "Destroy this temple, and in three days I will raise it up." It was as though He said, "You want a sign that I am the Son of God, that I am the One promised of the Father—you shall have a sign. In God's due time, destroy this temple, and in three days I will raise it up." They did not understand and they turned angrily upon Him, saying, "This temple was forty-and-six years in building, and would you raise it up in three days after it was destroyed!" He meant the temple of His body. But He did not explain. It was of no use to do so. Men get into such a state that there is no use trying to make clear spiritual realities to them.

So our Lord had nothing to say to them. They had chosen their own way and He did not attempt to explain the mystery of His words. But when He had risen from the dead, His disciples believed Him. We may consider those words today and we can see the meaning. "Destroy this temple." What was the temple? It was the building, as originally constructed, in which Jehovah manifested His presence. There in the holiest of all was that uncreated light, the Shekinah glory. That was the visible manifested presence of God on earth. The temple simply hid that glory from the eyes of the multitude outside. The high priest entered the holiest of all once every year. And so the Lord Jesus Christ's body, when He came into this scene, was the real temple of God. His body answers to the outer court, His soul to the holy place, and His spirit to the holy of holies. God was manifest in Christ. God Himself dwelt in Christ, reconciling the world to Himself, for He was God and Man in one Person. He spoke of the temple of His body, for God and Man were there in one Person. So He said, "Destroy this temple, and in three days I will raise it up." Notice, "I will raise it up." In other words, He was to die, but He died in perfect confidence that He would rise. Have you noticed how the resurrection of our Lord Jesus Christ is attributed to each Person of the blessed Trinity? In another place He says, "No man taketh My life from Me, but I lay it down of Myself. I have power to lay it down, and I have power to take it again." He laid down His life and He took His life again. He raised up the temple. But elsewhere we read that He was raised from the dead by the glory of the Father, and then we are told that the Holy Spirit raised up Jesus, our Lord, from the dead. Each

Person of the Godhead had His part in the resurrection of Jesus. And now He has been declared to be the Son of God with power by the resurrection of the dead. Apart from this we should have no gospel to preach to a lost world.

But Christ is risen, and we are told that, "If thou shalt confess with thy mouth the Lord Jesus, and shalt believe in thine heart that God hath raised Him from the dead, thou shalt be saved. For with the heart man believeth unto righteousness; and with the mouth confession is made unto salvation."

OUR LORD'S INTERVIEW
WITH NICODEMUS

✓   ✓   ✓

"Now when He was in Jerusalem at the passover, in
the feast day, many believed in His name, when they
saw the miracles which He did. But Jesus did not commit Himself unto them, because He knew all men, and
needed not that any should testify of man: for He knew
what was in man. There was a man of the Pharisees,
named Nicodemus, a ruler of the Jews: the same came
to Jesus by night and said unto Him, Rabbi, we know
that Thou art a teacher come from God: for no man can
do these miracles that Thou doest, except God be with
him. Jesus answered and said unto him, Verily, verily,
I say unto thee, Except a man be born again, he cannot
see the kingdom of God. Nicodemus saith unto Him,
How can a man be born when he is old? Can he enter
the second time into his mother's womb, and be born?
Jesus answered, Verily, verily, I say unto thee, Except
a man be born of water and of the Spirit, he cannot enter
into the kingdom of God. That which is born of the
flesh is flesh; and that which is born of the Spirit is
spirit. Marvel not that I said unto thee, Ye must be
born again. The wind bloweth where it listeth, and thou
hearest the sound thereof, but canst not tell whence it
cometh, and whither it goeth; so is every one that is born
of the Spirit. Nicodemus answered and said unto Him,
How can these things be? Jesus answered and said unto
him, Art thou a master of Israel, and knowest not these
things? Verily, verily, I say unto thee, We speak that
we do know, and testify that we have seen; and ye receive
not our witness. If I have told you earthly things, and
ye believe not, how shall ye believe, if I tell you of
heavenly things? And no man hath ascended up to
heaven, but He that came down from heaven, even the
Son of Man which is in heaven. And as Moses lifted up
the serpent in the wilderness, even so must the Son of
Man be lifted up: that whosoever believeth in Him should
not perish, but have eternal life" (John 2: 23-3: 15).

THE present section begins properly with the last three verses of chapter 2. We read, "Now when He was in Jerusalem at the passover, in the feast day, many believed in His name, when they saw the miracles which He did." A faith that rests upon miracles is not a saving faith. A faith that rests upon signs and wonders does not bring salvation to anyone. That is why it is not worth while for us to debate with unbelievers about their objections to the inspiration of the Bible. Jesus said, "Go ye into all the world, and preach the gospel to every creature." We are told, "The preaching of the cross is unto them that perish, foolishness." Paul says, "I am not ashamed of the gospel of Christ: for it is the power of God unto salvation to every one that believeth; to the Jew first, and also to the Greek." God gives miracles to authenticate the Word, but faith must rest on something far better than miracles. Here were people waiting for the Messiah to come and they said, "Well, now, if Messiah came, could He do any more miracles than Jesus did? He *must* be the One of whom the prophets have spoken." In that sense they believed that He was Messiah, but they did not confess that they were guilty souls needing salvation and they did not see in Jesus the Saviour whom they needed. They believed in His name when they saw the miracles; but the rest of the verse

says that Jesus did not commit Himself to *them*.
The words "commit" and "believe" are really just
the same in the original.   We might read it,
"Many believed in His name, but Jesus did not
believe in them."   He did not trust His interests
to them, because He knew they were not genuine.
He knew what was in man and needed not that
any should testify of man.   He knew the wickedness and unreliability of the human heart.   You
and I like to make out a good case for ourselves.
Scripture shows how little we have to boast of,
if we would be honest with God.   When we think
of the eyes of His Son looking down into our
hearts, what corruption, lusts, perversity, dishonesty He finds there!   "The heart is deceitful
above all things and desperately wicked.   Who
can know it? I, the Lord, search the heart, I try
the reins, even to give every man according to
his ways, and according to the fruit of his doings."   Because Jesus was God manifest in the
flesh, He knew what was in man.   He is as truly
omniscient as the Father.   He knows what is in
you and me and yet, knowing it all, He loved us
and gave Himself for us, but He does not trust
us, or rely upon these wicked hearts of ours.   He
knows that we cannot be depended upon.   We are
lost and ruined and undone; what we need, therefore, is a new life.   We need to be born again,
and that is the new life He gives us.

There is a little Greek word that has been dropped out in our English translation here. It sometimes is translated "and," though more generally, "but." It is the same word used in the beginning of verse 24 of chapter 2. So, if we put it in its right place at the beginning of verse 1 of chapter 3, we read, "But there was a man of the Pharisees." The Spirit of God thus puts this man in contrast with the people of verses 23 to 25. Here is a man whom Jesus recognizes as sterlingly honest in seeking after truth, and whenever our Lord finds a man who is really in earnest, He will see that that man will get the truth. You ask, Well, what about the heathen who have never heard? Will God condemn them to everlasting judgment for not believing in a Saviour of whom they have never heard? No, of course not. But what He will do is this: He will condemn the heathen for all the sins of which they have not repented, but He will see that every repentant soul gets light enough to be saved. He will not let a man be lost if he is seeking for the truth.

So here is Nicodemus, an honest seeker, and Jesus treats him as such. "There was a man of the Pharisees (the most religious group in Jerusalem) named Nicodemus, a ruler of the Jews." But this man, now face to face with the Christ of God, finds out he has a tremendous lack. A great many people are like Nicodemus. They are good folk, they reverence spiritual things, and yet there are many who have not confessed their sins before God and know not the second birth. Have you not often said, in the words of Tennyson. "Oh, for a man to arise in me, that the man that I am might cease to be?" You are dissatisfied with yourself, yet you have never turned to Christ that you may be born again. Let us follow our Lord Jesus' conversation with Nicodemus. Let us listen as though we had never heard it before.

Here is Nicodemus. "The same came to Jesus by night." I am not going to scold him for that. Some preachers do. I see no evidence of cowardice there. He does not act like a coward. I think Jesus was busy all day long, and Nicodemus says, "I would like to have a close-up talk with that man, and I cannot do it in a crowd. Perhaps if I ask Peter or James or John where He lives, I can have a private interview." And so he arranges to see and talk with Him at night after the Lord has withdrawn from the throngs. All honor to Nicodemus that he was interested enough to go. I am not going to find fault with him because he went by night.

Nicodemus began by saying, "Rabbi, we know that Thou art a teacher come from God: for no man can do these miracles that Thou doest except God be with him———." This was not the end of the sentence.   The Saviour interrupted him, and declared, "Verily, verily (truly, truly; amen, amen), I say unto thee, Except a man be born again, he cannot see the kingdom of God." "Born again," or "born from above"?   After all, I think the emphasis is on the newness of it.   That which made the impression on Nicodemus was not so much "born from above," but being born for the second time, "born *again*."   Jesus was saying, as it were, "It does not help to say nice things, Nicodemus.   You need more than a teacher, you need a Saviour—One who can give you a new life.   You need a second birth!"   "Except a man be born again, he cannot see the kingdom of God."

There is a widespread notion today that men may be educated into Christianity. *Religious Education* is one of the greatest abominations of the present day.   The idea is that you can take a child and instruct him along the lines of the Christian philosophy and thus educate him into salvation.   I do not object to the term *Christian Education*.   I believe that is a right and proper thing.   It is right and proper to instruct the Christian along Christian lines.   But Religious Education which simply tries to make people Christians by educating them into it, will, I believe, be the means of making tens of thousands of hypocrites instead of making them Christians. "Ye must be born again."   There must be the communication of a new life.

Nicodemus said, "But I don't understand it. How can a man be born when he is old? Can he go through the whole process of nature again? Why, that seems absurd. Just imagine! Can I go back and be born of my mother again?" And Jesus says to him, "Nicodemus, listen to Me; it would not make any difference if you could; you would be no better off the next time than you were before. The natural birth does not count; it must be a spiritual birth." "Verily, verily, I say unto thee, Except a man be born again, he cannot see the kingdom of God. That which is born of the flesh is flesh, and that which is born of the Spirit is spirit. Marvel not that I said unto thee, Ye must be born again." What weighty words are these! First the Saviour says, "Except a man be born of water and of the Spirit, he cannot enter into the kingdom of God." What did He mean? I know that there are those who tell us that to be born of water means to be born of baptism. But no one ever received the new life by water-baptism. You can search your Bible in vain for anything like that. It is not there. It is not in the Word of God. Nowhere is baptism in Scripture likened to birth. It rather speaks of death. We are buried with Him by baptism into *death*. Water-baptism is the picture of the burial of the old man, not a picture of a second birth. Well, then, what is the water

by which we are born again? Go through the
Word of God. Nowhere do we find people being
born of literal water. Trace "water" through
John's writings. You will find that it is the recognized symbol for the Word of God. David
asked the question, in Psalm 119 :9, "Wherewithal shall a young man cleanse his way? By
taking heed thereto according to Thy Word." And
in the fourth chapter of John, Jesus, speaking
to the woman of Samaria, said, "Whosoever
drinketh of this water shall thirst again: but
whosoever drinketh of the water that I shall give
him shall never thirst; but the water that I shall
give him shall be in him a well of water springing up into everlasting life." What is the water
that Jesus gives? It is the water of the Word. It
is the testimony of the gospel. "As cold waters to
a thirsty soul, so is good news from a far country." "Whosoever will, let him take the water of
life freely." What is the water of life? It is the
gospel message. We read in Ephesians 5: 25, 26,
"Husbands, love your wives, even as Christ also
loved the Church, and gave Himself for it; *that
He might sanctify and cleanse it with the washing of water by the Word,* that He might present
it to Himself a glorious Church, not having spot,
or wrinkle, or any such thing; but that it should
be holy and without blemish." And Jesus says to
His disciples, "Now are ye clean through the

Word." So we are to be born again by the Word
of God, brought home to our hearts and consciences by the Holy Spirit.

Here are two men sitting side by side as a
preacher, proclaiming the gospel of God, perhaps
quotes some such verse of Scripture as, "This is
a faithful saying, and worthy of all acceptation,
that Christ Jesus came into the world to save
sinners; of whom I am chief." One man pays no
attention; the other man looks up and says,
"What! He came to save sinners! I am a sinner. I will trust Him." What led him to do
that? The Holy Spirit using the Word as the
means of his second birth. "Except a man be
born of water and of the Spirit, he cannot enter
into the kingdom of God." The Lord makes it very
clear that there is a great distinction between
the flesh and Spirit. "That which is born of the
flesh is flesh, and that which is born of the Spirit
is spirit." You can do anything you like with
the flesh, but it does not turn it into spirit. If
you baptize it, it is baptized flesh. If you make
it religious, it is religious flesh. Flesh remains
flesh to the very end. "That which is born of the
flesh is flesh, and that which is born of the Spirit
is spirit. Marvel not that I said unto thee, Ye
must be born again." Nicodemus said, "How can
these things be?" The Lord explains that there
are mysteries in nature that we cannot under-

stand. "The wind bloweth where it listeth, and
thou hearest the sound thereof, but canst not tell
whence it cometh, and whither it goeth: so is
every one that is born of the Spirit." You cannot see the wind, but you recognize its power.
You cannot see the Holy Spirit, but you recognize
His power. He is invisible, but He makes His
presence felt in a mighty way as He convicts and
regenerates sinful men. He changes men completely. You recognize the power, although you
do not see it actually working. You see a vain
worldly woman, and suddenly she becomes a quiet
woman of prayer. You see a wicked, godless man
changed into a saint. That is the work of the
Holy Spirit. You do not see the Spirit, but you
see the power manifest in the life.

Nicodemus is still perplexed and says, "How
can these things be?" Jesus says, "Art thou a
master of Israel, and knowest not these things?"
He should have known about the new birth. He
had the Bible. In Isaiah 44: 3 we find these
words: "For I will pour water upon him that is
thirsty, and floods upon the dry ground: I will
pour My Spirit upon thy seed, and My blessing
upon thine offspring." What is this? Why, God
is saying, "By the water of My Word and by the
power of My Spirit I am going to work the miracle of the new birth."

In Ezekiel 36: 25 we have the same thing:

"Then will I sprinkle clean water upon you, and ye shall be clean: from all your filthiness, and from all your idols will I cleanse you." There you have it again, "Born of water and of the Spirit." "Why," He says, "Nicodemus, you are a master in Israel and you are surprised when I speak of being born of water and the Spirit! You should have known this." "If I have told you earthly things, and ye believe not, how shall ye believe, if I tell you of heavenly things?" What does He mean by this? Well, these earthly things were spoken of in the Old Testament. It was always necessary to be born again in order to come into God's kingdom. This kingdom was heaven's rule on earth. But Jesus knew that that earthly kingdom was, for the time being, set aside. He said, "I have other secrets, but you will not understand them, you do not even understand earthly things." I think the Lord meant that Nicodemus was not ready for a revelation of the heavenly kingdom, because he had not apprehended the truth of the earthly things.

"And no man hath ascended up to heaven, but He that came down from heaven, even the Son of Man which is in heaven." Let me say here, and I frankly say so, I do not know whether Jesus said that, or whether John, the apostle, wrote it as inspired of the Holy Ghost. If the text were written as ordinary literature, we might have a

quotation-mark at the end of verse 12, and then
verse 13 might come in as a parenthesis. I do
not know whether that is so or not. It may be
that Jesus said this, or it may be that John put
it in to explain a mystery. What is the mystery?
No one has ever ascended to heaven of his voli-
tion. Enoch was caught up; Elijah went up in
a whirlwind. If these words were spoken by the
Lord Jesus, He was looking into the future when
He should ascend. If they were written by John,
then he had in mind the ascension. But the wonder of it is this, that He who came down from
heaven and had the power to ascend into heaven,
was at all times the Son of Man in heaven, for He
was omnipresent.

In verse 14 we have our Lord's answer to Nicodemus' questions. He refers him to an incident
that occurred long years before in the wilderness,
and He says, "And as Moses lifted up the serpent
in the wilderness, even so must the Son of Man
be lifted up." That is your answer, Nicodemus.
It is as though Jesus said, "I am going to the
cross, and there on that cross I will become the
antitype of that brass serpent. There I will be
made sin in order that sinners may become the
righteousness of God through faith in Me." In
the wilderness it was the serpents that afflicted
the people. The poison of these dreadful creatures was in the blood of the dying Israelites.

The remedy was a serpent of brass uplifted, and all who looked to it were healed. It was sin that caused the trouble for humanity. The serpent was a type of Satan and sin. But what took place on the cross? The sinless One was made sin for us. He is the antitype of that brazen serpent. That serpent lifted up on the pole had no poison in it. It had never done anybody any harm. It was a picture of the great sin-offering. When they looked to it they were healed. The Lord Jesus Christ had no sin in Him, but in grace He took the sinner's place, and when people look to Him in faith they are born again; they have eternal life. Have you looked to Him? Have we all looked to Him? All who believe in Him shall never die, but have life eternal.

THE HEART OF THE GOSPEL

✓ ✓ ✓

"For God so loved the world, that He gave His only begotten Son, that whosoever believeth in Him should not perish, but have everlasting life. For God sent not His Son into the world to condemn the world; but that the world through Him might be saved. He that believeth on Him is not condemned: but he that believeth not is condemned already, because he hath not believed in the name of the only begotten Son of God. And this is the condemnation, that light is come into the world, and men loved darkness rather than light, because their deeds were evil. For every one that doeth evil hateth the light, neither cometh to the light, lest his deeds should be reproved. But he that doeth truth cometh to the light, that his deeds may be made manifest, that they are wrought in God" (John 3: 16-21).

✓ ✓ ✓

MARTIN LUTHER called this sixteenth verse the "Miniature Gospel," because there is a sense in which the whole story of the Bible is told out in it. "For God so loved the world, that He gave His only begotten Son, that whosoever believeth in Him should not perish, but have everlasting life." The verse negatives the idea that a great many persons seem to have; that God is represented in Scriptures as a stern, angry Judge waiting to destroy men because of their sins, but that Jesus Christ, in some way or other, has made it possible for God to come out in love to sinners; in other words, that Christ loved us enough to die for us and, having atoned for our sins, God can now love us and be merciful to us. But that is an utter perversion of the gospel. Jesus Christ did not die to enable God to love sinners, but "God so loved the world, that He gave His only begotten Son." This same precious truth is set forth in similar words in the fourth chapter of the First Epistle of John, "In this was manifested the love of God toward us, because that God sent His only begotten Son into the world, that we might live through Him. Herein is love, not that we loved God, but that He loved us, and sent His Son to be the propitiation for our sins." So the coming to this world of our Lord Jesus Christ and His going to the cross, there to settle the sin question and thus meet every claim of the divine righteousness against the sinner, is the proof of the infinite love of God toward a world of guilty men. How we ought to thank and praise Him that He gave His Son for our redemption! "God commendeth His love toward us, in that, while we were yet sinners, Christ died for us." It could not be otherwise, because He is love. We are taught that in 1 John 4: 8, 16. "God is love." That is His very nature. We can say that God is gracious, but we cannot say that God is grace. We can say that God is compassionate, but we cannot say that God is compassion. God is kind, but God is not kindness. But we can say, God is love. That is His nature, and love had to manifest itself, and although men had forfeited every claim that they might have upon God, still He loved us and sent His only Son to become the propitiation for our sins—"God so loved the world that He gave His only begotten Son, that whosoever believeth in Him should not perish, but have everlasting life."

Our Lord Jesus Christ is spoken of five times as the "only begotten" in the New Testament: twice in the first chapter of this Gospel. In verse fourteen we read, "The Word was made flesh, and dwelt among us, (and we beheld His glory, the glory as of the only begotten of the Father,) full of grace and truth." Also in verse eighteen, "No man hath seen God at any time; the only begotten Son, which is the bosom of the Father, He hath declared Him." Then here is this sixteenth verse of the third chapter, "God so loved . . . that He gave His only begotten . . ." Again in verse eighteen, "He that believeth not is condemned already, because he hath not believed in the name of the only begotten Son of God." The only other place where this term is used is in 1 John 4: 9, "God sent His only begotten Son into the world, that we might live through Him." It is a singular fact, and shows how wonderfully Scripture is constructed, that that term is not only used five times in the New Testament, but He is also called the "first begotten" or "the first born" exactly five times in the same book.

Now "only begotten" refers to His eternal Sonship. The term, "the first begotten," tells what He became, in grace, as Man, for our redemption. When He came into the world God owned that blessed Man as His first begotten, saying, "Thou art My beloved Son, this day have I begotten Thee." The term "only begotten" does not carry in it any thought of generation, but that of uniqueness—Son by special relationship. The word is used in connection with Isaac. We read that Abraham "offered up his only begotten." Now Isaac was not his only son. Ishmael was born some years before Isaac, so in the sense of generation you would not speak of Isaac as the only begotten son. He is called the "only begotten" because he was born in a miraculous manner, when it seemed impossible that Abraham and Sarah could ever be the parents of a child. In the Spanish translation we read that "God so loved the world that He gave His unique Son;" that is, our Lord Jesus Christ is the Son of God in a sense that no one else can ever be the Son of God—His eternal Son—His unique Son. Oh, how dear to the heart of the Father! And when God gave Him, He not only became incarnate to bear hardship and weariness and thirst and hunger, but God gave Him up to the death of the cross that there He might be the propitiation for our sins. Could there be any greater manifestation of divine love than this?

You remember the story of the little girl in Martin Luther's day, when the first edition of the Bible came out. She had a terrible fear of God. God had been presented in such a way that it filled her heart with dread when she thought of Him. She brooded over the awfulness of the character of God and of some day having to meet this angry Judge. But one day she came running to her mother, holding a scrap of paper in her hand. She cried out, "Mother! mother! I am not afraid of God any more." Her mother said, "Why are you not?" "Why, look, mother," she said, "this bit of paper I found in the print shop, and it is torn out of the Bible." It was so torn as to be almost illegible except about two lines. On the one line it said, "God so loved," and on the other line it said, "that He gave." "See, mother," she said, "that makes it all right." Her mother read it and said, "God so loved that He gave." "But," she said, "it does not say what He gave." "Oh, mother," exclaimed the child, "if He loved us enough to give anything, it is all right." Then the mother said, "But, let me tell you what He gave." She read, "God so loved the world, that He gave His only begotten Son, that whosoever believeth in Him should not perish, but have everlasting life." Then she told how we can have peace and eternal life through trusting Him.

Am I speaking to anyone today who dreads the thought of meeting God? Do you think of your sins and say with David of old, "I remembered God and was troubled"? Let me call your attention to this word: The love of God has been manifest in Christ. If you will but come as a needy sinner He will wash your sins away. "But," you say, "how can I be sure that it is for me? I can understand that God could love some people. I can understand how He can invite certain ones to trust Him. Their lives have been so much better than mine, but I cannot believe that this salvation is for me." Well, what else can you make from that word, "whosoever"? "God so loved . . . that He gave . . . that whosoever believeth in Him should not perish, but have everlasting life." He could not find another more all-embracing word than that. It takes you in. It takes me in. You have many another "whosoever" in the Bible. There is a "whosoever" of judgment: "Whosoever was not found written in the book of life was cast into the lake of fire." "Whosoever" there includes all who did not come to God while He waited, in grace, to save. If they had recognized that they were included in the

"Whosoever" of John 3:16, they would not be found in that of Rev. 20:15.

Somebody wrote me the other day and said, "A man has come to our community who is preaching a limited atonement. He says it is a wonderful truth that has been only recently revealed to him." Well, I could only write back that the term "limited atonement" has an uncanny sound to me. I do not read anything like that in my Bible. I read that "He tasted death for every man." I read that "He is the propitiation for our sins, and not for our sins only, but for the whole world." 1 read that "All we like sheep have gone astray; we have turned every one to his own way; and the Lord hath laid on Him the iniquity of us all." And here I read that "Whosoever believeth in Him should not perish, but have everlasting life." I say to you, as I said to the writer of that letter, that there is enough value in the atoning work of the Lord Jesus Christ to save every member of the human race, if they would but repent and turn to God; and then if they were all saved, there still remains value enough to save the members of a million worlds like this, if they are lost in sin and needing a Saviour. Yes, the sacrifice of Christ is an infinite sacrifice. Do not let the enemy of your soul tell you there is no hope for you. Do not let him tell you you have sinned away your day of grace; that you have gone so far that God is no longer merciful. There is life abundant for you if you will but look up into the face of the One who died on Calvary's cross and trust Him for yourself. Let me repeat it again, "Whosoever believeth in Him should not perish, but have everlasting life."

"Whosoever believeth." What is it to believe? It is to trust in Him; to confide in Him; to commit yourself and your affairs to Him. He is saying to you, poor needy sinner, "You cannot save yourself. All your efforts to redeem yourself can only end in failure, but I have given My Son to die for you. Trust in Him. Confide in Him!" "Whosoever believeth in Him should not perish."

A lady was reading her Greek Testament one day. She was studying the Greek language and she liked to read in the Greek Testament. She had no assurance of salvation. While pondering over these words, "whosoever believeth," she said to herself as she looked at the Greek word for *believeth*, "I saw this a few verses back." She went back in the chapter, and then back into the last verse of chapter two, and she read, "Many believed in His name when they saw the miracles which He did. But Jesus did not commit Himself unto them, because He knew all men." "Oh," she said, "there it is!" "Jesus did not commit Himself unto them," and she stopped and thought a moment, and light from heaven flashed into her soul. She saw that to believe in Jesus was to commit herself unto Jesus. Have you done that? Have you said,

> "Jesus, I will trust Thee, trust Thee with my soul,
> Weary, worn and helpless, Thou canst make me whole.
> There is none in heaven, or on earth like Thee;
> Thou hast died for sinners; therefore, Lord, for me."

Now, "whosoever believeth in Him should not perish." As you turn the pages of Holy Scripture you get a marked picture of those who refused this grace. To perish means to go out into the darkness; to be forever under judgment; to exist in awful torment. He wants to save you from that. "Whosoever believeth in Him should not perish, but have everlasting life."

"Have," that suggests present possession. He does not say, "*hope* to have everlasting life." You will have everlasting life right here and now when you believe in Jesus, when you trust Him. Somebody pondered about this one day and then he looked up and said, "God loved—God gave—I believe—and I have—everlasting life." Everlasting life, remember, is far more than life throughout eternity. It is far more than endless existence. It is the very life of God communicated to the soul in order that we may enjoy fellowship with Him. "This is life eternal, that they might know Thee, the only true God, and Jesus Christ, whom Thou hast sent. '

In verse 17, as though to encourage the guiltiest to come to Him, He says, "For God sent not His Son into the world to condemn the world; but that the world through Him might be saved."

I remember, years ago, a dear old man behind the counter in a big department store in Los Angeles, where I worked as a lad. The old man was very kind to me. He saw that I was very green and knew not what was expected of me. He took me under his wing and cared for me. I soon got interested in finding out whether he was saved or not. My dear mother was never with anybody very long before she asked them the question, "Are you saved? Are you born again?" I became so used to hearing her ask that question that I thought I ought to ask it of people too. I went to him one day and said, "Mr. Walsh, are you saved?" He looked at me and said, "My dear boy, no one will ever know that until the day of judgment." "Oh," I replied, "there must be some mistake; my mother knows she is saved." "Well, she has made a mistake," he said; "for no one can know that." "But the Bible says, 'He that believeth on Him . . . hath everlasting life.' " "Oh, well," he said, "we can't be sure down here unless we become great saints; but we must just do the best we can and pray to the Lord and the blessed Virgin and the saints to help, and hope that in the day of judgment it may turn out well and we will be saved." "But," I said, "why do you pray to the blessed Virgin? Why not go direct to Jesus?" "My dear boy, the Lord is so great and mighty and holy that it is not befitting that a poor sinner such as I should go to Him, and there is no other who has such influence as His mother." I did not know how to answer him then. But as I studied my Bible through the years, I could see what the answer was. Jesus unapproachable! Jesus hard to be contacted! Why, it was said of Him, "This Man receiveth sinners," and though high in heavenly glory, He still says to sinners, "Come unto Me all ye that labor and are heavy laden." Yes, you can go directly to Him and when you trust Him He gives you eternal life. He did not come to condemn the world. He came with a heart of love to win poor sinners to Himself.

And then the eighteenth verse is so plain and simple. Oh, if you are an anxious soul and seeking light, remember that these are the very words of the living God, "He that believeth on Him is not condemned: but he that believeth not is condemned already, because he hath not believed in the name of the only begotten Son of God." Now, do you see this? There are just two classes of people in that verse. All men in the world who have heard the message are divided into these two classes. What are they? First, "He that believeth." There are those who believe in Jesus. They stand by themselves. Now the other class, "He that believeth not." Every person who has ever heard of Jesus is in one of those two classes. You are either among those who believe in Jesus or among those who do not believe. It is not a question of believing *about* Him; it is a question of believing *in* Him. It is not holding mental conceptions about Him, mere facts of history; but it is trusting Him, committing yourself to Him. Those who trust Him and those who do not trust Him—in which of the two groups do you find yourself? "He that believeth in Him:" are you there? "He that believeth not:" are you there? Oh, if you are, you should be in a hurry to get out of that group into the other, and you pass out of the one and into the other by trusting in Jesus.

Are you in the first group? "He that believeth in Him is not condemned." Do you believe that? Jesus said that. "He that believeth in Him is not condemned."

I was in Kilmarnock three years ago and gave an address one night in the Grant Hall, and a number of people had come into the inquiry room and I went in afterwards to see how they were getting along. A minister called me over and said, "Will you have a word with this lad?" I sat down beside him and said, "What is the trouble?" He looked up and said, "I canna see it. I canna see it. I am so burdened, and canna find deliverance." I said, "Have you been brought up in a Christian home?" He told me he had. "Do you know the way of salvation?" He answered, "Well, in a way, I do; but I canna see it." I said, "Let me show you something." First I prayed with him and asked God, by the Holy Spirit, to open his heart. Then I pointed him to this verse and said, "Do you see those two classes of people? What is the first class? What is the second class? He answered clearly. "Now," I said, "which class are you in?" Then he looked at me and said, "Why, I am in the first class. I do believe in Him, but it is all dark. I canna see." "Now look again," said I. "What does it say about the first class?" He did look again and I could see the cloud lift, and he turned to me and exclaimed, "Man, I see it! I am not condemned." I asked, "How do you know?" He replied, "God said so." The minister said, "Well, lad, are you now willing to go home and tell your parents? Tomorrow when you go to work, will you be willing to tell your mates?" "Oh," he said, "I can hardly wait to get there."

Now, suppose you are in the other group. Listen, "He that believeth not is condemned already." You do not need to wait till the day of judgment to find that out. Condemned! Why? Because you have been dishonest? Because you have lied? Because you have been unclean and unholy? Is it that? That is not what it says *here*. What does it say? "He that *believeth not* is condemned already because he hath not believed in the name of the only begotten Son of God." That is the condemnation. All those sins you have been guilty of, Christ took into account when He died. "He was wounded for our transgressions, He was bruised for our iniquities: the chastisement of our peace was upon Him; and with His stripes we are healed." So, if you are condemned, it is not simply because of the many sins you have committed through your lifetime. It is because of spurning the revelation of the Saviour that God has provided. If you turn away from God and continue rejecting Jesus, you are committing the worst sin there is. He came, a light, into the world to lighten the darkness. If you turn away from Him, you are responsible for the darkness in which you will live and die.

"And this is the condemnation, that light is come into the world, and men loved darkness rather than light, because their deeds were evil." Is it not strange that men would rather continue in darkness than turn to Him, who is the light of life, and find deliverance. "For every one that doeth evil hateth the light, neither cometh to the light, lest his deeds should be reproved. But he that doeth truth (*i.e.,* he that is absolutely honest with God) cometh to the light, that his deeds may be made manifest, that they are wrought in God." Are you going to turn away from the light today or are you coming into the light? Will you trust the blessed One who is the light of the world, and thus rejoice in the salvation which He so freely offers you?

THE CLOSING TESTIMONY OF JOHN THE BAPTIST

✟ ✟ ✟

"After these things came Jesus and His disciples into the land of Judea; and there He tarried with them, and baptized. And John also was baptizing in Ænon near to Salim, because there was much water there: and they came, and were baptized. For John was not yet cast into prison. Then there arose a question between some of John's disciples and the Jews about purifying. And they came unto John, and said unto him, Rabbi, He that was with thee beyond Jordan, to whom thou barest witness, behold, the same baptizeth, and all men come to Him. John answered and said, A man can receive nothing, except it be given him from heaven. Ye yourselves bear me witness, that I said, I am not the Christ, but that I am sent before Him. He that hath the bride is the bridegroom: but the friend of the bridegroom, which standeth and heareth him, rejoiceth greatly because of the bridegroom's voice: this my joy therefore is fulfilled. He must increase, but I must decrease. He that cometh from above is above all: he that is of the earth is earthly, and speaketh of the earth: He that cometh from heaven is above all. And what He hath seen and heard, that He testifieth; and no man receiveth His testimony. He that hath received His testimony hath set to his seal that God is true. For He whom God hath sent speaketh the words of God; for God giveth not the Spirit by measure unto Him. The Father loveth the Son, and hath given all things into His hand. He that believeth on the Son, hath everlasting life: and he that believeth not the Son shall not see life; but the wrath of God abideth on him" (John 3 : 22-36).

"A FTER these things"—that is, after our Lord's ministry in the city of Jerusalem and His interview with Nicodemus, which we have considered already—"Jesus came, and His disciples, into the land of Judea." He went out of the city of Jerusalem into the surrounding country preaching and teaching. "There He tarried with them and baptized." Actually, we know from the fourth chapter, that it was not the Lord Himself who ministered the rite of baptism; but as He preached and the people believed His message, His disciples baptized them at His bidding.

Now, strikingly enough, not very far away, the forerunner of the Lord Jesus Christ was still continuing his ministry. We read that "John also was baptizing in Ænon near to Salim, because there was much water there, and they came and were baptized." Ænon is in the Jordan Valley about twenty miles north of where the Lord Jesus was at this time, and many people flocked there to hear John as he gave his great message of repentance with the view to the forgiveness of sin. He had already pointed out the Lord Jesus as the "Lamb of God that taketh away the sin of the world." The Saviour had gone away into the wilderness for forty days of fasting. There He had been tempted. He had returned to Jerusalem and begun His public testimony

there, rejected by most, but Nicodemus was one
honest soul who was interested in His message.
And now the Lord's own ministry was widening,
broadening out. But John continued preaching
at the same time, for he "was not yet cast into
prison."

Very shortly after this his arrest took place.
You remember the occasion of it. Herod had
been very much interested in John, sent for him
on a number of occasions, and was glad to hear
him preach. But Herod was guilty of a very
grave offence, both against the laws of God and
man: he was living in an adulterous relationship
with his own brother Philip's wife, Herodias.
Because of his place of power, very few dared to
criticize him, but John the Baptist stood before
him and fearlessly declared, "It is not lawful for
thee to have her." As long as he preached repentance in a general way, as long as he preached
forgiveness of sins in a manner that would apply
to everybody, Herod listened to him; but when
John made it as personal as that, and pointed out
his own sin and expressed the divine disapproval
of his iniquity, then Herod's indignation was
stirred and the Baptist was placed under arrest.
And you know that later on, in order to satisfy
the hatred of Herodias, a woman scorned, John
was put to death. But this had not yet taken
place, and he was preaching to multitudes and

baptizing those who gave evidence of repentance. The two ministries were going on at the same time, and evidently the Jews were surprised at this, for "there arose a question between some of John's disciples and the Jews about purifying." They saw in baptism a symbol of purification. Baptism does not actually cleanse the soul, but it is a symbol of the washing away of sin. And "so they came unto John and said unto him, Rabbi, He that was with thee beyond Jordan, to whom thou barest witness, behold, the same baptizeth and all men come to Him." As much as to say, "John, your star is sinking, His star is now in the ascendant. It will not be long until all will be going to Him and no one will be gathering to hear you."

How beautiful John's answer was! Not a bit of pride in this man, not a bit of self-assertiveness! He was not concerned about gathering disciples about himself. "John answered and said, A man can receive nothing except it be given him from heaven. Ye yourselves bare me witness that I said, I am not the Christ, but that I am sent before Him." We might paraphrase it like this: "I did not come to draw your attention to me. I only came as the forerunner of the promised anointed One. When you questioned me, 'Art thou that prophet that shall come into the world, of whom Moses spake?' I told you I

am not. When you inquired, 'Who art thou then
and why do you baptize?' I told you plainly. I
said, 'I am simply the voice of one crying in the
wilderness, Prepare ye the way of the Lord, make
His path straight.' It is honor enough for me to
herald the coming of God's Deliverer, the One
who is to bring redemption to Israel and to the
world."

And then he uses a very beautiful figure in
verse 29. He said, "He that hath the bride is
the bridegroom, but the friend of the bridegroom,
which standeth and heareth Him, rejoiceth greatly because of the bridegroom's voice. This my
joy, therefore, is fulfilled." In other words, John
refers to something they were all familiar with.
At a wedding, the bride is the one interested in
her bridegroom, and the bridegroom's joy is
found in his bride. But they had then, as we
have today, the "best man," as we call him, the
friend of the bridegroom. And the friend of the
bridegroom found his delight in the bridegroom's
joy. And so John says, "I am just like that. I
am the bridegroom's friend. The Lord Jesus
Christ Himself is the bridegroom; the bride belongs to Him, not to me. I rejoice in His gladness. I do not feel slighted, I do not feel set to
one side because I cannot claim the love and
allegiance of the bride."

Now John, of course, spoke from a Jewish

standpoint. According to the Old Testament, Israel was the bride, Jehovah was the bridegroom. Jehovah had become incarnate in the Person of the Lord Jesus Christ. John said, "I am simply here to announce His coming, and the bride belongs to Him." But God had other thoughts in mind that were not then made clear. Later on He showed that because of Israel's attitude toward His blessed Son they would be set to one side during a long period to be known as the "Times of the Gentiles;" and during this period God, by the Holy Spirit, is taking out a people for His Name, for the name of the Lord Jesus, and this people He designates as the Bride of the Lamb.

We have a heavenly Bride in the 5th chapter of the Epistle to the Ephesians, where the apostle sets forth the responsibilities of husband and wife in the marriage relationship. He directs our attention to that which took place at the very beginning, when God gave our first parents each to the other, and he says, "He that made them in the beginning said, 'For this cause shall a man leave his father and mother and shall be joined unto his wife, and they two shall be one flesh.'" And immediately he adds, "This is a great mystery, but I speak concerning Christ and the Church." He shows us that the marriage relationship is designed of God to picture the mystical union of Christ and the Church. The Church, therefore, is the "Bride, the Lamb's wife." We see her in the 19th chapter of the book of Revelation at the marriage supper of the Lamb. There we read, "His Bride hath made herself ready." You remember in that chapter we have two different groups at the marriage supper. We have the bridal company, and then we have the friends of the Bridegroom, just as John expressed himself here. We read, "Blessed are they that are called to the marriage supper of the Lamb." The Bride is not called to the marriage supper of the Lamb! How often we have a wedding and perhaps after the wedding a reception. Well, the friends who attend the reception are invited there. They receive invitations to be present; they are intimate friends of the bridegroom and the bride. But the bride does not receive an invitation; she is there by virtue of her character as bride. It is her wedding and it is her reception. She does not need to be called to the marriage supper. And so as we look at that wonderful picture in Revelation, we see the Bride herself (that is, the Church of the firstborn) united in that day to the Bridegroom, our Lord Jesus Christ. And then we see all the Old Testament saints of the Great Tribulation, who have been murdered under the Beast and the antichrist, but are raised at the close of that time of trouble, and they are all there, wedding guests, to rejoice in the joy of the Bridegroom and the Bride. And that is why our Lord Jesus said of those that are born of women, "There is none greater than John the Baptist, but he that is least in the kingdom of heaven is greater than he." John was the porter at the door of the kingdom, but he did not live to enter in himself. He did not become a member of the Church of the living God, though he heralded the coming of the One who is now the head of that Church. You say, "Do you mean to say that John was not a Christian?" Let us be careful to remember what the word "Christian" means. The word is not synonymous with "child of God." Old Testament saints were all saved, they were all God's children, but they were not Christians. The disciples were first called Christians in the new dispensation. A Christian is one united now to Christ in glory, and such are the ones who form the Bride of the Lamb.

So John took a subordinate place and rejoiced because of the Bridegroom's joy, and again he declared, as on a previous occasion, "He must increase, but I must decrease." The Apostle Paul expressed exactly the same thing when, in the first chapter of the epistle to the Philippians, he said that his great joy was that "Christ may be magnified in my body, whether by life or by death. For me to live is Christ and to die is

gain." I wonder if we, as children of God, today
can enter into this? Are we content to serve
without personal recognition, or are we ambitious
to be counted somebody or something in a world
that has rejected our Lord Jesus Christ? Are
we seeking places of power and authority, or
recognition even in the Church of God itself?
That is to deny the spirit that was seen in John
the Baptist and in the Apostle Paul. Their one
earnest desire was to make much of Christ, and
they themselves were willing to be lost sight of.
That comes out so beautifully in the second chapter of the epistle to the Philippians, where Saint
Paul, writing to these dear saints in that church,
says, "Yea, and if I be offered upon the sacrifice
and service of your faith, I joy and rejoice with
you all."

That word translated "offered" is really
"poured out" in the Greek. "Yea, if I be poured
out upon the sacrifice and service of your faith,
I joy and rejoice with you all." He is referring
to the burnt-offering. In Old Testament times,
whenever they presented a burnt-offering before
the Lord, all the parts of the victim were washed
and then placed upon the fire, and they were all
burnt as a sacrifice and went up before God, typi-
fying the offering up of His own blessed Son.
But just before the priest completed his part of
the service, he took a flagon of wine (that was

called a "drink-offering") and poured the wine all over the burnt-offering. Now that drink-offering pictured our Lord Jesus pouring out His soul unto death on our behalf. But, you see, if the worshippers were gathered about, they could see the burnt-offering on the altar, but if the wine had been poured out over it, they could not see that drink-offering. The wine was immediately lost sight of and only the burnt-offering remained. And Paul said, "I am willing," as he writes to these Philippians, "that your sacrifice and service should have, as it were, the place of the burnt-offering and that I, just like the drink-offering, should be poured out over the offering that you make." In other words, "I am willing to do my work, to serve the Lord Christ in my day and generation and then be lost sight of. I am willing that others shall get the glory, if there is any, for the work that is done." What a wonderful spirit that is! How we need to pray that we may learn more of the meekness and gentleness of Christ, the spirit that says, "Never mind me. If Christ is glorified, that is all I am concerned about. I do not want them to think of me. I do not want them to make anything of me."

When William Carey was dying, he turned to a friend and said, "When I am gone, don't talk about William Carey; talk about William Carey's

Saviour. I desire that Christ alone might be magnified." And so with John here: "He must increase, but I must decrease."

And then what a testimony he gives us! I often say I am afraid that many of us fail to realize how fully John the Baptist entered into the blessed Truth that came by Jesus Christ. We imagine sometimes that he had very little light, very little understanding of the Person of the Lord and of the full truth of redemption. But let us not forget, it was he who exclaimed, "Behold the Lamb of God that taketh away the sin of the world." It was he who said, "I saw and bare witness that this is the Son of God." And here in verse 31, we have this wonderful homage paid to the blessed Lord by John. He says, "He that cometh from above is above all." John knew that He came from above; John knew He did not begin to live when He was born of the blessed Virgin Mary; and John knew of His pre-existence with the Father before ever the world was. He says, "He that cometh from above is above all; he that is of the earth is earthly and speaketh of the earth." When men speak in a spirit of pride and vanity and rivalry they are speaking as of the earth. That kind of thing belongs to the earth and not to heaven.

"He that cometh from above is above all, and what He hath seen and heard, that He testifieth;

and no man receiveth His testimony." That is, the natural man, unaided by divine grace, never receives the testimony of God. That is why we are told in the third chapter of the epistle to the Romans, "They are all gone out of the way. They are together become unprofitable; there is none that doeth good, no not one. There is none that seeketh after God." If you ever find a soul seeking after God, you may know it is because the Spirit of God is working in that heart. A natural man goes his own way; he is not interested in divine things. And this, by the way, might help some who are troubled and concerned.

I have often had people come to me and say, "Oh, I do long for the assurance of my salvation. I have come to Christ, I have asked God to save me. I do believe that Jesus died for me. But I am so miserable about my sins. I have no assurance, I have no peace, I have no realization that God has accepted me." I say to people like that, "Don't you fear, dear friend; no natural man seeks after God. The fact that you are going through all these exercises is, in itself, a proof of your regeneration." Take a corpse lying here and put five hundredweight of lead upon the breast of that corpse. There is not a sign of distress. Why? Because the man is dead. But if you put that five hundredweight upon a living man, what then do you have? Groans of anguish, crying for deliverance. Why? Because there is life there. That is why people are so troubled about their sins. Because there is life there, divine life. God has already begun to work. Therefore, if that is your case, thank God that His Spirit has begun to work in your soul, and be persuaded that "He that hath begun a good work in you will perform it unto the day of Jesus Christ." Now take God at His word, believe what He has said about His blessed Son, and receive the peace that is rightfully yours. No natural man receives the testimony of God, but "He that hath received His testimony hath set to his seal that God is true." That is faith—nothing more nor less than believing that God means what He says.

So often we put a scripture before troubled souls and say, "Now, can't you believe this?" And they look up and say, "Well, I am trying to believe." Take a passage like this: "He came unto His own and His own received Him not; but to as many as received Him, to them gave He power to become the sons of God, even to them that believe on His name." "Don't you want to know Jesus? Are you seeking Christ? Are you ready to receive Him? Very well, what does it say— 'As many as received Him, to them gave He power to become the children of God.' Do you receive Him?" And the answer comes, "Yes, yes;

I believe I do." "Well, then, are you a child
of God?" "I don't know, I don't think I am. I
don't feel it. I am afraid to say that." Don't
you see what the trouble is? They are not taking
God at His word. Sometimes we say to them,
"Well, don't you see, dear friend? You must
have faith, you must believe what God has said."
And they look at you with the most amazing
effrontery and say, "Well, I am trying to believe."
What an insult to God! Trying to believe whom?
It is God who has spoken and you say, I am trying to believe. Why, I am only a frail, mortal
man, but if I told you something concerning some
place where I have been and you never have seen,
and you looked at me and said, "That is very
interesting, and I am trying to believe," I would
say, "Sir, you insult me. Do you think I am lying
to you? What do you mean by saying you are
trying to believe? I am telling the truth and I
expect you to believe my testimony." God has
spoken in His Word and He expects man to receive His testimony. That is all there is to faith.
It is believing what God has said. "If we receive
the witness of man (and we do), the witness of
God is greater. This is the witness of God, that
which He has testified concerning His Son." We
believe it, and believing it, we set to our seal that
God is true. "For He whom God hath sent—that
is, our Lord Jesus Christ—speaketh the words

of God, for God giveth not the Spirit by measure unto Him." The Spirit in all His fulness dwells in Christ, and the words that He spake were the words of God. "The Father loveth the Son and hath given all things into His hand." God has decreed that the Lord Jesus shall reign as Head of this universe, because, after all, He was its Creator. It was the Word Himself that brought all things into being and they have been created both by Him and for Him.

And now comes the greatest testimony of this section. And what a tremendous testimony it is! I am not exactly sure whether John the Baptist spoke all of these words or whether some of them, perhaps from about verse 34, are inserted in the record by inspiration through the hand of the Apostle John himself. Just where the testimony of John the Baptist ends and the testimony of the writer of the Gospel begins, we cannot always tell. But, at any rate, if we take verse 36 as spoken by John the Baptist, it is a marvelous testimony, or if we take it as penned directly by the Apostle John under divine inspiration, still it comes to us as the very word of the living God.

We noticed that verse 18 divided all mankind who have heard the gospel into two groups. This does not take in the heathen who have never heard the gospel; they will be dealt with according to the light they have, and will be judged for their own sins. Here again we have two classes. It says first, "He that believeth on the Son hath everlasting life." That is one group. "He that believeth not the Son shall not see life, but the wrath of God abideth on him." That is the other.

Let us look at the first statement for a moment or two. Could anything be clearer? Do you want to be certain that you have eternal life? Then I challenge you thus: "Do you believe on the Son of God? Do you put your trust in the Lord Jesus Christ? Do you rest your soul upon Him and His finished work, that work accomplished on Calvary's cross for our redemption? Then listen to what God Himself says: "He that believeth on the Son hath everlasting life." Now do not say, "Well, but I do not feel any different." It does not say "He that feeleth," but "He that believeth on the Son hath everlasting life."

A friend of mine, years ago, preached on that very text. At the close of the meeting, as preachers sometimes do in smaller places, he went down to the door to greet the friends. A lady troubled about her soul came along, and he reached out his hand and said to her, "Well, how is it with you tonight? Are you saved?" She said, "Oh, I don't know, sir; I hope so." He said, "Well, let me show you this verse, 'He that believeth on the

Son hath everlasting life.' Do you believe on the Son?" "Oh, I do, sir, I do believe on Him with all my heart." "Well, then, have you everlasting life?" "I hope so; I hope I have." "Read the verse again." She read it—"He that believeth on the Son hath everlasting life." "Do you believe on the Son?" "I do." "Then, have you everlasting life?" "I certainly hope so. I do hope so." "Read it again, please." She read it again —"He that believeth on the Son hath everlasting life." "Do you believe on the Son?" "I do." "Have you everlasting life?" "I hope so." "Well," he said, "I see what the trouble is." She said, "What is the trouble?" "Why, when you were a girl, they spelled very differently to what they did when I was a boy." She said, "What do you mean? I am not so much older than you." He said, "When you were a girl h-a-t-h spelled *hope;* when I was a boy, h-a-t-h spelled *hath.*" She exclaimed, "Hath! 'He that believeth on the Son *hath* everlasting life.' Why, of course, I have it. Yes, I see it. I believe on the Son of God and God says I have everlasting life." And so she entered into peace.

Again, I come back to the text, "He that hath received His testimony hath set to his seal that God is true." A little boy said to his school-teacher, "Faith is believing God and asking no questions." It is just taking God at His word.

Look at the other side of that verse. It is a very solemn side to the Truth indeed. "He that believeth not the Son." The word rendered *believeth* is different here. It suggests rather *obedience* in the Greek. "He that obeyeth not the Son." The Son's command is to believe. They came to Jesus and said, "What is the work of God, that we may do it?" And He said, "The work of God is to believe in the Son that was sent." "He that obeyeth not the Son shall not see life, but the wrath of God abideth on him." Oh, the hopelessness of that! Oh, the horror of it! Oh, the pity of it!—that men should hear the gospel over and over again, and hear it and turn away, and should live on rejecting, and die refusing to believe on Christ, and go out into a hopeless eternity! To die without Christ! See how this one verse cuts out by the roots the twin errors of the annihilation of the wicked and the universal salvation of all men sometime, somewhere. Take the question of universalism first. Listen to what it says: "He that believeth not the Son shall not see life." There is no thought there of a further hope if a man dies rejecting Christ. If a man does not have Christ in this world, he will never see life. Jesus has said, "Except ye believe that I am He, ye shall die in your sins." And He adds, "Whither I go ye cannot come." "He that believeth not the Son shall not see life."

But, on the other hand, there are many who think, "Even if I do live and die rejecting Christ, death will be the end to it all. I shall be utterly annihilated. There will be nothing more to me, and therefore I will pass out of existence and be as though I had never been." But Scripture says, "He that obeyeth not the Son shall not see life, but the wrath of God abideth on him." Notice the tense, *abideth* on him. You cannot logically couple the thought of abiding wrath with extinction of being. And so this verse solemnly warns us that if we do not put our trust in Christ in this life, the wrath of God must abide upon us in eternity.

But in order that this might never be, Jesus has died. He has settled the sin question for all who believe. God has given the record of it in His Word. The Holy Ghost has come from heaven to bear witness to it. And if you and I believe, we may know we have everlasting life.

CHRIST AND THE SAMARITAN WOMAN

⁂ ⁂ ⁂

"When therefore the Lord knew how the Pharisees had heard that Jesus made and baptized more disciples than John (though Jesus Himself baptized not, but His disciples), He left Judæa, and departed again into Galilee. And He must needs go through Samaria. Then cometh He to a city of Samaria, which is called Sychar, near to the parcel of ground that Jacob gave to his son Joseph. Now Jacob's well was there. Jesus therefore, being wearied with His journey, sat thus on the well: and it was about the sixth hour. There cometh a woman of Samaria to draw water: Jesus saith unto her, Give Me to drink. (For His disciples were gone away unto the city to buy meat.) Then saith the woman of Samaria unto Him, How is it that Thou, being a Jew, askest drink of me, which am a woman of Samaria? for the Jews have no dealings with the Samaritans. Jesus answered and said unto her, If thou knewest the gift of God, and who it is that saith to thee, Give Me to drink; thou wouldest have asked of Him, and He would have given thee living water. The woman saith unto Him, Sir, Thou hast nothing to draw with, and the well is deep: from whence then hast Thou that living water? Art Thou greater than our father Jacob, which gave us the well, and drank thereof himself, and his children, and his cattle? Jesus answered and said unto her, Whosoever drinketh of this water shall thirst again: but whosoever drinketh of the water that I shall give him shall never thirst: but the water that I shall give him shall be in him a well of water springing up into everlasting life. The woman saith unto Him, Sir, give me this water, that I thirst not, neither come hither to draw. Jesus saith unto her, Go, call thy husband, and come hither. The woman answered and said, I have no husband. Jesus said unto her, Thou hast well said, I have no husband: for thou hast had five husbands, and he whom thou now hast is not thy husband: in that saidst thou truly. The woman saith unto him, Sir, I perceive that Thou art a prophet. Our fathers worshipped in this mountain; and ye say, that in Jerusalem is the place where men ought to worship. Jesus saith unto her, Woman, believe Me, the hour cometh, when ye shall neither in this mountain, nor yet at Jerusalem, worship the Father. Ye worship ye know not what: we know what we worship: for salvation is of the Jews. But the hour cometh, and now is, when the true worshippers shall worship the Father in spirit and in truth: for the Father seeketh such to worship Him. God is a Spirit: and they that worship Him must worship Him in spirit and in truth. The woman saith unto Him, I know that Messias cometh, which is called Christ: when He is come, He will tell us all things. Jesus saith unto her, I that speak unto thee am He" (John 4: 1-26).

✓　✓　✓

IN tracing out the life of our blessed Lord Jesus Christ, we find it of great interest to note the way He dealt with different souls whom He interviewed. A great many books have been written on personal work for Christ, but there is no book in the world that is more helpful on that line than this Gospel of John. There are so many different records of those with whom the Lord Jesus Christ had conversations that we get a marvelous unfolding of His wonderful wisdom in opening up the Word of God to needy souls. One of the loveliest is this interview with the Samaritan woman.

We are told that the Pharisees were making much of the fact that Jesus was baptizing and making disciples, and it was reported that His

followers were out-numbering those of John.
When He heard that, because He did not want
anything that looked like rivalry, He left Judea
almost immediately and went to Galilee. Actually,
we read that Jesus Himself did not baptize, but
left that to His disciples.

An orthodox Jew would cross the Jordan near
Jericho and make his way up through Perea, and
then cross back near the Sea of Galilee in the
north.   But the Lord Jesus Christ did not take
that route. A stern legalist would not go through
Samaria; but the Lord Jesus Christ took that
direct road because of the very fact that He was
anxious to meet these poor Samaritan sinners
that He might reveal the truth to them.   "He
must needs go through Samaria."   Long before
the creation of the world it had been settled in
the counsels of eternity that He was to meet a
poor, sinful, Samaritan woman that day.   He
could not forego that appointment. So He went
until He came near the city of Sychar and there
by Jacob's well He stopped, and we read, "Jesus
therefore, being wearied with His journey, sat
thus on the well: and it was about the sixth
hour." The time here is not the same as in the
Synoptic Gospels.   The sixth hour was high
noon. It was an unusual thing for people to go
out at the noon hour to draw water. But there
sat the Lord, waiting to meet a thirsty soul, and

we are told, "There cometh a woman of Samaria to draw water." I can visualize that scene. My wife and daughter and I sat on the curbing of that very well and we looked off to the city of Sychar and, farther away, to the city of Shechem, and it was so easy to imagine that woman coming down the road, her water-pot on her head, and Jesus waiting to meet her. He sat, wearied, at the well. He had become tired, seeking for sinners! What wondrous grace that He, the eternal God, should have so linked Himself with our humanity that He should know what pain and weariness and toil meant!

She knew that He was a Jew by the ribbon of blue that went around the border of His robe. At once all her being would be stirred with indignation. What business did He have sitting there on their well? She probably said to herself, "If he dares to say anything insulting to me, I will give him back as good as he gives." But oh, how surprised she must have been when He looked up very kindly and said, "Give Me to drink." She knew that the ordinary Jew would have dashed the cup to the ground even if she had offered it; and here was a Jew asking drink of her. But she said, "How is it that Thou, being a Jew, askest drink of me, which am a woman of Samaria?" And then John puts in a little word of explanation. I do not think she said these next words, but the Spirit of God put them in that we might understand, "For the Jews have no dealings with the Samaritans."

Note the answer of our blessed Lord: "If thou knewest the gift of God and who it is that saith to thee, Give Me to drink; thou wouldest have asked of Him, and He would have given thee living water." What a wonderful revelation concerning the gift of God! Do you know the gift of God? Do you know that salvation is the gift of God? Do you know that eternal life is a gift? Do you know that God is not a merchant-man seeking to bargain with people, but God is a Giver, offering everything freely? It is so hard for people to understand that, and so they have devised all kinds of ways and means whereby they hope to earn salvation and thus to win, at last, a place in God's heaven. My dear friend, the God of this Bible is too rich to sell His salvation to anyone, and if He put a price on it in any degree comparable with its value, you and I are altogether too poor to purchase it. But, thank God, it is a gift. "If thou knewest the gift of God." How do you receive a gift? Suppose you wanted a Bible and you came to me and I said, "Let me give you this one," and you put your hand in your pocket and said, "I only have twenty-five cents." "My dear friend," I would say, "I don't want your money. I am offering this to you as a gift." What would you do? You would take it, I trust, and go away saying, "This book was given to me as a gift." So it is with God's salvation; you cannot do anything to earn it. "For by grace are ye saved through faith; and that not of yourselves: it is the gift of God; not of works, lest any man should boast." Have you come to Him and received His gift? "If thou knewest the gift of God." But notice also the other word, "and *who* it is that saith to thee, Give Me to drink." How little she recognized who it was. Who was it? The Son of God. We read, "In the beginning was the Word, and the Word was with God, and the Word was God." "The Word became flesh and dwelt among us, and we beheld His glory, the glory as of the only begotten of the Father, full of grace and truth." There He was, God and Man in one blessed, glorious Person, but she did not understand that. She had no conception of who He was, and He, on His part, did not try to amaze and astound, but He simply opened up in a wonderful way His stores of grace. She looked at Him doubtfully and said, "Sir, Thou hast nothing to draw with, and the well is deep: from whence then hast Thou this living water?" The well, as it is today, is about 78 feet deep. I saw them letting a candle down into it and they dropped it until it had gone down 78 feet. And the woman said, "The

well is deep, and you have nothing to draw with."
"From whence then hast Thou that living
water?" She was thinking only of that natural
water. He was thinking of spiritual water. The
well is deeper by far than that well in Samaria.
It is as deep as the heart of God with its infinite
love and affection. The water that He would
give was to be drawn from the depths of God's
love itself. But she inquired, wonderingly, "Art
Thou greater than our father Jacob, which gave
us the well, and drank thereof himself, and his
children, and his cattle?" Jesus might have said
to her, "Greater than Jacob! My poor woman,
did you ever read in the first book of Moses the
story of your father Jacob, as you call him, how
one night he had sent his family and flocks across
the ford, and he was bowed in prayer alone,
when there came to him a mysterious Personality,
with whom Jacob struggled all night. Then the
unknown one said, "Let Me go, for the day
breaketh," and Jacob said, "I will not let
Thee go except Thou bless me." Jesus might
have said to the woman, "Do you remember that
story? Well, I am the One who met Jacob there
in the darkness and overcame his stubborn will."
But I am afraid that if He had told her that, she
would have shrunk from Him, thinking that He
was insane. Instead of alarming her, He sought
to reach her heart and conscience. Without re-

plying directly to her question, Jesus answered and said, "Whosoever drinketh of this water shall thirst again." How well she knew that! Had she not time after time attempted to quench her thirst from that well, only to thirst again? And that may be said of everything that this scene offers as a palliative for the longings of the human heart. You may try everything that the world can give, but you will be unsatisfied still. Oh, I wish I could persuade some needy soul to take these words home to his heart, "Whosoever drinketh of this water shall thirst again." No one has ever yet found satisfaction in the things of the world. They cannot satisfy a heart that has been created for eternity.

"Whosoever drinketh of this water shall thirst again: but whosoever drinketh of the water that I shall give him shall never thirst; but the water that I shall give him shall be in him a well of water springing up into everlasting life," or literally, "a fountain of water springing up into everlasting life." What does He mean by that? Those who receive the message of His grace, who believe the revelation that God has given of Christ in this Word, will be born anew, and this fountain of living water will spring up within and they will find a satisfaction that none have ever been able to find in the things of earth.

Well, the woman, listening, finds her heart going to Christ. She feels He means what He says, so she timidly asks, "Sir, give me this water, that I thirst not, neither come hither to draw." She has not understood anything yet but the natural. The spiritual is hidden from her still. But the Lord Jesus Christ has won her confidence and this is a great thing. When that has been won, there is something else needed, that is, to reach the conscience. So the Lord, assured that He has won her heart, undertakes to grapple with her conscience. He overlooks her remark and says, "Go, call thy husband, and come hither." I can imagine she dropped her head, and with the color mantling her face, exclaimed, "I have no husband." "Jesus said unto her, Thou hast well said, I have no husband: for thou hast had five hus-bands, and he whom thou now hast is not thy husband." He drives the truth of her guilty past and sinful present home to her soul. She stands there, greatly moved, and for a moment does not know what to say. Who is this that could put His finger upon the black spot in her life? He looks so kind and considerate, and yet He has done the very thing that has stirred her con-science to the very depth. She blurts out, "Sir, I perceive that Thou art a prophet." A prophet is one who speaks for God. She realizes that this Man, who has never met her before, yet knows all about her sin, who knows all the evil of her

life, He must be a God-sent prophet. It was as
though she exclaimed, "I perceive that I am a
sinner." "Our fathers worshipped in this mountain (Mt. Gerizim); and ye say that in Jerusalem
is the place where men ought to worship"—I do
not think she ever finished the sentence. She
was ready to go into a long discussion, but I believe a question had been raised in her mind.
Where should she go to meet God with a sin-
offering? The Samaritans said, "Upon Mt. Gerizim." But the Jews said, "Oh, no, that will not
do. That temple God does not own. If you want
to meet with God, go to Jerusalem and prepare
your offering in the temple. There it will be accepted and there you can worship Jehovah." I
do not suppose that this age-long difference
meant much to her at the best, but now she sees
she is a sinner and she wants to get right with
God, and where shall she go? She wants to know
God that she may worship Him and receive forgiveness from Him. And Jesus said, "Woman,
believe Me, the hour cometh when ye shall neither
in this mountain, nor yet at Jerusalem, worship
the Father. Ye worship ye know not what: we
know what we worship: for salvation is of the
Jews. But the hour cometh, and now is, when
the true worshippers shall worship the Father in
spirit and in truth: for the Father seeketh such
to worship Him." What did He mean? He was

declaring that the hour had come when God is
putting to one side all earthly sanctuaries. It
is not a question now of going to either place.
You can meet with Him anywhere and everywhere if you are ready to take your right place
before Him, to confess your sin and own your
guilt. Then you can lift your heart to Him in
worship, recognizing Him as your Father, for the
moment you confess your sins He forgives. And
so you can be a worshipper, for the Father is
seeking such to worship Him. He has not left it
to you to seek Him first, but He is seeking you,
and you can find Him anywhere if your heart is
honest before Him. "They that worship Him
must worship Him in spirit and in truth."

While He was speaking she had been thinking,
"I wonder, could it be that this strange man,
whom I have never seen before, is really the
promised Messiah? He speaks as no man has
ever spoken before. I wonder if it could be He?"
And aloud she exclaims, "I know that Messias
cometh, which is called Christ: when He is come,
He will tell us all things." Oh, there were so
many questions, and she says, "I wonder, could
this be He? Some day He is coming, and when
He comes He will make all the dark things light
and the crooked things straight. When He comes
He will tell us all things." And Jesus says, "I
that speak unto thee am He." Then what hap-

pened? Did she start asking questions? Did she spread out all her perplexities? No, she had not a question to ask. She took one look into those wonderful eyes of His and every question was answered! She said in her heart, "Oh, this *is* He!" Her soul had found God in Christ. The effects of that is told us in the verses that follow. Am I speaking to anyone who has never found Him? Let me tell you, you need not seek Him anywhere else. He is waiting to reveal Himself to you if you will come to Him as a confessed sinner and trust His grace.

THE CONVERSION OF THE SAMARITANS

✦ ✦ ✦

"And upon this came His disciples, and marvelled that He talked with the woman: yet no man said, What seek-est Thou? or, Why talkest Thou with her? The woman then left her waterpot, and went her way into the city, and saith to the men, Come, see a man, which told me all things that ever I did: is not this the Christ? Then they went out of the city, and came unto Him. In the meanwhile His disciples prayed Him, saying, Master, eat. But He said unto them, I have meat to eat that ye know not of. Therefore said the disciples one to another, Hath any man brought Him ought to eat? Jesus saith unto them, My meat is to do the will of Him that sent Me, and to finish His work. Say not ye, There are yet four months, and then cometh harvest? Behold, I say unto you, Lift up your eyes, and look on the fields; for they are white already to harvest. And he that reapeth receiveth wages, and gathereth fruit unto life eternal: that both he that soweth and he that reapeth may rejoice together. And herein is that saying true, One soweth, and another reapeth. I sent you to reap that whereon ye bestowed no labor: other men labored, and ye are entered into their labors. And many of the Samaritans of that city believed on Him for the saying of the woman, which testified, He told me all that ever I did. So when the Samaritans were come unto Him, they besought Him that He would tarry with them: and He abode there two days. And many more believed because of His own word; and said unto the woman, Now we believe, not because of thy saying: for we have heard Him ourselves, and know that this is indeed the Christ, the Saviour of the world" (John 4: 27-42).

THERE are three distinct sections before us here. In verses 27 to 30 we have the return of the disciples from the city, where they had gone to buy food, and the return of the woman of Samaria to her home in Sychar, there to give testimony. In verses 31 to 38 we have our Lord's serious words in connection with the great harvest of souls and the necessity for more laborers. And in verses 39 to 42 we have the testimony of the Samaritans, who were brought to Christ by the woman to whom He had revealed His Messiahship, as recorded in the earlier part of the chapter.

We read in verse 27, "Upon this;" that is, just at the time that this Samaritan woman heard the Lord Jesus give that wonderful declaration, "I that speak unto thee am He," in answer to her doubtful, half-questioning word, "I know that Messias cometh, which is called Christ," just at that moment the disciples of the Lord returned. They marveled that He talked with the woman. Doubtless they knew her character, and that made them wonder all the more that their Lord should be found in conversation with her. But oh, how little people understood the love of His heart! Again and again we find certain ones surprised because of the depth of His interest in poor, sin-stained men and women. He loved to be with sinners; He loved to manifest His grace and compassion to them. But He never associated with sinners in order to go on with them in their ways; He sought them out in order to win them from their ways and to reveal to them the God of all grace.

And so here the disciples stood by, looking on in wonder and surprise, but nobody liked to speak out what was in his heart. They did not want to ask Him, "What seekest Thou? or, Why talkest Thou with her?" He could have answered readily. He could have replied, "I seek the salvation of her precious soul. I seek to give her the living water that she may never thirst again. I seek to make her My own and to cleanse her from all her sin." And if I am speaking today to anyone still living away from Him, let me say that is what He longs to do for you. "This Man receiveth sinners and eateth with them." The Pharisees said that, and they thought they were bringing an evil charge against Him when they used such language, but oh, it is to the very glory of His Saviourhood that He received sinners. I like those words of John Bunyan; he exclaims, "O this Lamb of God! He had a whole heaven to Himself, myriads of angels to do His bidding, but that could not satisfy Him. He must have sinners to share it with Him." We love to sing:

> "Sinners Jesus will receive;
> Sound the word of grace to all

Who the heavenly pathway leave,
    All who linger, all who fall.
Sing it o'er and o'er again,
Christ receiveth sinful men."

He received this poor sinner. He revealed Himself to her. He gave her the living Water. And then we read, "The woman left her waterpot and went her way into the city." Notice that. She came thirsty; she came to get the water from Jacob's well, but she found that in Christ which so satisfied the longing of her heart that she forgot her waterpot for love of Him, and off she hastened to the city. "She saith to the men, Come, see a Man which told me all things that ever I did. Is not this the Christ?" And so she who, a little while ago, had been a sin-stained, characterless woman, has now become an earnest evangelist. It is just what the Lord Jesus has been doing all down through the centuries, revealing His grace to needy souls, and it is what, if you do not know His saving power, He is waiting to do for you.

Then we read, "They (the people of Samaria) went out of the city and came unto Him," and in the meantime the disciples prayed their Master to eat. "But He said unto them, I have meat to eat that ye know not of." They were so concerned about meeting physical need. The Lord Jesus Christ was thinking of something very

much higher. His first thought was not of satisfying the cravings of physical appetite: His great
concern was a yearning love for poor, sinful men
and women, and a desire to deliver them from
their wretchedness and to cleanse them from
their iniquity and to make them pure and holy in
the sight of God.

"I have meat to eat." In other words, there
was nothing that gave Him such satisfaction,
there was nothing that meant so much to Him as
seeing anxious souls ready to receive His message. And oh, dear friends, I want to tell any
poor sinner, you need not hesitate about coming
to Jesus. He longs to have you come. People
say to me sometimes, "I fear I am almost too
great a sinner." You are not too great a sinner
for Him. He loves to take even the vilest sinners
and cleanse them from their sins. He is waiting
to do it for you. Yes, "I have meat," He says,
"that ye know not of."

And the disciples, who were thinking still on
the natural plane, turned to one another and
shook their heads and asked, "Whatever does He
mean? Has any man brought Him aught to eat?"
But Jesus knew what they were saying, and He
said, "My meat is to do the will of Him that sent
Me and to finish His work." It was in order to
do that will that He came from the glory He had
with the Father before the world was. We hear

Him say in Psalm 40, "I delight to do Thy will,
O My God; yea, Thy law is within My heart."
Doing that will meant assuming our humanity;
it meant coming to earth as a little babe born of
a virgin mother; it meant growing up in Nazareth, that mean, wicked and dirty city—growing
up there in holiness of life and purity of heart, a
Child without a stain of sin upon His conscience
and undefiled by any evil thought or by anything
unholy, a Man to whom the will of God was
utterly supreme, a Man whose hands were hardened as He used the carpenter's tools, who worked in the shop so that the people afterwards were
amazed when He went out preaching, and they
exclaimed, "Is not this the carpenter? How, then,
hath this Man these things, having never learned?" But in all this He was doing the will of
God, and He was ever looking forward to the
cross. In God's due time, He laid aside His carpenter's tools, left the shop and went out to
preach the gospel of the Kingdom of God and to
heal needy humanity of their ills, and the cross
loomed ever nearer before His face. In the seventeenth chapter of this very Gospel we see Him
in prayer, and He is bowed before the Father,
His heart going up to God who had sent Him into
the world and to whom He was soon going back
again. He cries, "I have glorified Thee on the
earth; I have finished the work which Thou

gavest Me to do." In this He was anticipating
the work of the cross, for the work that was
specially given Him to do was that of making
atonement for sin. He says, "The Son of Man
came not to be ministered unto, but to minister,
and to give His life a ransom for many." That
was the work that He had in view. That was the
work He must finish. He would not go back to
the glory until He had accomplished that for
which He had dedicated Himself from the very
beginning. And so at last, after those awful
hours of suffering on the tree, when God made
Him to be sin for us, though He knew no sin, that
we might become the righteousness of God in
Him, after He had drained the bitter cup of judgment to the dregs, the cup that our sins had filled,
after He had borne in His inmost soul all that our
iniquities deserve, when "He was wounded for
our transgressions, He was bruised for our iniquities; the chastisement of our peace was upon
Him and with His stripes we are healed"— then
we hear Him saying, "Father, into Thy hands I
commend My spirit," and He cried with a loud
voice, "It is finished," and He bowed His head
and yielded up His spirit to the Father. In the
Greek language that is only one word instead of
three. We say, "It is finished." He cried "Finished!" That means that the work that saves
was completed; it means that the work whereby

men and women may be cleansed from their sins and may stand justified from every charge before a holy God, had been fully done, and upon the basis of that finished work God can now be just and the Justifier of him that believes in Jesus.

A dear saint was dying, and somebody stood over him and asked, "Is all well?" He looked up and replied with a smile. "Yes, 'it is finished.' Upon that I can hang my whole eternity." Oh, do you realize the blessedness of that? "It is finished." You cannot add anything to a finished work. It is not a question of Christ having done His part and now you must do your part in order to put away sin: but the blessed truth is that Christ has forever put away sin by the sacrifice of Himself, and God wants us to receive the testimony of that, to believe it, and to give God glory for it. And the moment we do believe, all the work of the Lord Jesus Christ is put down over against our sin and our iniquity, and we are justified freely by His grace.

"My meat is to do the will of Him that sent Me and to finish His work." He came into the world for that express purpose, and He would not go back to heaven until it was accomplished.

But now, He thinks of the millions, the untold millions in the world who will have to wait so long before they hear the message, and so He says to His disciples, "Say not ye that there are yet four months and then cometh harvest?" This, evidently, was very early in the year and they could see the green fields about them, and they would make their calculations and say, "Well, in about four months it will be harvest-time." Jesus says, "Do not say that; do not say, There are yet four months, then cometh harvest. Behold, I say unto you, Lift up your eyes and look on the fields, for they are white already to harvest"— not the fields of wheat, not the fields of corn, but these great fields of the nations of men all about us everywhere in the world. They are white already to harvest, men and women everywhere who need Christ, men and women who are living in their sins, who are dying in their sins, who are crying out, "Who will show us any good?" and now it is the responsibility of the servants of Christ, of those who know Him, of those who have been saved by His grace, to give this message of His gospel to those still living in sin.

Here, I may say, is the challenge in regard to foreign missions. People say sometimes, "Well, I do not believe in foreign missions." You can be very thankful that somebody else did! If somebody had not believed in foreign missions long ago, you and I would be poor heathen still living in ignorance of God and in sin and corruption. But somebody was enough interested in foreign missions to come to our fathers in the various European lands from which our ancestors hail, and there to tell the story which turned them from darkness to light, and from the power of Satan unto God; and we today are enjoying the knowledge of Christ because of the faithfulness of those of bygone centuries. Oh, let us be as faithful today! Let us be as true today in heeding the command of our Lord Jesus Christ to get the gospel out to all the world in the shortest possible time! Do not let us put it off. Do not say, "Oh, well, some other day will do." He says here, "Say not ye, There are yet four months?" I think there are some to whom He might say today, if He were living in the earth, "Say not ye there is another dispensation, when the remnant of Israel will do the reaping and get the crop out of the world? Say not that, but lift up your eyes and look. The fields are white already to harvest, and it is your responsibility to do what you can to give them the truth." And be assured of this: If you and I do faithfully what we can, whether by going ourselves or by upholding in prayer and by our gifts those who do go, He will see that we are rewarded accordingly. The Lord adds, "He that reapeth receiveth wages and gathereth fruit unto life eternal: that both he that soweth, and he that reapeth may rejoice together. Herein is that saying true, One soweth and another reapeth. I sent you to reap that whereon ye bestowed no labor: other men labored and ye are entered into their labors."

The disciples were sent out into the land of Israel, to which prophets had been sent of God during other centuries, and they were going to reap where others had sown. And so today, He sends His servants, some to sow and some to reap, that all, at last, may rejoice together.

Now, in verses 39 to 42, we get the effect of that Samaritan woman's testimony. Whenever God saves a soul, it is in order that the saved one may give the ministry of His grace to somebody else. Has he saved you? Then are you trying to reach someone else? You have often heard the story of the life-saving crew that went out in a boat through a terrific storm and rescued a man who had been fastened to a mast on a wrecked ship caught in the rocks and visible clearly from shore through their glasses. They brought this man back, but he was utterly unconscious. They took him to the little hospital and they gave him some restorative to bring him to, and the first words he uttered when he came to consciousness, were these: "There is another man." They said, "What do you mean?" He said, "Another, another man." They said, "Do you mean there is another living man out on that wreck?" "Yes," he said, "another man." And so they went out again through the storm and this time they had to clamber aboard and search the ship, and, sure enough, they found another man in the ship lying there unconscious, and they brought him ashore in their boat and he was saved. Have you been brought to know the missionary grace of God in redeeming love? Well, there is another man, there is another woman, there is somebody else needing Christ. Do what you can to reach them.

The Samaritan woman was saved. She had found the living water. She had gone back to the village and she said to the men—I think that is significant; the men knew her pretty well—and she said to the men, "Everything is different now. Come, see a Man that told me all things that ever I did. Is not this the Christ?" And so we read, "Many of the Samaritans of that city believed on Him for the saying of the woman, which testified, He told me all that ever I did. So when the Samaritans were come unto Him, they besought Him that He would tarry with them, and He abode there two days, and many more believed because of His own word."

There was a wonderful awakening in that Samaritan city, all because of the devoted and faithful testimony of this poor woman, who had just newly come to know Him. "Many more believed because of His own word; and said unto the woman, Now we believe, not because of thy saying: for we have heard Him ourselves, and know that this is indeed the Christ, the Saviour of the world." It was she who aroused their interest; it was she who led the first to go out to Him. As a result of that, they invited Him into the city. But now they say, "We believe not just because of your testimony, but because we have seen Him and we have heard Him and He has spoken to our hearts, and He has moved our consciences, and He has won our love and affection, and we have put our faith in Him. We know He is the Christ, the Saviour of the world."

Do you know Him? What a blessed thing to be acquainted with Him, whom to know is life eternal, and then to endeavor to lead others to know Him too!

IN GALILEE

✓ ✓ ✓

"Now after two days He departed thence, and went into Galilee. For Jesus Himself testified, that a prophet hath no honor in his own country. Then when He was come into Galilee, the Galileans received Him, having seen all the things that He did at Jerusalem at the feast: for they also went unto the feast. So Jesus came again into Cana of Galilee, where He made the water wine. And there was a certain nobleman, whose son was sick at Capernaum. When he heard that Jesus was come out of Judea into Galilee, he went unto Him, and besought Him that He would come down, and heal his son: for he was at the point of death. Then said Jesus unto him, Except ye see signs and wonders, ye will not believe. The nobleman saith unto Him, Sir, come down ere my child die. Jesus saith unto him, Go thy way; thy son liveth. And the man believed the word that Jesus had spoken unto him, and he went his way. And as he was now going down, his servants met him, and told him, saying, Thy son liveth. Then inquired he of them the hour when he began to amend. And they said unto him, Yesterday at the seventh hour the fever left him. So the father knew that it was at the same hour, in the which Jesus said unto him, Thy son liveth: and himself believed, and his whole house. This is again the second miracle that Jesus did, when He was come out of Judea into Galilee" (John 4: 43-54).

✓ ✓ ✓

"NOW after two days He departed thence." We have been considering our Saviour's ministry in Samaria, that stretch of country that came in between Judea on the south and Galilee on the north. Down in Judea the people, as a rule, were very devoted, almost fanatically religious. Up in Galilee many of them were sinful, godless and ignorant, and there was a large group of Gentiles. In Samaria they had a religion which was based partly upon the law of Moses and partly taken from the heathen systems which their fathers had known before they were settled in that district, after the people in Israel proper were carried away by the King of Assyria.

The Lord Jesus had come to Sychar's well, there to minister in grace to a poor Samaritan woman. She had become an earnest evangelist after she knew Him as her Saviour, and as a result a multitude of people came out to listen to Him and believed His message. They invited Him to the village, and there He was two days, making known the precious things of grace and truth. Many of them believed and they said, "Now we believe, not just because of the testimony of the woman who said, 'He told me all things that ever I did,' but," they said, "we have seen and heard Him for ourselves." There was something about the words of Jesus that appealed to every honest, seeking soul.

But the Lord could not linger longer in Samaria. He must go on to Galilee. The prophet had predicted long ago that there would be the greater part of His ministry. In the ninth chap-

ter of Isaiah, in the opening verses, this is defi·
nitely referred to. There we read, "Neverthe·
less the dimness shall not be such as was in her
vexation, when at the first he lightly afflicted the
land of Zebulun and the land of Naphtali, and
afterward did more grievously afflict her by the
way of the sea, beyond Jordan, in Galilee of the
nations. The people that walked in darkness have
seen a great light: they that dwell in the land of
the shadow of death, upon them hath the light
shined." This prophecy had its gracious fulfilment when He, who is Himself the life and light,
went about healing the sick and working many
other signs of power and opening up the precious
things connected with the gospel to those needy
people, although the majority of them refused
to accept it. He lived in one of their cities, had
been brought up among them, and after He had
begun His ministry the family was removed to
Capernaum, and this was called His own city.
Both Nazareth and Capernaum were outstanding cities of Galilee. We say, "Familiarity
breeds contempt." Often the better you know
people, the less you think of them as being in any
sense remarkable and, unbelievably, that was
true in the case of our blessed Lord. As He
moved about in those places where the people
knew Him so well, they could not seem to recognize in Him the promised Messiah. Jesus Him-

self testified that a prophet has no honor in his
own country. He said this, you remember, when
He returned to Nazareth, where He had been
brought up, and went into the synagogue on the
Sabbath day, "as His custom was." I like that,
"as His custom was." Jesus of Nazareth, growing up in that city, set the example of regular
attendance upon the means of grace. There must
have been a lot about the service that was repugnant to Him, but it was the place where the name
of God was acknowledged. It was the place
where people gathered for prayer and praise on
the Sabbath, and Jesus, as a child, as a youth, as
a young man, always wended His way to the
village synagogue, for He recognized the place
where the things of God were acknowledged. "He
went, as His custom was, into the synagogue on
the Sabbath day." And He read, "The Spirit of
the Lord is upon Me, because He hath anointed
Me to preach the gospel to the poor; He hath
sent Me to heal the brokenhearted, to preach deliverance to the captives, and recovering of sight
to the blind, to set at liberty them that are
bruised, to preach the acceptable year of the
Lord." Luke tells us, "And He closed the book."
If you turn back to Isaiah you would think it was
a strange place for Him to read. The rest of
the sentence goes on like this, "And the day of
vengeance of our God." Why did He close the

book when He did? Why did He stop reading
at a comma instead of going on to the end of the
sentence? Because He had not come to declare
the "day of vengeance of our Lord." He came
to proclaim the acceptable year of our Lord, and
in accord with that He opened up God's message
of grace for the people of that day, and yet the
great majority of them turned away from Him
and they said, "Is not this the carpenter? Don't
we know His mother and sisters and brothers?"
"From whence hath this man these things?"
"Why doesn't He do some mighty works of
power?" They hoped to see some miracles
worked by Him. So the people rushed upon Him
and would have hurled Him over the cliff outside
the city, but He went His way, saying, "A
prophet is not without honor save in his own
country."

This gives us some little idea of the lowliness
of our Lord Jesus Christ. We might imagine
that such an one as He could not grow up in any
country but that people would realize instinctively that He must be Lord of all, but He "made
Himself of no reputation, and took upon Him the
form of a servant, and was made in the likeness
of men." Few realized who He was. I wonder
if we all have recognized Jesus of Nazareth as
the Eternal Son of God, who became Man for our
redemption?

We read then that when He was come into Galilee they received Him; that is, they thronged to hear Him, but they did not recognize Him as the Holy One of God. They received Him, having seen all the things that He did in Jerusalem at the feast. The Lord was just returning from Jerusalem. We need to realize that there were many, many things that Jesus did that were not recorded in this fourth chapter of the Gospel of John. They had seen Him, perhaps, give sight to the blind, cause the lame man to leap, etc., and now they hoped to see other miracles wrought, and so thronged about Him.

So "Jesus came again into Cana of Galilee, where He made the water wine." "There was a certain nobleman, whose son was sick at Capernaum," about twenty-five miles north-east of Cana of Galilee. This father had either come a long distance to find Jesus, or being there in Cana, he had received a message that his son was ill, and now he saw his opportunity to present the case to the great Miracle-Worker. He had no understanding of the true nature of the Lord Jesus Christ, but he did feel that He was one who could meet his need. How often, when men are in distress or in trouble, they feel that if they could get to Jesus, He would do something for them, and yet they do not really know Him as God the Son, manifest in the flesh, but they feel that He is able to do for man what no one else can do. Men invoke His name in times of distress. That seems to have been the case with this father. He heard that Jesus was come out of Judea, and so he came to beg Him to heal his son. You see what he is asking of Jesus: "Jesus, won't you take a journey of twenty-five miles and do something for my son? My son is dying and you have power to heal. You can work miracles. Won't you come and work a miracle upon him?" And you notice that Jesus answered him in what must have seemed almost a hard way. The Lord turned to him and said, "Except ye see signs and wonders, ye will not believe."

There are so many people like that, who want to see some outward demonstration of power, and then they think they will believe, but the Lord Jesus Christ wants to be received and trusted because of what He is in Himself, apart from any temporal benefit that might come from knowing Him. I wonder if there are not many who think of the Christ of God as though His great business is to help us. If we are sick or in financial trouble, maybe He will show us a way to get well or to make money. If members of our family are in some distressing circumstances and we are worried about them, perhaps if we go to Jesus He will do something for them. Oh, there is something higher than that! He wants us to learn to see in Him the blessed incarnate Son, who came in grace to reveal the Father and who asks our trust and allegiance because we ought to acknowledge and yield ourselves to Him, even if we never receive any temporal benefit whatever.

Real faith in Christ rests upon the fact that He who is God became Man; and in getting to know Him, the Son, we know the Father. I wonder if He could not say to us today, "Except ye see signs and wonders, ye will not believe." How different was the case of those Samaritans of whom we read in the former chapter! They saw no miracles wrought. We do not read that Jesus healed one of their sick or opened the eyes of one of their blind, but they heard His message and saw His behavior, and there was something that so impressed them that they said, "Oh, now we know Him, we have seen Him, we have heard Him for ourselves." This is the work of the Holy Spirit of God today, to make Christ known to men and women, in order that they may trust Him as Saviour and own Him as Lord of their lives. To know Him as God's Son, become Man for our redemption, is eternal life. In fact, Jesus Himself says, "This is life eternal, that they might know Thee, the only true God, and Jesus Christ, whom Thou hast sent."

But this poor father was so taken up with his

present need and so concerned about the state of
his son and so fearful he was going to lose this
boy, that he did not seem to take in exactly what
the Lord Jesus Christ was saying. The Lord
said, "Except ye see signs and wonders, ye will
not believe." But the man exclaimed, "Come
down, ere my child die." He did not realize
that Jesus did not need to go to Capernaum to
heal his son. Think of that Roman centurion,
not an Israelite, who came to Jesus and said, "I
have a servant who is very dear to me who is
sick. Speak the word only, and my servant shall
be healed." He realized that in the word of
Christ was power. But this Israelite, who ought
to know so much better than that Roman centurion, came far short of that simplicity of faith.
The Lord said of the Roman centurion, "I have
not met another who has refreshed Me like this
one who believes Me and knows that I have all
power." And yet the nobleman believed that
Jesus could do something if he could only get
Him to come in time to where his son was. That
is so often a question with us. If Jesus would
only hurry up! We may be praying for the salvation of someone, and we are so afraid that that
friend may pass into eternity before he is saved,
and we try to hurry the Lord up. So many
people write in and ask for special prayer for
some sick one, and they say, "Won't you please

hurry up and get this request before your people, for he is very, very sick." I just bow before the Lord and say, "Thou knowest I cannot get it before the people, but Lord, Thou hast all power, and right here I bring this request to Thee," and I know He will hear. You do not have to try to hurry Jesus. Those sisters in Bethany, how troubled they were! Their brother was so sick, and they thought if they just sent a message, that Jesus would drop everything and hurry to Bethany; but four days went by and Jesus had not come. Then He said, "Let us go to Bethany." And when He arrived the sisters thought it was too late, but Jesus had already told His disciples that He was glad He was not there earlier. You might have expected Him to say, "I am *sorry* I was not there." He never makes any mistakes, and He says, "I am glad I wasn't there, for God is going to be glorified in a way that He would not have been if I had hurried when I received the message to come." When He said, "Roll away the stone," they said, "Why, Master, there is no use rolling away the stone. He has been dead four days." But Jesus said, "Said I not unto thee that if thou wouldest believe, thou shouldest see the glory of God?" Then they rolled the stone away and He cried, "Lazarus, come forth." If He had not said "Lazarus" that day, He would have emptied the whole cemetery.

And just as Lazarus came forth, some day all His own will come forth and be caught up to meet Him in the air. We do not need to try to hurry Him. What we do need to learn is to rest in a sense of His love and wisdom and be able to say with the Psalmist, "My soul, wait thou only upon God."

But you see, this dear father did not understand Him. He only knew that his son was tossing in a fever and that any moment it might be too late, and he said, "Lord, come! Come twenty-five miles! Don't waste any time! Come down! Hurry! My child is dying!" But Jesus looked upon him with pity and compassion, and said unto him, "Go thy way; thy son liveth." He did not need to go down to Capernaum to raise him up. "Go home, thy son liveth. You will find him well again. You go back to Capernaum. Put away your dread and fear. It will be all right." And so the man believed the word that Jesus had spoken to him. Now he is growing in confidence. He first believed Jesus could heal the boy if He could get to him, but now he believes He can raise him up though so far away.

My dear friend, have you believed the word of Jesus? Do you know that salvation—not only healing of the body, if it please God—comes from believing the word of Jesus? "Verily, verily, I say unto you, He that heareth My word, and be-

lieveth on Him that sent Me, hath everlasting
life, and shall not come into condemnation; but
is passed from death unto life." We read of old,
"He sent His word and healed them," and the
Apostle Peter said, "Being born again, not of
corruptible seed, but of incorruptible, by the
Word of God, which liveth and abideth forever."

I can remember so well when I was a lad and
in great trouble about my soul. Now I had always read my Bible. I had read about angels
appearing to people and speaking directly to
them. I remember when about twelve, I went
to my room and got down on my knees and I
said, "O Lord, I have been reading the Word and
won't you please, when I open my eyes, have an
angel standing here? Won't you let that angel
tell me that my sins are forgiven?" I was almost
afraid to open my eyes. Finally I opened them.
He was not there, and I have never seen an angel
yet in all these years. But let me tell you something: I know beyond the shadow of a doubt
that my sins are all forgiven. How do I know?
I knew it when I took Him at His word, when
I accepted His testimony. The Book says, "If
thou shalt confess with thy mouth the Lord
Jesus, and shalt believe in thine heart that God
hath raised Him from the dead, thou shalt be
saved. For with the heart man believeth unto

righteousness; and with the mouth confession is made unto salvation."

O troubled soul, if you have said, "Oh, I wish that I knew that my sins were put away, that my heart was cleansed," let me urge you to believe the word of Jesus. Just trust Him. "He came unto His own and His own received Him not. But as many as received Him, to them gave He power to become the sons of God, even to them that believe on His name." And to believe is to trust, to confide in Him.

Well, this man believed the word and went back to Capernaum, and in all those twenty-five miles I fancy doubts would keep coming up: "I wonder about that boy of mine. Jesus said it was all right, that he lived, and that it was all right. I wonder if I shall find him alive!" But finally, how glad he was when he came in sight of Capernaum; for there, right ahead, was a messenger hastening to him, who cried joyously, "It is all right; thy son liveth." He believed before he got the testimony of his servant. He believed when Jesus said, "Thy son liveth," and now he had the corroborative testimony of his servants. "Then inquired he of them the hour when he began to amend. And they said unto him, Yesterday at the seventh hour the fever left him." They may have added, "We were watching him and suddenly—we just noticed the hour—the fever left him, a perspiration broke out all over him, and we put our hands on him, and from that hour on he has been getting stronger every hour." Then the father said, "The seventh hour! Why, that's the very time that I was talking to Jesus! It was that very hour that Jesus said, 'Thy son liveth.' "

"And himself believed, and his whole house." Oh, there is a higher faith now than before. First, he believed if Jesus could get there he could heal the lad; and, second, he believed *the word of Jesus,* and now he believes *in* Jesus. And his whole house believed with him. They said, "No one but the Son of God could work such a miracle as this, when He was twenty-five miles away." We are told, "This is again the second miracle that Jesus did, when He was come out of Judea into Galilee." He manifested Himself to the people of His own country as the Sent One of the Father. How blessed to realize that although He has been 1900 years in the glory, He is just as able to hear our cries of distress, just as able to heal our bodies today, just as able to meet our needs today, as "in the days of His flesh."

AT THE POOL OF BETHESDA

"After this there was a feast of the Jews; and Jesus went up to Jerusalem. Now there is at Jerusalem by the sheep market a pool, which is called in the Hebrew tongue Bethesda, having five porches. In these lay a great multitude of impotent folk, of blind, halt, withered, waiting for the moving of the water. For an angel went down at a certain season into the pool, and troubled the water: whosoever then first after the troubling of the water stepped in was made whole of whatsoever disease he had. And a certain man was there, which had an infirmity thirty and eight years. When Jesus saw him lie, and knew that he had been now a long time in that case, He saith unto him, Wilt thou be made whole? The impotent man answered Him, Sir, I have no man, when the water is troubled, to put me into the pool: but while I am coming, another steppeth down before me. Jesus saith unto him, Rise, take up thy bed, and walk. And immediately the man was made whole, and took up his bed, and walked: and on the same day was the sabbath. The Jews therefore said unto him that was cured, It is the sabbath day: it is not lawful for thee to carry thy bed. He answered them, He that made me whole, the same said unto me, Take up thy bed, and walk. Then asked they him, What man is that which said unto thee, Take up thy bed, and walk? And he that was healed wist not who it was: for Jesus had conveyed Himself away, a multitude being in that place. Afterward Jesus findeth him in the temple, and said unto him, Behold, thou art made whole: sin no more, lest a worse thing come unto thee. The man departed, and told the Jews that it was Jesus, which had made him whole. And therefore did the Jews persecute Jesus, and sought to slay Him, because He had done these things on the sabbath day" (John 5:1-16).

✶ ✶ ✶

WE are now to consider another of the signs and miracles, of which we have just eight in all, recorded in the Gospel of John. The apostle, in choosing, by the Spirit's

175

direction, the various miracles which he brings before us, was evidently seeking to illustrate in various ways the wonderful grace of God, as revealed in Christ, to needy sinners.

The background here is most interesting. We are told that after our Lord's ministry in Galilee there was a feast of the Jews. We do not know exactly what feast. It was probably the feast of the Passover, and the Lord Jesus, in accordance with the law, went down to participate in the feast. The Passover feast must have been of exceptional interest to Him, for He knew well that every paschal lamb that was sacrificed at that time pictured Himself, even as we are told in 1 Cor. 5:7, 8, "Christ our passover is sacrificed for us: therefore let us keep the feast, not with old leaven, neither with the leaven of malice and wickedness; but with the unleavened bread of sincerity and truth." The Lord Jesus then went to the feast, and as He moved in and out among the people He passed by the pool of Bethesda, which was near the sheep gate. We read, "Now there is at Jerusalem by the sheep market a pool, which is called in the Hebrew tongue Bethesda, having five porches." This was God's special provision for His people during the legal dispensation. Bethesda was a "house of mercy," where God was extending loving-kindness to an afflicted people. We need to realize that even before grace and truth came in all their fulness in the Person of our Lord Jesus Christ, the heart of God was toward every needy soul, and He made provision that all those who would turn to Him, might do so. There were certain regula. tions or requirements. They came to God, bring. ing their offerings, but these offerings all spoke of the Lord Jesus Christ and were accepted, not because of any intrinsic value they possessed, but because of that which they prefigured, and because of the faith and confidence that prompted the people to bring them. So all through the legal dispensation, God was reaching and saving man in His own wonderful way; and of that this scene is a picture.

Here was the pool of Bethesda, and around it "there lay a multitude of impotent people, blind, halt and withered." These expressions speak of the results of sin. It blinds our eyes to the truth of God and to the glory of God. It makes us lame, so that we cannot walk in the ways of God. It withers up all our strength, so that we are helpless and unable to do anything to save ourselves. Naturally, we are all like these impotent folk gathered there by the pool. We may say that all sickness and pain and suffering and warfare that distress mankind have come into the world, not through God's divine decision, but because of man's waywardness. They are the fruits of the fall, and our Lord Jesus Christ has come that He might destroy the works of the devil, and some day, thank God, He is going to undo completely all these effects of sin.

This motley, helpless throng were lying in the courts of Bethesda. What were they waiting for? Waiting for the moving of the water. Now I know there is a question among scholars as to the genuineness of verse 4, which tells of an angel troubling the water. In the most ancient manuscripts this verse is not found at all, and yet, as we read on in the story, there seems to be reference to it, so that one would think that it belongs to the original text. But many editors believe it was inserted in the margin by some copyist long years ago in order that we might understand why these people were gathered at the pool, and then some later scribes incorporated it into the text. At any rate, it explains the reason why the people were there. There was a spring, and at times it was perfectly quiet, and intermittently it bubbled up. Some of us have seen springs like that. The people understood that an angel went down into this spring at a certain season and troubled the water; so whosoever stepped in at that time was made whole of whatever disease he had. Here was the best that the law could do. The law had help for the one who needed it the least. The strong could get into the water first. But the worse he was, the more helpless and the more sinful, the more wretched his condition, the less likely he was to avail himself of the privileges that the law could offer him. Some of these people had lain there for not only weeks and months, but for years, and one man was there who had had an affliction thirty-eight years. He was paralyzed. He had lost the power to use his legs. How long he had lain at the pool of Bethesda we do not know, but his friends may have brought him there years before Jesus met him. He was a picture of a poor, helpless sinner. That is true of every one of us in our natural state.

Long years ago, out in San Francisco, a group of us were having a Sunday School outing down on the beach by the Cliff House. We used to go there on Washington's birthday. That morning when we got out to the beach at nine o'clock, the fog was just beginning to lift, and in a little while we were amazed to see all kinds of wreckage on the beach. We did not understand where it all came from. A little later we learned that a great ship, the "Rio de Janeiro," on its way home from China, had attempted to make the San Francisco harbor in a dense fog, and had run upon a rock and was broken to pieces. Hundreds of people were drowned; some had escaped. The paper told this story: Among the saved ones was a young American journalist; both of his legs had been broken, and in that condition he was thrown into the water. The cold water probably brought him back to consciousness and he began to float. Hours afterwards that utterly helpless man was drawn out of the water by a rescue party. I thought as I read that, what a picture of God's grace to needy sinners! There were others who swam for hours before they were picked up, strong and hearty men, and many others were drowned; but this man had no ability to swim. He was helpless and yet he was saved. What a picture of many of us! We read, "When we were yet without strength, in due time, Christ died for the ungodly," and we helpless sinners were saved and found life and peace.

Consider this helpless man at the pool. He did not seek the Saviour. He did not ask Jesus to heal him. We often turn things around, and plead with sinners to ask Jesus to save them, but nowhere in the Bible is man told to pray for salvation. Rather, we are told that God Himself is beseeching men to be reconciled to Himself. This man did not even know of Christ, but Jesus came seeking him. Oh, I like to tell, as I have often told, of the little boy's answer when someone said, "My son, have you found Jesus?" and he, looking up, said, "Why, sir, I didn't know He was lost; but I was, and He found me."

"The Son of Man is come to seek and to save

that which was lost." So He came to find this poor helpless man, who did not know anything about Him, not even His name. His need appealed to the tender, gracious heart of the Son of God. Oh, if I am speaking to anyone today who is lost and miserable be assured your very wretchedness and helplessness appeal to the heart of the Son of God. He wants to deliver you and save you.

See what it says in verse six: "When Jesus saw him lie, and knew that he had been now a long time in that case, He saith unto him, Wilt thou be made whole?" Jesus "knew that he had been now a long time in that case." Yes, eight years longer than Christ Himself had been on earth that man had been in this illness. Why did He wait so long? That the man might come to the end of himself. You and I would not have come to Christ if we had not been brought to see our insufficiency. You have heard of the poor man who fell into the water. Unable to swim, he went down once and came up again, and went down again. A strong swimmer stood on the pier, looking on, and the people cried, "Why don't you leap in and save that man?" He said nothing, but let the man go down again, and then he threw off his coat and plunged in and brought him safely to shore. They said, "Why did you wait so long before you went in to save him?" He answered, "He was too strong before. I had to wait till his strength was gone. I had to wait till he could do nothing himself, till he was helpless."

I think Jesus was waiting for that. When the man was brought to the pool first he had high hopes. "It won't be long till I can get in," he thinks, and then someone else got in before him. Over and over again he had gone through this disappointing experience, and now he is ready to give up in despair. It is the despairing soul that Jesus loves to meet in grace. He saves the one who admits, "I cannot do anything to deliver myself."

See how the Lord dealt with this man. "When Jesus saw him lie, and knew that he had been now a long time in that case, He said unto him, Wilt thou be made whole?" A very simple question. He puts it to everyone. Is my reader unsaved? The blessed Lord is saying, "Would you be made whole?" Do you want to find God's salvation? "Wilt thou be made whole?" Do you want to know the delivering grace of God? What is your answer? Do you want to be made whole?

The impotent man answered Him, saying, "Sir, I have no man, when the water is troubled, to put me into the pool: but while I am coming, another steppeth down before me." Oh, how many there are like that. "There is only one thing I

lack. If I could only get a man to help me."
How many people feel like that. Some say, "Oh,
if I could only find out the right church." My
friend, if you joined every church in Christen-
dom, that would not save you. "Well, if I could
only get instruction as to what principles I
should live up to." It is not doing that saves the
soul. The quicker we learn that lesson, the better.
"Now to him that worketh is the reward not
reckoned of grace, but of debt. But to him that
worketh not, but believeth on Him that justifieth
the ungodly, his faith is counted for righteousness."

The paralytic said, "I have no man to help
me." Seeing the deep need in which he was,
Jesus said unto him, "Rise, take up thy bed, and
walk." What a strange command to give a helpless man! Oh, but there is power in the words
of Jesus. We read, "Immediately the man was
made whole." There was something about the
word of Jesus that wrought faith in that man's
heart. Somebody says, "Well, I would like to be
saved and it takes faith, but I do not have faith."
But "faith cometh by hearing, and hearing by the
word of God." The man says, "I would like to
be made whole, but there is no way." Then he
hears the word of Jesus, "Rise, take up thy bed,
and walk," and he looks up and faith springs up
in his soul. I would like to have seen him leap

to his feet for the first time. He would say,
"Dear me, I can hardly believe it." Then he
looked down on that load of bedding and at the
command of Jesus took it under his arm, just a
pallet, and off he went rejoicing in his new-
found strength.

"Immediately the man was made whole, and
took up his bed, and walked; and on the same
day was the Sabbath." Now a sinister note comes
in "The same day was the Sabbath." Nothing
wrong with it, but there were critics sitting
there. "Doesn't He know this is the Sabbath
day?" It meant more to them than the healing
of a poor fellow-creature. They were far more
concerned about ceremony and ritual, so they
were ready at once to find fault. To the healed
man the Jews said, "It is not lawful for thee to
carry thy bed." Instead of rejoicing and saying,
"Why, friend, we have seen you lying there for
years, and we are so thankful you are now well!"
these legalists, like the elder son in the story of
the prodigal son, who would not go in when his
brother had come home and was forgiven, said,
"You have no business carrying this burden on
the Sabbath." The man might have said, "Burden! Why, this is no burden! It is a joy to carry
it." "It is not lawful for you," they cried, but
the healed man said, "He that made me whole,
the same said unto me, Take up thy bed, and

walk." As much as to say, "Go fight with Him now if you have any complaint." "Well," they asked, "who was it? What man was that?" "And he that was healed wist not who it was." He was so utterly ignorant that he did not even know the name of his deliverer. He only acted on what he was told.

This poor man did not know the name of the one who had healed him. We read, "Afterward Jesus findeth him in the temple, and said unto him, Behold, thou art made whole." He had not been in the temple for thirty-eight years and wanted to make up for lost time. People always do this when Jesus saves them. "Behold, thou art made whole: sin no more, lest a worse thing come unto thee." This man's illness was evidently a result of sin. Jesus warned him against falling into sin in the future. It was a timely admonition. Oh, young convert, do not trifle with sin. We may become cleared of the guilt of sin, but there are dire temporal consequences of certain sins that follow one all through life, though one may be forgiven.

Now the man found out who his Deliverer was. "The man departed and told the Jews that it was Jesus, which had made him whole." Oh, you would have thought that they would all have gone to Him and thanked Him for this deed of power, but instead of that, their cold legal hearts led them to act in the opposite way and we read, "Therefore did the Jews seek to slay Him, because He had done these things on the Sabbath day." Instead of recognizing the fact that that day, of all days, they should have expected God to work, they found fault with Jesus. They had no heart for the grace that could meet a poor sinner's need. Let us beware lest we too fall under the power of the same spirit of legality.

EQUAL WITH GOD

✦ ✦ ✦

"But Jesus answered them, My Father worketh hitherto, and I work. Therefore the Jews sought the more to kill Him, because He not only had broken the sabbath, but said also that God was His Father, making Himself equal with God. Then answered Jesus and said unto them, Verily, verily, I say unto you, The Son can do nothing of Himself, but what He seeth the Father do: for what things soever He doeth, these also doeth the Son likewise. For the Father loveth the Son, and sheweth Him all things that Himself doeth: and He will shew Him greater works than these, that ye may marvel. For as the Father raiseth up the dead, and quickeneth them; even so the Son quickeneth whom He will. For the Father judgeth no man, but hath committed all judgment unto the Son: that all men should honor the Son, even as they honor the Father. He that honoreth not the Son honoreth not the Father which hath sent Him. Verily, verily, I say unto you, He that heareth My word, and believeth on Him that sent Me, hath everlasting life, and shall not come into condemnation; but is passed from death unto life" (John 5: 17-24).

✦ ✦ ✦

WE have been considering the record of our Lord's healing of the impotent man at the pool of Bethesda, and closed by noticing the indignation of the legalistic Jews of that day who were distressed because the Lord did this upon the Sabbath day. They had added a great many of their own laws to those in the books of Moses. They were more concerned about

187

the technicalities of this case than they were in the blessing of the poor man who had waited so long for deliverance. "Therefore did the Jews persecute Jesus, and sought to slay Him because He had done these things on the sabbath day."

Note our Lord's defence. "But Jesus answered them, My Father worketh hitherto, and I work." Just what did He mean by this? Why, He would carry their minds back to creation. God created the heavens and the earth at an undetermined period, so far as man's records are concerned. We do not know how far back it may have been. Whenever that beginning was, God created the heavens and the earth. Then the earth fell into a chaotic condition, and God undertook to remake that earth that it might become the abode of man, and the stage upon which was to be enacted the great drama of redemption. So we have the six days' work in which the world was brought back from chaos to order, and we are told that God rested on the seventh day and that the seventh day was hallowed. It was the Sabbath of God. But, alas, God's Sabbath was a very brief one, for it was not long until sin came into that fair creation which but a little while before had been proclaimed as very good And when sin came in, God became a worker once more, and He never found rest again until at last He rested in the work of His own beloved

Son of Calvary's cross. During all the millenniums preceding the cross God never observed a Sabbath. He gave the Sabbath to man in the law for man's blessing and good. Jesus Himself says, "The Sabbath was made for man and not man for the Sabbath." But when God gave to man one day in seven, He had no rest Himself. It was unthinkable that He, the loving, holy, compassionate God, could rest as long as the sin question remained unsettled. So Jesus answered these men by saying, "My Father worketh hitherto, and I work." That is, because He was one with the Father, He did what His Father did, and so He was in the world working to undo the results of sin; and they found fault with Him because He delivered a man from sin's effect on the Sabbath day. It shows how little they comprehended the mind of the Father. "My Father worketh hitherto, and I work." They did not understand. Their indignation increased and they sought the more to kill Him because He not only had broken the Sabbath, but had said that God was His Father. The expression is a rather peculiar one. It implies that He Himself had implied that He had a right to use this name in a way that other men did not. He said that God was His own Father, making Himself equal with God. They understood that when the Lord Jesus spoke of Himself as the Son of the Father that He meant to say that He was one with the Father—one Person of the Godhead.

Jew and Gentile are both charged with the murder of the Son of God. The Jews dragged Him into Pilate's hall saying, "We have a law, and by our law He ought to die, because He made Himself the Son of God." That was their accusation, but Pilate gave sentence that it should be as they desired, so he stands as the representative of the Gentile world, accused before the bar of God of the murder of His blessed Son. Yet how gracious God is! He offers to both Jew and Gentile salvation through the One they rejected, although they spurned Him and united in crucifying the Son of God. The Jews would have stoned Him to death, but by driving Him to the Gentiles He was sent to the cross. However, in virtue of His sacrifice of Himself on the cross of shame, salvation can be offered to Jew and Gentile if they turn to God and believe on the Son. We need not be afraid then to admit that we have had a part in murdering the Son of God. But we can come to Him as repentant sinners and trust the One whom we have rejected, as our personal Saviour. "For there is no difference between the Jew and the Greek: for the same Lord over all is rich unto all that call upon Him."

Legalists of every kind always reject Jesus.

Legalists of every type, Jew or Gentile, would
crucify Him if He were here again. How can
you prove that? Why! They do not want Him
now. If they wanted Him they would accept
Him and believe in His name, but they refuse to
believe, showing that their hearts are just the
same today as the hearts of those who sought to
slay Him. They sought to slay Him because
they denied His Deity. He declared that He was
one with the eternal Father. He made Himself
equal with God. "Then answered Jesus and said
unto them . . ." Instead of trying to make things
easier for them, He makes them harder. If men
turn away and refuse to believe, then He will
give them something even more difficult to believe. But if they come to Him in repentance,
He will make things plain so that they can easily
understand. He said, "Verily, verily, I say unto
you, The Son can do nothing of Himself, but
what He seeth the Father do: for what things
soever He doeth, these also doeth the Son likewise." What a tremendous claim was this! Whatsoever the Son sees the Father do, He does.
Would ever mere man dare to say that? If he
did, would he not be branded as a paranoic? But
Jesus spoke as the Son of the Father. "The Son
can do nothing of Himself, but what He seeth the
Father do," He does. What does that really
mean? Some people imagine that He is saying,

"I have less power than the Father. I can only imitate." But it is the very opposite. He is saying, "It is impossible for the Son to act apart from the Father." Every Person of the Trinity might speak like that. The Father can do nothing without the Son, the Holy Spirit can do nothing without the Son, the Father can do nothing without the Holy Spirit, the Holy Spirit can do nothing without the Father, and the Son can do nothing without the Father, and the Son can do nothing without the Holy Spirit. In other words, the relationship of the three Persons in the Godhead is such that none can act apart from the other. Whatever the Spirit does, He does in the fullest fellowship with the Son and the Father, and so with every other Person of the Eternal Trinity. Here we have set forth in a marvelous way the reality of the unity and yet trinity of the Godhead. We sometimes speak of the three Persons of the Trinity as the Father, the first Person; the Son, the second Person; the Holy Spirit, the third Person. Scripture makes no such distinction. God the Father, God the Son, and God the Holy Spirit are one, coequal and coeternal, and neither can act without the full approval and fellowship of the rest. Here as a Man on the earth, the Lord Jesus could actually face His accusers in that day and say, "The Son can do nothing of Himself but what He seeth the

Father do." And then He added, "For the Father loveth the Son, and showeth Him all things that Himself doeth: and He will show Him greater works than these, that ye may marvel." Oh, how utterly impossible it is for us to understand the love of the Father for the Son as a Man here on the earth. Three times He rent the heavens above His head to declare His love for His Son, saying, "This is My beloved Son." "The Father loveth the Son and snoweth Him all things that He doeth." They are one in counsel and purpose and "He will show Him greater things than these that ye may marvel. He was looking on to His triumphs at the cross, and in His resurrection.

Our Lord Jesus claimed that He has exactly the same power to call man back from the dead as the Father has. "For as the Father raiseth up the dead, and quickeneth them; even so the Son quickeneth whom He will." To quicken is to impart life. The Son giveth life to whom He will. When we think of resurrection, we think of the omnipotent power of God put forth to bring the dead back from the grave. This power is attributed to the Father and to the Son and to the Holy Spirit. This is true in connection with our Lord's own resurrection. We read that He was raised up from the dead by the glory of the Father. He said, "Destroy this temple, and in three days I will raise it up again." He says elsewhere, "No man taketh My life from Me. I have power to lay it down, and I have power to take it again." And then we are also told that the Spirit of Him that raised up Christ from the dead shall quicken our mortal bodies. God the Father is said to have raised Him from the dead. The entire Trinity acted as one to raise the Lord Jesus, and the entire Trinity will have part in the resurrection of all them that are in Christ at His coming. It is God the Father and God the Holy Spirit and God the Son who will call the dead from their tombs.

Then the Lord Jesus said a tremendous thing: "For the Father judgeth no man, but hath committed all judgment unto the Son." What a stupendous claim is this! He who moved about over the hills and through the valleys of Palestine and, to all outward appearances, was just a Galilean artisan, says, "The Father . . . hath committed all judgment unto the Son." "He has given Him authority to execute judgment because He is the Son of Man." Scripture says that "God has appointed a day in the which He will judge the world in righteousness by that Man whom He hath ordained; whereof He hath given assurance unto all men, in that He hath raised Him from the dead." In the Bible we read that God is going to judge the world, but here we read that the Judge is He who became Man for c···

redemption. What a marvelous declaration! Are you out of Christ today? If you die like that, you will have to stand before the Great White Throne, where you will find yourself looking into the face of a Man. You will see upon that throne the Man Christ Jesus, the One who went to Calvary's cross to die for you. You will give an account of yourself to Him and His lips will proclaim the sentence of judgment. We who believe will not have to come into judgment for our sins, anɑ yet we will all stand before the judgment-seat of Christ. He will go over all our ways down here, since His grace brought us to know God as our Fathᴇr and Christ as our Saviour, and He will examine all our work and judge the deeds done in the body. Our Lord Jesus Christ will do this. He is the One who will call all the nations into judgment eventually: "When the Son of Man shall come in His glory, and all the holy angels with Him, then shall He sit upon the throne of His glory." "The Father hath committed all judgment unto the Son."

"That all men should honor the Son, even as they honor the Father. He that honoreth not the Son honoreth not the Father which hath sent Him." One of the first grave dissensions in thᴇ early Christian Church was the Arian contro‧ versy. Arius taught that it was unreasonablᴇ to believe that the Lord Jesus Christ was thᴇ

eternal, uncreated Son of the Father. He maintained that instead of that He was the first created being; that He was not eternal; that He was
not one with the Father from eternal ages. This
man was opposed by Athanasius, who maintained
the truth that the Lord Jesus, whose goings forth
are from everlasting to everlasting, was the eternal Son as God the Father is the eternal Father
and as the Holy Spirit is the eternal Spirit. That
controversy disrupted the Church for many
years, but finally at the Council of Nicæa it was
definitely declared that the Scriptures taught
that the Lord Jesus Christ was one with the
Father from all eternity. For a century afterwards, however, it was disturbed by the same
controversy.

On one occasion, Athanasius, the valiant de-
fender of the truth as to Christ's equality with
the Father, was summoned before one of the em-
perors who had given his own royal son the honor
of sharing the imperial power and sitting with
himself upon the throne. Athanasius bowed low
before the emperor, but utterly ignored his son.
"What!" exclaimed the angry ruler, "do you pretend to honor us while dishonoring and paying
no attention to our son, whom we have made the
sharer of our authority?" "Do not you," answered Athanasius, "profess to honor God the
Father, while refusing to give the same honor

to His coequal Son?" It was a word fitly spoken, but whether the emperor saw the truth or not we do not know.

Now we come to a verse which has been used as much as any other in the Gospel of John for winning souls: "Verily, verily, I say unto you, He that heareth My word, and believeth on Him that sent Me, hath everlasting life, and shall not come into condemnation; but is passed from death unto life." What a stupendous statement do we have here! Can any believer in the Lord Jesus doubt his eternal salvation with words like these before him, words that come to us directly from the lips of the Son of God Himself? He begins with the divine oath, "Verily, verily." We find that double "verily" only in John's Gospel. Again and again we find it there, and it always introduces a truth of tremendous importance. In the Douay Version the verse reads like this, "Amen, amen, I say to you, he who hears My word and believes Him who sent Me, has eternal life and comes not into judgment, but is passed out of death into life." Think of it! What a wonderful declaration! "Amen, amen!" "Verily, verily!" It means "without any possibility of controversy," "He that heareth My word . . ." Have you heard His word? There are many people who hear with the outward ear, but do not hear in the heart. He speaks of hearing the word in the sense of receiving it in the heart. He who receives and believes what God has said in His Word—what God has said about our lost condition—about redemption—he who hears the word of the Gospel, "and believeth on Him that sent Me"—it is not exactly *on* but "He that believeth Him." It is God who has spoken. When I stand up and give men something from that Book, I am preaching what God has said. Do you believe God? People say sometimes, "Well, I am trying to believe." Trying to believe whom? God has spoken. You either believe Him or you do not believe Him. If you believe what God has said, our Lord declares that you have eternal life. Now notice, it is not that you may *hope* to have it, providing that you continue faithful. It is not eternal life at the end of the way. It is the present tense: "He that believeth *hath*." There is a sense, of course, in which eternal life is at the end of the way. The reason is that if I am a believer in Jesus Christ today, I know that some day, when He comes again, my very body will be quickened into eternal life. But every believer, here and now, possesses life, eternal life. The very life of God is communicated to him who trusts the word of God.

Now look at this: "Shall not come into *condemnation*." The word is really *judgment*. There is no judgment to those who are in Christ. Why?

Because all our judgment was borne by the Lord Jesus Christ when His arms were outstretched on the cross. There all our sins deserved was poured out upon our blessed Substitute, and so we shall never have to go into the judgment for our sins. Our judgment-day was at the cross.

> "Jesus died, and we died with Him,
> Buried in His grave we lay."

All our sins were dealt with when He took oui place upon the tree, and so we shall not come into judgment, but already we have passed out of death into life.

ADDRESS SIXTEEN

THE TWO RESURRECTIONS

"Verily, verily, I say unto you, The hour is coming, and now is, when the dead shall hear the voice of the Son of God: and they that hear shall live. For as the Father hath life in Himself; so hath He given to the Son to have life in Himself; and hath given Him authority to execute judgment also, because He is the Son of Man. Marvel not at this: for the hour is coming, in the which all that are in the graves shall hear His voice, and shall come forth; they that have done good, unto the resurrection of life; and they that have done evil, unto the resurrection of damnation" (John 5: 25-29).

WE continue to examine our Lord's words uttered after the healing of the palsied man at the pool of Bethesda. Following that great gospel message of verse 24: "Verily, verily I say unto you, He that heareth My word and believeth on Him that sent Me, hath everlasting life and shall not come into condemnation (or judgment; this is exactly the same Greek word that is translated "damnation" in verse 29 and "judgment" in verse 27), but is passed from death unto life."

Now in verse 25 our Lord again used that solemn form of address by which He would challenge our most serious attention, "Verily, verily,

I say unto you, The hour is coming, and now is, when the dead shall hear the voice of the Son of God: and they that hear shall live." He is not speaking in this verse of the physically dead, but rather of the spiritually dead, of those who are dead in trespasses and sins, and this is true of all men out of Christ, all men who are in Adam by natural generation. Death passed upon all men when Adam sinned, and as God looks down upon the race today He sees it as a race of men and women dead to Himself and everything spiritual, and alive to what men call pleasure, alive to their own personal affairs, but with not one pulse-beat toward God—every one dead and utterly helpless, for, of course, a dead man cannot do anything to change his condition. He cannot help himself, and if those dead in trespasses and sin are to live, they must receive life through Another, even our Lord Himself. "The hour is coming, and now is." He is introducing this wonderful dispensation of the grace of God. The hour began when He came to earth, and has been in progress for over 1900 years—the hour when God is quickening dead souls and bringing men and women to find life in Christ. Millions have heard His voice and repented, and know what it is to have life eternal through receiving that Word. "The hour is coming, and now is, when the dead shall hear the voice of the Son of God."

That voice is a voice of power. It is a voice that can reach the heart that is utterly dead to everything holy. Remember Lazarus. He was physically dead and Jesus came to that graveside and said, "Roll away the stone." "But he has been dead four days and his body has become offensive." But Jesus commanded them to do as He said, and they did, and He called, "Lazarus, come forth!" and he came forth. That dead man heard the voice of Jesus because that voice was a life-giving voice.

I had a friend who was deep in sin, dead to God, living in the vilest corruption. One night in Fresno, California, as he passed a little open-air meeting he heard the group singing:

> "He breaks the power of cancelled sin,
>   He sets the prisoner free;
> His blood can make the foulest clean,
>   His blood availed for me."

Those words, sung over and over, went right home to his heart, and that man, dead in sin, heard the voice of the Son of God, and that night believed the message and became a new creature in Christ. The old sinful habits that had bound him so long dropped away. He was different because he had heard the voice of the Son of God.

I think of another, who came into a meeting a poor drunkard, utterly lost, but he heard someone repeat the words of Christ, "Come unto Me,

all ye that labor and are heavy laden, and I will
give you rest." He said, "Is that for me? Is He
inviting me to come?" That man was made to
live. He never touched a drop of liquor again.
He was through, because he had heard the voice
of the Son of God. Life is in His word.

"The hour is coming, and now is, when the
dead shall hear the voice of the Son of God: and
they that hear shall live." Notice, God does not
set people working in order to obtain life. We
could do nothing to deserve life, and we cannot
please God until we have received it. "The wages
of sin is death, but the gift of God is eternal life."
We cannot obtain life through subjection to certain religious ordinances or availing ourselves of
sacraments. Men do not get life through baptism or the Lord's Supper, or through doing
penance, attending church or giving money. They
receive eternal life through hearing and believing
the voice of the Son of God. "Hear, and your
soul shall live." Have you heard that voice? Men
turn away from it. Christ is speaking all the
time, down through the ages, but many turn
away and go on in their sins. They continue in
their state of death. But the moment a man
hears that voice in the depths of his heart, that
moment he receives life. This life is given by
the Son of God. He says, "As the Father hath
life in Himself; so hath He given to the Son to

have life in Himself; and hath given Him authority to execute judgment also, because He is the Son of Man."

If men refuse the message of the gospel, if they turn away from the Word of the Son of God and spurn His grace, then the same God, who has made Him a Giver of life to all who believe, has appointed Him as Judge of those who refuse Him, in the last day. The Father hath given to the Son to have life in Himself and hath given Him the authority to execute judgment. We had something like this in verse 22. There we read, "For the Father judgeth no man, but hath committed all judgment unto the Son." This gives us to know that the Son is God because Scripture declares that it is God who will judge the world. God will sit upon the Great White Throne and call sinners before Him to answer for the guilt of rejecting the salvation that He has provided, but the Person of the Godhead who will appear on that throne will be the Lord Jesus Christ. Men who stand before that throne in their sins will be judged by the Man, Christ Jesus. The Father has given Jesus authority to execute judgment because He is the Son of Man. When Job was utterly bewildered because of God's dealings with him, he said, "I look on my right hand and on my left hand, but He is not there. He is not a man as I am, that we might come together in judgment; neither is there any Daysman that might put His hand upon us both." But that for which Job longed, a man who could represent God to him, is found in the Person of our Lord Jesus Christ. He is as truly Man as He is God. "There is one Mediator between God and men, the Man Christ Jesus." If men refuse to trust that blessed Man, who bore our sins in His own body on the tree, they will be judged according to their works. In order that this might not be He died on that shameful cross: "He was wounded for our transgressions, He was bruised for our iniquities; the chastisement of our peace was upon Him; and with His stripes we are healed." If men refuse Him and turn away from Him now, some day they will have to meet Him. Some day they will have to face Him in their sins when it is too late to be saved. He who would have given life will then have to be their Judge.

But now, having spoken of one hour, the hour in which God is quickening dead sinners into life, He goes on to speak of another hour, the hour of the resurrection of dead bodies. For both are found in Scripture. He is quickening those dead in trespasses and sins in this hour. By-and-by He is going to quicken those whose bodies are in their tombs. "The hour is coming in the which all that are in the graves shall hear His voice, and shall come forth; they that have done good, unto the resurrection of life; and they that have done evil, unto the resurrection of damnation." "Marvel not at this." It is as though He said, Do not be surprised that I can quicken dead souls, that I can give eternal life to those who believe. Some day I am going to empty all the graves of earth. "There is an hour coming in the which all that are in the graves shall hear His voice, and shall come forth." "Well, how can that be?" you say. "Millions, untold millions, have died and their bodies have been dissolved into their chemical parts. How can they come back to life?" Nothing is impossible with God, who created these wonderful bodies. There will be a resurrection, both of the just and the unjust.

Yes, the hour is coming when all that are in the graves shall come forth. Notice that there will be two resurrections. Some people have imagined that both resurrections would take place in the same moment, that the Saviour would utter His voice and that all the graves would be emptied at once. This is not exactly what our Lord said. Scripture shows that there will be two resurrections: first, a resurrection unto life, the resurrection of the just. In Revelation 20 we read, "Blessed and holy is he that hath part in the first resurrection; on such the second death hath no power, but they shall be priests of God and of Christ, and shall reign with Him a thousand years." And then we read that after the thousand years are expired there will be the resurrection of the wicked dead, who will stand before the Great White Throne for judgment. Two resurrections, one resurrection to life of the just, and one resurrection to the second death of the unjust. And yet they both take place in one hour? Yes, in one hour. Remember though, how our Lord used this term. "The hour is coming and now is, when the dead shall hear the voice of the Son of God: and they that hear shall live." This hour began when Christ was here on earth and is still in progress. Nineteen hundred years have elapsed, and we are still living in the hour when Christ is quickening dead souls. Then we look on beyond this hour. The hour of resurrection will be at least a thousand years in length. At the beginning of that thousand years the righteous dead will be raised. At the close of the thousand years the wicked dead will be raised. The righteous dead stand before the judgment-seat of Christ to be rewarded. The wicked dead rise to stand before the Great White Throne, there to answer for the awful sin of rejecting the Lord Jesus Christ and to be judged for all the sins from which they might have been delivered. Someone says, "I am a bit perplexed about that 29th verse. It says, 'They that have done good, unto the resurrection of life; and they that have done evil, unto the resurrection of damnation.' Is salvation then after all based on what one does? Are we saved because we do good, and lost because we do evil?" Well, if men persist in their sins they will be judged for their evil-doing. All men are lost today not merely because of the sins they have committed, but because they have rejected the Lord Jesus Christ. "He that believeth on Him is not condemned: but he that believeth not is condemned already, because he hath not believed in the name of the only begotten Son of God." Elsewhere Jesus said the Holy Spirit would come to convict of sin because they believe not in Him. That is the one great damning sin that will ruin your soul for eternity if you persist in it. If you refuse the work of the cross, if you turn away from the One who died upon that tree, then the merits of that work can never be applied to you. In the day of resurrection you will come forth from the tomb as one who has done evil, and you will have to be judged for your sins.

But now, how about the rest? Who are those who have done good or, literally, those who have practised good? What does He mean by that? Are we saved because of our goodness? We know very well from other Scriptures that salvation is not based on human merit. "By grace

are ye saved through faith; and that not of yourselves, it is the gift of God: not of works, lest
any man should boast" (Eph. 2:8). And again
we are told, "To him that worketh is the reward
not reckoned of grace, but of debt. But to him
that worketh not, but believeth on Him that
justifieth the ungodly, his faith is counted for
righteousness" (Rom. 4:4). There is no contradiction. The minute a sinner believes on the
Lord Jesus Christ there is a change. That is
the outward sign that he is a Christian. Immediately following that verse in Ephesians 2,
we read, "For we are His workmanship, created
in Christ Jesus unto good works, which God hath
before ordained that we should walk in them."
If I tell you I am justified by faith, you cannot
see my faith. You have no other way of knowing whether my testimony is true than by watching my life. You wonder if my life corresponds
with my testimony. Do I live a Christ-like life?
And if I do not live such a life, you refuse my
testimony. God Himself does not accept any
man's testimony if his life does not correspond.
In that day it is those who have practised good
who will be raised and manifested as the children
of God.

Let me stress this: just as there are two ways
to live, so there are two ways to die, and there
are two resurrections, and following those two

resurrections there are two destinies. Have you received Christ as your Saviour? If so, death for you will mean to die in the Lord, and you will be raised in the first resurrection and enter into the blessings of heaven. On the other hand, if you continue to reject Him, then the day will come when you will die in your sins. Those who die in their sins will stand in the judgment and will be left in their sins through all eternity. In order that this might not be, our Lord Jesus Christ came to Calvary and gave Himself a ransom for all, a propitiation for each one who would trust in Him.

THE FIVE WITNESSES

✦ ✦ ✦

"I can of Mine own self do nothing: as I hear, I judge: and My judgment is just; because I seek not Mine own will, but the will of the Father which hath sent Me. If I bear witness of Myself, My witness is not true. There is another that beareth witness of Me; and I know that the witness which he witnesseth of Me is true. Ye sent unto John, and he bare witness unto the truth. But I receive not testimony from man: but these things I say, that ye might be saved. He was a burning and a shining light: and ye were willing for a season to rejoice in his light. But I have greater witness than that of John: for the works which the Father hath given Me to finish, the same works that I do, bear witness of Me, that the Father hath sent Me. And the Father Himself, which hath sent Me, hath borne witness of Me. Ye have neither heard His voice at any time, nor seen His shape. And ye have not His word abiding in you: for whom He hath sent, Him ye believe not. Search the Scriptures; for in them ye think ye have eternal life: and they are they which testify of Me. And ye will not come to Me, that ye might have life. I receive not honour from men. But I know you, that ye have not the love of God in you. I am come in My Father's name, and ye receive Me not: if another shall come in his own name, him ye will receive. How can ye believe which receive honour one of another, and seek not the honour that cometh from God only? Do not think that I will accuse you to the Father: there is one that accuseth you, even Moses, in whom ye trust. For had ye believed Moses, ye would have believed Me: for he wrote of Me. But if ye believe not his writings, how shall ye believe My words?" (John 5: 30-47).

THIS is a very interesting section, in which we have five distinct witnesses to the fact that our Lord Jesus Christ is the Sent One of the Father, who came into the world that through Him we might have life and have it in abundance, and that He might be the propitiation for our sins. He speaks to us as Man in the days of His humiliation here on earth. In verse 30 He says, "I can of Mine own self do nothing: as I hear, I judge: and My judgment is just; because I seek not Mine own will, but the will of the Father which hath sent Me." In this we see the Lord Jesus Christ taking the very opposite place to that which was aspired to by Lucifer of old. People often ask the question, "Why did God create a devil?" He did not create a devil. He created Lucifer, an archangel, but his heart was lifted up because of his beauty. Five times he set his will against God, saying, "I will." "I will be like the Most High. I will ascend unto the throne of God." That was his ruin. Because of asserting his own will, Lucifer, the archangel, became the Devil, or Satan.

Here, in contrast to this, we have One who was in the form of God from all eternity, and yet in grace renounced the glory that He had before the world was. As the lowly Man here on earth, He refused to put forth His own power, but undertook to do all His works in the energy of the Holy Spirit. He said, "I can of Mine own self do nothing: as I hear I judge, and My judgment is just." Why? Because His judgment was the judgment of God Himself. He did everything as under the authority of God, His Father. He alone of all men who have lived in this scene could always say, "I seek not My own will, but the will of the Father which hath sent Me."

The measure in which you and I as Christians imitate our Lord in this, will be the measure in which we too shall glorify God down here. We imagine sometimes that the greatest happiness we can have is to take our own way, but that is a mistake. The happiest man or woman on earth is the one who makes the will of God supreme. Jesus had no will of His own. His one desire was to do His Father's will, for which He had been sent into the world.

Having given this declaration, He goes on to say, "If I bear witness of Myself, My witness is not true." What does He mean? He has just declared that the Father had given everything into His hand. He has told us that some day His voice is going to cause the dead to come forth from the graves. He has declared that He is the One sent from the Father and now He says, "If I bear witness of Myself (the very thing He has been doing), My witness is not true." What does He mean by that? He means that if He alone bears witness of Himself, that testimony is not valid. We read elsewhere that "in the mouth of two or three witnesses every word shall be established." If anyone came bearing witness on his own behalf and speaking for himself and there were no others to accredit him, his witness would be ruled out of court and therefore would not be valid. He says, "Now if you have to depend only upon what I say, I recognize that that would not be valid as a testimony." Then He adds, "But I have other witnesses to corroborate what I have been telling you." He brings four additional witnesses that give absolutely clear testimonies to the fact that He is indeed the Sent One of the Father, and all these in addition to His own declaration. He is the first witness.

The second is John the Baptist. Now it was a singular thing that the great majority looked upon John the Baptist as a prophet. The leaders in Israel refused to accept his testimony because it condemned them, but the multitude of the people believed him to be sent of God. And so the Lord Jesus says, "If you will not receive My testimony unaccredited by another, then I will summon another witness into court." So He brings in the testimony of John. "There is another that beareth witness of Me; and I know that the witness which he witnesseth of Me is true." Here is now a second testimony, and therefore two

witnesses can be received in court. "I know
that the witness which he witnesseth of Me is
true." "Ye sent unto John, and he bare witness
unto the truth." To what truth? The same truth
that the Lord Himself declared. He presented
Jesus and said, "He that is preferred before me
. . . was before me." And John the Baptist on
another occasion pointed Him out and said, "Behold the Lamb of God, which taketh away the sin
of the world." He bore witness to the fact that
the Lord Jesus Christ was the appointed sacrifice
who was to give Himself for our sin upon that
cross of shame. And then again, John declared,
"I saw and bare witness that this is the Son of
God." Well, that is the very question. Is Jesus
the Son of God? Is He the Eternal Son sent into
the world to work out the plan of redemption?
Jesus answered, as it were, "If I were the only
one to say this you would not believe Me, but
here is the one whom you thronged to hear, and
recognized that he was a prophet. Well, he bears
witness to the same thing that I am telling you.
John the Baptist tells you that I am the Son of
God, the Lamb of God come to die for sinners.
I am the pre-existent Christ." "But," Jesus says,
"I am not dependent upon John. I do not need
his testimony to make these things valid. I am
not dependent upon man's testimony, but I say
these things that you might be assured of their

truth." The Lord wanted to cut out from under their feet any ground for unbelief. He desired to make it clear that He was the Saviour He professed to be. But He did not need John's testimony, no matter how good and great he was. The truth is the truth apart from any man's recognition of it. John was a wonderful man, "a burning and a shining light!" That witness had been silent for some time. Herod had slain him, but his testimony remained, and today we may hear the voice of John the Baptist declaring that Jesus is the Son of God, the Lamb of God, the pre-existent One.

But now the Saviour says, "I have another witness." What is the third witness? "The works which the Father hath given Me to finish, the same works that I do, bear witness of Me, that the Father hath sent Me." And that is the reason for the miracles of our Lord Jesus Christ. He wrought those mighty acts of power in order that He might prove that He was the Sent One of the Father. But Jesus never wrought a miracle simply to magnify Himself. They were performed to alleviate human suffering and help mankind. All this had been predicted beforehand in the Old Testament. The prophets had declared that the eyes of the blind should be opened, the ears of the deaf should be made to hear, the lame man should leap with joy, sorrow and sickness should flee away, and the prison-house of sin should be opened. These things the Lord Jesus Christ fulfilled during those three years. These wonderful works and miracles, these mighty acts of His, all bore testimony to the fact that He was indeed the Sent One of the Father. Look at that poor leper. He comes to Him all covered with sores. He cries out in agony, "Lord, if Thou wilt, Thou canst make me clean." Jesus looks upon him and He, the Holy One, is not afraid of being defiled by his unclean-ness, so He puts His hand on him and says, "I will; be thou clean." Do you think that man doubted that Jesus was sent from the Father? Would he raise any question as to the Deity of the Son of God?

Look at the sorrowing father at Capernaum. He comes to Jesus, pleading, "Master, my only child, my little daughter, is sick. Come and heal her." Jesus went to the home and the people came rushing out, saying, "There is no use; she is dead." But the Lord said, "Be not afraid. Only believe." He enters into that room and takes the hand of that little dead child and says to her tenderly in Aramaic, "Talitha cumi." That is, "Little maid, I say unto thee, arise," and she opened her eyes and sat up. Do you think Jairus and his wife had any difficulty in believing that He was the Sent One of the Father?

And that poor widow outside of the city of Nain, following the funeral procession of her only son, till Jesus came and stopped it all! Mr. Moody said, "You can't find any direction as to how to conduct a funeral service in the Bible. Jesus broke up every funeral He ever attended." So He interfered here, and said to the young man, "I say unto thee, arise," and Jesus gave him to his mother. Do you think she doubted that He was the Sent One of the Father?

"The same works that I do, bear witness of Me." Go over to Bethany by that grave in the hillside, and listen as Jesus cries with a loud voice, "Lazarus, come forth," and see him come shuffling out, bound by grave-clothes, and the two sisters rush to meet that beloved brother brought back from the dead. Any doubt there that Jesus is the Sent One of the Father? These were the works that bore witness of Him.

And then the most wonderful thing of all, when at last He Himself had died and yielded His spirit to the Father, and His body had been laid away in the tomb, and on the third day He came forth and was declared to be the Son of God with power. Yes, the works of Jesus bear witness to the fact that He is the Son of God.

We have had three witnesses. Now there is another, in verse thirty-seven, "And the Father Himself, which hath sent Me, hath borne witness of Me. Ye have neither heard His voice at any time, nor seen His shape. And ye have not His word abiding in you: for whom He hath sent, Him ye believe not." How did the Father bear witness to the fact that Jesus was His Eternal Son, sent into the world for our salvation? When the Saviour offered Himself at the Jordan to become the substitute for our sins, and John baptized Him there, when He came up from the watery grave, the heavens were opened and the Spirit of God was seen descending like a dove, and the Father's voice was heard saying, "This is My beloved Son, in whom I am well pleased" (or, in whom I have found all My delight). This was the Father's testimony. Not only then, but on the Mount of Transfiguration, once more the Father said, "This is My beloved Son; hear Him." And later on when Jesus on that other occasion lifted up His voice and said, "Father, glorify Thy name," a voice was heard from heaven saying, "I have both glorified it, and will glorify it again." Three times the voice of the Father was heard from heaven accrediting the Person and the mission of His blessed Son while here on earth, and yet these people who professed to believe in God as their Father did not hear His voice. The disciples heard it, but these hard, critical, legalistic men never heard the voice of the Father. Have you heard it? Have you heard the Father's voice speaking in your heart? Have you heard Him saying to you, "This is My beloved Son, I want you to find your delight in Him"? Oh, the Father still delights to accredit the Lord Jesus Christ.

Then there is a fifth witness. Verse thirty-nine says, "Search the Scriptures; for in them ye think ye have eternal life; and they are they which testify of Me." Most scholars, I think, understand that opening expression as a definite statement rather than a command, and they read it like this, as indicated in the margin, "Ye search the Scriptures." Whether they are right, or whether our translators were right, I do not pretend to say. Both might speak to our hearts. Certainly the Spirit of God again and again commands us to search this blessed Word. But if we take it as a statement rather than a command, it is the same in principle. He was talking to these leaders in Israel. They read and studied their Bibles, and He said to them, "Ye search the Scriptures, believing that in them ye have eternal life." That is, you take it for granted that you are going to have life by becoming familiar with and obeying the Scripture, but unless you trust the One of whom the Scripture speaks, you will not have eternal life. In 2 Tim. 3, when speaking to a man who had been brought up on the Word of God, the apostle said, "From a child thou hast known the Holy Scriptures, which are able to make thee wise unto salvation through faith which is in Christ Jesus." Notice that it is not simply familiarity with the Bible that will give you eternal life. It is becoming acquainted with the blessed Son, who is the theme of the story. So Jesus says, "You have the Bible. Go back into the Old Testament, and as you read the Old Testament you will find that there they are speaking of Me." He was the theme of the entire Old Testament. All the Levitical types spoke of Him. All the prophets gave witness to Him. He was the One who rebuked the adversary in the days of Zechariah, the prophet. All through the Old Testament we have Jesus preached in type and in prophecy. "They are they which testify of Me." The Scriptures tell of Jesus and Christ authenticates the Scriptures. Prophecy after prophecy was fulfilled in Him.

He shows that the entire Old Testament is the Word of the living God. Now He says, "You read your Bible, and yet you will not come to Me that you might have eternal life." My dear friend, do you know Christ? You are familiar with the Bible and I know some of you are depending upon that knowledge for salvation. Have you received the Christ of whom that Book speaks? Have you trusted the Saviour of whom the prophets wrote? Have you believed in the

One who came in grace to die for sinners? This is the theme of the whole Bible. It is a pitiful thing to pretend to honor the Bible while rejecting the Christ of the Bible.

His words imply that all men may come to Him if they will. There are some people who imagine that some are not welcome, but Jesus would not use language like this if it did not include everybody. "Whosoever will may come." If you are lost at last, it will be because you would not come: "Ye will not come to Me that ye might have life."

Now the Saviour says, "I receive not honor from men." He did not want their patronage, but He desired men to accept the salvation that He had come to provide. "But I know you (and He could say that as no other), that ye have not the love of God in you." He was here to do the will of the Father and yet they would not have Him. He warns them of the coming Antichrist, the false Messiah. He says, "If another shall come in his own name, him ye will receive." Who is this other? It is that wilful king of the eleventh of Daniel, that idol shepherd of Zechariah, the false prophet of Revelation, the lawless one of 2 Thess. 2, a sinister figure yet to arise in this world. Men who will not have Christ will bow down to him.

It is a very serious thing to reject Christ, to spurn the salvation that God has provided. How many a young man has sat in a gospel meeting, under deep conviction, but has thought of what this one and that one of his friends will think of him if he confesses Christ! How many a young woman has known that she should be saved, but someone whom she esteems very highly keeps her back, for she says, "What will he think of me if I do that?" Unless you put God first, you will never be able to believe. Once come to the place where you say, "I can't allow myself to be turned aside from that which is right and true because of any other interest, even the opinion of those nearest and dearest to me; I must seek first the kingdom of God and His righteousness, and then, the Lord Jesus says, the other things will be added to me." Have you been kept from confessing Christ because of the fear of man? Remember, that those who would hinder are just poor human beings like yourself and soon will have to give account to God.

"Well," you say, "then is He going to accuse us?" Oh, no. "Think not that I will accuse you to the Father." But He adds—and oh, it had point to those Jews—"There is one who accuseth you, even Moses." Moses accuse? How and whom does he accuse? Moses accuses all who reject his testimony, and he predicts dire judgment. And so Jesus adds, "Had you believed Moses, you would have believed Me." This is the answer to those who say, "Well, we do not believe that those first five books were written by Moses." But Jesus says, "Moses wrote of Me," and thus He puts His seal upon these books, declaring that Moses wrote them—"For he wrote of Me." Those prophecies written by Moses were written of Christ. Those types represented Christ. When Moses wrote, "The Lord thy God will raise up unto thee, a Prophet from the midst of thee, of thy brethren, like unto me; unto Him ye shall hearken," Moses was writing and speaking of the Lord Jesus Christ. And so the Saviour says, "If ye believe not his writings, how shall ye believe My words?" If men will not receive the testimony of the Old Testament they will not receive the testimony of Christ. The two are so linked together that they can never be separated.

So we have five witnesses. There is His own testimony, there is the testimony of John the Baptist, there are the miracles He performed, there is the witness of His Father's voice, and there is the Word of God, the Bible; and all agree in this, that Jesus is the Son of God, which should come into the world. Have you received Him?

✶ ✶ ✶

FEEDING THE MULTITUDE

"After these things Jesus went over the sea of Galilee, which is the sea of Tiberias. And a great multitude followed Him, because they saw His miracles which He did on them that were diseased. And Jesus went up into a mountain, and there He sat with His disciples. And the passover, a feast of the Jews, was nigh. When Jesus then lifted up His eyes, and saw a great company come unto Him, He saith unto Philip, Whence shall we buy bread, that these may eat? And this He said to prove him: for He Himself knew what He would do. Philip answered Him, Two hundred pennyworth of bread is not sufficient for them, that every one of them may take a little. One of His disciples, Andrew, Simon Peter's brother, saith unto Him, There is a lad here, which hath five barley loaves, and two small fishes: but what are they among so many? And Jesus said, Make the men sit down. Now there was much grass in the place. So the men sat down, in number about five thousand. And Jesus took the loaves; and when He had given thanks, He distributed to the disciples, and the disciples to them that were set down; and likewise of the fishes as much as they would. When they were filled, He said unto His disciples, Gather up the fragments that remain, that nothing be lost. Therefore they gathered them together, and filled twelve baskets with the fragments of the five barley loaves, which remained over and above unto them that had eaten. Then those men, when they had seen the miracle that Jesus did, said, This is of a truth that prophet that should come into the world. When Jesus therefore perceived that they would come and take Him by force, to make Him a king, He departed again into a mountain Himself alone. And when even was now come, His disciples went down unto the sea, and entered into a ship and went over the sea toward Capernaum. And it was now dark, and Jesus was not come to them. And the sea arose by reason of a great wind that blew. So when they had rowed about five and twenty or thirty furlongs, they see Jesus walking on the sea, and drawing nigh unto the ship: and they were afraid. But He saith unto them, It is I; be not afraid. Then they willingly received Him into the ship: and immediately the ship was at the land whither they went" (John 6: 1-21).

✦ ✦ ✦

THE miracle of the loaves, the feeding of the five thousand, is one of those signs which is recorded in all the four Gospels. There must be some very special reason for this, otherwise the Spirit of God would not have been so careful that each of the Evangelists should relate the account of this miracle. There are a few differences in the way the story is presented, such as we would expect from four independent writers, some of whom were eye-witnesses and some who heard of it through others. These diversities only make more evident the fact that the Bible is the inspired Word of God, for had the four men, Matthew, Mark, Luke and John, planned to make up a story about the Man called Jesus and foist it upon the world as a pretended divine revelation, they would have been very careful indeed to see that every incident was related in exactly the same way. But instead, there are differences according to the viewpoint of each one. Matthew, as we have seen, dwells upon the promised Messiah. Mark emphasizes those things that bring out the Servant character of our Lord Jesus, for that was the object he had in mind in writing, to show Christ as the Servant of the Godhead and of man. Luke emphasizes those things that speak of His holy humanity. John deals more particularly with that which would show that Christ is the Son of God, for this Gospel, as we have seen, is the Gospel of the Deity of our Lord Jesus Christ. We are not told in John exactly when these events took place. The Synoptics show us that they occurred just after the death of John the Baptist, as the Lord was beginning the last year-and-a-half of His ministry.

We read, "After these things Jesus went over the sea of Galilee, which is the sea of Tiberias." Tiberias is on the western shore of this lovely lake. Jesus crossed from there over to the opposite shore, where a multitude followed Him because they saw the miracles which He did. Everywhere He went there were throngs who followed Him because of the wonderful works of power which He wrought. That did not mean that they recognized Him as the Son of God, but they were stirred and their curiosity aroused, and sometimes there was heart interest. "Can He be some prophet raised from the dead? Is it Elijah who is to come, or is He indeed the promised Messiah?"

Jesus went up into a mountain, a high table-land by the Sea of Galilee, and there He taught the people. John tells us the Passover was nigh. It was called "a feast of Jehovah" in the Old Testament, but it is termed "a feast of the Jews." They had made it their own feast, because the One whom the Passover typified was right in their midst and they did not recognize Him. It had no real value any more.

In the evening, we read, that "when Jesus lifted up His eyes and saw a great company come unto Him, He saith unto Philip, Whence shall we buy bread, that these may eat?" They had been with Him all that day. They had listened to the marvelous words that came from His mouth. We know, from other records, that it was the disciples who took the initiative and said, "Send them home, for there is no possible way of feeding them." But John knew that the Lord Jesus had thought of that already. Jesus turned to Philip and said, "Whence shall we buy bread, that these may eat?" We can depend upon it that whatever interest the disciples had in the great throng of people, the interest of the Lord Jesus was much greater than theirs. That is a great encouragement to us who have so little concern and compassion for the throngs about us, but oh,

how wonderful that the compassions of Christ
are going out to men everywhere! He is far more
interested in their welfare than His servants can
possibly be! If we seem at times to fail to enter
into the seriousness of things, and our hearts are
not moved as they should be by humanity's crying
need, the great heart of the blessed Son of God
is throbbing with pity and compassion. He looks
upon the multitude with yearning love as He did
long ago. He looked at them and He said, "I
must feed them; I must meet their need"—He,
the blessed Bread of God that had come down
from heaven! So He asked, "Whence shall we
buy bread, that these may eat?" It was not that
He did not know what to do, but "this He said
to prove him: for He Himself knew what He
would do." What comfort in that! Here was an
emergency—thousands of people without any
food! If they had to seek it themselves they
would faint before they could get it. They were
a long way from home. But the Lord Jesus Christ
had already planned to meet that need.

Am I addressing someone who finds himself
in peculiarly difficult and trying circumstances,
and who is wondering if God has forgotten or if
He has lost all interest in you? Let me tell you
this: If you have trusted Him as your own
Saviour, His heart is always toward you, and He
knows what He is going to do. He is not going

to let you down. He is not going to leave you in the lurch. It may seem as though there is no possible way of meeting your present need, but He knows what He will do. We look at the things that we can see, and we can become so discouraged and disturbed as we take circumstances into account, but our blessed Lord Jesus Christ is never affected by circumstances.

> "He knows and loves and cares,
>   Nothing this truth can dim:
> He gives the very best to those
>   Who leave the choice with Him."

Go back into your Bible and see those Old Testament characters who had trials. Jacob was in trouble. There was famine over all the land. One of his sons had been held in captivity because Joseph wanted to see his brother, Benjamin, but Jacob was determined that Benjamin should not go down to Egypt. But in his distress he does not know what to do, and his other sons say, "We cannot go without Benjamin." Jacob throws up his hands and says, "All these things are against me." Why, you know, dear friends, at that very time God was planning for him in a wonderful way, and it was not long before the brothers came and took him and his family to Egypt, where he was provided for abundantly. Do you feel like wringing your hands and crying out in

despair, "Everything is going wrong. All these
things are against me." Oh, no; they are not;
God is for you, and if God is for you, who can
be against you? Our blessed Lord is for you.
"We have not a high priest which cannot be
touched with the feeling of our infirmities; but
was in all points tempted like as we are, yet apart
from sin;" and because "He Himself hath suffered being tempted, He is able to succor them that
are tempted." And He knows what He is going
to do. He is planning for you, my brother, at
this very moment. He is planning for you, my
sister. Believe it. Trust Him, and be assured
that He is going to undertake in His own good
time for you.

And so our blessed Lord here knew what He
was about to do. He was going to meet the need
in His own wonderful way. But Philip did not
understand, and he answered Him and said, "Two
hundred pennyworth of bread is not sufficient for
them, that every one of them may take a little."
Two hundred pennyworth—the denarius, called
the penny here, was a full day's wages for a man
in those days. While it was in value about an
English shilling or a little less, yet it had much
greater purchasing power in that land. So Philip
says, "Why, Lord, it would take about two hundred days' wages to provide bread enough so
that each one might take a little, and then where

would we get it out here?" It seemed they were
up against an insuperable difficulty. But there
are no insuperable difficulties with Christ. Two
hundred pennyworth of bread would not be sufficient that every one might take a little. Jesus
was not going to give them just a little bit of a
lunch, but He was going to give them a good full
meal that would satisfy them.

Just at that time Andrew came up. He seems
to be always the man who fits into the difficult
place. He has been scurrying around evidently
to see what he can find. He says, "I have run
across a lad with a little lunch." Yes, there
always is a lad in a big throng. He slips about
among the crowd. When the Lord wins the hearts
of the lads, you know what they are like. This
young lad was there that morning. He had said
probably, "Mother, I want to go to hear the great
Preacher." So she put a lunch together. And
Andrew says, "There is a lad here with five barley loaves and two small fishes, but what are they
among so many?" And yet I think that after all
Andrew was not hopeless. He is asking, "Is
there any way in which You can make these
enough?"

So Jesus said, "Make the men sit down." And
John tells us, "Now there was much grass in the
place. So the men sat down, in number about
five thousand." What a throng to be fed with

five loaves and two fishes, not even half a fish for a thousand. These are the people, and here is the banquet. "And Jesus took the loaves; and when He had given thanks (in perfect confidence that God would meet every need) He distributed to the disciples, and the disciples to them that were set down; and likewise of the fishes as much as they would." The supply seemed inexhaustible. Five thousand happy people were enjoying the feast Jesus had spread for them. Then He says, "Gather up the fragments, that nothing be lost." He gives freely, but will not waste anything. And so they went about and gathered up the fragments; twelve big baskets-full were the fragments of five barley loaves that remained. Why, to begin with they said, "We have nothing to feed this multitude with," and at the close they had a full basket for each of the twelve disciples! There was plenty for all. He does not do things in a niggardly way. My dear brother and sister, if you are in trouble, ask regally, for you are coming to a King. Do not be afraid to put Him to the test. He is able to meet every need. "My God shall supply all your need according to His riches in glory by Christ Jesus."

They filled the twelve baskets with the fragments which remained, and "then those men, when they had seen the miracle that Jesus did, said, This is of a truth that prophet that should come into the world." What made them say that? Well, these people knew their Bibles. They used the Book of Psalms in their homes, and they sang them at the temple services, and they knew that in Psalm 132: 15 it spoke of the Messiah of Israel, the Prophet and King who was to come into the world. It read, "I will abundantly bless her provision: I will satisfy her poor with bread." "Why," they said, "this must be He. That is the very thing He has done. See how He has satisfied us here with bread. This must be He indeed."

What prophet did they mean? The one of whom Moses spoke. "Him shall ye hear in all things." And so they said, "This must be the Prophet. This must be the coming Saviour." But the time had not come when Jesus was to fulfil all those Old Testament prophecies and take over the kingdom. He was going to do that in God's due time, but before that He was to go back to heaven and carry on a wonderful ministry as our great High Priest, and take out a people from the Gentiles to be His Bride in the day of His power.

So He withdrew Himself from the ship and went up into a mountain to pray. We have a beautiful picture of what He has been doing ever since He went back to heaven. They wanted to make Him King, but up into the heights He went. He went up there to talk to the Father, to intercede on behalf of His disciples, who were still in the world amidst the trials and difficulties. This is an illustration of the One who was on earth the Prophet, and who now has ascended to heaven to be our Intercessor, our Advocate with the Father.

"And when even was now come, His disciples went down unto the sea." The other Gospels tell us they went across the sea to Capernaum, but we are told the wind was contrary. John does not tell us that, but the other Gospels do. "And they entered into a ship, and went over the sea toward Capernaum." There is a kind of bay, and they are just crossing the bay when suddenly a storm came up. They come up very suddenly on the Sea of Galilee. "It was now dark, and Jesus was not come to them." In this you may see a picture of the people of God now going over the dark sea of time, and Jesus, while He is indeed present in the Spirit, is personally absent. "And the sea arose by reason of a great wind that blew." They could have turned about and been driven before the wind, but that would have taken them back, and Jesus had told them to go on. So on they attempted to go. The waves rose high and it looked as though they would be wrecked. Had Jesus forgotten? Was He indifferent? No, my brother and sister, no more than He is indifferent to your distress. No; He could see. Even in the dark, He could see. He even knows our thoughts. He knows our sorrows. He knows all about every difficulty we have to face.

There He was pleading and praying, and they were tossed on the sea, and His heart was concerned about them, and so at last He comes to them. And some day He is coming to us. Even now He comes in His loving care to give us just the help we need when we are in difficulty. We read that "when they had rowed about five and twenty or thirty furlongs, they see Jesus walking on the sea and drawing nigh unto the ship: and they were afraid." It takes faith to see Him like that today. They could see Him by sight. We cannot see Him with the natural eye, but we walk by faith and not by sight. No matter what the storms of life, no matter how high the waves, how serious the tempest, trust in Him, count on Him. and look out in faith, and you will see Him walking on the waves. We read, "Thou wilt keep him in perfect peace whose mind is stayed on Thee: because he trusteth in Thee." But you know it is possible to be so occupied with the things of earth that we do not even recognize Jesus when He comes to help us. We are so occupied with our own affairs, our own circum-

stances, that we do not know Him when He comes
to give deliverance.

They were afraid because they thought He was
a phantom or a ghost. Oh, now things are worse
than ever. Circumstances so blind the eyes that
we fail to discern it is really Jesus when He comes
to bring the rest we long for.

But the Saviour drew near and said, "It is I;
be not afraid." And so He speaks to every
anxious heart today who is crying for help, "It
is I; be not afraid." Do not allow yourself to be
oppressed with your difficulties. Once one man
asked another, "Well, brother, how are you getting along?" The other looked up with a gloomy
face and said, "Well, I am doing pretty well
under the circumstances." The other said, "Oh,
I am sorry to hear you are under the circumstances. Christ delights to lift us above all circumstances." That is just what He does. We do
not need to be under the circumstances. Paul the
apostle had more difficulties than we ever had to
suffer, but he said, "I have learned to be abased
and to abound." God says He will never leave
you nor forsake you.

Now Jesus says, "Poor, troubled souls, do not
be afraid, I have come to help you." "Then they
willingly received Him into the ship." They said,
"O Lord, if it be Thou, come into the boat with
us," and He did, and "immediately" everything

was changed and "the ship was at the land whither they went." You see, they were nearly at the port, and they did not know it. Dear friend, your ship is nearly at port; do not give up in despair. He is waiting to show you how marvelously He can meet your case. "Commit thy way unto the Lord, trust also in Him, and He shall bring it to pass." But am I speaking to someone today who says, "Yes, it is all very well to speak to those Christian people that way, but look at me, I do not know Him at all. I do not know how to be a Christian?" Well, dear friends, we have a message for you. Listen to this, "He came unto His own, and His own received Him not. But as many as received Him, to them gave He power to become the sons of God, even to them that believe on His name." Are you willing to receive the Lord Jesus Christ as your Saviour? Will you trust in Him as your Redeemer? Will you believe His Word, which tells you that He was delivered for your offences, and that He was raised again for your justification? Will you act on that word which says, "If thou shalt confess with thy mouth the Lord Jesus, and shalt believe in thine heart that God hath raised Him from the dead, thou shalt be saved." Why, you see, the moment you do that, He takes you in grace and saves you. "To Him give all the prophets witness, that through

His name whosoever believeth in Him shall receive remission of sins." And when you trust Him, then you will know that He came not only to forgive your sins, but to take charge of your life. Why not hand yourself over to Him today? Why not look up and say, "Lord Jesus, I give myself to Thee to be Thine, body and soul and spirit, and henceforth wilt Thou not undertake for me?" He will. He promises to take charge of those who put their trust in Him.

THE FOOD THAT ENDURES

✓ ✓ ✓

"The day following, when the people which stood on the other side of the sea saw that there was none other boat there, save that one whereinto His disciples were entered, and that Jesus went not with His disciples into the boat, but that His disciples were gone away alone; (howbeit there came other boats from Tiberias nigh unto the place where they did eat bread, after that the Lord had given thanks:) when the people therefore saw that Jesus was not there, neither His disciples, they also took shipping, and came to Capernaum, seeking for Jesus. And when they had found Him on the other side of the sea, they said unto Him, Rabbi, when camest Thou hither? Jesus answered them and said, Verily, verily, I say unto you, Ye seek Me, not because ye saw the miracles, but because ye did eat of the loaves, and were filled. Labour not for the meat which perisheth, but for that meat which endureth unto everlasting life, which the Son of Man shall give unto you: for Him hath God the Father sealed. Then said they unto Him, What shall we do, that we might work the works of God? Jesus answered and said unto them, This is the work of God, that ye believe on Him whom He hath sent. They said therefore unto Him, What sign shewest Thou then, that we may see, and believe Thee? what dost Thou work? Our fathers did eat manna in the desert; as it is written, He gave them bread from heaven to eat. Then Jesus said unto them, Verily, verily, I say unto you, Moses gave you not that bread from heaven; but My Father giveth you the true bread from heaven. For the bread of God is He which cometh down from heaven, and giveth life to the world. Then said they unto Him, Lord, evermore give us this bread. And Jesus said unto them, I am the bread of life: he that cometh to Me shall never hunger; and he that believeth on Me shall never thirst. But I said unto you, That ye also have seen Me and believe not. All that the Father giveth Me shall come to Me; and him that cometh to Me I will in no wise cast out. For I came down from heaven not to do Mine own will, but the will of Him that sent Me. And this is the Father's will which hath sent Me, that of all which He hath given Me I should lose nothing, but should raise it up again at the last day. And this is the will of Him that sent Me, that every one which seeth the Son, and believeth on Him, may have everlasting life: and I will raise him up at the last day" (John 6: 22-40).

✦ ✦ ✦

IN this somewhat lengthy section we have three distinct parts. In verses 22-25 the question is raised by the people as to how the Lord Jesus had conveyed Himself away from that part of the country where He fed the five thousand, and how He could be in Capernaum the following day. They knew, because it had been generally reported, that at the close of the day, after He had fed that great multitude, He had sent His disciples away, but He Himself had gone into a mountain to pray. They could not understand how He had travelled from that region to the place where they next found Him. "The day following, when the people which stood on the other side of the sea saw that there was none other boat there, save that one whereinto His disciples were entered, and that Jesus went not with His

disciples into the boat, but that His disciples were
gone away alone; (howbeit there came other
boats from Tiberias nigh unto the place where
they did eat bread, after that the Lord had given
thanks:) when the people therefore saw that
Jesus was not there, neither His disciples, "they
got into some of these other boats and came
"seeking for Jesus."

Now this looks like a movement of real interest,
but one cannot always depend upon outward appearances. It appeared encouraging to see a throng
of people seeking after Jesus in this way, who
were willing to go to the trouble of crossing the
sea to locate Him.   It seemed to indicate a real
deep and abiding interest.   But after all it was
a very shallow kind of thing.   They were not so
interested in Christ Himself, and they had no
sense of needing a Saviour, though they may have
hoped that He would prove to be the promised
Messiah, for they thought of Him as one who
could give them temporal blessings, could provide
them with bread to satisfy their hunger.

So they came seeking for Jesus, and when they
found Him they said, "Rabbi, when camest Thou
hither?"   They knew nothing about what had
taken place during the night; that is, His prayer
upon the mountain or the disciples tossing in the
midst of the sea, the Lord interceding for them,
then going to them on the water, and being re-

ceived by them into the ship, after which they soon reached their desired haven. All this was unknown to this throng who came seeking Jesus and asking, "Rabbi, when camest Thou hither?"

But Jesus used this opportunity to strengthen His testimony and to explain the real reason for His coming to earth. He saw through this apparent interest. He knew what was really in their hearts. Very often people come, for instance, to a gospel meeting, and will begin to talk very religiously, but it does not take long to find that what is really on their hearts is a temporal need, food or clothing, and somehow they feel that Christians ought to be interested in providing these things. And Christians are interested and are glad to minister to these needs, but their ability is often very small. When people come making a pretence of religion it is putting things on a very low level indeed. It would be far better for them to be frank and say, "It is not my soul that I am interested in, but my empty stomach, or it is a coat I need." Then one would know what to do for them, to the very best of his ability. It should not be necessary for people to pretend an interest in religion in order to get temporal help. But that is what these people did They pretended to a real interest in Christ, but He knew they were only thinking of loaves and fishes.

In the second section, verses 26 to 34, we have the answer of Jesus. He said, "Verily, verily, I say unto you, Ye seek Me, not because ye saw the miracles, but because ye did eat of the loaves and were filled." Not because the signs proved anything to them, but because they had a good meal! He provided what they needed yesterday and they would like Him to do the same today. They hoped He would continue to meet their temporal needs, but He was concerned about their spiritual need, for after all, temporal need is for only a little while, but if men live and die without their spiritual need being met, their distress will continue throughout eternity. So He said, "Labour not for the meat which perisheth, but for that meat which endureth unto everlasting life." What did He mean? Did He mean we are not to toil at our daily work to have the proper necessities of life? Not at all. Again and again we are urged to be diligent and careful about these things. Why, then, did He say, "Labour not for the meat which perisheth?" He meant that we are not to make it the supreme thing. The one great important thing to remember is that this life is but as a vapor and will soon be gone. "Labour not for the meat which perisheth, but for that meat (that spiritual food) which endureth unto everlasting life, which the Son of Man shall give unto you, for Him hath God the Father sealed."

Ungodly men of the world say sometimes, "Religion is just an opiate of the people to get them occupied with spiritual things and tell them about bread from heaven to satisfy their souls, so they will forget about the hunger of their bodies." But that is a libel on Christianity. All through the centuries no one has been more concerned about ministering to the temporal needs of men than those who have truly known and loved the Lord Jesus Christ. They have ever been the ones who have been most interested in relieving the circumstances of their fellow-men, and yet we would never want to put temporal relief before spiritual. We are to put first things first: "Seek ye first the kingdom of God and His righteousness, and all these things shall be added unto you"—these things that your heavenly Father knows you have need of. All of these things are important, tremendously important, in their place, but there is something of greater importance, and that is the "meat which endureth unto everlasting life." And He declares that it is only the Son of Man who can give this satisfying food for the soul. That is what He came for, to seek and to save that which was lost. He came from heaven in lowly grace and became the Son of Man in order that He might meet the needs of lost sinners.

"Him hath God the Father sealed." When He publicly dedicated Himself to give His life for us in His baptism in the Jordan, the Spirit of God was seen descending like a dove and abiding on Him, and the Father's voice said, "This is My beloved Son, in whom I am well pleased." That was His sealing.

He had spoken of not working simply for temporal things. Labor, He had commanded, for the food that endures unto everlasting life. They sought to parry this by inquiring, "What shall we do, that we might work the works of God?" They are thinking of the law that God gave at Sinai. They say, "Tell us what we must do in order that we may work the works of God, that we may obtain life eternal? What shall we do?" And Jesus answers, and opens up the truth of the grace of God. He answered and said unto them, "This is the work of God, that ye believe on Him whom He hath sent." "Well," you say, "believing is not working at all." No; but it is evidence of divine work in the soul. That is why we are told, "By grace are ye saved through faith; and that not of yourselves: it is the gift of God: not of works, lest any man should boast." What is the gift of God?—the salvation or the faith? We may include them both. We are told elsewhere that the gift of God is eternal life, but it is also perfectly clear that faith is the gift of God. No merely natural man has faith of himself. "All men have not faith."

But somebody says, "If faith is the gift of God and I, as a poor sinner, have no faith, how then can I believe?" Scripture says, "Faith cometh by hearing and hearing by the Word of God," or, "Faith cometh by a report, and the report by the Word of God." In other words, God has sent a message to man, and we are to have faith in the One of whom that message speaks, and so Jesus said, "If you speak of work, this is the work of God, that ye believe on Him whom He hath sent." There is no use talking about working to please God until you have received the gift of God. That is why we are told that salvation is "not of works, lest any man should boast." But immediately the Holy Ghost adds, "Created in Christ Jesus unto good works, which God hath before ordained that we should walk in them."

And so there is no such thing as meriting salvation by work. There is no such possibility as earning eternal life by effort. "This is the work of God, that ye believe." They were to take God at His word.

But these people were not serious. They were not really interested in their eternal welfare. They were concerned about getting a good meal, such as the Lord had spread for them the day before. So they asked, "What sign shewest Thou then? What dost Thou work?" They knew already. They knew He was going about healing the sick; that He was delivering men and women from all kinds of dire maladies; that He was unstopping the ears of the deaf. Some of them heard that He had raised the dead. But they were thinking of temporal benefit for themselves, just as a lot of people today think of Christianity as a means of bettering their worldly or physical circumstances.

They said, "What sign do you work?" And then they added (and thought that He did not see through it), "Our fathers did eat manna in the desert; as it is written, He gave them bread from heaven to eat." They can quote Scripture, you see. "What sign dost Thou work?" "Is there any manna around? We are looking for bread. Moses fed the people for forty years with bread from heaven. Can you do that? We heard that you did it yesterday. Could you do it today? Then we would believe that you are the Messiah. Is it not written of the Messiah that He will feed the people with bread? Well, here we are, give us bread from heaven." But He answered them, "Verily, verily, I say unto you, Moses gave you not that bread from heaven (in the sense of the true bread that is really worth while); but My Father giveth you the true bread from heaven. For the Bread of God is He which cometh down

from heaven, and giveth life unto the world."
Jesus came down from heaven. The manna sustained Israel for forty years in the wilderness.
Jesus is the Bread that sustains for time and
eternity. Consider the manna, how beautiful it
was, like the falling snow; and that speaks of
Jesus, the Holy One, the pure One, the unblemished One, in whom was neither sin nor flaw of any
kind. That manna fell upon the dew, which is
a type of the Spirit of God, speaking of the day
when God is going to pour out His Spirit upon
Israel. He says, "I will be as the dew unto Israel."
That is, the Spirit of God coming down in re-
freshing power upon them. The manna fell upon
the dew and Jesus came in the power of the Holy
Spirit. He was born of the Holy Spirit, of a virgin mother. His life was lived in the power of
the Spirit, and when at last He died, it was by
the Eternal Spirit He offered Himself without
spot to God. And then—oh, notice this—the
manna came not upon the high mountains where
the people had to climb up to get it, nor did it
fall into some deep ravine where they had to go
down hundreds of feet to find it, but it fell upon
the ground all around them and covered the plain
about the encampment of Israel, so that when an
Israelite stepped out of his tent-door in the morning, he either had to trample upon the manna or
stoop down and gather it as God's good gift!

It illustrates the place that Jesus has taken in lowly grace. Have you trodden ruthlessly upon His love? Or have you received Him into your heart in faith as your own personal Saviour? Rise and feed on Him, the Bread of God which came down from heaven. Which are you doing today? "As many as received Him, to them gave He power to become the sons of God, even to them that believe on His name; which were born, not of blood, nor of the will of the flesh, nor of the will of man, but of God."

And so Jesus puts to one side all their hinting about temporal food and bread to satisfy the natural man, and says, "There is something far more important than bread for the physical man, and that is bread for the spirit of man, the Bread of Life." But they were so dull, as men and women are today, as we all were once, until our eyes were opened. They said to Him, "Lord, evermore give us this bread," but they were only thinking of temporal help. They had not understood that which He had spoken to them.

In the third section, from verses 35 to 40, He makes it even clearer and says, "I am the Bread of life: he that cometh to Me shall never hunger; and he that believeth on Me shall never thirst." What a tremendous proclamation! He has been fulfilling this promise for nineteen hundred years. Many have gone to Him, hungry, distressed, dis-

couraged, and they have received Him in faith
and they have found heart-satisfaction.

Note the simplicity of it—"I Myself am the
Bread of life." Salvation is in a Person, our Lord
Jesus Himself. Remember when Simeon was
worshipping in the temple and Mary and Joseph
entered with the little Baby, and Simeon said,
"There is the salvation of God," and He hastened
to the Baby and took Him in his arms and he
said, "Lord, now lettest Thou Thy servant depart
in peace, according to Thy word: for mine eyes
have seen Thy salvation." Yes, God's salvation
is in a Person, and that Person His own blessed
Son. To receive Him is to be saved. To receive
Him is to have life eternal. But sad it is that
no matter how clearly the message is given, very
few believe: "But I said unto you, That ye also
have seen Me, and believe not."

Then He falls back on that great mystery of
the divine sovereignty of God. He says, "All
that the Father giveth Me shall come to Me: and
him that cometh to Me I will in no wise cast out."
Thank God for such an assurance as that! God
will never be defeated. His purpose will never
fail of accomplishment. All that the Father
giveth to Jesus shall come to Him. You do not
like that, perhaps. You say you do not believe
in election or predestination. Then you will have
to tear a number of pages out of your Bible, for

there are many of them which magnify God's
sovereign electing grace. But do not misunderstand them. Nowhere in the Bible are we told
that God has pre-determined before man is born
that he will be lost or saved, but Scripture says,
"For whom He did foreknow, He also did pre-
destinate to be conformed to the image of His
Son, that He might be the firstborn among many
brethren." Moody was right when he used to
say that, "The 'whosoever wills' are the elect and
the 'whosoever won'ts,' the non-elect." But there
it is, you cannot get around it, "All that the Father giveth Me shall come to Me; and him that
cometh to Me I will in no wise cast out."

But we must not overlook our personal responsibility, "And him that cometh to Me I will
in no wise cast out." Let no man say, "Well,
I am afraid I am not elected, and will not be
saved." The question is, Are you willing to come
to Jesus? He will in no wise cast out. Whoever
you are today, if you will come to Him, He will
take you in. You do not have to settle any question of predestination before you come to Jesus.
And when you come He receives you, and having
come, you may know that you are one whom the
Father gave to the Lord Jesus Christ.

In verse 38 He says, "I came down from heaven,
not to do My own will, but the will of Him that
sent Me." It was part of the Father's will that

Jesus should save eternally everybody who comes to Him. This is the Father's will, that He should lose nothing of all which He has given Him. And so, how sure we may be, how certain, as to our full, final salvation, if we but receive Him, the blessed Bread from heaven! "And this is the will of Him that sent Me, that every one which seeth the Son, and believeth on Him, may have everlasting life: and I will raise him up at the last day." "Every one." Notice the individuality of this. Every man, every woman, for himself or herself, "that every one which seeth the Son"— you see Him by faith, by the Word as He is made manifest by the Spirit—"every one that seeth the Son, and believeth on Him," that is, 'puts his trust in Him,' "may have everlasting life: and I will raise him up at the last day." What is it, then, to feed upon the Bread of Life? It is to receive Christ Jesus in faith as your own Saviour and then day by day to enjoy communion with Him. As you read this blessed Word, as it unfolds one blessed, marvelous truth after another, you are feeding on the living Bread as your soul makes these things your own. Are you still hungering, still thirsting? Do you want the living Bread? Well, then, receive Him now in faith, and if you will accept the testimony God has given, He will receive you, and He promises to give you eternal life and to raise you up at the last day.

EATING CHRIST'S FLESH AND
DRINKING HIS BLOOD

✓ ✓ ✓

"The Jews then murmured at Him, because He said, I am the bread which came down from heaven. And they said, Is not this Jesus, the son of Joseph, whose father and mother we know? How is it then that He saith, I came down from heaven? Jesus therefore answered and said unto them, Murmur not among yourselves. No man can come to Me, except the Father which hath sent Me draw him: and I will raise him up at the last day. It is written in the prophets, And they shall be all taught of God. Every man therefore that hath heard, and hath learned of the Father, cometh unto Me. Not that any man hath seen the Father, save He which is of God, He hath seen the Father. Verily, verily, I say unto you, He that believeth on Me hath everlasting life. I am that bread of life. Your fathers did eat manna in the wilderness, and are dead. This is the bread which cometh down from heaven, that a man may eat thereof, and not die. I am the living bread which came down from heaven: if any man eat of this bread, he shall live forever: and the bread that I will give is My flesh, which I will give for the life of the world. The Jews therefore strove among themselves, saying, How can this Man give us His flesh to eat? Then Jesus said unto them, Verily, verily, I say unto you, Except ye eat the flesh of the Son of Man, and drink His blood, ye have no life in you. Whoso eateth My flesh, and drinketh My blood, hath eternal life; and I will raise him up at the last day. For My flesh is meat indeed, and My blood is drink indeed. He that eateth My flesh, and drinketh My blood, dwelleth in Me, and I in him" (John 6: 41-56).

IT IS a very notable principle in connection
with the ways of our Lord Jesus Christ with
men that if a soul came to Him who was
honestly, earnestly, seeking to know the truth, He
undertook to make that truth just as simple as
possible so that the wayfaring man could understand. On the other hand, if the Saviour presented something which was difficult for the
natural mind to receive, and men, instead of recognizing their need and coming to Him for explanation, assumed a haughty, unbelieving attitude, He invariably seemed to make the truth
more difficult instead of making it simpler. That
is to say, if men will not have the truth of God
when it is presented to them but deliberately
choose to follow the path of error, they will be
blinded to the very truth itself. This principle
runs throughout Scripture. You remember how
Pharaoh set himself against doing the will of
God. We read that God hardened Pharaoh's
heart. He confirmed the haughty king in his very
wickedness. Later on, when the people of Israel
chose the path of disobedience, God said, "I will
choose their delusions." When we look on into
the future to the day when the Antichrist, that
last sinister enemy of God and man, shall arise,
we are told that in that time if men receive not

the love of the truth that they might be saved,
God will send them strong delusion.

There is something very serious in this. Great
responsibility is put upon the man and woman to
whom God's truth is proclaimed. That truth is
given us to be believed. It is not something with
which we may play fast and loose. We are called
upon to accept it. "Buy the truth and sell it
not," exclaims the writer of the book of Proverbs.
If there is anyone to whom I am speaking today
who has not opened his heart to the gospel and
received the Saviour, do not imagine that it is
a small matter if you turn away from that truth.
Do not try to persuade yourself that some other
day will do just as well. "Now is the accepted
time, now is the day of salvation." Do you imagine that it will be perfectly all right if you
wait to make up your mind to come to God when
you are ready? When your day comes, you may
find that God has withdrawn Himself. When you
at last come to knock on the door, you may find
that it has been shut and a voice will say, "Depart from Me; I never knew you."

Cowper has said,

> "Hear the just law, the judgment of the skies:
> He that hates truth shall be the dupe of lies;
> And he who will be cheated to the last,
> Delusions strong as hell shall bind him fast."

Oh, I beg of you, cherish every evidence that the Holy Spirit is working upon your heart and conscience. Thank Him for the opportunity of hearing the gospel. He has written, "Hear, and your soul shall live."

We have seen in our study of this sixth chapter of the Gospel of John that Jesus was dealing with a group of selfish people. They were not interested in spiritual realities. So instead of explaining things in a way they might easily take in, when He perceived that they were not interested or concerned about understanding Him, He seems to make things more and more difficult for the natural mind to comprehend.

The Jews murmured (ver. 41). They talked one to the other instead of coming to Him and saying, "Master, we are ignorant, our minds are darkened. We do not understand, but we long to do so. We do not know what you mean, but we want to know. Master, have pity upon our ignorance and enlighten us." They murmured and said, "Is not this Jesus, the son of Joseph, whose father and mother we know?" No; He was not. He was the son of Mary, but He had no human father. They knew Him as the son of Joseph in Nazareth and so they say, "Is not He our fellow-townsman? What does He mean by talking about coming down from heaven?" They did not address their questions to Jesus, but

He heard their murmurs because **He knows** what is in the **heart** of man.

"Jesus therefore answered and said to them, Murmur not among yourselves. No man can come to Me except the Father which hath sent Me draw him: and I will raise him up at the last day." Yes; that was as though He was deliberately turning away from them, saying, "You are not the people to whom I have come. I have no message for you. No man can come to Me except the Father draw him, and He is not drawing you." A little while before, He said, "All that the Father giveth Me shall come to Me." But they did not come, and therefore were not of those who are drawn of the Father.

Hear me, my friend, are you concerned as to whether you are one of those who are drawn of the Father? You can settle that very easily. Have you come to Jesus? Do you desire to come? If in your heart there is the least desire to come, it is the Father who is drawing you to His Son. Oh, cherish the work of the Holy Spirit and instead of resisting His pleadings yield to Him at once. Yield to Him and say, "Blessed Lord, there is so much I do not understand, but I seek enlightenment. Make clear to me the things that are dark, but give me to know that I have been born again in Jesus Christ, that I am to be saved eternally." You may depend upon it, you will not be left in darkness and perplexity. "It is written in the prophets, And they shall be all taught of God. Every man therefore that hath heard, and hath learned of the Father, cometh unto Me?" Have you heard? Have you learned of the Father? What is the lesson the Father is teaching? He is seeking to occupy people with the gracious provision He has made in the gift of His blessed Son. The Father sent the Son to be the Saviour of the world. In His infinite love He sent Him into the world, that we might live through Him. Listen, then, as little children, to the Father. Let Him be your instructor. Let Him teach you and open up to you from the Word the riches of His grace as revealed through His blessed Son. Thus you will be taught of God and you may know that you are numbered among those whose sins have been eternally settled for. It is not that you will be able to see the Father with your natural eyes, but with the eye of the heart. The only one who has ever actually seen the Father is our blessed Saviour Himself, for He says, "Not that any man hath seen the Father, save He which is of God, He hath seen the Father." But though you and I cannot see Him, we can believe His Word. We hear the message, we accept it in faith and we have life eternal. And so Jesus says, "Verily, verily, I say unto you, He that believeth on Me hath everlasting life."

Let that be an end of all controversy. Let that be an answer to every anxious questioner. How may I know that I am a child of God, that I am accepted of Him, that my sins are forgiven, that I have life eternal? "Believe on the Lord Jesus Christ, and thou shalt be saved." "He that believeth on Me hath everlasting life."

I heard Ira D. Sankey tell how he had been anxious for days and months for the assurance of salvation, and had sought for some internal evidence that might make him know that he had eternal life, but as he sat in a meeting he was led to turn to this sixth chapter of John and his eyes fell on this forty-seventh verse, and it came home to his soul with a strangely new and wonderful meaning, "He that believeth on Me hath everlasting life." Mr. Sankey told us that night long years ago in a meeting in San Francisco, that in a moment he saw it, and he looked up and said, "Lord, I believe. I dare to take Thee at Thy word." And that was the beginning of that great ministry of gospel song to hundreds of thousands of people, carrying the glad message of a full and free salvation.

"He that believeth hath everlasting life." Do not put anything between "believeth" and "hath." Not "hopes to have," but "He that believeth *hath* everlasting life." Take God at His word. "I," says Jesus, "am the Bread of life." "I am that

Bread of life. Your fathers did eat manna in the wilderness and are dead." He says, "Yes; your fathers ate that kind of bread in the wilderness that you long for, but they are dead. I am the Bread which cometh down from heaven that a man may eat thereof and not die." "I am the living Bread." It is not merely, "I have come to give you the living bread," but, *"I am* the living Bread. I must be received in faith, and the soul must feed upon Me as the body feeds upon natural bread, in order to be sustained." "I am the living Bread . . . if any man eat of this Bread, he shall live forever: and the bread which I will give is My flesh, which I will give for the life of the world." He is looking forward to the cross. In a little while He is to go to that cross. There He is to be immolated as the great sin-offering. The sacrifice of old was called the food of the altar, and He says, "There I am going to die, and in thus giving Myself, My body becomes the bread for poor starving souls to feed upon and live forever." "He that hath the Son hath life, and he that hath not the Son shall not see life." And so, dear friends, the great question for every one of us to decide is this, "Have I definitely received Christ?" When we eat our natural food it becomes part of us and gives new strength and life. In the same way when we receive the Bread of God, when we take the Lord Jesus Christ by faith and our hearts dwell upon the work that He did for us upon the cross, we gain new strength and life.

"I am the living Bread which came down from heaven: if any man eat of this bread, he shall live forever: and the bread that I will give is My flesh, which I will give for the life of the world. The Jews therefore strove among themselves, saying, How can this Man give us His flesh to eat?" They seemed to be unable to rise above the natural. Our Lord's words were clear enough. Anyone who comes to God as a repentant sinner will have no difficulty in understanding this. But the sneering legalist exclaims, "Eat His flesh! It is absurd! How can a man give us his flesh to eat?" So the Lord Jesus Christ seemed to say, "Well, if you refuse to believe Me, if you will not come to Me, I will tell you something even more difficult to believe." If men will not take what He has already told them, then He will give them something harder to comprehend.

So He said, "Verily, verily, I say unto you, Except ye eat the flesh of the Son of Man, and drink His blood, ye have no life in you. Whoso eateth My flesh and drinketh My blood, hath eternal life; and I will raise him up at the last day. For My flesh is meat indeed, and My blood is drink indeed. He that eateth My flesh and drinketh My blood dwelleth in Me, and I in him." What striking expressions these are, and how difficult

for an unbelieving Israelite to understand! What
did He mean by "eating His flesh and drinking
His blood?" Of course, the words cannot be taken
literally.   He certainly did not mean that they
were to feed upon His actual body and blood.   In
the law the children of Israel were forbidden to
eat blood in any form or manner.   Every kind of
flesh which they ate was to have every drop of
blood poured out.   Yet Jesus speaks of eating
blood and, amazing thought, His own blood—the
blood of a man!   He did not mean that literally.
He meant to challenge them, to make them see
their ignorance and need of enlightenment.   Apparently, His words had no such effect.   Neither
did He mean that He was to give His flesh and
blood in some mysterious sacrament.   I know
that many suppose He referred to the Lord's Supper, in which they tell us the bread and wine,
after the prayer of the officiating minister, pass
through some mysterious change, so that as people partake of it they will be partaking actually
of Jesus' body and blood.   But let me say this:
Millions of people have partaken of what is
known as the sacrament of the Lord's Supper,
the Holy Eucharist, the Communion, the Sacrifice
of the Mass—different names have been used—
millions of people have partaken of it who have
never received life through it.   They give no evidence of having received life through it.   They

can partake of it Sunday morning and live in sin
Sunday afternoon. There is no evidence whatever that they have been born again. Sacraments
do not give life. But let me tell you this: No one
ever ate and drank of the flesh and blood of Jesus
Christ without receiving life. He promised that,
and it is true. His word has been fulfilled down
through the centuries.

What did He mean? Well, throughout the
Church age He has shown us that to eat of the
Bread of life is to receive Him in faith. It is to
receive implicitly what Holy Scripture reveals
concerning the sacrifice of our Lord Jesus Christ
on Calvary's cross, that upon the tree His
precious body was given up for us and His blood
was poured out for our redemption. When we
recognize that His precious blood poured out on
the cross has atoned for our sins, then we are
eating His flesh and we are drinking His blood.
And it is practically true that in the regular observance of the Lord's Supper we do have that
which calls our minds back again to Calvary and
reminds us again of the price of redemption. We
may recognize the relationship between the communion and this precious truth. But do not confound the symbol with the reality. As we feed
in faith upon the body and blood of Jesus Christ,
we lose our appetite for everything unholy. That
same precious body and blood will be our meat

and drink through all the days to come, and when we get to yonder glory we shall still be occupied with Him, the Lamb that was slain. "Unto Him that loved us, and washed us from our sins in His own blood, and hath made us kings and priests unto God and His Father; to Him be glory and dominion forever and ever."

THE LIVING BREAD

✓ ✓ ✓

"As the living Father hath sent Me, and I live by the Father: so he that eateth Me, even he shall live by Me. This is that bread which came down from heaven: not as your fathers did eat manna, and are dead: he that eateth of this bread shall live for ever. These things said He in the synagogue, as He taught in Capernaum. Many therefore of His disciples, when they had heard this, said, This is an hard saying; who can hear it? When Jesus knew in Himself that His disciples murmured at it, He said unto them, Doth this offend you? What and if ye shall see the Son of Man ascend up where He was before? It is the spirit that quickeneth; the flesh profiteth nothing: the words that I speak unto you, they are spirit, and they are life. But there are some of you that believe not. For Jesus knew from the beginning who they were that believed not, and who should betray Him. And He said, Therefore said I unto you, that no man can come unto Me, except it were given unto him of My Father. From that time many of His disciples went back, and walked no more with Him. Then said Jesus unto the twelve, Will ye also go away? Then Simon Peter answered Him, Lord, to whom shall we go? Thou hast the words of eternal life. And we believe and are sure that Thou art that Christ, the Son of the living God. Jesus answered them, Have not I chosen you twelve, and one of you is a devil? He spake of Judas Iscariot the son of Simon: for he it was that should betray Him, being one of the twelve" (John 6: 57-71).

✓ ✓ ✓

THIS sixth chapter of John's Gospel with its seventy-one verses is the longest chapter in this marvelous book telling of the life and ministry of our Lord Jesus Christ. Someone has called John's Gospel the most wonderful book in the world, and perhaps this is its most wonderful chapter. It would have been more helpful if we could have taken the whole chapter at once, but there is so much in it that it is impossible to do this in thirty-five or forty minutes, so we have had to break it up. But I hope that this will not result in our losing sight of the setting. Jesus had fed the multitude and the next day people came to Him hinting that they would like to get another meal in the same way. They said, "What sign do you show? Our fathers did eat manna in the wilderness. We heard you did this yesterday. Are you prepared to do the same thing today?" But Jesus took the occasion to show them that there was something far more important than providing food for the body. We are told, "Man does not live by bread alone, but by every word that proceedeth out of the mouth of God." This was true even of the Son of Man who came to

Note—Owing to the fact that this address was given to many who were not present on earlier occasions, there is some repetition which I have thought best not to alter.
                  —H. A. I.

give His life a ransom for the world. And in this
chapter He expresses the mystery of His incarnation. The Bread of God is He who came down
from heaven. In other words, He did not just
begin to live when begotten in the womb of the
Virgin Mary. He was the pre-existent Son of
God who became Man for our redemption. And
it is in His incarnation, that is, God and Man in
the wonderful Person of our Lord Jesus Christ,
that He is presented to us as the Bread of God.
Then He speaks of something deeper, something
more serious. He says, "Except ye eat the flesh
of the Son of Man and drink His blood, ye have
no life in you." And in saying this, He used
terms that must at first have been abhorrent to
some of those Jews, for they knew that the law
said that man was never to eat blood. But He
declared, "You must eat My flesh and drink My
blood if you would have life, and I will raise you
up in the last day. If you do not eat and drink
My flesh and blood you will have no life in you at
all." This has no reference to what is called the
sacrament of the Lord's Supper. It had not been
instituted at this time, but He referred to His
sacrificial death when His blood was separated
from His body, His blood shed for sinners; and
men must eat His flesh and drink His blood, that
is, they must appropriate the value of His atoning
work, in order to avail themselves of God's sal-

vation. Eating the flesh of the Son of God and drinking His blood, are figurative expressions, and they mean laying hold of these precious truths by faith and making them our own. Eating is appropriating faith. Have you all done that? Have you received the Lord Jesus Christ in that way? Have you trusted Him for salvation? Do you recognize that His death was for you, that the shedding of His blood was that your sins might be put away? As you contemplate that cross—an empty cross now, He who hung suspended on the nails is now seated at God's right hand—and as you look from that empty cross to the throne of God can you say, "Lord Jesus, Thy blood was shed for me, I believe in Thee as my Saviour?" This is to eat His flesh and drink His blood. It is not simply a momentary thing. It is not that just at one particular time in our lives when troubled and convicted of sin we receive Him by faith, but it is living day by day in communion with Him, appropriating all that Christ is and all that He has done. This is indeed to feed upon the living Bread. And we do that as we meditate upon the Word of God. I do not know of any other way by which we may feed upon the living Bread. Those of us who have acquainted ourselves with the Word in the times of good health, find that memory will bring up the words when we are sick and thus we feed upon that which we have already learned. How important then when we are able to read the Word when we are strong and well, that we give ourselves to the extensive study of this Book, to meditate upon it, to build us up and nurture us, as Scripture puts it, in the words of faith and sound teaching. We need this in order to enter into and enjoy communion with our Lord.

In verse fifty-seven He says, "As the living Father hath sent Me, and I live by the Father: so he that eateth Me, even he shall live by Me." That is communion. The Lord Jesus Christ as a Man here in this world lived in daily communion with the Father, and it is wonderful to think that He studied His Bible just as He calls upon us to search the Scriptures. We read in Psalm 16 how the blessed Lord was speaking to the Father and He said, "My goodness extendeth not to Thee; but to the saints that are in the earth, and to the excellent, in whom is all My delight." There He was, as Man on earth, looking up to the Father, not pleading His own merit, save on behalf of others, and yet living in daily communion with God. And the prophet Isaiah (chapter 50) gives a wonderful illustration of His living by faith. There He says in verse 2, "Wherefore, when I came, was there no man? When I called, was there none to answer? Is My hand shortened at all, that it cannot redeem? or have I no power to

deliver? Behold, at My rebuke I dry up the sea,
I make the rivers a wilderness: their fish stinketh, because there is no water, and dieth for
thirst." Who is speaking here? The eternal
God, the Creator and Upholder of all things.
But which Person of the Godhead? Our blessed
Lord Jesus Christ, God the Son, for look at the
next verses (4-6), where He speaks as Man. In
verses 2, 3 He speaks as God. But now we hear
Him saying, "The Lord God hath given Me the
tongue of the learned, that I should know how
to speak a word in season to him that is weary:
He wakeneth morning by morning, He wakeneth
Mine ear to hear as the learned." This is the
same One who said, "I clothe the heavens with
blackness, and I make sackcloth their covering."
He took the place of a learner that He should
know how to speak a word in season to him that
is weary. I like Leeser's Jewish translation here
which reads, "That I should know how to comfort the weary with the Word." Think of it!
The Lord Jesus here on earth studying the Bible
day by day in order that He should know how to
speak a word in season to weary souls, for their
own comfort and help.

Then He adds, "Morning by morning, He
wakeneth Mine ear to hear as the learned." Three
times we read in Scripture of the pierced or
opened ear. There is that wonderful type of the

bondservant who had served out his time, and was now ready to go out free. But we are told in the Book of Exodus, "If that servant should say, 'I love my master, my wife and my children, I will not go out free,' " then he was to take him to the side of the door and pierce the servant's ear with an awl. Thus he became a perpetual servant. When one of his little ones would look at that ear and say, "Mother, why has father such an ugly hole in his ear?" she would say, "Oh, don't call that ugly! That tells how much he loves you and me! You see, he was a bondman and could have gone out free, but he would not leave us, so his ears were pierced with an awl." This is a picture of our blessed Lord in glory with the print of the nails still in His hands, the scars that tell of His unchanging love for His Father and His Church. Yes, He is the Servant with the pierced ear.

Then again He says in Psalm 40, "Mine ears hast Thou opened," and in the New Testament that is changed to, "Sacrifice and offering Thou wouldest not, but a *body hast Thou prepared Me.*" It meant this—when the Lord Jesus was one with the Father before the incarnation, He never had to take orders from anyone, He did not need the servant's ear; but when He became a Man, He took the servant's place and received instructions from the Father day by day. "For I came ... not

to do Mine own will, but the will of Him that
sent Me." And here in Isaiah 50 He says, "The
Lord God hath opened Mine ear, and I was not
rebellious, neither turned away back." Oh, we
get so rebellious. God begins to show what He
would have us do, and we become rebellious. It
was never so with Him, for He lived in daily,
hourly, momentary communion with the Father
and delighted in the will of God. See what it
brought Him. He says, "I gave My back to the
smiters, and My cheeks to them that plucked off
the hair: I hid not My face from shame and spitting." Think of it! The One who could say, "I
clothe the heavens with blackness, and I make
sackcloth their covering!" Now He says, "I hid
not My face from shame and spitting." So we
see Him in the two natures of God and Man. And
as Man here on earth He lived in communion with
the Father. "And I live by the Father." So he
who appropriates Him by faith day by day, even
he shall live by Him. Paul expresses this when
he says, "I have been crucified with Christ, nevertheless I live, yet not I, but Christ liveth in me."
That was eating Christ—that was making Christ
his own and part of himself, as it were—"Christ
liveth in me, and the life which I now live in the
flesh, I live by the faith of the Son of God, who
loved me, and gave Himself for me."

We become in large measure like the food we

eat. Someone has said, "What we eat, we are."
One who is really feeding on Christ will become
like Him. Such an one will manifest His purity,
goodness, tenderness, compassion, His kind interest in others. You take a professing Christian
who is hard and bitter and critical of others, and
you know he hasn't been feeding on Christ for
a long time. That tells the story. You take a
Christian who is drifting into worldliness and
carelessness, who is becoming vain and haughty
and self-centered—he has not been feeding on
Christ. The Word says, "Let this mind be in
you which was also in Christ Jesus." That is
the humble mind, the lowly mind. It is the mind
that thinks of others, and says, "Never mind me."
This is not natural to us, but it is developed in us
as we feed upon our blessed Lord. And this is
to be our portion forever. So He continues, "This
is that Bread which came down from heaven:
not as your fathers did eat manna, and are dead:
he that eateth of this Bread shall live for ever."

But when the people heard this, it troubled
them. Many had gone with Him that far and
had recognized in Him a wonderful prophet, and
they were asking themselves, "Is not this the
Messiah?" They were listening to His teachings
and following Him, but when He spoke of eating
His flesh and drinking His blood, when He opened

up this wonderful truth of His atonement, it began to trouble them. They were looking for a great world ruler who would deliver them from the Romans and make them the first nation in the world. They were not prepared for what He talked of—dying, giving His life for the world. When they heard this they said, "This is an hard saying; who can hear it?" There are many like that today. They are willing to take Jesus as a great Teacher. They are ready to acknowledge that in His life He has given us a wonderful example, and they talk about trying to follow in His steps, but they do not own His Saviourhood, they do not want His vicarious atonement, they are not willing or ready to believe that in Jesus we have God and Man in one blessed Person. They are ready to think of Him as a martyr for truth, but they are not ready to admit that Christ died for our sins according to the Scriptures. There is no life in them, for there is no new birth unless one receives Him as the incarnate Son of God, dying on the cross for our redemption. And so today there are many who would turn away from this truth saying, "This is a hard saying; who can hear it?"

Jesus knew what they were saying and He said, "Doth this offend you? Does this cause you to stumble because I have told you that I have come down from heaven and become Man? Because

I tell you that I am going to die that man might be saved; does this stumble you? I will tell you something more—some day I am going to ascend, as Man, into heaven." You see, when men resist the truth the Lord Jesus makes it harder for them, but when they will receive the truth, then He makes it very simple. So, now, He makes it far more difficult than before: "What and if ye shall see the Son of Man ascend up where He was before?" "Oh," they would say, "we can't believe that, that Jesus, as Man, should ascend up into heaven." Yet that is just what took place in God's due time. God raised Him from the dead and He was taken up. Four times in the first chapter of the book of Acts we get that phrase. And He sits now at the right hand of God. Some people believe that a great change took place in Christ's body as He was taken up after His death. They think of Him as some strange mysterious spirit without a material human body, but you remember He Himself said, "Handle Me, and see; for a spirit hath not flesh and bones, as ye see Me have." There was a physical form. He had poured out His blood for our redemption, but He is there in heaven in a body—in the same body that hung upon the cross. He is the Man Christ Jesus at God's right hand today, and when we see Him we shall look up into the face of a Man, we shall grasp the hand of a Man, but we

shall recognize a nail-print in that hand. He
will bear it through eternity.

"What and if ye shall see the Son of Man ascend
up where He was before?" Could you believe
that? But, He says, "It is the spirit that quickeneth: the flesh profiteth nothing: the words that
I speak unto you, they are spirit, and they are
life." It is only as we receive His words in faith
that we can lay hold of eternal truth. The flesh,
unless moved upon by divine grace, will not understand. His words are foolishness unto the
natural man, because they are supernaturally discerned. But these words are spirit and truth and
when you open your heart to receive them, a new
life is created, and you are able to take them in.

"But there are some of you that believe not.
For Jesus knew from the beginning who they
were that believed not." He knew what was going on in the hearts of men. He knew whenever
anyone made a profession that wasn't real. He
knows today. The Son of God knows whether you
are genuine or not. Your friends may not know.
Those you are close to may not know, but He
knows whether you have really put your trust
in Him, the Bread of God that cometh down from
heaven. Let us seek to be real before Him. Let
us not rely on mere profession, it will not avail
in that day. There must be reality. "And He
said, Therefore said I unto you, that no man can

come unto Me, except it were given unto him of My Father." And does that then shut anybody out? Does it make it impossible for some men to come? Does it mean then that there are some that God has decreed may come and some that may not? No. "Him that cometh unto Me, I will in no wise cast out." All may come if they will, but apart from the drawing of the Father none would come.

Well, this seemed like "strong meat" for many, and we read,"From that time many of His disciples went back, and walked no more with Him." They had kept company with Him up to that time. They hoped from day to day that He would put Himself at the head of the Jews, that He would lead them on to glorious victories, but now their hopes are dashed. They didn't understand His words about dying and ascending to heaven. This is not the Messiah that they were looking for. Then Jesus turned to the twelve whom He had officially selected and asked, "Will ye also go away?" They had seen Him in prayer. They had listened to His teaching and apparently had received His Word in their hearts. They knew His power. Alas, even of them there was one who had a devil.

"Will ye also go away?" or, "Do you desire to go away also? Are you ready to leave Me? Have I told you more than you are ready to receive?

Do you want to go away?" And then Peter speaks up—and we think of him as being so rash and speaking up out of place, and yet so many times he speaks up in such earnestness and faith that our hearts rejoice. How ready he was to speak out in Caesarea Philippi. And then he answered and said, "Lord, to whom shall we go? Thou hast the words of eternal life." As much as to say, "There is no one that we can go to, we can't turn to the sages of old or to the scribes. They cannot give us what You have given. "Thou hast the words of eternal life." Oh, hear it, dear friends! No one but Jesus can give us the knowledge of God. As you trust Him, as you receive Him and feed upon this living Bread, you shall have life eternal.

But now Jesus looks compassionately upon the twelve and He knows of the eleven that are genuine, and He knows of the one that is not real. And He says, "Have not I chosen you twelve, and one of you is a devil (or, is sold out to Satan)?" What privileges and opportunities they had, and yet one of them had never opened his heart to the truth. What a terrible thing! Dear friends, I wonder if there is anyone like that here today. You profess to be a Christian, and yet all through the years Jesus has never been to you a Saviour from sin. You have never definitely united your soul to Him. You have never bowed before God as a repentant sinner. Oh, I beg of you, before your doom is sealed, and you have to share the fate of Judas, I beg of you, come to His feet, confessing your sin and guilt. Judas never came. Judas never received the Word. So at last he went to his own place in everlasting darkness.

"He spake of Judas Iscariot the son of Simon: for he it was that should betray Him, being one of the twelve." Judas was one of those who kept company with Him so intimately through the years, but he will be separated from Him for eternity. Oh, God give us to be genuine, to feed upon the living Bread that cometh down from heaven.

THE ATTITUDE OF THE WORLD
TO GOD AND HIS CHRIST

✓ ✓ ✓

"After these things Jesus walked in Galilee: for He would not walk in Jewry, because the Jews sought to kill Him. Now the Jews' feast of tabernacles was at hand. His brethren therefore said unto Him, Depart hence, and go into Judæa, that Thy disciples also may see the works that Thou doest. For there is no man that doeth any thing in secret, and he himself seeketh to be known openly. If Thou do these things, shew Thyself to the world. For neither did His brethren believe in Him. Then Jesus said unto them, My time is not yet come: but your time is always ready. The world cannot hate you; but Me it hateth, because I testify of it, that the works thereof are evil. Go ye up unto this feast; I go not up yet unto this feast: for My time is not yet full come. When He had said these words unto them, He abode still in Galilee. But when His brethren were gone up, then went He also up unto the feast, not openly, but as it were in secret. Then the Jews sought Him at the feast, and said, Where is He? And there was much murmuring among the people concerning Him: for some said, He is a good man: others said, Nay; but He deceiveth the people. Howbeit no man spake openly of Him for fear of the Jews. Now about the midst of the feast Jesus went up into the temple, and taught. And the Jews marveled, saying, How knoweth this Man letters, having never learned? Jesus answered them, and said, My doctrine is not Mine, but His that sent Me. If any man will do His will, he shall know of the doctrine, whether it be of God, or whether I speak of Myself" (John 7:1-17).

✓ ✓ ✓

HAVING concluded our studies of that wonderful sixth chapter, in which our Lord presents Himself as the Bread of God, we proceed now to follow Him as He resumes His course traveling about from place to place, ministering the Word to believers and unbelievers alike, according to their needs.

We read, "After these things Jesus walked in Galilee." He preached that sermon on the Bread of God in Capernaum, in the northern section of Galilee, and from there He went about to other places in the same district, and later went down to Judea. Because the Jews sought to kill Him, He did not at first go to Judea. It is in the south. His foes were more violent there than in Galilee where the people did not take things as seriously as did the bigoted legalists of Judea, who were filled with pride and vain-glory and utterly intolerant of opposition to their views. They were very sure of their own position, and with that came an abhorrence of anything like consideration for the opinions of others who did not agree with them. They had decided already that the Lord Jesus Christ was a false prophet. They declared He deserved to be silenced, and drastically dealt with as one who sought to turn the people away from the law of God, which they confused with their own traditions. According to Deuter-

onomy, such an one was to be stoned to death. So
we can understand their attitude toward the
Lord Jesus Christ. They hated His teaching.
They thought it was contrary to the law of Moses.
In that they were mistaken, of course. "The law
was given by Moses, but grace and truth came
by Jesus Christ." He came to fulfil, in a marvelous way, that very law which was given to
show men that they needed a Saviour, to emphasize the exceeding sinfulness of sin. Paul says,
"The law is our schoolmaster until Christ." Now
we have the full revelation of the grace of God
as revealed in the gospel.

Our attention is next directed to the fact that
one of the last of the great annual festivals in
Judea was about to take place. We read, "Now
the Jews' feast of tabernacles was at hand. His
brethren therefore said unto Him, Depart hence,
and go into Judea." Notice the significant expression, "the Jews' feast of tabernacles." In
Leviticus 23 it is listed among the feasts of
Jehovah. Why the change? Because they had
missed the true meaning of it. They only observed
it in a cold, legal way; so the Lord refuses to associate His name with it. We can see the same
thing today. The Lord has given us the ordinances of baptism and the Lord's Supper. Now,
where they are observed according to the Word
of God their significance is very real, but where

people substitute baptism for regeneration, where they believe baptized children become members of the kingdom of God, or older people think that by baptism their sins are washed away, then this ordinance becomes an abhorrence in God's sight. The same thing is true of the precious observance of the Lord's Supper. When we come together to partake of the bread and the cup in remembrance of our blessed Saviour who gave Himself for us, it is precious in the sight of God. He delights to find His people coming together in a reverent manner to remember the One who has redeemed them. But when they make of the Lord's Supper simply a legal service and think that they are helping to fit themselves for heaven and to save their souls by observing it, then it becomes *their* feast and not the feast of the Lord. It becomes something that is human, of man, and not something that is of God.

Now this feast of tabernacles, as originally given, is most significant. We read in Leviticus 23: "These are the feasts of the Lord." The word *feast* does not exactly mean a festival in every instance, but a set time. In other words, they were the outstanding events in the Jews' ecclesiastical year, and you will find that there were four of them in the beginning of the year and three in the fall, and the feast of tabernacles was the last of them all. The first one is the feast of the passover, and in the fifth chapter of 1 Corinthians Christ, our passover, is said to be sacrificed for us. The passover was observed first in Egypt, when God visited the firstborn in judgment. There they divided the lamb into its parts and feasted upon it, but the blood was sprinkled outside on the door posts and lintels, and the people inside were safe from judgment; a wonderful picture of Christ—Christ the Passover Lamb—and as God said of old, "When I see the blood, I will pass over you," so it is today; when people put their trust in that precious blood they are safe from judgment, and then they feed, in spirit, upon the blessed Saviour who shed His precious blood for our redemption. That is the feast of the passover. And you know it was at the time of the feast of the passover that our Lord Jesus Christ died upon the cross. He, the Lamb of God, died on Passover day to put away our sins.

The second feast is that of unleavened bread. They began with passover day and continued for another seven days, eating only unleavened bread. Again in 1 Corinthians 5 we read, "Let us keep the feast, not with old leaven, neither with the leaven of malice and wickedness; but with the unleavened bread of sincerity and truth." Those people feeding upon that unleavened bread represent Christians feeding on Christ and living to the glory of God, putting out of their lives everything that is worldly, that is unholy, that is connected with the old life, and now walking in newness of life.

The third appointed festival was the feast of first fruits. It was celebrated on the first day of the week following the passover, when they took the first sheaf that was fully ripe. They brought it to God and presented it to Him. That represents our Lord Jesus Christ as the Risen One. This is made plain in 1 Corinthians 15. We read, "But now is Christ risen from the dead and become the firstfruits of them that slept." The corn of wheat had to die, but dying, it brought forth much fruit. And so as the priest brought and presented that sheaf to the Lord, it represented our blessed crucified Saviour rising from the dead on the morrow following the Jewish Sabbath. How perfectly the type fits the fulfilment, for it was on the first day of the week following the Passover-Sabbath that Christ rose from the dead. "He was delivered for our offences, and was raised again for our justification."

Then as we continue in the book of Leviticus, the people were to count fifty days until the morrow after the seventh Sabbath, when a new offering was to be brought to the Lord: two loaves of bread baked with leaven. Leaven was a type of sin, so there could be none of that in the bread that represented Christ. But on the fiftieth day, the feast of Pentecost, following the Jewish Sabbath, which has now been set aside, we find the two wave loaves presented before God, which were made of leavened dough. They picture Jew and Gentile saved by grace and they constituted a new meal offering. That pictures the beginning of the Church dispensation. All of these feasts have to do with the ground of our salvation, and have already been fulfilled.

Then in the fall of the year there were three other set feast types. First, the blowing of the trumpets, which speaks of the time when Israel will be brought back to God. Then came the great Day of Atonement, and we see it fulfilled, as pictured in Zechariah 12, when in the coming day Israel will "look upon Him whom they have pierced, and they shall mourn for Him, as one mourneth for his only son, and shall be in bitterness for Him, as one that is in bitterness for his firstborn." That will be the Jews' true day of atonement, when *they* find out at last that the Lord Jesus Christ who died on Calvary's cross was really the great sin offering who died to put away their sins, and they will recognize Him and, trusting Him, they will be able to say, "He was wounded for our transgressions, He was bruised for our iniquities: the chastisement of our peace was upon Him: and with His stripes we are healed."

Then the last appointed season of the seventh month was the feast of Tabernacles, and for eight days the people were to dwell in booths as a reminder of that which took place in the wilderness. Typically, it pointed to the time when the restored nation will dwell in peace, with nothing to make them afraid, with our Lord Jesus Christ reigning over them. For in Zechariah 14 we find that the true feast of Tabernacles will be when Israel and the world shall be brought to enjoy the saving grace of God and shall live under the glorious reign of our Lord Jesus Christ.

But, alas, the Jews of Christ's day did not realize that the King was among them already. Even the brothers of Jesus were unbelievers until after His resurrection. We have the names of some of them. We know that James, Jude, Simon and Joses were brothers of Jesus; whether they were full or half-brothers has been a debated question, but at any rate they belonged in the family in some sense and were related to the Lord Jesus Christ. Other scriptures show that there were sisters too. His brothers on this occasion were going up to the feast of Tabernacles. They say, "Are you going?" "Depart hence and go into Judea, that Thy disciples also may see the works that Thou doest." There is a sneer in that; it seems they would "put Him on the spot." "Why don't You go to Judea? You are a good Jew;

why don't You keep the feast of Tabernacles with
the rest instead of doing things secretly? If you
think You are the Sent One, if You di these
things, show Thyself to the world."

It must have been very hard to take that from
His own brethren, to find that those who had
grown up with Him did not believe in Him.
"Neither did His brethren believe in Him." Think
of it! It is very difficult sometimes to convince
people in your own household. Have not many of
us found out that it is easier to approach people
outside the members of the family? If you have
faults, every fault is magnified, it becomes so
manifest; and it is so much harder often to im-
press those of your own family with any spiritual
blessing that God has given. Jesus Himself, the
Holy One, endured that. He can understand the
trouble we have in our own homes because of our
Christian testimony.

The day came when these brothers believed in
Him, but it was after His resurrection, after He
rose from the dead. Then, eventually, they were
convinced, and James and Jude became two of
His outstanding disciples. And Simon, another
brother, was for many years revered as a devoted
servant of our Lord, as early Christian writers
tell. There was a fourth brother, Joseph, or
Joses, of whom we know nothing. We have their
names listed in Matt. 13: 55.

But now, instead of answering their sneer with a sneer, or reviling as they had reviled, He replies very kindly, "My time is not yet come." "I am waiting for word from My Father." You see, having come down and taken a servant's place, He would never move until He had the Father's word. "I came not to do My own will, but the will of Him that sent Me." We make so many mistakes as we act according to our own will. The Lord Jesus Christ never did that. He always waited for word from the Father. "My time is not yet come: your time is alway ready." That is, the time of man after the flesh is alway ready. "The world cannot hate you; but Me it hateth, because I testify of it, that the works thereof are evil." That is why men were displeased with the Lord Jesus Christ. If He had been willing to condone their sins and look kindly upon their evil doings, they could have tolerated Him, or even have become His enthusiastic adherents, but, no, He bare witness against the sin and corruption and iniquity of the world and therefore they hated Him without a cause, simply because of His holiness and purity, which was in contrast to their iniquity.

Now He says to them, "Go ye up unto this feast: I go not up yet unto this feast, for My time is not yet full come." And so His brethren went on without Him. "He abode still in Galilee."

Later on, after they were gone up, He went up alone secretly by Himself. Without any flourish of trumpets, without any public announcement, He went up to Jerusalem. Evidently the Jews expected Him to be present, for we are told that "The Jews sought Him at the feast, and said, Where is He?" Why did they expect Him to be there? Because He was always careful to observe the law, and the law said that every Israelite was to appear three times in the year before God at the place where He set His name; and so the Lord Jesus Christ would keep to that, the Passover, the day of Pentecost, and the feast of Tabernacles. So they had a right to expect Him. There was much murmuring. Not finding Him they began to talk about Him. "Some said, He is a good man: others said, Nay: but He deceiveth the people." His name was dividing the nation then as it divides the world today. Some recognized in Jesus a sincere man. They thought He was a good man, and if He was a good man it followed He would speak truthfully. But there were others who said, "No, He is a deceiver." Just so is the world divided today. Which side are you on? Are you among those who recognize His claims, or are you one of those who refuse Him?

Nobody spoke out openly, for they were afraid that some of the leaders might hear what was said and it might lead to difficulty. But now about the midst of the feast, Jesus suddenly appeared in the temple. It was customary of old for teachers to go into the courts of the temple. Different rabbis would take up their stand by various pillars. At a set time of the day you might have seen various groups gathered about their favorite instructors. You might have come to one pillar and found a Sadducee teacher with a group surrounding him. At another a Pharisee would be holding forth. Jesus would take His place by one of these pillars and the Jews who gathered around Him listened with amazement as He taught them. What a grasp of things He had! With what authority He set forth His teaching! They exclaimed, "How knoweth this Man letters, having never learned?" In other words, "Why, He has never been to college. He never sat at the feet of any of our great teachers. Where did He get all this? How did He learn these wonderful things?" One might have said, "Why, He is God." Why did not He tell them that? But that was not the answer. He was not to draw on His divine knowledge, but He chose to learn from the Word of God and to receive from His Father from day to day. Think of it! The blessed Son of God—the Eternal Wisdom—the Wisdom that created the heavens and the universe, now become Man on earth and poring over His Bible, as you and I are commanded to do, turning from page to

page in God's Word, as Man, learning from day
to day as a disciple. What an example to us!

And this was the thing that made His ministry
so rich and so full, and if I am speaking to any
today who would be a blessing to mankind, I emphasize, saturate yourself with this Book. Do not
waste your time simply on the works of man with
the thought that your understanding and vocabu-
lary will be enlarged. Live in your Bible! The
better you become acquainted with this Book, the
more you will be able to present the true Word
of God to mankind.

"How knoweth this Man letters?" He learned
at the feet of His Father, and we may learn in
the same way. Jesus answered them, "My doctrine is not Mine, but His that sent Me." "Doctrine" is "teaching." "I am not giving you My
own words," He says, "but My Father's." "My
teaching is not Mine, but His that sent Me." If
anybody says, "I wish I knew for sure whether
these teachings are really true," then He Himself
tells us how we may find out in order that we may
be absolutely certain. He says, "If any man will
do His will, he shall know of the doctrine, whether
it be of God, or whether I speak of Myself." It
may be easier understood if we say, "If any man
willeth to do His will." That is, if a man settles
it in his heart that he wants to know God's will,
and if he comes to God in repentance and says, "I

want to be delivered from my sins and I want to do the will of God"—if a man takes that attitude, you have the word of the Son of God for it that you will not be left in doubt as to what that will is. This is a test that any honest man may apply, and find out for himself whether the teaching of Jesus is true or not.

People come to me and say, "I wish I could believe as you do, but the trouble with me is that I am not sure whether the Bible is the Word of God or not. I do not know whether these things are true or not. If I could believe them it would be all right." My friend, here is Christ's own word, telling you how you may know for certain whether these things are true. Do you desire above everything else to do the will of God? Are you more concerned about this than about making money, getting on in life? Then He says, If you put that first, you will know of the doctrine. If you seek deliverance from your sins and you want to be right with God and ask Him by His Spirit to open up the truth, He declares in this verse that He will do just that. How many times people have come to me with that, and I always send them to the Gospel of John. In John 20: 30, 31 we read, "And many other signs truly did Jesus in the presence of His disciples, which are not written in this book: but these are written that ye might believe that Jesus is tne Christ, the Son of God; and that believing ye might have life through His name." If you really desire to do the will of God and you have any doubt as to that will, take this Gospel of John and read it quietly and reverently. Do not take too many verses at one time. Take it line by line, and as you read, lift your heart to God and say, "O God, above everything else, I desire to know Thy will, and since this book has been written to prove it, as I study, open Thy truth up to me and let me know whether Jesus is really Thy Son or not." Many people have gone to God in that way and have found out God's will for them, and their doubts have all been dissipated.

I used to have a cowboy friend out in Arizona. He had gotten far away from God, but a day came when God spoke in power to his soul. I have heard him tell how for years he did not believe the Bible and had ridiculed it and rejected its testimony. At last, when under deep conviction of sin, someone said, "Why don't you go to God yourself and ask Him to make it clear and real to you?" So one night he got down by his cot and he prayed, "O God, if there is a God and if Thou dost look down upon a poor sinner like me, and if Thou canst hear my prayer, if Jesus Christ is Thy Son, reveal it to me and I promise I will serve you the rest of my days." He began to search the Scriptures and he often told us afterwards, "I can't express or explain it, but I know that something took place, and within three days I knew beyond the shadow of a doubt that the Lord Jesus Christ was the Son of God and my Saviour." He was a faithful servant of God for years, until taken home to heaven. He died in the faith he had confessed for so long.

Now if you say, "I can't believe the Bible," I can tell you why. It is because you are living in some sin that that Book condemns. If you cannot believe the Bible, it is because you are living in sin. If you will face that sin honestly before God, He will give you light enough to be saved.

CHALLENGING THE LEGALISTS

1   1   1

"He that speaketh of himself seeketh his own glory: but he that seeketh his glory that sent him, the same is true and no unrighteousness is in him. Did not Moses give you the law, and yet none of you keepeth the law? Why do ye go about to kill Me? The people answered and said, Thou hast a devil: who goeth about to kill Thee? Jesus answered and said unto them, I have done one work, and ye all marvel. Moses therefore gave unto you circumcision; (not because it is of Moses, but of the fathers;) and ye on the sabbath day circumcise a man. If a man on the sabbath day receive circumcision, that the law of Moses should not be broken; are ye angry at Me, because I have made a man every whit whole on the sabbath day? Judge not according to the appearance, but judge righteous judgment. Then said some of them of Jerusalem, Is not this He, whom they seek to kill? But, lo, He speaketh boldly, and they say nothing unto Him. Do the rulers know indeed that this is the very Christ? Howbeit we know this Man whence He is: but when Christ cometh, no man knoweth whence He is. Then cried Jesus in the temple as He taught, saying, Ye both know Me, and ye know whence I am: and I am not come of Myself, but He that sent Me is true, whom ye know not. But I know Him: for I am from Him, and He hath sent Me. Then they sought to take Him: but no man laid hands on Him, because His hour was not yet come. And many of the people believed on Him, and said, When Christ cometh, will He do more miracles than these which this Man hath done? The Pharisees heard that the people murmured such things concerning Him; and the Pharisees and the chief priests sent officers to take Him. Then said Jesus unto them, Yet a little while am I with you, and then I go unto Him that sent Me.   Ye shall seek Me, and shall not find Me: and where I am, thither ye cannot come. Then said the Jews among themselves, Whither will He go, that we shall not find Him? will He go unto the dispersed among the Gentiles, and teach the Gentiles? What manner of saying is this that He said, Ye shall seek Me, and shall not find Me: and where I am, thither ye cannot come?" (John 7: 18-36).

✦   ✦   ✦

IT seems almost a pity that one is not able, because of the fulness of the narrative, to take up at one time, a complete account such as that which we have in this seventh chapter, because it all relates to our Lord's meeting with the Jews in the temple court at Jerusalem.   One incident follows another in rapid succession, but they are all connected.

In our last message we saw the Lord presenting Himself to the people and considered the beginning of His conversation with them.   Now, in verse eighteen we go right on with the same incident.   The Lord Jesus Christ had said, in verses sixteen and seventeen, "My doctrine is not Mine, but His that sent Me.   If any man will do His will, he shall know of the doctrine, whether it be of God, or whether I speak of Myself."   Now He adds, "He that speaketh of himself seeketh his own glory: but he that seeketh his glory that sent him, the same is true, and no unrighteousness is in him." The Lord Jesus always claimed to be the Sent One of the Father and then He says, "If any man will do His will." He means, of course, that if people are sincerely desirous of knowing and doing the Lord's will and will come to Him seeking the light, they will find out whether He, Himself, is just a self-seeking egotist endeavoring to gather men for His own glory or whether He is, as He said, the One sent from God as the Saviour and Redeemer. If He was only speaking of Himself He was simply seeking His own glory. We remember that passage in Proverbs 25: 27, "It is not good to eat much honey: so for men to search their own glory is not glory." The illustration that is there used is rather interesting. Solomon used it frequently. Honey is that which is naturally pleasant and agreeable, and I suppose that there is nothing more pleasant than to have people speak well of us. There is something in us that makes us really enjoy having people say nice things about us. Well, according to Scripture, that's honey. Don't get too much of it. Too much will upset us and cause trouble. So he says, "It is not good to eat much honey," and for many to attract attention to themselves is a dishonor. It is a shame for men to seek their own glory. You remember in Jeremiah 45: 5, God sends a special message to Baruch, *"And seekest thou great things for thy self?* *Seek them not*: for, behold, I will bring evil upon all flesh, saith the Lord: but thy life will I give unto thee for a prey in all places whither thou goest."

That is the path of blessing. Our Lord Jesus Christ came not to do His own will but the will of Him that sent Him. His forerunner was a man of like character. He said, "He must increase but I must decrease."

So our Lord Jesus here reminds us that if a man is constantly talking of his own work and his own ability and power, and that kind of thing, with the idea, of course, to get people occupied with himself, he is seeking his own glory. "But he that seeketh the glory of Him that sent Him, the same is true and no unrighteousness is in Him." And this is what the Lord Jesus came to do. Before He went away, as He prayed in that last night ere He went out to Gethsemane, He said, "Father, I have glorified Thee on the earth; I have finished the work which Thou gavest Me to do." And in this He becomes our great example. The one thing that men ought to be occupied with above everything else is bringing glory to the One who has redeemed them. I like that question in the Shorter Catechism of the Westminster Confession, "What is the chief end of man?" The answer is, "The chief end of man is to glorify God and enjoy Him forever." You see,

we make such a mistake when we put self first.
We tell ourselves that if we don't seek our own
interests, no one else will, but the Word declares
that is not true. "Seek ye first the kingdom of
God and His righteousness, and all these things
shall be added unto you." In other words, Put
God first and self last, and God will see that you
are honored in His own time.

And so the Lord Jesus made this the object of
His life—to seek to glorify the One who sent Him.
But then He turns to His opponents who accuse
Him of being false, and says, "Did not Moses
give you the law, and yet none of you keepeth the
law?" It was the glory of Israel that God had
given to them the law on Mount Sinai. No other
nation had such a revelation of the mind and will
of God as that which was given to them. "And
yet," Jesus says, "not one of you keepeth the
law." Not one man had been found, until Christ
came, who walked in complete obedience to that
law. Therefore the law could only condemn. It
said, "Cursed is everyone that continueth not in
all things which are written in the book of the
law to do them." And in the New Testament we
read, "For whosoever shall keep the whole law,
and yet offend in one point, he is guilty of all."
How that cuts out from under us any possibility
of justifying ourselves before God by obedience
to His law. No one but Christ has ever obeyed

perfectly. And yet He went to Calvary's cross and bore the curse of the broken law in order that we might be redeemed.

But these people in Israel were so occupied with their own special place and privileges that they gloried in that which could only condemn them. And the Lord Jesus put His finger at once upon a sore spot. He said, "Why go ye about to kill Me?" But of course the common people were not aware of all this, and the crowd answered and said, "Thou hast a demon. You are demon-possessed. Who goeth about to kill Thee?" Doesn't it show how lowly He had become? He is the Creator of heaven and earth, and He stands calmly there among His own people and allows them to bring a charge like this against Him, and yet He answered them so quietly. They said, "Thou hast a demon." And Jesus said, "I have done one work, and ye all marvel." To what was He referring? To the healing of the man at the Pool of Bethesda. They had never forgiven Him for healing that man upon the Sabbath. The word had gone out that He was a law-breaker, because He had found that poor soul, who had been thirty-eight years helpless, and He had made him whole on the Sabbath. They concluded that this was a violation of the law. Jesus showed them that there were certain things that had to be done on the Sabbath: circumcision of a child, for instance. Jesus declared, "Moses gave you this covenant." On the Sabbath day they carried out this requirement. On the Sabbath day they put the sign of the covenant upon the body of a child. And if a man on the Sabbath day received circumcision why were they annoyed with Him because He made a man every whit whole on the Sabbath? If God gave strength to a helpless cripple, a paralytic, and He chose to do it through Jesus on the Sabbath day should they not rather rejoice that God was visiting His people and pouring out blessing upon mankind? Then He adds, "Judge not according to the appearance, but judge righteous judgment." How we need to take that to heart! How quick we are to judge without knowing all the facts! That is what they did. They heard He had come and made the man whole on the Sabbath and they jumped to the conclusion that He was controlled by Satan and breaking the law of God, and so they condemned Him as if He had sinned against the law, and yet all the time it was God's own Son acting in grace toward needy souls!

Our blessed Lord said in another place, "Judge not that ye be not judged." And then He added solemnly, "For with what judgment ye judge, ye shall be judged: and with what measure ye mete, it shall be measured to you again." What did He really mean? There are times when Christians are called upon to judge. For instance, if evil breaks out among believers, Christians are called upon to judge the wicked person and put him away from their fellowship, and if they do not then God will hold the church responsible. How is that to be harmonized with these words, "Judge not that ye be not judged"? There our Lord was referring to motives. You and I are not competent to judge the underlying motives of the acts of others. Oh, how cruel we are at times! Perhaps I am prejudiced against someone and yet cannot find any fault in his outward life, but I am ready to attribute evil to anything he does. Perhaps a man gives a large contribution to the work of the Lord, and I say, "Oh, he is just doing that to make an impression." It is concerning such things that the Lord Jesus says, "It is not for you to judge." God reads the heart; you do not. "Judge not according to the appearance." "Man looketh on the outward appearance but the Lord looketh on the heart." "Judge righteous judgment," and righteous judgment, of course, is on the basis of that which is manifest and clear. This, you see, was not the case when they were judging Him for breaking the law.

But they were perplexed. "Then said some of them of Jerusalem, Is not this He, whom they seek to kill?" They knew that the leaders were trying to apprehend Him and put Him to death, and yet His words and bearing were so wonderful that they could not understand why anybody should hate Him and want to kill Him. So they asked wonderingly, "Is not this He, whom they seek to kill?" "Then why is He so bold and without fear? Does He not know they are lurking on the outskirts of the crowd, and yet He speaks so boldly. Do the rulers know who He is? After all, can it be that our leaders know in their hearts that He is the promised Messiah?" You know, of course, that the Greek word "Christ" and the Hebrew word "Messiah" are one and the same, and both mean, the Anointed. "Can it be that our rulers know that He is God's Anointed—the One who was to come into the world for the deliverance of Israel?" And yet they are puzzled. "After all, it can't be, because we know this Man and where He comes from." They knew He was born in Bethlehem. But they say, "When Christ cometh, no man knoweth whence He is." Why, the Word of God said, "But thou, Bethlehem Ephratah, though thou be little among the thousands of Judah, yet out of thee shall He come forth unto Me that is to be ruler in Israel; whose goings forth have been from of old, from everlasting." Who is this strange mysterious personality? They say, We can't understand that, but this Man we know all about. He was born in Bethlehem, He lived in Nazareth, and worked at the carpenter's bench. But Jesus took them up on what they were saying. He could hear the very thoughts of their hearts, and "He cried in the temple as He taught, saying, Ye both know Me, and ye know whence I am: and I am not come of Myself, but He that sent Me is true, whom ye know not." "You know that I was born at Bethlehem and lived in Nazareth, but you don't know My Father. You don't know the One who sent Me. If you did, then you would receive Me. But I know Him; I know who the Father is. I am from Him and He hath sent Me." And in this He was declaring His Deity, because you remember it says that He came from God and went to God, and He prayed, "Father, glorify Thou Me with Thine own self with the glory which I had with Thee before the world was." He was One with the Father from all eternity. He was conscious of that as a Man down here on earth. He knew the Father in a sense that no one else did.

But, in their minds, this was tantamount to blasphemy. They endeavored to arrest Him, but no man laid hands on Him because His hour was not yet come. That should make clear to us that Jesus was not subject to man's power. Jesus did not die on the cross because He was helpless in the hands of His enemies. Not until the appointed hour when He was to go out to die, was it possible for anybody to injure Him or for anybody to put

Him to death. "No man laid hands on Him, because His hour was not yet come." As a result of this we read that many of the people believed on Him. That does not necessarily mean that they trusted Him as Saviour, but they believed in His sincerity, that He was in all likelihood the true Messiah. They were waiting now to see how He would manifest Himself. For they said, "When Christ cometh, will He do more miracles than these which this Man hath done?" How could they credit any other person as Messiah if He was not the One predicted by the prophets who was to come for the deliverance of Israel?

But the Pharisees, the most strict of the Jews, who were looked upon as rigidly orthodox, who accepted all the great doctrines of the Bible and yet some way or other had refused to receive the Lord Jesus Christ, they heard that the people murmured concerning Him and these Pharisees and the chief priests sent officers to take Him, and He met them and said to them, "Yet a little while am I with you, and then I go unto Him that sent Me," as much as to say, "You cannot take Me, the hour is not come; I am not ready to be delivered into your hands. I am still going on with My ministry among you." "Yet a little while I am with you, and then I go (voluntarily of My own will) unto Him that sent Me." He knew that He was going by way of the cross, by way of the tomb. He had come into the world for that very purpose. But from the tomb He was to rise triumphant and to ascend into the presence of the Father. And to those to whom He had come and ministered, but who had set their hearts against Him, He said, "Ye shall seek Me, and shall not find Me: and where I am, thither ye cannot come." Solemn words, not only for them, but for people living today; for once more Jesus is presenting Himself to mankind through the preaching of the gospel, and is asking men to open their hearts to receive Him, but they refuse to do it. For them the time will come when they shall seek Him but shall not find Him. He meant that when He should go back to the Father, if they persisted in refusing obedience to His message they could never be with Him yonder.

Do you see how contrary that is to the conception that many have that no matter how folks live, everybody is going to heaven at last?

We would like to believe that there is something about death so purifying, that the soul would be made clean from sin, but we dare not believe it with the testimony of the gospel to the contrary. No, no. Jesus says, "If you refuse to accept My testimony, where I am, thither ye cannot come." Unless men receive Christ here on earth they will never be with Him in eternity. Have you trusted Him? Have you accepted Him as your own personal Saviour? **Or are you** still debating and saying, "Maybe some day I will settle this question." Be persuaded that your time is short. Your opportunity will soon be gone. Be sure you close with Him as He waits in grace, ere He says to you, "Ye shall seek Me and shall not find Me."

The Jews did not understand that He spake of His death. They said, "Whither will He go, that we shall not find Him? Will He go unto the dispersed among the Gentiles, and teach the Gentiles?" What did they mean by this? Well, you see, centuries had elapsed since Israel had been dispersed among the Gentiles. Year after year many came up to Jerusalem to keep the feasts, but their homes were among the Gentiles, and the Jews who lived in Palestine looked upon them with a measure of scorn. They asked, "Will He go out to these wanderers among the Gentiles and preach to them?" No, He did not mean that exactly and yet there was a sense in which that would be true, for after His resurrection His gospel was to be carried not only to the dispersed of Israel but to the Gentiles everywhere.

But that was not exactly what He meant when He said, "Where I am, thither ye cannot come." He was referring to His ascension into heaven. But they asked, "What manner of saying is this that He said, Ye shall seek Me, and shall not find Me: and where I am, thither ye cannot come?" And with this the present conversation broke up. The Lord Jesus apparently turned away and said no more to them, but left them to think it out and debate the question among themselves. Later on He appeared again among them on the last day, the great day of the feast, but this must be reserved for our next address.

Have we trusted Him? Have we opened our hearts to Him? Oh, if we have, let us seek to go on to serve Him better and let us seek, by grace, to become increasingly like Him by witnessing to a lost world.

THE PROMISE OF THE SPIRIT

✓ ✓ ✓

"In the last day, that great day of the feast, Jesus stood and cried, saying, If any man thirst, let him come unto Me, and drink. He that believeth on Me, as the Scripture hath said, out of his belly shall flow rivers of living water (But this spake He of the Spirit, which they that believe on Him should receive: for the Holy Ghost was not yet given; because that Jesus was not yet glorified) (John 7: 37-39).

✓ ✓ ✓

IN these verses our Lord was directing the minds of His listeners on to a new dispensation. He came, as we know, under the law. He came in exact accordance with all Old Testament prophetic Scripture. He came to magnify the law and to make it honorable. But throughout His glorious ministry, while pointing out the failures of the people under the law, He spoke constantly of that grace and truth which He came to make known. We have already considered His various interviews in the temple and now we come to something that took place on the last day, the great day of the feast of tabernacles.

It had been customary on the last day to have a special service called, "the pouring out of the water." On that day a company of white-robed priests went down to the Pool of Siloam. They filled their jars with water from the pool, and then walked back to the temple and poured out the water in the presence of the people. This was to call to their minds the marvelous provision that God had made for Israel during the days of their wandering in the wilderness. When they came murmuring to Moses he cried to God, and He said, "Thy rod, wherewith thou smotest the river, take in thy hand and go. Behold, I will stand before thee, there upon the rock in Horeb; and thou shalt smite the rock, and there shall come water out of it." Moses did so, and as the rock was cleft the water gushed out and the people had all they needed. On a later occasion, shortly before they entered into the land, when again they were in distress because of lack of water, God said, "Take the rod (Aaron's rod), and gather thou the assembly together, thou and Aaron thy brother, and speak ye unto the rock before their eyes; and it shall give forth his water." But Moses *smote* the rock twice. The water came out abundantly, but Moses had not followed God's directions. He was a bit troubled and irritated, and he made a great blunder. Sometimes, you know, God's servants do get troubled and upset. Moses actually lost his temper on this occasion. As a result he spoiled God's lovely type. The smiting of the rock in obedience to God, in Exodus 17, was a beautiful type of the smiting of Christ with the rod of judgment. When Moses lifted the rod up over the Red Sea, the waters parted asunder and the people went through on dry ground, so it was perfectly proper that he should use the same rod on the rock. That rock was Christ. Christ had to be smitten in judgment on Calvary's cross, and when the wrath of God that was our due fell upon Him and He bowed His head beneath that rod—when the Rock of Ages was cleft for us, the living water flowed forth for the refreshment of a famishing world. But you know He was only smitten once in judgment. Having died for our sins, He is never to die again, and will never have to know the smiting of the rod of judgment again. That question has been settled once for all.

God commanded Moses on the second occasion to take Aaron's rod and go out and *speak* to the rock and it should give forth its water. That is, He was to take the rod of priesthood, reminding us that our Saviour is now ministering in the presence of God as our great High Priest. He does not need to be smitten again to sustain our life. But we read in Numbers 20, "Moses lifted up his hand, and with *his* rod he smote the rock twice," after he had said to the people, "Hear

now, ye rebels; must we fetch you water out of
this rock?" And so he spoiled the type of God's
lovely picture of the present work of His Son.
But—oh, the grace of God!—in spite of the failure of the servant the water gushed out. God
still, in His infinite grace, meets people's need far
beyond their understanding. But read what
happened to Moses. God said, "Now because you
did not sanctify Me in the eyes of the people—
you smote the rock and were angry,—you will
not go into the land but will die in the wilderness." And oh, how Moses pleaded and prayed
that he might go in, but the Lord at last said,
"Speak to Me no more of these matters. You will
not go in, but you can go up and see the land;"
and so Moses' prayer, in that instance, could not
be answered. Afterwards, of course, fifteen hundred years afterwards, God did allow him to
enter the land. When the disciples were on the
Mount of Transfiguration, they looked up and saw
the Lord Jesus Christ, and with Him were Moses
and Elias. God let him go in, but it was when
he could be there as the companion of the Lord
Jesus Christ.

But now going back to the memorial of the
smiting of the rock,—the priests, in the observance of the feast of tabernacles, brought the
water from the Pool of Siloam (which means
"Sent"), and they poured that water out before

the Lord in the presence of the people. And on the last day Jesus stepped forward and cried, saying, "If any man thirst, let him come unto Me and drink." And today He stands crying the same wonderful words: "If any man thirst, let him come unto Me and drink." Note the universality of the message. Is there any man who does not thirst and who does not know what it is to yearn and long for that which is eternal? And Jesus says, "If *any man* thirst"—not just select cases, and He does not even indicate the nature of the thirst. He might have said, as He did once, "Blessed are they that hunger and thirst after righteousness." He might have said, "If any man thirst after goodness, after purity, after holiness, let him come unto Me and drink." But He makes it far wider than that. He says, "If any man thirst." That is for every one of us. You may say, "Yes, I am thirsting for pleasure. I want to find more joy and delight in living." Well, my dear friends, if any man thirst after real pleasure and lasting joy, Jesus says, "Let him come unto Me and drink." It is written, "At Thy right hand are pleasures for evermore." What Jesus said concerning the water of that well in Samaria is just as true of all that earth has to offer—"Whosoever drinketh of this water shall thirst again." You may try all of the different pleasures of earth, they will never quench your thirst. We grant that there is a measure of pleasure in sin, but you know Scripture says that, "Moses, when he was come to years, refused to be called the son of Pharaoh's daughter; choosing rather to suffer affliction with the people of God, than to enjoy the pleasures of sin for a season." That is all, they last only a little while. They are like some of these sweet drinks that you take in the summer, and every time you drink you become only the more thirsty. So it is with all that the world has to offer. But Jesus says to those who try the world but are thirsty still, "Come to Me and drink, and you will never thirst again."

Someone says, "Well I am not concerned about pleasure, but I thirst for wealth—for the means to make things comfortable for my family and myself." Yes, but the wealth of this world passeth away, but if you want pleasure that will last forever and the wealth that will abide, come to Jesus and heed His gracious invitation, and you will be wealthy forevermore.

Perhaps you thirst for the good opinion of others—to be well thought of. Oh, dear friends, there is nothing like having the good opinion of God Himself, and you get that when you trust His blessed Son, when you receive the Lord Jesus Christ as your own Saviour. Then God Himself guarantees that you shall participate with Him in glory—that shall last forever.

Jesus says of His own, "The glory which Thou gavest Me I have given them; that they may be one, even as We are one." We often sing that "Glory" song, and one verse goes,

> "When by His grace I shall look on His face,
> That will be glory, be glory for me!"

Some object to that phrase and say they would rather sing, "That will be glory for Him." Well, of course, that will be glory for Him, but on the other hand it will be glory for me to gaze on His blessed face and be with Him for all eternity. How perfectly satisfied we shall be in that day! Yes, "If any man thirst, let Him come unto Me and drink."

And then He adds, "He that believeth on Me, as the Scripture hath said, out of his belly shall flow rivers of living water." To come unto Him and drink is to believe Him and the message He has given, to put your trust in Him. "He that believeth on Me, as the Scripture hath said, out of his belly shall flow rivers of living water." Now where has the Scripture said this? Well, there may not be any exact verse of Scripture that says in so many words that he that believeth on Jesus from within him shall flow rivers of living water, but I take it that the Lord is refer-

ring to the general tenor of Scripture. The living
water flowing forth from the smitten rock—scripture after scripture indicates that truth.   In
Isaiah 41:17, 18 is a glorious promise which
really refers to the very same thing as that of
which our Lord Jesus Christ speaks. Refreshment and blessing spiritually is for those who put
their trust in this Saviour that God has provided.
"When the poor and needy seek water, and there
is none, and their tongue faileth for thirst, I the
Lord will hear them, I the God of Israel will not
forsake them. I will open rivers in high places,
and fountains in the midst of the valleys: I will
make the wilderness a pool of water, and the dry
land springs of water."

Then in chapter 43:19, 20 of the same book,
that of the prophet Isaiah, it is written, "Behold,
I will do a new thing; now it shall spring forth;
shall ye not know it? I will even make a way
in the wilderness, and rivers in the desert. The
beast of the field shall honour Me, the dragons
and the owls: because I give waters in the wilderness, and rivers in the desert, to give drink to
My people, My chosen."

And then again in Isaiah 44:3, "For I will
pour water upon him that is thirsty, and floods
upon the dry ground: I will pour My Spirit upon
thy seed, and My blessing upon thine offspring."

One other quotation from the same prophet,

chapter 58:11, "And the Lord shall guide thee continually, and satisfy thy soul in drought, and make fat thy bones: and thou shalt be like a watered garden, and like a spring of water, whose waters fail not." The heart of the believer is pictured there. The very inward being of the believer is as a watered garden with streams flowing out for the blessing of others.

Jeremiah uses the same figure in chapter 31:12, "Therefore they shall come and sing in the height of Zion, and shall flow together to the goodness of the Lord, for wheat, and for wine, and for oil, and for the young of the flock and of the herd: and their soul shall be as a watered garden; and they shall not sorrow any more at all."

And then in that lovely book, the Canticles, the holy of holies of the Old Testament, we have the believer typified by the bride, and pictured as one whose heart is a garden from which the water flows forth: "A garden inclosed is my sister, my spouse; a spring shut up, a fountain sealed. . . . A fountain of gardens, a well of living waters, and streams from Lebanon" (chap. 4: 12, 15). It is living water flowing out from the garden for the blessing of others.

And one other Old Testament scripture: "Drink waters out of thine own cistern, and running waters out of thine own well. Let thy fountains be dispersed abroad, and rivers of waters in the streets" (Prov. 5: 15, 16).

And so in all of these passages, to which many more might be added, we have the thought of the Spirit of God dwelling within the child of God as living water and flowing out in blessing to others.

This refers to the work of the Spirit of God in this present age as well as in the glorious kingdom age. This is clearly indicated in verse 39 of our text, "But this spake He of the Spirit, which they that believe on Him should receive: for the Holy Spirit was not yet given; because that Jesus was not yet glorified."

The Lord Jesus Christ was pointing on to a time when He was going back to the Father, after being smitten on the cross, when the Holy Spirit was to come in a new sense to take possession of and dwell within all believers, in order that they, by their testimony, might carry refreshment and joy to others. And, dear Christian, how concerned you and I ought to be as to whether we are allowing anything in our lives that is hindering the outflow of living waters. Just as a stream flowing out from a garden might become choked and hindered by stones and rubbish, so may unholy things in our lives choke and hinder the flow of blessing. I am afraid we Christians hinder the outflow by selfishness, by worldliness, by careless behavior, by unjudged sin, etc. All of these things hinder the outflow of the living water. If we have come to Christ, if we are living in the enjoyment of His love, and are not allowing anything to hinder our communion with Him then indeed we shall be channels of blessing from and through whom the living water shall flow forth constantly.

"NEVER MAN SPAKE LIKE THIS MAN"

✦ ✦ ✦

"Many of the people therefore, when they heard this saying, said, Of a truth this is the Prophet. Others said, This is the Christ. But some said, Shall Christ come out of Galilee? Hath not the Scripture said, That Christ cometh of the seed of David, and out of the town of Bethlehem, where David was? So there was a division among the people because of Him. And some of them would have taken Him; but no man laid hands on Him. Then came the officers to the chief priests and Pharisees; and they said unto them, Why have ye not brought Him? The officers answered, Never man spake like this Man. Then answered them the Pharisees, Are ye also deceived? Have any of the rulers or of the Pharisees believed on Him? But this people who knoweth not the law are cursed. Nicodemus saith unto them (he that came to Jesus by night, being one of them), Doth our law judge any man, before it hear him, and know what he doeth? They answered and said unto him, Art thou also of Galilee? Search, and look: for out of Galilee ariseth no prophet. And every man went unto his own house" (John 7: 40-53).

✦ ✦ ✦

IN the previous address we considered our Lord's wonderful declaration concerning the coming of the Holy Spirit when He cried on the last day of the feast of tabernacles, "If any

322

man thirst, let him come unto Me and drink." And then He added, "He that believeth on Me, as the Scripture hath said, out of his belly shall flow rivers of living water." The Evangelist explained the meaning of the living water when he said, "But this spake He of the Spirit which they that believe on Him should receive." The people who heard our Lord Jesus speaking in this way of the living water, naturally connected the Old Testament passages that told of the living water with the day of the Messiah, for they knew from the prophecies of Jeremiah and Isaiah that it was in His day when the gift of the living water would be given. So they at once jumped at the conclusion that our Lord was declaring His Messiahship, and indeed He was, and yet He knew that the time had not arrived when all this blessing should come to the nation of Israel, but the blessing that they refused was to go out to the Gentiles and was to be enjoyed by a remnant of Israel who would put their trust in Him.

Those who were listening to the Lord turned one to another and some said, "Of a truth this is the Prophet." What did they mean by The Prophet? They were thinking of the words of Moses in Deuteronomy 18. There, beginning with verse 15, we hear Moses speaking to the people of Israel as they were gathered about him on the plains of Moab before they entered the land of

Canaan. He said, "The Lord thy God will raise up unto thee a Prophet from the miast of thee, of thy brethren, like unto me; unto Him ye shall hearken; according to all that thou desiredst of the Lord thy God in Horeb in the day of the assembly, saying, Let me not hear again the voice of the Lord my God, neither let me see this great fire any more, that I die not. And the Lord said unto me, They have well spoken that which they have spoken. I will raise them up a Prophet from among their brethren, like unto thee, and will put My words in His mouth; and He shall speak unto them all that I shall command Him. And it shall come to pass, that whosoever will not hearken unto My words which He shall speak in My name, I will require it of him."

These words referred to our Lord Jesus Christ. In the Book of the Acts, chapter 3: 22, when the Apostle Peter was addressing the people, we read, "For Moses truly said unto the fathers, A Prophet shall the Lord your God raise up unto you of your brethren, like unto me; Him shall ye hear in all things whatsoever He shall say unto you. And it shall come to pass, that every soul, which will not hear that Prophet, shall be destroyed from among the people." So these Jews who were listening to the teaching of our Lord Jesus, by putting various things together that they had heard, and thinking of the marvelous signs He had performed among them, said, "This must be the One for whom we have waited." You see He was to come from among themselves; God "will raise up unto you of your brethren." They were terrified when God spoke in flaming fire in Mt. Sinai and they said, "Moses, you speak to us, but not God, lest we die." And God said, "Well, I will raise up a Prophet like unto Moses. He will be My messenger to them, but whosoever will not hear that Prophet I will require it of him," or "he shall be destroyed."

They were not quite sure, but they thought this must be He. And others said, "This is the Christ" —that is, "This is the Anointed One." They knew from their Bibles that the day would come when God's Anointed One should appear to them. That is why the Jews called Him the Messiah, for Messiah means the "Anointed One." In Psalm 2 we read: "Why do the heathen rage, and the people imagine a vain thing? The kings of the earth set themselves, and the rulers take counsel together, against the Lord, and against His Anointed, saying, Let us break their bands asunder, and cast away their cords from us." A little farther down in that same Psalm, in verse six, it reads, "Yet have I set My King upon My holy hill of Zion." "I have anointed My King upon My holy hill of Zion." The Lord Jesus Christ is God's Anointed. He is the One whom

God Himself has anointed by the Spirit and sent into the world to be the Redeemer of lost mankind.

But some curled the lip and asked sarcastically, "Shall Christ come out of Galilee?" These men of Judea despised the more ignorant and less religious folk of Galilee, and it was unthinkable to them that one who came from there could really be the Anointed One of God. Later on, in verse 52, we find them making a very false declaration about Galilee.

"Hath not the Scripture said, That Christ cometh of the seed of David, and out of the town of Bethlehem, where David was?" Yes, the Scripture said that. The prophet Micah plainly declared it, and his prophecy was quoted at the birth of the Lord: "Thou Bethlehem, in the land of Juda, art not the least among the princes of Juda: for out of thee shall come a Governor, that shall rule My people Israel." They knew that; it was in their Bibles. They knew Christ was to be born in Bethlehem. But they blundered now because they had never learned that He was born in Bethlehem, and that He did come from David through Mary, who was of the lineage of David. The birth of the Lord was a fulfilment, in all points, of prophecy. He was born of a virgin, He was born in Bethlehem, and He was born of David's line, but they did not take the trouble to find out if these things were true or not. When God gives His Word, ignorance of that Word does not excuse anyone. Many today are vastly ignorant of this Book, and perhaps imagine that in the day of judgment they can plead ignorance of it as an excuse for not understanding His will. But, remember, if you are ignorant of the Word of God, you are wilfully ignorant. You have the Bible in your homes. If you do not study your Bibles then you are responsible if you do not learn the mind of God. Jesus says, "Search the Scriptures, for in them ye think ye have eternal life." Oh, that there might come a great awakening of our responsibility to this! I am afraid there are thousands who rarely open their Bibles from one week-end to the other. They depend upon an occasional message from the pulpit or in the Sunday School, and, God knows, very often they get very little there. But there is no excuse, for you have the Bible, and you can read for yourselves. I am sure of this, if there would come a real sense of responsibility as to this and Christians would begin to read and study this Book to become familiar with the mind of God, we would soon have a great revival among the people of God and a great awakening among the Christless.

Sometime ago a dear missionary in England was telling us that he had left his station in India because of ill-health. He read us a letter from one of the native elders in the church in India. He was telling how much they missed him and yet, he went on to say, during his absence they were doing a great deal more praying and reading the Word, and in fact, they were having a real "re-Bible." And that missionary, when he read it to us, said, "I think what my Indian brother said is right, where we have 're-Bible' we will have revival." "For man does not live by bread alone, but by every word that proceedeth out of the mouth of God." But when people do not take the trouble to know, they will be held responsible for their ignorance.

We read that "there was a division among the people because of Him." There is still a division because of Him. Some said, "Is not this the Christ?" There were others who said, "Will the Messiah come out of Galilee; No; we cannot accept Him." So there are the two classes today. There are those who look up in faith and say, "We recognize in Him our Saviour and Redeemer," and there are those who spurn and refuse Him. But God has told us that there is no other name given among men whereby we must be saved, and if we will not accept God's testimony concerning Him, if we go on refusing to receive Him as Saviour and Lord, then His own solemn words will be fulfilled, "Whither I go ye cannot come, for except ye believe that I am He, ye shall die in your sins."

Yes, there is a division because of Him today, and may I ask you tenderly now, On which side are you? Are you among those who have trusted in Him and received Him; or are you numbered among those who have spurned Him and rejected His grace? Thank God, if you are among the latter, it is not too late to come to Him in repentance and to take Him as your Saviour. There was a division among the people because of Him. Some would have taken and arrested Him, but no man laid hands on Him. The hour was not come when He was to be offered up. The Pharisees had sent certain officers to Him to arrest Him and bring Him before the Sanhedrin, but we are told in verse 45 that they came back empty-handed, and the chief priest said, "Why have ye not brought Him?" "Why did you not arrest Him?" And the officers gave this wonderful answer, "Never man spake like this Man." Yes, there was something about Jesus, something about His very message, His manner of speaking, and the matter of His instruction that stirred the hearts of these officers, hard, ruthless men, so that they found themselves absolutely helpless and paralyzed, and they did not dare arrest Him. They went away baffled and amazed. Who is this One who speaks with such power? "Never man

spake like this Man." And as they answered the
chief priests and Pharisees like this, they thought
these officers must have been persuaded of the
Messiahship of Jesus. They said, "Are ye also
deceived?" They meant, "Are ye also deceived
so that you are not able to weigh things carefully
and thoughtfully?" Then they asked, "Have any
of the rulers or of the Pharisees believed on
Him?" The great ones, as a rule, are not given
to believing on Him. But God has chosen the
poor of this world, the people that are despised.
He uses the things that are not to bring to nought
things that are. The great ones seldom get in,
but yet, on the other hand, there have always
been those even in the higher ranks of life who
have discerned the beauty and blessedness of our
Lord Jesus, and so among the outstanding saints
of God have been men and women even in royal
or important families. God has saints even
among wealthy people, and that is a great thing,
you know.

They asked, "Have any of the rulers or of the
Pharisees believed on Him?" They declared that
these people who know not the law are given up
to judgment because they do not understand.
This was the opportunity for Nicodemus to show
where he stood. He was one of the Pharisees,
one of the doctors of the law, an authority on the
Scriptures. Nicodemus spoke right up (he that

came to Jesus by night, being one of them),
"Doth our law judge any man before it hear him,
and know what he doeth?" As much as to say,
"Have you heard Him yourself? Have you seen
His works of power? If you have not, then why
do you pass judgment? Why do you say He is a
deceiver?" In other words, Nicodemus is saying,
"Investigate before you judge." And we would
say that today to all those who try to refute the
claims of the Lord Jesus Christ, "Investigate before you judge." If you are an agnostic or infidel,
and you say, "I can't believe the story of Jesus
Christ, I can't believe He was the Son of God,
born of a virgin," let me ask you what investigation of the records have you made?

I think almost all well-educated ministers of
the gospel have read scores of books by men who
reject the Bible and refuse the testimony of the
Lord Jesus Christ. I can say that I have read
literally hundreds of such books written by unbelievers. "Have they not shaken your faith in
the Bible?" you ask. No, they only show me the
folly of unbelief. But having said that, let me
say this, I have never met an infidel yet who has
ever read one serious book on Christian Evidences. Now there may be some, but I have
never met one who has. Men read the arguments
from the other side, but the average objector does
not take the trouble to read the books written in

defense of the truth of God. I knew a lawyer who was an infidel by his own confession, for years. Finally, someone said, "But you haven't read the other side." "I have made up my mind," was the reply. "Yes, but you have never read the other side. There is an old book—it is called 'Nelson on Infidelity'—suppose you read it." "Well," he said, "I presume I ought to." He read it. Before he finished he was a Christian. There are many such books, as Dr. A. T. Pierson's "Many Infallible Proofs," and others one might speak of. The trouble is with the enemies of the cross of Christ, they are not willing to investigate because they do not want to give up some sin that the Bible condemns. They know that to become Christians would mean turning from sin and yielding their wills to Christ.

Nicodemus throws down the challenge and says, "Does our law judge any man before it hear him and know what he doeth?" Do they answer him? Oh, not at all. They answer, it is true, but their answer is an evasion. They said, "Art thou also of Galilee? Search, and look: for out of Galilee ariseth no prophet." And again they showed their ignorance. They thought they knew it all, these dignified doctors. They thought that "all scholars were agreed" with them, and when one of their own number comes out to speak for Him they say, "Art thou also of Galilee?" "Are

you also going to join that crowd? No prophet
ever came out of Galilee." They had not been
reading their Bibles very carefully. They forgot
that Jonah was from Gath-Hepher, a town in
Galilee (See 2 Kings 14: 25). Then, too, it is
generally believed that Nahum was a Galilean.
So at least one prophet had come out of Galilee,
perhaps two, and it was not impossible that another should. But they said, "Look, for out of
Galilee ariseth no prophet." That is the way
men do away with the truth of God today. Oh,
dear friends, do not be unfair to your own souls.
If you have never yet investigated the claims of
the Lord Jesus Christ, I beg of you to do so. It
is the height of folly to assume that His claims
are false, when you have never weighed the
evidence.

But now let us come back to those words used
by the officers. They said of Him, "Never man
spake like this Man," and I want you think of
those words as indicating the wonderful character of our Lord Jesus Christ. His words were
words of power. It was not merely the lovely
similes and beautiful illustrations that led them
to speak like that. They said, "Never man spake
like this Man." Think of some of His sayings.
He declares, "Now in the law i is written so and
so, but I say unto you." Surely never man spake
like this Man! And think of the power of His

words! When the people in distress came to Him
—the blind man said, "Lord, that I may receive
my sight!" and He put His hands upon his eyes
and said, "Be opened," and the blind man saw.
Look at the poor leper, so unclean and polluted
and defiled. "If Thou wilt Thou canst make me
clean," he said, and Jesus put forth His hand
and touched him and said, "I will; be thou clean,"
and as that leper looked at his clean flesh wonderingly, his heart said, "Never man spake like
this Man!" And then when Jesus stood by the
dead or by the grave, as when He went into the
house where the little daughter of Jairus was,
and took her by the hand said, "Little girl, I
say unto thee, Arise," and she arose. Her parents
must have thought, "Never man spake like this
Man." At the grave of Lazarus, when they had
rolled the stone away, He cried, "Lazarus, come
forth," and "he that was dead came forth." I
imagine that crowd must have said in their
hearts, "Never man spake like this Man." And
oh, dear friends, when He hung upon the cross
and He prayed for the transgressors and cried,
"Father, forgive them, for they know not what
they do," and then He exclaimed in triumph a
little later: "It is finished"—surely "never man
spake like this Man!" When He came forth in
resurrection and met His disciples and said, "All
hail!" and later appeared among them and said

"As My Father sent Me, even so send I you"—surely they must have gone away saying to themselves, "Never man spake like this Man." And now He has gone up to the glory of God and is sitting on the right hand of the Majesty in heaven, but in a little while He is coming back and He will call the dead from the tomb and cause the living to be changed—when He exclaims, "Arise, My love, My fair one, and come away," we will rise and go singing our way through the air crying, "Never man spake like this Man." And when at last the ages of time have run their course and the great white throne is set, and the dead are called from their tombs and they stand before Him for judgment and they look into the face of the One who walked the shores of Galilee, the One who spoke so tenderly to the troubled and distressed, when they see Him on the throne and they stand before Him to give account for their sins, and above all else, for the sin of rejecting His grace, and hear Him say (How I hope you will never have to hear Him say it!), "Depart from Me, ye cursed, into the everlasting fire prepared for the devil and his angels," they will turn away wringing their hands and crying, "Never man spake like this Man." "Oh, if we had only accepted His testimony when He called in grace and said, 'Come unto Me, all ye that labor and are heavy laden,' and we would have never had to hear Him say, 'Depart from Me.' "

Today He speaks, and He says, "Come unto Me . . . and I will give you rest." "Today, if ye will hear His voice, harden not your hearts, as in the provocation, in the day of temptation in the wilderness." He speaks to you who are in your sins and He promises you deliverance if you but trust Him. Let your hearts cry out: "Never man spake like this Man!" Say, "I will take Him now as my Saviour."

CHRIST AND THE ADULTERESS

✁ ✁ ✁

"Jesus went unto the mount of Olives. And early in the morning He came again into the temple, and all the peoole came unto Him; and He sat down, and taught them. And the scribes and Pharisees brought unto Him a woman taken in adultery; and when they had set her in the midst, they say unto Him, Master, this woman was taken in adultery, in the very act. Now Moses in the law commanded us, that such should be stoned: but what sayest Thou? This they said, tempting Him, that they might have to accuse Him. But Jesus stooped down, and with His finger wrote on the ground, as though He heard them not. So when they continued asking Him, He lifted up Himself, and said unto them, He that is without sin among you, let him first cast a stone at her. And again He stooped down, and wrote on the ground. And they which heard it, being convicted by their own conscience, went out one by one, beginning at the eldest, even unto the last: and Jesus was left alone, and the woman standing in the midst. When Jesus had lifted up Himself, and saw none but the woman, He said unto her, Woman, where are those thine accusers? Hath no man condemned thee? She said, No man, Lord. And Jesus said unto her, Neither do I condemn thee: go, and sin no more" (John 8: 1-11).

✁ ✁ ✁

THE last sentence in chapter seven properly belongs to the first verse in chapter eight. We should recognize at the very beginning that in the minds of many people, many Bible critics, many Christian scholars, this entire passage is considered questionable because in some of the older manuscripts you will not find these eleven verses. On the other hand, it is rather an interesting fact that in a number of very ancient manuscripts, while these verses are omitted, there is a blank space left on the page, showing that evidently the scribe meant to indicate that in some other manuscripts something came in between verse 52 of chapter seven and verse 12 of chapter eight. In other manuscripts this section is omitted altogether. Others again give us the passage, but do not place it here. They put it at the end of John's Gospel as a kind of postscript. On the other hand, we have very good authority for regarding it as genuine, for it is found in many old Greek manuscripts, and it seems very evident that it is part of this Gospel. The reason that it is omitted in many instances, I take it, is because some of the early Christians apparently felt that a story such as this, which seemed to suggest a lenient attitude toward immoral behavior, might be misunderstood, and particularly by a people just emerging from heathenism, with all its vile and impure practices, which were often connected even with the worship of their gods. It might have looked to some of these as though this passage implies that, after all, the sin spoken of here is nothing very heinous in the sight of God. But one only needs to read the rest of the Gospel to see how false such an assumption would be.

As we read on in this chapter we find many definite references to this very incident. There are passages that could not be clearly and properly understood if this story were missing. Personally, I think the translators did exactly right in including it as part of the sacred text without any marks of any kind to differentiate it from the rest of the Gospel. In the Revised Version it is set off by parentheses, and many do not consider it genuine. However, anyone who knows the grace of God as revealed in Christ, it seems to me, must recognize it as genuine, for it is so like Jesus to do what He is represented as doing here. And, after all, the sin of this poor woman is no worse than the sins of every one of us—"All we like sheep have gone astray, we have turned every one to his own way." The first clause there speaks of the sin of the race—the entire human race has gone astray. It has gone away from God. But then the second clause indicates our individual iniquities—"We have turned every one to his own way." There are people who have been kept from fleshly indulgences such as this, and yet are guilty in God's sight of sins of the mind and of the heart, that are just as vile, unholy and unclean in His sight as sins of the flesh. "Man looketh upon the outward appearance, but God looketh upon the heart." Pride is that abominable thing which God says He hates —jealousy, covetousness, the love of money, extortion, a wicked tongue that says unkind and untruthful things and spreads scandalous stories. All of these are numbered among the things that are wicked and hateful in His eyes. "We have turned every one to his own way." "He hath laid on Him the iniquity of us all." Here we contemplate the grace of God to one sinner and that same grace is extended to all sinners who will avail themselves of it. Now notice the passage somewhat carefully.

"Every man went to his own house, but—" How much we lose without that little word "but." The afternoon had passed away. The evening shadows were falling and the company broke up and every man went unto his own house, "but Jesus"—Jesus, the Creator of all things, had no house to which to go. He went out to the mount of Olives. His hearers had their comfortable beds. His hearers could go back to their families and their homes, but Jesus, a stranger in the world His own hands had made, sought repose on the slopes of Mount Olivet. Possibly He went, as He frequently did, to the Garden of Gethsemane. Oh, that blessed holy Stranger, the One who could say, "The foxes have holes and the birds

of the air have nests, but the Son of Man hath
not where to lay His head." How close He had
come to poor wandering, troubled, distressed men
and women. Think of the homeless men and
women in this world today. Remember that Jesus
was one like them—with no place to lay His head.
He went to the mount of Olives, and after spend-
ing the night out there on the mountainside, beneath the shelter of the olive trees, arising in the
morning He returned to the temple, and some
of the people came to Him and He sat down and
taught them.

I have mentioned before that it was customary
for teachers to go to the outer courts of the temple by one of the pillars, and there their disciples
gathered about to hear them. So Jesus took His
place by one of the pillars of the temple and began to teach the people. He was unfolding the
truth concerning the kingdom of God, when suddenly there was a disturbance and the Pharisees
came dragging a poor woman into the midst of
the assembled group. She is struggling and trying to hide her face. Indifferent to her shame
and to the ignominy they are heaping upon her,
they are bent upon putting the Lord Jesus Christ
into a position where He will have to take His
stand against the law of Moses, or else He will
have definitely to condemn a poor sinner who
needs His help. So they drag this woman before

Him—a woman taken in adultery. Where was the man? Had he, as such paramours generally do, fled away, leaving her to face the shame alone? It happens thousands of times in this world. The double standard that existed then, exists today. They brought her in to hold her up to the scorn of those who had gathered around, but the man, guiltier by far, is not there to face that crowd. He is not there to stand by the victim of his own sensual lust and to say, "It is by my wickedness that she has come to this terrible place." Poor, foolish women down through the ages have had to know that bitter experience, over and over and over again.

They said, "Master, this woman was taken in adultery, in the very act, and Moses in the law commanded us that such should be stoned: but what sayest Thou?" What did Moses in the law command? Did he command that in the case of two falling into sin like this the woman alone was to be stoned? No, nothing like it. He commanded that *both* should be stoned. He commanded that the guilty man as well as the woman should be punished.

But they came bringing her, the weaker of the two. Now what will Jesus do? Suppose He turns to them and says, "Why, yes; Moses commanded that such should be stoned, and the law is God's holy Word, and the only thing to do is to take this woman out and stone her; then, if you can ever find the man, arrest him and stone him too." Had He said that, oh, never again would a poor sinner, like the one in the seventh of Luke, come weeping to His feet! She would say, "Oh, no; He would have no mercy on such as I." Never again would a poor wretch, over-powered by temptation and sorrow, ever dare to go to Him for help. They would say, "No; He only condemns such as I am. He will give me up to judgment."

But, on the other hand, suppose He says, "Well, Moses said that, and of course it was God's Word, but I say unto you, let the woman go free. I am releasing you from obedience to the law." Why, they would have said at once, "He professes to be sent from God, a prophet of Jehovah, and He is teaching things contrary to the law of Moses, and therefore His teaching cannot be depended upon." They thought they had trapped Him, but oh, how wonderfully the Lord met them! They said, "Well, here she is; what do You say? There is no question about her guilt. The law says, Stone her. Now what shall we do?" Those self-righteous men! And what does He answer them? We read that Jesus stooped down and wrote upon the ground, as though He heard them not. Why did He do that? These men were familiar with the Scriptures, but it is sadly pos-

sible to be familiar with the Scriptures and have
a heart as hard as the nether millstone, ever
ready to heap condemnation upon other people,
forgetting that "all have sinned and come short
of the glory of God." Now because they knew
their Bibles, they must have known of the passage in the book of Jeremiah, which says, "O
Lord, the Hope of Israel, all that forsake Thee
shall be ashamed, and they that depart from Me
shall be written in the earth, because they have
forsaken the Lord, the fountain of living waters."
It might be translated, "written on the ground."
See them there gathered about Him, and He
stoops down and writes on the ground. They
turn one to the other, saying, "What is He doing,
writing on the ground? Writing on the ground!
—Isn't there something like that in our Bibles?"
Yes, there is. They will come down to the dust
of death eventually because of their sins. The
Lord was acting out a message from God that
should have gone home to every one of their
hearts, but instead of that, they continue pressing Him, asking, "What are we going to do with
her? No use of your stooping down there writing on the ground. We want to know what we
are to do." So hypocritical are they in their
pretence of being so zealous, when, after all, they
are only trying to put Him in a place where they
can discredit Him!

He lifted up Himself and faced that little group of hypocritical leaders of the people, who had never had to do with God about their sins in all their lives, but were trying to hide their own wickedness by zeal in condemning others. Looking them in the eyes, first one and then another, He said very quietly, but very decisively, "He that is without sin among you, let him first cast a stone at her." He did not say, "Do not carry out the law of Moses." He did not say, "I have come to repeal the law of Moses," but He put it up to them to carry out that law, if they dared. "He that is without sin among you, let him first cast a stone at her." They were utterly discomfited. He turned away, and again He wrote upon the ground. I wonder if that second writing might have suggested to them that verse in Psalm 22, "Thou hast brought Me into the dust of death." In a little while, He was going down to the dust of death, when all the trangressions and iniquity of sinners such as this woman would be charged against Him as He offered Himself a sacrifice for a world's redemption.

So He stooped down again and wrote on the ground, and while He was writing there was a movement going on among the accusers. They looked one at another, and then at Him and at the sinful woman, and before the oldest man there arose the memory of the sins which he had been trying to forget for years. Finally, he dropped his stone and went out, saying, "I don't dare cast a stone at her." And then the next, and the next, and finally the youngest of them all had slunk away. They had all gone; every one alike guilty before God. "There is none righteous, no, not one." We read, "They went out, being convicted by their own consciences, beginning at the eldest, even unto the last."

And Jesus was left alone (that is, the throng was still there), but Jesus was left alone in the midst of His disciples and those whom He had been teaching. There was the woman down on her knees, bowed in shame, doubtless her scalding tears falling down to the earth. Jesus turned to her. Oh, I should like to have heard Him speak that day. I am sure there was a tenderness, compassion and pity such as that poor woman had never heard in the voice of any man with whom she had held conversation. Jesus said, "Woman, where are those thine accusers? Hath no man condemned thee?" And she looked up and said, "No man, Lord." Notice how she addresses Him. She recognized something so superior about Jesus, something so different from any man she, poor, hunted creature, had ever met—Jesus, the Holy One of God. "No man, Lord, has ventured to stone me." Then Jesus answered and said unto her, "Neither do I condemn thee: go, and sin no more." This is doubtless why some of the older scribes kept this passage out of the Bible. They said, "What! Jesus, the Holy One! Does He not condemn a sin like that? Does not He anathematize adultery?" Oh, yes, He has spoken out very strongly against adultery. But He knew that poor woman recognized her sinfulness. She realized her uncleanness and pollution. He knew all that was going on in her heart of hearts, and He spoke to her heart and conscience as He said, "Neither do I condemn thee." And then He added, "Go, and sin no more."

I do not know the story of that woman's life afterwards. I do not know where she dwelt nor how she behaved after this episode, but I dare to believe she was never again taken in the same form of sin, for she had been brought into the presence of Christ. I feel sure something had taken place within her soul that day. I think He saw her going away from the temple that morning with the light of heaven in her countenance. I can imagine her friends saying to her, "What makes you look so glad today?" and she says, "Oh, I have been to the feet of Jesus and He has said, 'Neither do I condemn thee; go, and sin no more.'"

But how could He say, "Neither do I condemn thee?" Because of the fact that He was on His way to the cross, where in only a little while He was to take her sin upon Himself and to be dealt with as though He were the guilty one, to endure the wrath of God and to suffer, the Pure One for the impure, the Holy One to suffer for the unholy, He, the Righteous One, to suffer for the unrighteous. In view of the cross, He could say to that woman, "Neither do I condemn thee." He is ready to say that today. He does say it to any poor sinner who comes trusting His grace, who comes repentant and broken-hearted and dares to sue for mercy. In Romans 8:31 we read, "What shall we then say to these things? If God be for us, who can be against us? He that spared not His own Son, but delivered Him up for us all, how shall He not with Him also freely give us all things? Who shall lay anything to the charge of God's elect? It is God that justifieth. Who is He that condemneth? It is Christ that died, yea, rather, that is risen again, who is even at the right hand of God, who also maketh intercession for us." "There is therefore now no condemnation to those who are in Christ Jesus." How much we would lose if this story were left out of our Bibles. To how many poor sinners, to how many adulterers and adulteresses, has it brought a message of hope and peace and blessing when they came to the feet of Jesus and trusted Him as Saviour. And it seems to me it would speak to every sinner, for we are all alike, stained and polluted.

" Tell me what to do to be pure
   In the sight of all-seeing eyes;
Tell me, is there no thorough cure,
   No escape from the sins I despise?
Will my Saviour only pass by,
   Only show how faulty I've been?
Will He not attend to my cry,
   May I not this moment be clean?"

Yes, He who cleansed and saved this poor woman of the eighth of John, waits to save you if you will come and trust Him. "Neither do I condemn thee; go, and sin no more."

THE LIGHT OF THE WORLD

"Then spake Jesus again unto them, saying, I am the light of the world: he that followeth Me shall not walk in darkness, but shall have the light of life. The Pharisees therefore said unto Him, Thou bearest record of Thyself; Thy record is not true. Jesus answered and said unto them, Though I bear record of Myself, yet My record is true: for I know whence I came, and whither I go; but ye cannot tell whence I come, and whither I go. Ye judge after the flesh; I judge no man. And yet if I judge, My judgment is true: for I am not alone, but I and the Father that sent Me. It is also written in your law, that the testimony of two men is true. I am one that bear witness of Myself, and the Father that sent Me beareth witness of Me. Then said they unto Him. Where is Thy Father? Jesus answered, Ye neither know Me, nor My Father: if ye had known Me, ye should have known My Father also. These words spake Jesus in the treasury, as He taught in the temple: and no man laid hands on Him; for His hour was not yet come" (John 8:12-20).

✓ ✓ ✓

YOU will notice how definitely this portion of the Gospel links with that which we have been considering. I mentioned that in certain ancient manuscripts the story of our Lord's dealing with the adulterous woman and delivering her from condemnation, is not found, but if we should omit it, we should do violence to the text that follows.

These words, with which verse twelve begins, connect definitely with what has gone before. "Then spake Jesus again unto them," that is, immediately following some incident, which is clearly the story of verses 1 to 11. As we close chapter seven, "And every man went unto his own house," then verse one of chapter eight begins, "Jesus went unto the mount of Olives." Now if this 12th verse were the beginning of chapter 8, it would leave the Lord Jesus out on the mountain with no one to whom He was ministering, but it is clear that He is in the temple court, where some striking event has just taken place, which indicated that a light shone from Himself into the hearts of men, and He follows that up by saying, "I am the light of the world: he that followeth Me shall not walk in darkness, but shall have the light of life." When they brought that poor woman to Him and said, "Moses in the law commanded us, that such should be stoned: but what sayest Thou?" He stooped down and wrote on the ground, and then lifting up Himself, He said, "He that is without sin among you, let him first cast a stone at her." The light was shining out from His own blessed, holy personality, shining upon them and into their hearts, and making manifest all the hidden wickedness and corruption and hypocrisy. That was why not one of them dared to stone the poor,

sinful woman, but beginning with the eldest one
they all went out, one after the other, and the
woman was left alone with the Lord Jesus, who
spoke those wonderful words, "Neither do I condemn thee."

And so He says, "I am the light of the world."
Light reveals, light makes manifest, and that is
the first way in which we must all know the Lord
Jesus Christ.   There is no other like Him.   His
very presence among men was the condemnation
of all other men, for here, at last, was one Man
absolutely holy, utterly true, perfectly righteous.
Every other man was shown up alongside of Him
as sinful and full of iniquity.   "The light of the
world," and yet He was in the world and the
world knew Him not.   "The light shineth in darkness; and the darkness comprehended it not."
Men turned away from Him, fearing the illumi-
nation that His presence brings.   But nevertheless He is the light of the world and all men are
going to be judged by the light that the Lord
Jesus Christ brought into this scene.   He says,
"He that followeth Me shall not walk in darkness,
but shall have the light of life."   It is through
the knowledge of Christ and subjection to Him
that deliverance is given from darkness and its
awful power.   People talk about the problem of
Jesus, and we have had author after author writing books to try to explain the problem of Jesus.

But Jesus is not a problem, Jesus is the unraveler
of all problems and all the perplexities that face
us. Trust Him and receive Him as He is, God and
Man in one glorious Person, and your problems
are met. And so He says, "Follow Me, and you
will not walk in darkness. You will have the
light of life." But remember, it is only as the
Divine One that Jesus can say, "I am the light
of the world." In this Gospel, on many occasions,
we hear Him using that divine name "I AM."
Long ago, when God appeared to Moses in the
burning bush and sent him to Egypt to deliver
His people, Moses asked, "Whom shall I tell them
has sent me? What name shall I give to Thy
people Israel when I appear before Pharaoh to
tell him that Thou hast sent me to deliver them?"
God said, "Tell them that 'I Am' hath sent you.
I am that I am." That is really an explanation
of the name "Jehovah," "The eternally existing
One," "I am that I am." And so "I am" is a
divine title, and Jesus takes it on His lips again
and again in His walk on earth. He says, "I am
the bread of life," "I am the good Shepherd"—
that is, the Shepherd of Israel, "I am the door,"
and here, "I am the light of the world." If Jesus
Christ had been anything less than God it would
be blasphemy to speak like this. Think of any
servant of God you know. Think of the very
best man you have ever met or heard, the great-

est preacher, the truest follower of Christ, and imagine him standing up before men and saying, "Look at me, I am the light of the world. Follow me, and you will not walk in darkness, but have the light of life." Why, you would say, "Who does he think he is that he has grown so great, calling himself the light of the world?" You would put him down as a paranoiac. But there is no evidence of paranoia here. When Jesus contemplates the millions of people who have come into the world and says, "I am the light of the world," He is practically saying, "Look unto Me and be ye saved, for I AM God and there is none else," for we read elsewhere, "God is light, and in Him is no darkness at all." You take every faithful servant of Christ—they point you to Christ the Light. They say, "He is the light, look to Him and you shall find the light of life." But Jesus says, "Come to Me and believe in Me, for I am the light of the world." And notice the universality of it. He was not only the light of Israel, but a light to lighten the Gentiles also.

So Jesus moved among them there and they recognized Him not, because of their blinded hearts. So it is today. People say to us, "I do not see anything in it. I do not understand what you are talking about. I cannot comprehend all these things that you tell us about sin and salvation, about men's lost condition and God's provision for meeting their every need. I cannot understand it." Well, that is just what the Word says: "The natural man understands not the things of God, for they are spiritually discerned." It is like a blind man to whom you are trying to explain a sunset in all its glory in the western sky, and he turns his sightless eyes to you and says, "I cannot make it out." He needs sight to understand the sunset. O Christless soul, if I am addressing you today, you need to have your eyes opened by divine power in order that you may see the beauty and glory of our Lord Jesus Christ. But if you will come to Him, He will open your eyes and illumine your mind and you will understand the deep things of God. Think of the untold millions in the nineteen hundred years since Jesus uttered these words, who have found in Him the light of life.

Do you want to be delivered from the darkness? Do you want to know the light? Then go to Him, or you will never find it. Sometime ago a lady wrote me and she said, "I have been for years seeking after light. I am a searcher after truth, and if you can help me I will be glad." She said, "I have investigated Theosophy, Spiritism, New Thought, and other cults. I have studied all kinds of religions, and I am in the dark still." I wrote her and said, "My dear friend, you have been looking down blind alleys for years. Come

back to your Bible, read the Gospel of John, and
see the wonderful revelation of the Lord Jesus
Christ, and in Him you will find all your questions answered. Your soul will be satisfied when
you receive Him as your Saviour." We do not
need all these other things. Do you remember
that incident that took place here in Chicago during the World's Fair of 1893? They had a great
congress of religions, with the representatives
of most of the religions of the world there, each
one crying up the virtues of the particular system with which he was connected. One day
Joseph Cook, the great Boston preacher, gave his
testimony. He was to give an address setting
forth the Biblical view of salvation. He took his
text, not from the Bible, however, but from
Shakespeare's tragedy of Macbeth, for he knew
that those thousands were not interested in the
Bible, but probably had all read Shakespeare.
And he said, "See, here is Lady Macbeth. It is
after the death of Duncan, you remember. See
how she rubs her hands, saying, 'Out, damned
spot! Will these hands ne'er be clean? All the
perfumes of Arabia will not sweeten this little
hand.' And here is her husband, Macbeth, looking on and he cries out, 'Will all great Neptune's
ocean wash this blood clean from my hand? No,
this my hand will rather the multitudinous seas
incarnadine, making the green one red!' There

they rub and they rub, trying to wash out the stains of Duncan's blood, but it is impossible." And Joseph Cook said, "I will place Lady Macbeth on my right arm and her husband upon my left, and as I walk down the aisle of this great Congress of Religions I have only one question to put to you, 'Who will cleanse *our* red right hands? Our hands and hearts are stained with sin. Tell us how we may get rid of our sins!' No religious system on earth could give a satisfactory answer, but, he cried, "When I turn from all of these I hear the words rising from the Scriptures, 'The blood of Jesus Christ, God's Son, cleanses us from all sin.' "

Oh, that is the answer to all your spiritual problems and perplexities: Jesus the Light of the world, the Divine Saviour of sinners. But when men are determined to reject the truth of God and their hearts are filled with self-righteousness, they will go to any length to discredit the messenger. There is nothing more blinding than religious prejudice.

And so the Pharisees said to Jesus, "Thou bearest record of Thyself; Thy record is not true," or, "Thy record is not valid." They were referring to what He had said Himself (chap. 5: 37), "If I bear witness of Myself, My witness is not true." But after telling them of John the Baptist, and of His mighty works, He said, "The

Father Himself which hath sent Me, hath borne witness of Me." The law tells us, "In the mouth of two or three witnesses shall every word be established." The testimony of one man was not valid. So the Pharisees are quick to take Him up on that. But He answered by declaring that He was not alone, but the Father was with Him, and so the witness was true.

"And yet if I judge, My judgment is true: for I am not alone, but I and the Father that sent Me." "The law demands more than one to prove a testimony true. Very well, I am one that bears witness of Myself, and the Father that sent Me, He beareth witness of Me." How did the Father bear witness? When our blessed Lord was baptized there came a voice from heaven saying, "This is My beloved Son, in whom I have found all My delight." And then the works that Jesus did;—they were the works of the Father by the Holy Spirit through the Son, and all these bore testimony to the fact that He was indeed the light of the world. And so God has given abundant witness to the Deity of our Lord Jesus Christ, if men are willing to receive it, if they are not filled with prejudice, if they are not determined to reject the message of God.

"Then said they unto Him, Where is Thy Father?" I do not know how to put into that question the scorn and contempt that I am sure they put into it. Do you see what is implied there? It is said sometimes that John never referred definitely to the virgin birth of our Lord Jesus Christ, and so some have gone so far as to say that John knew nothing about it, that it is only mentioned in Matthew and in Luke, and therefore it may not be true. John deals with the full Deity of Christ. He traces Him back to the eternities (John 1:1), but you notice here that you have an intimation of the truth of the incarnation of our Lord Jesus Christ and His virgin birth. What was back of that scornful question of theirs? He had said, "I am one that bears witness of Myself and the Father beareth witness of Me." And they said, "Where is Thy father?" Do you get the point of that? Do you see the cruelty of it? Do you see the malice of it? Oh, they knew that it was reported that He had no human father, and they are intimating that He was born of fornication—conceived out of wedlock—and therefore it was absolutely false for Him to talk as though He knew His father. In verse forty-one they said, "We be not born of fornication: we have one Father, even God." See what they meant. Oh, yes; they had heard the story of the virgin birth, and that is the way they treated it.

But His Father was God. God was the Father of His humanity as truly as of His Divine nature.

And Jesus answered and said, "Ye neither know Me, nor My Father: if ye had known Me, ye should have known My Father also." Oh, weigh those words well. People sometimes say, "I wish I knew God and understood God. I wish I could know how God looks at things and how He feels about things, and what His attitude toward men really is, but God seems so far away and to me He is the Unknowable. Back of this universe, I take it, there must be some First Cause. He that formed the ear must be able to hear, and He that formed the lips must be able to speak. He that formed the brain must be able to think. Back of this universe there must be a personal God. But oh, He seems so far away! I wish I knew Him." Like Job, maybe you say, "Oh, that I knew where I might find Him." Listen to me! You may find Him in Jesus. Jesus said, "He that hath seen Me hath seen the Father." If you want to know God, get acquainted with Jesus. "And without controversy, great is the mystery of godliness: God was manifest in the flesh, justified in the Spirit, seen of angels, preached unto the Gentiles, believed on in the world, received up into glory." In the face of Jesus you will find the face of God; in the character of Jesus you will find the character of God.

But Jesus says sadly, "Ye neither know Me, nor My Father: if ye had known Me ye would

have known My Father also." Then we read
"These words spoke Jesus in the treasury, as He
taught in the temple: and no man laid hands on
Him; for His hour was not yet come." See again,
it is absolutely necessary that you recognize
verses 1 to 11 as part of the Gospel, otherwise
there would be no record of His entering the
treasury. "And no man laid hands on Him; for
His hour was not yet come." As we have seen
before in looking at some of the earlier passages,
it was impossible that any harm should come to
Jesus, that He should be injured in any way, or
that He should die, until the hour struck for
which He came into the world. Before He left
the Father's glory, it had been settled in the
counsels of eternity that on the Passover Day,
one particular, definite day, the Lord Jesus, the
Passover Lamb, was to be offered up. And until
His hour was come, men could not take Him. But
when that hour came, He put Himself into their
hands and allowed them to spit upon His blessed
face, to beat Him with their cruel rods, and, at
last, nail Him upon a cross of shame, and there
He made reconciliation for iniquity, and the light
never shone brighter than in the darkness of
Calvary. And now, because the sin question has
been there settled, God offers salvation to every
soul in all the world who will receive His Son
and trust in Him as Saviour. Those of us who

have trusted Him have found Him to be far
more than we ever dreamed He could be, and because of what He means to us we long to have
you know Him too. And so we plead with any
of you here who are out of Christ to come to Him
and to take Him as your Saviour.

ADDRESS TWENTY-EIGHT

IS THERE A SECOND CHANCE FOR SALVATION AFTER DEATH?

"Then said Jesus again unto them, I go My way, and ye shall seek Me, and shall die in your sins: whither I go, ye cannot come. Then said the Jews, Will He kill Himself? because He saith, Whither I go, ye cannot come. And He said unto them, Ye are from beneath; I am from above: ye are of this world; I am not of this world. I said therefore unto you, that ye shall die in your sins: for if ye believe not that I am He, ye shall die in your sins. Then said they unto Him, Who art Thou? And Jesus saith unto them, Even the same that I said unto you from the beginning. I have many things to say and to judge of you: but He that sent Me is true; and I speak to the world those things which I have heard of Him. They understood not that He spake to them of the Father. Then said Jesus unto them, When ye have lifted up the Son of Man, then shall ye know that I am He, and that I do nothing of Myself; but as My Father hath taught Me, I speak these things. And He that sent Me is with Me: the Father hath not left Me alone; for I do always those things that please Him. As He spake these words, many believed on Him. Then said Jesus to those Jews which believed on Him, If ye continue in My word, then are ye My disciples indeed; and ye shall know the truth, and the truth shall make you free" (John 8: 21-32).

THE question, "Is there a second chance for salvation after death?" is a very serious one. It is raised at times even by real Christians when some of their own loved ones close their eyes in death without giving any evidence of repentance or of personal saving faith in the Lord Jesus. No matter how orthodox one may be or how thoroughly one may be indoctrinated in respect to the hopelessness of the state of the unsaved dead, this question will come to the surface. People who have never thought of it before, think seriously of it when one of their own has gone out into eternity in this hopeless condition. And their hearts cry out, "May it not be true that after all, when men live and die out of Christ, there may be some way by which God will save men on the other shore after He has failed to reach them on this side?" The only way we can get a true answer to this question is by turning directly to the Word of God itself. And here we have the testimony of our Lord Jesus Christ, and it is very solemn and serious. "Then said Jesus again unto them, I go My way, and ye shall seek Me, and shall die in your sins: whither I go, ye cannot come."

He was addressing men who had seen His works of power, who had heard His marvelous teaching, who had been urged to receive Him in faith, the Living Bread, that they might find life eternal. And now He says to them, "I am not going to be here forever. I have come for an appointed service. The hour of My crucifixion is just before Me. I go My way back to the presence of the Father. I go My way through the gates of death into resurrection and up to the glory, and after I have left you, after I have gone, many of you will begin to be concerned. You will seek Me, and want to listen to My message, but you will not be able to. find Me.   You will not be able to hear Me.   Ye shall seek Me, but ye shall die in your sins."   And He adds, "And whither I go, ye cannot come."   There is something very, very tragic about that.   I have often said that every time I am asked to speak at a funeral service where the deceased has given no evidence of knowing Christ, I would like to believe that there is something so purifying about death, so wonderful about dissolution, that when men pass from this life into the next they will immediately have their eyes opened and they will see how foolish they have been in rejecting Christ, and then they will gaze upon His face and will trust Him.   I would like to believe that.   I would like to believe that no one will be lost.   So would any compassionate person.

We can enter into and sympathize with the thoughts of Richard Baxter, who used to pray, "O God, for a full heaven and an empty hell!" We would it might be, but when we turn to this blessed Book and are prepared to bring our thoughts to the test of "Thus saith the Lord," we do not find that this Word diffuses any ray of hope for the one who dies unsaved.   Nothing could be clearer than our Lord's words here. He says, "Ye shall die in your sins."

There are two ways to die. In the book of the Revelation we read, "Blessed are they that die *in the Lord. . . .* They shall rest from their labors and their works do follow them." It will be a blessed thing to die in the Lord. Millions have died in the Lord and are resting from their labors, and their works shall follow them. Their works did not save them; they were saved by the Lord Jesus Christ. But when they stand at the judgment-seat of Christ they will be rewarded for their works by the One who has saved them. But here is the awful contrast, "If ye believe not that I am He, ye shall die in your sins." See verse twenty-four, "I said therefore unto you, that ye shall die in your sins: for if ye believe not that I am He, ye shall die in your sins." And to all those who die in their sins Jesus says, "Whither I go, ye cannot come." He was speaking of going back into heaven. It is just another way of saying, if you die in your sins you will never enter heaven.

I do not think you can find a clearer passage than this. There are many others. It was the Lord Jesus Himself who said, "And these shall go away into everlasting punishment: but the righteous into life eternal." And it was Jesus who said, "Wherefore if thy hand or thy foot

offend thee, cut them off, and cast them from
thee: it is better for thee to enter into life halt
or maimed, rather than having two hands or two
feet to be cast into everlasting fire." Jesus said
that, and when He used language like that He
meant us to understand there is a possibility of
being eternally lost. In the epistle to the Hebrews
we read, "It is a fearful thing to fall into the
hands of the living God." Search this Book
throughout. Read it carefully, and you will find
that it does not offer the slightest hope of even-
tual blessing for anyone who leaves this world
impenitent.

But now having said that, I want to say something to comfort the hearts of some of you who
may be saying in your hearts, "Well, that may be
the truth. It must be the truth if Jesus said it,
but even so, it hurts my heart to think of loved
ones for whom I prayed for years and they died
unsaved." Let me say this to you: Do not jump
at conclusions. Who put it into your hearts to
pray for that loved one? Who laid the burden
for that soul upon your heart? It was the blessed
Holy Spirit of God. It was Christ Himself.
Often when God is going to do something for us,
He puts it on our hearts to pray for that very
thing. It is a great thing for anyone who has
a praying mother or praying friends. It is a great
thing for an unsaved wife to have a praying hus-

band, or *vice versa,* "For what knowest thou, O wife, whether thou shalt save thy husband? or how knowest thou, O man, whether thou shalt save thy wife?" If we bring our loved ones to God in prayer we can count on Him to work in His own way upon their hearts and consciences, and even though we may not get the evidence that our prayers have been answered, let us never give up, but let us believe that the God who taught us to pray for our dear ones has found a way of answering our prayers. Have you ever thought of the mother of the penitent thief, that one who hung by the side of our Lord Jesus Christ on the cross? I wonder if he had a praying mother, a mother who had again and again brought her son before God, and I wonder if by any chance she was in the crowd that day when Jesus was on that center cross and her son and another hung on either side of Him. What anxiety must have been hers if she was there, and if she was, I wonder if she got close enough to hear the colloquy that went on between her boy and that One who was "in the same condemnation." I wonder if she was off there somewhere in the crowd and doing her best to look over the heads of the others and saying, "Oh, there he is, my poor, lost boy, and I prayed for him and counted on God to save him, and there he is, dying a malefactor's death." I wonder if she might have been close enough to

have heard both of those robbers railing on Jesus,
and said, "Oh, there he is dying with curses on
his lips." But he did not die that way! I wonder if she was so far away that she did not hear
what went on during those last moments. "And
one of the malefactors which were hanged railed
on Him, saying, If Thou be Christ, save Thyself
and us. But the other answering rebuked him,
saying, Dost not thou fear God, seeing thou art
in the same condemnation? And we indeed justly;
for we receive the due reward of our deeds: but
this Man hath done nothing amiss. And he said
unto Jesus, Lord, remember me when Thou com-
est into Thy kingdom. And Jesus said unto him,
Verily I say unto thee, Today shalt thou be with
Me in Paradise." It was as though He said,
"You will not have to wait until I come in My
kingdom. You will be with Me in Paradise today." I wonder if his mother heard that. If she
did not hear she might have cried, "Oh, my boy!
Lost!" No; he was saved; though she may have
known nothing about what took place at that last
moment. God's ways are past finding out. So I
say to you who are praying: Do not let your faith
waver. Count on God to work in His own wonderful way. Sometime, somewhere, He will
answer you.

But to you who are Christless, I would say this:
Do not count too much on the patience of a holy
God. There is such a thing as sinning against

His mercy and goodness and grace to such an extent that the conscience becomes seared as with a hot iron. It is that against which Jesus warns us here. "If ye believe not that I am He, ye shall die in your sins."

The Jews did not understand Him and said, "Where is He going? Will He commit suicide?" He said, "You reason as men of the earth. I am from above and not of this world. I said to you, 'If ye believe not, ye shall die in your sins.'" "Then said they unto Him, Who art Thou? And Jesus saith unto them, Even the same that I said unto you from the beginning." He was the Eternal Son who came down into this world to be our Redeemer. He added, "I have many things to say and to judge of you: but He that sent Me is true; and I speak to the world those things which I have heard of Him. They understood not that He spake to them of the Father. Then said Jesus unto them, When ye have lifted up the Son of Man, then shall ye know that I am He, and that I do nothing of Myself; but as My Father hath taught Me, I speak these things." They lifted Him up on the cross, where He died for our redemption, and it was that to which He referred as He said to Nicodemus, "As Moses lifted up the serpent in the wilderness, even so must the Son of Man be lifted up." He has been lifted up.

> "Lifted up was He to die,
> 　It is finished, was His cry;
> 　Now in heav'n exalted high,
> 　　Hallelujah! What a Saviour!"

He concludes this address with these words, "He that sent Me is with Me: the Father hath not left Me alone; for I do always those things that please Him." No one else ever lived who could use such language as that in its entirety. God's most devoted servants have failed in something. We are all poor sinners saved by grace. But Jesus failed in nothing. He could say, "I do always those things that please Him." "As He spake these words many believed on Him." Then Jesus put a test to them by saying something like this, "Now it is not enough that you simply believe intellectually. You must prove the reality of your faith by obedience to My word." "Then said Jesus to those Jews which believed on Him, If ye continue in My word, then are ye My disciples indeed; and ye shall know the truth, and the truth shall make you free." And so we know Him who is the truth, and from His lips we receive the truth, and through His word that truth is opened up to us, and by the Spirit we are able to walk in that truth.

> "My sins laid open to the rod
> 　The back which from the law was **free;**
> And the Eternal Son of God
> 　Received the stripes once due to me."

IS THERE A PERSONAL DEVIL?

✦ ✦ ✦

"They answered Him, We be Abraham's seed, and were never in bondage to any man: how sayest Thou, Ye shall be made free? Jesus answered them, Verily, verily, I say unto you, Whosoever committeth sin is the servant of sin. And the servant abideth not in the house for ever: but the Son abideth ever. If the Son therefore shall make you free, ye shall be free indeed. I know that ye are Abraham's seed; but ye seek to kill Me, because My word hath no place in you. I speak that which I have seen with My Father: and ye do that which ye have seen with your father. They answered and said unto Him, Abraham is our father. Jesus saith unto them, If ye were Abraham's children, ye would do the works of Abraham. But now ye seek to kill Me, a Man that hath told you the truth, which I have heard of God: this did not Abraham. Ye do the deeds of your father. Then said they to Him, We be not born of fornication; we have one Father, even God. Jesus said unto them, If God were your Father, ye would love Me: for I proceeded forth and came from God; neither came I of Myself, but He sent Me. Why do ye not understand My speech? even because ye cannot hear My word. Ye are of your father the devil, and the lusts of your father ye will do: he was a murderer from the beginning, and abode not in the truth, because there is no truth in him. When he speaketh a lie, he speaketh of his own: for he is a liar, and the father of it" (John 8: 33-44).

✦ ✦ ✦

THIS portion of John's Gospel both suggests and answers the question, "Is There a Personal Devil?" Our Lord was still in controversy with the ritualistic and legalistic element of the Jewish people who were opposing His teaching in the courts of the temple, where He was ministering at this time. He had brought truth after truth to bear upon them, but on every occasion they had sought to argue Him down instead of opening their hearts to receive the message. And now in answer to what He had previously said, "Ye shall know the truth, and the truth shall make you free," they replied, "We are Abraham's seed, and were never in bondage to any man: how sayest Thou, Ye shall be made free?"

It is a striking instance of how men will bolster themselves up, even though their entire history proves far different conclusions. Imagine these men in Jewry saying, "We were never in bondage to any man!" Even as they spoke, the Romans had them in subjection, and ever since the captivity of Babylon they had been in bondage to one power after another. They may have meant, "While we have been subject to Gentile governments, yet our spirits are free, and therefore we have never been in bondage or been subject religiously to any system of man's devising." But the Lord Jesus sought to show them that this is not enough; there must be the impartation of divine life, and works accompanying it. And He knew, and they knew, that they were actually slaves to sin. So He answered and said, "Verily,

verily, I say unto you, Whosoever committeth sin is the servant of sin." Whosoever is given to the practice of sin, is the slave of sin. "And the servant abideth not in the house forever: but the Son abideth ever. If the Son therefore shall make you free, ye shall be free indeed." That is, He told them that it was not enough that they were literally descended from Abraham, but that they must know that deliverance from the power of sin that Abraham knew, if they were to be recognized as the children of God. And in contrast to their own condition, He dares to present Himself as the One who never came under the bondage of sin and He says, "The Son abideth forever." He was, in very truth, that promised Seed of Abraham through whom all nations were to be blessed. And though the nation as a whole had broken down, and in many cases the name of God was blasphemed among the Gentiles because of their sins and failures, yet He remained the one promised Deliverer of Abraham's lineage who was to bring salvation near. He offers freedom to us today: "If the Son therefore shall make you free, ye shall be free indeed."

Let me turn aside for the moment from the exposition of the passage to apply this to the many slaves of sin that are all about us, men and women struggling against evil habits, passions, desires, which hold them in absolute bondage. Again and again they have cried out,

> "Oh, for a man to arise in me,
> That the man that I am might cease to be!"

My dear friends, it is possible to be saved from sin, not only from the guilt of sin, but it is possible to be saved from the power of sin, through regeneration and the indwelling of the Holy Spirit. This is what Jesus meant when He said, "If the Son therefore shall make you free, ye shall be free indeed." The truth of which He spoke is the blessed program of regeneration given us in His holy Word. When men believe this message they are set at liberty because of the new birth, and as they go on in fellowship with God, walking in the power of the Holy Spirit, they are not dominated by the lust of the flesh, but they walk in the freedom of the children of God.

The ritualists and the self-righteous never understand this, but are always looking within for deliverance. But deliverance comes from without.

Now the Lord continues to speak to these controversialists. He says, "I know that ye are Abraham's seed." Naturally, they came from that particular line. "But ye seek to kill Me, because My word hath no place in you." And yet He was the One for whom Abraham looked, and

all down through the centuries the people of
Israel had been waiting for the promised Seed.
"And in thy Seed shall all nations be blessed." He
was present, and they knew Him not.

He had proven that He was indeed the promised One by the mighty works that He had
wrought, and yet here were these self-righteous
hypocrites and they did not recognize Him and
so refused to put their trust in Him, the One who
had come according to the promise. "But ye seek
to kill Me, because My word hath no place in you.
I speak that which I have seen with My Father:
and ye do that which ye have seen with your
father." He came down here to earth as the Son
of the Father, and day by day the Father opened
up His Word to Him to do and say the things
which He willed. "The words that I speak are
not Mine, but His that sent Me." "I speak that
which I have seen with My Father: and ye do
that which ye have seen with your father." Ah,
that was rather stinging, that was sharp indeed!
He was driving the truth home now—*your*
father: *My* Father. He puts the two in contrast.

Men speak very glibly today of the universal
Fatherhood of God and the universal brotherhood
of man. This Book does not speak that way.
Some people perhaps will take exception to that,
but read the Book and see if you can find such

expressions in it. Here are two families indicated: Jesus says, "I speak that which I have seen with My Father: and ye do that which ye have seen with your father." His Father was God: their father was—He will tell them in a moment—not God, but the great enemy of God and man. Here were two families then; His own redeemed ones constitute one family, and those who refuse His grace constitute another family; so we do not have either universal Fatherhood or universal brotherhood. It is perfectly true that one God is the Creator of all men, and God has made all of one blood; but, alas, sin has come in and alienated man from God, and that is why men need to be born again in order that we may be brought into the family of God, that we may look up into His face and say, "Our Father, which art in heaven." Do you know the blessedness of this? Do you know what it is to be born of God?

"Ye are of your father, the devil," He said, and oh, how that stirred their indignation! He knew it would, but it was the truth. Sometimes it is necessary to say the thing that will stir the indignation of men and women. Some say we should be very careful never to hurt people's feelings about their sins. For instance, we should be careful about mentioning divorce, for perhaps some of our listeners have been re-married a half-dozen times, and so their feelings are very easily stirred! We should be very careful not to refer to any differences in doctrine or anything of that kind! There would not be much to mention if one took note of all the prejudices people have.

You have heard of the evangelist who went to a town in Nevada to have some meetings, and the minister said to him, "Now, my good man, there are certain sins about which you will have to be very careful here: for instance, it would never do to talk about divorce or anything of that kind, for you know this is the great divorce center. You won't dare mention the liquor question, for some of our best-paying members are in the liquor business. A great many of our people earn their living by furnishing worldly amusements; so be careful about that." The poor evangelist looked at him and said, "Well, of whose sins may I speak?" "Go for the Piute Indians and their sins," was the reply; "they never go to church anyway." It would not do much good, would it, turning loose on people who never hear you? The Lord realized that the people had to be spoken to faithfully about their sins. Some of the greatest Christians I have ever known were first terribly stirred by the messages they heard from the platform, but they came back and heard more, till God spoke to them and brought them to Himself.

Jesus said to these objectors, "Ye do that which ye have seen with your father. They answered and said unto Him, Abraham is our father. Jesus saith unto them, If ye were Abraham's children, ye would do the works of Abraham." That is, morally and spiritually, they would do the works of Abraham. Abraham was justified by faith before God and by works before men. They claimed to be the children of Abraham, but were not characterized by righteous living. "Now ye seek to kill Me . . . ye do the deeds of your father." That gave them their opportunity. A second time He had spoken in this way. They said to Him, "We be not born of fornication; we have one Father, even God." What did they mean by that? They meant to imply that He was the illegitimate son of Mary of Nazareth. It was their way of throwing back at Him their vile insinuation because they had heard of the virgin birth, and they used it to taunt Him, God's holy Son.

People say to me that the doctrine of the virgin birth is not touched on in John. Well, you have it there. They were practically throwing it into His face—"We were not born of fornication." But the Lord Jesus said to them, "If God were your Father, ye would love Me." There is a wonderful test: if men love God they love His Son, or *vice versa*. "If God were your Father, ye would love Me: for I proceeded forth and came from God; neither came I of Myself, but He sent Me. Why do ye not understand My speech? even because ye cannot hear My word;" that is, you cannot hear, in the sense that you will not hear; you are allowing sin to come in and so you cannot hear.

Then He comes right out and speaks of that which He had previously indicated, "Ye are of your father the devil, and the lusts of your father ye will do. He was a murderer from the beginning, and abode not in the truth, because there is no truth in him. When he speaketh a lie, he speaketh of his own: for he is a liar, and the father of it."

Now notice how much our Lord has put into one verse in regard to the great doctrine of Satanology. Is there a personal devil, or is the devil simply the personification of evil? We are often told nowadays that the belief in a personal devil is a relic of the dark ages, and that it is absurd to believe there is such a being. But here is the testimony of Holy Scripture—please carefully consider these verses. He says, "I come forth from God." He declares Himself to be the Son of God. "Ye are of your father the devil." But might He not have meant, "Ye are overcome of evil?" Ah, but He goes further; He uses the personal pronoun and He says, "he was a murderer." He is speaking of a person, and of a person who was not always what he is now. In other words, Jesus is telling us that in this universe there is a foul, malevolent spirit who actuates and moves upon those who do not acknowledge the authority of God. And this evil, malevolent spirit was not always such; he was not always what he is now. "He abode not in the truth."

People often ask, "If there is a devil, why would a good God create him?" A good God did not create a devil. The being that God created was a pure and innocent angel. In Isaiah 14: 12 we read how this angel fell. Who is the one spoken of here? He is called "Lucifer, son of the morning." "Lucifer" means "the day star," a glorious being who dwelt in the presence of God. We read of only one archangel; that is Michael. Lucifer seems to have had a similar place before he fell. How did he fall? Through self-will. Five times he said, "I will;" "I will ascend into the heavens; I will exalt my throne above the stars of God; I will sit also upon the mount of the congregations in the sides of the north; I will ascend above the heights of the clouds; I will be like the Most High." This created angel dared to aspire to a place of equality with God, if not to crowd God Himself from His throne. And in answer to that fivefold "I will," the answer comes ringing down from the skies, "Yet thou shalt be brought down to hell, to the sides of the pit."

So a glorious angel was changed into the devil. It all began when he abode not in the truth.

In the book of Ezekiel we have another remarkable scripture. In chapter 28 God is speaking of the prince of Tyre, but back of the prince of Tyre is one whom He calls the king of Tyre, one who dominated the heart of this earthly prince, but who himself was more than man. "Thou hast been in Eden the garden of God; every precious stone was thy covering, the sardius, topaz, and the diamond, the beryl, the onyx, and the jasper, the sapphire, the emerald, and the carbuncle, and gold: the workmanship of thy tabrets and of thy pipes was prepared in thee in the day that thou wast created." "Thou hast been in Eden the garden of God." This was something that never could be said of any earthly ruler. These precious stones were used to represent the various aspects of his character. Here was the leader of the heavenly choir. This glorious being piped in the presence of God until sin came in. "Thou art the anointed cherub that covereth; and I have set thee so: thou wast upon the holy mountain of God; thou hast walked up and down in the midst of the stones of fire. Thou wast perfect in thy ways from the day that thou wast created, till iniquity was found in thee." And what that iniquity is, is told us in verse 17, "Thine heart was lifted up because of thy beauty, thou hast cor-

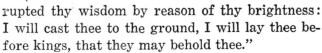

rupted thy wisdom by reason of thy brightness:
I will cast thee to the ground, I will lay thee before kings, that they may behold thee."

Lucifer fell through pride. Self-will was the
first expression of that pride, and so an angel
became the devil. He is called the devil and he is
called Satan. "Devil" means "the slanderer" and
"Satan" means "the adversary," and he combines
both in himself. He accuses man to God and God
to man; but he is the adversary particularly of
God Himself and His blessed Son, and then in a
more general way of everything that is of God
here on earth. He is not simply here to tempt
men; there is that within their own hearts which
leads them to sin, but the great work in which he
is engaged is in throwing evil reflections upon
that which is of God. He is called "the accuser
of the brethren." Let us be sure that we are not
found in his company. When I hear people making unkind reflections on the people of God, I say
to myself, They are doing the devil's work. That
is the work he has been engaged in all down
through the centuries. Let us seek to take a definite stand against all such evil behavior.

The devil then is an apostate; he abode not in
the truth. He turned away from it. And he is a
murderer from the beginning. The word translated "murderer" here really is "manslayer." It
is not that his malice is directed against men as

such, but he knows that God is a lover of men and it hurts God to see men turned away from Himself.

There is no truth in him, we are told. When he speaks of a lie, he speaks of his own, for he is a liar and the father of it. In the first epistle of Peter we hear the apostle saying, "Be sober, be vigilant; because your adversary the devil, as a roaring lion, walketh about, seeking whom he may devour: whom resist stedfast in the faith, knowing that the same afflictions are accomplished in your brethren that are in the world." If we walk in the truth, we need not fear the power of Satan. If we put on the whole armor of God, we can resist him successfully.

But let us not under-estimate the power of the enemy. There is a personal devil, he is the prince of this world, and men and women in their unsaved state are subject to his control. Christians are warned not to listen to his suggestions or to walk in his way. To be delivered from his power means to stand against him, faithfully battling for the truth which God has committed to us. When men and women are awakened about their sins they realize the power of Satan, but, thank God, our Lord Jesus Christ died that He might destroy him that had the power of death and might deliver those who put their trust in Him from the fear of death. Satan tempted man to sin, and by sin came death, and now Satan uses death to terrify and frighten the victims of his own wiles, who, in their folly, have turned away from the path of obedience to God. But the Lord Jesus Christ has abolished death by going through it and coming up in triumph, and now He delivers those who will trust Him from the fear of death.

Does the thought of death strike terror to your heart? Do you say, "Oh, if I only did not have to face that last great ordeal!" Listen to me: If you will put your faith in the One who died and rose again, you will know that death is just the door to life. Jesus says, "I am the Way, the Truth, and the Life: no man cometh unto the Father but by Me." "He that followeth Me shall not walk in darkness, but shall have the light of life."

> "A mighty fortress is our God!
>   A bulwark never-failing:
> Our helper He, amid the flood
>   Of mortal ills prevailing.
> For still our ancient foe
>   Doth seek to work us woe:
> His craft and power are great,
>   And armed with cruel hate;
> On earth is not his equal."
>
> —*Martin Luther.*

THE PRE-EXISTENT CHRIST

✓ ✓ ✓

"And because I tell you the truth, ye believe Me not. Which of you convinceth Me of sin? And if I say the truth, why do ye not believe Me? He that is of God heareth God's words: ye therefore hear them not, because ye are not of God. Then answered the Jews, and said unto Him, Say we not well that Thou art a Samaritan, and hast a devil? Jesus answered, I have not a devil; but I honor My Father, and ye do dishonor Me. And I seek not Mine own glory: there is One that seeketh and judgeth. Verily, verily, I say unto you, If a man keep My saying, he shall never see death. Then said the Jews unto Him, Now we know that Thou hast a devil. Abraham is dead, and the prophets; and Thou sayest, If a man keep My saying, he shall never taste of death. Art Thou greater than our father Abraham, which is dead? and the prophets are dead: whom makest Thou Thyself? Jesus answered, If I honor Myself, My honor is nothing: it is My Father that honoreth Me: of whom ye say, that He is your God: yet ye have not known Him; but I know Him: and if I should say, I know. Him not, I shall be a liar like unto you: but I know Him, and keep His saying. Your father Abraham rejoiced to see My day: and he saw it, and was glad. Then said the Jews unto Him, Thou art not yet fifty years old, and hast Thou seen Abraham? Jesus said unto them, Verily, verily, I say unto you, Before Abraham was, I am. Then took they up stones to cast at Him: but Jesus hid Himself, and went out of the temple, going through the midst of them, and so passed by" (John 8:45-59).

✓ ✓ ✓

WE have noticed that all these conversations took place in the temple following the wonderful words to that poor, sinful woman who was brought to Jesus by her accusers.

"Neither do I condemn thee; go, and sin no
more." Phase after phase of truth has been set
forth for the enlightenment of the Jewish leaders. Many and various claims had been put before the people, and one by one they had been
questioned by the majority who had listened to
Him. Now in the closing part of this chapter
there are really two outstanding themes. First,
the sinlessness of Jesus, and then, second, His
pre-existence, and both of these testify to His
Deity. He is God. On earth He was God manifest in the flesh, and because He was God in flesh
He was an absolutely sinless Man. He was the
One who had existed from all eternity. He was
the Son of the Father before He came into this
world through the gates of birth. He says, "Because I tell you the truth, ye believe Me not."
The truth was so utterly beyond anything that
they had known that they would not accept it.
It was a reminder that the natural man understandeth not the things of God. This explains why
men have so much difficulty with the teaching of
the Word of God. They are bereft of spiritual
discernment. What men need is a second birth.
You remember the story of the man who was
denying that God answers prayer. He said,
"There is no such thing as God-answered prayer
in this world," and an old Quaker was standing
there and asked, "Does thee not believe that God

answers prayer?" "No," said the man, "I don't."
"Did thee ever pray to God?" "No, I never did."
"Well then, friend, what does thee know about it?
Had thee not better be silent till thee has tested
it?" We need to test it for ourselves. We need
the reality of the second birth, for except a man
be born again he cannot see (that is, he cannot
understand) the things of the kingdom of God.

Here was Truth incarnate moving among men;
they listened and turned away incredulous. They
could not believe because their minds were
blinded on account of their sins. And so the Lord
Jesus says, "I tell you the truth, but ye believe
Me not." Then He puts this question, "Which of
you convinceth Me of sin?" They would not believe what He was telling them. Had they ever
known Him to commit a sin or any kind? That
question comes as a challenge to all the world
still, "Which of you convinceth Me of sin?" Men
have searched these records, they have tried to
find some fault or flaw in His character or something wrong in His behavior, but have not been
able to find one. He stands before us as the only
sinless character in all history and in all literature, and that in itself declares that He is more
than man. Of all men it is written, they have
sinned and come short of the glory of God. But
here was One who came to earth as man, and He

never sinned, but glorified God in everything He did.

Consider the prayer-life of our Lord Jesus and see how that demonstrates His sinlessness. Our Lord Jesus taught His disciples to pray, "Forgive us our trespasses as we forgive them who trespass against us," but He never prayed that prayer Himself. We never read of Him joining with anyone in prayer. He prayed *for* people, but not *with* them. Why? Because He prayed from an altogether different standpoint than others. He prayed as the Eternal Son of the Father whose communion had never been disturbed for an instant. When we come to God, we pray as forgiven sinners, or we pray for the forgiveness of sins. Jesus could not join in that. Some of our most blessed experiences have been when we have knelt with others and prayed with them. We pray with confidence and faith, believing that God is ready to forgive, for He says, "If we confess our sins, He is faithful and just to forgive us our sins and to cleanse us from all unrighteousness." Jesus never joined with any body to pray like that.

And then, again, consider the question of His piety. If you are a Christian, may I ask you this?—How did your life of piety begin? You were not always a Christian. You were not born a Christian, though you may have been born into a Christian family. How did your life of godliness begin? Did it not begin with the recognition of your own lost estate, and did not that lead you to see your need of salvation and bring you to God for pardon? Jesus knew nothing of this. In His life we see piety without one thought or mention of repentance. No tears of contrition ever fell from His eyes. If He wept, He wept for others' sins, as when He looked over Jerusalem and said, "O Jerusalem, Jerusalem, which killest the prophets, and stonest them that are sent unto thee: how often would I have gathered thy children together, as a hen doth gather her brood under her wings, and ye would not!" His tears were for others' sins and sorrow. He had none for His own, for He was the sinless One, and in this we recognize His Divinity and His Deity.

And so He speaks the truth and He challenges everyone by saying, "If I say the truth, why do ye not believe Me? He that is of God heareth God's words: ye therefore hear them not, because ye are not of God." If we reject the testimony of our Lord Jesus Christ, our very rejection declares that we are not subject to the will of God. But our Lord's hearers, on this occasion, were very indignant with Him. They resisted His testimony and answered, "Say we not well that Thou art a Samaritan, and hast a devil?" And for an orthodox Jew to call anyone a Samaritan was to use the most contemptuous expression possible, for if there was anyone the Jew detested, it was the Samaritan. So they said, "Say we not well that Thou art a Samaritan, and hast a devil?" (It is really "a demon." There is only one devil.)

Is it not a striking thing that in that parable of the man on the Jericho road, which we all love, He uses that name for Himself. He pictures Himself as a Samaritan. It is as such our blessed Lord has come from the heights of glory into this dark world, seeking those that are lost. How wondrous His grace!

But when they said, "Thou hast a demon," He replied, "I have not a demon, but I honor My Father, and ye do dishonor Me." And whenever we refuse His testimony we are dishonoring Him. In the next verse He explains that He was here to seek the glory of God, and He could commit this into the hands of Him who judgeth righteously. Then He adds something that astonished them, "Verily, verily, I say unto you, If a man keep My saying, he shall never see death." Now outwardly, of course, believers pass through the article of death as others do; that is, they die as others die. And yet the wonderful thing is that the words of Jesus are absolutely true: the believer does not see death. What does He see? He sees the entrance into the Father's house. Death, we are told, is our servant. How does death serve us? By ushering us into the presence of God.

I was with an evangelist in the South and we went to visit a friend who lived in a nice house, where we were met at the door by a kindly colored servant. "Oh," she said, "the mistress is waiting for you," and took us inside. The evangelist turned and said, "You know, that kindly colored servant reminds me of the scripture that says, 'Death is ours.'" Death stands by, death is just a servant who ushers us into the presence of the Lord. "He that believeth in Me shall never see death."

When Mrs. General Booth of The Salvation Army was dying, she looked up and said, "Is this death? Why, this is glorious!" Somebody said, "But you are suffering." She said, "Oh, yes; the waters are rising, but so am I."

Yes, death is only the means of entrance into eternal blessing—with Christ. But oh, what a sad thing if one does not know Christ! That will mean eternal banishment from God.

But the Lord's hearers did not understand, for they said, "Now we know You have a demon. Why, Abraham is dead, and he was the father of our nation, and the prophets are dead, and Thou sayest. 'If a man keep My saying, he shall never see death. Art Thou greater than our father Abraham, which is dead? and the prophets are dead: whom makest Thou Thyself?' " They could not conceive anyone greater than Abraham. Abraham was called the friend of God, and here was God standing among them in human guise. "Jesus answered, If I honor Myself, My honor is nothing: it is My Father that honoreth Me; of whom ye say, that He is your God." He added, "If I should say, I know Him not, I shall be a liar like unto you: but I know Him, and keep His saying. Your father Abraham rejoiced to see My day: and he saw it, and was glad." When did Abraham see His day? When God gave him the promise, "In thee and in thy Seed shall all the nations be blessed."

Abraham believed God and it was counted to him for righteousness. But the Jews could not understand this. They said, "Thou art not yet fifty years old, and hast Thou seen Abraham?" He did not say, "I have seen Abraham," but He said, "Abraham saw My day."

Jesus said unto them, "Verily, verily, I say unto you, Before Abraham was, I am." Again, He uses the incommunicable name of God. "Who shall I say has sent me?" said Moses. "Say I AM has sent thee." And Jesus says here, "Before Abraham was, I am." He speaks as the God of Abraham. Notice how He insists on His pre-existence. He is the ever-living Christ who came into this world as our Redeemer.

When He spoke like this, they counted it blasphemy. You remember how some of them came to the temple earlier, intending to stone that poor woman, but when Jesus thus declared His Deity they took up stones to cast at Him. But Jesus hid Himself, going through the midst of them, and so passed by, and they lost their opportunity. They refused to credit His testimony and He left them, "and so passed by."

FROM BLINDNESS AND PENURY
TO ETERNAL BLESSING

✟ ✟ ✟

"And as Jesus passed by, He saw a man which was blind from his birth. And His disciples asked Him, saying, Master, who did sin, this man, or his parents, that he was born blind? Jesus answered, Neither hath this man sinned, nor his parents: but that the works of God should be made manifest in him. I must work the works of Him that sent Me, while it is day: the night cometh, when no man can work. As long as I am in the world, I am the light of the world. When He had thus spoken, He spat on the ground, and made clay of the spittle, and He anointed the eyes of the blind man with the clay, and said unto him, Go, wash in the pool of Siloam, (which is by interpretation, Sent.) He went his way therefore, and washed, and came seeing. The neighbours therefore, and they which before had seen him that he was blind, said, Is not this he that sat and begged? Some said, This is he: others said, He is like him: but he said, I am he. Therefore said they unto him, How were thine eyes opened? He answered and said, A man that is called Jesus made clay, and anointed mine eyes, and said unto me, Go to the pool of Siloam, and wash: and I went and washed, and I received sight. Then said they unto him, Where is He? He said, I know not. They brought to the Pharisees him that aforetime was blind. And it was the sabbath day when Jesus made the clay, and opened his eyes. Then again the Pharisees also asked him how he had received his sight. He said unto them, He put clay upon mine eyes, and I washed, and do see. Therefore said some of the Pharisees, This Man is not of God, because He keepeth not the sabbath day. Others said, How can a Man that is a sinner do such miracles? And there was a division among them. They say unto the blind man again, What sayest thou of Him, that He hath opened thine eyes? He said, He is a prophet.

But the Jews did not believe concerning him, that he had been blind, and received his sight, until they called the parents of him that had received his sight. And they asked them, saying, Is this your son, who ye say was born blind? how then does he now see? His parents answered them and said, We know that this is our son, and that he was born blind: but by what means he now seeth, we know not; or who hath opened his eyes, we know not: he is of age; ask him: he shall speak for himself. These words spake his parents, because they feared the Jews: for the Jews had agreed already, that if any man did confess that He was Christ, he should be put out of the synagogue. Therefore said his parents, He is of age; ask him. Then again called they the man that was blind, and said unto him, Give God the praise: we know that this Man is a sinner. He answered and said, Whether He be a sinner or no, I know not: one thing I know, that, whereas I was blind, now I see. Then said they to him again, What did He to thee? how opened He thine eyes? He answered them, I have told you already, and ye did not hear: wherefore would ye hear it again? will ye also be His disciples? Then they reviled him, and said, Thou art His disciple; but we are Moses' disciples. We know that God spake unto Moses: as for this fellow, we know not from whence He is. The man answered and said unto them, Why herein is a marvellous thing, that ye know not from whence He is, and yet He hath opened mine eyes. Now we know that God heareth not sinners: but if any man be a worshipper of God, and doeth His will, him He heareth. Since the world began was it not heard that any man opened the eyes of one that was born blind. If this Man were not of God, He could do nothing. They answered and said unto him, Thou wast altogether born in sins, and dost thou teach us? And they cast him out. Jesus heard that they had cast him out; and when He had found him, He said unto him, Dost thou believe on the Son of God? He answered and said, Who is He, Lord, that I might believe on Him? And Jesus said unto him, Thou hast both seen Him, and it is He that talketh with thee. And he said, Lord, I believe. And he worshipped Him. And Jesus said, For judgment I am come into this world, that they which see not might see; and that they which see might be made blind. And some of the Pharisees which were with Him heard these words. and said unto Him, Are we blind also? Jesus said unto them, If ye were blind, ye should have no sin: but now ye say, We see; therefore your sin remaineth."— John 9.

IN considering the eighth chapter we have seen that the Lord Jesus Christ was acting in accordance with the special title that He gave Himself, "The Light of the World."

In this ninth chapter, He is still manifesting Himself as the light of the world, but the difference is this: in chapter eight we saw the light shining into the darkened hearts of those who were accusing the poor woman who had been brought in her sinful condition to Jesus that He might condemn her to death. He said, "He that is without sin among you, let him first cast a stone at her." And the light shone into their hearts and revealed their own personal guilt, so that not one dared to stone that poor sinner who knelt shamed at His feet. Now in this ninth chapter we have light entering a darkened heart in order to give the knowledge of the grace of God. We have a blind man, and the light shined through his darkened lids and enlightened his natural eyes, as well as the eyes of his soul. We read, "And as Jesus passed by, He saw a man which was blind from his birth." This was very shortly after the incident recorded in chapter eight, possibly on the same Sabbath day, though we are not sure. This man evidently occupied a special place in the courts of the temple. The people saw him from time to time as he sat there hoping to receive alms from them. Doubtless some were glad to help him. As they were passing by, the disciples of Christ turned to Him and said, "Master, who did sin, this man, or his parents, that he was born blind?" They knew that sickness and blindness and all the different things from which humanity suffers had come into the world because of sin. Now, like Job's three friends, they were trying to place the guilty one. Here was a man who was born blind. Was his punishment because of the sins of his parents, or his own sin? You might say, "How could it possibly be because he had sinned?" Well, there were many of the Jews who believed that even a child in the womb could sin. In Genesis we are told of Jacob, who "took his brother Esau by the heel in the womb." The Jews insisted that self-will could be manifested in an unborn child. They did not believe in the transmigration of souls; therefore that question does not imply the possibility of his having sinned in a former life. But they were perplexed and confused by the teaching of some of the Rabbis.

"Jesus answered, Neither hath this man sinned, nor his parents: but that the works of God should be made manifest in him." He was not saying these people had never sinned at any time, but He was answering their question.

Why was this man born blind? This naturally raises a question that troubles a great many peo-

ple. Why is it that infants have to suffer? Why
is it that some children are born into the world
with imperfect, maimed bodies? Some are blind,
some deaf and dumb. How can you account for
a God of infinite love and grace allowing an infant to suffer? Well, if you leave out the doctrine of the fall of man, I do not know of any
way in which you can reconcile an infant's suffering with a God of love, but when we realize that
all pain, suffering and sorrow have come into the
world because of sin, because man, in the beginning, turned away from God, we realize that these
things are the effect of man's disobedience. And
our Lord Jesus Christ makes something else clear,
and it is this: If an infant is born into the world
in such a condition as mentioned here, in some
way God is going to be glorified by that condition.
This man had lived to attain his majority, for we
are told that when his parents were questioned,
they said, "He is of age, ask him." All his years
had been spent in the dark. But now think of
this wonderful thing: the first person whose face
he ever saw was the Lord Jesus Christ! Surely
that was some compensation for all that he had
endured in those years of darkness!

Mr. Spurgeon used to tell of an aged Christian
who was born blind and yet he was a happy saint.
One day when speaking with another believer he
said, "You know, I have so much more to give

thanks for than you." "What! More than I?" the other exclaimed. "Why, I have been able to see for years!" The blind man looked up with those sightless eyes and said, "Oh, yes; but you have had to see so many things which have been disagreeable and distressing, so many faces which were unkind and angry and unholy, but the first face that I shall ever see will be the face of my blessed Saviour, who loved me and gave Himself for me. So," he said, "I have more to be thankful for than you." It takes the grace of God to enable one to speak like that. I know that many of you who read this have all your lives bewailed the fact that you have had to suffer in ways that others did not, possibly from babyhood, and you have said many a time, "The ways of God are hard to understand." Oh, let me assure you of this, if you will just settle it in your mind that God never makes any mistakes, that He is too good to afflict needlessly the children of men, and He is too loving to do anything unkind, you will then realize that as you study the Word and as you put your heart's trust in Him, some day you will have reason to thank and praise Him even for the things that have caused you the greatest sorrow and made you weep the bitterest tears.

Of this man Jesus said, "Neither hath this man sinned, nor his parents: but that the works of God should be made manifest in him." God sent

His blessed Son to him just at the right time to
make him a wonderful witness to His delivering
power. Do you notice this?—the Lord was interested in this man long before he was interested
in Jesus. He was there by the temple gate asking an alms and hoping that the people who
passed by would have mercy on him. He did not
know that there was One there who could do far
more than give him an alms,—One who could give
him his sight. But there was Jesus, and He was
talking to His disciples, and He said to them, "I
must work the works of Him that sent Me, while
it is day: the night cometh, when no man can
work." We need to take that to heart. Jesus said,
"As long as I am in the world, I am the light of
the world." But He said to His disciples, "Ye are
the light of the world," and to us also cometh the
night when no man can work. God give us to be
faithful while we have opportunity to make Christ
known.

"As long as I am in the world, I am the light of
the world. When He had thus spoken, He spat on
the ground, and made clay of the spittle, and He
anointed the eyes of the blind man with the clay."
This was a very simple thing. You might say it
even made conditions worse. Had there been the
least glimmer of light before, the clay would have
shut it all out. But there was something wonderful in that simple act. It was a picture of the in-

carnation of our Lord Jesus Christ. He had come
from heaven's glory and had taken a body of clay
and that only helped to make the darkness greater
for many people. They did not understand when
they saw Him going about. They could not understand, until the Holy Spirit showed them, that
He was the Sent One of the Father. And so He
anointed the eyes of this man with the clay and
said "Go, wash in the pool of Siloam (which is
by interpretation, Sent)." In other words, "When
you realize that I am the Sent One of the Father,
you will see." And he did, for he went and
washed, and came seeing.

What a wonderful experience it must have
been when he opened his eyes upon the beauty of
the world and came and gazed upon the face of
the Lord Jesus Christ! "He went his way therefore, and washed, and came seeing."

But the Saviour conveyed Himself away for
the moment. The neighbors crowded around and
looked at this man and saw that he could see, and
they said, "Why, this is amazing! Is this not he
who sat and begged?" "Some said, this is he:
others said, He is like him." They were not quite
sure. You know there is such a difference. There
is a sort of vacant look upon the countenance of
a blind man. They said, "Is this really our old
neighbor or not?" They were not certain. "But
he said, I am he." "Oh, yes; I am the man that

was born blind, and now I am able to see." Thank
God that is the kind of a miracle that Jesus works
even today. Oh, how many there are who have
been blind in their hearts; blind to eternal realities, but when they learned that Jesus was the
Sent One of the Father and trusted Him, they
were able to see. Everything was different.

And they turned to this man and said, "Well,
how were your eyes opened?" He answered, "The
Man that is called Jesus, made clay and anointed
my eyes and said to me, Go to the Pool of Siloam,
and I went and washed and I received sight." I
like the simplicity of this man's confession. He
knew how he had himself met the conditions—
"The Man that is called Jesus"—Do you know
that lovely name? "For there is one God, and one
Mediator between God and men, the Man Christ
Jesus." Do you know that blessed Man?

"Fairest of all the earth beside,
Chiefest of all unto Thy bride;
Fulness divine in Thee I see,
Beautiful Man of Calvary."

Oh, to know Him is to know God, for He is the
exact expression of the divine character. He
could say, "He that hath seen Me hath seen
the Father." Do you know Him? I am not asking
you if you profess to be a Christian or if you
belong to some Church, or if you from time to
time avail yourself of participation in the sacra-

ments of the Church, or if you are trying to live a good life. All these things have their places, but I am asking you this, Do you know the Man that is called Jesus? Have you trusted Him as your own Saviour? Till you know Him, you do not know God, you are still in your sins. But when you know Him your sins are put away and you have life eternal. When you know Him, the darkness is past and the true light shines.

This man had met Jesus and Jesus had given him sight. He says, "A Man that is called Jesus made clay, and anointed mine eyes." He heard His voice, who said, "Go, wash in the pool of Siloam." And he obeyed and received his sight. And so today the ultimatum goes out to everyone, "Wash, and be clean. Wash, and receive your sight. Believe the testimony that God has given concerning His Son, and you have life everlasting." You remember John 5: 24, "Verily, verily, I say unto you, He that heareth My word, and believeth on Him that sent Me, hath everlasting life, and shall not come into condemnation (judgment) : but is passed from death unto life." And so we are told elsewhere, "That if thou shalt confess with thy mouth the Lord Jesus, and shalt believe in thine heart that God hath raised Him from the dead, thou shalt be saved. For with the heart man believeth unto righteousness; and with the mouth confession is made unto salvation."

This man took Jesus at His word and he received his sight. There are thousands who read this who have taken Him at His word and who can give the same testimony, "I went and washed, and I received my sight." You who have not received Christ, I plead with you, do that which He asks you to do. Trust Him as the Sent One of the Father and you shall have light and life and peace.

"Then said they unto him, Where is He? He said I know not. They brought to the Pharisees him that aforetime was blind." And of course, the Lord Jesus is put right in conflict with their legalistic consciences. It was so much more important that one should believe their own man-made laws in regard to the observance of the Sabbath than to meet the need of a poor blind man. So Jesus has again exposed Himself to their criticisms. They asked the man how he had received his sight. He said, "He put clay upon mine eyes and I washed, and do see." The Pharisees immediately jumped to an unwarranted conclusion, and they passed on their judgment. They said, "This Man is not of God, because He keepeth not the Sabbath day." No matter what He does for suffering humanity, because He keepeth not the sabbath day, He is not of God. He was acting in utter disregard of the many hundreds of laws which they had made themselves. Jesus was quite indifferent to them, and when men and women were in distress He would help them, no matter what offense it gave to these legalists.

There were some among their number who said, "But how can a man who is a sinner do such miracles?" So there was division among them. They called the blind man again and said, "What sayest thou of Him, that He hath opened thine eyes? He said, He is a prophet." He is God's messenger. A prophet is a man who comes to act for God. "He said, He is a prophet."

"But the Jews did not believe concerning him that he had been blind." They said, "This is not the beggar who used to sit at the gate of the temple." So they called his parents and said, "Is this your son, who ye say was born blind?" What an implication there, as though they might have been deceiving all the way along. His parents answered them and said, "We know that this is our son, and that he was born blind: but by what means he now seeth, we know not; or who hath opened his eyes, we know not: he is of age; ask him: he shall speak for himself." And then the next verse tells us why they were so guarded. Already the word had gone around that the Jews would make trouble for anyone who bore witness to Christ. "For the Jews had agreed already, that if any man did confess that He was Christ, he should be put out of the synagogue," and they did not want to be put on the spot, as we say. If they were to be put out of the synagogue they would be absolutely on the outside of everything, so people dreaded this sentence of synagogue excommunication. These parents did not want to run the risk of confessing what they, in their hearts, had to believe. They said, "Ask him; he is of age." So again they called the blind man and said to him, "Give God the praise: we know that this Man is a sinner." "There seems no doubt that you were born blind, but do not give any credit to this Man, for He is a sinner." I like the testimony of this one-time blind man. Looking full upon them with those now-seeing eyes of his, he said, "Whether He be a sinner or no, I know not: one thing I know, that whereas I was blind, now I see." Oh, that is a great testimony, and I am sure that there are many of my readers who could give just the same witness, "This one thing I know, that whereas I was blind, now I see." "Whereas I was once a poor sinner, having the understanding darkened, now I know that my eyes have been opened."

"Oh, Christ, in Thee my soul has found,
    And found in Thee alone,
The peace and joy I sought so long,
    The bliss till now unknown.

"Now none but Christ can satisfy,
    None other name for me;
There's love, and life and lasting joy,
    Lord Jesus, found in Thee.

"The pleasures lost I sadly mourned,
  But never wept for Thee,
 Till grace my blinded eyes received
  Thy loveliness to see."

We who are saved are not simply resting on someone's say-so, nor even on believing the Word of God itself, but there has come within us an experience of an ever-deepening knowledge of the presence of the Lord Jesus Christ with us through the years, that enables us to say from the heart, "I know!" Paul could say, "I know whom I have believed, and am persuaded that He is able to keep that which I have committed unto Him against that day."

Well, this man gives his testimony and now his interrogators begin to quiz him a little further. "How opened He thine eyes?" I like the seriousness of the man. He looked up and said, "Well, I have already told you. Why are you asking me? If you would really like to know, I will tell you again." "Will ye also be His disciples?" But that angered them and they exclaimed, "Thou art His disciple; but we are Moses' disciples." But Jesus could say, "Moses wrote of Me." "Had you believed Moses you would have believed Me." Let me say to you who believe Moses to be a prophet of God and who accept the Old Testament as inspired, read those records, ask God to shed light from heaven on those passages, and if you are sincere you will see Christ Jesus in the testimony of Moses.

They said, "We know that God spake unto Moses: as for this fellow, we know not from whence He is." And then the man with the new eyes answered and said, "Why, herein is a marvelous thing, that ye know not from whence He is, and yet He hath opened mine eyes. Now we know that God heareth not sinners: but if any man be a worshipper of God, and doeth His will, him He heareth. Since the world began was it not heard that any man opened the eyes of one that was born blind. If this Man were not of God, He could do nothing." The thing that amazes me is how fast this man grew. Why, only a little while before he was a blind beggar. Doubtless he had meditated on a great many things, sitting there in his darkness. So many things became clear. When you get acquainted with Christ the veil is taken away from heart and mind.

But they, having no answer, became angry. That is generally true, you know, when a person cannot meet an argument, the natural thing is to speak loudly and shout down your adversary. They turned on him and said, "Thou wast altogether born in sins, and dost thou teach us?" Who were these men? They were the folk who said, "Lord, I thank Thee I am not like other men. I am not a drunkard. I am not an adulterer." And so they looked with contempt upon this poor man. Who is this man? He is born "in sins." No, the Bible does not say that. It says, "in sin." "I was shapen in iniquity and in sin did my mother conceive me," David says. We fall into sins after we are born.

But they cast him out. That was the greatest thing that could have happened to him. Some folk are so afraid of being cast out. Do you know where they cast him out? Right into the arms of Jesus! Jesus said to him, "Dost thou believe on the Son of God?" He answered, "Who is He, Lord, that I might believe on Him?" As much as to say, "I would believe in anyone of whom You tell me." Jesus said to him, "Thou hast both seen Him, and it is He that talketh with thee." And immediately the man worshipped and said, "Lord, I believe." Just think of it, in the beginning of the passage he is a poor blind beggar in great need, and in the end of the passage he is a happy worshipper, looking into the face of Christ. That is a wonderful "Pilgrim's Progress," from blindness and poverty to worshipping at the Saviour's feet, as one enlightened and enriched for eternity.

"And Jesus said, For judgment I am come into this world, that they which see not might see; and that they which see might be made blind. And some of the Pharisees which were with Him heard

these words, and said unto Him, Are we blind
also? Jesus said unto them, If ye were blind (if
you had been born that way and had never had
the light), ye should have no sin: but now ye say,
We see; therefore your sin remaineth." They are
convicted of deliberately rejecting the light.

The Lord Jesus is still the light of the world.
He is still opening blinded eyes, and if there are
those of my readers who have never yet come to
Him and have not proven to themselves what He
can do for the heart that trusts Him, I am glad
to commend Him to you. Bring your trials, your
sins, your tears, come in all your need, and be
assured that He is ready to meet it in His own
rich, wondrous grace.

"Come, ye disconsolate, where'er you languish;
　Come to the mercy-seat, fervently kneel;
　Here bring your wounded hearts, here tell your anguish;
　Earth hath no sorrow that heav'n cannot heal."

THE GOOD SHEPHERD

✓ ✓ ✓

"Verily, verily, I say unto you, He that entereth not by the door into the sheepfold, but climbeth up some other way, the same is a thief and a robber. But He that entereth in by the door is the shepherd of the sheep. To Him the porter openeth; and the sheep hear His voice: and He calleth His own sheep by name, and leadeth them out. And when He putteth forth His own sheep, He goeth before them, and the sheep follow Him: for they know His voice. And a stranger will they not follow, but will flee from him: for they know not the voice of strangers. This parable spake Jesus unto them: but they understood not what things they were which He spake unto them. Then said Jesus unto them again, Verily, verily, I say unto you, I am the door of the sheep. All that ever came before Me are thieves and robbers: but the sheep did not hear them. I am the door: by Me if any man enter in, he shall be saved, and shall go in and out, and find pasture. The thief cometh not, but for to steal, and to kill, and to destroy: I am come that they might have life, and that they might have it more abundantly. I am the good shepherd: the good shepherd giveth his life for the sheep. But he that is an hireling, and not the shepherd, whose own the sheep are not, seeth the wolf coming, and leaveth the sheep, and fleeth: and the wolf catcheth them, and scattereth the sheep. The hireling fleeth, because he is a hireling, and careth not for the sheep. I am the good shepherd, and know My sheep, and am known of Mine. As the Father knoweth Me, even so know I the Father: and I lay down My life for the sheep. And other sheep I have, which are not of this fold: them also I must bring, and they shall hear My voice; and there shall be one fold, and one shepherd" (John 10: 1-16).

WE really have two distinct sections in
this portion. The first five verses constitute a complete parable in themselves,
and then in verses six to sixteen we have added
instruction and a fuller opening up of the truth
of the Shepherd character of our Lord Jesus
Christ. He is emphatically the Good Shepherd.
It is a rather significant thing that the word
"good" here is one that really means "beautiful."
"I am the beautiful Shepherd." Of course, it
refers to beauty of character—the shepherd who
is absolutely unselfish and devoted to the will of
the Father. He presented Himself to Israel as
their Shepherd and this was in accordance with
many Old Testament Messianic scriptures. In
Genesis 49, when by divine inspiration Jacob is
speaking of Joseph, he concludes with these
words, "Joseph is a fruitful bough, even a fruitful bough by a well; whose branches run over the
wall: the archers have sorely grieved him, and
shot at him, and hated him: but his bow abode in
strength, and the arms of his hands were made
strong by the hands of the mighty God of Jacob;
(from thence is the shepherd, the stone of Israel),"
i.e., the Shepherd is from the mighty God of Jacob;
and He brings this in here because the experiences
that the true Shepherd, the Stone of Israel, was

destined to pass through were so nearly akin to those that Joseph had to endure, rejected and spurned, as he was, by his own brethren. Then we have the Messiah spoken of as Jehovah's Shepherd in Psalm 23, that beautiful gem which we love so much. Somebody has said that it is more loved and less believed than any other portion of Holy Scripture. "The Lord is my Shepherd, I shall not want." We love to repeat the words, but how many believe them? How often we get panicky when the purse is empty and we are out of employment! There is one thing to do, and that is turn to Him and leave all with Him. "The Lord is my Shepherd; I shall not want."

Then in Psalm 80:1, "Give ear, O Shepherd of Israel, Thou that leadest Joseph like a flock; Thou that dwellest between the cherubims, shine forth." The Shepherd of Israel was God Himself, who was watching over His people, and who some day was to come into the world in human form in order to guide them into blessing. Isaiah portrays Him in this way. In chapter 40:10, "Behold, the Lord God will come with strong hand, and His arm shall rule for Him. Behold, His reward is with Him, and His work before Him. He shall feed His flock like a shepherd: He shall gather the lambs with His arm, and carry them in His bosom, and shall gently lead those that are with young." This was the prophecy of the coming to this scene of the Lord's Anointed, Israel's Messiah.

Then in Jeremiah 31—that great chapter that tells of God's everlasting interest in His people Israel—in verse 10 we read, "Hear the word of the Lord, O ye nations, and declare it in the isles afar off, and say, He that scattered Israel will gather him, and keep him, as a shepherd doth his flock. For the Lord hath redeemed Jacob and ransomed him from the hand of him that was stronger than he." It was given to Ezekiel to confirm this, when in chapter 34: 12-15 he says: "As a shepherd seeketh out his flock in the day that he is among his sheep that are scattered; so will I seek out My sheep, and will deliver them out of all places where they have been scattered in the cloudy and dark day. And I will bring them out from the people, and gather them from the countries, and will bring them to their own land, and feed them upon the mountains of Israel by the rivers, and in all the inhabited places of the country. I will feed them in a good pasture, and upon the high mountains of Israel shall their fold be: there shall they lie in a good fold, and in a fat pasture shall they feed upon the mountains of Israel. I will feed My flock, and I will cause them to lie down, saith the Lord God."

We might turn to many other passages that depict the Lord as a shepherd; passages that were destined to have their fulfilment in the Person of our Lord Jesus Christ. So when He stood in the midst of Israel and declared Himself to be the Good Shepherd, they should have understood at once, for they were familiar with the Old Testament. These passages had been in their hearts and minds down through the centuries. They were looking for the coming of Jehovah's Shepherd, and now Jesus appeared and said, "I am the Good Shepherd." We noticed sometime ago, when speaking on the "I Ams" of Christ, that that expression is really a definite, divine title. Jesus takes that incommunicable name of God and He says, "I am the Good Shepherd."

He puts Himself in contrast with false shepherds who had appeared from time to time: "Verily, verily, I say unto you, He that entereth not by the door into the sheepfold, but climbeth up some other way, the same is a thief and a robber. But he that entereth in by the door is the shepherd of the sheep." I think these words are generally misapplied or given a wrong application. I do not mean that they are made to teach something that is false, but they are used contrary to what is taught in this particular verse. How often you hear people say, "If anyone tries to get into heaven in some other way than through Christ, he is a thief and a robber." But that is not what the Lord is speaking about

here, at all. It is perfectly true that if you try
to enter heaven by some other way than trusting
the Lord Jesus Christ, you will be like a thief
trying to break into a place to which you have
no title, "For there is none other name under
heaven given among men, whereby we must be
saved."

But that is not what the Saviour is speaking
of here. He is not talking about getting into
heaven. Heaven is not the sheepfold. Judaism
was the sheepfold, and in the half-century before
the appearing of our Lord Jesus Christ there
were many who came pretending to be Messiahs,
but they did not come in by the door—that is,
according to Scripture. They tried to climb up
some other way, and He berated them as thieves
and robbers. Then in contrast, He speaks of
Himself: "But He that entereth in by the door
is the shepherd of the sheep." He came in exact
accord with the prophetic Word. His life was
in exact accord with the predictions of Old Testament Scriptures. "To Him the porter openeth;
and the sheep hear His voice: and He calleth His
own sheep by name, and leadeth them out." John
the Baptist was the porter, who had been sent
of God to announce the coming of the Messiah.
He told of One whose shoe-latchet he was not
worthy to unloose. To him Jesus came for baptism. John said, "O Master, I am not worthy to

baptize You. I need rather to be baptized by
You. You are the Sinless One, and I am baptizing sinners. This is a baptism of repentance,
and You have nothing of which to repent." Jesus
said, "John, suffer it to be so now." And in His
baptism He pledged Himself to fulfil every righteous demand of the throne of God, to meet the
need of sinners. As He came forth from the
waters, a voice from the heavens declared, "This
is My beloved Son, in whom I am well pleased."
He had entered in by the door into the sheepfold. The porter had opened the way. And the
Spirit of God, descending like a dove, abode upon
Him, anointing Him as Messiah. That is what
the word "Messiah" implies, "the Anointed One."
He was anointed that day by the Spirit of God as
the true Shepherd of the sheep.

So He entered in by the door, and there were
those within the sheepfold who received Him.
These were those who were really God's children.
They had opened their hearts already to His
truth, and when Jesus came they said, "Why, this
is the Saviour for whom we have been looking!"
"The sheep hear His voice: and He calleth His
own sheep by name." He did not intend to leave
them forever in the fold of Judaism, but He was
to lead them into the liberty of grace and blessing
of Christianity. He entered into the Jewish
sheepfold to lead His Church outside of Judaism

into the liberty of grace. "When He putteth
forth His own sheep, He goeth before them, and
the sheep follow Him: for they know His voice."
This is the supreme test. Somebody says, "Well,
I think I am a Christian, but I do not see why
Christ had to come into the world and die to save
sinners. I do not understand." That proclaims
a very sad fact. It says that you do not really
know the Shepherd's voice. You have never
taken your place before God as a repentant sinner
and received Christ in simple faith. Those who
do are born again, they receive eternal life, and
with that new life is linked a new nature which
causes them to delight in obedience to His voice.
They know Him. They know the Shepherd's voice.
They will not follow a stranger.

And so we are told, "This parable spake Jesus
unto them: but they understood not what things
they were which He spake unto them." They
could not follow; their eyes were blinded; they
did not apprehend the meaning of this beautiful
little picture that He presented to them, so He
went on to open up things more fully. "Then
said Jesus unto them again, Verily, verily, I say
unto you, I am the Door of the sheep. All that
ever came before Me are thieves and robbers: but
the sheep did not hear them. I am the Door: by
Me if any man enter in, he shall be saved, and
shall go in and out, and find pasture."

Now He seems to change the figure here. Be-
fore He said, "I am the Shepherd, and I entered
in by the door." Now He says, "I am the Door."
Is it contradictory? Not at all. You may have
heard a little incident told by Dr. Piazzi Smith.
On one occasion he saw a shepherd leading his
flock up the hill. He led them into the fold and
made them comfortable, and then Dr. Smith said,
"Do you leave the sheep in this fold all night?"
"Yes." "But aren't there wild beasts around?"
"Yes." "Won't they try to get the sheep?" "Yes."
"Well, you have no door here; how can you keep
the wild beasts out?" But the Arab shepherd
lay down on his side, and as he settled himself
in that entry way, he looked up and smiled and
said, "I am the door." You see, no wild beast
could enter without awakening him, and no sheep
would go out over his body.

So Jesus said, "I am the Door. I am the One
through whom My sheep enter into blessing and
I am their guard and their guide." Then He says,
"I am the Door: by Me if any man enter in, he
shall be saved, and shall go in and out, and
find pasture." Oh, that is what David meant
when he said, "He leadeth me beside the still
waters, He maketh me to lie down in green pastures." The shepherd takes care of the sheep,
guides them to proper pastures, where they are
refreshed and fed. So our blessed Lord makes

Himself responsible for those who put their trust in Him.

Now in contrast to Himself, there were false teachers and prophets, who are only concerned about their own welfare. There have been such all down through the centuries and the Lord spoke of them in very strong language. "The thief cometh not, but for to steal, and to kill, and to destroy: I am come that they might have life, and that they might have it more abundantly." He came to give eternal life to all who put their trust in Him. And if we are walking in fellowship with God we have that abundant life. A great many Christians have life, but they do not seem to have abundant life. I was in a home lately where there were two children. One was sickly and pale, while the other was so lively that he was a constant annoyance to the little sickly one. As I looked at them I thought, "Well, they are like Christians." There are a lot of Christians who have life; they have trusted Jesus as Saviour, but they do not seem to count much for God—no testimony, no witness. And then there are others who are spiritually exuberant, bearing a great witness for the One who has redeemed them, radiant as they live in fellowship with the Lord.

First, Jesus says, "I am the Good Shepherd: the Good Shepherd giveth His life for the sheep."

Then He declares, "I am the Good Shepherd, and know My sheep, and am known of Mine." You see two sides of truth here. As the Good Shepherd He went to Calvary's cross and there laid down His life. There He was wounded for our transgressions and bruised for our iniquities and with His stripes we are healed. Oh, that wonderful Shepherd!

> "O Thou great all-gracious Shepherd,
>   Shedding for us Thy life's blood,
> Unto shame and death delivered,
>   All to bring us nigh to God."

Because, you see, there was no other way. In Gethsemane He prayed, "If it be possible, let this cup pass from Me." That is, "If it is possible to save sinners by any other means than by My drinking of the cup of judgment, then make it manifest." But there was no other way, and so the Good Shepherd went out to die.

But He who died lives again. He lives in glory, and He is the Good Shepherd still. He is called elsewhere the Great Shepherd and the Chief Shepherd. "Our Lord Jesus, that Great Shepherd of the sheep . . . make you perfect in every good work to do His will, working in you that which is well pleasing in His sight, through Jesus Christ; to whom be glory forever and ever." But this Great Shepherd is the Good Shepherd

still, and He knows His sheep, and He says, "I
am known of Mine." Does not that comfort your
heart, dear child of God? If I am speaking to
somebody who is lying on a sick bed—perhaps
some of you have not been able to leave your
bed for years, and the temptation would be to
feel so utterly forsaken and lonely and tired and
weary of it all—O dear, sick one, remember Jesus
says, "I am the Good Shepherd and I know My
sheep." He knows your struggles, disappoint-
ments, and the cup you have to drink. He drank
a more bitter one Himself.

> "If in thy path some thorns are found,
>   Oh, think who bore them on His brow!
> If grief thy sorrowing heart hath found,
>   It reached a holier than thou."

In His deep sympathy He enters into all your
trials and shares all your griefs. And then—is
it not blessed?—He says, "I know My sheep and
am known of Mine." And we say again with
David, "The Lord is my Shepherd, I shall not
want." "As the Father knoweth Me, so know I
the Father: and I lay down My life for the sheep."
And, of course, He was speaking primarily of the
sheep of the Jewish fold. But in the next verse
we read, "And other sheep I have, which are not
of this fold: them also I must bring, and they
shall hear My voice; and there shall be one fold,

and one Shepherd." The word "fold" here should really be "flock." You see, Judaism was a fold, a circumference without a center, but Christianity is a flock, where we have a center without a circumference. We have no wall about us, but we are gathered about Him, our Good Shepherd. Our Lord Jesus Christ is indeed our Good Shepherd, and "unto Him shall the gathering of the peoples be."

ADDRESS THIRTY-THREE

THE SECURITY OF CHRIST'S SHEEP

✦ ✦ ✦

"Therefore doth My Father love Me, because I lay down My life, that I might take it again. No man taketh it from Me, but I lay it down of Myself. I have power to lay it down, and I have power to take it again. This commandment have I received of My Father. There was a division therefore again among the Jews for these sayings. And many of them said, He hath a devil, and is mad; why hear ye Him? Others said, These are not the words of him that hath a devil. Can a devil open the eyes of the blind? And it was at Jerusalem the feast of the dedication, and it was winter. And Jesus walked in the temple in Solomon's porch. Then came the Jews round about Him, and said unto Him, How long dost Thou make us to doubt? If Thou be the Christ, tell us plainly. Jesus answered them, I told you, and ye believed not: the works that I do in My Father's name, they bear witness of Me. But ye believe not, because ye are not of My sheep, as I said unto you. My sheep hear My voice, and I know them, and they follow Me: and I give unto them eternal life; and they shall never perish, neither shall any man pluck them out of My hand. My Father, which gave them Me, is greater than all; and no man is able to pluck them out of My Father's hand. I and My Father are one" (John 10:17-30).

✦ ✦ ✦

THERE are two outstanding themes in these verses, and perhaps it may be well to say that verses 17 and 18 really belong to the previous paragraph, which sets forth our Saviour as the Good Shepherd who laid down His life for

425

the sheep. Our Lord stresses the fact that it was not man that forced Him to do that. In other words, He did not have to die. His humanity was different from ours in this, that we begin to die as soon as we are born. The seeds of death, as it were, are in the body of every child of Adam. We are all under that Adamic curse, "Dying, thou shalt die." These bodies of ours are mortal, that is, subject to death. It was otherwise with the body of our Lord Jesus. We are told that, "Sin, when it is finished, bringeth forth death." That is why we die, because we have all inherited the virus of Adam's sin. But our Lord Jesus Christ was the Sinless One, and therefore, while He came into the world with a body that could die, it was not necessary that it should die. He had in His own power the ability to die or to live on for endless years. But He died out of love for our guilty souls and out of love for the Father, because He came to do the Father's will.

In Psalm 118 we hear Him saying, through the psalmist, "God is the Lord, which hath showed us light: *bind the sacrifice with cords, even unto the horns of the altar.*" He Himself was the One whom all the sacrifices of the law typified; therefore this verse refers to Him. The altar of old had four brazen horns, and we might never have known what they were used for had it not been for these words. But we learn from this psalm that when they brought a beast, such as an ox or a lamb, for sacrifice, they bound it to the horns of the altar, and its blood was spilled about the altar, for "without shedding of blood there is no remission."

So our Lord Jesus Christ was bound with cords to the horns of the altar. What were the cords? We read in Hosea 11: 4 that God has drawn us with the cords of love: "I drew them with cords of a man, with bands of love." The cords of love have drawn our poor hearts to Christ and bound us to Him, and it was the cords of love that bound Him to the cross.

> " 'Twas love that sought Gethsemane,
> Or Judas ne'er had found Him;
> 'Twas love that held Him to the tree,
> Or iron ne'er had bound Him."

And there was not only one cord; there were cords. There was the cord of love to the Father, and the cord of love to us. We hear Him saying, "That the world may know that I love the Father, and as the Father gave Me commandment, even so I do. Arise, let us go hence." And He went out to the garden of sorrow and on to the cross of atonement. Love to the Father took Him there, thus to lay down His life for us. But it is also written that "Christ loved the Church and gave Himself for it, that He might sanctify and cleanse it." The apostle could say, "The Son of God, who loved me and gave Himself for me." So it was love for us, for our needy souls, that took Him there and led Him to die as a sacrifice for sin.

So He says, "Therefore doth My Father love Me, because I lay down My life, that I might take it again," though it is also perfectly true that sinful men laid hold of Him and nailed Him to the cross. The apostle Peter said to the Jews of his day, "Him, being delivered by the determinate counsel and foreknowledge of God, ye have taken, and by wicked hands have crucified and slain." And speaking of the Gentiles and their rulers, the apostle Paul says, "Which none of the princes of this world knew, for had they known it, they would not have crucified the Lord of glory." Man is held responsible for the rejection of Christ, but man was perfectly powerless to take His life. He laid it down of Himself. He says in verse 18, "No man taketh it from Me, but I lay it down of Myself. I have authority to lay it down" (*New Trans.*). That is, He had commandment from the Father to lay it down, and He came to do the Father's will, and that will involved His becoming the great sin offering.

Then observe, just as He had authority to lay down His life, so He had authority to take it again. "This commandment have I received of

My Father." The resurrection of the Lord Jesus Christ is attributed to each Person of the Holy Trinity. We read that He was "raised up from the dead by the glory of the Father." We read of the "Spirit that raised up Christ from the dead." The Holy Spirit then had His part in the resurrection. But Jesus also said, "Destroy this temple, and in three days I will raise it up." "He spake of the temple of His body." So the Father and the Son and the Holy Spirit were all concerned in the resurrection of our Lord Jesus Christ even as all were concerned in His death. It was the Father who gave the Son that He might die as our Redeemer. It was in the power of the Eternal Spirit that Christ offered Himself without spot unto God. And it was in His own love and grace that He laid down His life as the Good Shepherd, and rose again, that we might know redemption from the guilt and power of sin.

You remember we quoted several passages from the Old Testament, in which we saw that the Shepherd of Israel was the coming One, God Himself, who was to be manifested here on earth. So when Jesus said, "I am the Good Shepherd: the Good Shepherd giveth His life for the sheep," He was declaring that He was the One who would fulfil all these scriptures.

But the people were not ready to receive Him. Many declared that He had a demon. Others

said, "These words are not the words of one who
has a demon." They seemed to be so carefully
chosen, and so reverent and holy. They did not
sound to some of His hearers like the words of
one speaking under the power of an evil spirit.
Then they asked very sensibly, "Can a demon
open the eyes of the blind?" They remembered
that wonderful miracle that had been done among
them. It seemed that, after all, Jesus might be
the expected Messiah.

And now in verse 22 we are told that "it was at
Jerusalem, the feast of the dedication." This
was celebrated annually since the days of the
return under the leadership of Zerubbabel, of
David's lineage, and of Joshua, the high priest,
and the scribe Ezra and the governor Nehemiah.
It was winter, and Jesus walked in the temple in
Solomon's porch, or court. "Then came the Jews
round about Him, and said unto Him, How long
dost Thou make us to doubt?"

He had told them many times, but again they
put the question, and Jesus answered and said,
"I told you, and ye believed not: the works that
I do in My Father's name, they bear witness of
Me." Why did they not consider the signs, the
evidences? They seemed to be blind to these
things. And He gave the reason for this. "Ye
believe not, because ye are not of My sheep, as I
said unto you." They refused to believe His mes-

sage. His sheep are those who have turned to God in repentance and have accepted the message that He brought. He says, "My sheep hear My voice, and I know them, and they follow Me."

And now I have come to a rather crucial passage, about which there has been probably more controversy than concerning anything else in the Gospel of John. One is often asked: Do you think that this passage teaches that if a man is once saved, he is saved forever?—that it is impossible to fall from grace?—that a man will continue to be a Christian, no matter what sins he commits, if he has once professed faith in Christ? We need to be very careful here. It is good to follow the exact words of Jesus, and then we will not go astray.

First, He says, "My sheep hear My voice." John 5: 24 tells us, "He that heareth My word, and believeth on Him that sent Me, hath everlasting life." "Hear, and your soul shall live." So He says, "My sheep hear My voice." We cannot say that people are numbered among His sheep simply because they make a profession. There are people even in evangelical churches who are not numbered among the sheep of Christ, because actually they have never heard His voice. They are formalists, members of the church outwardly, but not of the Church which is His Body. Such people make a religious profession, maybe under emotion, and flock into the church and for a time they seem to go on very well, and then by-and-by the newness wears off and their enthusiasm disappears, and the hankering for the world wells up in their souls and then they begin to drift. We say, "Poor souls, they are backsliders." But, as one has well-said, "They were never frontsliders." They had turned from their sins, reforming themselves, but they had never heard the voice of the Son of God in their inmost souls. Their hearts were like that house that was swept and garnished, but left empty after the evil spirit had departed.

Such as these are those who bring reproach upon the doctrine of the eternal security of the believer in the Lord Jesus Christ. They were never real believers at all. No matter what people profess, if they do not hear the voice of the Son of God, they are not actually His sheep. I wish we may get that clear. Of all His sheep He says, "They follow Me and I know them." Now, will you put in contrast to that a passage in Matthew's Gospel, 7:21: "Not every one that saith unto Me, Lord, Lord, shall enter into the kingdom of heaven; but he that doeth the will of My Father which is in heaven." "He that doeth the will,"—Stop there for a moment. Are we saved by doing? No; we are saved by faith. What does He mean when He says, "Not every one that saith unto Me, Lord, Lord, shall enter into the kingdom of heaven; but he that does the will of My Father which is in heaven?" We are not saved by doing, but we manifest the reality of our faith by doing the will of God. You remember that passage again in Eph. 2, "For by grace are ye saved through faith; and that not of yourselves: it is the gift of God: not of works, lest any man should boast." But he immediately adds, "For we are His workmanship, created in Christ Jesus unto good works, which God hath before ordained that we should walk in them."

Be very clear about that. Our works have nothing to do with procuring eternal life, but no man has eternal life who is not manifesting good works.

> "I would not work my soul to save;
> That work my Lord has done;
> But I would work like any slave
> From love to God's dear Son."

"Not every one that saith unto Me, Lord, Lord, shall enter into the kingdom of heaven; but he that doeth the will of My Father which is in heaven. Many will say to Me in that day, Lord, Lord, have we not prophesied in Thy name? and in Thy name have cast out devils? and in Thy name done many wonderful works?" He is referring to the day of judgment, the day of manifestation. We might put that in modern language, "Have we not preached in Thy name?" Perhaps through their preaching men have been delivered from the awful power of Satan, for I believe that many an unsaved preacher has been used of God to save men, even though his own life was all wrong. *God uses His word by whomsoever proclaimed.* "And in Thy name cast out demons." "And then will I profess unto them, I never knew you: depart from Me, ye that work iniquity."

He will never say to anyone in that day of judgment, "I used to know you, but I do not know you any more." He says, "I *never* knew you." But of His own He says, "I know them."

Now if you will keep that in mind I do not think you will have any question about the eternal security of the believer. He never knew those who, though they seemed to be workers in His own vineyard, had never heard His voice.

So then, first, His sheep know His voice. Second, He says, "I know them." Notice the third thing, "and they follow Me." There is no use to profess to be a sheep of Christ's unless you follow Him. Christ means so much to those who are truly born again that their souls delight to follow Him. Do you follow Him? Is His will precious to you? We do not become sheep by following Jesus. It is the very opposite. We follow Him because we belong to His flock. Having been saved, we manifest that by following Him. There are a great many people who bear the Christian name who are not really born of God. This accounts for so many who at one time seemed to be Christians, but because there was no reality, they never knew the Lord, they never found any satisfaction in following Him and so they fell away.

Speaking of His own sheep, "I give unto them eternal life; and they shall never perish, neither shall any man pluck them out of My hand." What kind of life? Eternal life. My brother, my sister, you who have questioned the eternal security of the believer, how long is "eternal?" "I give unto them eternal life." Do you not see? It is not probationary life, it is not temporal life, it is *eternal* life.

A lady came to me in San Francisco, where I had been preaching on John 5: 24, and she said, "I agree with everything you said tonight except that doctrine, once saved, always saved. I have never found that in the Bible." I said, "Don't you believe the words of the Lord Jesus? Let me show you what He said." She replied, "I know where you are going to turn: John 10: 28, 29." "Well," I said, "you do know. But let me read the verses: 'And I give unto them eternal life; and they shall never perish, neither shall any man pluck them out of My hand. My Father, which gave them

Me, is greater than all; and no man is able to pluck them out of My Father's hand.' "

I inquired, "Do you believe that?" She said, "Not in your way." I said, "What is my way?" "Well," she said, "you believe that if a person is once saved he can never be lost." I read it again, "My sheep hear My voice, and I know them, and they follow Me: and I give unto them eternal life; and they shall never perish, neither shall any man pluck them out of My hand. My Father, which gave them Me, is greater than all; and no man is able to pluck them out of My Father's hand." I said, "Do you believe that?" "Not in your way." "But I am not telling you my way. I have not explained it at all. Do you not believe what the Son of God has said?" "Not the way you do." "Well, let me read it again." And I read it through once more, except for one change. I put "ten years" in place of "eternal life." I inquired, "What does that mean?" She answered, "Well, it would mean that if a person once got saved he would be saved for ten years." "Exactly; now let us stretch it a bit. 'I give unto them life for forty years.' What does it mean now?" She admitted it would imply that one thus saved would be secure for forty years. "Suppose it read, 'I give unto them life as long as they are faithful'." "That is what I believe," she replied. "But that is not what it says. It says, 'My sheep hear My voice, and I know them, and they follow Me: and I give unto them eternal life; and they shall never perish, neither shall any man pluck them out of My Father's hand.' How long does that mean?" She said, "As long as they remain His sheep." And she went out. She did not want light, so turned her back upon it. If one would only take God's Word at its face value. "I give unto them eternal life." It could not be eternal if it could ever come to an end, and He said, "They shall never perish." "No man can pluck them out of My hand." There could not be a stronger statement. His sheep are safe in the hands of the Father and the Son. There is no power in earth or hell that can pluck us out, and there is no power in heaven that would want to do so. You say, "Well, but you know I can take myself out." But you would perish then; wouldn't you? The marvelous thing is that when He saves a person He puts such a love for Himself in the heart that none would wish to be separated from Him.

I remember a dear friend of mine, a minister of the Gospel, a kindly, gracious man, who was reasoning with me about this. He said finally, "My brother, if I believed as you do, I could go out and sin all I want to, and it would not make any difference." I said, "My dear brother, do you want to sin?" "Oh, no!" he replied; "I do not want to sin." That's it. The Christian does not want to sin.   Nothing makes him more miserable than failure or falling into sin. His only joy is found in walking in fellowship with God.

What does Jesus mean when He says, "My Father is greater than all?" He was coequal with the Father from all eternity. But as Man here on earth, He could say, "My Father is greater than all." He was made a little lower than the angels for the suffering of death, that He by the grace of God should taste death for every man. He voluntarily took the subject place, in the days of His flesh.

But having said, "My Father is greater than all," He immediately adds, "I and My Father are one." What a proof of His true Deity we have right there! "I and My Father." Why, you would have thought He would have said, "My Father and I." It would be the natural thing—would it not?—for the subservient One. But there is no subserviency here; God the Son, and God the Father, and God the Holy Spirit are coequal; so He says, "I and My Father are one."

Isn't it marvelous grace! The Father, the Son, and the Holy Spirit are united in sending this gospel to the world and inviting sinners everywhere to put their trust in the work that Jesus did. And when you trust Him you have eternal life, and you will be as secure as God Himself can make you, even as we read elsewhere, "For I am persuaded, that neither death, nor life, nor angels, nor principalities, nor powers, nor things present, nor things to come, nor height, nor depth, nor any other creature, shall be able to separate us from the love of God, which is in Christ Jesus our Lord." What a gospel to proclaim to poor, dying men! If there is one who reads these words who has never trusted the Saviour, won't you come to Him today?

Years ago, there was a poor old man who lived in a miserable hovel and subsisted on what he could beg. Finally he was taken to a hospital, very ill, and when the nurse moved his clothes she found a worn paper that he had put away in an inner pocket. When she examined it she saw that it was an order on the Treasury of the United States to give him a pension because of his faithfulness in serving as a scout in the army during the war between the States. The poor old man said, "Oh, don't take that away from me! President Lincoln gave me that, and I value it above all else." And yet, he had never cashed in on it! He had never availed himself of his privileges.

Are you treating God's salvation like that? You have the right to come to Jesus and receive eternal life and forgiveness of sins. "Today, if you will hear His voice, harden not your hearts."

THE ETERNAL SON OF THE FATHER

✓ ✓ ✓

"Then the Jews took up stones again to stone Him. Jesus answered them, Many good works have I showed you from My Father; for which of those works do ye stone Me? The Jews answered Him, saying, For a good work we stone Thee not; but for blasphemy; and because that Thou, being a man, makest Thyself God. Jesus answered them, Is it not written in your law, I said, Ye are gods? If He called them gods, unto whom the word of God came, and the scripture cannot be broken; say ye of Him, whom the Father hath sanctified, and sent into the world, Thou blasphemest; because I said, I am the Son of God? If I do not the works of My Father, believe Me not. But if I do, though ye believe not Me, believe the works: that ye may know, and believe, that the Father is in Me, and I in Him. Therefore they sought again to take Him: but He escaped out of their hand, and went away again beyond Jordan into the place where John at first baptized; and there He abode. And many resorted unto Him, and said, John did no miracle: but all things that John spake of this man were true. And many believed on Him there" (John 10: 31-42).

✓ ✓ ✓

THE real object, as we have seen before, in the writing of this Gospel, is that men might believe that Jesus is the Son of God and that believing they might have life through His name. So we have had one incident after another, all intended to make clear the Deity of our Lord

440

Jesus Christ and His eternal relationship to the Father as the only begotten Son, who was ever one with the Father and the Spirit, both as to eternity of being and as to power and authority, wisdom, love and grace.

We closed our last chapter with the declaration of our Saviour, "I and My Father are one." Now whatever men today may understand that to mean, there can be no question that those to whom Jesus spoke understood that He was affirming definite equality with God. That was why they took up stones again to stone Him. In their eyes He was a blasphemer.

May I put it this way to you: if the Lord Jesus Christ is not God—God manifested in the flesh— then they were correct. If He is not truly God, He must have been a blasphemer, because He used language which no one but God should use, and He accepted worship which should be received by no one but God. The law said, "Thou shalt worship the Lord thy God, and Him only shalt thou serve," and the Lord Jesus allowed His disciples to worship Him, and therefore He took to Himself that which rightly belongs to God. Now He was either God manifest in the flesh, or else a gross deceiver.

Some take another view of it and say He was a paranoiac, who imagined He was divine while just a human being like others. But there was nothing about the behavior and the words of our Lord Jesus Christ to indicate one of unbalanced mind. His life was too pure, His words too wonderful, to allow us to accept that view for a moment, and we certainly cannot think of such a holy Person as a deceiver. Good men do not say that which is untrue, normally. He claimed over and over again to be the Son of the Father—"I and My Father are one."

It was because of this declaration that His enemies, in accordance with the law of Moses, which commanded that the blasphemer was to be stoned to death, took up stones to stone Him. He calmly said to them: "Many good works have I showed you from My Father; for which of those works do ye stone Me?" His works had manifested the truth of what He said of Himself. They had always been for the interest and good of mankind. What had He done that they should stone Him?

"The Jews answered Him, saying, For a good work we stone Thee not; but for blasphemy." What was the blasphemy? "Because that Thou, being a man, makest Thyself God." They said, "You are a man, and you declare yourself to be God, therefore you are a blasphemer." Well, the truth is that He was Man in all perfection, but He was also God—as truly Man as though He had never been God, and as truly God as though He had never become Man.

But now the Lord may seem to us to beg the question when He says, "Is it not written in your law, I said, Ye are gods? If He called them gods, unto whom the word of God came, and the scripture cannot be broken; say ye of Him, whom the Father hath sanctified, and sent into the world, Thou blasphemest; because I said, I am the Son of God?"

What is the Lord referring to here? In Psalm 82: 6, in addressing the judges of the people, who stood in the place of God to act for Him, we read these words, "I have said, Ye are gods; and all of you are children of the most High." It says, in the first verse of that psalm, "God standeth in the congregation of the mighty; He judgeth among the gods." What does He mean by this? God is the Judge over all, but He appointed in Israel men who were to represent Him. The people were to bring their questions and grievances to them and they were to judge in accordance with the Word. "I have said, Ye are gods;" That is, they were there to act for God. Today all judges do not act for God. But the thought is that these were to be righteous judges, and as such they were designated "gods."

This was in their Bibles, and they never thought of that expression as blasphemy.

Now why not inquire more definitely as to what the Lord Jesus meant when He said, "I and

My Father are one?" It was necessary to do this in order to understand it aright and so the Lord Jesus practically says, "Why not consider the works that I do? Why not study your own Bibles and see if the claims that I make are not borne out by the works that I perform and by the Scriptures?" But they were not willing to do this. They jumped at conclusions, as people so often do. We have our preconceived notions and are not willing to subject our thoughts to the declarations of the Word of God. We stress our own views and ideas and reject those of the Lord.

Thus they were ready to call Him a blasphemer, Whose one object in life was the glory of the Father. But now observe, this passage not only sets forth the Deity of the Lord Jesus and His equality with the Father, but it emphasizes the inspiration of the Holy Scriptures. We can be very grateful indeed to the Jews for having preserved for us the Bible. All the Old Testament was preserved by them, handed down through the centuries in manuscript form, translated into the Greek tongue later, and that by Jewish scribes, so that all the Old Testament Scriptures have come to us through the people of Israel. We will never be able to pay our debt to the Jews for that.

The Old Testament we have today is the Old Testament that Jesus had. He had it in both

Greek and Hebrew, and He read it in both of these versions, for He quoted from them both in His ministry here on earth, sometimes from the Hebrew, and at other times from the Greek text. There were flaws in that translation, but whenever He could He used that translation, because it was in the hands of the common people.

Notice what He says, "The Scripture cannot be broken." What rest that gives to heart and mind in these days when there are so many voices regarding the question of the inspiration of our Bible! They tell us that many of the books of the Old Testament have been discredited. The Lord Jesus says the Scripture cannot be broken and when He used that term "Scripture" He was using it as the Jews of His day used it, and they applied it to the books of their Old Testament, which were the Law, the Prophets and the Psalms. The whole volume was called "Scripture." Jesus says, "The Scripture cannot be broken." In other words, He authenticated the whole of the Old Testament.

This comes out very clearly as you go through the four Gospels, and see how Jesus puts His imprimatur on every part of the Law, the Prophets and the Psalms. If confused by evolutionary theories of creation and inclined to believe that men are only specialized brutes who have come up through the ages from a beast ancestry, we find that Jesus says, "From the beginning (of the creation) God made them male and female." Thus our Lord put His seal upon the doctrine of the special creation of man. He made them at the beginning, male and female. He also put His authorization upon the marriage relationship. "For this cause shall a man leave father and mother and shall cleave to his wife: and they twain shall be one flesh." This is the divine institution of marriage. So we have the Lord Jesus Christ Himself authenticating both special creation and the marriage relationship.

Then there are so many other things in the Old Testament to which modern teachers object. Is it true that there was once a great flood and that one family alone was saved out of that deluge? You turn to your New Testament and read, "For as it was in the days that were before the flood, they were eating and drinking, marrying and giving in marriage, until the day that Noe entered into the ark, and knew not until the flood came, and took them all away; so shall also the coming of the Son of Man be." I have no question about the universality of the flood in the face of words like these. Jesus knew, because He was God manifest in the flesh.

And so with the destruction of Sodom and Gomorrah. Again the Lord says, "Likewise also as it was in the days of Lot; they did eat, they drank, they bought, they sold, they planted, they builded; but the same day that Lot went out of Sodom it rained fire and brimstone from heaven, and destroyed them all. Even thus shall it be in the day when the Son of Man is revealed."

Scholars raise questions as to who wrote the first books of our Bible, Genesis to Deuteronomy, and they are willing to admit almost anybody but Moses, as their authors, and yet the Lord Jesus Christ says, "Had ye believed Moses, ye would have believed Me, for he wrote of Me." And He is speaking of the Law, and the Law was composed of those five books, and He says that Moses wrote them.

Was there ever such a man as Abraham? Was he but the imaginary character of a Hebrew myth? Or did he actually exist, and was he the father of the faithful, as Moses said? Jesus answers: "Your father Abraham rejoiced to see My day: and he saw it, and was glad." What did He mean? He was referring to that promise God gave to Abraham, "In thy seed shall all the nations of the earth be blessed." "And Abraham believed God and it was counted to him for righteousness." In the same way Jesus authenticates the story of Jonah and the repentance of Nineveh.

I confess I cannot understand how any man can profess to be a follower of the Lord Jesus Christ and recognize His true Deity and yet spurn any portion of His testimony, for we have the blessed Lord Himself declaring that the Scripture cannot be broken.

And then notice verse 36: "Say ye of Him, whom the Father hath sanctified, and sent into the world, Thou blasphemest?" The Father sanctified the Son and sent Him into the world. What does that tell us? It tells us that our Lord Jesus Christ did not become the Son when He was born of the Virgin Mary here on earth. It tells us He was the Son of the Father in the ineffable glory before He came down here at all. He was one of the Holy Trinity and the Father sanctified the Son and sent Him into the world.

What does that word "sanctify" mean? It really means, "to set apart." And so the Father set the Son apart and sent Him into the world that He might become the propitiation for our sin. This is the glorious truth here fully unfolded. "In this was manifested the love of God toward us, because that God sent His only begotten Son into the world, that we might live through Him" (1 John 4:9). He did not become the Son after He came to earth, but the Father sent the Son. "Herein is love, not that we loved God, but that He loved us, and sent His Son to be the propitiation for our sins." No wonder the apostle adds, "Beloved, if God so loved us, we ought also to love one another." The supreme example of the love of God is this—God sent His Son into the world, and He turned His back on heaven's glory, to be born a child here on earth, to grow up to manhood, living a holy, spotless life, and at last to go to Calvary's cross to offer Himself for our redemption. Is it blasphemy to believe this? On the contrary, it is an insult to God to deny it.

Jesus says, "Say ye of Him, whom the Father hath sanctified, and sent into the world, Thou blasphemest; because I said, I am the Son of God?" He told them to consider His works. Do not these accredit Him? "If I do not the works of My Father, believe Me not."

So we throw that challenge out today. If you have any doubt as to whether He was the eternal Son of God, read the record. See what He did when He was here. Can you explain His works in any other way? If you can, then you must reject Him. But if His works accredit Him, then be reasonable and accept Him.

If people would only read the Bible thoughtfully and face its testimony honestly, oh, how many would be delivered from the snare of unbelief!

So Jesus says, "If I do not the works of My Father, believe Me not. But if I do, though ye believe not Me, believe the works: that ye may know, and believe, that the Father is in Me, and I in Him." But, alas, though He was so tender and faithful, those who listened to Him were not willing to make the test.

"Therefore they sought again to take Him: but He escaped out of their hand." The hour had not come that He was to die, and they could not put Him to death, so He went away beyond Jordan, where John had baptized Him. "And there He abode. And many resorted unto Him, and said, John did no miracle; but all things that John spake of this Man were true."

"And many believed on Him there." To believe on Him is to put your trust in Him. I wonder if all who read this have really believed on Him. Have you put your trust in Him? Oh, read the record for yourselves. Face the testimony honestly and if the Spirit of God reveals to you that Jesus is indeed the Son of the living God, then receive Him as your Saviour and confess Him openly before men.

> "O for a thousand tongues to sing
> My great Redeemer's praise,
> The glories of my God and King,
> The triumphs of His grace!"

ADDRESS THIRTY-FIVE

THE RESURRECTION AND THE LIFE

✓   ✓   ✓

"Now a certain man was sick, named Lazarus, of
Bethany, the town of Mary and her sister Martha. (It
was that Mary which anointed the Lord with ointment,
and wiped His feet with her hair, whose brother Lazarus
was sick.) Therefore his sisters sent unto Him, saying,
Lord, behold, he whom thou lovest is sick. When Jesus
heard that, He said, This sickness is not unto death, but
for the glory of God, that the Son of God might be glorified thereby. Now Jesus loved Martha, and her sister, and
Lazarus. When He had heard therefore that he was sick,
He abode two days still in the same place where He was.
Then after that saith He to His disciples, Let us go into
Judea again. His disciples say unto Him, Master, the
Jews of late sought to stone Thee; and goest Thou thither
again? Jesus answered, Are there not twelve hours in the
day? If any man walk in the day, he stumbleth not, because he seeth the light of this world. But if a man walk
in the night, he stumbleth, because there is no light in
him. These things said He: and after that He saith unto
them, Our friend Lazarus sleepeth; but I go, that I may
awake him out of sleep. Then said His disciples, Lord if
he sleep, he shall do well. Howbeit Jesus spake of his
death: but they thought that He had spoken of taking of
rest in sleep. Then said Jesus unto them plainly, Lazarus
is dead. And I am glad for your sake that I was not
there, to the intent ye may believe; nevertheless let us go
unto him. Then said Thomas, which is called Didymus,
unto his fellow-disciples, Let us also go, that we may die
with Him. Then when Jesus came, He found that he had
lain in the grave four days already. Now Bethany was
nigh unto Jerusalem, about fifteen furlongs off: and many
of the Jews came to Martha and Mary, to comfort them
concerning their brother. Then Martha, as soon as she
heard that Jesus was coming, went and met Him: but
Mary sat still in the house. Then said Martha unto Jesus,

451

Lord, if Thou hadst been here, my brother had not died. But I know, that even now, whatsoever Thou wilt ask of God, God will give it Thee. Jesus saith unto her, Thy brother shall rise again. Martha saith unto Him, I know that he shall rise again in the resurrection at the last day. Jesus said unto her, I am the resurrection, and the life: he that believeth in Me, though he were dead, yet shall he live: and whosoever liveth and believeth in Me shall never die. Believest thou this? She said unto Him, Yea, Lord: I believe that Thou art the Christ, the Son of God, which should come into the world. And when she had so said, she went her way, and called Mary her sister secretly, saying, The Master is come, and calleth for thee. As soon as she heard that, she arose quickly, and came unto Him. Now Jesus was not yet come into the town, but was in that place where Martha met Him. The Jews then which were with her in the house, and comforted her, when they saw Mary, that she rose up hastily and went out, followed her, saying. She goeth unto the grave to weep there. Then when Mary was come where Jesus was, and saw Him, she fell down at His feet, saying unto Him, Lord, if Thou hadst been here, my brother had not died. When Jesus therefore saw her weeping, and the Jews also weeping which came with her, He groaned in the spirit, and was troubled, and said, Where have ye laid him? They said unto Him, Lord, come and see. Jesus wept. Then said the Jews, Behold how He loved him! And some of them said, Could not this Man, which opened the eyes of the blind, have caused that even this man should not have died? Jesus therefore again groaning in Himself cometh to the grave. It was a cave, and a stone lay upon it. Jesus said, Take ye away the stone. Martha, the sister of him that was dead, saith unto Him, Lord, by this time he stinketh: for he hath been dead four days. Jesus said unto her, Said I not unto thee, that, if thou wouldest believe, thou shouldest see the glory of God? Then they took away the stone from the place where the dead was laid. And Jesus lifted up His eyes, and said, Father, I thank Thee that Thou hast heard Me. And I knew that Thou hearest Me always: but because of the people which stand by I said it, that they may believe that Thou hast sent Me. And when He thus had spoken, He cried with a loud voice, Lazarus, come forth. And he that was dead came forth, bound hand and foot with graveclothes: and his face was bound about with a napkin. Jesus saith unto them, Loose him, and let him go.

Then many of the Jews which came to Mary, and had seen the things which Jesus did, believed on Him. But some of them went their ways to the Pharisees, and told them what things Jesus had done" (John 11: 1-46).

ᚵ ᚵ ᚵ

THE main theme of this eleventh chapter is the raising of Lazarus from the dead. In Romans 1: 4 we are told that our Lord Jesus Christ is "declared to be the Son of God with power . . . by the resurrection from the dead." That is the way the sentence reads in our Authorized Version. Greek scholars have pointed out the fact that the word for "dead" there is actually in the plural. We might think that the passage simply meant that the Lord was declared to be the Son with power by His own resurrection from the dead. But the passage might better be translated "through the resurrection of dead persons." That includes, of course, His own triumph over death, but it takes in also those other raisings from the dead of which we read in the Gospels. Three times our Lord exerted this marvelous resurrection power, and the three cases are all different and each I think, very significant.

In the first instance we have the daughter of Jairus, the ruler of the synagogue at Capernaum.

That was a little child who had died, and the Lord
Jesus went into the room where she lay, and He
said to her so tenderly, "Little one, arise," and
she arose. He awakened her from the sleep of
death, and that may suggest our Lord's gracious
way of dealing with children who are dead in
trespasses and sins and need to hear His voice
as truly as older ones today.

And then we have the instance of the raising of
the son of the widow of Nain. The Lord Jesus
and His apostles were approaching the village
when out came that sad funeral group bearing
the dead body of this young man, and his poor
mother following. The Lord Jesus stopped that
funeral procession, and touched the bier and said
to the young man, "I say unto thee, Arise," and
we read that "he that was dead sat up and Jesus
delivered him to his mother." That again, I think,
has a spiritual lesson. Many a young man, dead
in trespasses and sins, or possibly a young woman,
is causing grief to a godly father and mother. Oh,
how that mother and father are yearning for the
time when the hand of Jesus will be placed upon
those dear ones, raising them to life everlasting!
Mr. Moody once said, "It is a peculiar thing, you
cannot get any instruction in the Bible as to how
to conduct a funeral, for Jesus broke up every
funeral He ever attended, by raising the dead."

Now the third instance is that which is before

us, the raising of Lazarus, and here may I say we
have a picture of one who has spent years in sin,
and is utterly corrupt and beyond all human hope.
Yet Jesus came and raised Lazarus from the dead
after four days had gone by. Let us consider this
passage somewhat carefully.

We are told, "Now a certain man was sick,
named Lazarus, of Bethany, the town of Mary
and her sister Martha." That is interesting; is it
not? I am sure there were a great many other
people living in Bethany. But to the Lord who
looked down upon that city, to God Himself, it
was the town of Mary and Martha. What does
that mean? There were two devoted hearts there,
and that meant more to God than all the other
people who lived in that village. I wonder about
your community. Are you so devoted to the Lord
Jesus Christ, so living for the glory of God, that
He thinks of your community as the particular
place where you live? Does He pass by the rich
and great, the powerful and noted, from a worldly standpoint, and say of you, "That is one of
My friends, who loves Me," and therefore thinks
of it as your town or your locality?

I think that this is most significant. "Bethany,
the town of Mary and her sister Martha. It was
that Mary which anointed the Lord with ointment, and wiped His feet with her hair, whose
brother Lazarus was sick." And so the sisters,

when they saw their brother drooping and dying, sent a message to the Lord Jesus, who was some distance away. He was at Bethabara, near to what is now called Allenby's Bridge. Ordinarily, it would have taken two full days to come from there to Bethany; or perhaps three days if walking, and two if riding.

And so they sent a message. And how brief it was: "Lord, behold, he whom Thou lovest is sick." They felt that was enough. They knew He loved Lazarus. They knew their brother was very dear to His heart, and they felt sure that if Jesus understood that he was ill, He would come immediately and cure the disease and save the life of His friend.

But singularly enough, He said when He heard it, "This sickness is not unto death, but for the glory of God, that the Son of God might be glorified thereby." That is, death is not going to claim and keep this man at the present time, but God is going to be glorified in some wondrous way in his particular case. So there was no hurry on the part of Jesus. That is so trying for us who profess faith in Him. When we come presenting some problem we hope that He will intervene immediately and answer our prayer in the way we would like to have Him do it without any delay. But often He seems to wait so long and apparently appears to be so indifferent. He is never indifferent; He is always interested. And we may be sure of this: if He permits delay in the answer to prayer, it is because there is some plan that He desires to work out in connection with that answer, and it should be ours to wait in faith for Him to act. You know Scripture speaks of waiting *on* God and waiting *for* God. It is a wonderful thing to learn to wait *on* God. We may come to Him in every time of difficulty and perplexity in accordance with His Word, which says, "Be careful for nothing; but in everything by prayer and supplication, with thanksgiving, let your requests be made known unto God." "My soul," says David, "wait thou only upon God, for my expectation is from Him."

But then it requires even more faith to wait *for* God. After you have presented your petition to God, just leave everything in His hands, assured that in His own good time, He will act in the way that is best.

These sisters, I fancy, watched for the Lord every moment after they thought the message had had time to reach Him, but hour after hour went by, even day after day, and still Jesus did not come. And then Lazarus passed away. They must have said, "How strange it is! Not a word from Jesus, not a message of any kind! And He is not here, and He could easily have hindered all this, but He has not come." Did it mean He was not interested, that He did not love Lazarus, and was not concerned about their breaking hearts? Not at all. But they were going to learn lessons that they would never have learned in any other way.

We are told that "Jesus loved Martha, and her sister, and Lazarus. When He had heard therefore that he was sick, He abode two days still in the same place where He was. Then after that saith He to His disciples, Let us go into Judea again." He had been bitterly persecuted in Judea, and the disciples would rather have had Him turn His face northward and go back where the people heard Him gladly. When He spoke of returning to Judea, they said, "Master, the Jews of late sought to stone Thee; and goest Thou thither again?" But "Jesus answered, Are there not twelve hours in the day? If any man walk in the day, he stumbleth not, because he seeth the light of this world. But if a man walk in the night, he stumbleth, because there is no light in him."

He meant this, "I know what My path should be. The Father hath made it perfectly clear to Me where I should go, and in returning to Judea I am walking in the light that shines upon My steps." Then He adds, "Our friend Lazarus sleepeth; but I go, that I may awake him out of sleep." After all, this is what death is for the believer. It is just a sleep. "Oh," you say, "the entire man, spirit, soul and body?" Oh, no; but the sleep of

think, that in the last day saved and unsaved will all be raised.

But Jesus had a sweeter message than that for her. He said unto her, "I am the Resurrection, and the Life: he that believeth in Me, though he were dead, yet shall he live: and whosoever liveth and believeth in Me shall never die. Believest thou this?"

What is He telling her? Oh, He is telling her, "You do not have to wait till the resurrection on the last day. I Myself am the Resurrection and the Life, and when I come into the scene death is at an end." And He adds, "He that believeth in Me, though he were dead, yet shall he live." When will that be? At His own return from heaven, when He shall descend with a shout and empty all the graves where lie the Christian dead. "Whosoever believeth in Me, though he were dead, yet shall he live." Then He looks on to the time when those who have never died at all, but will be living on the earth when He returns, will be changed without dying and says, "Whosoever liveth and believeth in Me shall never die." What a wonderful revelation! And then He puts the question, "Believest thou this?"

I think she was a bit puzzled. She said, "Yea, Lord: I believe that Thou art the Christ, the Son of God, which should come into the world." And therefore, of course, she implies, "Whatever You say must be true." Whether she could understand it or not, it must be true, for it came from the One she recognized as the Son of God.

She went and called her sister. Mary met with them outside the town. The Jews saw her leave and said, "She goeth unto the grave to weep there." But, no, on the way out she met Jesus, and she said to Him also what Martha had said, but I wonder if there was not a different tone than what Martha had used. "Lord, if Thou hadst been here, my brother had not died." Jesus looked upon her in her grief, and His heart went out to her. The Jews who had followed behind were weeping and Jesus groaned in the spirit and was troubled. He was a real man. It was not merely Deity inhabiting a human body, but He had a true human spirit and soul as well as a human body. And so He groaned in the spirit and was troubled.

And He said, "Where have ye laid him? They said unto Him, Lord, come and see."

And now we have the shortest verse in our English Bible. Literally translated it is "Jesus shed tears." Tears, as He contemplated the awful ravages that death had wrought because of sin. "Then said the Jews, Behold how He loved him. And some of them said, Could not this Man, which opened the eyes of the blind, have caused that even this man should not have died? Jesus therefore again groaning in Himself cometh to the grave. It was a cave, and a stone lay upon it." It was a singular thing. I always thought of it as a cave in the side of the hill, as in the case of the tomb where our Lord Jesus Christ was buried, until I was in Bethany and saw a similar tomb. You went down into the cave and a stone lay over it. And thus it was here. The stone lay over the tomb.

"Jesus said, Take ye away the stone. Martha, the sister of him that was dead, saith unto Him, Lord, by this time he stinketh: for he hath been dead four days." Her faith did not rise to the glorious thing that was about to take place. "Jesus saith unto her, Said I not unto thee, that, if thou wouldest believe, thou shouldest see the glory of God?" Faith triumphs over all conditions, depending upon the living God.

"Then they took away the stone from the place where the dead was laid. And Jesus lifted up His eyes, and said, Father, I thank Thee that Thou hast heard Me." What sweet communion this, between the Father and the Son! "And I knew that Thou hearest Me always: but because of the people which stand by I said it, that they may believe that Thou hast sent Me." He prayed in this way that they might be edified by His prayer, that they might believe. "And when He thus had spoken, He cried with a loud voice, Lazarus, come forth!"

Oh, that voice of power some day will be heard, and all the dead in Christ will come forth. That day in Bethany He singled out one person. If He had left out the word *Lazarus* He would have emptied the whole cemetery! But He said, "Lazarus, come forth! And he that was dead came forth." And it says he was "bound hand and foot with graveclothes; and his face was bound about with a napkin." That was the way the Jews buried their dead; they wrapped them completely in linen cloths.

"Jesus saith unto them, Loose him, and let him go." There is a lesson here too—life first, and then liberty. All who hear the voice of Christ have life—"He that believeth on the Son hath everlasting life." But many a believer does not yet know liberty. Many are still bound by the graveclothes of tradition, or of misunderstanding, or unbelief. Oh, how wonderful when Jesus says, "Loose him and let him go." "Ye shall know the truth, and the truth shall make you free."

So Lazarus was raised and loosed. "Then many of the Jews which came to Mary, and had seen the things which Jesus did, believed on Him. But some of them went their ways to the Pharisees, and told them what things Jesus had done." It would almost seem that they were His enemies, and that they reported these things, seeking to stir up the Pharisees against Him.

Satan is the one who has the power of death, and by sin came death. Jesus is the One who has power to deliver from sin and from death itself. I wonder if we have all trusted Him. He is declared to be the Son of God with power by resurrection of dead persons. He is still the same, and He delights to impart life to all who hear His voice.

ONE MAN TO DIE FOR THE NATION

ᕯ ᕯ ᕯ

"Then gathered the chief priests and the Pharisees ⸿
council, and said, What do we? for this Man doeth many
miracles. If we let Him thus alone, all men will believe
on Him: and the Romans shall come and take away both
our place and nation. And one of them, named Caiaphas,
being the high priest that same year, said unto them, Ye
know nothing at all, nor consider that it is expedient for
us, that one man should die for the people, and that the
whole nation perish not. And this spake he not of himself: but being high priest that year, he prophesied that
Jesus should die for that nation; and not for that nation
only, but that also He should gather together in one the
children of God that were scattered abroad. Then from
that day forth they took counsel together for to put Him
to death. Jesus therefore walked no more openly among
the Jews; but went thence unto a country near to the
wilderness, into a city called Ephraim, and there continued with His disciples. And the Jews' passover was
nigh at hand: and many went out of the country up to
Jerusalem before the passover, to purify themselves.
Then sought they for Jesus, and spake among themselves,
as they stood in the temple, What think ye, that He will
not come to the feast? Now both the chief priests and
the Pharisees had given commandment, that, if any man
knew where He were, he should show it, that they might
take Him" (John 11: 47-57).

ᕯ ᕯ ᕯ

WE have considered the raising up of
Lazarus, that greatest of all our Lord's
signs and miracles, indicating His power
over death, proving that He was indeed the Mes-

siah who was to come into the world not only to deliver Israel, but to be a means of blessing to all nations and the fulfilment of the promise made to Abraham.

One would have thought that surely so marvelous a sign would have spoken to the hearts of even the worst enemies of the Lord Jesus Christ, proving to them that this Man who was going about among them in so lowly a way, doing such wondrous works of mercy, was truly Immanuel. But no; if men's consciences are not awakened, if men are determined to resist the truth, miracles will not win them to Christ.

Do you remember the story that Jesus told concerning the rich man? We read that he died and went to hell, and in hell he lifted up his eyes— that man who had enjoyed every privilege and opportunity on earth, but who had only lived to gratify his own desires—and began to pray for his five brethren. What a family: six brothers, one in hell and five on the way! And he cried and prayed to Abraham, whom he could see in Paradise, and said, "Send Lazarus that he may dip the tip of his finger in water and cool my tongue, for I am tormented in this flame." When told that was impossible, he said, I pray thee then, send him to my five brethren, that they come not to this place of torment." And Abraham said, "They have Moses and the prophets, let them hear them."

That is, they have the Word of God, the Old Testament. Let them read and believe their Bibles.
But the rich man replied, "Nay, Father, Abraham,
but if one went to them from the dead, then would
they repent." But the answer came back with
crushing force: "If they hear not Moses and the
prophets, neither will they be persuaded, though
one rose from the dead."

What a solemn truth we have unfolded here! If
men are determined to take their own way, if they
will not bow to the testimony of the Word of God,
then signs and wonders will never reach their
hardened hearts and bring them to repentance.
These scribes and Pharisees had set themselves
against the Word of God. They had rejected every
message, and the raising of Lazarus only stirred
them up to make them feel they were likely to
lose their hold on the people. They foresaw a
possible uprising among the populace to make
Jesus King, and the result would be the sending
of the Roman legions to enforce Caesar's will
upon them at the point of the sword.

They said, "Now, what are we going to do
about it?" You would have thought they would
have said something like this: "We must turn to
God and confess our sins and face our iniquity.
We must get right with God. The resurrection
power of Jesus proves that He is one with the
Father." But no; they said, "This thing is likely

to draw men after Him.   We must take an active stand against this man and His miracles."

"For this Man doeth many miracles."   They had already dared to tell the crowd that He did the miracles by the power of Beelzebub, thus blaspheming against the Holy Spirit, who was working through Him. Now they said, "If we let Him thus alone, all men will believe on Him." Just think of it! They were afraid to have people believe in Jesus.

I invited a lady sometime ago to a gospel meeting. She said, "I am afraid to go for fear I will be converted." Afraid! Afraid that one might get right with God! I remember a gentleman, well up in business circles, out on the West Coast. I said to his wife one day, "I have not seen your husband for quite a while. Has he lost his interest?" She said, "Well, he is afraid to come; for when he comes and hears the Word, it takes him nearly two weeks to get over it." How we ought to cherish the least evidence that the Spirit of God is speaking to any of us! There are people in this world today, I am afraid, who have heard the last message from the Word of God they will ever hear. It is a solemn thing when God ceases to speak to a soul.

But these Pharisees were determined to have their own way and to reject Christ. They said, "We must break His influence over the people;

otherwise the Romans will destroy our city and
nation." And notice this, the very thing they
dreaded was the thing that happened. But it happened, not because the people believed on Jesus,
but because they refused His grace. They spurned
Him when presented as the Prince of Peace. When
Pilate said, "Shall I crucify your King?" and they
said, "We have no King but Caesar," what happened? Jesus was crucified, rejected of men, died
there on Calvary's cross for a world's redemption.

But what about the nation? Not long after the
Romans did indeed come and take away their
place and scattered them throughout the world.
And all the suffering and the sorrows they have
gone through have been the sad result of their not
knowing the day of their visitation.

So the very thing that these Pharisees thought
they would avoid by rejecting Jesus, was the
thing that came upon them because they refused
Him. So short-sighted are men, so unable to see
into the future, that they spurn the testimony that
God Himself has given.

As they were debating this thing, one of them
took the leadership—Caiaphas, who was the high
priest that year. That in itself indicates the ob-
jection of the people to the Roman authority.
According to God's original institution, when a
son of Aaron was inducted into the office of high-
priest, he remained in it until his death. But the

nation had fallen so low that the Romans sold the office of high-priest from year to year to the highest bidder. At this particular time Caiaphas was high-priest. There were several other men who had been high-priests, but had been set to one side.

So now Caiaphas, the high-priest that year, said unto them, "Ye know nothing at all." That is a good way, somebody has said, when you want to shut out any argument. Just begin, "You know nothing at all. You don't know what you are talking about." You cannot reason with folks like that. They know it all, and they won't admit for a moment that you have any information which might be of any value to them. I think Job's friends were something like that. You recall he answered them on one occasion, "Ye are the people, and wisdom shall die with you." That is, "You think no one knows anything but you."

That was the stand Caiaphas took—"You know nothing at all, nor consider that it is expedient for us, that one man should die for the people, and that the whole nation perish not." And in this you hear the voice of a contemptible, dastardy politician. He knew that Jesus was innocent of the charges that were being brought against Him. He should have been the deliverer of the innocent, but he, for policy's sake, was against Jesus. He reasoned, "We must get Him

out of the way or we shall suffer, so the best thing
is to get rid of Him. Bring false charges. if need
be, in order that the nation may be saved." It
was dastardly advice, and yet the marvelous thing
is that God was behind it all, and overruled it to
work out His own plan. We do not for one moment condone the speech of Caiaphas, but, on the
other hand, we have the testimony of the Holy
Spirit here to tell us that he was saying more than
he really knew. The reason he spoke as he did
was because of selfishness, but that which he
thereby proposed, in a higher sense than he could
ever understand, was to work out the purpose of
God in the redemption not only of Israel, but of
a needy world.

We read here, "This spake he not of himself,"
that is, he thought he was giving them advice of
a political nature, but the Spirit of God was
overruling and controlling him beyond his own
thought. To think the Spirit of God could use a
wicked man like that! In the case of Balaam, who
loved the wages of unrighteousness, we have three
chapters in the book of Numbers containing some
of the most glorious prophecies in the Bible,
which came from his unhallowed lips. God was
overruling for blessing.

So God was overruling here, and He used a bad
man, a time-serving politician, to utter a tremendous truth. "This spake he not of himself;

but being high-priest that year, he prophesied that Jesus should die for that nation." He did not know it, but the Spirit of God was speaking through those unclean lips. "He prophesied that Jesus should die for that nation," though not in the sense that he meant. He meant that the death of this innocent man would be used to save the nation from the Romans. It did not do that, for the Jews were carried away in due time. But the prophecy was true in the sense that He was to become the great sin-offering, taking the blame for that nation's guilt upon Himself, that load of sin, and bearing it before God and enduring the judgment that sin deserved. This was what Isaiah saw, when, looking down through the ages with the eyes of faith, he said, "He was wounded for our transgressions; He was bruised for our iniquities: the chastisement of our peace was upon Him; and with His stripes we are healed. All we like sheep have gone astray; we have turned every one to his own way; and the Lord hath laid on Him the iniquity of us all."

"One man should die for the people." Here was the great Kinsman-Redeemer, who looked upon His own nation, sold under sin, and said, "I will pay the price in My own precious blood," and so He gave Himself a ransom for all. But His death was not only for that nation. We read: "That Jesus should die for that nation, and not for that nation only, but that He should gather together in one the children of God that were scattered abroad." That is, the work of our Lord Jesus Christ on Calvary was not to be simply for the nation of Israel. It was for that nation, He did come to bear the sins and guilt of that nation, He did come to redeem His own people; but He also said, "Other sheep I have, which are not of this fold: them also I must bring, and they shall hear my voice; and there shall be one flock, and one shepherd." Those "other sheep" are the Gentiles, the nations outside of Israel, the nations which at that time did not have any written revelation from God. They had no Bible, they had no prophets and teachers. They had the testimony of creation, and they had turned away from that, and because of this God had given them up to all kinds of sin and uncleanness and yet His heart went out to them and He had settled it that His blessed Son would give Himself a ransom for all. Oh, the amazing grace, that God should send Jesus, and that Jesus should gladly come to die for a guilty world. We read, "This is a faithful saying, and worthy of all acceptation, that Christ Jesus came into the world to save sinners;" (and the apostle Paul could add) "of whom I am chief."

We sing today,

"Saved by the blood of the crucified One,
Ransomed from sin and a new life begun;

Sing praise to the Father, and praise to the Son,
I'm saved by the blood of the crucified One."

We dare to say that there is no sinner in all the world today so vile and guilty, but if he will come in the merit of that sacrifice on the cross, God will receive him to Himself, freely forgive him and give him a new life. Am I addressing anyone who has not realized that He died to "gather together in one the children of God that were scattered abroad." Wherever you are today, if you are bowed down beneath the sense of your sin and guilt, if your conscience is accusing you before a holy God and you are saying, "Oh, that I knew how I might make my peace with God, how I might get right with Him," you do not have to make peace with Him yourself. Jesus made peace by the blood of His cross. Come to Him with a broken and a contrite heart. Confess your iniquity, and trust Him as your Saviour. You may know His redeeming grace today. You may come just as you are.

But notice further;—in connection with the account of this effort to railroad the Son of God to a felon's death on the part of men who knew Him to be innocent, we read, "Then from that day forth they took counsel together for to put Him to death." There was no softening of the heart, nor any sense of their own wickedness. Sin is

such a hardening thing. We are warned against
the danger of being hardened by the deceitfulness
of sin. The only way to deal with sin is to face
it honestly before God, who alone can give salvation from its power, through faith in the Lord
Jesus Christ.

Following this, we are told that "Jesus walked
no more openly among the Jews; but went thence
unto a country near to the wilderness, into a city
called Ephraim, and there continued with His disciples." The hour had not yet come that He was
to be delivered up to death, so He labored on,
ministering in another district.

And we are told the Jews' passover was at
hand. That is a strange expression as we noticed
before—the Jews' passover. It was originally a
feast of the Lord, but they were going on with
the outward observances while rejecting the
Christ of whom the feast spoke. I think we see
something like this at the present time. I am
afraid that there are thousands of people who are
very punctilious about church-membership and
attendance on divine service, who lay great
stress on Christian ordinances such as the sacred
ordinances of baptism and the Lord's Supper, and
yet are in their hearts rejecting the Saviour of
whom these things speak. God, who looks down
upon them, sees them as empty rites and ceremonies that men in the flesh are carrying out and

which avail them nothing because they are refusing the Lord Jesus Christ.

Think of the solemnity, for instance, of observing the Lord's Supper and taking the bread and wine that speak of a crucified Saviour, while rejecting that Saviour, refusing to trust Him, spurning His grace, eating and drinking judgment to one's own soul, not discerning the Lord's body. Let us be honest, and face things as they actually are before Him.

The Jews' passover was nigh at hand. Many went out of the country up to Jerusalem to purify themselves. These were country people, not the people of the city who had rejected Him, and it is of some of these we read, "The common people heard Him gladly."

And as they came to keep the feast of the passover, they wondered, "Shall we get an opportunity to see Him?" They were anxious to see Him and listen to His teaching. They sought for Him and spoke among themselves: "What think ye, that He will not come to the feast?" Oh, yes; He would be there. In a little while they would see Him, but alas, all His wondrous grace would not change the attitude of the leaders.

We read, "Now both the chief priests and the Pharisees had given a commandment that if any man knew where He were he should show it, that they might take Him." What for? That they might test His claims and face things honestly before God and decide whether this was really the Messiah or not? Oh, no; not that. They gave "commandment that, if any man knew where He were, he should show it, that they might take Him" and arrest Him, and thus bring about His death. How little they realized that one was yet to come forward who would betray Him to them, and that one numbered among His own!

THE HEART'S APPRECIATION OF CHRIST

✦ ✦ ✦

"Then Jesus six days before the passover came to Bethany, where Lazarus was which had been dead, whom He raised from the dead. There they made Him a supper; and Martha served: but Lazarus was one of them that sat at the table with Him. Then took Mary a pound of ointment of spikenard, very costly, and anointed the feet of Jesus, and wiped His feet with her hair: and the house was filled with the odour of the ointment. Then saith one of His disciples, Judas Iscariot, Simon's Son, which should betray Him, Why was not this ointment sold for three hundred pence, and given to the poor? This he said, not that he cared for the poor; but because he was a thief, and had the bag, and bare what was put therein. Then said Jesus, Let her alone: against the day of My burying hath she kept this. For the poor always ye have with you; but Me ye have not always. Much people of the Jews therefore knew that He was there: and they came not for Jesus' sake only, but that they might see Lazarus also, whom He had raised from the dead. But the chief priests consulted that they might put Lazarus also to death; because that by reason of him many of the Jews went away, and believed on Jesus" (John 12:1-11).

✦ ✦ ✦

WE are now approaching in our study the closing hours of our Lord's ministry here on earth. He had come to Jerusalem for the last time to give His final testimony,

knowing well that rejection and crucifixion await-
ed Him, for none of these things took Him by
surprise. He had come from heaven for the express purpose of dying for lost men. We read
that very definitely. He said, "The Son of Man
is come not to be ministered unto, but to minister,
and to give His life a ransom for many." He had
declared this from the very beginning. He is
represented in Psalm 40 as saying, "Lo, I come:
in the volume of the book it is written of Me, I
delight to do Thy will, O My God." The doing
of that will meant His going to the cross. But as
He got nearer and nearer to the cross, because
He was perfect man as well as true God the
horror of it all grew upon His own soul until at
last we see Him (recorded in other Gospels, not
in John in the same full way) bowed in agony
in Gethsemane's garden, praying, "If it be possible, let this cup pass from Me." And yet He
says, "If this cup may not pass except I drink it,
Thy will be done." And a little later we hear
Him saying to Peter, who had cut off the servant's ear, "Put up thy sword . . . the cup that
My Father hath given Me, shall I not drink it?"
That cup was the cup of wrath, the cup of divine
judgment that our sins had filled, the cup that
was overflowing with the indignation of a holy
God against iniquity. Jesus could not have been
perfect, holy Man if He had not shrunk from the

drinking of that cup. To be made sin meant to be dealt with by God as though He were the one great sinner of all the ages. All our iniquities were laid upon Him. It meant a horror and darkness of soul that our poor finite minds cannot understand. It meant bearing there upon the cross, in the depths of His own spotless spirit, what lost men who reject Christ will have to endure in the pit of woe for all eternity. He realized the awfulness of sin; the dreadfulness of having to do with a holy God in regard to it. In Ps. 69: 20 it is written, "I looked for some to take pity, but there was none; and for comforters, but I found none." He was so intensely human that He longed for those who could enter with Him into His sorrows. We feel like that. We look to our dear ones for comfort, to express the love that they feel for us. And Jesus longed for human fellowship and was glad when He found it. We have a beautiful picture of that in this twelfth chapter.

He had come to Judea, and He and His little company were now at Bethany, the city of Mary, Martha and Lazarus. We have already considered His raising of Lazarus from the dead. We read here, "Jesus, six days before the passover, came to Bethany, where Lazarus was which had been dead, whom He raised from the dead. There they made Him a supper." In Mark's Gospel we read that it was actually two days before the passover that this supper was given to Him. He came to Bethany six days before the passover. Four days went by, and then they made Him this supper. It was a testimony on the part of His loving friends, an evidence of their affection for Him.

We learn from Matt. 26: 6 that this took place in the house of Simon the leper. He could not have been a leper still, for then it would have been impossible for him to have dwelt there. "The leper shall dwell alone," the Scripture says. He was to have a covering upon his lip, and he was to cry out, "Unclean! Unclean!" if anyone drew near. This must have been the past state of Simon the leper—for how long we do not know. But we gather from this scripture that one day a wonderful event occurred in Simon's life. He met with Jesus and everything was different. Have you had a meeting like that? Have you been affected with the leprosy of sin, utterly lost and ruined? Have you had a meeting with Jesus? That changes everything! To hear Him say, "Be thou clean;" to have Him speak peace to the troubled heart; to know He has cleansed the guilty soul—what an experience that is! Simon must have had an experience like that; otherwise he would not have been there in Bethany.

Among those who were participating that evening besides the blessed Lord and His apostles, there are three who stand out prominently; the three who had so often entertained Jesus in their home. We read, "Martha served: but Lazarus was one of them that sat at the table with Him. Then took Mary a pound of ointment of spikenard, very costly, and anointed the feet of Jesus." These set forth three aspects of the Christian life. We see in Martha, service; in Lazarus, fellowship; in Mary, worship. Service, fellowship and worship—how much do we know of these aspects of the Christian life? Service here comes first— "Martha served." When we are saved we are no longer our own. How natural it is to yield ourselves to Him as those alive from the dead, that we may serve the Master who has done so much for us. I do not understand those who profess to be saved but give no evidence of a desire to be of service to the Lord Jesus Christ. That should be the first proof of the new birth: "He saved me; now what can I do to show my love for Him?" We are not saved by our service. Salvation is not of works, lest any man should boast. No effort of ours can cleanse our guilty souls.

> "Not the labor of my hands
> Can fulfil Thy law's demands;
> Could my zeal no respite know,
> Could my tears forever flow,
> All for sin could not atone:
> Thou must save, and Thou alone."

But does that mean that we make light of service or that we are indifferent to good works? Not at all. We recognize that when one is regenerated, when he has been justified from all things, when he has become a child of God, he is responsible to work and labor for the One who has done so much for him.

And we serve Him as we minister to those for whom He died. Service for Christ is not some mysterious thing that is not practical. If I give a cup of cold water in the name of Jesus, I am serving Him. And if I refuse to give the cup of cold water, then I am drawing back from service for Him. If men are in distress and I minister to them, giving clothing to the naked, food to the hungry, sharing the troubles and sorrows of others, I am serving Him. When He shall sit upon the throne of His glory when He shall return to this earth, the standard of judgment will be this: "I was sick, and you ministered to Me; I was hungry, and you fed Me; I was naked, and you clothed Me." Some say, "When did we see you sick and hungry and naked?" And He says, "Inasmuch as you did it unto one of the least of these, you did it unto Me." And others say, "But when did we ever see you in such circumstances and did not minister unto you?" "Inasmuch as you did it not to the least of these, ye did it not unto Me." Do not let us overlook the importance

of that Scripture by seeing only its dispensational
aspect. It has a very practical lesson for all ages.
It sets before us the standard that every one of us
will have to face when we stand before the judgment-seat of Christ. He is going to credit us
with all service done for His own as service done
for Himself. This is a very serious thing. Do
you treat coolly some fellow-Christian? Do you
call on some poor, needy ones whose distress you
might alleviate, or do you pass them by indiffer-
ently? Do you harden your heart against the
needy? Then listen! He says, "Inasmuch as
you did it not unto one of the least of these, ye
did it not unto Me." But when you share what
you have with those in trouble, when you minister
to those afflicted, when you try to manifest the
grace of Christ to those who are suffering, He
accounts it as done unto Himself.

Do not let us make light of service. It is very
important. It comes first here . "Martha served."
It was not grudging service now. There was a
time once before when Martha was cumbered
about her service, but it was not so on this occasion. Martha served, and evidently she did it
gladly. Only a few days before, her brother lay
cold in death. Then she had gone with Jesus to
yonder tomb and heard Him cry, "Lazarus, come
forth!" And he that was dead came forth bound
hand and foot with the graveclothes. Martha

had seen all that and her heart swelled with gratitude to the Lord, and she was so glad to be able
to serve. I imagine that if somebody had said,
"Let me serve," she would have refused and said,
"He has done so much for me that I want to do
everything I can for Him."

I heard once of a dear old brother who belonged
to a group who ran a little mission hall. He
wanted to preach, but had no gift for it. He
helped open up this mission hall. This man used
to go down there after his office closed on Satur-
day noon. He would roll up his trousers, and take
a bucket of water and brush, and clean the chairs
and scrub the floor. No one of the rest of the
company knew of his service. You know how
careless people are. They never thought to ask
who did the cleaning. But it happened one day
that a couple of the young men went over in the
afternoon to get some song-books. Just as they
opened the door they saw the old man scrubbing
away. They threw up their hands and said, "Oh,
we never knew you were doing this! You must
not do this. We will scrub this floor." "Oh," he
said, "please let me do it for Jesus' sake." He
pleaded not to be robbed of the privilege of doing
it for Christ's glory. So they had to leave it to
him.

But now the next one. "But Lazarus was one
of them that sat at the table with Him." That

means fellowship. Lazarus, the risen cne, sits
at the feast with Jesus and enjoys hallowed communion with Him. Get together with people of
like mind and how they enjoy a great repast together—not merely because of that which is set
before them, but they delight in the exchange of
thoughts in regard to the things that are precious
to them all. Sometimes we speak of the Lord's
Supper as the Communion. We meditate together
upon His loveliness. So here they were occupied
with Him whom they loved. I am sure that wherever Jesus sat was recognized as the head of the
table. It was in Simon's house, but He would
be the Host.

So Lazarus sat at the table with Jesus, Lazarus,
who had been dead, and lived again! You and I,
who are saved, are men and women of the resurrection, and it is our blessed privilege to have fellowship and communion with the Lord Jesus Christ as
our glorious Head. It takes two to have fellowship. One speaks and the other responds. We have
fellowship with Him when we get before Him
over His own Word and He speaks to us, and when
we draw near to Him in prayer and pour out our
hearts to Him.

Worship is the next thing. "Then took Mary
a pound of ointment of spikenard, very costly,
and anointed the feet of Jesus, and wiped His feet
with her hair: and the house was filled with the

odour of the ointment." I wonder if she was thinking of the verse in the Song of Solomon, "While the king sitteth at his table, my spikenard sendeth forth the smell thereof." She looked at Jesus and said, "Oh, He is my King, and I must show Him how much I love and adore Him." She remembered that she had a pound of spikenard, very precious. It would have taken one year's labor to pay for it. She may have kept it for a long time, perhaps using a little of it on special occasions. But now she knows Jesus is going out to die. He tells us that a little later. She says, "I want to give Him the best I have." And she broke the alabaster box and poured its contents on His feet. In Matthew and Mark we read it was, "on His head." There is no contradiction. She did both. It was the expression of her heart's adoration, for that is what worship is. We worship as we give back to Him of that which He has given to us. In the Old Testament God is worshipped as the Creator. That is very precious, but oh, it is when you come over to the New Testament that you will find the Lord Jesus the object of the worship of His beloved people as they cry, "Thou art worthy . . . for Thou wast slain, and hast redeemed us to God by Thy blood out of every kindred, and tongue, and people, and nation." How Jesus covets that! How He loves to have the hearts of people lifted up in worship before Him!

But the unsaved cannot understand that. The one who was to betray Him said, "Why was not this ointment sold for three hundred pence, and given to the poor?" Had Jesus ever been indifferent to the needs of the poor? Had Mary? Not at all. Give Christ the first place, and everything else will come out all right. He who worships and adores the Lord Jesus Christ as the pre-eminent One, will not forget the poor and needy.

But Judas cannot understand. "This he said, not that he cared for the poor; but because he was a thief, and had the bag, and bare what was put therein." Jesus and the disciples had appointed Judas to carry the bag and we read he "bare what was put therein." Literally it is, "he bare away." He was a covetous man. He felt Mary was wasting her treasure on Jesus.

But the Saviour understood and knew what was going on in the heart of Judas. And He said, "Let her alone: against the day of My burying hath she kept this. For the poor always ye have with you; but Me ye have not always." We do not want to forget those words of His. In Mark He says, "Whensoever ye will ye may do them good."

Now in the closing verses we read, "Much people of the Jews therefore knew that He was there: and they came not for Jesus' sake only, but that they might see Lazarus also, whom He had raised from the dead. But the chief priests consulted that they might put Lazarus also to death." They said, "We would rather he were dead once more than that people, through him, should believe in Jesus." "Because that by reason of him many of the Jews went away, and believed on Jesus."

Oh, the evil of the human heart! Listen, if you will not believe in Jesus because you know you need a Saviour, if you will not come to Him through the Holy Spirit, you would not come to Him no matter what miracle was wrought.

THE TRIUMPHAL ENTRY

✦   ✦   ✦

"On the next day much people that were come to the feast, when they heard that Jesus was coming to Jerusalem, took branches of palm trees, and went forth to meet Him, and cried, Hosanna: Blessed is the King of Israel that cometh in the name of the Lord. And Jesus, when He had found a young ass, sat thereon: as it is written, Fear not, daughter of Sion: behold, thy King cometh, sitting on an ass's colt. These things understood not His disciples at the first: but when Jesus was glorified, then remembered they that these things were written of Him, and that they had done these things unto Him. The people therefore that was with Him when He called Lazarus out of his grave, and raised him from the dead, bare record. For this cause the people also met Him, for that they heard that He had done this miracle. The Pharisees therefore said among themselves, Perceive ye how ye prevail nothing? behold, the world is gone after Him. And there were certain Greeks among them that came up to worship at the feast: the same came therefore to Philip, which was of Bethsaida of Galilee, and desired him, saying, Sir, we would see Jesus. Philip cometh and telleth Andrew: and again Andrew and Philip tell Jesus. And Jesus answered them, saying, The hour is come, that the Son of Man should be glorified. Verily, verily, I say unto you, Except a corn of wheat fall into the ground and die, it abideth alone: but if it die, it bringeth forth much fruit. He that loveth his life shall lose it; and he that hateth his life in this world shall keep it unto life eternal. If any man serve Me, let him follow Me; and where I am, there shall also My servant be: if any man serve Me, him will My Father honour. Now is My soul troubled; and what shall I say? Father, save me from this hour: but for this cause came I unto this hour. Father, glorify Thy name. Then came there a voice from heaven, saying, I have both glorified it, and will glorify it again" (John 12: 12-28).

THERE are really two distinct incidents recorded in these verses, either of which might serve as the theme for a complete address; but I want to try to combine the two incidents.

First, we have the Lord riding into Jerusalem and hailed as the Son of David, and then we have the Greeks coming with their quest, "We would see Jesus."

Our Saviour's mission is rapidly drawing to a close. For three and one-half wonderful years He had been moving about through the land of Palestine, doing mighty works of power, bearing witness to the testimony which He came to give. Now He had come to Jerusalem in order that He might die, that He might give Himself a ransom for our sins there. At the first it looked as though the people were ready to receive Him as King, and that He would not be rejected as He Himself had predicted. But this proved to be just an ephemeral movement, largely participated in by children and those who had been especially benefited by His ministry, who loved Him because of what He was and what He did. On the next day, the day following the visit in the house of Simon the leper, much people were come to the feast of the Passover, which was soon to be celebrated. When they heard that Jesus was coming to Jerusalem they went out to meet Him and took branches of palm trees, the

palm being the well-known symbol of victory,
crying "Hosanna!" or, "Save now." That is
quoted from Psalm 118, which is a Messianic
Psalm, setting forth the Lord Jesus as the blessed
Son of David. "Hosanna! Blessed is the King
of Israel that cometh in the name of the Lord."

One might say, "Well, at last the Saviour is
being recognized for what He is, and will be able
to take the throne and reign in righteousness,
overthrowing all iniquity." It was just a little
remnant of people who really acknowledged Him.
The majority of the religious leaders had com-
bined to refuse His claims, and it was not very
long after the cries of "Hosanna," before these
same leaders stirred up the people in Pilate's
judgment-hall to cry, "We have no king but
Caesar." And so He was definitely rejected when
He came as king.

He entered as predicted in the prophetic Word.
We are told, "Jesus, when He had found a young
ass, sat thereon, as it is written." Step by step,
from His birth right to the very last, the Lord
has moved on in exact accord with prophecy. This
very last week there were scores of prophecies
fulfilled, made many hundreds of years before.
In Zechariah's prophecy we have Him depicted
riding into Jerusalem upon an ass, and upon a
colt, the foal of an ass. It is from this book that
the Spirit of God now quotes: "As it is written,

Fear not, daughter of Sion: behold thy King cometh, sitting on an ass's colt." There was something striking even in that. Why? We are told in another Gospel that the Lord was seated on·a colt on which man had never ridden, an unbroken colt. It is not the easiest thing ordinarily to ride an unbroken colt, but this colt seemed instinctively to recognize its Master. Jesus was the Creator of all things, who had stooped in grace to become Man, and so He took control of the colt and rode triumphantly into the city as the people spread their garments before Him and shouted their welcome. Neither were these things understood by His disciples at first, but when Jesus had been glorified, when He had come through the agony of the cross, when He had been raised from the dead, and ascended to God's right hand in heaven, and the Holy Spirit had come, as He did at Pentecost, and opened their eyes to an understanding of the truth they never had before, then remembered they that these things were written of Him, and that they had done these things unto Him. It is the work of the Holy Spirit of God to bring to mind the things that God has written in His Word for our instruction, for He wrote the words: "Holy men of God spake as they were moved by the Holy Spirit." And so it is a very simple thing for the Holy Spirit to take these things and open them up to the people of God, calling to mind prophecies and promises that have been long since forgotten until He brings them back to the sphere of consciousness.

"The people therefore that was with Him when He called Lazarus out of his grave, and raised him from the dead, bare record. For this cause the people also met Him, for that they heard that He had done this miracle." The raising of Lazarus seemed to have a greater effect on the people than any of His other miracles. We need not wonder at that, for it certainly was His greatest physical miracle, as that of stilling the tempest was the greatest in connection with inanimate nature. By calling forth that man from the grave, who had been four days dead, Jesus demonstrated Himself to be the Resurrection and the Life. The people who had never considered His claims before began to wonder if He were the promised Messiah which was to come, when He rode into Jerusalem on this occasion. But there were those who dissented and who eventually succeeded in alienating many of these people from Him. "The Pharisees therefore said among themselves, Perceive ye how ye prevail nothing? Behold, the world is gone after Him." And so Isaiah's words, spoken seven hundred years before, as he contemplated the coming of the Messiah, were now being fulfilled: "Who hath believed our report, and to whom is the arm of the

Lord revealed?" Those who should have believed, who should have been the first to receive Him, were actually the first to reject Him.

We pass on to the next incident. When the Pharisees were thus deliberately and wilfully rejecting the claims of Christ, it must have been a great joy to His heart to meet this first token of interest of the Gentile world in Him and the message He came to bring. We read, in verse 20, "And there were certain Greeks among them that came up to worship at the feast." Now, sometimes when in our English Version we read of Greeks, the word is one that means not people who were actually Greeks by nature, but Jews who were born out among the Greeks in the Gentile world. But here it is really Greeks that are mentioned. These Gentiles had come up to the Jews' feast, the Passover. They were perhaps proselytes. They may have recognized in Judaism a much purer, holier, and better religious system than that to which they had been accustomed among the pagan peoples of whom they formed a part. There were a great many at that time who were dissatisfied and who were turning away from the gods their fathers had worshipped. Their hearts were yearning for something better, nobler, purer and truer. And so as the Jews were scattered over all the world, where they had their synagogues and places of prayer, many of

these inquiring Gentiles visited the Jewish meet-
ing-places and learned something of the one true
and living God, and the promise that He had
made to Abraham that a Seed was coming
through whom the world should be blessed. These
Greeks may have been among them. They had
come up to the Passover. They came to worship,
we are told, and when in Jerusalem they heard
about Jesus, They heard of this marvelous One
who had lived among the people three and one-
half years, who had gone about doing good, healing the sick and opening the eyes of the blind.
Doubtless they put many questions to those who had
heard Him and they would be asking themselves,
"Could He be the promised One?" As they listened to the stories about Jesus, one can imagine
them comparing notes and saying, "Could this
be the Logos for whom Plato longed, and could
this be the One that the Jewish Scriptures, which
we have been reading, promised, testifying of
the coming into the world of the Messiah?"

And so, learning that Jesus was already in the
city, they sought out the company of the disciples.
They came to Philip, who was of Bethsaida. Why
to Philip? Well, his very name would appeal to
them. Philip was a Greek name, meaning "a
lover of horses." A great Greek king, Philip of
Macedon, had made a wonderful name for himself, and this Philip, they may have thought,

would have some link of understanding with them. They did not go to Peter, John, James, or to the other disciples. They went to Philip, who bore a Greek name, and they said, "Sir, we would see Jesus." The thing they desired must have delighted Philip's heart, for these Greeks were strangers. Gentiles from the outside, that longed to see and know Jesus. Philip must have felt, "Oh, the day of our Lord's triumph must be near, the Gentiles are already coming, just as the Old Testament said, to recognize His claims."

Philip called Andrew, and Andrew and Philip together went to the Lord Jesus, and I fancy they were most eager as they said, "Master, will you come and meet some Gentiles who are here, who want to see and to know You, and who are interested in the message You give?" I have no doubt Jesus revealed Himself to these Greeks, but we are not told that He did. We are told that He answered saying, "The hour is come, that the Son of Man should be glorified." He recognized in this request of these Gentiles a kind of first-fruits of the great harvest from among the nations. He was about to be rejected by His own people, but the Scripture had said that if Israel rejected Him, He should become a light to lighten the Gentiles. So here is the first evidence of it in these Greeks with their request, "We would see Jesus."

He saw in their request an evidence of what will take place in the whole Gentile world in the years to follow. He then told the disciples very seriously and very solemnly that He could not fully reveal Himself either to Jew or Gentile until He had passed through death and resurrection. "Verily, verily, I say unto you, Except a corn of wheat fall into the ground and die, it abideth alone: but if it die, it bringeth forth much fruit." What does He really mean? Well, He was the corn of wheat, and if He did not die there would be no salvation for any poor sinner. Jesus did not come to save men by His instruction; He did not come to save men by His example. He is not saying to men: "If you will try to live in the way that I live, and follow My steps, you will be saved." Let me say again—as I have said many a time before, and that at the risk of being misunderstood—no one was ever saved by following Jesus. It is after we are saved that we begin to follow Him. He left us an example that we should follow, but we need to know Him as Redeemer, we need to receive divine life from Him before we can follow Him.

Jesus is not simply the great Teacher, nor Example. Jesus must suffer and die in order that men and women might be saved. "Except a corn of wheat fall into the ground and die, it abideth alone: but if it die, it bringeth forth much fruit." Apart from His death, the beautiful life of Jesus could not have saved one poor sinner. Instead of that, it would only condemn men. If there is anything that would show men how sinful they are, it would be to line up alongside the Lord Jesus. If you are pretty well satisfied with yourself, and want to see how wicked and corrupt and sinful you are in the sight of God, read these four Gospels, consider the life that Jesus lived, and you will soon see how far short you come. "He abideth alone." He was the sinless One, the spotless One, the only begotten Son of the Father, and the One who could say, "I do always those things which please Him." He was the only Man who could turn to His worst enemies and say, "Which of you convinceth Me of sin?" His humanity was absolutely holy, and so He abode alone in His life here on earth.

He added, "But if it die, it bringeth forth much fruit." He went to the cross, and upon that cross He gave Himself a ransom for our sins; He died that He might redeem us; He poured forth His most precious blood that we might be cleansed from all our iniquities. And now think of the millions down through the so-called Christian centuries who have found life and peace and salvation through His atoning death. The corn of wheat has indeed fallen into the ground in death, and there has been a great harvest. "If it die, it bringeth forth much fruit."

Notice the challenge to those who trust Him, in the verses that follow. If we profess to receive Him and take Him as our Saviour, naturally we follow Him, and we become His disciples. And so He tells us, "He that loveth his life shall lose it, but he that hateth his life in this world shall keep it unto life eternal."

To the worldling it always looks as though a Christian is throwing away his life when he gives up worldly follies and pleasures and devotes himself to the glory of the Lord Jesus Christ. But he who does throw away his life in this respect actually finds it. The worldling thinks he knows life at its best, but it is only the Christian who really enters into and enjoys the more blessed, deeper life. He enters into life at its highest, its richest and its best.

Jesus said, "If any man serve Me, let him follow Me; and where I am, there shall also My servant be." There is a promise for every believer. You and I are given the privilege of not only believing in His Name, but suffering for His sake, following in His steps, bearing shame and ignominy for Jesus' sake, and some day God the Father is going to honor all of those who have borne shame for the Name of His blessed Son.

Now, having spoken of the work of the cross, it would seem as though the soul of Jesus already began to enter into the dark shadow that was involved in His being made sin, for He said, "Now is My soul troubled." What troubled Him? The fact that there on the cross He was to endure the pent-up wrath of God, that He was to be dealt with in judgment in order that we might be dealt with in grace. And all that disturbed His soul. He could not have been man in perfection and holiness if He did not shrink from being made sin for us. "Now is My soul troubled; and what shall I say? Father, save Me from this hour: but for this cause came I into the world. I came into the world to die, to give Myself a ransom for all." And so instead of asking to be saved from that hour He prays that the Father's Name might be glorified. Then, we are told, there came a voice from heaven, and this is the third time in the experience of our Lord Jesus that there came such a voice from heaven, saying, "I have both glorified it, and will glorify it again."

When Jesus passed through the cross God glorified His Name by raising Him from the dead. He has glorified His Name by setting His own Son at His right hand in highest heaven. He will yet glorify His Name when He sends Jesus back into this scene to reign as King of kings and Lord of lords.

"WALK WHILE YE HAVE THE LIGHT"

1   1   1

"The people therefore, that stood by, and heard it, said that it thundered; others said, An angel spake to Him. Jesus answered and said, This voice came not because of Me, but for your sakes. Now is the judgment of this world: now shall the prince of this world be cast out. And I, if I be lifted up from the earth, will draw all men unto Me. This He said, signifying what death He should die. The people answered Him, We have heard out of the law that Christ abideth forever: and how sayeth Thou, The Son of Man must be lifted up? Who is this Son of Man? Then Jesus said unto them, Yet a little while is the light with you. Walk while ye have the light, lest darkness come upon you: for he that walketh in darkness knoweth not whither he goeth. While ye have light, believe in the light, that ye may be the children of light. These things spake Jesus, and departed, and did hide Himself from them" (John 12: 29-36).

1   1   1

AS we closed the previous address we were considering those words of the Saviour recorded in verses 24-28: "Except a corn of wheat fall into the ground and die, it abideth alone: but if it die, it bringeth forth much fruit." He was speaking of Himself, for He came into this world, the incarnate Son of God, a Man of a different order to any other, absolutely sinless, holy and without blame. Had it not been that in grace He went to the cross and died for us, He must have remained alone as Man for eternity. But as a result of His death there is now a glorious harvest of redeemed men and women. The corn of wheat fell into the ground and died, and millions have been saved through His death.

To those who are saved there comes the challenge, "If any man serve Me, let him follow Me," and then our Lord, realizing that the cross was just before Him and that on that cross He was to drink the cup of judgment that our sins had filled, said, "Now is My soul troubled; and what shall I say? Father, save Me from this hour?" No; He did not ask that. He said, "But for this cause came I unto this hour. Father, glorify Thy name. Then came there a voice from heaven (in immediate response), saying, I have both glorified it, and will glorify it again." God was glorified in the perfect life of the Lord Jesus Christ. He would be glorified in His sacrificial death and in His wondrous resurrection.

The people heard the noise of the voice but they could not make out the words, and so they said it thundered. There are only a very few who have an ear for the voice of God. It is just the same today as it was then. When God is speaking in power, possibly through one of His servants in some great gathering where the message is gripping individuals who are in earnest about spiritual realities, the great majority say, "It's only a noise, just thunder; nothing to it." They don't hear the voice of God. Other people rise a little higher. There were those who said, "An angel spake to Him." But it was neither thunder nor an angel; it was the Father Himself.

Long before this, after His baptism in Jordan, the Father's voice was heard, saying, "This is My beloved Son in whom I am well pleased; hear ye Him." And again on the Mount of Transfiguration that same voice may be heard authenticating the works and the message and the perfection of the Son, in almost the same words: "This is my beloved Son; hear Him." And now He speaks of Jesus in connection with the glory of His Name, and says, "I have both glorified it, and will glorify it again," that is, through the work that He was about to accomplish on the cross. Jesus answered and said, "This voice came not because of Me, but for your sakes." And then He made the tremendous statement, "Now is the judgment of this world: now shall the prince of this world be cast out. And I, if I be lifted up from the earth, will draw all men unto Me."

There are really four parts to this great statement of His. He speaks of a judged world, a vanquished prince, a lifted-up Saviour, and a coming Judge. The first thing is, "Now is the judgment of this world." What was He referring to? The judgment of this world was expressed in the cross of Christ. The world said of the Lord Jesus, "We don't want Him." He came and presented Himself as the King who would have set everything right if men would have received Him, but they cried, "We have no king but Caesar," so they refused Him, and in refusing Him they brought judgment upon themselves, and the entire world has been under judgment ever since.

Do you wonder sometimes why God permits certain dreadful things to happen in this world? It is because people rejected the Prince of Peace. Think how different it might have been if Jesus had been received, had the men of His day accepted Him, had He set up His kingdom in power and glory. Then wars would long since have disappeared from the earth, sorrow and sighing and sickness would be done away with, and millennial blessings would have been enjoyed during these past centuries. By rejecting Christ men brought judgment on themselves, and so no one need be surprised at the dire things that are coming on the world. The surprise, rather is, that God holds back His wrath and does not deal in summary judgment with men because of their sins. The world is like one condemned to die, out still permitted to live on until that sentence will be executed. Soon the day of God's red heavens will come; soon the vials of the wrath of God will be poured out upon this world, and then indeed will men know its judgment to the full.

But now grace is mingled with judgment. God is sending out a message of mercy. He is calling upon people to repent and to receive the Saviour they once rejected. Have you done that? Have you accepted the Lord Jesus? Do you remember those striking words of the Apostle Peter to the Jews: "Save yourselves from this untoward generation?" What does he mean? Somebody might well ask, "We cannot save ourselves; can we?" No, we cannot save ourselves, so far as salvation from hell is concerned. We can only be saved from that through the finished work of Christ on the cross. "For there is none other name under heaven given among men, whereby we must be saved." What, then, did Peter mean when he said, "Save yourselves from this untoward generation?" It is just another way of saying, "Break with the world that is under judgment; step out from that world and take sides with the One who is now rejected. If you do that, then you are secure from the judgment that is coming upon the world." One often grieves to see Christians who seem to enter so feebly into this. Why

is it that some Christians are not interested in
separation from the world? It is because they
have never realized that the world is a judged
scene, that all that men delight in will soon be
burned up in the day of Jehovah's wrath, and
that God is calling His people to walk in separation from the world. Sometimes our dear young
people think their godly pastors and teachers and
parents are too severe and strait-laced because
they try to warn them against things that are of
a worldly character. Remember, from this
blessed Book of God they have learned the end
of all these things, and it is in order that youth
may be spared the sorrows of the coming judgment that they call upon them now to separate
themselves from the world. "Save yourselves
from this untoward generation." One thing I
know—in that day when the seven vials of the
wrath of God will be poured out upon this world,
nobody will be sorry that he lived a separated life
and that he walked apart from the world that
God is going to judge. "Now is the judgment of
this world." It is already judged, but the judgment is not yet executed.

The second thing the Saviour says is, "Now
shall the prince of this world be cast out." Who
is the prince of this world? Satan. How did he
become the prince of this world? He is a usurper.
God put this world under the charge of our first

parents. He said to Adam, "Have authority over
the world; I have given it all to you, and you are
to take charge of it for Me." But Adam gambled
away his title as prince of this world to the devil,
and ever since then Satan has been the prince,
and not only the prince but the god of this world.

But you remember the promise when the Lord
said, in pronouncing judgment upon the serpent,
"The Seed of the woman shall bruise thy head,
and thou shalt bruise His heel." In the cross of
Christ the heel of Jesus, the Seed of the woman,
was bruised, but in that same cross the head of
the serpent was bruised. And so Satan is now
a vanquished prince, and yet there are still thousands and millions of people who own his authority, and in the coming day when he is to be cast
down from heaven into the bottomless pit, and at
last into the lake of fire, God's full judgment
will be carried out upon him.

Now notice the third thing. "And I, if I be
lifted up from the earth." What was the Lord
referring to there? The sentence as a whole
reads like this: "And I, if I be lifted up, will
draw all men unto Me." I think this verse is
often entirely misapplied. I have frequently
heard it used in this way: "If the preacher lifts
up Jesus, all men will be drawn unto Him." We
all believe that the only way to draw men to
Christ is to preach the gospel, and that is our

mission—to preach the gospel. But did one ever know *all* men to be drawn to Jesus through the preaching of the gospel? I have had a continual sorrow in my heart for fifty years because men are not all drawn when I lift up Jesus in preaching. I remember over fifty years ago when I accepted Christ on my knees in my own room in Los Angeles, and how three nights later I stepped out with a group in the open air to give my first testimony for Christ. Some way or another as I began to speak I forgot all circumstances. I hadn't studied any sermon, but I found I had preached a half-hour when the leader of the meeting stopped me and said we should have been in the hall twenty minutes ago.

I had to stop, but my heart was full. I thought, "These people only need to know about Jesus, and they will all be saved." I remember my text as though it was yesterday—"He was wounded for our transgressions; He was bruised for our iniquities: the chastisement of our peace was upon Him: and with His stripes we are healed." Oh, how I preached with all the fervor of my young heart, and I thought, "They only need to know, and they will come to Jesus." But they didn't come. There was a great crowd gathered around and some of them looked on curiously and said, "What's that youngster talking about? What does a lad of fourteen know about this?" And they turned and went away and only one came to me and said, "My boy, you seem to have found something that I have been looking for all my life, and never been able to get." He was an aged colored man, with snow-white hair crowning his black face, and I led him to Christ—my first convert. But the rest passed on and seemed totally indifferent, and for fifty years I have been trying to lift up Jesus, and I hope I can say before God I have had no other message. I recognize there are a great many different lines of truth in this blessed Word, and my commission is not merely to preach the gospel but to preach the Word, for all these different lines of truth center in Jesus. I hope I can say with Paul, "Whom we preach."

I trust the day will never come when I will be found preaching "what" instead of "whom." But I testify to this, that after fifty years of trying to lift up Jesus in preaching, I haven't seen all men drawn unto Him. Sometimes as I look out over the audience here on Sunday night with 3500 to 4000 people present, my heart trembles, and I say to myself, "What an opportunity!" And again I think that in that great multitude there are only about 200 or 300 who do not believe in Jesus—the great majority are already Christians. But the others, where are they?—the people you would like to reach. They are on the streets, in the theatres and other places of worldly amusement. They don't care. Lift up Jesus? Yes; but that does not draw all men to Him. You say, Well, then, is the Bible wrong? No; but sometimes our interpretation of it is wrong. It does not say here, that if the preacher lifts up Jesus all men will be drawn unto Him. Note carefully what it does say, "And I, if I be lifted up from the earth will draw all men unto Me." And then look at the Holy Ghost's explanation in verse 33—"This He said, signifying what death He should die."

There you have it. The lifting up here is not referring to preaching. That lifting up is a reference to Calvary. It's the same thing as that which was brought before Nicodemus when Jesus said, "And as Moses lifted up the serpent in the wilderness, even so must the Son of Man be lifted up: that whosoever believeth in Him should not perish, but have eternal life." When the people of Israel were bitten by the fiery serpents in the wilderness, God said to Moses, "Make thee a fiery serpent, and set it upon a pole: and it shall come to pass, that every one that is bitten, when he looketh upon it, shall live." And Jesus practically says to Nicodemus, "That serpent of brass is a picture of Myself." A writhing, twisting serpent a picture of Jesus? Yes, of Jesus made sin for us, that we might become the righteousness of God in Him. You see, it was the serpent that caused the trouble. They were bitten by the fiery serpent, and the serpent is the recognized symbol in the Bible of Satan and sin, and that is how all the trouble began in the world. We are all infected by the poison of sin, the poison of asps is under our lips. Every one of us has been infected by the serpent's poison, but Jesus came, and when He was lifted up on the cross He was made sin for us.

> "He took the guilty's sinner's place,
>   And suffered in our stead;
>   For man—oh, miracle of grace!—
>   For man the Saviour bled!"

The serpent in the wilderness was made of brass, and brass is the symbol of judgment. It spoke of Christ bearing our judgment. It was a serpent that had no poison in it. It could not injure anyone, and Jesus, holy, harmless and undefiled, has been lifted up, and He says, "And I, if I be lifted up from the earth (that is, on the cross) will draw all men unto Me."

Jesus is the uplifted Saviour. Of course, the preacher is to tell all men that Jesus died for them. Of course, he is to point to the crucified One.

> "There is life in a look at the Crucified One,
>   There is life at this moment for thee;
>   Then look, sinner, look, unto Him and be saved,
>   Unto Him who was nailed to the tree.

Oh, why was He there as the Bearer of sin,
    If on Jesus thy guilt was not laid?
Oh, why from His side flowed the sin-cleansing blood,
    If His dying thy debt has not paid?"

"And I, if I be lifted up, will draw all men unto
Me." But it is not now that all men are drawn
to Him. The great majority pass on their way
unheeding. The Son of God seems to cry, as it
were, to mankind: "Is it nothing to you, all ye
that pass by? Behold, and see if there be any
sorrow like unto My sorrow, which is done unto
Me, wherewith the Lord hath afflicted Me in the
day of His fierce anger." What is your answer?
Do you go on your way, saying, "It's nothing to
me."

"I'll live for myself, for myself alone,
    For myself and none beside—
Just as if Jesus had never lived,
    And as if He had never died."

You can turn away from Him if you desire. You
can refuse His grace and spurn His love and
trample on His gospel, if that's what you want
to do. Nobody is ever going to force you to accept Christ. You can go on in your sins and be
lost forever. But one thing you can't do—you
can't evade Him at the end.

"If I be lifted up from the earth will draw all
men unto Me." Some day the One who was lifted

up on the cross will sit on the throne of judgment. Some day the One who took our place in grace on the tree will be the occupant of the Great White Throne, and then all men will be drawn to Him. The word translated "drawn" here suggests compelling power. It's exactly the same word that is used in the last chapter of this Gospel, where it speaks of the net enclosing one hundred and fifty-three great fishes, and they came, we are told, *dragging* the net to the land. You see, the fish were helpless; they were dragged in the net to land. "I, if I be lifted up, will draw (drag) all men unto Me." Men may say, "But I don't want to come to Him; I don't want to face Him; I don't want to give an account to Him." But you will not be asked if you want to or not; you will have to face Him and stand in the presence of Him who says, "If I be lifted up, I will draw all men unto Me."

Oh, how much better to be drawn by love divine and come to Him in the day of His grace, than to wait to be drawn to Him in judgment when it will be too late to be saved!

But now we must notice our responsibility in view of all this. We read, in verse 34: "The people answered Him, We have heard out of the law that Christ abideth for ever: and how sayest Thou, The Son of Man must be lifted up? Who is this Son of Man?" They practically say, "We don't know what you are talking about. We are looking for a Messiah who is coming on earth to destroy our enemies, and the one you are talking about is the Son of Man. We don't understand that. You speak of the Son of Man. Who is this Son of Man?" It is Jesus, who is "God over all, blessed forevermore," who became man in grace for our redemption. Jesus said to them, "Yet a little while is the light with you." He had told them before, "I am the light of the world. I am only going to be here a little while and then I am going out to die. Walk while ye have the light, lest darkness come upon you: for he that walketh in darkness knoweth not whither he goeth. While ye have light, believe in the light, that ye may be the children of light. These things spake Jesus, and departed, and did hide Himself from them."

These words should come home to our hearts today. We have every evidence that we are getting near the close of the present dispensation of the grace of God, to be succeeded by the darkest night this world has ever known. Our Lord's words may well have a special message for all of us. "Walk while ye have the light." Accept the truth of God while ye have the opportunity; believe the message while it is still being proclaimed, for darkness is coming, and "he that walketh in darkness knoweth not whither he goeth. While ye have light, believe in the light, that ye may be the children of light." We are told that "Thy Word is a lamp unto my feet, and a light unto my path," and again, "The entrance of Thy Words giveth light." And so the light is shining today, and all men who will may walk in the light. "If we walk in the light as He is in the light, we have fellowship one with another, and the blood of Jesus Christ His Son cleanseth us from all sin."

> "Come to the light, 'tis shining for thee,
> Sweetly the light has dawned upon me;
> Once I was blind, but now I can see,
> The light of the world is Jesus!"

But it is not only to men outside that the message comes: "Walk while ye have the light," but oh, Christians, this Word was given to shed light on your path, and yet how many believers there are who are opposing the light, who are going on in ways of their own devices, refusing to submit to the truth of the Word of God. We only have a little while longer in which to be faithful to the Lord who saved us. Let us yield ourselves wholly to Him to walk in the light while we have the light. "The night cometh when no man can work."

CONFESSING OR REJECTING CHRIST

ʃ   ʃ   ʃ

"But though He had done so many miracles before them, yet they believed not on Him: That the saying of Esaias the prophet might be fulfilled, which he spake, Lord, who hath believed our report? and to whom hath the arm of the Lord been revealed? Therefore they could not believe, because that Esaias said again, He hath blinded their eyes, and hardened their heart; that they should not see with their eyes, nor understand with their heart, and be converted, and I should heal them. These things said Esaias, when he saw His glory, and spake of Him. Nevertheless among the chief rulers also many believed on Him; but because of the Pharisees they did not confess Him, lest they should be put out of the synagogue: for they loved the praise of men more than the praise of God" (John 12: 37-43).

ʃ   ʃ   ʃ

THE first part of this passage suggests truth that is exceedingly solemn, something we are very apt to forget. It reminds us that God's Word has a softening or hardening effect upon the souls of those who hear it. It has been well said, that just as the same sun softens the wax and hardens the clay, so the same gospel message may soften the heart of one and bring him to repentance and to definite faith in the Lord

Jesus Christ, or it may harden the heart of another and put him into that condition of soul where he will never yield or break down before God and receive Christ, but will die in his sins and be banished from the presence of God for all eternity. It is not a question of the purpose of God, nor even of the method in which the truth is presented. It is not that God has designed that some men should accept it while others reject it, that some should receive it while others refuse, some be softened and others hardened, but it is a question of the individual's own attitude toward that truth.

When God spoke to Israel of old the words quoted here, "Lord, who hath believed our report? and to whom hath the arm of the Lord been revealed?" He drew their attention to the fact that He had given them clear instruction concerning the wickedness of idolatry. He had pleaded with them to give Him the first place in their hearts as the one true and living God. They turned away. He sent His prophets to call them back, but the testimony was spurned, and the time came when the message had no effect upon their consciences at all. So God gave them up to hardness of heart because they themselves preferred it. They chose to disobey God. You have something like that in 2 Thess. 2, where we have that awful picture of the man of sin yet to arise in this world in the dark days of the tribulation just ahead of us, which may be much nearer than any of us realize, which, however, cannot break upon the world until the Church of God has been taken up. We read of people then who will be left behind in this scene; some who have heard the gospel over and over again, but only to refuse it. And we are told that, "For this cause God shall send them strong delusion, that they should believe a lie: (that is, the lie of the antichrist) that they all might be damned who believed not the truth, but had pleasure in unrighteousness."

God's heart goes out to all men everywhere. He does not desire the death of the sinner, but that all should turn to Him and live. He cries, "Turn ye, turn ye from your evil ways; for why will ye die, O house of Israel?" But if men refuse to heed His word they will be given up to hardness of heart. The conscience, stirred by the Word, may respond at first and one may feel in his very soul that he should yield to Christ, but it is possible to stifle the voice of conscience, to refuse to heed, until at last conscience no longer speaks but becomes seared as with a hot iron and men are hardened in their sins and die without hope.

Our Lord Jesus Christ had been ministering in grace for about three-and-a-half wonderful

years, and had given evidence through signs and
wonders which He wrought and the marvelous
message He brought to man, that He was the
Messiah and Redeemer of Israel, but we read
though He had done so many miracles, yet they
believed not on Him. Miracles alone will never
convince if people refuse the Word. No signs,
no wonders, no miracles, will ever reach their
consciences, if they are determined to go on in
their sins and refuse to repent.

Abraham reminded "a certain rich man who
died and was buried" of this, when he said of
his still-living brothers: "If they hear not Moses
and the prophets, neither will they be persuaded,
though one rose from the dead."

What a solemn responsibility that puts upon
every one of us who hear the Word of God as
recorded here in His blessed Book. If men reject
this testimony, signs and wonders and miracles
will not convince them. They become hardened in
their sins. These people refused to hear the word
Jesus brought, and so the saying of Isaiah was
fulfilled when he cried out (chapter fifty-three),
"Lord, who hath believed our report? and to
whom hath the arm of the Lord been revealed?"
He was implying that the great majority would
reject the testimony of Jesus when He came, and
they did. Only a little group received Him. And
today that question still comes to us, "Who hath

believed, and to whom is the arm of the Lord revealed?" Have you believed, dear friend? Have you opened your heart to the Word of God? Has His mighty saving power been revealed to you? Do you know Him as the One who has delivered you from going down to the pit, and has given you a place in Christ, free from all condemnation? If you spurn the Word, God has no other message for you.

Thus we read that they could not believe, because "He hath blinded their eyes, and hardened their heart; that they should not see with their eyes, nor understand with their heart, and be converted, and I should heal them." Was it that God was not willing they should be converted? Not at all. He yearned for their conversion. He entreated them to return to Himself, but they refused the message and hardened their own hearts against Him, and God said, "Very well, you can remain hardened in your sins," and the day came when the Word made no more impression on them.

Years ago, I was talking to a little group of boys and girls in a Sunday School in San Francisco. I was trying to illustrate like this, "How sad to know, dear girls and boys, each time you say, 'No' to the Lord Jesus, your heart gets a little harder, and if you keep on saying 'No,' the heart gets harder and harder and harder until

by-and-by God calls it a heart of stone, and you
no longer care about the things of God, but persist in spurning His grace, and you will therefore die in your sins." So I was pleading with
those boys and girls to give their hearts to Jesus
in their early days. There was one dear little
tot there, only five years old (and we sometimes
think these little folk take nothing in), whose
eyes were fastened on me as I spoke. Her mother
brought her to Sunday School and then took her
home, and on the way home she had not a word
to say. She was thinking of her own dear father
who never went to Church or Sunday School,
who never went to hear the Word of God, and
when she got to the house, there sat the father
smoking his cigar, with the Sunday paper spread
around him. The little thing darted in ahead of
her mother and up into her father's arms she
leapt, and said, "Daddy, Daddy, feel your heart!
Is it getting like stone?" He said, "What are
you talking about?" She said, "Well, the man at
Sunday School said if you say 'No' to Jesus, you
are going to get a stone in your stomach! Have
you got a stone there? Oh, Daddy, I hope you
haven't, for if you have, you can't be saved." The
father turned to her mother and said angrily,
"What have they been telling this child, anyway?" Then the mother explained a little more
fully, and when he saw the tears in the wife's

eyes and felt the arms of his little girl about his neck, and heard her saying, "Oh, Daddy, don't go on saying 'No' to Jesus," he looked up and said, "Well, I think I had better settle this thing," and he got down on his knees and yielded his life to Christ. What a mercy he came in time! What a solemn thing it is to say "No" to the voice of the Lord Jesus Christ.

That explains the strong delusion of the last days, and why men and women are given up to hardness of heart. They turn away from God, and at last the time comes when God says, "Very well, Ephraim is joined to his idols: let him alone." God grant that this may not be true of any to whom these pages come. If you are still in your sins, and you hear the voice of Jesus calling today, will you not bow before Him in repentance and faith, and tell Him that at last you yield your heart to Him and come to Him in all your sin and need, that you will trust Him as your Redeemer?

Isaiah gave this special word of warning, we are told, when he "saw His glory." "These things said Esaias, when he saw His glory, and spake of Him." When was that? Well, you remember the incident recorded in the sixth chapter of Isaiah, when he said, "In the year that King Uzziah died I saw also the Lord sitting upon a throne, high and lifted up, and His train filled the temple. Above it stood the seraphims: each one had six wings; with twain he covered his face, and with twain he covered his feet, and with twain he did fly. And one cried unto another, and said, Holy, holy, holy, is the Lord of hosts: the whole earth is full of His glory." Do you realize who it was whom the seraphim adored? The Holy Spirit says, "Isaiah saw *His* glory and spake of Him." Our Lord Jesus Christ was with the Father there in brightest glory. He who was yet to come in to this earth to save sinners, was the object of angelic adoration, and Isaiah looked on through the ages and saw Him coming down to die on Calvary's cross, and he cried, "He was wounded for our transgressions, He was bruised for our iniquities: the chastisement of our peace was upon Him; and with His stripes we are healed."

Isaiah saw Him in faith, and that blessed One stood in the midst of Israel, and His own people did not recognize Him. He came to His own, and His own received Him not. What about you? Have you received Him? Has the message gone in one ear and out of the other? Or has it bowed your heart in repentance before Him? The trouble is, you know, many do believe, but they do not have the courage to come right out and confess their faith.

We read in verse forty-two, "Nevertheless among the chief rulers also many believed on Him; but because of the Pharisees they did not confess Him, lest they should be put out of the synagogue: for they loved the praise of men more than the praise of God." What a foolish thing! Men's praises will pass away. What difference does it make whether men praise or not if one does not have the approval of God? Men cannot do anything for you along spiritual lines. How foolish for people to be concerned as to what others think about it, and yet how many people have refrained from taking a definite step for Christ because the thought comes of some friend or companion, some pal whose good will they esteem. They say, "Oh, I am not prepared to commit myself definitely. What will this one, or that one think?"

I remember when I was a little boy, how my mother would draw me to her knee and speak to me so solemnly of the importance of trusting the Lord Jesus Christ as my Saviour, and I would say, "Well, mamma, I would like to do it, but the boys will all laugh at me." Mother used to say, "Harry, remember, they may laugh you into hell, but they can never laugh you out of it." And oh, how that used to go home to me, and it stayed with me all through the years! Yes, men may sneer and ridicule and not understand us as we come out for Christ, but after all, His is the only approval worth having.

Long years ago I read of a conflict which took place between two Indian Rajahs. The one defeated the other and took captive the son of his rival, and the day he was to return to his own palace he prepared to march into the city in triumph. There was a great procession of elephants, cavalry, infantry and a long line of captives. Among them was the young prince. He was told that he was to walk bare-footed and bare-headed. He was indignant and said, "What! Go in like that! What will the people think? What kind of faces will they make?" The rajah said, "You haven't heard all yet. You shall carry a bowl of milk in your hand, and if you spill so much as a drop, you will lose your head at the close of the procession." In a few minutes they had brought that bowl of milk, and two guards walked with him, one on either side, and the procession started to move. On and on they went, for perhaps a mile or more, into the presence of the rajah. And that young prince walked along, holding the bowl of milk. It seemed as though he would never finish without spilling some of it, but he completed the ordeal safely. Finally he stood before the rajah, "Well, Sir Prince, what kind of faces did the people make?" He looked up and said, "Your majesty, I did not see the faces of the people. I saw only my life, which I held in my hands, and I knew one false step would make me lose my life."

These people of old loved the praise of men more than the praise of God, and because of that they did not have courage enough to confess the Lord Jesus Christ before their fellows. They knew He was the Sent One of the Father. They knew He was the Shepherd of Israel, Redeemer of sinful men, but the good opinion of their companions meant more to them than the favor of God. How is it with you today? You remember the Word says, "If thou shalt confess with thy mouth the Lord Jesus, and shalt believe in thine heart that God hath raised Him from the dead, thou shalt be saved." And again, our Lord Jesus has said, "Whosoever therefore shall confess Me before men, him will I confess also before My Father which is in heaven. But whosoever shall deny Me before men, him will I also deny before My Father which is in heaven."

If you do believe in your heart that God gave Jesus for you, if you have trusted Him, oh, then, do not hesitate to confess Him openly before men. I believe a great many secret believers are without the peace they might have because they do not confess Christ openly. You say, "Do you think there really are secret believers?" Yes, the Word tells us that Joseph of Arimathea was one, but oh, how much he lost! He came at the last, and offered his new tomb that they might bury the body of the Son of God there. Nicodemus was a secret believer, and once he tried to speak out, but did not say definitely, "He is my Lord and Saviour," but he sent a hundred pounds of spices for the burial of the body of the Lord Jesus, and thus identified himself with the Christ who had died, but how much more blessing would he have enjoyed if he had come right out with it while Jesus lived! I believe that many people today, deep in their hearts, believe in Christ, and in their homes tell Him they love and trust Him, but they are not honoring Him by making confession before men. They do not have the joy and victory in their lives that they might have if they came out openly and let others know.

> "Jesus, and shall it ever be,
> A mortal man ashamed of Thee?
> Ashamed of Thee, whom angels praise,
> Whose glories shine thro' endless days?
>
> Ashamed of Jesus! sooner far
> Let evening blush to own a star;
> He sheds the beams of light divine
> O'er this benighted soul of mine.
>
> Ashamed of Jesus! Yes, I may,
> When I've no guilt to wash away,
> No tear to wipe, no good to crave,
> No fear to quell, no soul to save.

Till then, nor is my boasting **vain,**
Till then I boast a Saviour slain;
And oh, may this my glory be,
That Christ is not ashamed of me."

NOT JUDGE, BUT SAVIOUR

✓ ✓ ✓

"Jesus cried and said, He that believeth on Me, believeth not on Me, but on Him that sent Me. And he that seeth Me seeth Him that sent Me. I am come a light into the world, that whosoever believeth on Me should not abide in darkness. And if any man hear My words, and believe not, I judge him not: for I came not to judge the world, but to save the world. He that rejecteth Me, and receiveth not My words, hath One that judgeth Him: the word that I have spoken, the same shall judge him in the last day. For I have not spoken of Myself; but the Father which sent Me, He gave Me a commandment, what I should say, and what I should speak. And I know that His commandment is life everlasting: whatsoever I speak therefore, even as the Father said unto Me, so I speak" (John 12: 44-50).

✓ ✓ ✓

THERE are some very important truths brought before us in these few verses. They give the conclusion of our Lord's presentation of Himself to the world. We have already pointed out that the book really divides into two parts, the first twelve chapters giving the presentation of the Lord Jesus Christ to the world, and in this part He is set forth in every possible way that unsaved men could apprehend Him.

Then beginning with the first verse of chapter thirteen and going on to the end of the book, we have His presentation to the hearts of His own beloved people. In these first twelve chapters we have, "He came unto His own," but we read that "His own received Him not" (chap. 1:11). As we open chapter thirteen we read, "Having loved His own which were in the world, He loved them unto the end." In the first instance the term "His own" applies to all those whom He Himself had brought into the world by His power. "He came unto His own—but His own received Him not." But in the thirteenth chapter, "His own" refers to a distinct company, taken out of the world, who had received Him as Saviour and owned Him as Lord.

We have seen Him as the Eternal Word, as the Light come into the world, as the Lamb of God that taketh away the sin of the world, as the great Sin-offering, as the Giver of eternal life, as the Living Water, as the One who has power to quicken the dead, as the Truth and the Life, as the Bread of Life come down from heaven, as the Judge of living and dead, and in many other aspects. And in concluding His presentation in these various aspects, He says, "He that believeth on Me, believeth not on Me, but on Him that sent Me. And he that seeth Me seeth Him that sent Me." In these words our Lord Jesus Christ seeks to turn the attention of the people away from His mere humanity. He would not have men and women simply occupied with that, blessed as it is. If Jesus is only a man, it is impossible that He should be the Saviour of sinners. He did become true Man; the title that He delighted to use was "The Son of Man," and as Son of Man He came to seek and to save that which was lost, but He could not have saved the lost if He had not been more than Son of Man. He was true Man and true God. In Psalms 146: 3 it is written, "Put not your trust in princes, nor in the son of man, in whom is no help." Even though He were the best of men, if Jesus were not more than man He would be powerless to save sinners.

Therefore He turns our attention away from His humanity and fixes our minds upon the fact that He was God manifest in the flesh. He says, "Put your trust not in Me only, but in Him that sent Me." "He that seeth Me, seeth Him that sent Me." The Old Testament insists upon this in the book of Isaiah. After that wonderful promise in chapter seven that a virgin should conceive and bear a Son, and His name should be called Immanuel, which is, God with us, we read in chapter 9: 6: "For unto us a Child is born (that is His humanity), unto us a Son is given" (that is His Deity). He was the child of Mary, born by divine generation; but He was also the Eternal

Son of God who came into this world as Man, through the gate of birth. "The government shall be upon His shoulder: and His name shall be called Wonderful, Counsellor, The mighty God, The everlasting Father, The Prince of Peace." It seems to me that every enlightened Jewish reader, pondering these words, could not fail to see that the promised Messiah must be a supernatural being. These words could not apply rightfully to some great man, a prophet who came to do Jehovah's bidding. They tell us clearly that the Son given is "The Mighty God."

And then again, in the announcement of His birth, as found in Micah 5: 2, we have the insistence upon His eternity of being as the Son of God, "But thou, Bethlehem Ephratah, though thou be little among the thousands of Judah, yet out of thee shall He come forth unto Me that is to be ruler in Israel; whose goings forth have been from of old, from everlasting." How could these words ever find their fulfilment in one who was simply man and not also God? He was born in Bethlehem as man, it is true, but His goings forth have been from of old, from everlasting. And the Lord Jesus Christ insisted on this. In chapter 10: 30 of this Gospel we hear Him say, "I and My Father are one," and when Philip said to Him, "Show us the Father, and it sufficeth us" (chap. 14: 8), Jesus said to him, "He that hath seen Me hath seen the Father; and how sayest thou then, Show us the Father? Believest thou not that I am in the Father, and the Father in Me? The words that I speak unto you I speak not of Myself: but the Father that dwelleth in Me, He doeth the works. Believe Me that I am in the Father, and the Father in Me: or else believe Me for the very works' sake." That is, His works proved that He was the divine, eternal Son of God. Who else could have had power to still the waves, or who else could have robbed the grave of its victim? Only One could say, "I and My Father are one." And from the beginning this has been the confession of the Church of God; the Lord Jesus has ever been recognized as God manifest in the flesh.

In 2 Cor. 5: 18 we read, "And all things are of God, who hath reconciled us to Himself by Jesus Christ, and hath given to us the ministry of reconciliation." Now what is that ministry? "That God was in Christ reconciling the world unto Himself, not imputing their trespasses unto them and hath committed unto us the ministry of reconciliation." God was in Christ, not in the sense simply of empowering Christ or taking possession of Christ, but in His very nature, He was God and Man in one Person.

So again in 1 Tim. 3: 16 we are told, "And without controversy great is the mystery of godliness: God was manifest in the flesh, justified in the Spirit, seen of angels, preached unto the Gentiles, believed on in the world, received up into glory." And in the opening verses of Hebrews 1, we are told, "God, who at sundry times and in divers manners spake in time past unto the fathers by the prophets, hath in these last days spoken unto us by His Son, whom He hath appointed heir of all things, by whom also He made the worlds." Could that ever be said of a mere man? "By whom also He made the worlds; who being the brightness of His glory, and the express image of His person, and upholding all things by the word of His power, when He had by Himself purged our sins, sat down on the right hand of the Majesty on high." Let me read those words in a slightly different translation—"Who being the effulgence of His excellence and the exact expression of His character, and sustaining all things by the word of His might, when He had made purification for sins, sat down on the right hand of the Majesty in heaven." This is our Lord Jesus Christ, and therefore, he that believeth on Him believeth not only on the Man, Christ Jesus, but also on Him that sent Him, God, our Father, for Jesus could say, "He that seeth Me seeth Him that sent Me."

And then He goes on to tell us, "I am come a light into the world, that whosoever believeth on

Me should not abide in darkness." That is one of the outstanding things of John's Gospel; it is the gospel of the light and life of man. We read in the first chapter, "The life was the light of men. And the light shineth in darkness; and the darkness comprehended it not." Light is that which makes manifest, and we are told that God is light and in Him is no darkness at all. Jesus says, "I am the Light of the world. He that followeth Me shall not walk in darkness, but shall have the light of life." Therefore to turn away from Him is to turn away from the light. To follow Him and listen to His Word is to walk in the light. We read that, "If we walk in the light, as He is in the light, we have fellowship one with another, and the blood of Jesus Christ His Son cleanseth us from all sin."

Our Lord Jesus Christ is not only the light of the world, but He is the light of heaven. In Revelation 21, where we have that glorious description of the new Jerusalem, the city that hath foundation, whose Builder and Maker is God, we read in verse 22, "And I saw no temple therein: for the Lord God Almighty and the Lamb are the temple of it. And the city had no need of the sun, neither of the moon, to shine in it: for the glory of God did lighten it, and the Lamb is the light thereof." Jesus is the light of all heaven as well as the light of the world. And, thank God, many

of us can say that "God, who commanded the
light to shine out of darkness, hath shined in our
hearts, to give the light of the knowledge of the
glory of God in the face of Jesus Christ."

I am wondering if there is someone among my
readers who is perplexed by present world conditions; troubled and distressed as you think of
the misery and sorrow which are all about you.
In doubt and perplexity you are asking continually, "Why, and what, and wherefore?" Oh,
dear friend, the answer to all your questions may
be found in the knowledge of our Lord Jesus
Christ, for when you know Him, He opens everything up, He explains everything. In Him are
hid all the treasures of wisdom and knowledge.
Listen to His words again, "Whosoever believeth
in Me shall not abide in darkness." When you
put your trust in Him, when you receive Him in
faith as your own Saviour, when you yield yourself to Him, recognizing Him as your Lord, when
you take Him as your divine Teacher, He opens
up all the mysteries that perplex you. His light
shines upon the darkness and drives it away. In
Daniel 2 we read, "He knoweth what is in the
darkness, and the light dwelleth with Him." And
when you trust Him, you come into the light and
His light makes everything clear.   "The darkness
is passing," says the Apostle John in his First
Epistle, "and the true light now shineth."

In verse 47 the Lord says, "And if any man hear My words, and believe not, I judge him not: for I came not to judge the world, but to save the world." The Lord Jesus Christ came into this scene as the expression of God's matchless, sovereign grace. He bore all the shame that men heaped upon Him. He permitted them to turn away from His testimony. Some day He is going to appear as the Judge, and then if men have spurned His grace they will have to know the wrath of the Lamb. When the 6th Seal is broken, as set forth in Rev. 6, John sees the collapse of what we call civilization in the day of tribulation that is going to follow this wonderful dispensation of the grace of God. We read in verses 15, 16, "And the kings of the earth, and the great men, and the rich men, and the chief captains, and the mighty men, and every bondman, and every free man, hid themselves in the dens and in the rocks of the mountains; and said to the mountains and rocks, Fall on us, and hide us from the face of Him that sitteth on the throne, and from the wrath of the Lamb: for the great day of His wrath is come; and who shall be able to stand?" What a remarkable expression, "the wrath of the Lamb!" We do not associate the thought of wrath with a lamb; we think of a lamb as the very symbol of gentleness and meekness, and it is right that we should. We read,

"As a sheep before her shearers is dumb, so He openeth not His mouth." He allowed sinful men to blindfold and buffet Him with their hands, to cause Him intense anguish, and at last nail Him to a cross of shame. But the days of His lowliness, as the rejected One on earth, are over, and He sits exalted on the Father's throne. He is now speaking peace to all who will trust in Him. But if men persist in refusing the message, if they will not hear, the Scripture speaks of the wrath of the Lamb as that which succeeds the day of grace. Oh, how foolish it is for people to turn away from Him. He tells us in verse 48, "He that rejecteth Me, and receiveth not My words, hath one that judgeth him: the word that I have spoken, the same shall judge him in the last day." Oh, the folly of rejecting Christ! If men would only realize that in rejecting Him they are sinning against their own best interests!

In Proverbs 1 we hear Wisdom pleading with man to leave the path of folly and hearken to her voice. Who is Wisdom? It really speaks of our Lord Jesus Christ, for He is the wisdom of God. Will you turn away from that which is wisest and best? Wisdom says, "If ye turn away from Me, the day will come when you will plead in vain for mercy, for I have called, and you have refused." In verse 26, He says, "I also will laugh at your calamity; I will mock when your fear cometh; when your fear cometh as desolation, and your destruction cometh as a whirlwind; when distress and anguish cometh upon you." When will this be? When at last the great day of God's wrath has come. Now, in this day of His grace, Wisdom pleads with men to take the path of repentance, to receive the message of grace, to believe in the Lord Jesus Christ. But if men reject Him and His Word, then the very message that they have heard will rise up against them in judgment in that coming day.

There is another very striking verse in Proverbs 8: 16. (It is Wisdom speaking) "By Me princes rule, and nobles, even all the judges of the earth. I love them that love Me; and those that seek Me early shall find Me." Wisdom, that is Christ, says, "I love them that love Me." "Well," you say, "does He not love those who do not love Him?" Yes; He loves all men and gave Himself for them, but in a very special way, He loves them who love Him. But in righteousness He must judge those who spurn His grace. "He that rejecteth Me, and receiveth not My words, hath one that judgeth him: the word that I have spoken, the same shall judge him in the last day." When we reject Christ we are really sinning not only against Him and God, but against our own souls.

In the Gospel of Luke 7: 30, we read, "But the
Pharisees and lawyers rejected the counsel of
God against themselves, being not baptized of
him." And when, today, men refuse the full,
clear gospel message, sent out in the power of the
Holy Spirit, concerning our Lord Jesus Christ,
they are sinning against their own souls. If you,
my reader, have been thus acting toward Christ,
I plead with you to turn to Him and find a satisfying portion for your soul, lest someday you
will be found among them who cry in vain for
mercy. "When once the master of the house is
risen up, and hath shut to the door, and ye begin
to stand without, and to knock at the door, saying
Lord, Lord, open unto us; and He shall answer
and say unto you, I know you not whence you
are."

And now the last two verses, 49 and 50, of Chap.
12: "For I have not spoken of Myself; but the
Father which sent Me." Our Lord Jesus Christ,
when He left the Father's glory and came down
to this world, did not cease to be God; He did not
cease to be the omnipresent One; He did not cease
to be the omnipotent One; He did not cease to be
the omniscient One, but He chose not to use His
divine omniscience, but to learn of the Father. He
chose to be localized in a given, definite place, as
a Man, here on earth. And He chose not to use
His own omnipotence. but to take His place

as Man, subject to God. Therefore we are told that the works that He did, He did in the power of the Holy Spirit, and the words that He spoke, He spoke as the Father gave them to Him. This was predicted of Him long years before He came to the world, for Isaiah 50: 2 sets Him forth as to both His Deity and His humanity. We read, "Wherefore, when I came, was there no man? When I called, was there none to answer? Is My hand shortened at all, that it cannot redeem? or have I no power to deliver? Behold, at My rebuke I dry up the sea, I make the rivers a wilderness: their fish stinketh, because there is no water, and dieth for thirst." Who is the Speaker here? Anyone reading it must recognize the fact that it is God Himself. It is the Creator of all things, for it is only God who can say, "I clothe the heavens with blackness, and I make sackcloth their covering." It was God who caused the blackness to fall upon Egypt. It is God only who can say, "At My rebuke I dry up the sea" (the Red Sea). God only could say, "I make the rivers a wilderness." No one but God could do these things.

But notice the next verses. It is the same Person, but how different the language! "The Lord God hath given Me the tongue of the learned, that I should know how to speak a word in season to him that is weary: He wakeneth morning by morning, He wakeneth Mine ear to hear as the

learned." In Leeser's beautiful Jewish translation it reads, "The Lord God hath given Me the
tongue of the disciple." Notice, there is no change
in the Speaker. The One who could say, "I
clothe the heavens with blackness," now says,
"The Lord God hath given Me the tongue of the
learned, that I should know how to speak a word
in season to him that is weary." Here you have
His humanity. The Creator has come unto His
own creation. Oh, how many millions of weary
souls have heard His voice! How many have
heard Him say, "Come unto Me, all ye that labor
and are heavy laden." And they have come and
have proven how wonderfully He can fulfil the
promises He has made.

Continuing the reading in Isaiah 50:5, "The
Lord God hath opened Mine ear, and I was not
rebellious, neither turned away back. I gave My
back to the smiters, and My cheeks to them that
that plucked off the hair: I hid not My face from
shame and spitting." It is Jesus speaking through
the prophet seven hundred years before He came
into the world.

And so He says, "I have not spoken of Myself;
but the Father which sent Me, He gave Me a
commandment, what I should say, and what I
should speak." Day by day, the blessed Lord
learned of the Father what He should say to
those who heard Him preach. "He gave Me a

commandment, what I should say, and what I should speak." Thus, life everlasting is found in receiving the Word. "Verily, verily, I say unto you, He that heareth My Word, and believeth on Him that sent Me, hath everlasting life, and shall not come into condemnation; but is passed from death unto life."

"And I know that His commandment is life everlasting: whatsoever I speak therefore, even as the Father said unto Me, so I speak." And this concludes the Lord's presentation of Himself to the world. If men refuse the testimony of these first twelve chapters of John's Gospel, God has no more to say to them. He has given His full revelation. Have you received Him, or are you still rejecting Him?

CLEANSING BY WATER

✦   ✦   ✦

"Now before the feast of the passover, when Jesus knew that His hour was come that He should depart out of this world unto the Father, having loved His own which were in the world, He loved them unto the end. And supper being ended, the devil having now put into the heart of Judas Iscariot, Simon's son, to betray Him; Jesus knowing that the Father had given all things into His hands, and that He was come from God, and went to God; He riseth from supper, and laid aside His garments; and took a towel and girded Himself. After that He poureth water into a basin, and began to wash the disciples' feet, and to wipe them with the towel wherewith He was girded. Then cometh He to Simon Peter: and Peter saith unto Him, Lord, dost Thou wash my feet? Jesus answered and said unto him, What I do thou knowest not now; but thou shalt know hereafter. Peter saith unto Him, thou shalt never wash my feet. Jesus answered him, If I wash thee not, thou hast no part with Me. Simon Peter saith unto Him, Lord, not my feet only, but also my hands and my head. Jesus said to him, He that is washed needeth not save to wash his feet, but is clean every whit: and ye are clean, but not all. For He knew who should betray Him; therefore said He, Ye are not all clean. So after He had washed their feet, and had taken His garments, and was set down again, He said unto them, Know ye what I have done to you? Ye call Me Master and Lord: and ye say well; for so I am. If I then your Lord and Master, have washed your feet; ye also ought to wash one another's feet. For I have given you an example, that ye should do as I have done to you. Verily, verily, I say unto you, The servant is not greater than his lord; neither he that is sent greater than he that sent him. If ye know these things, happy are ye if ye do them" (John 13: 1-17).

W E begin, with this 13th chapter, the study of the second part of John's Gospel. We have seen how in the first twelve chapters the Lord Jesus presented Himself to the world in every possible aspect that the Holy Spirit could portray Him to men and women, in order that they might be convicted of their sin and brought to know Him as their Saviour. Now as we enter upon the second great division of the Gospel, we see our Lord manifesting Himself to His disciples and to those who have received His testimony and accepted Him as Lord and Saviour. It is they who are referred to in this verse as "His own."

We read, "Now before the feast of the passover, when Jesus knew that His hour was come." All the way through He has been looking forward to this hour; the hour when He was to go to the cross to be made sin for us, and when He was to pass on from the cross and the tomb, up yonder to the glory. Jesus, knowing that the set time had arrived when He was to go to the Father, "having loved His own which were in the world, He loved them unto the end." We have seen how in chapter 1, that expression, "His own" is found. "He came to His own, and His own received Him not," that is, He came to His own country, His own city, His own temple where

everything spoke of His glory, but His own covenant people, the majority of Israel, received Him
not. "But as many as received Him, to them gave
He the power to become the sons of God." And
these are the ones spoken of now as "His own."
"Having loved His own which were in the world."
They are His own in a five-fold sense: (1) They are
His own by creation; He brought them into being.
The very life we have comes from Him. (2) But
then more than that, they are His own by redemption; He went to the cross to purchase them. Of
course, He had not yet died on the cross when He
contemplated this little group in the upper room,
but He looks at the cross as though it were in
the past. He had come for that purpose. In the
next place (3) they are His own by the Father's
gift. In the 17th chapter of this book, seven times
over Jesus speaks to the Father of the "men that
Thou gavest Me out of the world." We who are
saved have been given to the Son by the Father.
In that sense we are His own. More than that,
(4) we are His own by right. He had to work
in our hearts and consciences convicting us of
sin, and that led to repentance toward God, and
faith in the Lord Jesus Christ. So we were born
of the Spirit and made the children of God. (5)
Then we are His own by subjugation: It was His
own grace that ended our rebellion and brought
us in chains of love to His feet. So we belong to
Him in this five-fold sense.

All believers are included in this number of whom the Spirit says, "Having loved His own which were in the world, He loved them unto the end." Someone has translated that last expression, "He loved them all the way through." Through what? Through everything. He loved Peter all the way through his boasting and failure, and He loved him back to victory and faithfulness. And, thank God, when once He takes up a poor sinner in grace, He loves him all the way through. It can be said of every Christian, "Having loved His own which were in the world, He loved them unto the end." "For He which hath begun a good work in you will perform it until the day of Jesus Christ."

And now we learn from this chapter something of how He cares for His own. After His grace has saved us from judgment, we see how He watches over His saints and keeps their feet clean as they go through a defiling world. In other words, we have here an acted parable. He is picturing that service with which He has been occupied now for 1,900 years since going back to the glory.

"And supper being ended." That word "ended" might be left out, for it is clear that the translators have placed it there without authority. The supper was not ended. It should read, "And supper being," or "during supper." "The devil having now put into the heart of Judas Iscariot, Simon's son, to betray him." Oh, the pity of it! Judas, who had walked with Him for three-and-a-half years, had heard His words of grace, seen His works of power, beheld His wonderful life and yet his heart was never won for Christ. Jesus knew all about him; He was not deceived. The Lord said of him, "Have not I chosen you twelve, and one of you is a devil?" Judas had never been regenerated. His hard heart had never glowed with love for Christ. He was one of the twelve, but he was not one who had been actually born again. It shows how one may be temporarily religious and be under the best of instruction and see the most marvelous evidences of the working of divine power and yet after all never truly turn to God as a repentant sinner and own Christ as Lord. The ways of Judas might well speak to everyone of us, warning us to examine ourselves to see whether we be in the faith or not.

Judas is about to betray Him. In the light of this, we read, "Jesus knowing that the Father had given all things into His hands, and that He was come from God, and went to God." Let those words sink into the heart. Jesus knew that the Father had given all things into His hands. Later on we hear Him saying, "All authority is given to Me in heaven and earth." He says, "Go and disciple all nations, baptizing them in the name of the Father, and of the Son, and of the Holy Spirit, teaching them to observe all things, whatsoever I have commanded you, and lo, I am with you alway."

You remember of old, in Genesis, the servant who went down to get a bride for Isaac, said to the parents of Rebecca, "My master has given all that he has unto Isaac," and so God has put everything into the hand of the Lord Jesus Christ. "Now Jesus knew that He had come from God and went to God." In His great high-priestly prayer He said, "And now, O Father, glorify thou Me with Thine own self with the glory which I had with Thee before the world was." He came from the Father. As Micah puts it, "His goings forth have been from of old, from everlasting." He came from God's fullest glory to the cross of Calvary, and then back to God He went, and there He sits at the right hand of the Father to make intercession for us.

In view of all this, He takes the servant's place. "He riseth from supper, and laid aside His garments; and took a towel and girded Himself. After that He poureth water into a basin, and began to wash the disciples' feet, and to wipe them with the towel wherewith He was girded." Our blessed Lord, He who is sovereign of the universe, takes the place of a slave. He went to one after another to wash the defiled feet of His disciples. It was customary in homes in those days to do that when a guest was entertained. A servant would come and wash his feet. But there was no one to do that for the disciples or for Jesus, and so Jesus takes the servant's place. He who had deigned to take upon Him the form of a poor man, girds Himself with a towel, and goes from one to the other and washes their feet. And as He does this, Simon Peter is watching Him. He sees Him go first to one and then another of his fellow-disciples, washing and wiping their feet. Peter's heart is filled with indignation. "Why, will John allow Him to do anything so lowly as that, And Thomas, and Matthew! Wait till He comes to me. I will never let the Lord humiliate Himself like that at my feet." Finally He came to Simon Peter, and Peter said, "Lord, dost Thou wash my feet?" In the original, he uses two emphatic pronouns here, "Dost *Thou* wash *my* feet?" And in those two words Peter puts himself in vivid contrast with the Lord Jesus Christ. But listen to the answer of Jesus. He uses two emphatic pronouns also. "Jesus answered and said unto him, What *I* do thou knowest not now; but *thou* shalt know hereafter." "Peter, I am doing something that you do not understand now." If it was simply a matter of washing the disciples' feet in literal water—that was clear to Peter. He was doing the work of a servant, cleansing their feet. But Jesus says, "No, Peter; there is a picture here. You do not yet comprehend." "What I do thou knowest not now; but thou shalt know hereafter." When was that "hereafter" to be? When would Peter really enter into the meaning of this and understand what it meant for Jesus to wash his feet? It was after he fell into the muck and mire of sin, after he, because of cowardice, denied his Lord and declared that he never knew the Man. Then it was that Jesus sought him and applied the water of the Word to Peter's defiled feet, and made him fit once more to walk in fellowship with the Lord. But right now Peter did not understand, and Jesus indicates that the understanding is to be in the future. Peter, not realizing, said to Him again with greater emphasis, *"Thou* shalt never wash *my* feet." You know it does not do to be too positive. "Thou shalt never wash *my* feet." But Jesus answered, and I think there was wonderful tenderness in His voice as He met Peter's loud affirmation in His own quiet tender way, "If *I* wash thee not, *thou* hast no part with Me." Shall we not take those words home to ourselves?—for they are not only for Peter, they are for all believers to the end of time. Jesus says to you, my friend, to me, to everyone of us, "If I wash thee not, thou hast no part with Me."

Now notice what Jesus did *not* say, and then notice what He *did* say. He did not say, "If I wash thee not, thou hast no part *in* Me." He did say, "If I wash thee not, thou hast no part *with* Me." What is the difference between "part *in* Him," and "part *with* Him?" Well, "part *in* Him," is life, and Peter already had divine life. He was already *"in* Him." To be *in* Christ is just the opposite of being in Adam. We are in Christ by new birth. And Peter had been already born of God. He had already received Him as his Saviour, and so he was in Him. But now Jesus says, "If I wash thee not, thou hast no part with Me," and *with* Him is communion. *With* Him is fellowship. Every believer is linked up with the Lord Jesus Christ by two links. There is the link of union, and the link of union is so strong that the weight of a world could not break it. He says, "My sheep hear My voice and I know them, and they follow Me, and I give unto them eternal life, and they shall never perish, neither shall any man pluck them out of My hand." It might be translated. "They shall never, by any means, perish, neither shall any pluck them out of My hand." That is the link of union.

But there is also the link of communion, and the link of communion is so fragile that the least unconfessed sin will break it in a moment. and

the only way it can be reformed is by confessing
and forsaking the sin that snapped it.

And so Jesus says, "If I wash thee not, thou
canst have no part with Me." He means, "If I
am not daily washing thee from the defilement
that continually clings to one's feet you cannot
have fellowship with Me." Is there anything more
precious than knowing that you can go to Him
about everything? You can tell Him all your
trials and difficulties, your joys, etc. You can go
to Him with thanksgiving and praise. It is so
easy to go to Him with our troubles and distress
and spread our sorrows and worries before Him
—and we should do that. He enters into them
all with us. It is written, "In all their affliction
He was afflicted." But He would have us share
our joys with Him too when things are bright and
glad, and tell Him all about those things that fill
our hearts with cheer. But we can't do this and
have fellowship with Him if we are defiled by
unconfessed sin. We must be clean to enjoy communion with Christ. "If I wash thee not, thou
canst have no part with Me."

Now Peter goes to the other extreme. He says,
"Lord, not my feet only, but also my hands and
my head." As much as to say, "Oh, Lord, I did
not understand, but if having part with Thee
means being washed by Thee, I won't resist any
more. You can give me a full bath if you want

to." But Jesus says, "No, Peter; you are wrong again. He that is bathed needeth not save to wash his feet, but is clean every whit: and ye are clean, but not all. For He knew who should betray Him; therefore said He, Ye are not all clean." He knew who should betray Him, so He said, "You are not all clean." Judas had never known that first cleansing of regeneration. What is it the Saviour is telling us here? Why, this: When a Christian fails and becomes defiled in thought or deed or word, he does not thereby cease to be a Christian; he does not cease to be a child of God and have to begin all over again, but he simply needs to have his feet washed—he needs to have his walk cleansed.

So many dear Christians with sensitive consciences feel that if they sin, it is all over with them and they are lost again. The enemy of our souls comes to us and says, "It's all up with you now. You will have to start all over again." Some dear people are always getting saved over and over again! I remember an incident which would have been almost amusing if it had not been so sad. A dear young fellow came out to the front of the church where I was preaching. He made a profession and we thought we had a new convert and rejoiced over him as such. After we had prayed with him and given him encouraging and assuring scriptures one of his friends came up to

him and said, "Well, I am glad to see you out here
at the front again. How many times have you
been converted now?" "Oh," he said, "this makes
ninety-nine times." Poor, dear fellow! He had
such a tender conscience that he thought that
every time he sinned that he had to get regenerated all over again. In other words, he was trying to get a full bath everytime he became defiled!
"He that is washed needeth not save to wash his
feet, but is clean every whit."

You see, in those days, a rich householder had
a large bath in the center court and when he
rose in the morning he would step down into the
bath and have a complete cleansing. Then he
went out with his open sandals, and as the streets
of those oriental cities were very filthy, when he
came back to the house, one of his servants came
and washed his feet. He did not have a bath every
time he came in, but he did need to have his feet
washed.

When we are cleansed by the precious blood of
Christ we are washed all over, once for all. That
does not have to take place again. "The blood of
Jesus Christ His (God's) Son cleanseth us from
all sin." That is, it cleanseth us continually. We
are always clean in that sense.

But now, "He that is bathed needeth not save
to wash his feet," and feet speak of our walk. We
read, "He will keep the feet of His saints," so

every time we fail, as believers, we are to go to
our blessed Lord, and say, "Cleanse me now by
the washing of water by the Word." We read in
Ephesians 5: 25, 26, "Husbands, love your wives,
even as Christ also loved the Church, and gave
Himself for it; that He might sanctify and cleanse
it with the washing of water by the Word." You
see the Word of God is likened to water. In Psalm
119: 9 we read, "Wherewithal shall a young man
cleanse his way? By taking heed thereto according to Thy Word." Suppose my hand becomes defiled and unclean. What do I do? Why, I go and
apply the water, and after I apply the water, the
uncleanness disappears. When my heart and conscience have become defiled, what do I do, I let
the blessed Lord apply the water of the Word.
"For if we confess our sins, He is faithful and
just to forgive us our sins, and to cleanse us from
all unrighteousness." The Word of God is the
water which is applied to our hearts and consciences and cleanses us from all defilement.

Jesus recognized the fact that they had not all
had the initial cleansing. Judas had not known
that cleansing. "He knew who should betray
Him." Judas had never been washed by Christ
at all. Then after He had washed their feet and
had taken His garments and sat down, He said,
"Know ye what I have done to you?" Well, of
course they saw what He had done, but they had

not learned the hidden lesson yet. So He said, "Know ye what I have done to you?" "Ye call Me Master and Lord: and ye say well; for so I am. If I then, your Lord and Master, have washed your feet; ye also ought to wash one another's feet."

Will you notice one thing here that I am afraid many Christians overlook. He says, "You call Me Master and Lord, and ye say well; for so I am." What do you call Him? He approved these disciples calling Him "Master" and "Lord." Have you ever noticed this in reading the New Testament, that no lover of the Lord Jesus Christ is ever represented as addressing Him individually by His proper name? We never read that Peter said, "Jesus" when addressing Him. We never read that John said it. You never read of anyone saying, "Lovely Jesus," "Sweet Jesus," etc. That is very significant; is it not? How do they speak of Him? "Master," "Lord," "My Lord," "My God," etc. And He commends them for that. "Ye call Me Master and Lord: and ye say well; for so I am." Whenever the Holy Spirit is guiding us in our prayers when we address Him, we will magnify Him. He will lead us to recognize Him as Lord. Some people address our Saviour in a way that they would not address the President of the United States. If you were presented to the President you would not call him by his given name. You would not dare do that. You would use some expression of appreciation of the dignity of his office. You would be afraid to do otherwise. Well, when you address your Saviour next time, just remember that, while His name is Jesus, He is our Master and our Lord, and the Holy Spirit loves to glorify Him.

"Ye call Me Master and Lord: and ye say well: for so I am. If I then, your Lord and Master, have washed your feet; ye also ought to wash one another's feet." Now what is He telling us here? Some dear people, some of the most godly people I have ever met, believe that the Lord was instituting a third Christian ordinance, and so they observe from time to time what they call the "Washing of Feet." But I am afraid sometimes one forgets that Jesus said, "What I do thou knowest not now, but thou shalt know hereafter." If it was a matter of literally washing feet in water they knew all about it. But it is easy to miss the real meaning of this act.

How do we wash one another's feet? What was the water? The water was the Word. Of what do our feet speak? Our ways. We wash one another's feet when we apply the Word of God to our ways. When a Christian slips a bit you say, perhaps, "He was a wonderfully fine out-and-out Christian, but now he is getting a bit worldly." But what are you going to do about it? You can

just ignore it and pass it by, or you can criticize
and say very unkind things; but neither of these
methods will help very much. You can go to the
dear brother or sister and tenderly point out from
the Word of God the mistake they are making,
the sin into which they are falling. You can show
them how their lives are becoming defiled. Thus
you wash their feet. Did you every try to wash
your brother's feet? There is a Scripture which
reads, "Thou shalt not hate thy brother in thine
heart: thou shalt in any wise rebuke thy neighbor, and not suffer sin upon him" (Lev. 19: 17).
It takes grace to be kindly faithful. Some say
to me, "Oh, well, I have tried it, but it doesn't
do any good." We need much grace ourselves to
wash another's feet. If you are going to wash
your neighbor's feet, you ought to be careful
about the temperature of the water. You would
not go to anyone and say, "Put your feet into this
bucket of scalding water, and I will wash them
for you." Ice-water is just as bad. Some people
go at you in such a way that you just shrink back
from them. Some are so hot, and some are so
cold and icy and formal. You don't appreciate
either; do you? The proper thing is this, when
you see your brother going wrong, get into the
presence of the Lord about it. Then remember
the word that tells us, as recorded in Gal. 6: 1:
"Brethren, if a man be overtaken in a fault, ye

which are spiritual, restore such an one in the spirit of meekness; considering thyself, lest thou also be tempted." When you go to your brother like this seeking to apply the Word of God faithfully. He must be in a very bad state indeed if he will not listen. If he is not ready, you can continue to pray and wait for the time when God may permit you to help him.

"Verily, verily, I say unto you, The servant is not greater than his lord; neither he that is sent greater than he that sent him. If ye know these things, happy are ye if ye do them."

THE TRAITOR EXPOSED

✓ ✓ ✓

"I speak not of you all: I know whom I have chosen:
but that the scripture may be fulfilled, He that eateth
bread with Me hath lifted up his heel against Me. Now I
tell you before it come, that, when it is come to pass, ye
may believe that I am He. Verily, verily, I say unto you,
He that receiveth whomsoever I send receiveth Me; and
he that receiveth Me receiveth Him that sent Me. When
Jesus had thus said, He was troubled in spirit, and testified, and said, Verily, verily, I say unto you, that one of
you shall betray Me. Then the disciples looked one on
another, doubting of whom He spake. Now there was
leaning on Jesus' bosom one of His disciples, whom Jesus
loved. Simon Peter therefore beckoned to him, that he
should ask who it should be of whom He spake. He then
lying on Jesus' breast saith unto Him, Lord, who is it?
Jesus answered, He it is, to whom I shall give a sop,
when I have dipped it. And when He had dipped the sop,
He gave it to Judas Iscariot, the son of Simon. And after
the sop Satan entered into him. Then said Jesus unto
him, That thou doest, do quickly. Now no man at the
table knew for what intent He spake this unto him. For
some of them thought, because Judas had the bag, that
Jesus had said unto him, Buy those things that we have
need of against the feast; or, that he should give something to the poor. He then having received the sop went
immediately out: and it was night" (John 13: 18-30).

✓ ✓ ✓

T HE central theme of this particular section
is the treachery of Judas. When one considers the privileges that Judas had enjoyed

and realizes how little impression they made upon his heart and mind and what the final result was, these things might well cause each one of us individually to examine ourselves and search our hearts in the presence of God. Here was a man, who, for three-and-a-half wonderful years, walked with the blessed Son of God. He had opportunities to see His wondrous works of grace, heard the marvelous things that came from His lips, saw His life—(he could see what others could not see)—and surely must have known that here was one who was evidently a superhuman Person moving among them. John said, you remember, "We beheld His glory, the glory as of the Only Begotten of the Father, full of grace and truth." Judas had the opportunity of thus beholding Him. He must have had many a quiet talk with Him, and he must have been highly esteemed by the rest of the disciples, and yet all the time he had never yielded his heart to the Lord Jesus Christ. You remember the Saviour said, "Have not I chosen you twelve, and one of you is a devil?" He did not say, "one of you shall become a devil," but, "one of you *is* a devil." And when He speaks to the Father, as in the seventeenth chapter, He says, "Those that Thou gavest Me I have kept, and none of them is lost, but the son of perdition; that the scripture might be fulfilled." We might think perhaps, reading that verse carelessly, that He meant, "Those that Thou gavest Me I have kept and have only lost one, the son of perdition." But that is not what He said. The son of perdition was not one of those who had been given to Christ by the Father. He was in Christ's company but he was never of that company. It is quite possible to have an interest in Scripture, to be exercised to a certain extent about a needy world, to act and talk like a Christian, and yet never be born of God. This ought to challenge us to face the questions, "Have I ever honestly come to God as a repentant sinner? And have I put my trust in Him, and yielded my heart and life to Him?"

I said a moment ago that Judas was evidently very highly respected by the disciples. You might ask, "On what do you base that supposition?" He was the chosen one to be the treasurer of the little company. When you choose a treasurer you always want a man of probity and of integrity, of good reputation, one whom you can confide in as one above suspicion of dishonesty. So the impression that Judas made on the disciples in those early days, at least, was that of a man of absolute reliability. We may almost say, in fact, Judas was the real gentleman of all the twelve. Most of them were hard-working men. They came from the region about the Sea of Galilee where the poorer class of people dwelt, but Judas came from

Judea, from a town called Kerioth and he was perhaps the most distinguished man of the entire apostolic company. And yet he was the one man whose heart Jesus never won and whose conscience Jesus never truly reached. In our last message we noticed that Jesus said, "He that is bathed needeth not save to wash his feet, but is clean every whit, and ye are clean, but not all." And the Holy Spirit explains why He said that, "for He knew who should betray Him, therefore He said, Ye are not all clean." That is a marvelous thing. The Son of God saw through this man during those three-and-a-half years, and He sees through hypocrites today. He sees into the very heart of people who are not real. Outwardly they may appear to be true and genuine, but Christ sees into the heart and He knows if any are not clean.

He tells us in verse eighteen, "I know whom I have chosen; but that the scripture may be fulfilled, He that eateth bread with Me hath lifted up his heel against Me." He knows all those who have put their heart-trust in Him. Judas' treachery was foreknown, but this does not mean that he was foreordained to do that dreadful thing. Nothing of the kind. There is a great deal of difference between God's foreknowledge and God's foreordination. He looked down through the ages and knew what Judas would do, but He never foreordained it. If you can think of a man as free who is led captive by the devil, Judas was free. He was free to yield to Christ or to Satan, and so you and I can choose. We should not blame our failures and sins on any predetermined fate. God has never decreed that any man or woman should live in sin, or that anyone should be lost. The Lord Himself said, "Ye will not come to Me that ye might have life," and to all men He says, "Whosoever will, let him take the water of life freely." So Judas could have been saved, but he would not trust Jesus; and God foreknew this, and so his sin was spoken of beforehand in the Book of Psalms. The Lord Jesus knew it. All the time He was with him, Jesus knew what was going on in his heart, and He knew he was to be the agent of the devil to deliver Him to wicked men.

He said, "Now I tell you before it come, that, when it is come to pass, ye may believe that I am He." In other words, He says, "I don't want you to think that I was helplessly put into the hands of my captors, that I was taken by surprise. I have foreseen all this. I know what is going to take place; I must be crucified." But He told them that the third day He would arise again from the dead. "When that time comes," He says, "you will understand that I am." Again He uses the Divine Name, "I Am." "Verily,

verily, I say unto you, He that receiveth whomsoever I send receiveth Me; and he that receiveth Me receiveth Him that sent Me." It was of comfort for the apostles, as a little later they were to commence the work of the evangelization of a lost world. They were to go as His representatives. Paul said in after years, "We are ambassadors for Christ." An Ambassador speaks for his Government, and as Christ sends His servants into the world they go out to witness for Him. That's why He could say, "Whose soever sins ye remit, they are remitted unto them; and whose soever sins ye retain, they are retained." This is not some peculiar priestly function, but it means that every servant of Christ can go to any sinner and say, "I come proclaiming the remission of sins if you come to Christ, and if you refuse to come to Christ for the remission of sins then they cannot be remitted." This authority have all His servants. Whosoever receives them, receives Him. "When Jesus had thus said, He was troubled in spirit." Though He was God, our Lord was a true Man. He was not only God but God manifest in flesh. In becoming man He took a human spirit, a human soul and a human body. Here we read, "He was troubled in spirit." As He looked forward to what was ahead, He groaned in anguish as He thought of the judgment that the treachery of Judas was to bring down upon that guilty man. No soul will ever be lost without filling His soul with grief. "Verily, verily, I say unto you, That one of you shall betray Me (one of you who has been so close to Me, who has shared so many things with Me, one of you who has failed to believe Me and trust Me)—one of you shall betray Me." Oh, I wonder if He looks down from heaven today and if His holy eyes can discern here and there among those who read these pages one who is unreal and hypocritical, and I wonder if He is saying, "One of you shall betray Me." For, if one professes the Christian name only and does not have genuine heart trust in Him, there is no telling to what depths of iniquity he may sink.

The disciples were troubled, and doubted of whom He spoke. They could not trust themselves. They each wondered, "Could it be I?" They asked one of another, "Is it I?" On His bosom was leaning one of His disciples, John, the human author of this book, who never refers to himself by name. He was the youngest of the Apostles. One of the Early Church writers, Tertullian, says John was an adolescent when called by Jesus. This lad was very dear to the Son of God. Oh, how Jesus loves to see young men and women giving themselves to Him, yielding themselves wholly to Him. Young people, there is nothing greater on this earth than to

bring your young lives to Christ. You can be
sure of this, that He will indeed love you as an
individual. You remember that young man who
came to Him with his question about eternal life,
and Jesus put him to the test—"Sell all that thou
hast . . . and come, follow Me," and the young
man turned away sorrowful for he had great
possessions. Jesus, looking upon him, loved him.
He saw the possibilities in that youth. He saw
what might be if he would yield himself to Christ.
Here was young John whose affectionate heart
went out to Christ in a way which older ones
perhaps would not have felt like expressing. He
lay with his head upon the bosom of the Lord.
Simon Peter beckoned to him and said, "Ask Him
to tell you of whom He speaks." "John saith
unto Him, Lord, who is it?" And Jesus, in a
very low voice, said, "He to whom I shall give a
morsel." It was customary in those days to hand
a morsel to some special one as a token of real
affection. And Jesus said, "John, notice the
one to whom I give this morsel; he is the one
who will betray Me." So Jesus dipped the morsel
and handed it to Judas. Judas! Will he receive
it? Judas had the impudence to reach out and
take it from the One for whose arrest he had
already been bargaining. And we read, "After
the sop Satan entered into him"—in a new way
now. Judas, by this further act, had put himself

absolutely under the domination of the devil.
Now it is all over with Judas and there is no
more possibility of repentance. Jesus recognized
that he had crossed the dead-line. So the Lord
Jesus turned to him and said solemnly, "What
thou doest, do quickly." As much as to say,
"Judas, you have sold yourself to the devil. You
have despised every opportunity of mercy. You
have trampled on My love and grace. You have
hardened your heart against the goodness of God.
Now, Judas, make an end of it. What thou doest,
do quickly." No one at the table understood
what He meant. Some of them thought because
Judas was the treasurer of the company that
Jesus may have meant, "Go buy those things that
we have need of against the feast." They did
not know that the traitor was about to sell the
Lord for thirty pieces of silver. Some thought
perhaps Jesus had told him to give something to
the poor. Is not that interesting? Would they
have thought that if such had not been a common
thing in the life of our Lord? Don't you see, He
was accustomed to do that. He always thought
of the poor. He said, "Ye have the poor always
with you." It was very natural for them to
think, "Now He has learned of some poor needy
one, and He is sending Judas out to minister to
him." That was the heart of the Son of God.
Oh, what a contrast to the heart of Judas! His

heart was filled with covetousness. He was going out to line his purse with the silver which came from the sale of the Son of God.

"He then having received the sop went immediately out: and it was night." It is always night when people turn their backs on God. It is always night when they trample the goodness of Jesus beneath their feet. And if you are doing that today, the sun may be bright outside, but it is night inside your heart until Jesus, the light of life, comes in. For Judas, there was never again to be light. He went out and it was night in his poor dark soul, and, for him, the beginning of the blackness of darkness which goes on forever. Oh, how many of us can thank God that in the riches of His grace, He has won these poor hearts of ours. Why did Judas trample on all His love? We cannot understand it, but we may be sure He had every opportunity to be saved.

THE ELEVENTH COMMANDMENT

✓ ✓ ✓

"Therefore, when he was gone out Jesus said, Now is the Son of Man glorified, and God is glorified in Him. If God be glorified in Him, God shall also glorify Him in Himself, and shall straightway glorify Him. Little children, yet a little while I am with you. Ye shall seek Me: and as I said unto the Jews, Whither I go, ye cannot come; so now I say to you. A new commandment I give unto you, That ye love one another; as I have loved you, that ye also love one another. By this shall all men know that ye are My disciples, if ye have love one to another. Peter said unto him, Lord, whither goest Thou? Jesus answered him, Whither I go, thou canst not follow Me now; but thou shalt follow Me afterwards. Peter said unto Him, Lord, why cannot I follow Thee now? I will lay down my life for Thy sake. Jesus answered him, Wilt thou lay down thy life for My sake? Verily, verily, I say unto thee, The cock shall not crow, till thou hast denied Me thrice" (John 13: 31-38).

✓ ✓ ✓

OUR Lord and His disciples were still in the upper room where they had observed that last passover together, as we learn from the other Gospels, that had been followed by the institution of the Lord's Supper, that sacred feast of love which has been kept by God's beloved people all down through the centuries since. Judas had left the little company. Moved by the worst of motives, controlled by covetousness, he had gone out to meet the chief priests and to receive the money they had promised him in view of a little later betraying the Lord Jesus into their hands. And now as the Saviour was left alone with the eleven whose hearts were strangely troubled because of certain things He had already told them, He spoke with a new joy and said, "Now is the Son of Man glorified, and God is glorified in Him."

It did not look as though God was about to be glorified, and during the next three days they must have had plenty of doubts indeed as to God being glorified in the events that took place. The Lord had said that He was going out to die, that He was to be betrayed into the hands of sinners. Could that glorify God? He had said that He was to be buried and then raised again, and it was in this, His death and His resurrection, that God was to be glorified. For in His sacrificial death upon the cross, He was to settle the sin question in a way that would meet every claim of the holiness of God's nature and the righteousness of His throne. And we may say that in that death of His upon the tree, God has received more glory than He ever lost by Adam's sin and by all the guilt and enmity and iniquity that came into the world since.

For after all, men are but finite—finite sinners it is true—and as such have dishonored God. It could be said of every man, "God, in whose hand thy breath is, hast thou not glorified." But the Lord Jesus was the infinite One who had linked Deity with humanity in order that He might give Himself a ransom for our souls. And because He was Himself infinite, the work He did upon Calvary's cross had infinite value, and therefore we are right in saying that God received more glory out of that work than He ever lost by finite man's sin. And as proof that He has been glorified, God raised His Son from the dead, glorifying Jesus, the One who had accomplished the work. "If God be glorified in Him, God shall also glorify Him in Himself, and shall straightway glorify Him."

The thought of the Father's glory was very much in the heart of Jesus at this time. In fact— it may seem strange to some of us to say it—but our Lord apparently was far more concerned about glorifying God than He was about saving sinners. How we like to think the opposite! We like to think that our salvation was the important thing, that the great thing Jesus came to do was to save our souls. And He did come for that. "The Son of Man came," He said, "not to be ministered unto but to minister and to give His life a ransom for many." "Christ also loved the

Church and gave Himself for it." But there was something greater than the salvation of sinners that occupied His heart, and that was glorifying the Father. So in the seventeenth chapter when we see Him before God as our great High Priest, anticipating the work of the cross, we hear Him saying, "I have glorified Thee upon the earth, I have finished the work that Thou gavest Me to do." God's glory is first, and then that finished work of the cross by which our souls are saved.

I remember hearing of a Universalist, a man who believed that all men will eventually be saved, saying once to an earnest Christian, "I have a far higher conception of the work of the atonement than you have, for you believe that even though Christ died on the cross there are thousands upon thousands, perhaps millions of men who will be lost forever. I have a far higher view of the atonement than that. I believe that if one soul were ever lost since Christ has died, His atonement would be the greatest failure that has ever taken place in the universe."

The Christian replied, "Oh, no. I have a higher conception of it than that. I dare to say even though not one soul were ever saved, the atonement has been the greatest success of anything that has ever taken place in the universe, for in that atoning work God has been honored and glorified as He never could have been otherwise."

But now the wonderful thing is that our salvation is linked up with God's glory. You see, God's heart went out to sinful man, but He could not save sinners till sin was settled for, for it would violate the righteousness of His throne. He could not save sinners if it involved His acting in a way that was contrary to the holiness of His nature. So His own beloved Son, the Eternal One, the One whose goings forth have been from of old, from everlasting, became incarnate. In humility He became Man and went to that cross, paid the full price of our redemption, and every claim that God had against a sinner was met, and now God can be just and the Justifier of him that believeth in Jesus. So our salvation and God's glory stand or fall together. Christ has given Himself for us, an offering and a sacrifice of a sweet smelling savor unto God, and because of God's satisfaction in the work His Son has accomplished, He can now open His arms and invite every guilty sinner to come to Him and offer full, complete pardon and justification from all things; yes, cleansing from every guilty stain to those who come in the name of Jesus. Have you come?

A lady on one occasion came to a servant of God. When asked if she was saved, she replied, "I don't understand it. I see that Jesus died for me, but surely there is something I must do. That seems too simple a way for anyone to be saved."

And the other said, "My dear friend, it was God who sent His Son to die. It was God who put on Him all that our sins deserved. Christ has borne that judgment for you, and now God is satisfied, and if God is satisfied surely you should be."

She looked up somewhat startled as she said, "I had never seen it that way before. Surely I should be satisfied with that which satisfies God. Yes, I can trust Him, I can take Him at His Word."

Have you done that? Do you realize that on the cross the sin question has been settled? Now when you receive the Lord Jesus, you stand cleared of every charge.

He who glorified God on the cross has been raised from the dead, taken up to the Father's right hand, and there God has glorified Him with His own self with the glory which He had with the Father before the world began.

Jesus was looking upon all this as an accomplished fact when He spoke as He did as recorded in verses thirty-one and thirty-two. And then He added, "Little children"—only a few more hours and then He was going out to die—"yet a little while I am with you. Ye shall seek Me: and as I said unto the Jews, Whither I go, ye cannot come; so now I say to you." He was going away and He was going to leave His disciples in the world to be witnesses for Himself. While He was here, He said, "I am the Light of the world." But He was going back to the heavens from whence He came, and the disciples, after He left here, were to shine as lights in this gloomy world. It was then He gave this new commandment. "A new commandment I give unto you, That ye love one another; as I have loved you, that ye also love one another. By this shall all men know that ye are my disciples, if ye have love one to another." It was His last charge to His saints before He went to the cross. Looking down through the years, He knew they would be in a hostile world and be hated of all men for His name's sake, and He pleaded with them, "Don't hate one another. Don't be ungracious and unkind and quarrelsome and discourteous to each other. You who have been redeemed by the same precious blood, indwelt by the same Holy Spirit, be ye kind one to another, tenderhearted, forgiving one another, even as God for Christ's sake hath forgiven you. A new commandment give I unto you, that ye love one another." May we not well challenge ourselves and each one ask the question in his or her own heart, "How have I answered to this command of my Saviour? Am I characterized by love for my brethren in Christ? Or have I so far forgotten my responsibility as a Christian that I have permitted malice and envy and jealousy and even hatred to well up in my heart? Have I cherished these evil things?" There are children of God who are cold and hard and indifferent and critical and unkind. We may well face these things in the presence of God.

How much bitterness has been engendered through the years by religious controversy! I remember reading of a striking incident in the life of that wonderful man of God, Samuel Rutherford, whose last words are embodied in that beautiful hymn, "Immanuel's Land." Rutherford, the author of a whole volume of heavenly letters that bear the celestial aroma, was a Church of Scotland minister, and his place of ministry a little Scottish town known as Anwoth. There he labored among a happy group of earnest believers. But there were troubles in connection with the Government. The British Government had declared that the Scottish Church must no longer follow the Presbyterian order, which was that which Rutherford used, and sought to impose an altogether different, and as the Scots thought, foreign order of things upon them. And Rutherford was one of those devoted ministers who for conscience' sake refused to admit and would not acknowledge the authority of the king's bishops.

Because he refused to conform, Rutherford was banished to Aberdeen and put in prison there. He always said he would not permit a bishop of any kind to stand in his pulpit. But before he left, while he was still pastor in the church, there came one night to the manse a stranger. Knocking at the door, Rutherford himself welcomed him. The stranger did not give his name, but said he was on his way, and would be glad of accommodations for the night. They ate together. Afterwards, Rutherford took up the Word of God and then he said, "Now we have the catechism, the reading of the Scriptures and prayer, and we expect every visitor to participate with us." It was a good old-fashioned custom. I wish we had more like it today. So the servants were called in and Rutherford read the Scripture. Then he began to catechise the whole house and turned eventually to the stranger, and he said, "How many commandments are there?"

The stranger looked up, and without batting an eye, answered, "Eleven."

Rutherford looked abashed. "I asked how many commandments there are."

"Yes, I understood. Eleven."

"I am surprised that in all the Scottish realm there should be found a man so ignorant that he doesn't know there are only ten commandments."

And then the stranger looked up and said, "A new commandment I give unto you, that ye love one another."

"Oh," said Rutherford, "what is your name, stranger?"

He said, "My name is Usher. I am archbishop of Ireland."

An archbishop in Rutherford's home! The man who had said he could have no fellowship with anyone who held to another ecclesiastical order than his own. Broken, ashamed of his harshness, Rutherford begged the stranger to lead them all in prayer, and responded fervently as the archbishop bore them all up before God.

Oh, how we need to be reminded of this eleventh commandment, "A new commandment give I unto you, that ye love one another." It is not enough, my brethren, to know that you are saved. It is not enough that you stand firmly, as I hope you do, for the fundamental truths. Back of all fundamental truth there is a great fundamental experience that everyone of us should have.

"Though I preach with the tongue of men and of angels and have not love, it profiteth me nothing. And though I give my body to be burned, and though I understand all mystery and all knowledge and have not love, I am nothing." It would be well for every one of us to test ourselves every little while by the thirteenth chapter of First Corinthians. "Love suffereth long and is kind. Love envieth not. Love is not boastful. Love is not conceited. Love doth not behave itself discourteously. Love is not self-seeking. Love is not quickly angry. Love thinketh no evil." That is, love doesn't impute evil and try to judge people's motives. "Love rejoiceth not in iniquity but rejoices in the truth. Beareth all things, believeth all things, hopeth all things, endureth all things."

We might take these words as a character sketch of our Lord Jesus Christ. You could put in His name here, and they all would be true of Him. "Christ suffereth long and is kind. Christ envieth not. Christ vaunteth not Himself. Christ is not puffed up. Christ does not behave Himself unseemly. Christ sought not His own. Christ was not easily provoked. Christ thinks no evil. Christ rejoices not in iniquity. Christ beareth all things, Christ believeth all things, Christ hopeth all things. Christ endureth all things. Christ never fails." And if you and I have the mind of Christ, this divine love will be manifested in us. If it is not then all our talk about being fundamentalists, all our talk about standing for the truth, goes for very little indeed. We may be tremendously in earnest in contending for certain great outstanding facts, but if we contend in a bad spirit, we only harm the cause that we rep-

resent. And if back of our contention for the
faith there is no sincere love for our brethren,
yea, love for all men, then we dishonor the One
who Himself is the Way, the Truth, and the Life.
He has said, "By this shall all men know that ye
are My disciples if ye have love one to another."
That is, we do not prove we are His disciples by
striving for a creed, however great and exact it
may be. We do not prove we are His disciples by
insisting on the fact that we believe in an inspired
Bible, blessed as that is. We do not prove that
we are His disciples by loudly proclaiming our
faith in the virgin birth and perfect humanity of
our Saviour, His atoning work, His physical
resurrection and His present intercession at God's
right hand. We do not prove to men and women
that we are really Christians by insisting that we
believe in the pre-millennial coming of our Lord
Jesus and all these great and precious verities,
but, "By this shall all men know that ye are My
disciples, if ye have love one to another." Let us
not forget this, and let us examine ourselves faithfully and honestly and see if we are allowing
hatred and malice in our hearts while presuming
to be holding to our Lord Jesus Christ.

Not only here does He speak of this, but in
chapter fifteen, verse twelve, He says, "This is
My commandment, That ye love one another, as
I have loved you. Greater love hath no man than

this, that a man lay down his life for his friends.
Ye are My friends, if ye do whatsoever I command you." You see, real love is unselfish. Love
delights to bear and do. Do not talk about loving
one another if you are not concerned about serving one another as God enables.

Look at the First Epistle of John. The beloved
disciple who heard our Lord utter these words
never forgot them. We are told that when he
was an old man, after he was too feeble to walk,
he used to be carried into the assembly of the
saints at Ephesus, and then two of the elders
would assist him to his feet while he gave a few
words of godly counsel to the people of God. And
it is said that he always ended with this expression, "Little children, love one another." And
here it is written in First John 2: 7, and following, "Brethren, I write no new commandment
unto you, but an old commandment which ye had
from the beginning. The old commandment is
the word which ye have heard from the beginning. Again a new commandment I write unto
you, which thing is true in Him and in you: because the darkness is past and the true light now
shineth. He that saith he is in the light and
hateth his brother, is in darkness even until now.
He that loveth his brother abideth in the light,
and there is none occasion of stumbling in him."

Look at verse seventeen of chapter three: "But whoso hath this worlds good, and seeth his brother have need, and shutteth up his bowels of compassion from him, how dwelleth the love of God in him? My little children, let us not love in word, neither in tongue; but in deed and in truth."

Love is a very practical thing. To what extent are we manifesting it toward those in more difficult circumstances than ourselves? To what extent are we manifesting it to those who have failed and sinned? Are we content simply to point out their faults and criticize and say hard, unkind things? Or do we love them enough to go to them in the Spirit of Christ and seek to recover them to Himself? "A new commandment I give unto you, That ye love one another."

But now Simon Peter for the moment listens but does not hear. What our Lord has said, recorded in these two verses, appears to make no impression upon him at all. He is still thinking of what the Saviour said a little while before, "Whither I go, ye cannot come." And with that in mind, he breaks in and destroys for the moment the continuity of thought. "Simon Peter said unto Him, Lord, whither goest Thou? Jesus answered him, Whither I go" (that is to death) "thou canst not follow Me now; but thou shalt follow Me afterwards." Our Lord was speaking as a prophet. He was going to be crucified. Peter was not ready for that, though he did not realize it. But Jesus said, "Some day you will follow Me even in that," and he did. For in his old age we are told Peter, too, was crucified. Peter laid down his life on a cross as a martyr for the gospel of the Lord Jesus Christ.

But Peter did not understand, did not recognize his own limitations. Peter said unto Him, "Lord, why cannot I follow Thee now? I will lay down my life for Thy sake." He meant every word of it. Evidently he thought he was prepared for that. But he did not know the deceitfulness of his own heart.

"Jesus answered him, Wilt thou lay down thy life for My sake? Verily, verily, I say unto thee, The cock shall not crow, till thou hast denied Me thrice."

In the original text there is no break between the last verse of chapter thirteen and the first verse of chapter fourteen. What is Jesus really saying? Listen to it, and be encouraged if you have failed.

"Verily, verily, I say unto thee, The cock shall not crow, till thou hast denied Me thrice. Let not your heart be troubled; ye believe in God, believe also in Me."

"Peter, I know you are going to fail Me. You do not realize how untrustworthy your heart is, but, oh, Peter, when at last you discover the corruption that is there and you are broken-hearted to think of what you have done, I want you to remember, Peter, I love you still, and I am going to prepare a place for you."

Do you know this Saviour? Oh, if you do not, I would plead with you, acquaint thyself with Him and be at peace. He wants you to know Him, and He bids you come to Him today. He says, "Him that cometh to Me, I will in no wise cast out."

THE FATHER'S HOUSE AND THE LORD'S RETURN

✓ ◄ ✓

"Let not your heart be troubled: ye believe in God, believe also in Me. In My Father's house are many mansions: if it were not so, I would have told you. I go to prepare a place for you. And if I go and prepare a place for you, I will come again, and receive you unto Myself; that where I am, there ye may be also. And whither I go ye know, and the way ye know. Thomas saith unto Him, Lord, we know not whither Thou goest; and how can we know the way? Jesus saith unto him, I am the Way, the Truth, and the Life: no man cometh unto the Father, but by Me" (John 14: 1-6).

✓ ✓ ✓

IN these verses, there are two outstanding truths emphasized: first, that of the Father's house, and second, our Lord's personal return for His own.

We are all familiar with the fact, I presume, that the Bible was not written in chapters and verses. These breaks in the text were put in by editors, and that in rather recent years, some of them as late as the time of the Protestant Reformation. And sometimes the chapter-breaks seem to come at rather unfortunate places, and I think

it is the case here. Who, for instance, beginning
to read the first verse of chapter fourteen, connects it in his mind with our Lord's words to the
Apostle Peter at the close of chapter thirteen?
And yet, there is a very real connection, as we
have seen. The Lord Jesus had been giving His
last messages to His disciples. He had intimated
that soon they would forsake Him and flee. He
had told them that He was going away and for
the present they could not come where He was to
go. He was going home to God by way of the
cross and resurrection, and told questioning Peter
that he could not follow immediately. But the
Lord says, "Thou shalt follow Me afterwards."
Peter did not understand that, and said: "Lord,
why cannot I follow Thee now? I will lay down
my life for Thy sake. Jesus answered him, Wilt
thou lay down thy life for My sake? Verily,
verily, I say unto thee, The cock shall not crow
till thou hast denied Me thrice." And then he
immediately adds: "Let not your heart be
troubled: ye believe in God, believe also in Me."

You see, the Lord Jesus is addressing these
words, of course, to all His disciples, but directly
to the disciple who was to deny Him in so short
a time. And this is surely very comforting for
our hearts. Peter was to fail the Lord—Jesus
knew he would fail—but deep in Peter's heart
there was a fervent love for the Lord Jesus. And

when he said, "I will lay down my life for Thy
sake," he meant every word of it.   But he did
not realize how untrustworthy his own heart was.
It was a case of the spirit being willing, but the
flesh weak.   And Jesus knew the fearful dis-
couragement that would roll over the soul of
Peter when he awoke to the realization of the
fact that he had been so utterly faithless in the
hour of His Master's need.   In the very time that
Jesus needed someone to stand up for Him and
to say boldly, "Yes, I am one of His, and I can
bear witness to the purity of His life and to the
goodness of His ways," at that time Peter, fright-
ened by the soldiers gathered about, denied any
knowledge of his Saviour.   And, oh, the days and
nights that would follow as he would feel that
surely he must be utterly cast off, surely the Lord
could never put any trust in him again!   But if
he remembered the words of our text, what a
comfort they must have brought to his poor
aching heart!   For Jesus is practically saying,
"I know all about it, Peter.   I know how you are
going to fail, but I want you to know that in My
Father's house are many mansions, and you are
going to share one of those mansions with Me
some day.   I am not going to permit you, Peter,
to be utterly overcome.   I am not going to permit
you to go into complete apostasy.   You will fall,
but you will be lifted up again, and you will share
with Me a place in the many mansions."

When He says, "Let not your heart be troubled," He does not mean, "Do not be exercised about your failure," for He Himself sought to exercise the heart of Peter, and in a wonderful way restored him by the Sea of Galilee later on. But He means this: "Do not be cast down. Do not allow the enemy of your soul to make you feel there is no further hope, there is no opportunity for you."

I wonder if some who read this have failed, perhaps, as Peter failed. Under the stress of circumstances you, too, have denied your Lord, denied Him in acts if not in words, and the adversary of your soul is saying to you now, "It is all up with you; your case is hopeless. You knew Christ once, but you have failed so miserably, He would never own you again." Oh, let me assure you His interest in you is just as deep as it ever was. If you truly trusted Him as your Saviour, the fact that you failed so grievously, and the fact that you mourn over it, only emphasizes the truth that you belong to Him. Still He says, "Return, O backsliding children, unto Me; for I am married unto you"—not, "I am divorced from you." And therefore He waits for you to come back and confess your failure and your sin, and He has promised complete restoration, for, "If we confess our sins, He is faithful and just to forgive us our sins, and to cleanse us from all unrighteousness."

And some day for you, too, there will be a place in the Father's house.

"Let not your heart be troubled: ye believe in God, believe also in Me." In the days gone by before Jesus came to them at all, the people of Israel did have faith in the one true and living God. Now they had never seen Him, and Jesus is saying to His disciples, "You have believed in God when you could not see Him, now I am going away in a little while and you will not be able to see Me, but I want you to trust Me just the same as when I was here. Just as you have believed in the unseen God through the years, I want you to put your faith in Me, the unseen Christ, after I have gone back to the Father." Do we have that implicit trust and confidence in Him, realizing that He is deeply interested in every detail of our lives? The Word says, "Casting all your care upon Him, for He careth for you." There is absolutely nothing that concerns His people that He Himself is not concerned about. And therefore He would have us put away all the stress and all the anxiety. He says, "Be not anxious about anything, but in everything by prayer and supplication and thanksgiving, let your requests be made known unto God." "Ye believe in God, believe also in Me."

And then He adds, "In My Father's house are many mansions." "My Father's house," and by that of course He means Heaven, and He is speaking of a place to which He was going, a place into which some day He will take all His own. I often hear people say, "Heaven is a condition rather than a place." Heaven is both a place and a condition. It is true we do not read a great deal about Heaven in the Bible. Somebody has said, "Heaven is the land of *no more*." We have more in the Bible about what will not be in Heaven than about what will be there. Remember in the book of Revelation we read that there will be no more sin, there will be no more tears, there will be no more pain, there will be no more sorrow, there will be no more curse, there will be no more darkness, there will be no more distress of any kind in the Father's house. The Father's house is the place where Christ is, and that is the place to which the redeemed are going.

Some may have thought the expression here, "In My Father's house are many mansions" is rather peculiar. Somehow or other, the word *mansion* to most of us has an accustomed meaning that it did not have originally. When we see a great building we call it a "mansion." But the word as originally used had rather the meaning of an apartment, as we use that word today, a splendid apartment. So one building might have many mansions in it. And Jesus is telling us, "In My Father's house are many apartments, many resting-places." There is a place, an individual place, for every one of His own, all in that Father's house.

"If it were not so, I would have told you." The Jews believed in a heaven of bliss after death, and Jesus said, "If you had been wrong in that, I would have corrected you." But because He did not correct it but rather affirmed it, we know that it is true, that there is a glorious home beyond the skies for the redeemed which we shall share with Him by-and-by.

He adds, "I go to prepare a place for you." You see the mansions are different from what they were before He went back there. Before He returned to the Father's house, the sin question had never been settled. Before He went back to the Father's house, the veil not been rent, the blood had not been sprinkled on the mercy-seat. So the saints of old went to Paradise on credit. They did not have the same blessed access into the immediate presence of God that the saints have now. We read in the Epistle to the Hebrews that we have now come "to the spirits of just men made perfect." They were the spirits of just men of all the centuries before the cross; God had saved them and taken them to Paradise, but they were not yet made perfect. They could not be until the precious blood of Jesus was shed on the cross. Now, having settled the sin question. He entered into the holiest with His own blood in antitypical fashion, sprinkled His own blood on the mercy-seat above, and now a place is prepared in the holiest for all of His own, and the spirits of just men of the past have been perfected, and we who believe now are perfected forever. So we are all suited to that place to which we are going. "I go to prepare a place for you."

And then He said, "And if I go and prepare a place for you, I will come again, and receive you unto Myself; that where I am, there ye may be also." A great many people think this passage relates to death, and of course, when a believer dies, that believer goes to be with Christ. But we are never told in Scripture that in the hour of death Christ comes for His people. If we may draw an analogy from something our Lord said when He was here on earth, we gather that this is hardly true. We are told that a dear child of God was dying—he was a beggar, it is true. He was an outcast, lying at the rich man's gate, but he was a real son of Abraham. He had faith in the God of all grace. And the beggar died, we are told, and was carried by the angels into Abraham's bosom. Angels carried the poor beggar— poor no longer—into Paradise. What I gather from that is, that the last ministry of angels, who are ever keeping watch over the people of God, will be to usher them into the presence of God.

He is yonder in the Father's house, and His angels usher His saints into His presence.

But He is speaking of something different here. Death is the believer going to be with Christ. That is what the Scripture tells us—"absent from the body, present with the Lord," "to depart and be with Christ which is far better." But a believer going home to be with Christ is spoken of as being unclothed, having laid his body aside. He is there in the presence of the Lord a glorified spirit, but he is there waiting for his redeemed body. When the Lord Jesus fulfils that which is spoken here in the fourteenth chapter of John, then believers will receive their glorified bodies and will be altogether like Him. This coming, referred to here, is developed for us more fully in the fourth chapter of the First Epistle to the Thessalonians. There we read in verse thirteen: "I would not have you to be ignorant, brethren, concerning them which are asleep" — that is, saints whose bodies are sleeping in the graves but whose spirits are with Christ—

"I would not have you to be ignorant, brethren, concerning them which are asleep, that ye sorrow not, even as others which have no hope. For if we believe that Jesus died and rose again, even so them also which sleep in Jesus will God bring with Him. For this we say unto you by the word of the Lord, that we which are alive and remain unto the coming of the Lord shall not prevent them which are asleep. For the Lord Himself shall descend from heaven with a shout, with the voice of the archangel, and with the trump of God: and the dead in Christ shall rise first: then we which are alive and remain shall be caught up together with them in the clouds, to meet the Lord in the air: and so shall we ever be with the Lord."

This is the coming our Saviour refers to when He says: "If I go and prepare a place for you, I will come again and receive you unto myself." It is at that coming that the expectation of our completed redemption will be fulfilled. In Romans eight the Apostle Paul tells us: "For the earnest expectation of the creature waiteth for the manifestation of the sons of God. . . . For we know that the whole creation groaneth and travaileth in pain together until now. And not only they, but ourselves also, which have the firstfruits of the Spirit, even we ourselves groan within ourselves, waiting for the adoption to wit, the redemption of our body." What does he mean by that?

Our spirits have already been redeemed, we have already received the salvation of our souls, but we are waiting for the complete salvation of the body, the redemption of the body at the coming of the Lord Jesus Christ.

"For we are saved by hope: but hope that is seen is not hope" (Rom. 8:24).

What hope is it then? The hope of the coming of our Lord. And to this He refers again in the third chapter of the Epistle to the Philippians, where we read in verse twenty:

"For our conversation (really citizenship) is in heaven; whence also we wait for a Saviour, the Lord Jesus Christ: who shall fashion anew the body of our humiliation, that it may be conformed to the body of His glory, according to the working whereby He is able even, to subject all things unto Himself" (R.V.).

This is the glorious event that will take place when the Lord comes back again, when He comes back for us.

There is the widest difference, you see, between this and the time when He is manifested as the Son of Man to deal in judgment with the godless world and eventually to set up His kingdom. This was a secret the Lord was revealing to these apostles that night in the upper room. In the three Synoptic Gospels it was not mentioned. It was the Apostle Paul who was the chosen instrument to develop it, but it seems that the Lord Jesus, just before He went away, had a secret welling up in His heart as it were, which He could not hold back any longer and He must tell them a little about it, so He says, "I am going away, but I am going to prepare a place for you. But if I go and prepare a place for you, I will come again and receive you"—not, "I will send the death angel for you," or any other angel, but, "I will come again and receive you unto Myself, that where I am there ye may be also."

You see, He will never be satisfied until every one of His redeemed people is with Him in the glory in the Father's house. His heart is yearning for that.

Now a word about the Father's house. Notice it is the Father's house, and the Father's house is for all the Father's children. We fear a great many strange things these days. Some people would try to tell us that it is only the deeply spiritual people of God that will be caught up with the Lord Jesus at His coming. When people talk like that, how little understanding they have of the Father's heart! Think of a normal father and mother here on earth, with say, eight or ten children, and that is quite a family; is it not? The father's house is open to all the children. I pity the home, and pity the children, where the father or the mother makes distinctions among their children. I think it is a sad thing when out of a number of children one perhaps occupies a special place in the heart of the father and the others are held at a distance. "Oh," but you say, "maybe one or two are naughty children. Of course the father could not love naughty children as much as he loves the good children." Is that true? Why even the naughty children are so dear to the father's heart that they give him many sleepless nights as he thinks about their naughtiness. He loves them and truly longs to see them all that they ought to be. There is always a welcome for them at the father's house.

We need to remember, too, that in the Father's house above, there is no distinction. People often say to me, "Oh, if I can just get into Heaven and get a seat behind the door, I can be satisfied. I know I don't deserve anything better."

My dear friend, you don't deserve to get there at all. I don't deserve to go there. But I am not going there because I deserve to go, but I am going to Heaven because I have been born again and the Lord Jesus Christ is preparing a place for me, and the Father's house is for all the Father's children.

Another thing is this: There are no seats behind the door over yonder! I wish everybody would realize this. There are no distinctions in the welcome that believers will have in the Father's house. I repeat, the Father's house has the same welcome for all the Father's children.

You say, "Well, but doesn't the Bible indicate some will have greater rewards than others?" Oh, yes, but rewards have nothing to do with the welcome into the Father's house. The rewards specially have to do with the coming glorious kingdom, of course given in Heaven, given at the judgment-seat of Christ, but the differences are in the kingdom. For instance, look at the Second Epistle of Peter: "So an entrance shall be ministered unto you abundantly into—" Into what? Into Heaven? No, it is not true that some people will get an abundant entrance into Heaven and other folk will not have anything like so warm and cordial a welcome. What does it mean? It says that some people have an entrance ministered unto them abundantly. Yes, but into what? "Into the everlasting kingdom of our Lord and Saviour Jesus Christ." Don't confuse, don't confound in your thinking, the Father's house with the everlasting kingdom. The Father's house is the home of the saints; the everlasting kingdom is the sphere of service and rewards, where through all eternity, first in the millennium and then in the ages to come, we shall be serving our blessed Lord who has prepared a place for us in the Father's house.

Will you allow me to use an old illustration? Suppose here is a good old-fashioned family, with ten or a dozen children. Now the children are scattered all over. Christmas is drawing near, and there is going to be a home-gathering. The invitations have gone out to all the children to come home for Christmas and the family is gathering. Very well, they are all coming in. Some are coming by automobile, some by Pullman coach, some by airplane, some by bus, and perhaps one is even obliged to come on foot. But there they come from all over, coming home to the father's house for Christmas.

I can just imagine the great table loaded with all the wonderful dainties kind hands have been preparing. I can imagine father and mother coming in for a last look, to see if everything is right. There is mother's place and father's place. Here is where the great big platter will be with a couple of big fifteen-pound turkeys, and all the rest of the good things that have been prepared are there on the table. Father and mother come in, and mother says, "Now father, I have put Bob right beside you."

Bob is out in the world, he is a senator, he has made a great place for himself, but he is just Bob at home.

"And here is the place for Mary."

I think Mary is the president of a woman's college or something like that. You know, she is very dignified when she gets on her cap and gown, but at home she is just Mary; that's all.

"Then here is the place for Tom."

Let's see, who is Tom? I think Tom is an officer in the army, but he is just Tom at home.

"And here is a place for Anna."

Anna? Who is Anna? Perhaps she is a physician, and very distinguished in her profession, and she is Dr. Anna outside, but she is just Anna at home, you know.

And so down the line she goes. And mother says, "I put a place right here by my right hand for Jim."

Who is Jim? Well, Jim is the ne'er-do-well of the family. Poor Jim! He has tried a number of things.

I generally think of Jim as an inventor. He has invented so many different things, but there is always something that doesn't work right. If he could only get things going, there would be millions in it, but he has used up everything he had and everything he could borrow, and still he gets nowhere. Poor Jim!

He wouldn't be home at all if mother hadn't slipped in a twenty-dollar bill to get an extra suit of clothes so he would be presentable enough to come. And I can imagine one of the brothers saying, "You know, mother, there's Jim—I don't know whether we had better let Jim sit at the table with the rest of us. Our family has done so well, and Jim has failed so miserably. Wouldn't it be better to put Jim in the kitchen? He could eat with the servants out in the kitchen."

And mother flares up: "What is that? Jim shall
have the very best we can give him! I want him
to know if there is any place on earth where he is
welcome it is his father's and mother's house.

You see, at home in the father's house, they are
all welcome and they are all treated as well as the
father and mother can treat them.

But by-and-by the big day is over and they are
separating and Mary goes back to the college, and
Bob goes back to Washington to the senate. And
Anna goes back to her practice in the big city,
and Tom goes back to the army, and so on. By-
and-by poor Jim goes back to his little room yonder in the city. But I see the mother giving him
a last good-bye kiss, and what is that she is slip-
ping into his hand? It is a fifty-dollar bill. And
off he goes, with such happy memories of the
father's house!

That is only a very human illustration, but perhaps it will show what I mean when I say that
the Father's house is one thing and the kingdom
is another. The Father's house is the home of all
the Father's children. But we make our own
places in the kingdom by our own devotedness to
the Lord Jesus Christ. Do you get the difference?
So there is a place for all in the Father's house.

About the way there. Will everybody get to
the Father's house? I wish that they would. But
alas, alas, many persist in rebellion against God

so that prayer can never be answered! There nly one way to the Father's house. And what that way? I have had people say to me so many times, "We are travelling different roads, but we will all get to Heaven at last." No, no. I don't find that in my Bible. My Bible says, "There is a way that seemeth right unto a man, but the end thereof are the ways of death" (Prov. 14:12), and it warns me against taking the broad way that leads to destruction and tells me to take the narrow way that leads to life.

And so here Jesus says, "And whither I go, ye know, and the way ye know. Thomas saith unto Him—" Thomas was honest and he was never afraid just to blurt out all the truth. He said, "We do not know what You are talking about. We have to confess we are ignorant, and we don't know where You are going, and how can we know the way."

Jesus said unto him, and, oh, dear friends, do get what He said, for it is for you as well as for Thomas. "Jesus saith unto him, I am the Way, the Truth and the Life. No man cometh unto the Father but by Me."

Oh, do not talk about many ways. There is only one—Jesus is the only way. There is none other name under heaven given among men whereby we must be saved, but the name of Jesus. Have you come to Him? Are you trusting Him? If you

are, you are on the way to the Father's house, and
now you can wait with equal glad expectation for
the hour of His return, for He said, "If I go, I
will come again and receive you unto Myself."
When will He come? We cannot tell that, but we
are waiting for Him day by day.

> "I know not when the Lord will come
>   Or at what hour He may appear,
>   Whether at midnight or at morn,
>   Or at what season of the year.
>
> "I only know that He is near,
>   And that His voice I soon shall hear.
>   I only know that He is near,
>   And that His voice I soon shall hear."

THE FATHER MANIFESTED IN THE SON

✓   ✓   ✓

"If ye had known Me, ye should have known My Father also: and from henceforth ye know Him, and have seen Him. Philip saith unto Him, Lord, show us the Father, and it sufficeth us. Jesus saith unto him, Have I been so long time with you, and yet hast thou not known Me, Philip? He that hath seen Me hath seen the Father; and how sayest thou then, Show us the Father? Believest thou not that I am in the Father, and the Father in Me? the words that I speak unto you I speak not of Myself: but the Father that dwelleth in Me, He doeth the works. Believe Me that I am in the Father, and the Father in Me: or else believe Me for the very works' sake. Verily, verily, I say unto you, He that believeth on Me, the works that I do shall he do also; and greater works than these shall he do; because I go unto My Father. And whatsoever ye shall ask in My name, that will I do, that the Father may be glorified in the Son. If ye shall ask any thing in My name, I will do it" (John 14: 7-14).

THERE are seven things which this portion suggests, and the first is this: The Father is only known through the Son. Notice verse seven: "If ye had known Me, ye should have known My Father also: and from henceforth ye know Him, and have seen Him." Now it is perfectly true that God may be known through creation. We are told that in the first chapter of the Epistle to the Romans. There we read that "the invisible things of Him from the creation of the world are clearly seen, being understood by the things that are made, even His eternal power and Godhead; so that they are without excuse:" so men who deny God, who refuse to believe in a God, who live as if there were no God, are without excuse. We are often asked, "Will God condemn the poor heathen because they have not had the gospel?" No; but He will condemn us because they have not heard the gospel. We are responsible to get it to them. We have been so selfish and content to enjoy our morsel alone. We have paid so little attention to the Lord's command, "Go ye into all the world." We have quibbled so much about whether the command belongs to our dispensation or to another, and have professed to have so much light and knowledge, so we have sat at home and let the heathen die in their sins. We shall have to answer to God for it some day. The heathen are lost, that is why they need a Saviour. That is why you and I needed a Saviour. "The Son of Man came to seek and to save that which was lost." If the heathen were not lost they would not need a Saviour, but they are lost because they did not want to keep God in their knowledge. They are condemned by their own consciences because of the sins of which they are guilty. They will not be charged for the sin of rejecting Christ of whom they never heard, but for the sins that they have actually committed. As they look into the heavens they must know there is a God. As they see the wonderful things He has prepared for man, as they consider their own bodies and all their marvelous functions they cannot help but realize that back of all this there must be a Creator to whom men are responsible. So His eternal power and Godhead are known through creation. "The heavens declare the glory of God; and the firmament showeth His handywork. Day unto day uttereth speech, and night unto night showeth knowledge." But the Fatherhood of God could only be revealed through the Lord Jesus Christ. Nature tells me there is a God, that He must be infinite in wisdom and power, but it does not tell me He has a Father's heart. I would not know that except from the revelation He has given in His blessed Son. How thoughtless we are about that revelation sometimes.

I remember a lady with whom I was speaking at one time, and if there is any one on earth who ought to thank God for the Christian revelation, it is the women of the world, for how marvelously their status has been changed in all lands where the gospel is known. But this lady said to me, with a toss of her pretty head, "I am not interested in the gospel. I never read the Bible. It is enough for me to know that **God is love.**" I said, "Do you know that?" "Why, certainly," she said. "You really know that God is love?" "Why, of course I do." "Well," I inquired, "pardon me. Madam, but how did you find that out?" "Why. everybody knows that God is love." Oh, no: everybody does not know it. They do not know it in India, in Africa, in lands where the gospel has not yet gone. They did not know it in the Islands of the Sea in the old cannibal days. No one knew that till Jesus came to declare the heart of God to needy men. And it is the Holy Spirit who told us God is love, and the evidence He gave of it was this, "Herein is love, not that we loved God, but that He loved us, and sent His Son to be the propitiation for our sins." Oh, we could have known that God was great, that God was powerful. that God was wise. We might even have known or gathered from the abundant provision He has made for His creatures that He is good, but we would never have known that He is love if Jesus had not come to reveal the Father. "The Word became flesh and tabernacled among us, and we beheld His glory, the glory as of the Only-begotten of the Father, full of grace and truth." And so I repeat, we would never have known the Fatherhood of God apart from the revelation given us in our Lord Jesus Christ.

Then in the second place I would like to remind you of this, Christ is the exact expression of the Father. Do you say to yourself sometimes, "Oh, I wish I understood God better. I wish I could know just how God the Father looks at things, and how He feels about things, and what His attitude is toward men in general, and His people in particular." Well, all you need to do is read the four Gospels and get better acquainted with the Lord Jesus Christ, for He has made the Father known in all His fulness.

I love those verses with which the Epistle to the Hebrews opens: "God, who at sundry times and in divers manners spake in time past unto the fathers by the prophets, hath in these last days spoken unto us by His Son, whom He hath appointed Heir of all things, by whom also He made the worlds (or ages) ; who being the brightness of His glory, and the express image of His Person, and upholding all things by the word of His power, when He had by Himself purged our sins, sat down on the right hand of the Majesty on high." Those words, "the express image of His Person" might well be rendered the "exact expression of His character."

He is speaking about Jesus who is the exact expression of the Father's character. So if you want to know what God, the Father, is like, just get better acquainted with the Lord Jesus Christ.

The better you know Him, the better you know
the Father. Everything in the character of Christ
tells out that which is in the heart of God; His
love for holiness, His delight in righteousness,
His interest in men—even unconverted men—His
deep tender affection for His own as evidenced by
His love for that little company of disciples who
walked with Him three-and-a-half years, of whom
we read, "Having loved His own who were in the
world, He loved them unto the end," His sweet
gracious interest in the little children, His love
for the girls and boys, so that they delighted to
come to Him and sit upon His knee. He took them
in His arms and put His hands on them in blessing. All this tells us of God the Father's love for
the children.

Then on the other hand, the scorn of Jesus for
sins such as hypocrisy, deceit, disobedience, etc.,
expresses the scorn of the Father Himself for
everything unreal and consequently unholy. And
then the glorious anger of Jesus! "Oh," you say,
"I don't like to think that Jesus ever became angry." There are some people who insist that we
should not get angry about anything. But scripture says, "Be ye angry and sin not." Think of
the anger of Jesus as He stood in the temple with
flashing eyes and said, "It is written, My house
is the house of prayer: but ye have made it a
den of thieves." And remember that day in the

synagogue in Capernaum when that poor woman, nearly bent double with her misery, came. The Scribes and the Pharisees were watching. They were saying, "Will He dare to heal her on the sabbath day?" Jesus said, "Is it lawful to do good on the sabbath days, or to do evil? to save life, or to kill?" He looked round about upon them with anger, as He asked "Which of you shall have an ass or an ox fallen into a pit, and will not straightway pull him out on the sabbath day?" And He said, "Ought not this woman, being a daughter of Abraham, whom Satan hath bound, lo, these eighteen years, be loosed from this bond on the sabbath day?" Glorious indignation! Glorious anger! And the anger of Jesus is the anger of God. How is it that we are afraid of the wrath of God and yet we don't like to think of our Lord Jesus ever being angry? There is a time coming when men shall flee to the rocks and the mountains and shall cry to the rocks and the hills, "Fall on us, and hide us from the face of Him that sitteth on the throne, and from the wrath of the Lamb!"—the wrath of the Lord Jesus Christ! Yes, the Lamb's indignation with men who have spurned His grace, refused His mercy, turned down every opportunity of salvation. I repeat, the anger of Jesus is the anger of God. If you want to know God just get better acquainted with Jesus.

Philip came to Him and said, "Show us the Father, and it sufficeth us." You see it was a new thing to Philip. Jesus talked so quietly and with such full knowledge of the Father. Philip says, "Well, what do You mean, Lord? Show us the Father, and it sufficeth us." And Jesus said, "Have I been so long time with you, and yet hast thou not known Me, Philip? He that hath seen Me hath seen the Father." That is, you see, the Father's character was fully told out in Jesus.

But now this involves the third thing I want to emphasize, and that is the unity of the Father and the Son. The unity of the Father and the Son does not involve the thought that Father and Son were exactly the same Person. They were two Persons, and yet one in the unity of Deity with the Holy Spirit—the Father, the Son and the Holy Spirit. Joseph Cook used to say, "The Father without the Son and the Holy Spirit would not be God in His fulness. The Son without the Father and the Holy Spirit would not be God. The Spirit without the Father and the Son would not be God. But the Father and the Son and the Holy Spirit together are one God in three blessed, adorable Persons." So Jesus was here on earth, the Man, Christ Jesus, and yet He was the Son of the Father. The Father was in the heavens, and of course, omnipresent in the whole universe. Jesus said, "He that hath seen Me hath seen the Father. Believest thou not that I am in the Father and the Father in Me?" The union is an indissoluble one. "I speak not of Myself, but the Father that dwelleth in Me, He doeth the works." Everything that Jesus did as Man here in this world, He did in fellowship with the Father. That is why He could say that the Son could do nothing of Himself but whatsoever He seeth the Father do. It was not possible that He, as the Son of the Father, should do anything that was not in harmony with the will of the Father: two Persons and yet one in Deity.

Then notice in the fourth place that the works that He did were a testimony to this truth. Verse eleven reads, "Believe Me that I am in the Father, and the Father in Me: or else believe me for the very works' sake." It is as though He challenged them, saying, "If you are not prepared to take My declaration of My oneness with the Father, if there is still a question in your mind, see what I have done. Did any man ever do the works that I have done? Has any man ever been able to accomplish what I have accomplished? Be convinced by these works that God the Father is working through Me." If any other man had touched the leper he would have been defiled, but when Jesus touched him, He said, "Be thou clean." His hands were not defiled. His hands healed the leprosy instead of the defilement of leprosy cleaving to Him. No mere man ever had power over the tempest, but Jesus could turn to the wind and the waves and say, "Peace, be still!" Man sows the seed and cultivates the ground, and eventually through the mercy of God, whose sunshine and rain falls on it and whose chemical action takes place beneath the sod, the earth brings forth the grain from which he can make his bread. But Jesus took five loaves and a few fishes, and after giving thanks, produced food for over 5,000 people. Why did He do these things? Not that people might look on with amazement or to attract attention to Himself, but in order that He might manifest the heart of God.

So the miracles of Jesus are a challenge to us. We see in them the evidence that He is the Eternal Son of the Father.

But now He was going away, and in the fifth place we notice a wonderful promise He makes to us which He would fulfil in His absence. Verse twelve reads, "Verily, verily, I say unto you, He that believeth on Me, the works that I do shall he do also; and greater works than these shall he do; because I go unto My Father." Now there are some people who say that He makes a promise here which He never fulfilled. They declare that no man has ever done greater works than these miracles. But He was not speaking of miracles. His chief work was not performing miracles but revealing the Father, bringing knowledge of the Father. It is that of which He was speaking. As a result of His three-and-a-half years of ministry, when He left this scene He said goodbye to a group of about five hundred disciples. There were, doubtless, a few more scattered about but not very many. Very few saw in Him the revelation of the Father. But go on a few days—fifty days later. Ah, then Peter and the rest of the eleven stand up on the day of Pentecost and the third Person of the Trinity comes upon them in power and they are prepared to witness for Him. They preached a crucified and risen Christ, and what happened? Three thousand believed! Probably more in that one day than in all the three-and-a-half years of our Lord's ministry. Oh, it is not miracles of which He is speaking. If it were miracles, what was the greatest? Of the miracles concerning the body, was it not when He went to that tomb at Bethany and stood and cried, "Lazarus, come forth!" and he that was dead came forth—the man of whom his sister said, "Lord, he has been dead four days." That was Jesus' greatest work in regard to the body. Has anyone excelled that?

What was greatest in regard to the powers of nature? Was it turning the water into wine or multiplying the loaves and fishes? Or was it not perhaps in controlling the wind and the waves? No one else has been able to do that.

But His greatest work of all was to reveal the Father. When you realize that when Jesus left this scene, committing His gospel to a little group of eleven men in order that they might carry it to the ends of the earth, at that time the whole world, with the exception of a few in Israel, was lost in the darkness of heathenism. But in three hundred years Christianity closed nearly all the temples of the heathen Roman Empire, and numbered its converts by millions. These were the greater works, and down through the centuries He still carries on this ministry.

In the sixth place, notice His promise to hear the prayers of His servants. "Whatsoever ye shall ask in My name, that will I do." "If ye shall ask any thing in My name, I will do it." Now somebody speaks up and says, "Well, I asked God for something in the name of His Son, Jesus Christ, and He did not do it." Oh, but that was not necessarily asking in His Name. To ask in His Name is to ask by His authority; that is to pray in accordance with His revealed will. It is as though He said to us, "Whatever you ask by My authority, I will do." And so what you and I need is to be sure that we understand His will and that we have His authority for the requests that we make.

The seventh thing is this: our Lord's one purpose. The last part of verse thirteen reads, "That the Father may be glorified in the Son." It was the delight of the Lord Jesus, while here on earth, to glorify the Father, and now it is the joy of His heart to see His people carry on the mission He has given. Every time a soul is saved, it is to the glory of the Father and this is the joy of the Son. Every thing we do in loving obedience to His Word is that the Father may be glorified.

THE PROMISED COMFORTER

✓ ✓ ✓

"If ye love Me, keep My commandments. And I will pray the Father, and He shall give you another Comforter, that He may abide with you for ever; even the Spirit of truth; whom the world cannot receive, because it seeth Him not, neither knoweth Him: but ye know Him; for He dwelleth with you, and shall be in you. I will not leave you comfortless (orphans): I will come to you. Yet a little while, and the world seeth Me no more; but ye see Me; because I live, ye shall live also. At that day ye shall know that I am in My Father, and ye in Me, and I in you. He that hath My commandments, and keepeth them, he it is that loveth Me: and he that loveth Me shall be loved of My Father, and I will love him, and will manifest Myself to him. Judas saith unto Him, not Iscariot, Lord, how is it that Thou wilt manifest Thyself unto us, and not unto the world? Jesus answered and said unto him, If a man love Me he will keep My words: and My Father will love him, and We will come unto him, and make Our abode with him. He that loveth Me not keepeth not My sayings: and the word which ye hear is not Mine, but the Father's which sent Me. These things have I spoken unto you, being yet present with you. But the Comforter, which is the Holy Ghost, whom the Father will send in My name, He shall teach you all things, and bring all things to your remembrance, whatsoever I have said unto you" (John 14: 15-26).

✓ ✓ ✓

THERE is such richness and fulness in this particular section of John's Gospel that I hesitate to try to take it up in one address, and yet it is all so intimately linked together that

I feel as though it would be doing violence to it if divided.

There are a number of things that require to be emphasized. First of all, we have the promise of the Comforter. That word "Comforter" is interesting. It is used to translate a Greek word, *Parakletos*, which is a compound word meaning, one who comes to the side of another, that is a helper in time of need. In the First Epistle of John (chap. 2:1) we have "Advocate," which is exactly the same word in the original.

There is a sweetness and preciousness about that word "Comforter" that appeals to the heart. After all, we cannot use any other word in our language that would so adequately represent the Greek word, for the Paraclete is in very truth the Comforter. Our English word "Comforter" is also a compound. "Comforter" comes from two Latin words—*con,* and *fortis,* the one meaning "to be in company with," and the other "to strengthen," so that actually the Comforter is one who strengthens by companionship. That is one of the great ministries of the Holy Spirit. The Paraclete is one who comes to your side to help, to give aid, and so the word is properly used. An attorney-at-law, or an advocate, is one who comes to help you in your legal difficulties, and the Holy Spirit is all this. He has come from heaven, as promised by our blessed Lord, to assist us in every crisis, in every time of difficulty that may arise in our Christian lives—He strengthens by His companionship.

Let us notice how definitely the Lord Jesus points out, or insists upon, the personality of the Comforter, the Holy Spirit. Consider the last part of verse 17: "But ye know *Him;* for *He* dwelleth with you, and shall be in you." And again, the previous verse, "And I will pray the Father, and He shall give you another Comforter, that *He* may abide with you for ever."

Our Lord would never have used this masculine pronoun if He did not mean us to understand that just as God the Father is a Person, and God the Son is a Person, so God the Holy Spirit is a Person—Three Persons in one God. I emphasize this because I am afraid many real Christians, otherwise sound and orthodox enough, have very imperfect thoughts in regard to the Holy Spirit. So often we hear people speaking of the Holy Spirit as "It," and it is perfectly true that in Romans 8 we read: "The Spirit itself beareth witness with our spirit, that we are the children of God." But that is because in Greek the word for "Spirit" is in the neuter, and therefore a neuter pronoun goes with it. But in conveying it exactly in English it might have been rendered: "The Spirit Himself beareth witness with our spirit, that we are the children of God."

What the Lord Jesus teaches is that the Holy Spirit is not an impersonal influence, and above all, the Holy Spirit is not simply a wave of emotion pouring through the heart and mind of a man, but the Holy Spirit is a divine Person. Just as God the Father sent the Son, and the Son had a certain ministry to perform for thirty-three wonderful years in this world, so now the Father and the Son have sent the Holy Spirit, and He has been performing His ministry for something like 1,900 marvelous years, in which the gospel of the grace of God has been going out into all the world, working miracles and transforming the lives of men and women everywhere it has been received in faith.

Then, notice the dispensational distinction that the Lord makes here in regard to the Spirit's ministry. He says, "I will pray the Father, and He shall give you another Comforter, that He may abide with you for ever; even the Spirit of truth; whom the world cannot receive, because it seeth Him not, neither knoweth Him: but ye know Him, for He dwelleth with you, and shall be in you."

Note that expression: "He dwelleth with you." That was true all through the centuries before that wonderful day of Pentecost when the Spirit of God came down to form the Church of the new dispensation and to indwell all believers. In all

past centuries the Holy Spirit was working in
the world and He dwelt with believers. The Apostle Peter tells us how Noah preached by the Spirit
while the ark was preparing. The Holy Spirit
was with the patriarchs in their particular dispensation. The Holy Spirit was with the people
of God in the wilderness in the days of Moses,
and all through the legal dispensation He was
with the saints on earth. David prayed, "Take
not Thy Holy Spirit from me"—a prayer very
appropriate for the age and dispensation in which
he lived, but not an appropriate prayer for Christians today, for Jesus said, "When He is come He
will abide with you for ever." But in the Old
Testament dispensation the Holy Spirit came and
abode upon people, wrought in and through them,
and with them. "He hath been with you." That
was true particularly when Jesus was here on
earth because the Holy Spirit was given without
measure to Him.

Now Jesus looks forward into the new age, the
new dispensation, which was to begin at Pentecost, and He says, "He shall be *in* you." And this
is the glorious distinctive truth of the dispensation in which we live. The Holy Spirit in this
age dwells in every believer in the Lord Jesus
Christ. "Upon your believing, you were sealed
with that Holy Spirit of promise." It can now be
said, "If any man have not the Spirit of Christ,

he is none of His." That does not mean that if
any man have not the disposition of Christ he is
none of His, but the apostle there is speaking of
the Person, the Holy Spirit. Therefore, in this
age of grace we do not need to go to God and ask
Him to give us the Holy Spirit. The Holy Spirit
dwells within us. He has sealed us as believers in
the Lord Jesus Christ. What we do need, and
need very much, is to recognize the indwelling of
the Holy Spirit and allow Him to have His way
in our hearts and lives, that we may be filled with
the Spirit and controlled by Him.

Then, notice that the Holy Spirit dwelling within makes Christ real to us. The Lord Jesus Christ
was going away, but He said, "I will not leave you
comfortless (orphans), I will come to you." He
was coming Himself in the Spirit to dwell in the
believer. "Yet a little while, and the world seeth
Me no more, but ye see Me." They would see Him
by faith, they would recognize His presence by
faith. We are told that Christ may dwell in our
hearts by faith, and "at that day ye shall know
that I am in the Father, and ye in Me, and I in
you."

Notice the intimate union of believers with the
members of the Godhead—"Ye in Me, and I in
you." As we walk in obedience to Him He says
He will manifest Himself to us in a precious and
wonderful way. "He that hath My command-

ments, and keepeth them, he it is that loveth Me: and he that loveth Me shall be loved of My Father, and I will love him, and will manifest Myself to him."

Judas, not Iscariot, but Judas the faithful apostle, did not understand this, and he inquired, "Lord, how is it that Thou wilt manifest Thyself unto us, and not unto the world?" Jesus replied, "If a man love Me, he will keep My words: and My Father will love him, and We will come unto him, and make Our abode with him." In other words, the obedient believer enjoys communion with the Father and the Son in the power of the indwelling Holy Spirit.

"He that loveth Me not keepeth not My sayings"—that is the disobedient one. "The word which ye hear is not mine, but the Father's which sent Me." Notice two things dwelt on here. I go back to verse 15: "If ye love Me, keep My commandments." Now verse 23 again; "If a man love Me, he will keep My words." What is the difference between keeping Christ's commandments and keeping His words? Well, there are a great many things concerning which our Lord has spoken very definitely, either personally or by the Holy Spirit, a great many things in which He has revealed His will very clearly, showing us just exactly what He would have us do and how to live. Take, for instance, "Love not the world, neither the things that are in the world. . . . For all that is in the world . . . is not of the Father, but is of the world. And the world passeth away, and the lust thereof: but he that doeth the will of God abideth for ever." A Christian cannot go after the things of the world and love the world without going into the path of disobedience, because there is a very definite command concerning this from the Spirit of God. Or again: "Be ye not unequally yoked together with unbelievers: for what fellowship hath righteousness with unrighteousness? and what communion hath light with darkness?" There you have a very distinct command of the Spirit of God.

Now Jesus says, "If ye love Me, keep My commandments." So as we search our Bibles, we see where the Lord has expressed His will, either personally, as in the Gospels, or by the Spirit, as in other parts of the New Testament, and the obedient believer gladly walks in accord with what is there written. When he gets a direct command from the Lord he says, "It is not for me to argue, nor to reason about it; as a Christian, for me it is to do what my Master tells me."

But the Lord Jesus goes even farther than this. "If a man love Me, he will keep My words." What does He mean by that? This is more than just keeping a direct commandment. I will try to illustrate. Here is a young girl whom we will call

Mary, a loved daughter of a widowed mother. She is attending school and the mother is considerate; ʋhe knows that Mary has a lot of heavy lessons and responsibilities, and so tries not to put upon her any more work at home than is necessary. But as a wise mother she realizes that her daughter should have certain duties to perform, so she says, "Daughter, you can look after your own room; hang up your own clothes." (You have seen some daughters did not.) "And I will expect you to do thus-and-so."

Mary loves her mother, so she obeys her. She is about to leave her room for school one morning and notices that things are in an untidy state. "Mother says I must always make up my room before I leave. I may be late, but I shall have to fix up my room." She must keep her mother's command in order to be an obedient girl. So she tidies up her room and then runs off to school with a light heart.

One day Mary has her heart set on going out for a game of tennis in the afternoon as soon as she returns from school, so she hurries home. Entering the house she hears her mother talking to a neighbor and happens to hear her say, "Oh, dear, I feel so badly. I have company coming this evening and I've had such a sick headache all day, and have the dinner all to prepare, and I'm hardly able to do it." Then Mary says, "What is it,

Mother? You have the dinner to get and you're
not feeling well? Mother, you go and lie down
and I'll peel the potatoes, put the meat on, and
I'll get everything ready." But mother says, "You
had planned to meet your friends and play tennis
this afternoon; don't let me keep you from it."
But Mary answers, "Why, Mother, I wouldn't be
happy playing tennis knowing that you are sick
with all this work to do; and it's because you need
me that I want to do this for you."

Do you see the difference? In the morning
Mary kept her mother's commandment; now she
is keeping her word. She realizes, from what her
mother said, how glad she would be to have somebody help, and she says, "It's my privilege; I
would rather help my mother than spend my time
in pleasure." And so off comes the coat and on
goes the apron, and Mary is in the kitchen keeping her mother's word.

With the Christian it is not always a matter of
getting a definite command. He reads his Bible,
and as he reads he sees that God has expressed
His mind in such a way that the obedient Christian can discern what the will of the Lord is, and
so he is glad to keep His word and thus render
devoted service.

The last thing I want to dwell on is found in
verse 26. The blessed Holy Spirit is the power for
all this, the revealer of God's truth, and through

Him the love of God is shed abroad in our hearts. The Holy Spirit is now the teacher, for Jesus said, "But the Comforter, which is the Holy Ghost, whom the Father will send in My name, He shall teach you all things, and bring all things to your remembrance, whatsoever I have said unto you."

That is His special ministry to the people of God as they go through this scene. It means far more to sit down over the Bible and have the Holy Spirit open up its precious truths, than to have some kind of an ecstatic thrill in an exciting meeting. There are many Christians who spend a lot of time looking for thrills. They think when they become excited or stirred up in a meeting that such an experience is a special manifestation of the ministry of the Holy Spirit. The fact of the matter is that the great ministry of the Spirit is to take of the things of Christ and reveal them to us, to open up His truth, to make His holy Word clear and plain and real to our souls. The more we read this Word in dependence on the teaching of the Holy Spirit, the more it will be opened up to us and the more precious it will become.

THE FATHER'S PEACE

✓ ✓ ✓

"Peace I leave with you, My peace I give unto you: not as the world giveth, give I unto you. Let not your heart be troubled, neither let it be afraid. Ye have heard how I said unto you, I go away, and come again unto you. If ye loved Me, ye would rejoice, because I said, I go unto the Father: for My Father is greater than I. And now I have told you before it come to pass, that, when it is come to pass, ye might believe. Hereafter I will not talk much with you: for the prince of this world cometh, and hath nothing in Me. But that the world may know that I love the Father; and as the Father gave Me commandment, even so I do. Arise, let us go hence" (John 14: 27-31).

✓ ✓ ✓

IT was possibly at this point that our blessed Lord and His disciples rose from the supper table where they had been observing the Passover, followed by the institution of that most sacred of all feasts of the Church, called the Lord's Supper. He had washed their feet, told them of His coming again, of the Father's love, and of the coming of the Comforter. And now they rose up together and started on the way to Gethsemane where the blessed Lord was to enter into that hour of sorrow before going on to the judgment-hall and the cross.

His words have peculiar force as we think of the circumstances under which they were spoken. "Peace," He says, "I leave with you, My peace I give unto you: not as the world giveth, give I unto you. Let not your heart be troubled, neither let it be afraid." When He came to earth, He was presented to man as the One who was to bring peace. The prophet Isaiah, seven hundred years before the birth of Christ, the Saviour, had predicted that His name should "be called Wonderful, Counsellor, the Everlasting Father, the Mighty God, the Prince of Peace." Angels sang at His birth, "Glory to God, in the highest, and on earth peace, good will toward men." And yet the sad thing that cannot but occupy our hearts today is this, that after nineteen centuries—nineteen centuries of gospel preaching—this world knows less of peace than it has ever known. Our Lord indicated that such would be the case before He went away, and the reason He gave was this, "Because thou knowest not the time of thy visitation and the things that belong to thy peace." "He came unto His own, and His own received Him not." He presented Himself to them as their King and they said, "We will not have this Man to reign over us." In Pilate's judgment-hall He was rejected in this specific character—that of king. Pilate asked, "What! Shall I crucify your King?" And the Jews replied, "We have no king but Cæsar," and oh, how they have suffered under the "Cæsars" since! And all because of that dreadful mistake. The Saviour said before He went away, "Think not that I am come to send peace on earth: I came not to send peace, but a sword." That is, if man did not receive Him and the truth He brought which was to make them free, then they must still remain in bondage to sin with all its dreadful consequences.

He foresaw all these scenes of strife and bloodshed, and when they asked Him, "What shall be the sign of Thy coming?" He replied, "And ye shall hear of wars and rumors of wars: . . . for nation shall rise against nation, and kingdom against kingdom . . . but the end is not yet."

The little children sang as He rode into Jerusalem that last time, "Blessed be the King that cometh in the name of the Lord: peace in heaven, and glory in the highest." Notice the difference. The angels said, "Peace on earth," and the children, divinely taught, sang, "Peace in heaven," for He was going back to heaven, taking with Him the peace that He would so gladly have shared with the people of the world. And now He sits at the right hand of God—the Man of peace. And before He went away He said to His disciples, "Peace I leave with you, My peace I give unto you: not as the world giveth, give I unto you. Let not your heart be troubled."

I take it we have two distinct characters of peace in that verse: First, the peace that Jesus left—"Peace I leave with you." That, I believe, has to do with the question of sin. There could be no peace between God and man as long as sin came in as a barrier. Twice in Isaiah we read this, "There is no peace, saith Jehovah, to the wicked." First it follows Jehovah's controversy with idols. There is no peace to those who put something else in place of the one true and living God.

And in the second place, Isaiah pictures the coming into the world of the Saviour, Jehovah's Servant, our Lord Jesus Christ, and he says, "He was despised and rejected of men. . . . He was wounded for our transgressions, He was bruised for our iniquities: the chastisement of our peace was upon Him; and with His stripes we are healed." He told how God's blessed Son was to be rejected by His own people and he ended up that section of prophecy with these words, "There is no peace, saith my God, to the wicked," no peace for those who reject the Lord Jesus Christ who alone can give peace. But though the rejected One, He went to the cross to make atonement for sin, and there was fulfilled the prophecy concerning the chastisement by which our peace is made. So in Colossians 1 we read, "Having made peace through the blood of His cross, by Him to recon-

cile all things unto Himself." I think that is what
He was referring to when He said, "Peace I leave
with you." He did not go back to heaven until
He had settled the sin question and made it possible for man to be at peace with God, and that on
a righteous basis, for remember there cannot be
peace with God apart from righteousness. "The
effect of righteousness shall be peace, quietness
and assurance forever." Jesus is "a high priest
forever after the order of Melchisedec, king of
Salem." Melchisedec means "king of righteousness;" Salem means "peace." And the Spirit of
God says, "First being by interpretation King of
righteousness, and after that also King of Salem,
which is, King of peace"—no peace apart from
righteousness. For that reason, you and I as sinners could never make our peace with God.

Away back in the Old Testament God challenged man to make peace with Him, but no one
could ever do it. Why cannot I make peace with
God? Because I have no ability to put away my
sin. No efforts of mine could make satisfaction
for sins.

But the Lord Jesus Christ, as our representative, went to the cross and made peace—made
peace by blood of His cross. In Zechariah 6: 13
we read, "He shall be a priest upon his throne
. . . and the counsel of peace shall be between
them both." That is, the covenant of peace is

made between the Father and the Son. The Son took our place, settled the sin question and so made peace for poor guilty men and everyone who will, may come to God as repentant sinners, and the moment we trust Him, we can say, "Therefore being justified by faith, we have peace with God through our Lord Jesus Christ."

At the close of the war between the States, we are told that a troop of Federal cavalry were riding along a road between Richmond and Washington. Suddenly they saw a poor wretch, clothed in the ragged remnants of a Confederate uniform come out of the bush. He hailed the Captain who drew rein and waited for him. He gasped out, "I am starving to death. Can you help me? Can you give me some food?" The Captain said, "Starving to death! Why don't you go into Richmond and get what you need?" The other answered, "I dare not, for if I did I would be arrested. Three weeks ago I became utterly disheartened and I deserted from the Confederate army, and I have been hiding in the woods ever since waiting for an opportunity to get through the lines to the north, for I knew if I were arrested I would be shot for deserting in time of war." The Captain looked at him in amazement and said, "Haven't you heard the news?" "What news?" the poor fellow gasped. "Why, the war is over. Peace has been made. General Lee surrendered to General Grant at Appomattox two weeks ago. The Confederacy is ended." "What!" he said, "peace has been made for two weeks, and I have been starving in the woods because I did not know it?" Oh, that was the gospel of peace to him. Sinner, listen to me! Peace was made nineteen hundred years ago and millions today are dying in their sins because they do not know it. You do not have to make your peace with God. You do not have to atone for your sins. You could not do it, but Jesus has done it all and you may come to God in His name. All that He accomplished at Calvary will be put down to your account. The One who died on the cross to make propitiation for your sins has been raised again and sits today at God's right hand speaking peace to all who turn to Him, who trust in Him as their Redeemer—

> "Peace with God is Christ in glory,
>   God is light and God is love;
> Jesus died to tell the story,
>   Foes to bring to God above."

So Jesus said, "Peace I leave with you." Have you availed yourself of it? Can you say "I thank God I am justified by faith and I have peace with God through the Lord Jesus Christ?"

But that is only one side of it. There is another aspect of peace. "My peace I give unto you: not

as the world giveth, give I unto you." Now Jesus
says, "I am going to give you a peace which will
keep you from heart-trouble." We are living in
such strenuous days and times. There is a heart-
trouble which may cause great sorrow and distress even though the physical heart may be in
very good condition, and that is when one has to
endure pain because of bereavement, financial
trouble, family trials, and perhaps saddest of all,
church troubles. I think sometimes the greatest
sorrow people have to endure is trouble among
Christians who do not trust each other or love
one another any more, who instead of being help-
ers to one another are really hinderers of one another's progress. And yet how often we come up
against that very thing. Some time ago a brother
came and began telling another an unkind thing
about a third Christian brother. "Wait a minute," said the person addressed; "are you telling
me this because you love this man?"

Then there are the sorrows we have to endure
out in the world. There are indeed things going
on everywhere that are enough to break a sensitive heart. Yet Jesus says, "Peace I leave with
you, My peace I give unto you." He speaks rest
to troubled hearts.

"My peace I give unto you!" He could say,
"Reproach hath broken My heart," and yet His
spirit was in perfect peace. And the same peace

that possessed the heart of the Son of God, He desires to impart to us. How may we obtain it? We read in Isaiah 26:3, "Thou wilt keep him in perfect peace, whose mind is stayed on Thee: because he trusteth in Thee." There is the secret— trust and confidence in a God of love, a God of infinite power who worketh all things in accordance with His will. We are bidden to come to Him as He says, "Be careful for nothing; but in every thing by prayer and supplication with thanksgiving let your requests be made known unto God. And the peace of God, which passeth all understanding, shall keep your hearts and minds through Christ Jesus." The real meaning of that passage is this: the peace of God shall "garrison" your heart, or "keep" your heart, or "protect" your heart. This is the peace which Jesus would share with His own.

> "Oh, the peace my Saviour gives,
>   Peace I never knew before,
> And the way has brighter grown
>   Since I've learned to trust Him more."

In the 28th to the 31st verses, with which this chapter concludes, we see how our blessed Lord was kept in peace in the face of the most adverse circumstances. He said, "Ye have heard how I said unto you, I go away, and come again unto you. If ye loved Me, ye would rejoice, because I said, I go unto the Father: for My Father is greater than I." "If ye loved Me, ye would rejoice!" Is there not a word of comfort there for those of us who have lost dear ones down here? He said, "I told you I am going away. You should be so glad that I am going to the Father." Oh, these loved ones in Christ who have left us. Where have they gone? They have gone to the Father. Surely it should rejoice our hearts that they have entered into the Father's house. "My Father is greater than I." Remember He who is God, the Son, became Man, and as Man on earth, He takes the place of subjection and He says, "My Father is greater than I." As the Eternal Son, He is one with the Father and the Spirit. "Who, being in the form of God, thought it not robbery to be equal with God: but made Himself of no reputation, and took upon Him the form of a servant, and was made in the likeness of men: and being found in fashion as a man, He humbled Himself, and became obedient unto death, even the death of the cross." He took the place of recognized subjection to the Father.

"And now I have told you before it come to pass, that, when it is come to pass, ye might believe." This might be applied to many things going on in the world today. If we did not have the witness of Holy Scripture as to the conditions that were to prevail in the world, we might become discouraged. Nineteen hundred years of gospel preaching, and such dreadful things going on that we might say the gospel is a failure. Oh, no; it is not failure. People will not receive the gospel. Someone said, "Don't you think that Christianity has failed miserably?" and the other answered, "Christianity has not failed. It has never been tried." You see, God has shown us beforehand the conditions that will prevail until the return of the Lord. So you see, all is known to Him and He will overrule all for good.

"Hereafter I will not talk much with you: for the prince of this world cometh, and hath nothing in Me." Neither you nor I could say that. I have been a Christian for fifty years but I would not dare say that. The prince of this world is the devil and there is still something in me that responds to the prince of the world, but Jesus had nothing like that in Him. He knew no sin. So when the prince of the world came to Him there was no traitor inside waiting to throw open the door. I have to be on guard against Satan's wiles, but there was no such thing in His case. He was ever the sinless, spotless, unblemished Son of God.

"But that the world may know that I love the Father; and as the Father gave Me commandment, even so I do. Arise, let us go hence."

"Arise, let us go hence." Go where? To Gethsemane, out to Golgotha. What for? "That the world may know that I love the Father and as the Father gave Me commandment, even so I do." This is the burnt-offering aspect of the work of Christ. He died, not only to put away sin, but to glorify the Father. God had been so dishonored in this world by man's wickedness and disobedience and then the Son of God became Man and was obedient even to the death of the cross. He has glorified the Father in such a way that God has received more glory through that sacrifice than He ever lost by all of man's sin. It is of this that the burnt-offering speaks. Christ offered Himself, a sacrifice and a sweet-smelling savor to God.

But then God's glory and our salvation are linked up together and now since God has been glorified in the work of the cross, He can be just and the Justifier of all who believe in Jesus.

> "I hear the words of love,
>   I gaze upon the blood;
>   I see the mighty Sacrifice,
>   And I have peace with God.
>
>   'Tis everlasting peace,
>   Sure as Jehovah's name;
>   'Tis stable as His steadfast throne,
>   For evermore the same.

The clouds may go and come,
  And storms may sweep the sky,
This blood-sealed friendship changes not,
  The cross is ever nigh.

I change, He changes not,
  The Christ can never die;
His love, not mine, the resting-place,
  His truth, not mine, the tie."

THE TRUE VINE

❧ ❧ ❧

"I am the true Vine, and My Father is the husbandman. Every branch in Me that beareth not fruit He taketh away: and every branch that beareth fruit, He purgeth it, that it may bring forth more fruit. Now ye are clean through the word which I have spoken unto you. Abide in Me, and I in you. As the branch cannot bear fruit of itself, except it abide in the vine; no more can ye, except ye abide in Me. I am the Vine, ye are the branches: he that abideth in Me, and I in him, the same bringeth forth much fruit: for without Me ye can do nothing. If a man abide not in Me, he is cast forth as a branch, and is withered; and men gather them, and cast them into the fire, and they are burned. If ye abide in Me, and My words abide in you, ye shall ask what ye will, and it shall be done unto you. Herein is My Father glorified, that ye bear much fruit; so shall ye be My disciples" (John 15: 1-8).

❧ ❧ ❧

IT has been suggested, and probably with good reason, that our blessed Lord uttered these words as He and His disciples were passing through the city of Jerusalem, having left the upper room to go out to Gethsemane. As they went by the Temple they noticed a beautiful golden vine sculptured upon one of the Temple gates, and the Lord Jesus turned to His disciples and said, "I am the true Vine." The emphasis would be on the word "true." Israel was Jehovah's vine. In the 80th Psalm we read, "Thou hast brought a vine out of Egypt." That picture of the vine is used frequently in the Psalms and in the Prophets to represent the people of Israel. In separating Israel from the Gentile world it was the will of God that they should be His testimony in the earth, to bear fruit for Himself.

A vine is of very little use other than as a fruit-bearer. You can not build houses with the wood of a vine. You can not make furniture from it. It is of very little use even as fuel, for when cast into the fire it flames up a moment or two, and then it is gone. A vine was intended to bear fruit. God intended Israel to bear fruit for Him to glorify His Name before all the nations of the world. But He says sadly, through the prophet Hosea, "Israel is an empty vine, he bringeth forth fruit unto himself." That is, he had gone all to wood and leaves, but there was no real fruit for God. Isaiah pictures the vine in chapter 5, and Jehovah says, "I looked that it should bring forth grapes, and it brought forth wild grapes."

And so God rejected that earthly vine. It is no longer His specific testimony to the world. It is perfectly true that through all the centuries, in spite of their sufferings since Jerusalem was destroyed and the people of Israel have been scattered among the Gentiles, they have borne testimony to the unity of the Godhead. They have acknowledged the one true and living God, and *that* in spite of the sufferings that idolatrous nations have heaped upon them. But as to being Jehovah's witnesses to the truth of the Messiah, the Saviour that He had sent into the world, they have had no testimony. They have borne fruit unto themselves.

The Lord Jesus, foreseeing all this, says, "I am the true Vine." All else had failed, but He was to be the witness for God in the world. He was to bear fruit for Him. But He was going away; He was on His way already to the garden of sorrow, and then to the judgment-hall, the cross, and then back to the glory. How should He take Israel's place in testimony and bear fruit in the world?

Well, He says, "All my own are branches in the Vine, and will bear fruit for God here in the world," and so He pictures Himself as the Vine proper, and then all those redeemed to God by His precious blood who have found in Him their Saviour and Lord, as the branches in that living Vine here in the world to bear fruit for the Father.

Now mark, the great theme of these eight verses is fruit-bearing, which is conditioned upon communion or fellowship with the Lord. It is a common thing for people who have certain doctrinal views in their minds, to try to read those doctrines into every part of Scripture. For instance, the hyper-Calvinists, the extreme Calvinists, take it for granted that almost everywhere Scripture is treating of their five points. Recently I heard the 15th of Luke turned from its proper meaning, and the parable of the Prodigal Son made to represent the recovery of a backslider. They said the son was always a son, and no matter how far down he got among the swine he remained a son still, until eventually he repented and returned to his Father. The Lord Jesus was not talking about the doctrine of eternal security in Luke 15. Personally I have no question of the scripturalness of that doctrine, but in Luke 15 we read that the scribes and Pharisees murmured and said, "This Man receiveth sinners, and eateth with them," and He showed it is His glory to do that, for He came to seek sinners and to save them. He then gave the threefold parable of the lost sheep and the shepherd going out after it; the lost coin and the woman seeking it, and the lost son and the father's welcome when he returned. All these were meant to indicate heaven's interest in sinners repenting. What does it say? "There is joy in heaven over one sinner that repenteth, more than over ninety and nine just persons, which need no repentance." He was not talking about the recovery of the backslider, but of the salvation of the sinner.

Well, the hyper-Calvinist's mind was so occupied with the one side of the doctrine of the eternal security of the believer that he could think that even in Luke 15 Christ was dealing with that question.

Our dear Arminian friends, who take the other extreme, are afraid, that once being saved, if they are not careful, something might come up to destroy their relationship with God, so they say, "Don't you see, if the branch doesn't bear fruit it is cut off from the vine," and so they picture the Christian as lost forever if he does not bear fruit. In one case the Lord was showing the grace of God to sinners, and in this case He was telling of the importance of fellowship on the part of the saints, and fruit-bearing as the result of fellowship. So the Lord Jesus says, "I am the true Vine, and My Father is the husbandman." The Vine is up yonder, but we are linked with Him who is in heaven.

He says, "Every branch in Me that beareth not fruit He taketh away: and every branch that beareth fruit, He purgeth it, that it may bring forth more fruit." "Fruit," and "more fruit." If we are branches in the living Vine, if we have trusted the Lord Jesus Christ as Saviour, then the one great thing for which we are left in this world is to bear fruit to the glory of God. But someone says, "What do you mean by fruit?" We may think of it in a number of different ways. In

Galatians 5: 22 we see the fruit of Christian character which the Spirit of God produces in the life of the believer; love, joy, peace, longsuffering, gentleness, goodness, faith, meekness, temperance (self-control). All of these constitute fruit for the glory of the Father. You profess that you have been saved through faith in the Lord Jesus? Is the fruit of the Spirit seen in your life? It will be if you are living in fellowship with Christ. If the contrary to these is manifest, then you may be sure of this, that even though you may have trusted Christ for salvation you are not living in fellowship with God. If instead of love there is bitterness, malice, unkindness; if instead of joy there is gloom; if instead of peace there is unrest; if instead of longsuffering there is impatience; if instead of gentleness there is harshness; if instead of goodness there is moral evil beginning to be manifested; if instead of faith, worry and lack of confidence; if instead of meekness, pride and haughtiness; if instead of temperance or self-control you are subject to the lusts of the flesh— then that tells the story that, no matter what you profess, you are not living in fellowship with God. Because as we live in fellowship with Him and walk in the power of the Spirit, the fruit of the Spirit is manifest in the life.

But then, fruit is also seen as the result of service. Sometimes we have heard it said we must

distinguish between fruit and service, and that is
perfectly true in one sense of the word, but you
remember the Apostle Paul in writing to the
Romans said, "I want to visit you that I might
have some fruit among you also." He is thinking of the winning of precious souls and building
up of the believers, and so this too is fruit for the
glory of God. Surely if we have been saved ourselves we ought to be very much concerned about
this aspect of fruit. We ought to be seeking so
to honor God that we will have the joy of winning
others to the Lord Jesus Christ. Service is one
thing and fruit is another, but the results of
faithful service will be precious fruit that will
abide the coming day when we shall stand at the
judgment-seat of Christ. As branches in the Vine
we are responsible to bear fruit. We ought to be
exercised as to our true state or condition. We
ought to be careful about the profession we make
if our lives are not backing that profession. If
people hear us talking about being saved by grace,
and there is no evidence of it, men will indeed cast
us into the fire and we will be burned, so far as our
testimony is concerned.

Somebody says, "I do hope through grace I
have been bearing a little fruit for God, but it
seems so little." Yes, the humbler we are, and
the more we realize it, the more we will feel
there has been very little fruit indeed compared

with what there might have been. Let us take
heart from this: "Every branch that beareth
fruit, He purgeth it, that it may bring forth more
fruit." The Father is the Husbandman, and He
is constantly looking after the branches of the
living Vine, and if He sees a little fruit He says,
as it were, "So far, so good, but I want a little
more fruit." So He prunes and purges with the
spray of affliction and deep sorrow and grief, in
order to draw our hearts to Himself so that there
may be increased fruit to His glory.

I suppose if a branch were a conscious thing,
as it is a living thing, and the husbandman drew
near with the big shears to clip and cut, and then
to spray with some poisonous solution in order
that all kinds of evil insect-life might be destroyed, it might say, "Oh, dear, it's all up with
me now. What suffering I have to endure. What
sorrow I have to go through. What pain is caused
by the pruning, and then in what danger am I
myself because of the spray!" But the branch
would learn in due time that it was for increased
blessing and for better fruit.

So it is in all God's dealings with us. We should
not be discouraged if we are called upon to pass
through some very severe trials. You said you
wanted to walk with God, you wanted to live for
Him, you wanted Christ to be magnified in your
experiences, whether by life or by death. God

may give you some very strange and bitter and peculiar experiences in order that this wish of yours might be fulfilled.

> "I asked the Lord that I might grow
>   In life and faith and every grace,
> Might more of His salvation know
>   And seek more earnestly His face.
> 'Twas He who taught me thus to pray,
>   And He I trust has answered prayer,
> But it has been in such a way
>   As almost drove me to despair."

We hear the voice of the Spirit of God saying "Beloved, think it not strange concerning the fiery trial which is to try you, as though some strange thing happened unto you: but rejoice, inasmuch as ye are partakers of Christ's sufferings." It is a very interesting thing, a remarkable thing, that in this world God sometimes seems to treat His best friends worst, and He treated His own Son worst of all. And so when we have to pass through great trials, deep waters and many sorrows, it is not an evidence that He does not love us, that He does not care for us. He loved His own Son—shall I say?—if it were possible, more than He had ever loved Him when Jesus cried, "My God, My God, why hast Thou forsaken Me?" But, oh, the precious fruit of,

> "His death of pain and sorrow,
>   So like unto His birth,
> Which would no glory borrow,
>   No majesty from earth."

And so the Father prunes and purges the branches of the living Vine that we may bring forth more fruit. Jesus said, "Now ye are clean through the word which I have spoken unto you." He was addressing His disciples. They were clean through the washing of water by the Word, through the washing of regeneration and renewing of the Holy Ghost. They were clean, and now they were to abide in Him, cleansed by the Word, made conscious of the importance of fellowship. "Abide in Me, and I in you." "Abiding" speaks of "communion." "As the branch cannot bear fruit of itself, except it abide in the vine, no more can ye, except ye abide in Me."

How forgetful we are of that! The preacher goes out to face his audience to whom he has preached so frequently through the years, perhaps often from the very same passage of Scripture. He goes out with self-confidence, forgetting the need of prayer, of being before God for a time of heart-searching lest anything, any root of bitterness, might have come up which might hinder the work of the Spirit of God. He rushes to the platform and delivers his sermon—but nothing happens. Nothing happens because he was not consciously abiding in the living Vine.

You have possibly heard the story of a young minister who had been called to be pastor of his first church. He was just out of Seminary and he had much confidence in his own ability. He had graduated with honors, and everybody felt sure that he was going to be a second Henry Ward Beecher. The people were watching him as he entered the pulpit with an air of self-importance. He read his text, and then his whole sermon went from him. The whole thing was gone. He read the text again, and still he could not recall the sermon he intended to preach. He tried the third time and said, "I want to read my text again," hoping the sermon would come back to mind. But all was a blank so far as the sermon was concerned, and looking at his audience he said, "I am sorry; but I can't speak to you this morning." Down the stairs he went with bowed head and broken step. At the close an old church officer came to him and said, "Laddie, if you had gone up the way you came down, you might have come down the way you went up!"

You see, it is so easy to be self-confident and to believe that because we have done it before, of course we can do it again, and so we forget the need of constantly abiding, of ever being before Him in communion. And it is the same in every detail of Christian life. We have had a great blessing and a wonderful day of victory, and in the power of that we try to live the next day, forgetting in the rush of things the necessity of being before God, of having a quiet time before

Him. Then comes a crash and a failure, and we are heartbroken and wonder what is the matter. Jesus gives the answer, "As the branch cannot bear fruit of itself, except it abide in the Vine; no more can ye, except ye abide in Me. I am the Vine, ye are the branches: he that abideth in Me, and I in him, the same bringeth forth much fruit."

Now notice the order in verse 2: "Every branch that beareth fruit," and then in the next clause: "He purgeth it that it may bring forth more fruit." See verse 5: "He that abideth in Me, and I in him, the same bringeth forth much fruit." It is "fruit," "more fruit," "much fruit."

How often we have known those who walked with God in early days, lived in a sense in dependence upon the Lord, enjoyed communion and fellowship with Him in a wonderful way, manifested the fruit of the spiritual life, were used cf God, won souls for Christ, and so had the fruit of a life which glorified the Father. Then something happened. No one else, perhaps, knew what it was. Outwardly the life was just as correct, the sermons were just as clear, but there was no longer that savor of Christ about them, no longer that evidence of walking in fellowship with Him; no power, no blessing. Why, it is the will of God that as the years go on there should be increased fruit, not less. Of the aged saints who walked with God through the years it says in the Psalms, "They shall still bring forth fruit in old age." But this will only be as we continue to walk humbly before God.

What a lovely thing it is to see a saint of God, a man or woman, grow old gracefully. There are some who, as they grow old, seem to take age and its infirmities as an excuse for short tempers and unkind criticism, and all those things that make it so hard to get along with them. But what a lovely thing to see people going down the valley looking beyond the river to the Celestial City with the glory of heaven shining in their faces, the faith of God possessing their hearts, and the grace of Christ manifested in their lives! Bearing fruit in old age. "Fruit," "more fruit," "much fruit."

Now if one fails here, if there is no communion, if fellowship is not maintained, if the spirit of prayer is lacking, if the Word of God is neglected, then the testimony soon counts for nothing. "If a man abide not in Me, he is cast forth as a branch (keep that in mind, for a branch should bear fruit), and is withered; and men gather them, and cast them into the fire, and they are burned." Men utterly ignore the testimony of those who profess to be Christ's, but do not live in fellowship with God, do not manifest the Spirit of Christ. Their testimony counts for nothing.

I was trying to talk with a dear lad who had been brought up in what I supposed was a Christian home, and I said, "Isn't your father a Christian?" He answered with a sarcastic twist of his lip, "Well, he says he is; but he ain't working at it." It was evident that that father's testimony had no weight whatever with his boy. How often people try to say something for Christ, urged by the desire to help a needy soul, they want to say the right word, but if the life is not in harmony, it as as Emerson said once, "What you are speaks so loud that I can't hear what you say."

A life lived in fellowship with God gives power to the message. "But if a man abide not in Me, he is cast forth as a branch," and men spurn such profession and refuse his testimony.

On the other hand, "If ye abide in Me, and My words abide in you"—that's the secret—"My words abide in you." Where do we get those words? Right here in God's blessed Book. And so the believer who is abiding in Christ is the one who is feeding upon the Word, and does not have just a headful of truth. Some people, if they were cut off at the neck, would lose all the truth of God; but take off the heads of others and the truth would still be in the heart!

"If ye abide in Me, and My words abide in you, ye shall ask what ye will, and it shall be done unto you." Here, then, is the secret of answered prayer. Why is it we ask God for so many things that we never receive? Why is it that so many of our prayers never seem to reach heaven? Well, it is because we are not abiding in Christ. God has never promised to answer the prayers of those who are out of communion.

"Herein is My Father glorified, that ye bear much fruit; so shall ye be My disciples." Shall we not challenge our own hearts, "Am I really abiding in Christ? Am I conscious of anything that is hindering communion, anything that comes up when I kneel in prayer that makes it hard to pray, that makes it seem as though the heavens are brass?" If so, then may God give us grace to judge it, and no matter if it is as near or dear as the right eye or the right hand, to pluck it out, that nothing may be allowed in the life that will in any way hinder fellowship with Christ; that thus we may bear much fruit to the glory of the Father.

ABIDING IN LOVE

✦ ✦ ✦

"As the Father hath loved Me, so have I loved you: continue ye in My love. If ye keep My commandments, ye shall' abide in My love; even as I have kept My Father's commandments, and abide in His love. These things have I spoken unto you, that My joy might remain in you, and that your joy might be full. This is My commandment, That ye love one another, as I have loved you. Greater love hath no man than this, that a man lay down his life for his friends. Ye are My friends, if ye do whatsoever I command you. Henceforth I call you not servants; for the servant knoweth not what his lord doeth: but I have called you friends; for all things that I have heard of My Father I have made known unto you. Ye have not chosen Me, but I have chosen you, and ordained you, that ye should go and bring forth fruit, and that your fruit should remain: that whatsoever ye shall ask of the Father in My name, He may give it you. These things I command you, that ye love one another" (John 15: 9-17).

✦ ✦ ✦

THE Holy Spirit has given us a wonderful privilege in allowing this last marvelous discourse of our Lord Jesus Christ to be put on record and preserved throughout all the centuries, that we might listen today to the tender gracious things that He said to His disciples just before He went out to Gethsemane and from there to the judgment-hall and the cross.

Did you ever stop to ask how it was that after something like forty or fifty years the Apostle John was able to give us a discourse like this in such detail? These words were spoken about A.D. 30, and John is supposed to have written this Gospel somewhere within the eighth or ninth decade of the first century of the Christian era when he was an old man living in Ephesus. I have mentioned before that one of the old Church fathers tells us that John was an adolescent when Jesus called him, and therefore we are not surprised to learn that he outlived all his fellow-disciples. Peter, for instance, had been with Christ for some thirty or forty years when John wrote this Gospel. Paul, who did not know Jesus on earth, died by martyrdom a year or two before. We are told that Matthew was slain by a lance in Scythia, and Thomas was killed in India where he had gone to preach Christ. All the others of the apostolic band had gone to be with Christ long ago. John was the only one left, and he could look back and think of the time when he was associated with the Lord Jesus Christ here on earth. Impressed by the Spirit he sat down to write this wonderful record.

He says, "The Word was made flesh, and dwelt among us, (and we beheld His glory, the glory as of the only begotten of the Father,) full of grace and truth." John gives us details as to the Sav-

iour's conversations such as we get nowhere else;
His long conversation with Nicodemus, with the
woman at the well, and with many other characters. And now in these marvelous chapters, 13
to 16, we have His last discourse, and His high-
priestly prayer in chapter 17, all recorded with
such remarkable detail after the lapse of nearly
a half-century. Have you ever said to yourself,
"How could he do it?" We need to remember the
words of the Lord Himself, "But the Comforter,
which is the Holy Ghost, whom the Father will
send in My name, He shall teach you all things,
and bring all things to your remembrance, whatsoever I have said unto you." So when John sat
down to write, doubtless these things which had
become dim through the years were brought anew
to his mind through the guidance of the Holy
Spirit of God, who could reproduce them exactly
as they were spoken by the Lord.

We are permitted, as it were, to sit in that
upper room with the Lord and His disciples and
to tread the way out to the garden of sorrows.
And here we listen to these blessed unfoldings of
His tender heart. Notice verses 9 and 10, as He
sets before them the love of the divine Saviour.
He says, "As the Father hath loved Me, so have I
loved you: continue ye in My love. If ye keep My
commandments, ye shall abide in My love; even
as I have kept My Father's commandments, and

abide in His love." Jesus says, "I love you just as the Father loves Me." We get the other side in chapter seventeen when He said, "That the world may know that Thou hast sent Me, and hast loved them, as Thou hast loved Me." God, the Father, loves us—who believe in the Lord Jesus —just as much as He loves His Son. And the Lord Jesus Christ loves us as much as He loves His Father. What a wonderful circle that is!

> "In that circle of God's favor,
>   Circle of the Father's love;
> All is rest and rest forever,
>   All is perfectness above."

It is one thing to talk about love and another to manifest it. I may say I love my mother, and yet refuse to do anything for her when she is sick. Such love counts for very little. I am a father, and I say I love my children, but I may be so taken up with the things of the world that I don't lift my hand to help them when they need it. Love is manifested by active benevolence and by obedience. The Lord Jesus says, "If ye keep My commandments, ye shall abide in My love," that is, dwell consciously in the sense of His love. It was the delight of His heart to do the will of the Father. It will be the delight of our hearts to do the will of the Lord Jesus Christ if we really love Him.

We have already heard Him say, "My peace I give unto you." Now in verse eleven, He speaks of sharing His joy with us. "These things have I spoken to you, that My joy might remain in you, and that your joy might be full." We are told in the Old Testament that the joy of the Lord is our strength. Joy is more than peace. Joy is peace bubbling up. The Lord would have us to be a joyful people. He Himself was like that. While it is true that He was the suffering One, the Man of Sorrows, yet we never feel, as we read the records penned by Matthew, Mark, Luke and John, that we are reading of a sad man, but all the way through we are reading of One in whose heart there was fulness of joy. No matter how things went outwardly He could always find His joy in the Father, and the very time when He had to pronounce judgment upon the cities wherein most of His mighty works were done, we read "at that time Jesus rejoiced in spirit and said, I thank Thee, O Father, Lord of heaven and earth, that Thou hast hid these things from the wise and prudent, and hast revealed them unto babes." He says, in effect, "If you abide in fellowship with Me, and make it the object of your life to glorify Me, you shall share My joy; the very joy that is Mine will be yours, that your joy may be full." You say, "What commandment does He mean?" What commandment? "This is My commandment,

That ye love one another, as I have loved you." You see, if we keep that commandment, everything else will be all right. You will never grieve the heart of God if you love one another. Love is the fulfilling of the law. Oh, if we would only test ourselves more. If we would ask ourselves, "Now am I doing this because I love my brother? Would I say that because I love my brother, or am I allowing myself to do things that are incompatible with love?" Love covers a multitude of sins we are told. If I really love my brother I shall never want to hurt him, or to shame and disgrace him. Even if he has been guilty of what is wrong, I will go to him and seek to restore him in tender love. We forget this so much, and deal with each other in such a reckless way. If God dealt with us as we deal with each other, it would go very hard with us. But, ah, His abounding love!—love that covers, love that, in grace, has overlooked so much in our life! Did you ever stop to think, if every hidden thing you ever did was blazed abroad, whether you would feel like facing the world again? So many things you have had to go to Him about, and He has kept them covered up. What a mercy! Do we deal with our brethren that way? Love covereth. "This is My commandment, That ye love one another, as I have loved you. Greater love hath no man than this, that a man lay down his life for his friends." Here, then, is the supreme test of his love. John, the Apostle, says, "We ought to lay down our lives for the brethren." It is our duty to go so far as even to lay down our lives for them. Do we act on that? That is what Jesus did. Paul could say, "I live by the faith of the Son of God, who loved me, and gave Himself for me."

Long years ago a missionary over in China was engaged in the work of translating the New Testament into Chinese. He had an eminent scholar to assist him, a Confucianist who had never heard of Christianity until this missionary had engaged him to help in the translation. He sat with him day after day, and together they went over the New Testament page by page and verse by verse. The Chinese scholar would suggest the proper Chinese word in order to make the meaning plain. The missionary was a painstaking person and anxious to produce a splendid translation. One thing he thought he had better not do, was to talk religion with his helper. So he was very careful, and never said a word to the man about his need of Christ and the salvation of his own soul. But finally when they had finished, he thought he ought to say something. He said, "You have been a great help to me. I could not have gotten along without you, and now I would like to ask, as we have come along through the New Testament, has not the beauty of Christianity appealed to you?

Would you not like to be a Christian?" The scholar looked at him and said, "Yes, it does appeal to me. It is the most wonderful system of ethics and philosophy I have ever known. I think that if I could once see a Christian I might become interested." "But," said the missionary, "I am a Christian!" "You," said the Chinese scholar, "are you a Christian? Oh, no. Pardon me, I don't want to offend you, but I have observed you and listened to you all the way along. You are not a Christian. If I understand aright, a Christian is a follower of Jesus, and Jesus says, 'A new commandment give I unto you, that you might love one another.' But I have listened to you talk about others who were not present, saying unkind things about them. You are not a Christian. And then I have noticed too that Christianity teaches perfect trust, and I translated for you a passage that says, 'My God shall supply all your need according to His riches in glory by Christ Jesus,' and you are told to trust and not be afraid, but you don't do that. If your check is a little late in reaching you, you are dreadfully worried and you wonder what you are going to do." And he went on with a number of things like that, ending with, "I have had to conclude that you are not a Christian. I think if I could see a Christian, I would like to be one."

The **poor** broken-hearted missionary! He sobbed **before** the Lord and said, "Oh, I have been so **careless.**" He just broke down and had to ask **forgiveness** for his coldness and neglect. The **scholar** went away and said, "Well, I wonder if, after all, I haven't seen a Christian." You see Christians are not perfect as the world expects perfection, but we should grow more like our Master every day.

"Greater love hath no man than this, that a man lay down his life for his friends." Jesus says, "You are My friends if you do whatsoever I have commanded you." We do not become Christians by doing His commandments, but we become manifestly His friends by obeying His words. We show that we are really friends to Christ by walking in obedience.

"Henceforth I call you not **servants**; for the servant knoweth not what his **lord doeth**: but I have called you friends; for all things that I **have** heard of My Father I have made known unto you." (The word for servants is "bondmen.") Jesus says, in effect, "I love to take you into My confidence." "I have called you friends; for all things that I have heard of My Father I have made known unto you." You know how you feel about your friends. Most of us do not have a great many friends. There are just a few folks whom we take right into our hearts, and we talk of them as our friends. We do not like to share our secrets with everyone. But when we get a real, intimate friend, we love to share the secret things of our heart with that friend. So the Lord Jesus Christ says, "I am calling you My friends." Oh, how He opens up His heart and makes known His precious things to His friends.

And then another thing, we give our friends privileges that we do not give to strangers. So He says, "For all things that I have heard of My Father I have made known unto you. Ye have not chosen Me, but I have chosen you, and ordained you, that ye should go and bring forth fruit, and that your fruit should remain: that whatsoever ye shall ask of the Father in My name, He may give it you." In other words, He wants His own to enter into such an intimate sense of fellowship and communion with Himself that they may go to the Father in His name and, as friends, offer their petitions in that name and the Father will delight to hear and fulfil, because it glorifies the name of Jesus.

I may have a friend and I write a little note and say, "This will introduce you to so-and-so, who is also a friend of mine. If you can do what he or she desires, I shall esteem it as though it were done for me." And that one goes to my friend, who says, "I am a friend of his, and I will be a friend to you." That is what Jesus says.

He means; "Tell the Father I sent you." You see some people believe that to pray in Christ's name merely means to close by saying, "These things we ask for the name and sake of the Lord Jesus Christ." If you are not saved you are not authorized to go to God in Christ's name, and if you are not in fellowship with God neither are you authorized to go to God like that. People who are living selfish, worldly lives are not authorized to go to God in this way. If you are abiding in Him you can go to the Father by His authority and He will guide your petitions. He delights to answer, because in answering He is showing His love for and confidence in His own blessed Son.

But there is something here in verse sixteen I must not pass over. What does He say? "Ye have not chosen Me, but I have chosen you." Did not they choose Him? Did not you choose Christ? Yes, but not before He chose you.

> " 'Tis not that I did choose Thee,
>   For, Lord, that could not be;
> This heart would still refuse Thee,
>   But Thou hast chosen me.

> " 'Twas the same love that spread the feast,
>   That gently forced me in,
> Else I had still refused to come,
>   And perished in my sin."

Long before my heart was inclined to come to
Christ, He touched me by the blessed Holy Spirit,
and at last when I was utterly broken down and
brought to repentance, and cried to Him in
shame, "Save, Lord, or I perish," He took me in
and made me His own.

And then when it is a question of service, it is
He who chooses for this or that special work.
And it is He who selects our sphere of ministry,
whether at home or abroad. You remember the
man who wanted to follow the Master, and the
Lord said, "No; go home, and show how great
things the Lord has done for thee." We can glorify Christ in whatever place we may be and we
must recognize that He chose that task for us.
"Ye have not chosen Me, but I have chosen you,
and ordained you."

Many people are troubled about ordination.
Folks ask, "Has any one a right to preach who
has not been ordained?" In this Book you do not
read of people being ordained to preach the gospel. You never get the word "ordination" connected with the actual setting apart of a man to
preach the gospel. What about Timothy? The
word "ordained" was not used in Timothy's case.
"Well," you say, "did you forget about Paul and
Barnabas?" No, but they had been preaching a
long time in Antioch before the elders laid their
hands on them. Nobody authorized them by any

service of ordination to go out and preach. That
is the Lord's prerogative. He said, "I have chosen
you, and ordained you, that ye should go and bring
forth fruit." The word "ordained" means "set
apart." "I have chosen you." It is good to be
able to say,

> "Christ, the Son of God, has sent me,
>   Through the midnight lands;
> Mine the mighty ordination
>   Of the piercèd hands."

That is the ordination that counts. All that the
elders or others can do is to recognize what God
has done already. The Lord said in regard to
Paul, when he was still Saul of Tarsus, "He is a
chosen vessel unto Me, to bring My name before
the Gentiles, and kings, and the children of
Israel." And to Paul himself He said, "I have
appeared unto thee for this purpose, to make thee
a minister and a witness both of these things
which thou hast seen, and of those things in the
which I will appear unto you." It is the Lord
Himself who makes ministers, who gives men first
to know Christ as their own Saviour, and then
sends them forth to preach. "I have chosen you
and ordained you, that ye should go and bring
forth fruit, and that your fruit should remain:
that whatsoever ye shall ask of the Father in My
name, He may give it you."

He concludes this particular section with these words, "These things I command you, that ye love one another." Ah, that is the final test. Love is the evidence of grace working in our souls. So the passage closes as it began.

NOT OF THE WORLD

✦ ✦ ✦

"If the world hate you, ye know that it hated Me before it hated you. If ye were of the world, the world would love his own: but because ye are not of the world, but I have chosen you out of the world, therefore the world hateth you. Remember the word that I said unto you, The servant is not greater than his lord. If they have persecuted Me, they will also persecute you; if they have kept My saying, they will keep yours also. But all these things will they do unto you for My name's sake, because they know not Him that sent Me. If I had not come and spoken unto them, they had not had sin: but now they have no cloke for their sin. He that hateth Me hateth My Father also. If I had not done among them the works which none other man did, they had not had sin: but now have they both seen and hated both Me and My Father. But this cometh to pass, that the word might be fulfilled that is written in their law, They hated Me without a cause. But when the Comforter is come, whom I will send unto you from the Father, even the Spirit of truth, which proceedeth from the Father, He shall testify of Me: and ye also shall bear witness because ye have been with Me from the beginning" (John 15: 18-27).

✦ ✦ ✦

THESE words acquire a peculiar solemnity when we recall the fact that they were uttered by our Lord Jesus Christ when the dark shadow of the cross, which expressed the world's hatred toward Him, was already falling athwart His pathway. On ahead He saw Calvary where He, the sinless One, was to be made sin

for us. And there He was to experience all the
hatred and malignity that man, activated by
demon power, could heap upon Him. He had no
illusions as to His future. He knew from the first
just how His earthly ministry would end. He came
from heaven to close it in that very way. He said,
long before, "The Son of Man came not to be
ministered unto, but to minister, and to give His
life a ransom for many." He knew that He would
meet with rejection on every side, but He came
to die for those who hated Him, for those who
trampled upon the love and grace of God, as seen
in Him.

And now He calls upon those who trust Him to
walk with Him, recognizing the fact that this
world-system is incurably evil, that it can never
be improved but that it will ever stand in opposition to God. Many Christians have imagined that
it can be improved. Many have supposed that it
was the program of the Church to make the world
over, and so, to make it better; but as you look
out upon this world today after nineteen hundred
years of gospel preaching it is still the most
wicked of all possible worlds. And it is just as evil
now as it ever was. People ask, "But is not the
world better, because of so many millions of
Christians in it?" They forget that Christians
are not of the world, for the Lord Jesus Christ
tells us right here that He has chosen us out of

the world. So when you want to see whether the world is any better than it was when it crucified the Lord of glory, subtract the Church and everything connected with it, and all you have left is the world in its stark hideousness and hatred of God—just the samè wicked world today as when its representatives cried in Pilate's judgment-hall, "We have no king but Cæsar," and as for Jesus, "Crucify Him! Crucify Him!" And so these words come down to us, "If the world hate you, ye know that it hated Me before it hated you." And we need to remember that we begin our Christian life by choosing One whom the world rejects. We identify ourselves with Him, by faith. That is why the Spirit of God elsewhere says, "Love not the world, neither the things that are in the world. If any man love the world, the love of the Father is not in him. For all that is in the world, the lust of the flesh, and the lust of the eyes, and the pride of life, is not of the Father, but is of the world. And the world passeth away, and the lust thereof: but he that doeth the will of God abideth forever."

Some people are perplexed when we use this term, "the world," and they ask the question, "Just what do you mean when you speak of Christians not loving the world and Jesus choosing us out of the world. What world do you mean? Do you mean the universe as such?" No "Do you

mean the globe?" No; not that. "What, then?"
This order or system of humanity that has turned
its back on God. That is the world. And that
world, I repeat, is just the same today as it ever
was, and when a Christian tries to be a friend of
the world, he constitutes himself, at least in that
act, into an enemy of God. Scripture uses strong
language for those of His children who try to be
friends of the world. In James we read, "Ye adulterers and adulteresses, know ye not that the
friendship of the world is enmity with God? Whosoever therefore will be a friend of the world is
the enemy of God." We have pledged ourselves
to the One whom the world rejects. Therefore,
we are guilty of spiritual adultery if we throw
our arms about the world that has refused Him.
Oh, if every Christian could realize that he is
called out of the world. If we only understood the
heavenly nature of our calling we would not raise
so many questions as to whether there is any
harm in this or that. The one great question
would be, "Is this of the Father, or is it of the
world?" If it is for the glory of God, I can go
on with it gladly, but if not, then it should have
no place in my life as a Christian.

This world hates Christianity. We see many
examples of that today. How Christians are suffering in various parts of the world where once
they seemed to have a welcome! Only a few years

back Japan was heartily patronizing Christianity, and today they are declaring that it is an enemy of the State. The last word we hear is that all Christian missionaries are ordered to leave the land. Why? Because they know that Christianity is the very antithesis of the theories that they are now advocating, and by which they hope to dominate eastern Asia. We see the same attitude on the part of other great world-powers. Christ is still the hated One. The opposition to Him becomes more and more intense. It behooves us to ask ourselves if we are really prepared to stand with and for Him no matter what attitude men may take round about us. They hate our Lord. They hate His very grace and lovingkindness because it is such a reflection upon their pride and spirit of warfare which is opposed to the humility of Jesus. Men detest Him for His very lowliness.

He says, "If ye were of the world, the world would love his own: but because ye are not of the world, but I have chosen you out of the world, therefore the world hateth you." What a wonderful thing to be chosen out of the world! I am sure when we look forward and think of the judgment, we can thank God that we have been chosen out of the world.

But what shall we say of those who hope to be delivered and who profess to be Christians, but who are now seeking to get all the pleasure and good times the world can give them. One thinks of Lot and his family so long ago. They moved down to Sodom in order that they might participate in worldly things, tired of the life of separation lived up there on the hills of Palestine. Step by step downward, until they became ensconced in Sodom. Then came the day when the judgment of God was about to fall upon that guilty city and the angels came to bring the message, "Escape for thy life; look not behind thee, neither stay thou in all the plain; escape to the mountain, lest thou be consumed." We are told the angels commanded Lot to go to his relatives in the city, men who had married his daughters, and tell them that tomorrow the judgment was to fall But they mocked Lot when he talked to them about judgment. Why? Because he had lived so much like the rest of them. And now they thought he was demented. Are you and I so living that our testimony really counts when we warn men to flee from the wrath to come, or are we living so near to the edge of the world, are we so much like those around us, that others question whether we really believe what we are professing. Oh, if there ever was a day when God is calling to absolute separation from this world, this is the time!

"Remember the word that I said unto you, The servant is not greater than his lord. If they have persecuted Me, they will also persecute you; if they have kept My saying, they will keep yours also." There you have the two classes, those who are subject to Him and those who refuse to own His authority. The lines are being drawn closer and closer, and will be drawn more and more definitely. As we read our Bibles and the news-papers, and look around about us, we can not help but believe that even now perhaps we are mov-ing right on toward the darkness and horrors of the great tribulation. And if that be so, the hour when the Lord Jesus Christ shall descend from heaven with a shout, with the voice of the arch-angel, and with the trump of God: and the dead in Christ shall rise first, must be very close at hand. Let us see that we so live, so behave our-selves, so use the talents that God has entrusted us with in order that our actions towards those about us, in the family, in the professing church and in the world around, will carry weight, and that when we hear that voice, that shout, that trump, we will go with gladness and not be ashamed before Him at His coming. One thing I am sure of is, that there will never be a Chris-tian in that day who will wish he had been a lit-tle more worldly or enjoyed more of the frivolity of the present moment. But there will be tens of thousands of believers who will in that day be willing to give almost anything if they had been more interested in the things of the Lord during the little time that they spent in this scene. God give us to live as those who have been chosen out of the world! When we came to Christ we said farewell to the world. We left it all for His name's sake. Oh, how can we then go back on that which meant so much to us in the hour of our first love.

Let us search our hearts, and if we find that the world means more to us now than it did then, let us repent and "do our first works over again" that we may have His approval in the coming day.

The world hates God; it will hate us. If we are seeking its love it will only be at the cost of faithfulness to Christ. That is the trouble with the world. It does not know God. Do we know Him? We never can know Him if we reject Jesus Christ. He says, "I am the Way, the Truth and the Life; no man cometh unto the Father, but by Me." "There is none other name under heaven given among men, whereby we must be saved." He came to reveal the Father. He has told out all that God is, and if men spurn Him, it is because they know not God. When we receive Him, we receive eternal life—"And this is life eternal, that they might know Thee, the only true God, and Jesus Christ, whom Thou hast sent."

"If I had not come and spoken unto them, they had not had sin: but now they have no cloke for their sin." Responsibility increases with knowledge. People have said to me, "If that is true, then what about the heathen? Are not the heathen all right just as they are? Why should we go to them with the gospel? For if we do not go they will not have sin. Does that mean that the heathen are saved without the gospel?" Not at all. The first chapter of the Epistle to the Romans explains that. It is not because of what they do not know—not because of the rejection of the Saviour of whom they have never heard—but because of what they do know, because of the light of conscience which they already have that they are condemned. They are doing day by day the things that their own consciences tell them are wrong. The Christian is to go to them with the gospel and proclaim a full and free salvation through the finished work of the Lord Jesus Christ, bringing a message of joy and happiness such as they never have known in their idolatry. When they hear, they are responsible to accept the gift of God. Every time we preach the gospel here at home we must remember that to some it is the savor of death unto death; and to others the savor of life unto life. Men, hearing the message either accept Christ as Saviour, or spurn the word and increase their condemnation. It is a solemn thing when life is offered and men refuse it. That is what we are told in the earlier part of this book when Jesus was speaking to Nicodemus. He said, "This is the condemnation, that light is come into the world, and men loved darkness rather than light, because their deeds were evil. For every one that doeth evil hateth the light, neither cometh to the light, lest his deeds should be reproved. But he that doeth truth cometh to the light, that his deeds may be made manifest, that they are wrought in God."

And so the greatest condemnation rested upon those who heard and rejected Christ when He came. He came, He revealed God, they rejected Him and thus rejecting Him they had no cloke for their sin, for in hating Him, they hated His Father also.

"If I had not done among them the works which none other man did, they had not had sin: but now have they both seen and hated both Me and My Father." That is, the Lord Jesus Christ not only ministered by word of mouth but He authenticated His teaching by His acts of power, and every miracle wrought by Christ proved that He was what He professed to be, the holy, spotless Son of God. The people went in crowds to see His miracles, but they rejected the One who wrought these works, and therefore added to their own condemnation. Of this He says, "But this cometh to pass, that the word might be fulfilled that is written in their law, they hated Me without a cause." He quotes from Psalm 69, where we have a wonderful prophetic picture of His dying on the cross for our sins. It is in that connection we read, "They hated Me without a cause." There was no reason why Jesus should be hated. He came with a heart full of love for mankind, and went about doing good. Men spurned Him because His very purity brought their impurity out into the light; His very holiness accentuated their unholiness; His perfect righteousness but manifested their unrighteousness. They said, "Get Him out of the way!"

There is a story told of an African chiefess who happened to visit a mission station. The missionary had a little mirror hung up on a tree outside his cabin. The chiefess happened to look into the mirror and saw herself reflected there in all her hideous paint and evil features. She gazed at her own ugly, grotesque countenance and she started back in horror and said, "Who is that horrible-looking person inside that tree?" "Oh," they said, "it is not in the tree; the glass is reflecting your own face." She could not believe it until she held that mirror in her hand. She said, "I must have the glass. How much will you sell it for?" "Oh," he said, "I don't want to sell it." But she insisted and begged, till finally he thought it might be best to sell it to her to avoid trouble. So he named the price and she took it. Then as she said, "I will never have it making faces at me again," she threw it down and broke it to pieces.

That is the way people treat the Bible and Jesus Christ. The Word of God shows up men's wickedness. They say, "Down with Christ! We don't want your Bible and we don't want your Christ."

But now, what is our power for testimony as we go to meet a world like this? In the last two verses Jesus again refers to that blessed One whose coming He had promised in the earlier part of His discourse. "But when the Comforter is come, whom I will send unto you from the Father, even the Spirit of truth, which proceedeth from the Father, He shall testify of Me! and ye also shall bear witness, because ye have been with Me from the beginning." We have no power in ourselves. As Chritsians we are weak, and have no ability to stand against the enemy, but, "Greater is He that is in you than he that is in the world." And so our reliance is upon the Divine Comforter, the third Person of the Trinity, who has come to take the Saviour's place and to empower us to go forth and bear witness, that through this testi-mony, men may be saved.

THE MISSION OF THE COMFORTER

✦ ✦ ✦

"These things have I spoken unto you, that ye should not be offended. They shall put you out of the synagogues: yea, the time cometh, that whosoever killeth you will think that he doeth God service. And these things will they do unto you, because they have not known the Father, nor Me. But these things have I told you, that when the time shall come ye may remember that I told you of them. And these things I said not unto you at the beginning, because I was with you. But now I go my way to Him that sent Me; and none of you asketh Me, Whither goest Thou? But because I have said these things unto you, sorrow hath filled your heart. Nevertheless I tell you the truth; It is expedient for you that I go away: for if I go not away, the Comforter will not come unto you; but if I depart, I will send Him unto you. And when He is come, He will reprove the world of sin, and of righteousness, and of judgment: of sin, because they believe not on Me; of righteousness, because I go to My Father, and ye see Me no more; of judgment, because the prince of this world is judged. I have yet many things to say unto you, but ye cannot bear them now. Howbeit when He, the Spirit of truth, is come, He will guide you into all truth: for He shall not speak of Himself; but whatsoever He shall hear, that shall He speak: and He will show you things to come. He shall glorify Me: for He shall receive of Mine, and shall show it unto you. All things that the Father hath are Mine: therefore said I, that He shall take of Mine, and shall show it unto you. A little while, and ye shall not see Me: and again, a little while, and ye shall see Me, because I go to the Father" (John 16: 1-16).

✦ ✦ ✦

IN verses 1-6 the Lord emphasizes what He has already been putting before His followers as recorded in the last part of the previous chapter; that is, the Christian as a stranger in the world and the unchanging state of this world during all the years since Christ went to be at the right hand of God. He says, "These things have I spoken unto you, that you should not be offended (stumbled)." If the disciples of the Lord Jesus felt that they had reason to expect that the attitude of the world as such was going to be changed through the preaching of the gospel, they might well be stumbled by what they see as they look back and about them at the present time. For instance, take our own day. Suppose we really believed that the whole world was to be converted in this age and that all men everywhere were eventually to be changed in attitude toward the Lord Jesus Christ, how discouraged we might well become, for we have seen in our day whole nations turned against the Lord Jesus Christ that once professed to honor Him. And we have seen other lands where the gospel was once permitted, banning everything of a Christian character. They have used methods worse than pagan or papal Rome ever tried, to rout Christianity out of their dominions. But the Lord Jesus Christ told us to expect these things. The attitude of the world as such has never changed. The world hates Christ, the world hates God, and the world hates the gospel of God.

And so Jesus warned His disciples about this, and even pointed out that men would be so dominated by a lying spirit that they would actually think that in opposing Christianity they would be glorifying God. He says here, "Yea, the time cometh, that whosoever killeth you will think that he doeth God service." Saul of Tarsus is a sample of this. Saul said when he stood before the council, "I verily thought within myself that I ought to do many things contrary to the name of Jesus of Nazareth, which thing I also did in Jerusalem." Which thing he did until God, in His grace, stopped him on the Damascus Road, revealed Christ to him, and sent him out to preach the faith he had once destroyed. Men of the world, religious men, have often assumed, that they were really honoring God in trying to destroy evangelical Christianity. "These things," said Jesus, "will they do unto you, because they have not known the Father, nor Me. But these things have I told you, that when the time shall come, ye may remember that I told you of them. And these things I said not unto you at the beginning, because I was with you." He was going away. He knew that the centuries would roll by during which He would be sitting on the Father's Throne in heaven interceding for His disciples here on earth. So He would have them understand just what they would be expected to go through in this world because they belonged to Him.

He says, "Now I go My way to Him that sent
Me; and none of you asketh Me, Whither goest
Thou? But because I have said these things unto
you, sorrow hath filled your heart." They took
it for granted that He was indeed the Messiah of
Israel, and that the Messiah came to abide with
them here on the earth, bringing in the blessing
so long predicted by the prophets. And now He
speaks of going away, and is unfolding to them
that another work of God is to be carried on in
His absence—not now the deliverance of Israel,
as such, not now the fulfilment of blessing for
God's earthly people, but a special message of
grace going out to the Gentiles, calling upon all
men everywhere to face their sins in the presence
of God and find in the Lord Jesus Christ an all-
sufficient Saviour. His apostles are to be their
missionaries.

He tells them of the power by which they will
be endowed—the One who is to come upon them
and dwell in them, who will enable them to speak
for God and bear witness in such a way that
many will believe and live. "Nevertheless," He
says, "I tell you the truth; It is expedient for you
that I go away: for if I go not away, the Comforter will not come unto you; but if I depart, I
will send Him unto you." If you had said to one
of them, "Do you think it will be well for your
Master to leave you?" I am sure he would have

replied, "Oh, no; the best thing for us would be
that He should tarry with us."

But you see, if that had been so, He would not
be in a position to carry on His world-wide program. As Man, in grace, He must necessarily be
localized where His body is. But He was going
away, and another Person of the Godhead was
now to be sent to the earth who was not to become
incarnate in one Person, but who was to work
through the whole Church, empowering the servants of God as they proclaimed His message. "It
is expedient for you that I go away: for if I go
not away, the Comforter will not come unto you;
but if I depart, I will send Him unto you."
Notice, that during the Old Testament dispensation we have God the Father working. God the
Son was working directly in the days of His
flesh. Now, since Christ has returned to the right
hand of God, and has taken His place as Mediator,
the Father and the Son have sent another Person
of the Godhead, and He is here working in this
world, and will remain here carrying on this glorious work until the consummation of this age. Notice, incidentally, how the Deity of our Lord Jesus
Christ is implied in these words. Can you think
of any man, no matter how good, no matter how
godly, no matter how powerful, daring to say of
the blessed Holy Spirit, "I will send Him?" Why,
we see the very opposite in Scripture. The Holy

Ghost sends men out into the world, men do not send Him. But Jesus was more than man, He was God and Man in One adorable, wonderful Person, and therefore He could say with confidence, "I will send the Comforter, the Paraclete, to bear witness, when I have gone back to the glory."

Now, notice the mission of the Comforter: "When He is come, He will reprove the world of sin, and of righteousness, and of judgment." That word "reprove," is sometimes translated "convince," and sometimes "convict." The Spirit of God is in the world and working through the servants of God in this scene and His special mission is to convict, to convince, to prove to man three great facts—sin, righteousness and judgment. Sometimes when you speak of the convicting work of the Holy Spirit, people have the idea that it simply means the stirring of the emotions of men and making them sorry because they sin. Undoubtedly when men recognize their lost condition, their emotions are stirred. But it is not a question of working upon the emotions of mankind. It is far more than that. The Holy Spirit has come to convince the mind, to exercise the conscience, and to cause the will to act in accordance with the desires of our blessed Lord Jesus Christ. The Holy Ghost, in other words, has come to give such power to the Word that men will believe it and act upon it. You remember we read in Acts 14 : 1 : "And it came to pass . . . that they . . . so spake, that a great multitude both of the Jews and also of the Greeks believed." If it is possible to so speak that many believe, it is also possible to so speak that nobody will believe. And a great deal of the present-day preaching is of that character. Men are not filled with the Spirit of God and they are not proclaiming the truth of God. But those early servants of the Lord went forth preaching the word in the power and energy of the Holy Spirit, and the result was that many believed on the Lord Jesus Christ. Oh, that the Spirit of God might so fill and control every minister today that as the message is proclaimed it would go home to the hearts and consciences of Christ-rejecting men and women, that they might be brought to face these things in the presence of the Lord,—sin, righteousness and judgment.

Of what is He speaking? What does He mean when He says that the Holy Spirit has come to convince of sin? Some of us may think that the Spirit of God has come to make men feel terribly sorry because of their unrighteousness, because of their intemperance, because of their hatreds, lasciviousness, covetousness, malice, and other evil things which are rightly classed as sinful. But we are not told that it is the purpose of the Holy Spirit to convict men of sins, but of *sin*. Every man who thinks at all, knows that it is wrong to lie and steal and be intemperate and wicked. We all know these things, and if conscience becomes so numb by sinning against light, then God's holy law given at Sinai convicts of the sinfulness of such things as these. Of what sin does the Holy Spirit come to convict? Listen, "Of sin, because they believe not on Me." That is the great outstanding, damning sin which, if not repented of, is going to sink men to the depths of perdition for all eternity. Remember the Lord's words, "He that believeth on Him is not condemned: but he that believeth not is condemned already, because he hath not believed in the name of the only begotten Son of God." Oh, hear me, my friend, if you stand, at last, condemned before the Almighty God and hear Christ say, "Depart from Me, I never knew you," it will not be simply because of the sins of your daily life, many of which you declare you are overtaken in and are powerless to resist, but the outstanding sin which will separate you from God forever will be that you rejected the Saviour Whom He has provided. When He hung on the cross, God laid on Him the iniquity of us all. It has often been said that the great question between God and man today is not so much the sin question as the Son question. It is not so much what we have done as sinners, but how we respond to the fact that Christ has died as a ransom for sinners, and now God says,

"What will you do with My Son?" If you trust Him, then the value of His atoning work goes over against your sins and iniquity, but if you refuse Him and turn away, then you must face God at last about your own sins, and the crowning sin of all will be that you rejected the Saviour who died to deliver you. "Of sin, because they believe not on Me."

So I press the question home for your consideration. Have you trusted the Lord Jesus Christ as your Saviour? If you have not trusted Him and turned to Him in faith and yielded your heart to Him, remember you are guilty of the worst sin that any man can possibly commit. You are insulting the Father who gave Jesus to die for you. You are saying, "I count His blood an unholy thing. I want no Christ. I want no Saviour." And if you continue thus to reject the Lord Jesus Christ, some day you will stand naked and alone at the judgment bar to receive your due reward. But it need not be thus. You can trust Him today and know that the blood of Jesus Christ, God's Son, cleanseth you from all sin.

But notice that the Comforter will also reprove the world of righteousness. "Of righteousness, because I go to My Father, and ye see Me no more." After He had completed the work of atonement, God raised Him from the dead on the third day, and took Him up to His own right hand in heaven. Sin put Jesus on the cross; righteousness put Him on the throne. And now, you see, I need a righteousness which He only can provide in order that I might stand before God uncondemned. I must have a righteousness which I cannot provide myself. Paul says, "That I might be found in Him, not having mine own righteousness, which is of the law, but that which is through the faith of Christ, the righteousness which is of God by faith." So Christ Himself exalted in Heaven, is the righteousness of all who put their trust in Him. The Spirit delights to point men who are destitute of any righteousness of their own to a Seated Christ in heaven, who is "made unto us righteousness."

"Of judgment, because the prince of this world is judged." I do not know how it is, but I find that men generally mis-quote verse eight and make it read like this, "Of judgment to come," etc. But that is not what it says. You do not get those words "to come." He is speaking of present judgment. The thought is this: When Satan stirred that crowd in Jerusalem to send the Lord Jesus Christ to the cross, he sealed his own condemnation. It was said of old that the serpent should bruise the woman's Seed and her Seed should bruise its head. And at the cross Satan's head was bruised and he has been judged by God, because of his attitude towards God's blessed Son, and the world has been judged in its prince. But now through grace, all who trust in the Lord Jesus Christ have come out from under that judgment and are delivered from a world over which hangs the wrath of God. We are saved out of that world. That is what Peter meant when he said, "Save yourselves from this untoward generation."

Have you ever turned from this world and found your heart-satisfaction in the Lord Jesus Christ? This is more than accepting a doctrinal statement. It is a practical experience of separation.

In the last four verses He speaks of the special ministry of the Holy Spirit to the people of God. When the Spirit of truth is come, He will guide us into all truth. When you sit down over your Bible and study this blessed word, do you lift up your heart to Him and pray, "Blessed Comforter, interpret the Word to me, and reveal Thy mind as I read." You know He delights to do it. It is His joy to open up the Word and lead us into all truth. He is not working independently of the Scriptures but He opens up the truth as we have it in the Book. "For He shall not speak of Himself." He is not here to glorify Himself. "But whatsoever He shall hear, that shall He speak: and He will show you things to come." We have the marvelous privilege of knowing the things which are to come, when all the world is wondering what the future has in store. The man of God who knows his Bible can look ahead and know just what is coming. He knows that all evil will be put down when Jesus returns to reign over this universe, and righteousness will cover the earth as the waters cover the sea. And he knows what will take place in eternity. The special mission of the Spirit of God is to magnify the Lord Jesus. "He shall glorify Me: for He shall receive of Mine, and shall show it unto you." A Christ-centered ministry is a Spirit-given ministry. The Spirit of God delights to make much of Christ. Paul said he desired Christ to be magnified in him. Every true servant of God will say "Amen" to that.

"All things that the Father hath are Mine: therefore said I, that He shall take of Mine, and shall show it unto you." He opens up the riches of grace and love, and gives us to know the wealth of the realm over which Christ is set and which we are to share with Him.

And so He says, "A little while, and ye shall not see Me: and again, a little while, and ye shall see Me, because I go to the Father." And we live in the interval between His going to the Father and that "little while" when we shall see Him again.

"Jesus, Thou joy of loving hearts,
  Thou Fount of life, Thou Light of men!
From the best bliss that earth imparts,
  We turn unfilled to Thee again.

Thy truth unchanged hath ever stood;
  Thou savest those that on Thee call:
To them that seek Thee, oh, how good,
  To them that find Thee, All in All!

We taste Thee, O Thou living Bread,
  And long to feast upon Thee still:
We drink of Thee, the Fountain Head,
  And thirst our souls from Thee to fill!

O Jesus, ever with us stay;
  Make all our moments calm and bright;
Chase the dark night of sin away,
  Shed o'er the world Thy holy light."

"A LITTLE WHILE"

✓ ✓ ✓

"Then said some of His disciples among themselves, What is this that He saith unto us, A little while, and ye shall not see Me: and again, a little while, and ye shall see Me: and, Because I go to the Father? They said therefore, What is this that He saith, A little while? We cannot tell what He saith. Now Jesus knew that they were desirous to ask Him, and said unto them, Do ye enquire among yourselves of that I said, A little while, and ye shall not see Me: and again, a little while, and ye shall see Me? Verily, verily, I say unto you, That ye shall weep and lament, but the world shall rejoice: and ye shall be sorrowful, but your sorrow shall be turned into joy. A woman when she is in travail hath sorrow, because her hour is come: but as soon as she is delivered of the child, she remembereth no more the anguish, for joy that a man is born into the world. And ye now therefore have sorrow: but I will see you again, and your heart shall rejoice, and your joy no man taketh from you" (John 16: 17-22).

✓ ✓ ✓

ALREADY in this closing address of our Lord Jesus Christ to His disciples He had spoken to them of His coming again. He said, "I go to prepare a place for you. And if I go and prepare a place for you, I will come again, and receive you unto Myself; that where I am, there ye may be also." But they seemed to have been as blind as a great many of our modern apostles and preachers. They could not understand that He meant that He was going away literally and He was coming back literally. He was going away in the body and He was coming back in a glorified body. One would suppose that the Scripture teaching as to the second coming of our Lord Jesus Christ is so plainly expressed that it would be impossible for any ordinary mind to misunderstand. And yet, what weird things people have made out of our Lord's promise that He will come again! Some people think that He had in mind that great event which took place very shortly after He spoke these words—the coming of the Holy Spirit to build the Church and carry on the work of God in this scene. But that is not a reasonable explanation of His words, because it was after the Holy Spirit came that all the New Testament was written, and all through its books the second coming of the Lord Jesus Christ is set forth an event still in the future, a blessed hope for which believers are to wait and toward which they are to look.

And then again many people imagine that when the Lord spoke of His second coming that He meant when a believer comes to die, at the end of life, that in the hour of death, the Lord will come for him in the guise of death. But that will not stand because, as we turn page after page in the New Testament dealing with this subject, we find that death is going to be swallowed up in

victory at the coming of our Lord Jesus Christ.
In another passage of scripture we are told that:
"The Lord Himself shall descend from heaven
with a shout, with the voice of the archangel, and
with the trump of God, and the dead in Christ
shall rise first: then we which are alive and remain shall be caught up together with them in
the clouds, to meet the Lord in the air: and so
shall we ever be with the Lord." It is impossible
that death and the second coming of Christ should
be synonymous expressions, for death for the
believer will be ended when the Lord comes again.

Then there are a great many other foolish ideas.
I picked up a Sunday School quarterly the other
day, and the writer of the lessons ridiculed the
old-fashioned idea of the second coming of Christ,
and undertook to show that the only second coming that the Bible teaches is His coming in the
providential affairs of life, in the political and
economic clouds, and by the Spirit to comfort and
help in the hour of trial. "But as to His personal
coming, it is a vain hope," said this writer.

I am thankful we do not have to depend on
those who edit the Sunday School lesson for our
enlightenment. Jesus said, "I will come again,
and receive you unto Myself; that where I am,
there ye may be also." And here He speaks very
definitely, both of His going away and His coming back. Verse 16 reads, "A little while, and ye

shall not see Me: and again, a little while, and ye
shall see Me, because I go to the Father." That
was all a settled thing so far as He was concerned.
He was speaking of leaving this world by way of
the cross and the ascension, and going back to
the Father, and the interval was but "a little
while." So just as in a few days He would go to
the Father, so in a few days more He would be
back again!

"But," you say, "countless years have come and
gone since He went away." Yes, but "the Lord is
not slack concerning His promise, as some men
count slackness; but is longsuffering to us-ward,
not willing that any should perish, but that all
should come to repentance." And we are told that
one day is with the Lord as a thousand years,
and a thousand years as one day. So, really, according to the Lord's reckoning, He has not been
away two days yet, so shortly when that "little
while" closes, He will come again.

Notice how frequently He speaks of the "little
while." In Chapter 7: 33 Jesus said, "Yet a little
while am I with you, and then I go unto Him that
sent Me." He was speaking here to His enemies,
those who were seeking His destruction. He was
going to the cross to die, but going voluntarily,
and then someday He was going to the throne.
"Ye shall seek Me, but ye shall not find Me." He
explains what He means by that. He says, "If ye

die in your sins, whither I go, you cannot come."
He was going back to the Father, and only those
can join Him who know Him as Saviour and Lord
here on earth.

Then in the twelfth chapter of this same Gospel once more He speaks of the "little while." The
people said, "We have heard out of the law that
Christ abideth forever: and how sayest Thou, The
Son of Man must be lifted up? Who is this Son
of Man? Then Jesus said unto them, A little while
is the light with you. Walk while ye have the
light, lest darkness come upon you: for he that
walketh in darkness knoweth not whither he
goeth. While ye have light, believe in the light,
that ye may be the children of light. These things
spake Jesus and departed, and did hide Himself
from them." That is, as long as He was in the
world, He was the light of the world, and God was
speaking directly through Him. "A little while
is the light with you," and then He was to go to
the Father.

And in chapter thirteen, verse thirty-three, He
says, "Little children, yet a little while I am with
you." He was speaking to His own beloved disciples who had trusted Him and accepted Him
as their promised Redeemer. "Yet a little while
I am with you . . . and as I said unto the Jews,
Whither I go, ye cannot come; so now I say to
you." Oh, but He means something different

when He speaks thus to them. The Jews who rejected Him will be unable to find Him. But He says to His own, "I am going back to the glory. You will not find Me here on earth, but I will come and get you, and take you to be with Me. "Yet a little while I am with you."

The fourteenth chapter and nineteenth verse reads, "Yet a little while, and the world seeth Me no more; but ye see Me: because I live, ye shall live also." What does He mean by this? Well in the time of His absence He has gone unto the far country, where He is seated on the Father's throne waiting to receive for Himself the kingdom. The world knows nothing of Him, but His own have the eyes of faith, and they are able to look into the heavens and say, with Paul, "We see Jesus, who was made a little lower than the angels for the suffering of death, crowned with glory and honor."

> "We love to look up and behold Him there,
>   The Lamb for His chosen slain;
> And soon shall His saints all His glories share,
>   With their King and their Lord shall reign."

He is absent actually as to the body, but we behold Him by faith, and we know He sits exalted at God's right hand, and we are waiting for Him to come back again in person, as He went away.

And so this sixteenth chapter connects with all that has gone before. "A little while, and ye shall not see Me: and again, a little while, and ye shall see Me, because I go to the Father."

It has been suggested by some that it might be rendered, "I go back to My Father," implying that He was the One who came from the Father. He left His Father's bosom and came down in order to be our Saviour, and then, having finished our redemption, returned to His Father. Even His disciples did not understand and did not like to ask. It suggests something of the reverent awe in which they held Him. There was something about Him that stirred their hearts to the deepest depths. They knew that His heart was saddened as He said it, and they hesitated to ask, but they might as well have done so, for He knew their very thoughts.

But as they walked along, they turned one to the other. and said, "What does it mean?" "What is this that He saith, A little while?" "And then, what does He mean by saying, 'Because I go to My Father?'" They were still looking for Him to raise up a standard here on earth, to call all who were faithful to God to follow Him and lead a revolt against the Roman power and set up the kingdom of Israel, long predicted by the prophets here in this world. "When Messiah comes He is going to abide forever. What does He mean?"

And He heard them just as though they had asked Him, and said to them, "Do ye enquire among yourselves of that I said . . . Verily, verily, I say unto you, That ye shall weep and lament, but the world shall rejoice: and ye shall be sorrowful, but your sorrow shall be turned into joy."

He knew that they loved Him. He knew that with all their infirmity, their hearts were really true to Him. And He realized that His leaving them was going to disturb them greatly. The entire program they supposed would be thrown out of joint. They did not understand that God was working everything according to His own will.

So He knew that they would weep. This has been true ever since, for He told them, "In the world ye shall have tribulation." And while He is absent we can not expect fulness of joy down here. Think how God's people are suffering in Europe, Great Britain and China—real Christians who, if they had their way, would not have seen the nations plunged into war, for they love the Prince of Peace and they love His gospel of peace and they would have been willing to do anything to keep the nations from bloody conflict. But they have to suffer with the rest. Oh, how many Christian homes have been broken up! How many Christian wives and children as well as men in

arms have had to suffer, and many to die, because
of the terrible conditions prevailing. And all of
this just because those to whom He came did not
know the time of their visitation. When He came,
who alone could have brought in peace and blessing, they rejected Him and said, "We will not
have this Man to reign over us." So they have
had to suffer and endure pain and agony and the
horrors of warfare, and bitter persecution, and
no one has suffered more than His own people.

There is one sense in which His absence glad-
dens the heart of the world. The world does not
want Him. Suppose He came back today. He
would interfere with all the plans of the world.
"Ye shall sorrow," He says, "but the world shall
rejoice." The world rejoices now in the day of
His absence. The world's sorrow in fulness will
be when He returns again, taking vengeance on
them that know not God. But in the meantime,
God's plans are working out.

He uses the picture of an expectant mother in
the twenty-first verse: "A woman when she is
in travail hath sorrow, because her hour is come:
but as soon as she is delivered of the child, she
remembereth no more the anguish, for joy that a
man is born into the world." And so the church
is going through its travail-pains now, but oh,
the joy when at last the new age comes in with
the return of our Lord Jesus Christ, when sin and

righteousness and malice will be forever put down, and when Jesus will have all authority in this scene, and shall reign in righteousness, speaking peace to all people.

In the meantime, while He is away, this blessed hope is put before us in many different aspects, in order that He may reveal to us His grace. We read in the Epistle to the Hebrews, "For yet a little while, and He that shall come will come, and will not tarry." The hope of His coming is put before us as an incentive to purity of life. We are told in the First Epistle of John, "And every man that hath this hope in him purifieth himself, even as He is pure." Are you waiting for the coming of the Lord? You are a Christian. You are trusting Him as your Saviour. Well, then, are you allowing anything in your life that is unclean, anything that is impure, anything that is unholy? Oh, if so, then the hope of the coming of the Lord has never yet really gripped your soul. "Every man that hath this hope in him purifieth himself, even as He is pure." If I am living day by day in expectation of His return I will see to it that I put out of my life everything that is contrary to His will. Just imagine if I am allowing myself in something impure and Jesus should come at that very moment, how ashamed I would be at His coming. No; if the coming of the Lord is to be truly a blessed hope, I will not want to tolerate anything that would be offensive to Him.

Then you notice the coming of the Lord is put before us as an incentive to service, because at His coming, the rewards will be given out. In I Thess. 2: 19 we read, "For what is our hope, or joy, or crown of rejoicing? Are not even ye in the presence of our Lord Jesus Christ at His coming? For ye are our glory and joy." What does he mean? He says (and Paul is writing to some of his own converts), "I have given up everything on earth to preach Christ, and I have the privilege of winning souls to Him. Now at last, when He returns, I am looking forward to meeting Him with all that great company that I have led to His feet." Think what it will be for Paul! Think of the thousands who were saved through him when he was here. Think of the millions since then who have read the messages he left behind. Finally, think of him coming before the Lord Jesus Christ when He returns with these great throngs surrounding Him and saying to His Father, "Behold, I and the children whom Thou hast given Me." It will be then that Paul will get his reward.

And so the hope of the coming of the Lord Jesus Christ should stir us up to devoted service. He says, "Behold, I come quickly, and My reward is with Me, to give to every man according as his work shall be." Everything that is really done for Him will bring a reward in that day. Everything that is a result of that old corrupt nature will go for nothing in that day, and will cause us to suffer loss rather than to obtain a reward. I listened to a Christian berating another believer some little time ago, and oh, the unkind things he said. I inquired, "Would you like the Lord Jesus to come and find you talking so of your brother?" "Oh," he answered, "it is all true." "Well," I said, "Love covereth a multitude of sins. Now tell me, which nature is it that is working now? We have the divine nature if we are born again. Is that what leads you to speak unkindly of your brother?" Oh, the coming of the Lord should be that which tests all our behavior. Is it such that He would approve of when He returns for us?

In this same Epistle to the Thessalonians you will find that the Apostle is urging upon the Christians the importance of holiness. He links it with the coming of the Lord. In verses twelve and thirteen we read, "And the Lord make you to increase and abound in love one toward another, and toward all men, even as we do toward you: to the end He may stablish your hearts unblameable in holiness before God, even our Father, at the coming of our Lord Jesus Christ with all His saints." I don't wonder that Satan likes to becloud this truth of the second coming, because it means so much to God's people from a practical standpoint. If it really grips my soul, I will want to increase and abound in love to the brethren. I will want to walk in holiness of life. And, oh, what a comfort in the hour of bereavement, is the coming of the Lord. When our dear ones in Christ are taken away from us,

> "When their words of love and cheer,
> Fall no longer on our ear,
> Hush, be every murmur dumb,
> It is only till He come!"

Then will come the glad re-union when we all meet in His presence.

And so the fourth chapter of I Thess. connects intimately with the sixteenth of John. "But I would not have you to be ignorant, brethren, concerning them which are asleep, that ye sorrow not, even as others which have no hope." Mark, he does not say we are not to sorrow. He does not call upon us to be hard and cold and stoical. He doesn't forbid our tears. Tears often ease the heart. He has bidden His people to weep with those who weep. When He was here, He Himself wept at the grave of His friend, Lazarus. He does not tell us we are not to grieve for loved ones taken from us; but He does say we are not to sorrow as others who have no hope. Oh, we have a blessed and wonderful hope! We know we shall meet them again. So He tells us there will be the voice, the shout, the trump, and we shall

be caught up together to meet the Lord in the
air. I love that word, "together," in that connection. You see, there will be wonderful recognition. We were heirs together of the grace of life.
We had fellowship together here on earth. We
were laborers together in the things of God. We
shall be caught up together when Jesus comes.

> "Down Life's dark vale we wander,
>   Till Jesus comes.
> We watch and wait and wonder
>   Till Jesus comes.
> All joy! His loved ones bringing,
>   When Jesus comes.
> All praise through heaven ringing,
>   When Jesus comes.
> All beauty bright and vernal,
>   When Jesus comes.
> All glory grand, eternal,
>   When Jesus comes!
>
> He'll know the way was dreary,
>   When Jesus comes.
> He'll know the feet grew weary,
>   When Jesus comes.
> He'll know what griefs oppressed us,
>   When Jesus comes.
> Oh, how His arms will rest us,
>   When Jesus comes.
> Oh, let my lamp be burning,
>   When Jesus comes.
> For Him, my soul be yearning,
>   When Jesus comes."

And so we turn now to the last verse of the section we are considering. "And ye now therefore have sorrow: but I will see you again, and your heart shall rejoice, and your joy no man taketh from you." It must be so long as we are in a world filled with pain and suffering, that we must suffer with the groaning creation. But soon we shall behold Him when He returns to take us Home. Then our joy will be complete.

So the "little while" will soon be past, and we shall see Him face to face. Meantime, be it ours to work and labor for Him till He comes.

PRAYER IN THE NAME OF THE LORD JESUS

✦ ✦ ✦

"And in that day ye shall ask Me nothing. Verily, verily, I say unto you, Whatsoever ye shall ask the Father in My name, He will give it you. Hitherto have ye asked nothing in My name: ask, and ye shall receive, that your joy may be full. These things have I spoken unto you in proverbs: but the time cometh, when I shall no more speak unto you in proverbs, but I shall show you plainly of the Father. At that day ye shall ask in My name: and I say not unto you, that I will pray the Father for you: for the Father Himself loveth you, because ye have loved Me, and have believed that I came out from God. I came forth from the Father, and am come into the world: again, I leave the world, and go to the Father. His discipies said unto Him, Lo, now speakest Thou plainly, and speakest no proverb. Now are we sure that Thou knowest all things, and needest not that any man should ask Thee: by this we believe that Thou camest forth from God. Jesus answered them, Do ye now believe? Behold, the hour cometh, yea, is now come, that ye shall be scattered, every man to his own, and shall leave Me alone: and yet I am not alone, because the Father is with Me. These things I have spoken unto you, that in Me ye might have peace. In the world ye shall have tribulation: but be of good cheer; I have overcome the world" (John 16: 23-33).

✦ ✦ ✦

IN the first part of this section our Lord brings before us in a truly illuminating way, the privilege now extended to us, as believers, to go directly to the Father in prayer, in the name of our Lord Jesus Christ. I do not think that

714

there is any subject on which there seems to be
more confusion than that of prayer. So many
people have an idea that prayer is the effort to
overcome God's unwillingness; to make Him willing to do something for us which He does not
desire to do. That is not the case. We are not told
to pray in order to overcome God's unwillingness.
Our God delights to bless, but He chooses to bless
in answer to prayer, and that for a number of
reasons. You see, when I go to God directly,
when various things are pressing upon heart and
mind, and they drive me to Him, I find that just
speaking to Him of the things that burden me
has a sanctifying effect upon my own soul. The
Psalmist said, "It is good for me to draw nigh to
God." If some of us did not have some special
exercises to make us go to God, we would probably move on from day to day forgetting the
privilege of speaking to the Father. Our needs
send us to Him, and if we talk things over with
Him, oh what blessing it gives, what a change a
little time in His presence will make! Perhaps
pressure has been brought to bear. You have been
worried and anxious about many things, concerned about loved ones going astray perhaps,
and the more you have thought about these things
the more distressed you have become. And then
you have said, "How foolish I am to be worried.
Why not act upon that verse which reads, 'Be

careful for nothing; but in everything by prayer and supplication with thanksgiving let your requests be made known unto God. And the peace of God, which passeth all understanding, shall keep your hearts and minds through Christ Jesus'." And so you have pressed into His presence and poured out your heart to Him. You have told Him about the financial worries, family affairs, the loved one whose salvation you long for, and as you unburdened your heart, He drew near. Then you went out to take up the affairs of life again with a lightened heart and mind, and more than that, such a spiritual sense of blessing, for as you were pouring out your heart, you felt constrained to talk about yourself and confessed your own failure and your own sin. And after you had confessed, you had the joy of knowing that He forgave.

So prayer was meant to be a means of sanctification, but more than that, God chooses to give, in answer to prayer, what He may not give apart from prayer, in order that we may have constant proof that we have to do with a living God. You see, when I go to God in secret and tell Him my story and then go forth to meet the world and see Him working in His wonderful way, I know by practical experience that I have to do with a living God.

I read a remarkable testimony which I think
will be a blessing to all who hear it. It had to do
with a money matter. Down in Columbia, S. C.,
is located the Columbia Bible College of which
Dr. Robert McQuilken is the president. Some
time ago they started to buy a large building to
be used as a men's dormitory. They put the
amount of money needed before the Lord and it
came in, and then the next year they were to pay
ten thousand dollars on October 1. This letter
came telling us that on the last day of September,
singularly enough, the balance needed was exactly
$2,121.21. They took it to the Lord in prayer,
and then went out and opened a little box into
which donations had been dropped. When they
counted the money put in that morning, it was
$21.21. That left 2,100.00 to be made up. They
had a day of prayer, and as they waited before
the Lord that day, from different sources gifts
began to come in. The largest gift that morning
was one hundred dollars. Later a gift of five
hundred was received. By evening they had received in all, exactly $2,121.22, just one cent more
than they needed. What a wonderful bookkeeper
God is. He gave all they needed and one cent more
toward the next ten thousand dollars! How could
anyone doubt but that they had to do with a living
God. It was as they were gathered together waiting upon God, that the money came from different

places, from people who did not know they were praying for it at that time. Prayer then is a God ordained method of demonstrating the reality of God and His definite interest in the affairs of His people.

Now see how our blessed Lord puts it in this passage in verse 23, "And in that day ye shall ask Me nothing. Verily, verily, I say unto you, Whatsoever ye shall ask the Father in My name, He will give it you (He will give it you in My name)." Notice, I have changed the position of "in My name," and I will explain why. It says in our Authorized Version, "Whatever you shall ask the Father in My name." Another verse shows us we are to pray in the name of Jesus Christ, but the best MS read this way, "Whatever you ask the Father, He will give you in My name." Notice then what the Lord is saying: "In that day," that is, after His death, when the Comforter has come, when the present day of grace is brought in—the day in which we are living—"ye shall ask Me nothing. Verily, verily, I say unto you, Whatsoever ye shall ask the Father in My name, He will give it you."

Now it is very interesting to note that there are two different Greek words here that are translated "ask" and they have quite different meanings. In the first place where He says, "In that day ye shall *ask* Me nothing," the word means literally "familiar entreaty," as you might go to a very loved friend and put a case before him definitely, whereas in the other sentence, "Verily, verily, I say unto you, Whatsoever ye shall *ask* the Father in My name, He will give it you," the word there means literally, "petition," "taking the place of a suppliant," "begging for the help you need." And you notice the difference. The Lord says, "In that day ye shall ask Me nothing." You see, when here on earth, they went to Him and He answered their questions and made things clear. Now He says, I am going away and I won't be here for you to come to Me in that free, familiar way, and ask for My personal help in the way you could then. For nineteen hundred years our Lord has been absent in heaven. You take some of the questions that have troubled the Church. Would it not be delightful if we could go to Him and ask, saying, "Master, there has been a great deal of difference in the Church concerning baptism. Would you tell us plainly whether you mean we are to sprinkle or baptize by immersion, or whether we should immerse only once, or three times? Should we put them in forward or backward?" Now wouldn't it be delightful if we could just go to Him and ask Him? Why, He could tell us in a moment. But He isn't here, and so we have to study His Word and act in accordance with what we gather from our meditations upon it.

Though we can not go directly to Him, He says there is something even better than that. "In that day ye shall make no 'familiar entreaty' of Me. Verily, verily, I say unto you, Whatsoever ye shall ask (and here the word means to plead for something you need) the Father in My name, He will give it you." So we are invited there to go directly to God, the Father, with our petitions. Are you in need of financial help, comfort and health, etc.? What is there that is pressing upon your heart? He says, "You cannot come to Me personally, but you can go to the Father and bring your request to Him, and He will give you what you ask for in My name. He will do it for Me." The Father loves the Son and hath committed all things into His hand, and He delights to do things for us because it pleases His blessed Son, our Lord Jesus Christ. He does it in His name.

You may have heard the story of that poor boy who was dying on the battlefield after one of the great conflicts in the war between the States. Another soldier nearby crawled to him and found this poor boy in a dreadful condition and did everything he could to help him. They talked together, and then the other said, "Now, if I get out alive, is there anything I could do for you?" "Well," he said, "maybe I can do something for you. My father is wealthy, and if you get through this conflict alive, and are ever in need, take this little card (and he wrote a few words upon it) and go to see my father, and I know he will be ready to help you out." The soldier did not think he would ever use the card, but the time came when he was in dire need, and he remembered the conversation. He went and found this wealthy man. Through the underlings and secretaries, he sent in his own card and got no response. And then he thought of the other card and got it out, and on it was written these words, "Father, if you can ever do anything for my friend who helped me when I was dying, please do so." And it was signed "Charlie." In a moment, out came the big business man and he said, "Oh, why didn't you send that in before? I will do anything that I can for you for Charlie's sake!"

That is the way God feels about His Son. He wants us to come with our questions, our sorrows, our heartbreak, and our need. He will do anything for us for Jesus' sake, anything, of course, which is consistent with His righteousness and holiness. So how encouraged we ought to be to draw near to God in prayer.

Then, notice, the Lord continues to open up this subject. Now He uses that word which means to beg for something: "Ask, and ye shall receive." While He was here on earth they could come directly to Him, and He did not urge them to go to the Father in His name. Even the Lord's

Prayer (really the Disciples' Prayer), does not conclude in the name of the Lord Jesus. He did not ask them to do that when here on earth, but now He was going away, and He says, "Ask, and ask in My name, and ye shall receive, that your joy may be full." It means to ask by His authority. He has authorized me to come to the Father and present His name and say, "Father, Thy Son, the Lord Jesus Christ, told me to come, and so I am coming in His name to present my petition."

That was difficult for them to understand. "These things have I spoken unto you in proverbs: but the time cometh, when I shall no more speak unto you in proverbs, but I shall show you plainly of the Father," because God the Father and the Son are One. He does not mean that they are not to address Him in prayer. The disciples called on the name of the Lord Jesus. Stephen cried, "Lord Jesus, receive my spirit!" Paul, when he had the thorn in the flesh, said, "I besought the Lord three times that it might depart from me." It was perfectly right and proper for him to go to Jesus. The last prayer in the Bible is addressing Him; "Even so, come, Lord Jesus."

But that our finite minds might grasp it, He uses this allegory of going to the one Person of the Godhead in the name of the other. "These things have I spoken unto you in proverbs: but the time cometh, when I shall no more speak unto you in proverbs, but I shall show you plainly of the Father." That was the time of resurrection when He said, "I ascend to My Father and your Father, to My God and your God." He would have us understand that we can go to God the Father, just as you go to your own father.

"At that day ye shall ask in My name; and I say not unto you, that I will pray the Father for you: for the Father Himself loveth you, because ye have loved Me, and have believed that I came out from God." Do you get the implication of it? Do you know, if we could just see this, it would do away with all intermediaries and we would go directly to God for whatever we want. It is a strange thing, that very early in the history of the Church people began to feel that God was so great and far removed from us, and that we are such sinful people that we dare not call on the Father directly and so men thought of our Lord Jesus Christ as an intermediary who seeks to persuade the Father to help us. We hear people pray in this way, "We ask, Lord Jesus, that Thou wilt entreat for us." Or, "We pray that Thou wilt plead with the Father for us." Why, you need not do that! You don't need to go to the Lord Jesus and say, "Won't you please ask the Father to do something for me?" No; because the Son and the Father are really One, not in Person, but in essence.

And if we should not even go to Jesus as an intermediary in this sense, then what shall be said of those who have put a whole lot of mere creatures in between the soul and God? Did you ever hear this? "Holy Mary, pray for us. St. Jude, pray for us. St. Mark, pray for us. St. Paul, pray for us." Did you ever hear people pray like that? What does that imply? That they do not realize that the veil has been rent. We do not need any intermediaries. "Well," you say, "isn't the Lord Jesus Christ our Mediator?" Oh, yes; that is what we are told. "For there is one God, and one Mediator between God and men, the Man Christ Jesus." But that does not mean that we have to go to Him about our ordinary affairs of life and ask Him to persuade the Father to do something for us. He is there ever bearing us up before God, but we are invited to bring our petitions as to the details of life directly to God Himself in the Name of the Son.

Look at the verse again and get the good of it. "I say not unto you, that I will pray the Father for you: for the Father Himself loveth you." Are you afraid of God then? Afraid to go to Him direct? Why, the Father Himself loveth you.

Suppose here is a family with a loving father, a wayward son and a sweet daughter. This son comes to his sister and says, "Mary, I wish you would go to Dad and ask for money for a new suit of clothes for me." What would that imply? Why, that the son did not have confidence in his father's love, and so he says, "Mary, won't you please go in and plead with father to give me the money." If he had confidence in his father's love he would go to him direct and confess his sin and say, "But, Dad, look at my suit of clothes. I need new ones:" And then father would say, "Come, my boy, we will go down and get a suit." He would not need anybody to go to his father for him. You and I should understand that we need not go to the Son to pray to the Father for us. "The Father Himself loveth you." And notice why, "Because ye have loved Me, and have believed that I came out from God." That is what the world does not believe. "I came forth from the Father, and am come into the world: again, I leave the world, and go to the Father."

And they were quite sure now that they understood but they did not really see what He meant. "His disciples said unto Him, Lo, now speakest Thou plainly, and speakest no proverb. Now are we sure that Thou knowest all things, and needest not that any man should ask Thee: by this we believe that Thou camest forth from God." Well, they did understand later on, but actually at that time, they were over-confident, as their future behavior shows. "Jesus answered them, Do ye now believe? Behold, the hour cometh, yea, is now come, that ye shall be scattered, every man to his own, and shall leave Me alone: and yet I am not alone, because the Father is with Me." Who would have thought that such a thing would be true?—and yet, within a very few hours' time His words were fulfilled.

He says, "And yet I am not alone, because the Father is with Me." The time soon came when they all forsook Jesus, but even in that dark hour He was conscious of the Father's will and His presence with Him.

And now He closes His valedictory discourse which has covered chapters fourteen, fifteen and sixteen, and says, "These things I have spoken unto you, that in Me ye might have peace. In the world ye shall have tribulation: but be of good cheer; I have overcome the world."

It took some of us a long time to find that peace. We tried to find it ourselves and could not, but at last we turned to Him, confessing our sin, and we found peace with God. We came to Him about our care and found the peace of God filling our hearts. Have you learned that? God is light and love. Trust in Him and you will have peace, a peace that the world knows nothing of. In the world you will have tribulation. You will have your share of it. And yet, think of it, you can go through every trial triumphantly. He says, "Be of good cheer; I have overcome the world."

Just trust Him, and everything will come out right at last. Does the present war condition trouble you? Do you ask, "Why does not God stop it all?" Listen, God is taking everything into consideration. These conditions are the direct result of sin. God did not bring them about. They were brought about by the devil. God is letting them go on and on until they come to their fulness. Soon He is going to send His Son back again who will reign for a thousand glorious years. Be of good cheer; Christ has overcome the world! And we can take everything to God in prayer.

> "Its hours all have fled, dear Lord,
>   I bring the day to Thee.
> Wilt Thou in love cleanse of its sin
>   And give new strength to me.
> Forgive its failures, its defeats,
>   Its sorrow, and its loss,
> When I would prideful be, dear Lord,
>   Show me Thy shameful cross.
> May I in gentleness and love
>   Walk patiently my way,
> And live Thy glory from this hour
>   To everlasting day."

—Lucille Anderson Trimmier.

OUR LORD'S HIGH-PRIESTLY PRAYER (I)

✓ ✓ ✓

"These words spake Jesus, and lifted up His eyes to heaven, and said, Father, the hour is come; glorify Thy Son that Thy Son also may glorify Thee: as Thou hast given Him power (authority) over all flesh, that He should give eternal life to as many as Thou hast given Him. And this is life eternal, that they might know Thee, the only true God, and Jesus Christ whom Thou hast sent. I have glorified Thee on the earth; I have finished the work which Thou gavest Me to do. And now, O Father, glorify Thou Me with Thine own self, with the glory which I had with Thee before the world was" (John 17:1-5).

✓ ✓ ✓

WE are told in the Epistle to the Hebrews that God "is able to save them to the uttermost that come unto God by Him, seeing He ever liveth to make intercession for them."

Have you ever wondered how our blessed Lord speaks to the Father when He makes intercession as our High Priest? What does He have to say? This question is largely answered in this seventeenth chapter. We have here what has well been called the high-priestly prayer of our Lord Jesus Christ.

We have seen that the Gospel of John is divided into two parts. The first twelve chapters give the presentation of our Lord to the world; from the thirteenth on, we have His manifestation to His own. Even the chapter which speaks of His crucifixion is presented from the standpoint of the burnt-offering—that aspect of His work which is entered into only by those already in living relationship with God. In chapter 13 He appears as our Advocate, keeping His people fit and clean as they travel through this world. In chapter 14 He is the Coming One, the object of His people's hope. In chapter 15 He is the living Vine, and we the branches. So that the Christian is one whose roots are in Heaven, but the branches fall down to the earth, and from the branches, fruit is produced. In the sixteenth chapter, our blessed Lord is specifically the Giver of the Holy Spirit. In the seventeenth, He is presented as our great High Priest with God. It is as though we have been allowed to enter actually within the now rent veil and listen to the pleadings of the Son with the Father, to listen to the intercession of our great High Priest as He speaks to God on our behalf.

This chapter is rightly called the Lord's Prayer. We generally use that term for the beautiful prayer that He taught His disciples when they came to Him and said, "Lord, teach us to pray." He replied, "When ye pray, say, Our Father which art in Heaven, Hallowed be Thy name. Thy kingdom come. Thy will be done in earth as it is in Heaven. Give us this day our daily bread. And forgive us our debts, as we forgive our debtors. And lead us not into temptation, but deliver us from evil; for Thine is the kingdom, and the power, and the glory, for ever. Amen."

But that is not really the Lord's prayer. It is a prayer given by the Lord, but He Himself never prayed that prayer. In the very nature of things He could not do so. It is one of the evidences of His sinlessness that He never prayed with anyone. He prayed *for* people, but not *with* them. He could not say, "Forgive us our debts as we forgive our debtors," for He had no debts. He could not say, "Forgive us our trespasses as we forgive those who trespass against us," for He had no trespasses. This is not His prayer, but an outline putting before His disciples the petitions they might well bring to God, and indicating the lines of approach to God. The Lord's prayer, recorded in the seventeenth chapter of John, gives us His own blessed utterances. Have you ever wondered what He said, when He was out on the hillside all night in prayer, while His disciples slept? You can get an idea of the petitions He brought to the

Father from this prayer. Remember, our blessed
Lord was as truly Man as if He had never been
God, and as truly God as if He had never become
Man. He was the only absolutely sinless One, yet
He took the place of dependence as a humble sup-
pliant in prayer.

In this seventeenth chapter we have Him praying largely for His own.

"These words spake Jesus, and lifted up His
eyes to Heaven, and said, Father, the hour is
come; glorify Thy Son, that Thy Son also may
glorify Thee."

Toward that hour He had been looking, not
only ever since the beginning of the world, but
before the world began, when He said, in eternity past, "Lo, I come: in the volume of the book
it is written of Me, I delight to do Thy will, O
My God: yea, Thy law is within My heart." He
was willing to come into the world, to go to the
cross, to settle the question of redemption. Now
the cross is before Him. In a few hours more He
will be hanging on that tree in the sinner's place,
bearing the sinner's judgment, and yet He looks
on to it in perfect confidence, for He knows that
He cannot be holden of death. He is looking on
to resurrection. When the Greeks came saying:
"We would see Jesus," He said, "Father, glorify
Thy name." Then came a voice from Heaven,
saying, "I have both glorified it, and will glorify

it again." God was glorified in resurrection, in the triumph over the tomb at Lazarus' grave. God is about to be glorified in the resurrection of His Son. When the sin question is settled to the divine satisfaction, the glory of God demands the resurrection of the One who settled that question.

We have here the glory of our Lord presented in two very distinct ways—His essential glory and His acquired glory. When He says in the first verse, "Glorify Thy Son, that Thy Son may also glorify Thee," we have His acquired glory. In verse five, He says, "O Father, glorify Me with Thine own self with the glory which I had with Thee before the world was." He speaks here of His essential glory. He was one with the Father from all eternity. Yet in infinite grace He laid aside the outward signs of glory and came into this world and trod the path as a stranger and a pilgrim. Now He is going back whence He came, and all that has been hidden will be fully manifested, His essential glory as one with the Father. In verse one we have those glories He acquired by coming into the world, and doing His work down here. He never could have been a Saviour if He had not gone through suffering. The glory of Saviourhood came only through the cross. In Hebrews we read, "He was made perfect through suffering," not as to character, for He was always perfect in character. but He could not be the Captain of our salvation, except through the suffering of the cross.

Then we have His glory as Head of the Church. He was ever the Head of creation. In Colossians we read that He brought everything into existence, but it is in resurrection that He is the First-born from among the dead, and that He becomes the Head of the Church. The risen Man in glory is the Head of the Church.

Then there is His glory as the coming King who will reign over Israel, and over all peoples to the ends of the earth. This depends on His obedience to the Father's will down here. He must tread the path from the manger to the cross, and in view of this He is to be proclaimed Jehovah's King over all the earth.

We shall share with Him in all of His acquired glory, but not in His essential glory. We shall never become part of Deity. He remains alone therefore, the only One in all the universe who is both God and Man. But we shall share the fruits of His saving work. We are saved, and what He did on the cross has made us members of that Body of which He is the Head. We shall reign with Him. We share His acquired glory, but we worship and adore in the presence of His essential glory.

He is still speaking as a Man when He says, "Glorify Thy Son, that Thy Son may glorify

Thee." If our Lord had not come from the tomb, then the whole divine program would have been ruined, would never have been carried out.

In verse two we read, "As Thou hast given Him power over all flesh, that He should give eternal life to as many as Thou hast given Him."

This is in accordance with His declaration made in the last chapter of Matthew, "All authority is given unto Me." God has committed all authority unto the risen Christ. "As Thou hast given Him authority over all flesh."

Fancy anyone professing to believe that this is a reliable record of the utterances of our Lord Jesus Christ on that last night, questioning His Deity. Just imagine any man saying, "Thou hast given Me authority over all flesh, that I should give eternal life to as many as Thou hast given Me." This statement involves His own recognition of His Deity, because it is as the divine One that He gives eternal life.

Notice, too that expression, "As many as Thou hast given Him." Seven times that expression or a similar one is used in this chapter. What does this suggest? It clearly indicates that He thinks of all His reedemed as the Father's love gift to His Son. That is one reason I have no difficulty about the question of the eternal security of the believer. Every believer has been given to the Lord Jesus Christ, and I read, "The gifts and calling of God are without repentance." He never changes His mind. As children, we sometimes gave things to others and then wanted them back after a while. When God gave the Church to Jesus long before the world began, He gave every individual who would believe on His Son to Christ for all eternity. "That He should give eternal life to as many as Thou hast given Him." We shall notice that expression from time to time. The blessed Lord gives eternal life to as many as the Father has given Him. How many does He give to the Lord Jesus Christ? All who will come to Him. "All that the Father giveth Me shall come to Me; and him that cometh to Me I will in no wise cast out."

I have known some troubled souls who have been brought up under a hyper-Calvinism, who were distressed about this. One young lady came to me weeping and said, "It says, 'All that the Father hath given Me shall come.' If the Father has not given me to Jesus, I cannot come to Him. I do not know if I am one of those given by the Father to the Son."

I inquired, "Do you want to come?"

She replied, "With all my heart."

I told her, "All you need to do is to come, and when you come, you can say, I am one of those whom the Father has given to the Son. The fact that anyone wants to come tells its own story.

It is the beginning of a work of grace in the soul. You would not want to come if He were not working within you. You would be entirely indifferent."

Now verse three: "And this is eternal life, that they might know Thee, the only true God, and Jesus Christ, whom Thou hast sent." This is not a definition of eternal life. I do not know how to give a definition of eternal life that would be satisfactory. I do not know how to give a definition of natural life. I know what it is to be alive, but I cannot define life. Neither can I define divine life, or eternal life. Verse three gives us the manifestation of eternal life, and shows that for which it gives ability. "That they might know Thee, the only true God, and Jesus Christ whom Thou hast sent." That is, we cannot know God the Father and God the Son apart from having eternal life. The natural man understands not the things of God, but God gives eternal life when we believe on His Son, that we might know God the Father and the Lord Jesus Christ. That life introduces us into a blessed sphere of relationship where we enjoy communion with the Father and with the Son. No man can enjoy fellowship with the Lord Jesus Christ until he possesses eternal life.

In verse 4 the blessed Lord presents two things

that may well speak to our hearts. He goes back
over His sojourn here on the earth, and says, "I
have glorified Thee on the earth: I have finished
the work which Thou gavest Me to do." He had
not one regret. If anyone doubts the Deity of
our Lord, let him think of Christ's record. He
lived down here and never had one regret, never
said one word He had to apologize for, never did
one thing He later wished He hadn't done, never
made one mistake, never stumbled once on all the
rocky pathway from the manger of Bethlehem to
the cross of Calvary. How different from ourselves!

Bushnell calls attention to the fact that in
Christ you have piety without one dash of repentance. Think of it. How did your life of piety
begin? I am speaking to Christians. Did it not
begin with tears of contrition and repentance as
you bowed in the presence of the blessed Lord?
He was one who never had any failures to confess, never wept over His sins, for He had none,
though He did weep over the sins of others. Looking back over His life He said, "I have glorified
Thee on the earth." In everything He said and
did, He had the Father's glory in view. "I have
glorified Thee on the earth. I have finished the
work Thou gavest Me to do." What blessed title

He had to say, "Glorify Thou Me, for I have glorified Thee." He spent His entire sojourn on the earth seeking the Father's glory.

Notice the second thing: "I have finished the work Thou gavest Me to do." The order here is most instructive. He has left us an example that we should follow in His steps. In 1 John 2:6 we read, "He that saith he abideth in Him ought himself also so to walk, even as He walked." I can never walk perfectly as He walked; I am full of failure. But I can at least follow in His steps, and seek to walk as He walked, characterized by the same spirit of devotion to God and of separation from all evil. Let me first have before my soul the glory of God, and second, the work committed to me. There is something more important than working. As soon as a man is converted we say, "Put him to work. Give him something to do." Some people do things they are not prepared for, and work becomes legality. They do not know the blessedness and fulness of grace. There is something that comes before working, that is, the glory of God. It is more important that God be glorified than that I accomplish certain things in the line of service. I can well understand a dear invalid whom I went to see some years ago. A gentleman who gave much time to visiting among the poor and sick said to me, "I want you to go with me to see one of my

pets." I went with him. We came to a tenement
house set back from the street. We climbed the
stairs to a little room. There was a dear mother
and her daughter, a young woman of perhaps
thirty-two. She was sitting in a child's high-
chair. She had been afflicted with infantile par-
alysis many years before. For twenty-two years
that had been her throne, that little high-chair.
She sat near the window with a little desk before
her. She wrote letters to people in affliction and
trial all over the world. I began to express my
sympathy. She looked at me with the sweetest
smile, and said, "I believe God gets more glory
out of my being here in this chair than He would
if I could run around. I am content to be here
to glorify God." Then she began to talk of service. I found she was doing a wonderful service
sending out letters to other sick ones. She could
say, "I know all about what it means to be shut
in. I know what it means to be unable to walk,
unable to carry out my most cherished ambitions.
But I know, too, how wonderfully the blessed
Lord can come in and fill the soul; and so I commend Him to you." She glorified God on the
earth, and did the work He gave her to do. This
is ever the order, but we often reverse it, and put
work first. The Lord says, "I have glorified
Thee," first; then, "I have finished the work."

Observe from this point on how our Lord
speaks as though the cross were already in the

past. You see He has said, "I have finished the
work Thou gavest Me to do." In His own mind
that evidently took in the entire work of making
atonement. He takes on beyond the cross and
up to the glory. We are listening to the High
Priest within the veil in the Holiest of All, interceding in behalf of His own. It is a resurrection
priesthood. After the completion of the work of
making atonement, He takes His place as our
High Priest in glory. And so He anticipates the
cross in these words, "I have finished the work
which Thou gavest Me to do." In other words,
"I have accomplished that for which I came to
the earth, for which I laid aside my robes of
glory. Now I am going back to receive them
again."

When He was here on earth He did not lay
aside His Deity. He remained what He had ever
been, the Eternal Son, but He took a human
body, a human spirit, and a human soul, into
union with His Divine nature. He remained
what He had ever been, though now with all a
Man's nature added, thus fitting Him to be the
Daysman who could lay His hand upon both God
and man.

Some who reject the full truth of the incarnation of the Lord Jesus Christ, and yet hesitate
about giving up altogether His divine Sonship,
have invented a theory which is commonly called

Kenoticism. It is based on Philippians 2: 7, "He made Himself of no reputation," literally, "emptied Himself" (*ekonosin*). Men who otherwise seem to be good men, seem to believe in the divine Sonship of our Lord, can through this theory fit in with a lot of teaching of the day. They say when the Lord Jesus came down to earth He emptied Himself of His divine attributes, and though they confess His pre-existence and His divine Sonship, yet they say while He was here on the earth He was just like any other Galilean peasant. They call Him a peasant, though He was really a mechanic. They admit He lived a pure and beautiful life. But they insist that He had laid aside His Divine Omniscience and accepted all human limitations. So when He said, "God in the beginning made them male and female," He did not know any better. He had no schooling beyond His village, and believed what the rabbis said. When He spoke of Jonah, He was speaking just as any other uninstructed Galilean would. He made mistakes because He had emptied Himself! What these men overlook is that while He walked this earth the Holy Ghost said of Him, "He knew what was in man. He knew all things." He was God manifest in the flesh. Now when the work is finished, He goes back to take the glory He had left, not to be re-absorbed into Deity, but to go back into glory as One with the Father.

We have an illustration in history that may help us understand this. Peter the Great, when Czar of Russia, wanted to build a navy. But the Russian people were not a maritime people. As the result of wars he got a seaport for Russia on the Baltic Sea. He said, "I will build a navy." But his people knew nothing about ships. What did Peter do? He laid aside his royal robes and crown, and invested Katherine, his czarina, with the regent's authority over the Russian dominion. He dressed as a common working-man, and made his way to Holland and England. There he veiled his identity and wrought as an apprentice to a ship's carpenter, and learned how to build ships. Then he went back to Russia, laid aside his workman's garb, and arrayed himself once more in his royal robes. He was the same person when he was in Holland and in England as he was in Russia. He had simply emptied himself of the outward dignity of his royal estate. So our Lord, when He came to this earth, laid aside His glory, and came as God clad in robes of flesh. He glorified God, finished the work, and then said, "O Father, glorify Thou Me with Thine own self with the glory which I had with Thee before the world was."

And so He returned to the Father's presence, whence He had come, and now abides in the heavenly sanctuary as our High Priest, ever living to intercede for us.

OUR LORD'S HIGH-PRIESTLY PRAYER (II)

✻ ✻ ✻

"I have manifested Thy name unto the men which Thou gavest Me out of the world: Thine they were and Thou gavest them Me: and they have kept Thy Word. Now they have known that whatsoever Thou hast given Me are of Thee. For I have given unto them the words which Thou gavest Me; and they have received them, and have known surely that I came out from Thee, and they have believed that Thou didst send Me. I pray for them: I pray not for the world, but for them which Thou hast given Me; for they are Thine, and all Mine are Thine, and Thine are Mine; and I am glorified in them" (John 17: 6-10).

✻ ✻ ✻

AS He continues His prayer to the Father, Jesus has in mind particularly the company of His disciples, those who have continued with Him in His trials, who believed in His message and are now to be left behind to work for Him upon the earth.

First, we have the manifestation of the Father's name. "I have manifested Thy name unto the men which Thou gavest me out of the world." That wonderfully sweet and precious

743

name "Father," came as a new revelation. The
Fatherhood of God is not revealed in the same
way in the Old Testament. He was a Father to
Israel. When Malachi wrote, "Have we not all
one father; hath not one God created us?" he
referred not to God, in the first instance, but to
Abraham. Advocates of the modern theory of
the universal Fatherhood of God and brotherhood of man often cite this passage as a proof
text. But it is altogether beside the mark.

It remained for the blessed Lord to reveal the
Father's name, to show that God is the Father
of each individual believer in His blessed Son.
In olden days, He made Himself known as "Elohim," the Creator; "Jehovah," the God in covenant relation with men; "El-Shaddai," the all-
sufficient One, able to meet every need of His
people; as "God most high," supreme Ruler of
the universe; but we have to come to the pages
of the New Testament to get the revelation of
the Father's name from the lips and life of the
Lord Jesus Christ.

You remember that word in John 1:14: "The
Word became flesh and tabernacled among us,
and we beheld His glory, the glory as of the only
begotten of the Father, full of grace and truth."
As we become intimately acquainted with Him
we realize we are walking and talking with the
Man who was the only begotten, living in un-

broken fellowship with the Father. It is thus He made known the Father's name. Do you want to know the Father's heart? Get better acquainted with the Lord Jesus. "Show us the Father," said Philip. Jesus answered, "Have I been so long time with you, and yet hast thou not known Me, Philip?" It is not that He confounded the persons of the Trinity. He Himself distinguished them carefully when He commanded His disciples to "baptize in the name of the Father, and of the Son, and of the Holy Spirit." In the baptismal formula the persons are distinguished without denying the unity of the Godhead. But in Him we see the Father's heart, the Father's mind, and the Father's character. He is Himself the exact expression of the divine character.

So He says, "I have manifested Thy name" (but not to everybody) "to the men which Thou gavest Me out of the world." What men are these? "No man cometh to Me except the Father draw him, and I will raise him up at the last day. All that the Father giveth Me shall come to Me, and him that cometh to Me I will in no wise cast out." If I have come to Him, I am one of those whom the Father gave to the Son long before the world began.

I heard Sam Hadley say once in a great meeting in Oakland, California, after listening to a number of testimonies, "Many of you have been telling how you found Jesus. I have no such story to tell. I never found Him, for I was not looking for Him, but He found me, and drew me to Himself from a life of sin and shame." And he quoted the lines of the old hymn:

> "Jesus sought me when a stranger,
>   Wandering from the fold of God;
> He to rescue me from danger,
>   Interposed His precious blood."

You have heard the story of the little boy who was asked by a Christian worker if he had found Jesus. Looking up in wonder, he said, "Please, sir, I did not know that He was lost; but I was, and He found me." And so may every redeemed one say.

How precious to the heart of the Son of God must be the Father's gift of His redeemed. He says, "Thine they were, and Thou gavest them Me and they have kept Thy Word." He will be able to say that of every one of us when He brings us home at last, in spite of all our blunders, our failures, and our sins. As possessors of the divine nature, there is in every Christian a desire to do the will of God and to keep His Word. One who lacks this has never been regenerated.

In verse 7 He says, "Now they have known that all things whatsoever Thou hast given Me are of Thee." He takes the place of the distributor of the Father's bounty, like Joseph and David. Both of these young men were sent by their fathers to minister to their brethren, and yet both of them were grievously misunderstood and rejected. But the Lord looks with joyous complacency upon those who receive the blessing He brought, knowing surely that He came out from God, and so they believed that God had sent Him.

For them He prays. It is not for the unsaved that our Lord is carrying on His High-Priestly intercession in heaven, but for those who have been given to Him out of the world. On the cross He prayed for sinners; in heaven, He prays for saints. How sweet the words, "All Thine are Mine, and Mine are Thine, and I am glorified in them." What perfect security and what blessed communion! In spite of all our failures, He will be glorified in all His own, for He will make even these failures a means of teaching us our weakness and helplessness and our need of relying upon His unfailing love and power.

Literally, the word rendered "pray" here means to make request. Some day Jesus will make request concerning the world, and it will be given to Him as it is written in the second psalm: "Ask of Me, and I will give Thee the heathen for Thine inheritance, and the uttermost parts of the world for Thy possession." Then He will take His great power and reign, when "the Kingdoms of this world become the Kingdom of our God and His Christ." Now He is taking out from among the nations a people for His Name and it is on behalf of these that He makes request to the Father.

These are bound up in the bundle of life with the Father and the Son. He says, "All Mine are Thine, and Thine are Mine." Could anything be more precious? It is another way of saying what He had declared previously in John 10, when as the Good Shepherd He said of His sheep, "No man is able to pluck them out of My hand. My Father which gave them me is greater than all; and no man is able to pluck them out of My Father's hand." Every believer is held securely in the hands of the Father and the Son. We may well sing,

> "I'm safe in such confiding,
> For nothing changes there."

If He had not said it Himself we would never have dared assert that He is glorified in all His own. There has been such gross failure in many of us. We have followed afar off, so many times. Our careless ways and thoughtless words have brought dishonor upon His Name many times.

But as He looks upon us, cleansed by His blood and born of His Spirit He says of all who are saved "I am glorified in them." There is that in the life and experience of every Christian which is pleasant to Him and brings glory to His name.

It is hard for our poor legal hearts to abide in a sense of what grace really means. In a general way we confess that we are saved by grace, justified freely by His grace, and that the same grace that saved shall carry us on to the end. But practically we are ever ready to seek to build up some claim of personal merit. The blessed fact remains that we are maintained by grace all along the way, and so there will be in each one of us that in which He will be glorified. It is His own work in us by the power of the Spirit that makes this a reality. His very intercession is to that end. He saves evermore because He ever liveth to make intercession for us.

OUR LORD'S HIGH-PRIESTLY PRAYER (III)

✓ ✓ ✓

"And now I am no more in the world, but these are in the world, and I come to Thee. Holy Father, keep through Thine own name those whom Thou hast given Me, that they may be one, as We are. While I was with them in the world, I kept them in Thy name; those that Thou gavest Me I have kept, and none of them is lost, but the son of perdition; that the Scripture might be fulfilled. And now come I to Thee; and these things I speak in the world, that they may have My joy fulfilled in themselves. I have given them Thy Word, and the world hath hated them, because they are not of the world, even as I am not of the world. I pray not that Thou shouldest take them out of the world, but that Thou shouldest keep them from the evil. They are not of the world, even as I am not of the world" (John 17: 11-16).

✓ ✓ ✓

IN this section our Lord continues His intercession in behalf of His immediate disciples. They had walked with Him for three-and-a-half wonderful years. They had listened to the gracious words proceeding out of His mouth, and had been thrilled by His mighty works. Confidently they had looked forward to the proclamation of His kingly authority and the setting up of a new dynasty in Judea. Now they dimly apprehended that He was about to leave them and go back to the glory from which He came, and they were bewildered and troubled. He Himself knew, as none but He could know, what the world would mean to them after He had gone; what its attitude would be to them as they went forth carrying the message of the gospel, so He tenderly committed them to the keeping power of the Father. "Now I am no more in the world," He says, "but these are in the world and I come to Thee. Holy Father, keep through Thine own name those whom Thou hast given Me, that they may be one, as We are." Remember that all the way through this prayer He is anticipating the work of the cross. He speaks as though that were already in the past, and He looks at everything from the standpoint of His resurrection and ascension. It is as though He had already taken His place in the holiest as the great interceding High Priest. How blessedly He enters into the experience of His people. As on an earlier occasion He looked down upon them from the mountain-top while they were toiling in rowing across the stormy sea, so now He sees them exposed to trials and temptations of every kind, but He "ever liveth to make intercession for them."

There is a wonderful sense in which the saints are viewed even now in the heavenlies. We are told in Ephesians 2 that "He has raised us up together, and made us sit together in heavenly places in Christ Jesus." Christ is our Representative and God sees us in Him. Eventually we shall be with Him as an actual experience. But now we are like the children of Israel treading the sands of the wilderness. We need divine help to sustain us in a land of drought and desolation. There is nothing here that can minister to our needs. We are like David, who said, "All my springs are in Thee." We must draw from the Lord Himself that which will build us up in the spiritual life, and He pleads with the Father on our behalf that we may be sustained as we tread our pilgrim way.

Moreover, He is concerned that we be kept in the realization of our unity one with another. "Keep through Thine own name those whom Thou hast given Me, that they may be one as We are." It is sometimes said that this prayer of our Lord's has not been answered, because Christians are so scattered and divided. This, however, is not true. The unity of which He here speaks is the unity of life—family unity; and all believers are one in this sense. But it is a blessed thing to manifest this practically. It is as you and I realize our relationship to the

Father that we are kept in the manifestation of this unity. Then there will be unity in testimony. We see how this prayer was answered from that standpoint in the early days of the Church, when the apostles went forth witnessing to Christ the Lord, confirming the Word by signs. Thus with great power gave the apostles witness to the death, burial, and resurrection of our Lord Jesus Christ. It was unified testimony based upon a common life in Him.

Then in verse 12 He says, "While I was with them in the world, I kept them in Thy name: those that Thou gavest Me I have kept and none of them is lost, but the son of perdition; that the Scripture might be fulfilled." He had revealed the Father's name to them, and nurtured them in the blessedness of their divine relationship and responsibility. While He was with them, He guided, advised, corrected, and chastened, if need be, in order to keep from turning from the right hand to the left, and now He had brought them all safely through, losing none that the Father had given Him. We are not to understand that He had actually lost one, namely Judas, the son of perdition, for this is not what He says. In the original, "the son of perdition" is in the nominative case, therefore it is as though He said, "Those that thou gavest Me I have kept and none of *them* is lost, but the son of perdition; that

the scripture might be fulfilled." Judas had
never been given to the Son by the Father. He
walked in company with the rest: was even
trusted as their treasurer, but long before his
manifest defection, the Lord had said, "Have
not I chosen twelve, but one is a devil?" You
may be sure that whenever the Father gives any
one to Jesus, He gives him for time and eternity.
Such an one will never be lost. "Being confident
of this very thing, that He which hath begun a
good work in you will perform it until the day
of Jesus Christ." People call this the doctrine
of the perseverance of the saints, but I rather
like to think of it as the perseverance of the
Saviour. He says, "Those that thou gavest Me *I*
have kept." If I had to keep myself, I would be
hopeless of getting through. I would be sure that
something would happen some day which would
cause me to lose my hold on Christ and be lost.
But it is His hold upon me on which I rely. None
can pluck the believer out of His hand. I receive great comfort from these words. When He
gives His account to the Father, when the last
believer of this dispensation is safely arrived in
heaven, He will be able to say of the entire elect
Church, "Those that Thou gavest Me I have kept,
and none of them is lost." You may think you
know of exceptions to this; but it will be made
manifest in that day that these apparent excep-

tions were like Judas himself, never really born of God. It is said of him that he was lost, "that the scripture might be fulfilled." Does that mean that Judas could not have been saved had he honestly desired to be? No. But we need to distinguish between God's foreknowledge and His predestination. It was foreknown that Judas would betray the Lord Jesus Christ. It was foretold in the Word of God, but this does not mean that God had foreordained it. He permitted Judas to take his own way unhindered by divine grace, and Judas went wrong. God foreknew that he would do this, so the Scripture was fulfilled in his doom.

In verse 13 we read, "And now come I to Thee; and these things I speak in the world, that they might have My joy fulfilled in themselves." Our English word "fulfilled" is really two words turned around. To get the exact meaning, reverse the syllables, and you have, "filled full." And that is what our Lord has in mind. It is as though He said to the Father, "Now I am coming to Thee, and I am leaving them down in that world of trial, but I pray that their hearts may be filled full of joy. I want to share My joy with them. I would have them filled with that." In what did He find His joy? In doing His Father's will and communing with Him. As we trust and obey, this joy will fill our hearts to overflowing.

There is a great deal of difference between joy and happiness. Happiness comes from the old English word "Hap." A hap is a chance. If happenings are pleasant, a worldling is happy. If the happenings are unpleasant, such an one is unhappy. But the Christian has a deep-toned joy as he walks in fellowship with God which no happiness can ever affect or change. This was what gave such power to the testimony of the early disciples. Men could beat them, put them in prison, fasten their feet in stocks, condemn them to death, but they went through it all with songs on their lips. This is not of the world. It is the manifest joy of the Lord.

Then He says, "I have given them Thy Word, and the world hath hated them, because they are not of the world, even as I am not of the world. I pray not that Thou shouldest take them out of the world, but that Thou shouldest keep them from the evil. They are not of the world, even as I am not of the world." How slow we are sometimes to recognize the reality of our "strangership" down here. We know theoretically that we are not of the world; and yet how much like the world we are in our tastes, in our ambitions, and in our behaviour. The trouble is we are not occupied enough with the land to which we are going. No one can really put this world beneath his feet until he has seen a better world above his head. We are called to separation from that system which has no place for Christ, and our sustenance, as we pass on to our heavenly goal, is the Word which He has given us.

Notice that our Lord Jesus never expressed opinions concerning anything. Strictly speaking, He had no mere ideas to give out. People talk of Jesus' views, of Jesus' ideas, of His conceptions of things. But this is all wrong. When He spoke, it was God speaking. He gave forth the Father's Word, and that Word is far above all mere opinions or notions. Let us cling to it, let us hold it fast, and as we walk in obedience to it, prove that we do not belong to the world, but that as a pilgrim people, we are pressing on to the rest that remains for the people of God.

OUR LORD'S HIGH-PRIESTLY PRAYER (IV)

✹ ✹ ✹

"Sanctify them through Thy Word: Thy Word is truth. As Thou hast sent Me into the world, even so have I also sent them into the world. And for their sakes I sanctify Myself, that they also might be sanctified through the truth. Neither pray I for these alone, but for them which shall believe on Me through their word; that they all may be one; as Thou, Father, art in Me, and I in Thee, that they also may be one in Us: that the world may believe that Thou hast sent Me" (John 17: 17-21).

✹ ✹ ✹

THERE are two distinct lines of truth brought before us in these verses: first, our practical sanctification, and second, our unity of life and nature with all the people of God in the Father and the Son, a unity which forms the basis of Christian testimony to a lost world.

Note our Lord's petition, "Sanctify them through Thy truth; Thy Word is truth." What does He mean by this? There are three distinct aspects of sanctification in the New Testament: sanctification by the Holy Spirit; sanctification by the blood of Christ; and sanctification by the Word of truth. The first refers to the work of the Holy Spirit within us, cleansing us from all impurity and setting us apart to God practically. The second has to do with our judicial cleansing, fitting us for entrance to the heavenly sanctuary; and the last has to do with our daily walk.

We must never confuse justification with sanctification. To justify is to clear from every charge of guilt. To sanctify is to set apart for a holy purpose. Because we were guilty sinners we needed to be justified. Because we were unclean and defiled by sin, we needed to be sanctified. Positionally, we are set apart to God in Christ, in all the value of His precious blood, the moment we trust the Saviour. But practically, we are being sanctified day by day by the Spirit and the Word. In 1 Corinthians 6: 11, we read, "And such were some of you; but ye are washed; but ye are sanctified, but ye are justified in the name of the Lord Jesus, and by the Spirit of our God." In the previous verses, the apostle was speaking of a number of ungodly people, who, he said, "shall not inherit the kingdom of God." But Christians were once just as bad as they, but they have been washed, sanctified, and justified. The washing is the application of the water of the Word to our hearts and consciences, and that must be in the power of the Holy Spirit. This simply suggests two different aspects of one truth. The emphasis here is upon sanctification rather than justification. The Spirit had to do His work in me, awakening me, convicting of sin, before I ever put my trust in the Lord Jesus Christ.

I remember years ago going into a mission in San Francisco, and listening to some striking testimonies. People told how marvelously God had saved them from lives of sin and debauchery. I was to give the final message. As I listened to them, this verse came to me, and I took it for my text. "Such were some of you." When the meeting was over, one of the workers came to me and asked me, "May I have a word with you?" I said, "Certainly."

Then he told me, "You had your theology terribly mixed tonight."

I replied, "Did I? Won't you please straighten me out?"

"Yes," he answered, "that is what I want to do. You put sanctification before justification. Now justification is the first blessing and sanctification is the second, but you reversed this."

"You are mistaken," I replied. "I did not put sanctification before justification."

"You most certainly did," was his emphatic answer.

"No," I told him, "you are wrong. I did nothing of the kind. It was the apostle Paul that put sanctification before justification, and I simply quoted what he had written."

He insisted that I had misquoted it, but when we looked into the Bible, he had to admit I was right, but he was sure the translation was wrong. We consulted the Revised Version. The same order was there. Then he exclaimed in confusion, "Well, all I have to say is that Paul was not yet clear on holiness when he wrote that!"

But this is not the only Scripture where we have sanctification of the Spirit coming before justification. In 2 Thessalonians 2:13 we read: "But we are bound to give thanks alway to God for you, brethren beloved of the Lord, because God hath from the beginning chosen you to salvation through sanctification of the Spirit and belief of the truth." It is the Spirit's sanctification, you see, that leads to belief of the truth. And then again in 1 Peter 1 and 2 we have the same order. Through sanctification of the Spirit, we come in the obedience of faith to the sprinkling of the blood of Jesus Christ. It is by His blood we are justified from all our guilt, and by that same precious blood, we are sanctified, set apart to God in Christ, "who is made unto us wisdom and righteousness, sanctification and redemption." *

Here in our Lord's prayer, He asks the Father to "sanctify them through Thy truth." That is, the Word of God is to be applied to the lives of His people, and as they obey that Word they will be practically sanctified and cleansed from defilement. In Ephesians 5: 25, 26 we read: "Husbands, love your wives, even as Christ also loved the Church and gave Himself for it, that He might sanctify and cleanse it by the washing of water by the Word." You see the Word of God is likened unto water because of its cleansing efficacy. When I trusted Christ, I was cleansed by His precious blood once for all. This is a cleansing that never needs to be repeated, for the blood abides upon the mercy-seat, and it ever cleanseth us from every sin. But the washing of water by the Word is something I need daily. It is illustrated by our Lord's action in washing the feet of His disciples in John 13. Our feet become defiled with the things of this world, but the Word of God is applied and we are made clean. You will realize that in this sense, we could never speak of ourselves as whollyist, ctified. Positionally we know it is true that "By

---

* I have tried to go into all this very fully in my book, "Holiness, the False and the True," and if you are troubled about the question of sanctification, I would urge you to get a copy and read it carefully. I cannot go into it now with the fulness that I would like, as it would lead us too far away from our subject.

one offering He hath perfected forever them that
are sanctified." Christ is my sanctification and
that is complete and eternal, but so far as my
practice is concerned, I need the Word of God
applied every day, and thus I am being sanctified.

Now observe our blessed Lord says to the
Father, "As Thou hast sent Me into the world,
even so have I also sent them into the world.
And for their sakes, I sanctify Myself, that they
also might be sanctified through the truth." To
sanctify is to set apart. He was the holy, spotless Son of God, but He set Himself apart to go
to the cross, there to die for our sins, and then
to take His place at God's right hand in heaven.
As we are occupied with Him, we become like
Him. Our sanctification progresses as we are
taken up with Christ through the Word.

"Fix your eyes upon Jesus,
    Look full in His wonderful face,
And the things of earth will grow strangely dim,
    In the light of His glory and grace."

Now notice in verse 20, His thoughts go down
through the ages, reaching even to you and to
me, and to all in every place who shall ever put
their trust in Him. He says, "Neither pray I
for these alone, but for them also which shall believe on Me through their word." It is in this
way that we come to believe; is it not? And so

we are included in those for whom He prays. And what is it for which He makes request? Notice His words, "That they all may be one; as Thou, Father, art in Me and I in Thee, that they also may be one in Us: that the world may believe that thou has sent Me." Here we have a second prayer for unity. It is the unity of fellowship, on which, of course, our testimony to the world is based.

People say sometimes that this prayer of our Lord has not been answered and they point to the many different sects and denominations among professed Christians. Of these we very well are ashamed. And yet, despite them all, wherever real Christians get together they enjoy fellowship in the precious things of Christ. It is when we allow ourselves to be occupied with minor questions which do not profit, that our differences come in. We are all one in Christ. The fact that Satan, our great adversary, has set members of the same family to quarrelling with each other is sad indeed, and should cause us to bow our heads in humiliation and self-judgment before God. As our unity is manifested in a practical way our testimony has power with men. On the other hand nothing is so calculated to stumble the unsaved as finding that Christians are unkind and quarrelsome in their dealings with each other.

How quickly we realize that we are one when the hour of trouble and persecution comes. A fine old Armenian Christian who was greatly grieved by the divisions among Christians in America, said to me one time, as the tears started in his eyes, "They need the Turks. If they were exposed to the awful persecutions we had to know in Armenia, they would learn to value one another more."

A missionary wrote to me lately and spoke of meeting another missionary of an altogether different group of believers in a foreign land where he was laboring. He said, "Any kind of a Christian looks mighty good to me down here."

May we realize more and more our unity and act in accordance with it, that thus the world may believe that God sent Jesus to be the Saviour of men. Every time a worldling hears you making an unkind remark about another Christian, you are stultifying your own testimony. Of old, when believers were characterized by love of the brethren, Tertullian tells us that even the heathen exclaimed with admiration, "Behold how these Christians love one another."

The following lines are most suggestive and form a fitting commentary on our Saviour's prayer, "That they all may be one."

THEY'RE DEAR TO GOD

Oh that when Christians meet and part,
These words were graved on every heart—
    They're dear to God!
However wilful and unwise,
We'll look on them with loving eyes—
    They're dear to God!
Oh, wonder!—to the Eternal One,
Dear as His own beloved Son;
Dearer to Jesus than His blood,
Dear as the Spirit's fixed abode—
    They're dear to God!

When tempted to give pain for pain,
How would this thought our words restrain
    They're dear to God!
When truth compels us to contend,
What love with all our strife should blend!
    They're dear to God.
When they would shun the pilgrim's lot
For this vain world, forget them not;
But win them back with love and prayer,
They never can be happy there,
    If dear to God.

Shall we be there so near, so dear,
And be estranged and cold whilst here—
    All dear to God?
By the same cares and toils opprest,
We lean upon one faithful Breast,
We hasten to the same repose;
How bear or do enough for those
    So dear to God!

ADDRESS FIFTY-NINE

OUR LORD'S HIGH-PRIESTLY PRAYER (V)

"And the glory which Thou gavest Me I have given them; that they may be one, even as We are one: I in them, and Thou in Me, that they may be made perfect in one; and that the world may know that Thou hast sent Me, and hast loved them, as Thou hast loved Me. Father, I will that they also, whom Thou hast given Me, be with Me where I am; that they may behold My glory, which Thou hast given Me: for Thou lovedst Me before the foundation of the world. O righteous Father, the world hath not known Thee: but I have known Thee, and these have known that Thou hast sent Me. And I have declared unto them Thy name, and will declare it: that the love wherewith Thou hast loved Me may be in them, and I in them" (John 17: 22-26).

SOME very wonderful truths are brought before us in these verses. In verse 22 our Lord speaks of sharing His acquired glories with His own. You remember we saw that there is a difference between the essential glory of the Lord Jesus Christ and His acquired glory. When He spoke in verse 5 of the "glory which I had with Thee before the world was," and back into which He was going, He was speaking of *His* essential glory which you and I will never share. He is God—God the Son, with God the

Father, and God the Spirit. He is God, and we, of course, will never be exalted to Deity. We do not in any sense share that glory, but we are to behold that glory when we see Him. We shall see Him in all His glory as the Eternal Son. There are other *glories* which He won by His cross, that accrued to Him because of the work He did when down here in this world of sin, and those glories we shall share. He speaks of the glory which He had won when He says, "**The glory which Thou gavest Me.**" He has given us a share in all that He won by His death on the cross. In view of that, He prays a third time for the unity of His people. In verse 11 He prays for a unity in testimony: "And now I am no more in the world, but these are in the world, and I come to Thee. Holy Father, keep through Thine own name those whom Thou hast given Me, that they may be one, as We are." Thank God, through His grace they are kept in unity of testimony. In verse 21 He has in view unity in fellowship, and this, of course, is based upon the unity of life, which is shared by all saints; for, after having prayed for those with Him at that time, He says, "Neither pray I for these alone, but for them also which shall believe on Me through their word." There is a unity of life. We today have exactly the same divine life that He had, so that prayer has been answered. The people of God are one. It is perfectly true we do not always act as though we are one, but we are all members of His blessed family.

He desires us to so live in that unity that the world may believe. When people cf the world see that we Christians love one another they are impressed with the reality of our profession. When they see us quarreling, it gives them a reason to question the reality of our profession.

Now in the verse before us He says, "The glory which Thou gavest Me I have given them; that they may be one, even as We are one (as the Divine Trinity are one) : I in them, and Thou in Me, that they may be made perfect in one (that they may be perfected into one)." What is this? It is *displayed* unity at the coming again of the Lord Jesus Christ. "That they may be made perfect in one; and that the world may know that Thou hast sent Me." During the present time, as we manifest our unity, the world believes. At His coming, it will no longer be possible to question the fact. The world will know this unity when all the saints are revealed in the same glory as the Lord Jesus Christ. "That the world may believe that Thou hast sent Me." In that day the world will awaken to the realization of the fact that Christ is indeed the Sent One. It will then be too late for many of them who refused to believe to come into harmony with Him.

The second part of this verse is so marvelous that if it were not in the Word of God we would not believe it. "Thou hast loved them, as Thou hast loved Me." Just suppose somebody stood up and declared this without Scriptural authority. It would be too much to take in! "That the world may know that Thou has sent Me, and hast loved them as Thou hast loved Me." Is that really true? Does God the Father love me as much as He loves Jesus Christ? Do you believe it, my sister? Does he love you, my brother, as much as He loves Jesus Christ? What an amazing truth this is! I can understand that because He loves His Son He will take me into favor and give me a measure of affection because I believe in His Son. But here I find there is no difference between the love the Father has for His own Son, the Lord Jesus Christ, and the love He has for His children of faith in Jesus Christ.

> "So near, so very near to God,
>   Nearer I could not be;
> For in the person of His Son,
>   I am as near as He.
>
> "So dear, so very dear to God,
>   Dearer I could not be;
> The love wherewith He loved His Son,
>   Such is His love to me."

There is a verse in John's first epistle that long puzzled me. It contains just nine monosyllables.

We like to use big words, with which to set forth our poor poverty-stricken thoughts. But when the Holy Spirit sets forth the most profound truth He often clothes it in the very simplest language. He wraps it up in little words, so easy and plain that all can take it in. In the latter part of 1 John 4:17, we read, "As He is, so are we in this world." Look at that. Nine monosyllables, and some of them contain only two letters. *"As He is."* I could not make that out. I wondered if that were the correct translation. Might it not mean, "As He is, so *ought* we to be in this world?" I read the context and looked it up in the original. No; that was not it. Could it be that this is to be carried into the future? Could it mean, "As He is, so *will* we be when we get through with this world?" No; that was not it. "As He is, so are we in this world." But I am not pure in thought and word and deed as He is. I am not as considerate of the feelings of others as He. I do not love God as He does. I do not love the lost world as He does. There must be something wrong. Then my attention was directed to the fact that John had just been talking of the day of judgment. I used to be afraid of the day of judgment. How terrible it would be after many years of service to come to the judgment and find I had failed and might be lost after all! But I read, "Herein is our love made

perfect, that we may have boldness in the day
of judgment; because as He is, so are we in this
world (literal rendering)." It began to open up
to me. My relationship to the coming judgment
is the same as His. Is He ever coming into judgment for sin? He has been judged already in my
place. Is He to give an account for the sins laid
on Him at Calvary's cross? No. Then what
about me? "As He is, so are we in this world."
"Perfect love casteth out all fear." I had been
looking for perfect love in myself, trying to
pump it up; looking for perfect love, but never
finding it. The Lord led me to look for perfect
love in the blessed Lord Jesus Christ. I found it
there, the love that brought Him to Calvary's
cross. Perfect love is there and only there. It
casts out all fear. It was on my behalf He suffered.

> "Death and judgment are behind me,
>   Grace and glory are before;
>   All the billows rolled o'er Jesus,
>   There they spent their utmost power."

He took my place; He bore my judgment.
"There is no condemnation to them which are in
Christ Jesus." "Verily, verily, I say unto you,
He that heareth My Word, and believeth on Him
that sent Me, hath everlasting life, and shall not

come into condemnation; but is passed from death unto life." My fears are gone. "As He is, so are we in this world."

An English brother said:

"John's nine monosyllables all in a row,
  Are my joy and my comfort while here below."

Suppose I am passing the court-house and see the police taking in different ones. I ask, "What is going on here?" "Oh," they say, "they are trying a lot of gangsters." I say, "I think I'll go in." They tell me, "You had better stay out; you may get into trouble." "What for?" I ask, "My case is not coming up." I have boldness in the day of judgment. So it is here; I have boldness in the day of judgment because my case is not coming up. I have been judged in my Substitute. All my sins are settled for. I do not mean that I will not be judged for my works. That is a different occasion. We stand now before God in relation to the judgment in the same place as His blessed Son stands. He has made us "accepted in the Beloved." We are accepted in Him. Don't let any one cheat you out of the joy of that. The Father loves me as much as He loves the Lord Jesus Christ. Isn't it wonderful to be a Christian? "That the world may know that Thou hast sent Me, and hast loved them, as Thou hast loved Me."

Now notice the next portion. "Father, I will" (that is, "I desire") ; you know the Lord Jesus said, "I came not to do My will, but the will of Him that sent Me." He never asserted His will. He says, "I desire that they also whom Thou hast given Me, be with Me where I am; that they may behold My glory, which Thou hast given Me, for Thou lovedst Me before the foundation of the world." Do you think the Father will grant Him His desire? Do you think when the saints are gathered the Lord will be looking around and saying "Some I thought the Father had given Me are missing?" No, they will all be there. "I will that they also whom Thou hast given Me"—seven times He uses that expression—"be with Me where I am; that they may behold My glory which Thou hast given Me; for Thou lovedst Me before the foundation of the world." There is one glory we shall share, another glory we shall behold. We shall behold the glory of the only begotten Son, one who was loved of the Father before the world was created. "Thou lovedst Me before the foundation of the world." This tells not only of the pre-existence of the Lord Jesus Christ, but also of the blessed fellowship of the Persons of the Trinity.

Now the Lord closes His prayer thus: "O righteous Father, the world hath not known Thee: but I have known Thee, and these have known that Thou hast sent Me." When He speaks of God in view of the world, He says, "Righteous Father." When thinking of His own relationship, it is simply, "Father," or "Holy Father." What blasphemy it is to call any man on earth "Holy Father," when the blessed Lord reserves that title for God the Father! Here He says, "O righteous Father, the world hath not known Thee." How true it is, "the natural man understandeth not the things of God, but they are spiritually discerned." The world imagines it knows God. The unsaved talk about God, but know not the One revealed by the Lord Jesus Christ.

I was reasoning with a man who called himself a Unitarian. I gave him Scripture to prove the pre-existence and Deity of the Lord Jesus Christ. He did not accept the testimony of the Scripture. As he left me, he said, "Well, goodbye, brother; I cannot accept your faith, but we can shake hands because we both believe in God the Father, if we do not agree about Jesus." I answered, "If you had offered your hand simply as a man, I could shake hands with you. I do not want to be discourteous, but I cannot shake hands with you on your statement that we have the same Father, but disagree about the Lord Jesus Christ."

The world does not know the Father. The world has many lords and gods, but only in the Lord Jesus Christ has the Father been revealed. "The world hath not known Thee, but I have known Thee." He knew the heart of God, for He came from God and went back to God. He was one with the Father. Now this wonderful Lord is revealed by the Spirit to every one of us, His own. "These have known that Thou has sent Me." Here on earth He took the place of the Sent One. He said, "I am not alone, but I and the Father that sent Me." "As Thou has sent Me into the world, even so have I also sent them into the world." We can go into a lost world with the consciousness of being sent by the Son to carry the gospel to lost men and women.

In verse 26 He says, "I have declared unto them Thy name, and will declare it." In verse 6 He said, "I have manifested Thy name." Here He says, "I have declared unto them Thy name." That was a part of His mission, to make known the Father's name. He manifested it in His life, for He was "the only begotten of the Father, full of grace and truth." He manifested it by His doctrinal statement: "I have declared unto them Thy name, and will declare it." What does He mean? He is just going to the cross to die, to seal His testimony by giving His life for the redemption of mankind.

In resurrection, what is the first thing He does? He appears to Mary and says, "Go to My brethren, and say unto them, I ascend unto My Father and your Father; and to My God and your God." He had declared the Father's name here on the earth. He declares it again in resurrection. So we have a double testimony as to our relationship to God.

"I have declared unto them Thy name, and will declare it; that the love wherewith Thou hast loved Me may be in them, and I in them." How is that love in us, the love wherewith the Father loved the Son? Turn to Romans 5:1 and read, "Therefore being justified by faith, we have peace with God through our Lord Jesus Christ: by whom also we have access by faith into this grace wherein we stand, and rejoice in hope of the glory of God. And not only so, but we glory in tribulations also; knowing that tribulation worketh patience; and patience experience, and experience hope; and hope maketh not ashamed; because the love of God is shed abroad in our hearts by the Holy Ghost which is given unto us." The Spirit of God has come down from glory to witness to the acceptance of our blessed High Priest, the Lord Jesus Christ, who is entered into the holiest, and He it is who sheds abroad the Father's love in our hearts. That love is not merely human; it is that which is divine.

That is why the Scripture says, "Whosoever loveth is born of God." It does not mean, if you are an affectionate person you are born of God. We have such a low conception of love.

I remember hearing of a young man who came to his pastor as he was leaving for another field, and said, "Before you came here I did not care for God, man, or the devil. Now I have learned to love them all." That is the idea some people have of love! But divine love is holy love, the love of God to sinners, the love the Holy Ghost puts in the heart. It is this love that enabled Christ to triumph over all circumstances, and to love lost men, no matter how they treated Him. May we all enter into it more fully for His Name's sake.

IN THE GARDEN

✐ ✐ ✐

"When Jesus had spoken these words, He went forth
with His disciples over the brook Cedron, where was a
garden, into the which He entered, and His disciples.
And Judas also, which betrayed Him, knew the place:
for Jesus ofttimes resorted thither with His disciples.
Judas then, having received a band of men and officers
from the chief priests and Pharisees, cometh thither with
lanterns and torches and weapons. Jesus therefore,
knowing all things that should come upon Him, went
forth, and said unto them, Whom seek ye? They answered Him, Jesus of Nazareth. Jesus saith unto them,
I am He. And Judas also, which betrayed Him, stood
with them. As soon then as He had said unto them, I
am He, they went backward, and fell to the ground.
Then asked He them again, Whom seek ye? And they
said, Jesus of Nazareth. Jesus answered, I have told
you that I am He: if therefore ye seek Me, let these go
their way; that the saying might be fulfilled, which He
spake, Of them which Thou gavest Me have I lost none.
Then Simon Peter having a sword drew it, and smote
the high priest's servant, and cut off his right ear. The
servant's name was Malchus. Then said Jesus unto
Peter, Put up thy sword into the sheath: the cup which
My Father hath given Me, shall I not drink it? Then
the band and the captain and officers of the Jews took
Jesus, and bound Him, and led Him away to Annas first;
for he was father-in-law to Caiaphas, which was the
high priest that same year. Now Caiaphas was he, which
gave counsel to the Jews, that it was expedient that one
man should die for the people" (John 18: 1-14).

✐ ✐ ✐

WE come now to consider the closing hours of our blessed Lord's life upon this earth. All through the time of His sojourn in this scene He had been looking forward to that hour when He was to give Himself a ransom for our sins upon the cross.

Now He had enjoyed a season of hallowed fellowship with the little company whom He had called out of the world to be the companions of His lonely life. They had heard Him lift His heart to God in intercessory prayer, and now they walked over the brook Cedron, crossing by a small bridge, and then up the slope of the Mount of Olives to a garden, the garden of Gethsemane. Gethsemane is said by some to mean "oil-press." The olives were thrown into the press that the rich, golden oil might be expelled from them. It was there that our blessed Lord, the Son of God, was to go through the oil-press, as it were, the awful pressure that was to be put upon His heart and mind in view of the coming sacrifice He was about to offer on Calvary.

The three Synoptic writers, Matthew, Mark and Luke, all tell us that at this point, in the great agony that He went through in the Garden, His prayer was, "O My Father, if it be possible, let this cup pass from Me: nevertheless not as I will, but as Thou wilt."

Luke tells how, under that awful pressure, the blood burst from the pores of His forehead and fell in great drops to the ground, and how an angel came and strengthened Him. We do not have a word of that from John. Why not? John was one of the three who went with Him into the garden. He left eight of them by the gate of the garden and He took Peter and James and John deeper in. And He went forward a little farther and fell on His face, and endured that awful period of anguish of soul. And yet John does not say a word about it. Why? Oh, in this, as all else, we see the perfection of Holy Scripture. The four Gospels are not mere human records, they are divinely-given accounts of the Lord's life and death and resurrection. Each presents Him from a special viewpoint, according to the Spirit. It has often been noticed, as we have stated before, the subject of Matthew is Christ as the King of the Jews; the object of Mark is to present Him as the great Servant-Prophet, doing the will of the Father at all times. Luke presents Him in all the perfection of His Manhood, the Son of Man who gave Himself for us. But John's special object is to present His Eternal Sonship. He brings Him before us as the Divine One. And so in this Gospel there is no scene of agony in the Garden, for it was not the Deity of Christ that was concerned in that scene. But on the other hand neither is there any account of the transfiguration, because in John's Gospel the glory is shining out all the way through. So here we have the agony omitted. But it is well for us to think of it and remember what the other Gospels tell us.

What was really involved in that prayer of His?—"O My Father, if it be possible, let this cup pass from Me." What was that mystic cup of which He speaks? As we turn back to the Old Testament (and we must remember that our blessed Lord, as Man, was nourished on the Old Testament; it was His Bible), we find some very solemn references to the cup of judgment. In Psalm 11: 6 we read, "Upon the wicked He shall rain snares, fire and brimstone, and an horrible tempest: this shall be the portion of their cup." In Psalm 75: 8, we find these solemn words, "For in the hand of the Lord there is a cup, and the wine is red; it is full of mixture; and He poureth out of the same: but the dregs thereof, all the wicked of the earth shall wring them out, and drink them." In these passages we read of a cup, a cup of divine judgment, a cup filled with the wrath, the indignation of God against sin. And when we come to the last book of the Bible, that great prophetical book, we read of those who worship the Beast and his image, "If any man worship the Beast and his image, and receive his mark in his forehead, or in his hand, the same shall drink of the wine of the wrath of God, which is poured out without mixture into the cup of His indignation; and he shall be tormented with fire and brimstone in the presence of the holy angels, and in the presence of the Lamb" (Rev. 14: 9).

We are safe in saying that it was that cup of wrath that our Lord Jesus saw before Him as He prayed, "Father, if it be possible, let this cup pass from Me." Either you and I had to drink that cup, or He must take it in our room and stead. And that cup involved His being made sin upon the cross. It involved God dealing with Him as though He were guilty of all the sin, all the wickedness, all the corruption that men and women have been guilty of all down through the millenniums. All our sins were to be laid upon Him, and He was to bear, in His own body and His own spirit there upon the cross all that those sins deserved. This was the cup from which He shrank. He could not have been the absolutely Holy One if He had not dreaded the drinking of this awful cup. And so the three Synoptics tell us how He agonized, how His body was so racked with pain as He faced this time, that the sweat fell to the ground as great drops of blood.

But He was not bearing sin there in Gethsemane. He was not made sin there. All this was before Him. He was anticipating this and looking forward to it. Only on the cross did He settle the sin question. And so we hear Him say at last, "Father, if this cup may not pass away from Me, except I drink it, Thy will be done." And from that moment the struggle was over. He prepared, in perfect calmness, to meet His enemies and to face Judas, the traitor, and then to go on to the judgment-hall and to death.

And so we see that this entire scene of His agony comes in between the first and second verses of this 18th chapter. "When Jesus had spoken these words, He went forth with His disciples over the brook Cedron, where was a garden, into the which He entered, and His disciples." And the agony immediately followed.

Now we read, "And Judas also, which betrayed Him, knew the place: for Jesus ofttimes resorted thither with His disciples." He had often been there to pour out His heart in prayer in fullest, happiest communion with the Father. Now He went through a very different experience. In deepest distress of soul He poured out His heart to the Father, but with no rebellion. When there was no other way He accepted the cup with perfect submission.

"Judas then, having received a band of men and officers from the chief priests and Pharisees, cometh thither with lanterns and torches and weapons." Christ had arisen from His knees and come back to the three, Peter, James and John, and gently rebuked them for sleeping. And then He said to them, "Rise up now, Let us be going. He that betrayeth Me is at hand." Then they met the officers and Judas, coming to take Him.

"Jesus therefore, knowing all things that should come upon Him, went forth, and said unto them, Whom seek ye?" Nothing took Him by surprise. He knew all that was coming and He went forth voluntarily to meet them, asking, "Whom seek ye?" And the answer came, "Jesus of Nazareth." And Jesus said, "I am He." Really, what He said was this, "I am." He used the very name of Deity, "I am," as He had done so often before.

We read, "And Judas also, which betrayed Him, stood with them," Judas, who knew Him so well, Judas, who had been with the company for those three-and-a-half years, and yet whose conscience had never been really reached, Judas who had never truly yielded his heart to Christ. It shows how possible it is for people to keep company with those who are God's children and frequent the house of God, and yet never open the heart to the Saviour.

"As soon then as He had said unto them, I am He, they went backward, and fell to the ground," bowing at His feet. Then as they rise, He turned

again and said, "Whom seek ye?" And once more
they replied, "Jesus of Nazareth." "Jesus answered, I have told you that I am He: if therefore ye seek Me, let these go their way." His
heart went out to His disciples. He would not
have them arrested with Him. He would not
have them go through a martyr's death at this
time. He undertook to protect His own. He had
said to His Father, "Those that Thou gavest Me
I have kept, none of them is lost." And if He
can keep their souls for eternity, He can keep
their lives in this world. And so He says, "Let
these go their way."

But then at this moment, activity began among
them. It was very fleshly activity. "Simon
Peter, having a sword drew it, and smote the
high priest's servant, and cut off his right ear."
What a foolish thing to do, flashing about without any commandment from the Lord! And
after all, just injuring a poor servant who was
not responsible for what went on. We are not
told the sequel here, but if we turn to the other
Gospels we learn that Jesus healed the wounded
man. Somebody has said, "How often we are
like Peter. How busy we keep the Lord putting
on ears that we cut off." We do not mean to do
it, perhaps, but we go around saying such unkind, foolish things that we injure people instead
of helping them. I am sure that Peter would

have had great difficulty in leading Malchus to
Christ after cutting off his ear! Don't cut people's
ears off and then expect them to hear your message. Peter forgot that grace and truth came by
Jesus Christ. He was going to fight for His Lord
but it was in a very carnal way. It got him into
trouble afterwards, for it added to his difficulties
when the time of testing came. "Then said Jesus
unto Peter, Put up thy sword into the sheath:
the cup which My Father hath given Me, shall I
not drink it?" Before, in His agony, He prayed,
"Let this cup pass," and later, "If this cup may
not pass away from Me, except I drink it, Thy
will be done." Now He goes forth in perfect
serenity of spirit. The battle is over, the victory
is won, and He says, "I am going out to take that
cup, not from man, but from the hand of My
Father." In the fifty-third chapter of Isaiah we
read, "Yet it pleased the Lord to bruise Him; He
hath put Him to grief." I am afraid sometimes
we have a very shallow conception of the work
of the cross. It was not merely the physical
sufferings of Jesus which made atonement for
sin. He did suffer in His body more than anyone, for as He hung upon that cross, every nerve,
every fibre of His being must have been affected,
but it was not that which settled the sin question.
It was when Jehovah made His soul an offering
for sin; when it pleased God to bruise Him. In

other words, it was not what Jesus suffered at
the hands of man that made atonement for sin, it
was what He suffered at the hands of God. It
was God who put to His lips the cup of judgment. He received that cup from the Father's
hands and drained it to the dregs.

> "Death and the curse were in that cup,
>   Oh Christ, 'twas full for Thee;
> But Thou hast drained the last dark dregs,
>   'Tis empty now for me."

And this is what we remember when we gather
at the table of the Lord. We think of Him, our
blessed Saviour, going to that cross and draining
the cup of judgment to the dregs. If that cup
had been placed at our lips, it would have taken
all eternity to empty it, but He drank it all in
those three hours of darkness on the tree. "The
cup which My Father hath given Me, shall I
not drink it?"

He put Himself into their hands and allowed
them to take Him captive. "Then the band and
the captain and officers of the Jews took Jesus,
and bound Him. And led Him away to Annas
first; for he was father-in-law to Caiaphas, which
was the high priest that same year." Such a
midnight session of the Sanhedrin was absolutely unlawful but they did not stop to consider
that. "Now Caiaphas was he, which gave counsel to the Jews, that it was expedient that one

man should die for the people." And, thank God, the words he spoke were blessedly true. It was necessary that one man should die for the people and that the whole nation perish not. This he said indicating that Jesus should die not for that nation only, but for the whole world. Through that death all who will may have life everlasting and peace with God.

We remember Him today as the One who died for us and we, who have a saving interest in His blood, we who have trusted Him as our Saviour, will never have to drink the cup of judgment, for He took it for us, and gives to us the cup of salvation.

> "When I survey the wondrous cross
>   On which the Prince of glory died,
>   My richest gain I count but loss,
>   And pour contempt on all my pride."

PETER'S DENIAL

✓ ✓ ✓

"And Simon Peter followed Jesus, and so did another disciple: that disciple was known unto the high priest, and went in with Jesus into the palace of the high priest. But Peter stood at the door without. Then went out that other disciple, which was known unto the high priest, and spake unto her that kept the door, and brought in Peter. Then saith the damsel that kept the door unto Peter, Art not thou also one of this man's disciples? He saith, I am not. And the servants and officers stood there, who had made a fire of coals; for it was cold: and they warmed themselves: and Peter stood with them, and warmed himself. The high priest then asked Jesus of His disciples, and of His doctrine. Jesus answered him, I spake openly to the world; I ever taught in the synagogue, and in the temple, whither the Jews always resort; and in secret have I said nothing. Why askest thou Me? ask them which heard Me, what I have said unto them: behold, they know what I said. And when He had thus spoken, one of the officers which stood by struck Jesus with the palm of his hand, saying, Answerest Thou the high priest so? Jesus answered him, If I have spoken evil, bear witness of the evil: but if well, why smitest thou Me? Now Annas had sent Him bound unto Caiaphas the high priest. And Simon Peter stood and warmed himself. They said therefore unto him, Art not thou also one of His disciples? He denied it, and said, I am not. One of the servants of the high priest, being his kinsman whose ear Peter cut off, saith, Did not I see thee in the garden with Him? Peter then denied again: and immediately the cock crew" (John 18:15-27).

✓ ✓ ✓

IN this section we have two narratives enfolded together in a very striking way. The Apostle Peter's great failure, his denial of his Lord, and our Lord's trial—His mock trial—before the high priest, Caiaphas.

First, we are concerned with the Apostle Peter. What a wonderful man Peter was! As we read all that the Word tells us of him, and then add some few instances that have come down to us through what seems to be reliable Church history, we cannot help but be filled with admiration for this bold, energetic man who loved his Lord so loyally and yet who failed so terribly at times, but who eventually became the most outstanding of all the Apostles until Saul of Tarsus was converted and given his special ministry to the Gentiles.

We last considered the scene in the Garden, closing with the arrest of our blessed Lord and His being taken away to Annas and Caiaphas. The Lord Jesus had foretold that Peter would forsake Him, but Peter declared, "Though all men forsake Thee, yet will not I." But Jesus said to him, "Simon, behold, Satan hath desired to have you, that he may sift you as wheat: but I have prayed for thee, that thy faith fail not. . . . The cock shall not crow this day, before that thou shalt thrice deny that thou knowest Me."

This is a very interesting statement—"Satan hath desired (it is literally, *demanded*) to have thee that he may sift thee as wheat." Satan, then, is the sifter of God's wheat. In other words, when some of God's children need to have the chaff and the wheat separated, the Lord turns them over temporarily to Satan. You remember in 1 Corinthians 5 we read of a man who was delivered unto Satan, for the destruction of the flesh, that the spirit might be saved in the day of the Lord Jesus. This man, a professing Christian, had failed so terribly and had brought such grief and dishonor upon the Name of the Lord that the Spirit, through the Apostle Paul, commanded the church at Corinth to refuse to have any further Christian fellowship with him. They were to put him back into the world from which he once professed to be separated, and there he would be in Satan's realm, who would put him through a course of trouble and sorrow, and we know what the result was: the man broke down before God and confessed his sin and failure. He no more thought himself worthy of Christian fellowship, and would not have come back had not the people of God been careful to show him special grace and favor. Paul wrote again urging them to this, in 2 Cor. 2: 4-11.

We have often heard people ask, "Why does God not kill the devil?" Well, God has use for him. When God has no longer use for him, He will do away with him in the lake of fire. But until that time, God not only makes the wrath of man to praise Him, but there is a certain sense in which He even makes Satan to serve His purpose. When He sees pride and self-sufficiency in believers He permits Satan to sift them, even to causing some grievous fall that they may be awakened and brought to their senses. Jeremiah says, "Thine own wickedness shall correct thee, and thy backsliding shall reprove thee" (Jer. 2: 19). God allowed Israel to fall so grievously that they would realize as never before how far from Him they had wandered and how they needed to get right.

And so in Peter's case the Lord permitted the failure to take place that he might be corrected and He has related it here that it might be a warning and an encouragement for us at the same time.

We read, "And Simon Peter followed Jesus, and so did another disciple: that disciple was known unto the high priest" (this "other disciple" is undoubtedly John himself. He used this expression as a means of keeping himself in the background), "and went in with Jesus into the palace of the high priest. But Peter stood at the door without." There he was in the place of danger. If he had been inside with John and

Jesus he would have been safe. How was it he chose to stay there instead of definitely identifying himself with Christ? Backsliding is never a matter of a moment. Sometimes one whom we have esteemed as a Christian seems to suddenly fall into some grievous sin. We throw up our hands and say, "What a shame, that that one should have suddenly stumbled so terribly!" We are wrong in thinking of it in that way. It is never sudden. Backsliding is always a gradual declension.

Now with Peter, his backsliding really began immediately following one of his greatest experiences. Often when God has dealt with us in some special way, it proves to be the time of the greatest danger. Sometimes with a servant of God, when the Lord gives him special victory, uses him in an unusual way for the salvation of souls, that is the time when he is in the greatest peril. There is the danger of spiritual pride; the danger of self-occupation; the danger, in other words, of confidence in the flesh.

In the sixteenth chapter of Matthew we hear the Lord saying, "Whom do men say that I the Son of Man am?" They answer, "Some say you are Elias, some, John the Baptist." Jesus then said, "But whom say ye that I am? And Simon Peter answered and said, Thou art the Christ, the Son of the living God."

That was a wonderful confession. Up to that moment no one else had ever made such a fervent and complete confession. The Saviour turns to Peter and says, "Blessed art thou, Simon Barjona: for flesh and blood hath not revealed it unto thee, but My Father which is in heaven." If Christ is ever made known to any human soul as the Son of the living God, it is not simply through the intellect. It must be a divine revelation. That is why you cannot convince men of the Deity of Christ by argument. You may marshall scripture after scripture and down all their objections, and yet if the Spirit of God does not reveal the Deity of God, people will go away just as unbelieving as before. It is the work of the Holy Spirit to make the truth real to the hearts and consciences of men. So the Lord Jesus says, "Flesh and blood hath not revealed it unto thee, but My Father which is in heaven."

Then the Lord said, "And I say also unto thee, That thou art Peter, and upon this rock (the great truth that Christ is the Son of the living God) I will build My Church." Now do not misunderstand the Lord there. Strange that anybody would think that our Lord meant He would found His Church on a mere man. Not Peter, but Christ is the "Rock," and Peter agrees with this, for in his first epistle, he speaks of Christ as the living stone and of himself and all believers as living stones who have come to Christ and are built upon Him.

And so the Lord says, "I will give unto thee the keys of the kingdom of heaven: and whatsoever thou shalt bind on earth shall be bound in heaven, and whatsoever thou shalt loose on earth shall be loosed in heaven." That was a wonderful honor, which many have misunderstood. You have often seen pictures—have you not?—of Peter with a key at the gate of heaven. But Jesus did not give Peter the keys of heaven. Jesus gave to Peter the keys to the kingdom of heaven. The kingdom of heaven is not heaven, it is that sphere on earth where Christ is owned as Lord. On Pentecost Peter used the keys to open the door of the kingdom of heaven to the Jews. In the house of Cornelius he used them to open the door to the Gentiles.

In Matthew 18 we learn that all the disciples were given the power of binding and loosing. That is, they were authorized to go to men, in the name of the Lord Jesus Christ, and say, "If you believe in the Lord Jesus Christ, you are loosed from your sin, and if not, your sin remains upon you." That commission is given to all of Christ's servants.

That was indeed a wonderful revelation which the Father gave to Peter and the Lord recognized it in a very special way. But it is a remarkable fact that in the same sixteenth chapter of Matthew you hear the Lord say a little later to that very man, Peter, "Get thee behind Me, Satan . . . for thou savorest not the things that be of God, but those that be of men." He had been telling them of His coming trial and crucifixion and Peter turned to Him and dared to counsel the Son of God, as though he were wiser than He. He said, "Be it far from Thee, Lord: this shall not be unto Thee." And Jesus said, "Get thee behind Me, Satan." What does this mean? Why, Peter was so carried away, so lifted up and self-exalted, he became spiritually proud and dared to rebuke the One whom but a short time before, he had confessed as the Son of God.

Suppose the Lord had acted on that, and said, "Well, I won't go out and die." What a condition Peter would have been in! Jesus realized it was the devil speaking through Peter. We trace the record of Peter from that time on, and find that every time he opens his mouth he says the wrong thing. It was on the Mount of Transfiguration that he said, "Let us make here three tabernacles; one for Thee, and one for Moses, and one for Elias." And God then said, "This is My beloved Son, in whom I am well pleased; hear ye Him." Then when Jesus said to His disciples, "All ye shall be offended because of Me," Peter said, "Oh, no, Lord; not I. Though all men shall be offended because of Thee, yet will I never be offended." This man did not really know his own weakness. He loved his Lord and meant to be true to Him. But he failed his Master in the garden. He slept when he should have prayed. He used the sword in fleshly energy when he should have been quiet. He followed afar off when he should have been close to the Lord. Backsliding always begins with neglect of prayer. If you want to be kept from backsliding, then you want to be sure you spend much time in secret with God.

We read that, "Peter stood at the door without. Then went out that other disciple . . . and spake to her that kept the door." Now he is just inside on the porch. And the girl took a good look at Peter and said, "Art not thou also one of this Man's disciples? He saith, I am not." He never meant to say that, but when he thought of all the people looking on when this girl challenged him, suddenly his courage failed him, and out came the lie—he who had said, "Though all men forsake Thee, yet will not I forsake Thee." How good that God did not take him at his word! God knew Peter and allowed him to go down deeper yet.

The servants and the officials stood there who had made a fire of coals. Remember that fire of coals. When you come to Peter's restoration it is at a fire of coals. And Peter stood with them —stood with the world, stood with the enemies of His Lord—and instead of speaking up for Christ, he was silent. And the high priest asked Jesus of His disciples and His doctrine. "Jesus answered him, I spake openly to the world; I ever taught in the synagogue, and in the temple, whither the Jews always resort; and in secret have I said nothing." Everything with Christ was like an open book. He had nothing to hide, nothing that could only be whispered in dark places, but everything was open and above-board. "In secret have I said nothing." "Why askest thou Me? ask them which heard Me, what I have said unto them; behold, they know what I said." "And when He had thus spoken, one of the officers which stood by struck Jesus with the palm of his hand, saying, Answerest Thou the high priest so?"

But on the part of the Lord Jesus there is no anger, no retaliation, but perfect lowliness. "Jesus answered him, If I have spoken evil, bear witness of the evil: but if well, why smitest thou Me?" "Now Annas had sent Him bound unto Caiaphas the high priest. And Simon Peter stood and warmed himself. They said therefore unto him, Art not thou also one of His disciples?" There was something strange about this man, Peter. He might be one of the company, but they felt that after all, there was something different about him. So they asked again but "he denied it, and said, I am not." What an opportunity! He could have said, "Yes, I am one of His; and if need be, I am ready to die for Him." But he had not the courage for it now in the hour of testing. He denied and said, "I am not."

Now there was another in the crowd who was particularly interested in Peter, for it was this man's relative whose ear Peter had cut off in the Garden. Jesus had said, when He took Peter and James and John into the Garden with Him, "Sit ye here, and watch and pray," and He went on, and then He bowed before God in that time of agony. Then He came back and found them sleeping for sorrow. There they were prayerless, when they should have been alert. Then when the Lord so quietly put Himself into the hands of the soldiers, Peter drew his sword and cut off the ear of the servant of the high priest. That was the activity of the flesh, and now that comes back to him. The relative of this man said, "Did I not see thee in the Garden with Him?" Now Peter is down to the very lowest depth the Lord will allow him to go. Three times he denied his Lord, and, as other Gospels tell us, even with oaths and curses.

But there is a great difference between a backslider and an apostate. A backslider is really a child of God who has failed, and eventually the Lord will restore him. An apostate is one who is never re-born at all. Judas was an apostate; Peter was a backslider.

Oh, if there is any backslider reading this today, let me say to you that He who restored Peter is waiting to restore you. He says, "Return, O backsliding children, saith the Lord; for I am married unto you." If you confess your backsliding, you can be sure He will restore. He did it for Peter, He will do it for you.

In another Gospel we are told that the Lord turned and looked on Peter and Peter went out and wept bitterly. Those tears indicated the beginning of his restoration and in the last chapter we shall see how wonderfully the Lord restored him.

> "Return, O wanderer, return,
>   And seek an injured Father's face;
>   Those warm desires that in thee burn
>   Were kindled by reclaiming grace.
>
> "Return, O wanderer, return,
>   And seek a Father's melting heart;
>   His pitying eyes thy grief discern,
>   His hand shall heal thine inward smart.

"Return, O wanderer, return;
  Thy Saviour bids thy spirit live;
Go to His bleeding feet, and learn
  How freely Jesus can forgive.

"Return, O wanderer, return,
  And wipe away the falling tear;
'Tis God who says, 'No longer mourn;'
  'Tis mercy's voice invites thee near."

CHRIST BEFORE PILATE

❡ ❡ ❡

"Then led they Jesus from Caiaphas unto the hall of judgment: and it was early; and they themselves went not into the judgment hall, lest they should be defiled; but that they might eat the passover. Pilate then went out unto them, and said, What accusation bring ye against this Man? They answered and said unto him, If He were not a malefactor, we would not have delivered Him up unto thee. Then said Pilate unto them, Take ye Him, and judge Him according to your law. The Jews therefore said unto him, It is not lawful for us to put any man to death: that the saying of Jesus might be fulfilled, which He spake, signifying what death He should die. Then Pilate entered into the judgment hall again, and called Jesus, and said unto Him, Art Thou the King of the Jews? Jesus answered him, sayest thou this thing of thyself, or did others tell it thee of Me? Pilate answered, Am I a Jew? Thine own nation and the chief priests have delivered Thee unto me: what hast Thou done? Jesus answered, My kingdom is not of this world: if My kingdom were of this world, then would My servants fight, that I should not be delivered to the Jews: but now is My kingdom not from hence. Pilate therefore said unto Him, Art Thou a king then? Jesus answered, Thou sayest that I am a king. To this end was I born, and for this cause came I into the world, that I should bear witness unto the truth. Every one that is of the truth heareth My voice. Pilate saith unto Him, What is truth? And when he had said this, he went out again unto the Jews, and saith unto them, I find in Him no fault at all. But ye have a custom, that I should release unto you one at the passover: will ye therefore that I release unto you the King of the Jews? Then cried they all again, saying, Not this Man, but Barabbas. Now Barabbas was a robber" (John 18:28-40).

A ND so, we have read the first half of the greatest trial, or mock trial, that ever took place in human history, when before Pontius Pilate, our Lord witnessed a good confession.

Some very striking things are brought to our attention in this passage, and first of all we observe how very punctilious men may be in regard to the outward observance of what they call religion, while utterly bereft of any true spirituality and definite knowledge of relationship to God. We read here that the accusers of our blessed Lord led Him from the judgment hall of Caiaphas, the high priest, unto the Roman hall of judgment. While they had their own court to deal with cases that had to do with their own religion and their own customs and traditions, yet they were denied the right to deal with cases that involved crimes against the government or to carry out the death penalty. The Jewish way of executing capital punishment was by stoning to death, but they were not permitted to deal thus with their criminals. The Roman method was by crucifixion.

So, having decided on perjured evidence that our Lord Jesus Christ was guilty of blasphemy, the chief priests took Him before Pilate that He might be condemned to death. They led Him there early in the morning but they, themselves, went not into the judgment hall lest they should be defiled, that they might eat the feast of the passover. If they went two steps over the threshold of a Gentile hall on the passover day they were unclean ceremonially, and could not participate in that annual service of the Jewish congregation. And these men who were bent upon the murder of the Son of God, were so punctilious about the little things of the law that they did not dare pass over the threshold of Pilate's hall lest they should be defiled. And yet, there before them stood the One of whom every passover lamb that had ever been sacrificed, from that first passover in Egypt right down to their own day, was a type. We read, "Christ, our passover, is sacrificed for us: therefore let us keep the feast, not with old leaven, neither with the leaven of malice and wickedness; but with the unleavened bread of sincerity and truth."

For fifteen hundred years, except for occasional times when they were out of the will of God or away from their land, the Jewish people had been faithful in the observance of the passover. As those lambs were slain year by year, they pictured the Lamb of God which taketh away the sin of the world. As their blood was shed, it pictured the precious blood of Christ that cleanseth from all sin those who put their trust in Him. God declared in Egypt, on the night of the first passover, "When I see the blood I will pass over you." This was a gospel type. The blood over the lintel that night secured Israel's safety. The destroying angel could not enter in. And so today, those, whether Jew or Gentile, who put their trust in this true passover Lamb, our Lord Jesus, will find shelter beneath His precious blood and be absolutely secure from judgment. The Lord Jesus, Himself, has said, "Verily, verily, I say unto you, He that heareth My word, and believeth on Him that sent Me, hath everlasting life, and shall not come into condemnation; but is passed from death unto life." Notice that expression, "condemnation." I like the Catholic rendition of that verse. Listen to it, "Amen, amen, I say to you, He who hears My word and believes Him who sent Me, has eternal life and comes not into judgment, but is passed out of death into life." That is from the Douay Version. What a wonderful statement that is! That is the declaration of the Son of God that all who trust in Him are forever shielded from judgment. And those who thus trust Him know that the destroyer shall never touch them.

But here, you see, were people who were very conscientious about the outward things of the law and yet failed to recognize the One of whom the type of the law spoke, the Lord Jesus Christ.

And so they did not pass over the threshold of this court room lest they should become cere-

monially defiled, and yet, in a little while we hear
them demanding the death of the Son of God. Of
course, we hasten to say what Scripture affirms,
they did not know He was the Son of God. Peter
said after Pentecost, "I know, brethren, that
through ignorance ye did it." And because of
that, a city of refuge had been opened to them,
and God will deal with them, not as murderers,
but as unwitting man-slayers, if they will flee to
the refuge He has provided—but that refuge is
found in the same Saviour whom they crucified.

But let not us who are Gentiles think we are
any less guilty in the crucifixion of the Son of
God. The Gentiles too were linked with that
solemn event, but even there God shows mercy.
The Apostle Paul says, "Which none of the
princes of this world knew: for had they known
it, they would not have crucified the Lord of
glory." So here, you see, Jews and Gentiles
united in their ignorance and misunderstanding
to reject the One who came to save.

Well, here is the crowd waiting, and Pilate
graciously concedes to their demand. Recognizing their conscientious scruples, he went out to
them and said, "What accusation bring ye against
this Man?" Instead of presenting any very definite accusation, they said, "If He were not a
malefactor, we would not have delivered Him up
unto thee." They meant, "The fact that we

brought Him, declares that He is deserving of judgment." "Then said Pilate unto them, Take ye Him, and judge Him according to your law." But they said, "No; we cannot do that. It is not lawful for us to put any man to death. He deserves to die, but the Roman government has taken the power of life and death away from us."

But all this was done "that the saying of Jesus might be fulfilled, which He spake, signifying what death He should die." For on many occasions our blessed Lord had foretold His death. He had forewarned His disciples of what was coming. He said, "The Son of Man is delivered into the hands of men, and they shall kill Him; and after that He is killed, He shall rise the third day." Nothing was unforeseen. He knew exactly what was before Him when He came from heaven as the Son of God and in divine grace was born as a Child here on earth. He came, saying, "I delight to do Thy will, O My God," and He knew that the doing of that will meant going to the cross of Calvary. All through His life that was before Him. He was the only Israelite growing up in that land who knew the exact meaning of the Passover. He was the only Israelite who knew to what all those sacrifices of the temple referred. He knew that He was the One who was to fulfil them all and offer Himself, without spot, to God. But He never hesitated, and when at last this ministry of grace was coming to an end, we read, "He set His face like a flint to go to Jerusalem." He was steadfast in that which He came to do. Even in Gethsemane's Garden, when His holy humanity shrank from the awfulness of becoming the great Sin-bearer, yet He said, "My Father, if this cup may not pass except I drink it, Thy will be done."

So here He stands in Pilate's judgment hall, led as a lamb to the slaughter. He made no effort to clear Himself. He was ready to die, ready to go to the cross in order that we might live.

Pilate entered into the judgment hall again, and called Jesus to him and said unto Him, "Art Thou the King of the Jews?" They had brought this charge against Him, that He had declared Himself to be the King of the Jews. Pilate was used to different ones rising up with claims to be the Messiah. They had been dealt with very severely by the Roman Government.

"Art Thou the King of the Jews?" "Jesus answered him, Sayest thou this thing of thyself, or did others tell it thee of Me?" As much as to say, "Are you asking this question because of a sincere desire to know the truth, or is it simply a rumor that has come to you and you want to trace it down?" You see, whenever men honestly wanted to know the truth, the Lord Jesus was ready to clarify it but never to satisfy some indifferent questioner. So, I say to you, if you really wish to know if Jesus is the Son of God, if you are saying to yourself, "I wish I knew if He is really the Messiah of Israel. I wish I knew if He is really the promised King who is to bring in blessing for this poor world," let me tell you how you may know. "If any man will to do His will, he shall know of the doctrine, whether it be of God, or whether I speak of Myself." If you honestly desire to know, if you will go to God, take your place before Him as a sinner, confess your sin and guilt and cry to Him for the way of deliverance and look to Him to give you light, He has pledged Himself to do so.

Oh, if Pilate had only been in earnest that day! But we see him convicted as a trifler with eternal verities: He is not really interested to know if Jesus is King. In Pilate's eyes He is just some queer, fanatical Jew who has done nothing particularly worthy of death but is some sort of a public nuisance and must be dealt with in a way that will quiet the people.

So Pilate asks contemptuously, "Am I a Jew? Thine own nation and the chief priests have delivered Thee unto me: what hast Thou done?" In other words, "Tell me now, what is your error? What is your misdemeanor? What have you done?" One can readily imagine the scornful curl of his lip as he asked these questions.

Jesus looked up quietly and said, "My kingdom is not of this world," that is, "It is not of this order," or, "I do not pretend to be a King in the sense that those who fill the thrones of earth are kings. My kingdom is not of this universe, but of another order altogether. My kingdom is of heaven." That is really what He meant. He left Pilate to inquire, if he were earnest enough to do so. "If My kingdom were of this world, then would My servants fight, that I should not be delivered to the Jews: but now is My kingdom not from hence."

He is not denying that some day His kingdom is going to be set up in this world. Some day all the prophecies regarding Him will be fulfilled. But when that day comes, His kingdom will not be of this earthly order; it will be a heavenly kingdom set up here on earth.

So He disclaims all suggestions of expecting to overthrow Roman power. Pilate looks at Him contemplatively and says, more to himself than to Jesus, "Art Thou a king then?" Oh, there was something so striking about this lowly Carpenter from Nazareth, as He stood there unafraid and looked into the face of the representative of the greatest power on earth, and talked about a kingdom that is not of this world. Pilate wonders who this strange mysterious Man could be. "Art Thou a king then?"

Then Jesus answered and said, "Thou sayest that I am a King." He was indeed a King; a King without a kingdom here; a King without a host of subjects to acknowledge His authority, but the One of whom God, the Father, had said, "Yet have I set My King upon My holy hill of Zion." "To this end was I born, and for this cause came I into the world, that I should bear witness unto the truth," or, "that I might be a martyr to the truth." And some have said that that is all that Jesus was, simply dying as a martyr to the truth. He did so die, but that was not all. He died as the great sin-offering, yielding Himself without spot unto God for our redemption.

But there He stands in Pilate's judgment hall, a witness to the truth. He was, Himself, truth incarnate. He said, "I am the Way, the Truth and the Life." So now He says, "Every one that is of the truth heareth My voice." Do you see the challenge in that sentence? He is practically saying, "Every honest man and woman will listen to Me when they hear Me." Don't say, "I wish I knew whether Jesus was the Son of God," and then turn away and refuse the test that He gives in the Word, for everyone who is absolutely honest in seeking to know, will know. "Every one that is of the truth heareth My voice."

"Pilate saith unto Him, What is truth?" And there you have the question of the cynic. His restless mind and heart had not found satisfaction in anything, and he had come to the place where he feels that no one knows where we came from or where we are going. "Who can tell?" "What is truth?"

Oh, if Pilate had but been in earnest in asking that question! There stood One who could have told him; One who could have opened up all the things that were perplexing him. Lord Bacon wrote: " 'What is truth?' said jesting Pilate, and waited not for an answer." Oh, that is the pity of it! He might have had the answer. But this man was a trifler. This man was not in earnest. This man did not really want to know the truth. O God, give us to be honest and in earnest, and if we are, we shall soon find ourselves at the feet of the Lord Jesus Christ.

"Pilate saith unto Him, What is truth? And when he had said this, he went out again unto the Jews." He does not wait for an answer to his question, and so he is left in doubt and in darkness. He said to the Jews, "I find in Him no fault at all." In other words, "I see no reason to put this Man to death."

Then it occurred to him that there was a way by which he could placate the people and yet save Jesus from death. It had been arranged some years before that some prisoner of state should be set free at each passover season in order that the people might feel that Rome was considerate of their national prejudices. It came to his mind that he might put up the name of Jesus and they would let Him go free. So he said, "Ye have a custom that I should release unto you one at the passover: will ye therefore that I release unto you the King of the Jews?" (Listen to the irony in this question.)   But at this they cried out, "Not this Man, but Barabbas." Barabbas was a robber in the eyes of the law, it is true, but he was a Jewish patriot.   The very thing they charged against Jesus was true of Barabbas. He was an insurrectionist. They would let Barabbas go free and let Jesus be crucified. "Not this Man, but Barabbas."   And that has been the voice, not only of the Jews, but of the world down through the centuries.   They have chosen the robber and the murderer, and the world has been dominated by the robber and the murderer, and Jesus is still rejected.

Have you made your choice?   Are you saying in your heart, "Not this Man, but Barabbas?" "Not this Man, but"—what are you putting in the place of Jesus in your heart?   Oh, that you might reverse your decision.

Some years ago in an eastern city, a well-known Jewish merchant had a warm-hearted

Christian friend. These two business men used
to meet together at lunch time and talk things
over together, and the Christian frankly put forward the claims of the Lord Jesus Christ. His
Jewish friend would listen politely but never
make any comment. By-and-by, this Jewish
merchant was taken very ill, and word came that
he was dying. The Christian friend wanted to
go to see him, but was told he could not do so.
Word came that he could not live much longer,
and his friend made another effort to see him.
The doctor said, "Let him in; he cannot do him
any harm now." He promised not to talk to
him, and went into the room and slipped to the
bedside and knelt there, taking his friend's poor,
thin hand in his own, and silently lifted his heart
to God on behalf of the dying Jewish merchant.
Then as the sick man lay there with closed eyes,
breathing heavily, there was a change. His eyes
opened and turned to his friend and looked kindly
upon him. Then the lips parted, and he said
just before he slipped into eternity, "Not Barabbas, but this Man."

See what that meant. He had reversed the
sentence of his people in Pilate's judgment hall.
What would you say? "Not this Man, but Barabbas?" What would you say? "Not any other
but this Man, Christ?"

"Have you any room for Jesus,
  He who bore your load of sin;
As He knocks and asks admission,
  Sinner, will you let Him in?

"Room for pleasure, room for business,
  But for Christ the crucified,
Not a place that He can enter,
  In the heart for which He died?

"Have you any room for Jesus,
  As in grace He calls again?
Oh, today is time accepted,
  Tomorrow you may call in vain.

"Room and time now give to Jesus,
  Soon will pass God's day of grace;
Soon thy heart left cold and silent,
  And Thy Saviour's pleading cease."

PILATE BEFORE CHRIST

✌   ✌   ✌

"Then Pilate therefore took Jesus, and scourged Him. And the soldiers platted a crown of thorns, and put it on His head, and they put on Him a purple robe, and said, Hail, King of the Jews! and they smote Him with their hands. Pilate therefore went forth again, and saith unto them, Behold, I bring Him forth to you, that ye may know that I find no fault in Him. Then came Jesus forth, wearing the crown of thorns, and the purple robe. And Pilate saith unto them, Behold the Man! When the chief priests therefore and officers saw Him, they cried out, saying, Crucify Him, crucify Him. Pilate saith unto them, Take ye Him, and crucify Him: for I find no fault in Him. The Jews answered him, We have a law, and by our law He ought to die, because He made Himself the Son of God. When Pilate therefore heard that saying, he was the more afraid; and went again into the judgment hall, and saith unto Jesus, Whence art Thou? But Jesus gave him no answer. Then saith Pilate unto Him, Speakest Thou not unto me? knowest Thou not that I have power to crucify Thee, and have power to release Thee? Jesus answered, Thou couldest have no power at all against Me, except it were given thee from above: therefore he that delivered Me unto thee hath the greater sin. And from henceforth Pilate sought to release Him: but the Jews cried out, saying, If thou let this Man go, thou art not Cæsar's friend: whosoever maketh himself a king speaketh against Cæsar. When Pilate therefore heard that saying, he brought Jesus forth, and sat down in the judgment seat in a place that is called the Pavement, but in the Hebrew, Gabbatha. And it was the preparation of the passover, and about the sixth hour: and he saith unto the Jews, Behold your King! But they cried out, Away with Him, away with Him, crucify Him. Pilate saith unto them, Shall I crucify your King? The

817

chief priests answered, We have no king but Cæsar. Then delivered he Him therefore unto them to be crucified. And they took Jesus, and led Him away" (John 19: 1-16).

✶   ✶   ✶

IN the last section of the previous chapter we had a view of Christ before Pilate. In the present portion the conditions are reversed. Now it is really Pilate who is on trial before Christ. What will this pusillanimous Roman politician do with One whom he knows to be absolutely innocent of all the charges brought against Him? Will Pilate acquit the innocent, as a righteous judge should? Or will he condemn Him as guilty in order to protect himself against the evil insinuations of the leaders in Judea who threaten him with political ruin if he does not accede to their wishes? We know the answer well, but let us consider the entire case anew as we meditate upon the most unrighteous trial in all human history.

In this section, then, we have Pilate before Christ. In the previous chapter we had the Lord Jesus dragged before Pilate's judgment bar. But the trial was practically over when the judge himself went out to the people and said, "After careful examination, and after hearing all of the charges, I find in Him no fault at all." That was really a judgment of acquittal. Jesus had been tried and found innocent of the charges brought against Him, and according to all righteousness, Pilate should then have dismissed the case, and Jesus should have gone out free. But we know that in the purpose of God it had been settled from eternity that He who was born at Bethlehem was to die upon the cross to make propitiation for our sins. And God, therefore, so overruled and so permitted things that the mock trial should still go on.

Now Pilate is on trial. What about this Roman judge? What is his attitude? What is God's thought of him? What does this scene reveal concerning him?

In the first place, it reveals Pilate as a weakling who knew what was right and did it not. He knew he should have freed the Lord Jesus Christ. He knew after investigating and pronouncing Him innocent that he should have ended the case right there. But he did not act upon his own deepest convictions because he was not true to his own conscience. We may see in the first five verses how he stifled the voice of conscience. We are told that "Pilate therefore took Jesus and scourged Him." Why should he scourge Him? He has just declared Him innocent, and yet he permits Him to submit to the most ignominious punishment that involves terrible physical suffering. For that Roman scourge was made of a number of thongs in which sharp pieces of metal were set every few inches, so that when the scourge was brought down upon the bare back of the victim, the flesh was literally stripped into ribbons, and the blood poured forth. Why cause an innocent Man, an admittedly innocent Man, to submit to suffering like that? It was because Pilate wanted to appease the Jews. He wanted their favor even though it meant that the Man whom he had pronounced innocent should have to suffer. On the other hand, he hoped that the accusers of Christ would be satisfied with this punishment.

The soldiers having carried out the scourging, platted a crown of thorns and put it on His head, and they put on Him a purple robe—some old discarded garment, and thus they decked Him up as a pretended king, and they said, "Hail, King of the Jews!" and they smote Him with their hands. How little they realized that though what they did was done in sport, the day would come when before that Blessed One every knee should bow and every tongue confess that He is Lord of all, and when He will indeed be acclaimed as King of the Jews as well as King of all the nations of the earth. For in God's purpose it is declared that eventually Jew and Gentile will recognize in Him the One who is King of kings and Lord of lords.

"Pilate," we are told, "therefore went forth again and saith unto them, Behold I bring Him forth to you, that ye may know that I find no fault in Him." This reiterated the judgment already given. "Then came Jesus forth, wearing the crown of thorns, and the purple robe. And Pilate saith unto them, Behold the Man." In his own conscience he knows that Christ should go free, but debates within himself what is to be done, how to placate these ruthless persecutors! And doubtless back of it all was the thought of the insecurity of his own position. Pilate had done many things that had aroused the antagonism of the Jews and there was always a party working against him to unseat him as governor of Judea. And so he presents Christ again and cries, "Behold the Man." One would have thought the sight of that patient, suffering One standing there with the thorny crown pressed on His brow and the purple robe on Him and with a reed in His hand and blood pouring down his face would have been enough to soften the hardest heart and break down the strongest opposition. But there is that in the heart of the natural man which leads him to hate that which is holy, to hate perfect righteousness.

Many years ago at a great meeting of the Synod of the Free Church of Scotland, one minister was asked to preach the synodical sermon on Sunday morning. He gave a marvelously beautiful discourse on the beauty of virtue, and wound up with a great peroration in which he exclaimed, "Oh, my friends, if virtue incarnate could only appear on earth, men would be so ravished with her beauty they would fall down and worship her." People went out saying, "What a magnificent pulpit oration it was!"

But on the night of the same Lord's Day, another minister stood in that pulpit and he preached Christ and Him crucified, and closed his sermon with these words: "My friends, Virtue Incarnate has appeared on earth, and men instead of being ravished with His beauty and falling down and worshipping Him, cried out, 'Away with Him! Crucify Him! crucify Him! We will not have this Man to reign over us!' " That tells the wickedness of the natural heart—of your heart, of my heart—for those Jews that day were but representative men. They were not different men to others. "There is no difference, for all have sinned and come short of the glory of God." But they told out the hatred of the natural man to the holiness of God.

"When the chief priests therefore and officers saw Him, they cried out, saying, Crucify Him, crucify Him. Pilate saith unto them, Take ye Him and crucify Him: for I find no fault in Him." Think of it! For the third time this judge declares the innocence of the prisoner who stood before him, and yet he was himself utterly vacillating. Instead of standing for the innocent as justice should, he puts Him in the hands of His enemies.

"The Jews answered him, We have a law, and by our law He ought to die, because He made Himself the Son of God." This is something it is well for us to remember—they had no delusions regarding the claims of the Lord Jesus Christ. They understood perfectly by things He said that He meant men to know that He was indeed the Son of the living God. And because of that, they charged Him with blasphemy. If He had only meant that inasmuch as all men have been created by God, there is a certain sense in which all are His offspring, there would be no blasphemy in that according to their own standard. But they knew, they understood that He claimed equality with God, as the Son of the Father who came from Heaven and became incarnate here on earth, and they charged Him therefore with blasphemy against the unity of the Godhead.

"When Pilate therefore heard that saying, he was the more afraid." We are told that "the fear of man bringeth a snare," and this man, always politic, always concerned as to what others might think and what others might do,

and what effect it might have upon him, was
more afraid "and went again into the judgment
hall, and saith unto Jesus, Whence art Thou?"
Was he now really concerned? A little while
before he had asked the question, "What is
truth?" and did not even wait for an answer.
Now when he hears the charge, "He made Himself the Son of God," is he really a bit concerned?
Is he saying in his heart, "Can it be that this
strange Man before me is more than man, that
there is something supernatural about Him?"
Was he for the moment in earnest when he asked
the question, "Whence art Thou?" At any rate,
there was no evidence of repentance, there was
no evidence of self-judgment, no evidence of
integrity of heart. So Jesus gave him no answer.
Had he been earnestly desirous of learning the
truth, we may be absolutely certain Christ would
have answered his question in such a way as to
have made clear to him who He really was. But
Jesus never answers the caviller. He never at-
tempts to explain to the man who is determined
to refuse the truth. He does not attempt to make
clear the things that are dark to those who have
no desire to submit themselves to the will of
God. He says, "If any man willeth to do His
will, he shall know of the doctrine, whether it be
of God or whether I speak of Myself." He knew
that Pilate did not will to do the will of God.

And Pilate was nettled because Jesus did not
reply, because He stood there as predicted in
Isaiah, chapter 53, where we read, "He is led
as a lamb to the slaughter, and as a sheep before
her shearers is dumb. so He openeth not His
mouth."

Then Pilate said unto Him, "Speakest Thou not
unto me? knowest Thou not that I have power to
crucify Thee, and have power to release Thee?"
and in that he spoke his own condemnation.
But Jesus answered, "Thou couldest have no
authority at all against Me, except it were given
thee from above." He recognized that the powers
that be are ordained of God, and Pilate therefore
was set in that position as governor to do the
will of God, and to administer justice. "Thou
couldest have no power at all against Me except
it were given thee from above: therefore he that
delivered Me unto thee hath the greater sin."
There are, then, differences in guilt, and Jesus
is saying that the chief priests and Judas and
those who had to do with delivering Jesus over
to judgment before Pilate were the guiltier. "He
that delivered Me unto thee hath the greater sin.
And from thenceforth Pilate sought to release
Him." But he seeks to release Him in a way
that will please the people. He is not ready to
do the thing that he knows is right because it is
right.

You and I need to face that question—Are we doing the thing that is right because we know it is right? Here is a man who all his life has known of the Lord Jesus Christ, and he knows that he should open his heart to receive that Christ as his own personal Saviour, and yet the years go by and he does not act upon his convictions. In what sense is he different from Pilate, this vacillating man, this man who hadn't the courage of his convictions, this man who knew he should clear Jesus and yet eventually condemned Him to death? May we not ask ourselves the question —What is my attitude toward the Lord Jesus Christ today? Have I received Him? Am I confessing Him as Saviour and Lord? The Scripture says: "If thou shalt confess with thy mouth the Lord Jesus, and shalt believe in thine heart that God hath raised Him from the dead, thou shalt be saved." Have you confessed Him? "Whosoever confesses Me," He says, "before men, him will I confess also before My Father which is in heaven." And He solemnly adds, "But whosoever shall deny Me before men, him will I also deny before My Father which is in heaven."

Pilate denied Him, and Pilate has to face that for eternity. What is our attitude? What is your attitude? Have you confessed Him? Will you today confess Him as your Saviour and your Lord?

"From thenceforth Pilate sought to release Him: but the Jews cried out, saying, If thou let this Man go, thou art not Cæsar's friend: whosoever maketh himself a king speaketh against Cæsar."

And were they such ardent admirers of Cæsar as their words would seem to imply? Not at all. They hated the very name of Cæsar, and being under subjection to the Roman governor. They knew Pilate's weak point. They knew he wanted to keep in favor with Cæsar. "This Man is a traitor in opposition to the Roman Government. If you let this Man go, you are not Cæsar's friend." And "when Pilate therefore heard that saying," because he was a political opportunist rather than a conscientious judge, "he brought Jesus forth, and sat down in the judgment seat in a place that is called the Pavement, but in the Hebrew, Gabbatha. And it was the preparation of the passover, and about the sixth hour: and he saith unto the Jews, Behold your King! But they cried out, Away with Him, away with Him, crucify Him." Now ironically Pilate asks, "Shall I crucify your King?" as though he would insult them to their faces, because deep in his heart he despised them as much as they hated him. And the chief priests, almost unthinkingly for the moment, I am sure, put themselves on record, "We have no King but Cæsar." And, oh, what they have suffered under the Cæsars all through the centuries since.

Thus Pilate's last effort to save Jesus was ended. "Then delivered he Him therefore unto them to be crucified." Pilate has sold his soul for the approval of the world. Take care that you do not do the same. For Jesus Himself has asked, "What shall it profit a man if he shall gain the whole world, and lose his own soul?" (Mark 8:36). "And they took Jesus and led Him away." And so we see Him going out to die, to die as the Lamb of God for our sins. But, oh, thank God, for the untold millions who through the centuries since have found in Him a Saviour, have found in His death redemption; and in His blood cleansing from all sin. A great host have already been gathered about Him in yonder glory to acclaim Him as King of kings and Lord of lords. Thousands more on earth love and honor Him.

But, alas, alas, Pilate is in the outside place! If we can trust early history, he died a suicide, still rejecting the One whom he had condemned to death that day in Jerusalem so long before.

THE FINISHED WORK OF CHRIST

ᕓ   ᕓ   ᕓ

"And He bearing His cross went forth into a place called the place of a skull, which is called in the Hebrew Golgotha: where they crucified Him, and two other with Him, on either side one, and Jesus in the midst. And Pilate wrote a title, and put it on the cross. And the writing was, JESUS OF NAZARETH THE KING OF THE JEWS. This title then read many of the Jews: for the place where Jesus was crucified was nigh to the city: and it was written in Hebrew, and Greek, and Latin. Then said the chief priests of the Jews to Pilate, Write not, The King of the Jews; but that He said, I am King of the Jews. Pilate answered, What I have written I have written. Then the soldiers, when they had crucified Jesus, took His garments, and made four parts, to every soldier a part; and also His coat: now the coat was without seam, woven from the top throughout. They said therefore among themselves, Let us not rend it, but cast lots for it, whose it shall be: that the scripture might be fulfilled, which saith, They parted My raiment among them, and for My vesture they did cast lots. These things therefore the soldiers did. Now there stood by the cross of Jesus His mother, and His mother's sister, Mary the wife of Cleophas, and Mary Magdalene. When Jesus therefore saw His mother, and the disciple standing by, whom He loved, He saith unto His mother, Woman, behold thy son! Then saith He to the disciple, Behold thy mother! And from that hour that disciple took her unto his own home. After this, Jesus knowing that all things were now accomplished, that the scripture might be fulfilled, said, I thirst. Now there was set a vessel full of vinegar: and they filled a sponge with vinegar, and put it upon hyssop, and put it to His mouth. When Jesus therefore had received the vinegar, He said, It is finished: and He bowed His head, and gave up the ghost" (John 19: 17-30).

ᕓ   ᕓ   ᕓ

IT is very interesting to note the way in which the crucifixion of our Lord Jesus Christ is set forth in each of the four Gospels. In the Old Testament ritual there were four bloody offerings which the people of Israel were commanded to bring to God, and each of these presented the work of the cross from a different standpoint. When you turn to the opening chapters of Leviticus you read of the burnt-offering, the peace-offering, the sin-offering, and the trespass-offering. There is also the meal-offering, but the meal-offering was not a blood offering. It consisted of the presentation of certain cakes of fine flour and oil before God. It typified the perfect humanity of our Lord Jesus Christ, and of course that comes out in all the four Gospels. As you trace the footsteps of the blessed Lord through this scene, as pictured for us by the four different writers, Matthew, Mark, Luke and John, you see in Jesus absolute perfection. He was the only Man who ever trod this earth who never had one word to take back, never had one sin to confess. His was a life in which there was nothing to be repented of—the Man Christ Jesus, God's perfect, spotless Son, of whom He could say, "This is My beloved Son, in whom I have found all My delight."

The meal offering tells of the character of Jesus, and emphasizes the fact that He had to be who He was in order to do what He did. No other could have taken His place, no other could have made atonement of our sins, but the offerings in which blood was shed pictured the work of the cross in four different aspects. The burnt-offering presented the Lord Jesus dying to glorify God in the scene where He had been so terribly dishonored.

In John's Gospel we get this thought in His words as He was going out to die: "But that the world may know that I love the Father; and as the Father gave Me commandment, even so I do. Arise, let us go hence." He took the way to the cross, and in the cross through His sacrificial death God has received more glory than He ever lost by Adam's fall and by all the sin that has come into the world since. So that we may say that if not one human soul were ever saved as a result of the death of the Lord Jesus, still God's character has been vindicated, God's majesty has been sustained, God has been fully glorified.

But in the other three Gospels we have the offerings that have to do more particularly with man and his sin. The peace-offering presents Christ making peace by the blood of His cross. That is the way Christ is shown in Luke's Gospel. The sin offering presents the Lord Jesus Christ as being made sin for us; who died not simply for what we have done but for what we are; our doings only manifest our true character as sinners. As has been said often, I am not a sinner because I sin, but I sin because I am a sinner. Therefore, the sin-offering is not merely for the acts that I have done, but because of an evil, corrupt nature which unfits me for fellowship with God. So, "He who knew no sin was made sin for us." That is the way the work of the cross is presented in Mark's Gospel. But there is something more.

The Lord Jesus not only died for our sin, but He died for our sins. Our actual guilt had to be atoned for. He had to make up to the divine majesty for the wrong that we have done, and that is the trespass-offering. It is that which is set forth in Matthew's Gospel.

So, then here in the record given us by John it is particularly the burnt-offering of our Lord, dying to glorify the Father, which is set forth, and that explains why the three hours of darkness are not mentioned here. God's Word is written with marvelous precision. In the other Gospels we have those three dark hours in which the soul of the Lord Jesus was made an offering for sin, and we hear His awful cry, "My God, My God, why hast Thou forsaken Me?" The answer to that cry is that He was forsaken that we might not be forsaken. He took my place,

> "For man—oh, miracle of grace!—
> For man the Saviour died."

But that cry of anguish is not recorded in John's Gospel. We simply see the blessed Lord, in perfect subjection to the will of His Father, yielding Himself without spot to God in His death upon the tree.

"And He bearing His cross went forth into a place called the place of a skull." Many think that to be the little skull-shaped hill outside the Damascus Gate. Those of us who have been in Jerusalem and have stood on or beside that hill, have found our hearts more deeply moved perhaps than by any other scene, unless it be indeed the Garden tomb on the side of the knoll. It was on that skull-shaped hill that, as many Protestant scholars believe, our Lord Jesus Christ died for us. "The place of a skull; where they crucified Him, and two other with Him, on either side one, and Jesus in the midst." It had been written in Isaiah 53—"He was numbered with the transgressors"—and so we see Him on that central cross in the midst of transgressors. Two thieves crucified with Him—He in the center, as though of them all He was the worst! That is the chief sinner's place.

"And Pilate wrote a title, JESUS OF NAZARETH THE KING OF THE JEWS." The charge that the high priests of Jerusalem had made against Him was that He declared Himself to be King of the Jews. Pilate had asked Him, "Art

Thou the King of the Jews?" It was necessary
that Pilate, as the one who condemned Jesus to
die, should make out a placard that should indicate the crime of which the crucified one was
guilty. And so he wrote on this placard, "JESUS
OF NAZARETH THE KING OF THE JEWS"
—in Hebrew, the language of religion; in Greek,
the language of culture; and in Latin, the language of government. The charge against Jesus
was: "This is Jesus of Nazareth, the King of the
Jews." That was meant to say, "He is being crucified as a rebel, as an insurrectionist against the
Roman Government." Pilate did not believe that
for one moment, as we saw very clearly in the
previous chapter, but on his part it was an iron-
ical, sardonic thing. He wanted to taunt these
chief priests and scribes who had hounded him
until at last he had condemned an innocent Man
to death.

It is remarkable how the cross of Christ brings
out all that is in the heart of man, shows men up
as they really are. In the light of that cross
Pilate comes before us in all his cynicism and his
lack of conscience. In the light of that cross the
chief priests were manifested in all their hypocrisy and bitterness and their hatred of the holy,
spotless Son of God. And as we follow the story,
in the light of that cross we see the callousness,
indifference, greed and covetousness of the sol-

diers who were gambling for the clothing of the crucified One at the foot of the cross; but, thank God, we see brought out in beautiful relief the loyalty, the faithfulness, the tender love of Mary, the mother of Jesus, and the other women, her companions, who had been blest through the ministry of Christ, and also the fealty of his devoted follower, the apostle John, the author of this book. Where were the other apostles? They had fulfilled the Word that said, "They all forsook Him and fled." But John was there at the cross. Mary, the mother, was there, and Mary Magdalene and Mary the wife of Cleophas, were there, looking on with loving eyes and breaking hearts as they saw the Saviour dying on that tree, to glorify the Father and to save a guilty world.

And so Pilate designates Him as King of the Jews, and some day it will be found that the title Pilate put over the cross was more true than he or the world realized. For this One who has gone to His Father's throne in heaven will return again, and when He returns He will be welcomed by some from that very people who rejected Him, for a remnant in Jerusalem will be found whose hearts will be won for Him, the Messiah, and we are told that "they shall look upon Him whom they have pierced." They will recognize Him, when He comes again, as the true King of the Jews, "great David's greater Son," who will fulfil all the Old Testament prophecies and bring in that righteous kingdom so long predicted.

But when Pilate wrote this title—THE KING OF THE JEWS—it stirred the chief priests to indignation, and they came to him and said, "Write not, The King of the Jews; but that He said, I am the King of the Jews." But Pilate, looking at them with a hard, sardonic kind of smile, says, "What I have written I have written." As much as to say, "You forced me long enough, I'll go no further with you; that placard remains just as I have written it."

> "So He died, a King crucified,
> To save a poor sinner like me."

But notice, though Pilate put over His head the placard that designated His supposed crime —that He made Himself the King of the Jews— actually God saw another placard over that cross. That other placard was unseen by mortal eyes. It is referred to in Colossians 2:13-17: "And you, being dead in your sins and the uncircumcision of your flesh, hath He quickened together with Him, having forgiven you all trespasses; blotting out the handwriting of ordinances that was against us, which was contrary to us, and took it out of the way, nailing it to His cross; and having spoiled principalities and powers, He made a show of them openly, triumphing over them in it. Let no man therefore judge you in meat, or in drink, or in respect of an holyday, or of the new moon, or of the sabbath days: which are a shadow of things to come; but the body is of Christ."

What is the apostle Paul telling us here? Man was guilty before God, violating that holy law which He gave at Sinai, "For it is written, Cursed is every one that continueth not in all things which are written in the book of the law to do them." But there upon that cross Jesus is seen taking the law-breaker's place, and God sees, nailed on that cross, those ten ordinances given at Sinai, the law which God gave upon that mount, the law which was just and good, but which man had violated. Because of the transgression of that law Jesus died. But had He violated it? No! That law was against us because we were the law-breakers, but Jesus upon that cross died under the judgment of that broken law. Because of what He endured when He took my place in judgment, God can now say to me: "You go free," and through faith in His blessed Son I am justified from all things. And so we who believe are

> "Free from the law! Oh, happy condition!
> Jesus hath bled, and there is remission,
> Curs'd by the law and bruised by the fall,
> Christ hath redeemed us once for all."

But now we pass on with this most wonderful story that ever was written. "Then the soldiers, when they had crucified Jesus, took His garments, and made four parts, to every soldier a part; and also His tunic: now the tunic was without seam, woven from the top throughout. They said therefore among themselves, Let us not rend it, but cast lots for it, whose it shall be." They had no idea when they said this, when they gambled for His clothing, when they determined not to tear the tunic in four places that every one should have a part, that they were actually fulfilling a prophetic utterance made a thousand years before in Psalm 22: 18; "They part My garments among them, and cast lots upon My vesture." "These things therefore the soldiers did." Psalm 22 is a prophecy of the sufferings of our Saviour on that cross and of the glories that should follow, and when we turn back to it we see it begins with His cry of distress, and it closes with a shout of triumph. It pictures the Saviour suspended on that cross—"I may tell all My bones: they look and stare upon Me. They part My garments among them, and cast lots upon My vesture." And then in that hour of darkness He cries, "My God, My God, why hast Thou forsaken Me?" for with these words the psalm begins. Then it goes on, "But Thou art holy, O Thou that inhabitest the praises of Israel. But I am a worm, and no

man; a reproach of men, and despised of the
people." It tells of the place He took in lowly
grace for our redemption.

The figure He uses is a very striking thing!
"A worm," was the "tola," a little insect like the
cochineal found in Mexico. From the blood of the
crushed cochineal we get a beautiful crimson dye.
In the same way, from the tola was made a scarlet
dye with which the great ones of this world colored their garments. Jesus was practically saying, "I am like the tola; I am to be crushed to
death that others may be robed in glory." So we
see Him on that cross, bleeding and dying for
our sins. But as we read on in Psalm 22 we
come to the last verse where, in our Authorized
Version, we get this, "They shall come, and shall
declare His righteousness unto a people that shall
be born, that He hath done this," but in a more
literal translation you find it reads, "They shall
declare that it is finished." So the psalm begins
with the cry of distress, "My God, My God, why
hast Thou forsaken Me?" and ends with the cry
of triumph, "It is finished."

Continuing in our chapter, we read: "Now
there stood by the cross of Jesus His mother, and
His mother's sister, Mary the wife of Cleophas,
and Mary Magdalene. When Jesus therefore saw
His mother, and the disciple standing by, whom
He loved, He saith unto His mother, Woman, be-

hold thy son! Then saith He to the disciple, Behold thy mother! And from that hour that disciple took her unto his own home." We scarcely know which to admire most—the faithfulness, the devotedness of these dear women, and the beloved young disciple, or the tender, compassionate love of the blessed Lord Jesus Christ and His consideration for the dear mother that bore Him. He recalls the prophecy, "Yea, a sword shall pierce through thy own soul also," and He knows that sword is indeed piercing her mother heart as she sees her Son suffering in such awful agony hanging there upon the nails, and He would have her know that He is concerned about her and anxious to relieve her agonies. So He points her to John and says, "Behold thy son!" and to John He says, "Behold thy mother! And from that hour that disciple took her unto his own home." During the last of her sojourn here on earth, John became to her as a tender, loving son, and she to him as a loving mother.

"After this, Jesus knowing that all things were now accomplished that the scripture might be fulfilled, saith, I thirst." He knew that all things up to that present moment had been accomplished, but there was one scripture yet to be fulfilled. That was found in Psalm 69: 21: "They gave Me also gall for My meat; and in My thirst they gave Me vinegar to drink." That 69th Psalm also

portrays Him as the Sufferer upon the cross, and
so that that prophecy might not go unfulfilled,
Jesus cried, "I thirst." "Now there was set a vessel full of vinegar: and they filled a sponge with
vinegar, and put it upon hyssop, and put it to
His mouth." That vinegar told out all the malice
and hatred of man's heart, but Jesus took the
vinegar at the hand of the soldier and drank it.
A little earlier He had refused the wormwood
and gall, for that typified the wrath of God and
He would take that only from the hand of His
Father. Man had no right to press that cup to
His lips.

"When Jesus therefore had received the vinegar, He said, It is finished: and He bowed His
head, and gave up the ghost." "It is finished!"—
three words in our English Bible, only one in the
Greek Testament. *"Tetelestai!"*—that was His
cry of triumph. He had finished the work the
Father gave Him to do. He had glorified God to
the full in the place where He had been so terribly dishonored, and now because of that finished
work God can "be just, and the Justifier of him
which believeth in Jesus."

And so the message of the gospel that goes out
to all men everywhere today is this: "The work
that saves is finished! Jesus did it all upon the
cross."

Have you met with God at the foot of that cross where full settlement was made for sin? When Jesus cried, "It is finished," He bowed His head and gave up the ghost. He did not die from exhaustion. He dismissed His spirit. We can not do that. How many suffering ones have wished that they might. But when Jesus settled the sin question, when He had drunk the cup of judgment, when He had glorified God in the putting away of sin, He cried, "It is finished," and He dismissed His spirit. "Father, into Thy hands I commend My spirit." His spirit went to Paradise. The precious body of the Redeemer hung there upon the cross, soon to be quickened into new life on the day of His glorious resurrection.

Do you know this blessed Saviour? Have you trusted Him for yourself? Oh, if you have not trusted Him, I plead with you, bow now at the foot of that cross, confess yourself a sinner, tell Him that you will put your heart's confidence in Him who died to redeem you, and go forth to own Him henceforth as your Lord and Master as well as your Saviour.

THE BURIAL OF THE KING

✓ ✓ ✓

"The Jews therefore, because it was the preparation, that the bodies should not remain upon the cross on the sabbath day (for that sabbath day was an high day), besought Pilate that their legs might be broken, and that they might be taken away. Then came the soldiers, and brake the legs of the first, and of the other which was crucified with him. But when they came to Jesus, and saw that He was dead already, they brake not His legs: but one of the soldiers with a spear pierced His side, and forthwith came there out blood and water. And he that saw it bare record, and his record is true: and he knoweth that he saith true, that ye might believe. For these things were done, that the scripture should be fulfilled, A bone of Him shall not be broken. And again another scripture saith, They shall look on Him whom they pierced. And after this Joseph of Arimathea, being a disciple of Jesus, but secretly for fear of the Jews, besought Pilate that he might take away the body of Jesus: and Pilate gave him leave. He came therefore, and took the body of Jesus. And there came also Nicodemus, which at the first came to Jesus by night, and brought a mixture of myrrh and aloes, about an hundred pound weight. Then took they the body of Jesus, and wound it in linen clothes with the spices, as the manner of the Jews is to bury. Now in the place where He was crucified there was a garden; and in the garden a new sepulchre, wherein was never man yet laid. There laid they Jesus therefore because of the Jews' preparation day; for the sepulchre was nigh at hand" (John 19: 31-42).

✓ ✓ ✓

THE Spirit of God has been at great pains to
bring before us a number of most interesting and instructive details not only concerning the sufferings of our blessed Lord Jesus when
He took our place upon the cross to make expiation for our iniquities, but of the events that took
place afterwards in connection with His burial.

First we read of what happened while His body
was still upon the cross. The Jews, we are told,
because it was the sabbath, could not let the body
remain there. It was a high day in connection
with the passover celebration and the Jews besought Pilate that in order to hasten the death of
the three, their legs might be broken. In Deuteronomy we read, "If a man have committed a
sin worthy of death, and he be to be put to death,
and thou hang him on a tree: his body shall not
remain all night upon the tree, but thou shalt in
any wise bury him that day; (for he that is
hanged is accursed of God;) that thy land be not
defiled, which the Lord thy God giveth thee for
an inheritance" (Deut. 21: 22, 23).

Here we have a peculiar evidence of the perversity of the human heart. The very men who
had shown their utter indifference to the One
who came to be the Saviour of sinners, those who,
in fact, had not only been indifferent to Him, but
had hated Him and who had insisted upon His
crucifixion, were now very punctillious to carry

out the letter of the law. They did not realize that their rejection of Jesus was far worse than leaving His body upon the cross on the sabbath. They had already committed the greatest crime anyone could commit. In the sight of God there is noth‚ ing worse than rejecting His Son. How many there are today who pride themselves on their loyalty and responsibility, who are guilty of this most terrible of all sins. You remember the Lord Jesus Christ said, of the Holy Spirit, "When He is come, He will reprove the world of sin, and of righteousness, and of judgment: of sin, because they believe not on Me." That is the sin of all sins, the sin that will send men down to eternal perdition if it is not repented of. In the third chapter of John we read, "He that believeth on Him is not condemned: but he that believeth not is condemned already, because he hath not believed in the name of the only begotten Son of God." Observe, it does not say he is condemned because he is a drunkard, because he is a thief, because he is immoral. These things are wicked in God's sight, but for all of these Christ died on Calvary's cross, and he who turns to God in repentance and trusts that blessed Saviour for cleansing from every stain, stands cleared of every charge, but the sin that will never be for‚ given is the final rejection of the Saviour whom God has provided.

Here were men rejecting that Saviour and yet so careful about carrying out the letter of the law which said no body was to hang upon the tree overnight. So they went to Pilate and besought him to hasten the death of these poor victims that their legs might be broken. The Roman soldiers came and broke the legs of the two thieves, one on either side of the Lord; but when they came to Jesus, though He had been there but a few hours, and we are told that sometimes men hung suspended as much as three or four days before they died, they were amazed to find Him already dead. But as if to make it doubly sure, one of the soldiers pierced the side of the blessed Christ of God and blood and water flowed forth, giving evidence that He had pierced the heart-sac itself. John took special note of that; he said, "Forthwith came there out blood and water. And he that saw it bare record, and his record is true: and he knoweth that he saith true, that ye might believe." That is, John would have us understand very definitely that he knew the Son of God was already dead before the Roman spear-point was inserted into the heart. Then the amazing thing was that blood and lymph flowed forth freely from the body of the dead Man. Physicians say it would seem to indicate that Jesus died of a broken heart, but He died when He dismissed His own spirit to the Father, so it would be incorrect to say that a broken heart was the *cause* of His death, but Scripture tells us that He died *with* a broken heart. In Psalm 69 He says, "Reproach hath broken My heart; and I am full of heaviness."

Oh, dear unsaved friend, if you are reading these words today, it was because of your sins and mine that the heart of the Son of God broke in agony as He endured the wrath of God that we so richly deserved. And that blood and water that flowed from His side, John draws special attention to, because it has a typical meaning. Long years afterwards, when John himself was an old man, the memory of that scene was before him. He wrote, "This is He that came by water and blood, even Jesus Christ; not by water only, but by water and blood. And it is the Spirit that beareth witness, because the Spirit is truth. For there are three that bear record . . . and these three agree in one" (1 John 5: 6).

What is involved typically in the water and the blood coming from the side of the Lord Jesus Christ? It suggests two different aspects of our cleansing. When a poor sinner, stained with guilt and polluted by sin, utterly unfit for God, has need for judicial cleansing the Word tells me, "If we walk in the light, as He is in the light, we have fellowship one with another, and the blood of Jesus Christ His Son cleanseth us from all

sin." The blood of Jesus cleanseth us judicially;
that is, it frees us from every charge that could
ever be brought against us.

> "Once we stood in condemnation,
>   Waiting thus the sinner's doom.
> Christ in death hath wrought salvation,
>   God hath raised Him from the tomb.
> Now we see in His acceptance
>   But the measure of our own,
> He who lay beneath our sentence,
>   Seated high upon the throne."

If you are a Christian, think back to those
hours when you were troubled about your sins.
You realized your guilt, you felt how unclean, how
unholy you were, how unfit for the presence of
God. But oh, the joy that came to you when you
learned that the precious blood would wash you
from every stain. You remember when your
heart saw the meaning of those words,

> "Lord, through the blood of the Lamb that was slain,
>   Cleansing for me, cleansing for me;
> From all the guilt of my sin now I claim,
>   Cleansing from Thee, cleansing from Thee!"

And then when you trusted in the Lord Jesus
Christ, you knew on the authority of the Word
of God that all your sins were put away, and you
stood perfect and clear before God as though you
had never sinned. This is what it means to be
cleansed by the blood of the Lord Jesus Christ.
You remember it is written, "The life of the flesh

is in the blood, and I have given it to you upon the altar, to make an atonement for your souls." And so the Lord Jesus, by shedding His precious blood, giving up His holy, spotless life for us, bearing our judgment, has made full expiation for iniquity.

"Oh, why was He there as the Bearer of sin,
   If on Jesus thy guilt was not laid?
  Oh, why from His side flowed the sin-cleansing stream,
   If His dying thy debt has not paid?"

This is the very heart of the gospel, deliverance through His blood from every charge that could be brought against us.

Now, that is one aspect of our cleansing. But there is another. If we are going to have fellowship with God, there must not only be judicial cleansing, there must be practical cleansing. It will never do to point back to the cross and say, "There at the cross my sins were put away," if I am daily living in sin. It will never do to talk of justification by faith and redemption through His blood, if my daily life is unholy and bringing dishonor on the name of Christ. I am called to walk with God day by day. I am called to walk before Him in purity of heart, and this is where cleansing by water comes in. "Christ also loved the Church, and gave Himself for it; that He might sanctify and cleanse it with the washing

of water by the Word." By the precious blood of
Christ I am justified before God. By the water
I am practically sanctified. The water is a type
of the Word of God, which is likened to water
for practical cleansing in Ps. 119:9; "Wherewithal shall a young man cleanse his way? By
taking heed thereto according to Thy Word."

Let us imagine a young man who has been
away from God, a stranger to His grace, and he
is troubled because of his sin. He comes confessing his sin, and if he is intelligently instructed,
he comes to understand that his past sin is all
put away and he stands complete in the sight of
God, as if he had never sinned at all. Now is that
young man to go on living the way he did before?
Oh, no. Now he studies the Word of God and the
Holy Spirit opens it up and reveals its truths to
him. Thus, he is cleansed by taking heed to the
Word.

And so Jesus said to His disciples, "Now ye are
clean through the Word that I have spoken unto
you." This is cleansing by water. He illustrated
it, you remember, by washing the feet of His disciples, and He said to reluctant Peter, "What I
do thou knowest not now; but thou shalt know
hereafter." When did Peter find out its meaning?
It was after he had slipped and fallen into sin
and his feet became defiled, and later the blessed
Lord applied the Word to Peter and he was re-

stored to fellowship with God. Then he was made clean by the washing of water by the Word. You see why the Word is likened to water. It is because of its practical cleansing effect. I am to judge anything that God shows me to be wrong and then I am to seek, by grace, to walk as that Word indicates. What happens? Why, those things are literally washed away out of my life by the Word. My mind is purified by the Word, my heart is made clean by the Word. All this then is suggested by that which John saw on Calvary that day. The very spear that pierced the side of the Son of God drew forth the blood that saved, but not only the blood, there was also the water.

> "Let the water and the blood,
>   From Thy riven side which flowed,
>   Be of sin the double cure,
>   Save from wrath and make me pure."

John next calls our attention to two scriptures that were in process of fulfilment that day. He says, "These things were done, that the scripture should be fulfilled, A bone of Him shall not be broken." Those soldiers had no idea they were fulfilling anything in Scripture when they forebore to break His legs, but long years ago Moses gave instructions concerning the first passover. We read in Exodus 12: 43, 46: "And the Lord said unto Moses and Aaron, This is the ordinance of the passover: . . . In one house shall it be eaten; thou shalt not carry forth ought of the flesh abroad out of the house; neither shall ye break a bone thereof." So God had commanded that not one bone of the passover lamb should be broken, and there hung upon the cross the true Passover.

> "No bone of Thee was broken,
> Thou spotless Passover Lamb."

God's Word was fulfilled even though the soldiers did not realize it.

But another scripture had to be fulfilled; in Zechariah 12:10 it was written of Messiah, "And they shall look upon Me whom they have pierced, and they shall mourn for Him, as one mourneth for his only son, and shall be in bitterness for Him, as one that is in bitterness for his firstborn." And so when this other Roman soldier, without realizing that his act had anything to do with the Word of God, thrust that spear into the side of the Lord Jesus Christ, he too was simply carrying out what had been predicted long before.

But now, observe this, so long as our blessed Lord was in the sinner's place, so long as He was viewed by God as the great trespass-offering, God permitted every kind of indignity that Satanic malignity could suggest to be heaped upon the body of His Son. That blessed Head

was crowned with thorns. They smote Him in
the face with their hands. They spit upon that
lovely countenance. They beat Him with the cruel
scourge until the blood poured down His back.
They took Him out to Calvary and nailed Him to
the cross. And then at last, they pierced His side,
and God did not interfere. He permitted it all,
and yet it was not what man did to Jesus that
put away sin. It was not that which settled the
sin question. It was what Jesus endured at the
hand of God when His soul was made an offering
for sin. But it pleased God that all the worst
that was in man's heart should be there told forth
and the best that was in the heart of God. Man's
hatred and God's love met there.

God did not interfere as long as Jesus suffered
in the sinner's place. But just the moment after
the blood and the water flowed forth from that
wounded side, it was as though God said, "Now,
hands off! The sin question is settled. My Son is
no more in the sinner's place." And from that
moment on, no unclean hand touched the body of
the Son of God. Not one person was allowed to
do anything that would in any sense dishonor
that sacred corpse. Loving hands took Jesus
down from the cross, drawing out those dreadful
nails and removing His hands and feet from the
wood. Joseph of Arimathaea who had for sometime been convinced in his own heart that Jesus

was the Christ, came forth openly. We read, "And after this Joseph of Arimathaea, being a disciple of Jesus, but secretly for fear of the Jews, besought Pilate that he might take away the body of Jesus: and Pilate gave him leave. He came therefore and took the body of Jesus." Joseph and the friends of Jesus gathered round that cross and took that sacred body down, and then just at the appointed moment there came also Nicodemus, the man who had come to Jesus by night; the man who had spoken up in the Sanhedrin, and brought a mixture of myrrh and aloes, about an hundred pound weight, a vast amount. They took the body of Jesus and wound it in linen cloths. The Jews would dip these cloths in an ointment and spices, and then they would wind them round the arms, the lower limbs and the torso, and then bind them altogether. You remember Lazarus came forth bound in the grave clothes.

And where did they lay Jesus? Well, in the place where He was crucified, a garden at the side of Calvary. We walked around there a few years ago, and oh, how our hearts were moved as we went from the place of the cross to the garden tomb. "Now in the place where He was crucified there was a garden; and in the garden a new sepulchre, wherein was never man yet laid." And in that new sepulchre they laid Him.

They took the rest of the spices that were not needed for the body and they made a bed in the crypt. They gave Him the burial of a King. We read that when King Asa died, they laid him on a bed of spices. And God seemed to say, "While My Son was in the sinner's place, I allowed everything to be done to Him that Satanic minds could think of. Now He must be recognized as the King that He is, and He must be given the burial of a King." So He was laid upon a bed of spices. "There laid they Jesus therefore because of the Jews' preparation day; for the sepulchre was nigh at hand." And until the resurrection morning He was to remain in that new tomb and then come forth in triumph, the Conqueror of death. How our hearts rejoice in Him today!

THE EMPTY TOMB

✓ ✓ ✓

"The first day of the week cometh Mary Magdalene early, when it was yet dark, unto the sepulchre, and seeth the stone taken away from the sepulchre. Then she runneth, and cometh to Simon Peter, and to the other disciple, whom Jesus loved, and saith unto them, They have taken away the Lord out of the sepulchre, and we know not where they have laid him. Peter therefore went forth, and that other disciple, and came to the sepulchre. So they ran both together: and the other disciple did outrun Peter, and came first to the sepulchre. And he stooping down, and looking in, saw the linen clothes lying; yet went he not in. Then cometh Simon Peter following him, and went into the sepulchre, and seeth the linen clothes lie. And the napkin, that was about His head, not lying with the linen clothes, but wrapped together in a place by itself. Then went in also that other disciple, which came first to the sepulchre, and he saw, and believed. For as yet they knew not the scripture, that He must rise again from the dead. Then the disciples went away again unto their own home. But Mary stood without at the sepulchre weeping: and as she wept, she stooped down, and looked into the sepulchre. And seeth two angels in white sitting, the one at the head, and the other at the feet, where the body of Jesus had lain. And they say unto her, Woman, why weepest thou? She saith unto them, Because they have taken away my Lord, and I know not where they have laid Him. And when she had thus said, she turned herself back, and saw Jesus standing, and knew not that it was Jesus. Jesus saith unto her, Woman, why weepest thou? whom seekest thou? She, supposing Him to be the gardener, saith unto Him, sir, if Thou have borne Him hence, tell me where Thou hast laid Him, and I will take Him away. Jesus saith unto her, Mary. She turned herself, and saith unto Him, Rabboni; which is to say,

Master. Jesus saith unto her, Touch Me not; for I am
not yet ascended to My Father: but go to My brethren, and
say unto them, I ascend unto My Father, and your
Father; and to My God, and your God. Mary Magdalene
came and told the disciples that she had seen the Lord,
and that He had spoken these things unto her" (John
20: 1-18).

꜀   ꜀   ꜀

OUT of the different accounts which we
have in the Gospels of the events connected with the resurrection of our Lord
Jesus Christ, this is one of the most graphic, one
of the most interesting and one of the most compelling. When rightly understood, I do not see
how anyone desiring to know the truth, can meditate on this passage without being brought to
saving faith in the risen Christ.

Our Lord had told His disciples on a number
of occasions that He was to be crucified, but that
the third day He would rise again. It is a singular fact that they had never seemed to grasp
what He was saying. They were not looking for
Him to rise again, so when they saw His head fall
forward as He hung there on that cross, after hearing Him pray, "Father, into Thy hands I commit
My spirit," their hopes were dashed in pieces, and
they felt that all His Messianic claims were dissipated. But there were those who still loved to
linger about the tomb in which His body had
been placed. A great stone fitted into a groove

was rolled across the door of that tomb and then sealed. A Roman guard was set to watch that sepulchre, for the enemies of our Lord remembered what His disciples had forgotten, and they came to Pilate and said, "Sir, we remember that that deceiver said, while He was yet alive, After three days I will rise again. Command therefore that the sepulchre be made sure until the third day, lest His disciples come by night, and steal Him away, and say unto the people, He is risen from the dead: so the last error shall be worse than the first." And Pilate said to them, a bit sarcastically, "Ye have a watch: go your way, make it as sure as ye can!" And they did make it as sure as they could, but no human effort could hinder the working of omnipotent power when the hour came that God's Son was to come back in triumph from the grave.

And so here we are told that on "the first day of the week"—the new day of the dispensation of the grace of God—"cometh Mary Magdalene early, when it was yet dark, unto the sepulchre, and seeth the stone taken away from the sepulchre." Love drew her to that tomb. She and the other women hoped to go in and take care of the body in a way it had not been taken care of when it was hurriedly removed from the cross and placed in the crypt. So they were waiting for a time when they could perform this last sad office for Him whom they had loved so tenderly; whom they thought had been taken from them in death until the end of time.

But as Mary drew near, she was amazed to see that great stone rolled back, no one on guard, and the body of Jesus evidently removed. Apparently she did not go in and make a careful investigation, but ran immediately "and cometh to Simon Peter, and to the other disciple, whom Jesus loved" (that is the disciple, John, who wrote this book. John never speaks of himself as the disciple who loved Jesus—he did love Him, but felt his love was nothing of which to boast, but he could boast in the love of Jesus). So to Peter and John went Mary. She cried when she saw them and said, "They have taken away the Lord out of the sepulchre, and we know not where they have laid Him."

Immediately Peter started for the tomb and with him John—"Peter therefore went forth, and that other disciple, and came to the sepulchre." Peter had doubtless passed many an anxious hour since the death of his blessed Master. He could not forget that he had acted the part of the coward—he who had said, "Though all men forsake Thee, yet will I not forsake Thee." Yet he had denied with oaths and cursing that he ever knew Jesus Christ. But deep in his heart he loved his Lord. He had been overcome by fear and cowardice and when this word came he hastened to see if it were really true.

We read that they both ran together, Peter, a man of mature years, John, a sturdy youth. "The other disciple," John, "did outrun Peter." One would expect that. He soon outdistanced the older man and so reached the sepulchre before Peter did. We read that he stooped down and looked in, but did not go in.

Outside the city of Jerusalem, near the Damascus Gate is that remarkable skull-shaped hill which most Protestant Christians believe to be the actual Calvary. Many, of course, still insist that the Calvary is found in the Church of the Holy Sepulchre, which seems entirely inconsistent with this record. But this skull-shaped hill outside seems to be the very Calvary where Jesus died. "In the place where He was crucified was a garden and in the garden a sepulchre." In that sepulchre they laid the body of the Lord Jesus. Today you can see this skull-shaped hill and on one side of it there is a garden where a few years back they uncovered a sepulchre cut into the face of the cliff and it answers in every detail to the tomb described in the Word of God. As you draw near, it is natural to stoop down, as John did, and look in. The entrance, originally, was very low. Near this doorway there is a little window which throws the light upon an empty crypt, plainly visible as you peer through the entrance. The crypt is about twenty-four inches high, cut out of the limestone rock, and in that crypt the body would have been easily seen, lying upon its bed of spices, if it were still there.

John drew near and stooped down and looked into that entrance way but he did not go any further. Why? Because as he looked in he thought he saw that which proved that what Mary had told them was wrong. He evidently thought he saw the body lying there. So he did not go in. He doubtless said to himself, "Oh, poor Mary Magdalene, she made a mistake after all, they haven't removed the body. There it is plainly visible in the early dawn." But then came Peter, and he went into the sepulchre and he saw the linen cloths lying and the turban which was about His head not touching the linen cloths but wound together in a place by itself. The whole body had been swathed in these linen cloths. Peter did not stoop to look, like John, but rushed inside, and when he stood looking down upon that crypt he saw that which told a wonderful story. He saw the linen cloths just as they had been wrapped around the body, like the shell of the chrysalis after the butterfly has emerged. The cloths were there, but the body had gone! Between the turban and the linen cloths there was an empty space where the face should have been.

Peter looked on in wonder. "Oh," he said, "My Lord is risen!" for he knew that no power on earth could have taken that body out of those linen cloths and left them in the condition in which they were, but the almighty God. Peter turned around and beckoned to John. And we read, "Then went in also that other disciple, which came first to the sepulchre, and he saw, and believed." He could not do anything else! I think I can see Peter calling him in, and they stand there looking down upon those linen cloths, noticing that turban, the head no longer in its folds, and then they looked at one another and said, "He is risen!" "They saw and believed," and we would have believed, if we had been there. We would have known that Jesus had been raised from the dead by the omnipotent power of God. They were compelled to believe, even though they did not understand. "For as yet they knew not the scripture, that He must rise again from the dead." But they had positive proof that He had risen, and we read, "Then the disciples went away again unto their own home." They were not concerned now about anyone stealing away the body. They knew that was an impossibility. The body of Jesus had been raised from the dead.

And then a few minutes later, Christ manifested Himself to Mary, who stood without the sepulchre weeping, and as she wept she stooped down

And now the message that we are to give to sinners everywhere is this, "That if thou shalt confess with thy mouth the Lord Jesus, and shalt believe in thine heart that God hath raised Him from the dead, thou shalt be saved. For with the heart man believeth unto righteousness; and with the mouth confession is made unto salvation."

I am wondering if among my readers there are not numbers of people who perhaps have for years never definitely settled the matter of committing their souls to Christ. Will you not do so now?

"Low in the grave He lay—
  Jesus, my Saviour!
Waiting the coming day—
  Jesus, my Lord!
Up from the grave He arose
With a mighty triumph o'er His foes;
He arose a Victor from the dark domain,
And He lives forever with His saints to reign:
  He arose! He arose! Hallelujah! Christ arose!"

JESUS IN THE MIDST

✦ ✦ ✦

"Then the same day at evening, being the first day of the week, when the doors were shut where the disciples were assembled for fear of the Jews, came Jesus and stood in the midst, and saith unto them, Peace be unto you. And when He had so said, He showed unto them His hands and His side. Then were the disciples glad, when they saw the Lord. Then said Jesus to them again, Peace be unto you: as My Father hath sent Me, even so send I you. And when He had said this, He breathed on them, and saith unto them, Receive ye the Holy Ghost: whose soever sins ye remit, they are remitted unto them; and whose soever sins ye retain, they are retained. But Thomas, one of the twelve, called Didymus, was not with them when Jesus came. The other disciples therefore said unto him, We have seen the Lord. But he said unto them, Except I shall see in His hands the print of the nails, and put my finger into the print of the nails, and thrust my hand into His side, I will not believe. And after eight days again His disciples were within, and Thomas with them: then came Jesus, the doors being shut, and stood in the midst, and said, Peace be unto you. Then saith He to Thomas, Reach hither thy finger, and behold My hands; and reach hither thy hand, and thrust it into My side: and be not faithless, but believing. And Thomas answered and said unto Him, My Lord and my God. Jesus saith unto him, Thomas, because thou hast seen Me, thou hast believed: blessed are they that have not seen, and yet have believed. And many other signs truly did Jesus in the presence of His disciples, which are not written in this book: but these are written, that ye might believe that Jesus is the Christ, the Son of God; and that believing ye might have life through His name" (John 20: 19-31).

✦ ✦ ✦

NO one Gospel gives us all the various appearances of the Lord Jesus Christ to His disciples after His resurrection. In fact, all of them together do not give us every such appearance, for while we have a number of instances mentioned in each of the different Gospels, we are told that our Lord "showed Himself alive by many infallible proofs after He was raised from the dead," and that for forty days He continued with His disciples, teaching them, instructing them pertaining to the Kingdom of God, so that on many other occasions than those definitely mentioned in the Gospels the Saviour appeared to them and outlined the marvelous program with which He expected them to cooperate as they went forth as His messengers into all the world.

But of these instances that are recorded we might say that each one seems to have some special lesson for us. Here we have two definite appearances of the Lord Jesus Christ in the same place, an upper room in Jerusalem, possibly in the home of Mary, the mother of John Mark. And on these occasions He appeared, first of all, to ten of the apostles and then to eleven, Thomas being absent the first time but present the second time. And He gave them, in a very definite way, their commission to go out as His representatives.

We are told in verse nineteen, "Then the same
day (that is, the day on which John, Peter and
Mary Magdalene had visited the sepulchre early
in the morning) at evening, being the first day
of the week (for, as the seventh day was the
Sabbath of the old dispensation, the memorial of
creation, so the first day of the week became the
rest day of the new dispensation, the memorial
of new creation, the day on which our Lord Jesus
Christ arose from the dead) when the doors were
shut where the disciples were assembled for fear
of the Jews," suddenly they looked up and there
stood the blessed Lord in their midst. Not a door
had been opened to admit Him. That gives us
some idea of the difference between the resurrection body and these present bodies which are
subject to their various limitations. When our
Lord Jesus was here on earth, He allowed Himself
to be self-limited, but after resurrection, He came
out of the grave cloths, as we have seen, without
disturbing them, and we might even say He left
the tomb without opening the door, for the stone
was not rolled away to let Him out, but to let the
women and the disciples in.

Now He is able to present Himself in a material
body of flesh and bones, but no longer subject to
the former laws, appearing in a room without
coming through a door or entryway! Some day
we shall have bodies like His, and throughout the

glorious kingdom age we shall be able to flit from place to place at His command, unhindered by what men call "the law of gravitation."

"Jesus came and stood in the midst." This was His rightful place. What infinite grace! He took the place in the midst on the cross. There, we read, they crucified Him, and two thieves with Him, on either side one, and Jesus in the midst. He was numbered among the transgressors, and He took the central place as though of all of the malefactors He was the worst. There He was bearing our sins in His own body on the tree.

But before He went away He gave this promise to His disciples, "Where two or three are gathered together in My name, there am I in the midst." This was the first time since His resurrection that His disciples were gathered together, and they were there because of their mutual love for Him. They were met in His name, and suddenly He manifested Himself among them, fulfilling His words. So, though now we cannot see Him with the mortal eye, whenever we are gathered together in His name, He is always in the midst. We do not need to ask Him or plead with Him to be in our midst. He says He *is* there. What we do need to ask for is opened hearts that we may discern Him.

Why is He in the midst of His friends? In the second chapter of Hebrews He says, "I will de-

clare Thy name unto My brethren; in the midst
of the Church will I sing praise unto Thee." That
is one reason He is in the midst. He is in the
midst of His saints in order to draw out their
thanksgiving and praise. I love to think of Him
as the great Choir Leader. These hearts of ours
are the instruments with which we make melody
to the Lord, and it is He who touches the strings
of one heart after another. He is in the midst
as our great Intercessor. It is His presence in
the midst of the gatherings of His people in the
power of the Holy Spirit, that gives each meeting
its peculiar character. I think that if we always
remembered this it would have a very sobering
influence upon us. It would make us realize that
in the holy assembly of the saints of God nothing
should be done or said or sung that could not have
His approval. By and by when we gather Home
to glory, He will still be in the midst.

John tells us that he looked up into heaven and
that he saw the throne of God surrounded by the
living creatures and the twenty-four elders, rep-
resenting all the ransomed saints. He says, "And
I beheld and, lo, in the midst of the throne and
of the four beasts, and in the midst of the elders,
stood a Lamb as it had been slain, having seven
horns and seven eyes, which are the seven Spirits
of God sent forth into all the earth." Jesus in
the midst in the glory, bearing upon His glorified

body the marks of His passion, the reminder of all He suffered for sinners when He died on Calvary's cross!

And so we see Him on this resurrection evening in the midst of His gathered people. They were not very clear as to what had taken place and did not understand very much, but they loved Him, and when they were thus together He fulfilled His word and manifested Himself to them.

And now He speaks, and what is His word of greeting? "Peace be unto you." That is the way one oriental greets another even today—"Peace be unto you." But oh, how much meaning there was in this salutation coming from the lips of our precious Lord. He had just been to Calvary, where He made peace by the blood of His cross. He said to them before He went away, "Peace I leave with you, My peace I give unto you: not as the world giveth, give I unto you. Let not your heart be troubled, neither let it be afraid." And as He stood in the midst of them He seems to say, "It is all done. I have been through the sorrows of the cross. I have made peace, and now it is yours. Enter into and enjoy it." Do you enjoy the peace which has been made? "Therefore being justified by faith, we have peace with God through our Lord Jesus Christ," a peace we did not make, a peace He made for us, and which we enter into and enjoy when we believe the word of the truth of the gospel. We are told, "He is our peace." Oh, the blessedness of knowing Him, who is our peace! Peace in the midst of all the trials of earth. Peace in the day when everything that men have counted upon is being shaken. If you do not enjoy this peace, it is for you. But in order to enjoy it, you must receive the One who made it. You must trust Christ for yourself.

He said to them, "Peace be unto you." He showed them His hands and feet, the wound in His side. "Here are the wounds that tell you it is I, and not another, and I have borne all this for you!"

We too may see those marks of His love in the glory, and when we look upon those pierced Hands and upon the wound in His side, how they will speak to us and move our hearts. We will say to ourselves, "That is the most lovely thing about Jesus, for those wounds tell what He thought of us. He might have gone out free when He finished those wonderful years of service here, He might have gone back to the glory from which He came." But He went to that cross of shame and there he received those wounds which tell of a love that was stronger than death. And He will bear the scars for all eternity.

You say, "But how do you know that He still has those wounds upon His body, that He still bears those scars?" I know because in Zechariah we read, "And they shall look upon Me whom they have pierced, and they shall mourn for Him, as one mourneth for his only son, and shall be in bitterness for Him, as one that is in bitterness for his firstborn. . . . And one shall say unto Him, What are these wounds in Thine hands? Then He shall answer, Those with which I was wounded in the house of My friends."

And so those wounds will be the perpetual token of His love for the Church and His love for Israel.

"He showed unto them His hands and His side." Have you not sometimes gone to a gathering of the Lord's people feeling depressed, troubled? You had wondered whether to go or remain at home. But you went and took your place with them, and as the hymns were sung and the Word was read, and God's truth declared, your eyes were opened and you looked up and saw the Lord Jesus, and you went away refreshed, saying, "I have seen the Lord." We do not just come together to meet with one another. It is a great mistake if we think we come together merely for a social time. We come to meet Him.

Then Jesus again said, "Peace be unto you: as My Father hath sent Me, even so send I you." Why did He say it again? Well, I do not think it is too far-fetched to say that it was because He knew they were going into the world and they would meet with suffering, persecution and disillusionment. Paul could say, "And the peace of God, which passeth all understanding, shall keep your hearts and minds through Christ Jesus." The Father sent the Son to be the Saviour of the world. Now He sends His servants to tell the story to lost men everywhere, and as they go He will keep their hearts in peace, if they but confide in Him.

"And when He had said this, He breathed on them, and saith unto them, Receive ye the Holy Ghost." That carries our minds back to the creation of man in the first place. God formed man from the dust of the earth, and He breathed into the man the breath of the spirit of life, and man became a living soul. Now here are the disciples of the Lord Jesus Christ, born again, it is true, but going forth upon that great mission, and the Lord breathed upon them. Just as of old, God breathed upon Adam and he became a living soul, so it was when the Holy Ghost came on the Day of Pentecost. The first Adam was a living soul; the last Adam, we are told, is a quickening spirit. And here the Lord Jesus Christ breathes upon them. It was not that He actually gave them the Spirit at that time, but they would understand when, later at Pentecost, the Spirit actually descended and abode upon them and dwelt with them, that He was given by their exalted Lord.

With this He gives them a marvelous word of authority: "Whose soever sins ye remit, they are remitted unto them; and whose soever sins ye retain, they are retained." What does this mean? It has been claimed by some that these disciples were the first bishops of the Church, and the Lord was giving them the authority to remit sin and retain sin, and that they were to go out into the world and people were to confess sins to them and they would tell them what penance to do and thus obtain remission of their sins. I do not find anything like that here.

One of the most important of the group, the Apostle Peter, was there that day and Peter went forth in the name of the Lord to proclaim remission of sins. How did he do it? Did he say, "You come to me and confess your sins to me and I will forgive them?" Did he say anything like that? Let us see. In Acts 10 we find Peter preaching the gospel in the household of Cornelius. He tells of Christ's wonderful life "The word which God sent unto the children of Israel, preaching peace by Jesus Christ: (He is Lord of all) . . . To Him give all the prophets witness, that through His name whosoever"—confesseth his sins to a priest—"shall receive remission of sins." Is that right? Do you have your Bible open? What does it say? "That through His name whosoever *believeth in Him* shall receive remission of sins." Believe on Jesus and you will get remission. That is the commission that every servant of Christ has. We go out to the world and say, We are commanded by Jesus Christ to offer you remission of sin if you will believe on Jesus. And when they do, we dare to say, "Your sins are forgiven or remitted." And if they will not believe, what then? We say to them, "Your sins are retained." How do we know it? Because He said so. There is nothing sacramental here. This is just a clear, definite gospel statement.

But we are told that Thomas was not present. You know, sometimes people do not realize what they lose by not attending where God's saints are gathered together when Jesus comes to take His place in the midst. They lose out. We can imagine the disciples saying to Thomas when they again see him, "Oh, Thomas, we have had a wonderful time! We have seen the Lord!" Thomas looks up in a hopeless kind of way, and replies, "Except I shall see in His hands the print of the nails, and put my finger into the print of the nails, and thrust my hand into His side, I will not believe." And so Thomas goes on all through the week without getting any assurance, until eight days. "And after eight days again His disciples were within, and Thomas with them: then came Jesus, the doors being shut, and stood in the midst," He knows what Thomas said. He heard him. And

He turns to him and says, "Reach hither thy finger, and behold My hands; and reach hither thy hand, and thrust it into My side: and be not faithless, but believing." We do not read that he attempted to reach out his hand, but the sight of the risen Christ was apparently enough, and he exclaimed with adoring love, "My Lord, and my God!"

And what did Jesus say? Did He say, "You must not call me God. I am only the Son of God. Don't do that. That is a great mistake?" Did He do that? That is what He ought to have said if the Unitarian is right. But what did He say? Thomas had called Him, "My Lord and my God." Jesus said, "Thomas, because thou hast seen Me, thou hast believed: blessed are they that have not seen, and yet have believed." Is that blessing yours? We have never seen Him with mortal eyes but we gladly confess Him as our Lord and our God.

John closes this section by saying, "And many other signs truly did Jesus in the presence of His disciples, which are not written in this book: but these are written, that ye might believe that Jesus is the Christ, the Son of God; and that believing ye might have life through His name."

The selected instances recorded here are written that we might know who Jesus is. And if you

have any doubt about it, read John's Gospel over
and over again.

"Peace, perfect peace, in this dark world of sin?
The blood of Jesus whispers peace within.

Peace, perfect peace, by thronging duties pressed?
To do the will of Jesus, this is rest."

PETER CONFIRMED IN THE
APOSTOLATE

✓ ✓ ✓

"After these things Jesus showed Himself again to the disciples at the sea of Tiberias; and on this wise showed He Himself. There were together Simon Peter, and Thomas called Didymus, and Nathanael of Cana in Galilee, and the sons of Zebedee, and two other of His disciples. Simon Peter saith unto them, I go a fishing. They say unto him, We also go with thee. They went forth, and entered into a ship immediately; and that night they caught nothing. But when the morning was now come, Jesus stood on the shore: but the disciples knew not that it was Jesus. Then Jesus saith unto them, Children, have ye any meat? They answered Him, No. And He said unto them, Cast the net on the right side of the ship, and ye shall find. They cast therefore, and now they were not able to draw it for the multitude of fishes. Therefore that disciple whom Jesus loved saith unto Peter, It is the Lord. Now when Simon Peter heard that it was the Lord, he girt his fisher's coat unto him (for he was naked), and did cast himself into the sea. And the other disciples came in a little ship; (for they were not far from land, but as it were two hundred cubits), dragging the net with fishes. As soon then as they were come to land, they saw a fire of coals there, and fish laid thereon, and bread. Jesus saith unto them, Bring of the fish which ye have now caught. Simon Peter went up, and drew the net to land full of great fishes, an hundred and fifty and three: and for all there were so many, yet was not the net broken. Jesus saith unto them, Come and dine. And none of the disciples durst ask Him, Who art Thou? knowing that it was the Lord. Jesus then cometh, and taketh bread, and giveth them, and fish likewise. This is now the third time that Jesus showed Himself to His disciples, after that He was

risen from the dead.   So when they had dined, Jesus
saith to Simon Peter, Simon, son of Jonas, lovest thou
Me more than these?   He saith unto Him, Yea, Lord;
Thou knowest that I love Thee.   He saith unto him,
Feed My lambs.   He saith to him again the second time,
Simon, son of Jonas, lovest thou Me?   He saith unto Him,
Yea, Lord; Thou knowest that I love Thee.   He saith
unto him, Feed My sheep.   He saith unto him the third
time, Simon, son of Jonas, lovest thou Me?   Peter was
grieved because He said unto him the third time, Lovest
thou Me?   And he said unto Him, Lord, Thou knowest
all things; Thou knowest that I love Thee.   Jesus saith
unto him, Feed My sheep.   Verily, verily, I say unto
thee, When thou wast young, thou girdest thyself, and
walkedst whither thou wouldest: but when thou shalt be
old, thou shalt stretch forth thy hands, and another shall
gird thee, and carry thee whither thou wouldest not. This
spake He, signifying by what death he should glorify
God.   And when He had spoken this, He saith unto him,
Follow Me.   Then Peter, turning about, seeth the disciple whom Jesus loved following; which also leaned on
His breast at supper, and said, Lord, which is he that
betrayeth Thee?   Peter seeing him saith to Jesus, Lord,
and what shall this man do?   Jesus saith unto him,
If I will that he tarry till I come, what is that to thee?
Follow thou Me.   Then went this saying abroad among
the brethren, that that disciple should not die: yet Jesus
said not unto him, He shall not die; but, If I will that
he tarry till I come, what is that to thee?   This is the
disciple which testifieth of these things, and wrote these
things: and we know that his testimony is true.   And
there are also many other things which Jesus did, the
which, if they should be written every one, I suppose
that even the world itself could not contain the books
that should be written.   Amen" (John 21: 1-25).

✓   ✓   ✓

WITH these words we come to the close of
the Gospel of John, the book in which we
have been revelling for so long.   I trust
that our souls have been blessed as we have followed the pathway of our Lord Jesus Christ all

the way from the past eternity, as the One who
dwelt in the bosom of the Father, down to Bethlehem's manger, through the valleys and over the
hills of Galilee, Samaria and Judæa, at last to the
Garden of Gethsemane, the judgment hall and
cross, to the borrowed tomb, and now, in resurrection life.

The outstanding theme of this chapter is the
public restoration of the Apostle Peter. He who
had failed the Lord so sadly in the hour of need
might have thought he would never again be recognized as one of the apostles. But he was just
as tenderly loved by the Lord after his failure as
before. I wish we could take that in. I contact
so many people who tell me more or less the same
story. In some way or other they failed to stand
the test, and they are conscious of having sinned
against the Lord and though truly penitent, they
feel that it is all over with them, that the Lord
has given them up and that they are hopelessly
lost. Some say, "I wonder if I have committed
the unpardonable sin? I cannot get the witness
of the spirit any more. I have prayed and prayed
but do not get peace." Such souls forget that the
witness is the testimony of Holy Scripture and
that the Word of God has told us that if we confess
our sins He is faithful and just to forgive us our
sins and to cleanse us from all unrighteousness.
That is the witness of the Spirit given through

the Word of God, and no matter who the sinner is, when he comes to God confessing his failure, acknowledging and judging it, he may be absolutely certain that God will never go back on His declaration that the sin is put away, that the failing believer who has confessed his sins is cleansed from all unrighteousness, and that communion is restored.   Happy is the soul who enters into that by faith and goes on rejoicing in fellowship with his Saviour.

Now I have no doubt that the Lord had actually restored Peter's soul before this public event took place. We are told that when those disciples came from Emmaus on that first Lord's Day evening they found the disciples gathered together, saying, "The Lord is risen indeed, and hath appeared unto Simon."   Just where that appearance took place we do not know, but there had been a secret meeting between Peter and the Lord he had denied, and as a result of this, I am sure Peter's soul had been restored.   But you see it was one thing for a man like him to be personally restored to the Lord and another thing to be confirmed for public service, and in such a way as would be in harmony with the consciences of his brethren. Many a servant of Christ has failed and brought grave distress upon himself and others.   He has been, in the secret of his own room, restored to communion, but so far as launching out in public testimony again, his brethren do not have the confidence to accredit him or extend their fellowship for they do not know what has taken place in his heart.

The Lord Jesus dealt in this public way with Peter in order that the others might realize that Christ had confidence in His servant and sent him forth again in obedience to the Word to feed the sheep and lambs of the flock. The instance is said to be the third occasion on which the Lord appeared to the apostles.

We read, "After these things Jesus showed Himself again to the disciples at the sea of Tiberias; and on this wise showed He Himself. There were together Simon Peter, and Thomas called Didymus, and Nathanael of Cana in Galilee, and the sons of Zebedee, and two other of His disciples." And so they were in the will of the Lord in having made their way back from Judea to Galilee. But it is very evident they were restless. They were still not quite clear as to the meaning of the events of the past few days, such as those appearances of the Lord down there in the upper room in Jerusalem, and to the women, and so on. They haven't sensed the place that is to be theirs in the evangelization of the world and the carrying to all men the story of the risen Christ.

Peter, in his restlessness, thinks of his old occupation. There was nothing sinful about fishing, but it does seem as though going fishing at this time, when they should have been waiting for the manifestation of the Lord, implies the activity of the flesh. It is so much easier to go fishing than to give yourself to prayer! You know how that is. When the Spirit of God would call you to a season of waiting on the Lord, it is so much easier to get up and do something. We would rather do almost anything than wait quietly on God. That is the flesh. And so it was the flesh here that led Peter to say, "I go a fishing." It is a long time since he had an opportunity to visit the old haunts, perhaps not since he was called to become a fisher of men. And perhaps he thought, "There is not much chance of that now. It might have been different if I had proved true when the time of testing came. I can hardly expect Him to trust me now to fish for men, so I had better go back to my old occupation."

The others spoke up and said, "Well, we will go with you." And they toiled all night and caught nothing. That must have reminded Peter of another occasion—that time, over three years before, when the Lord had called him from his boat. Their labor was fruitless. There were no results. "But when the morning was now come, Jesus stood on the shore: but the disciples knew not that it was Jesus." They were drawing near the shore with their empty nets and suddenly they saw a strange figure emerging from the mists. They did not recognize Him. He called to them as they were still some little way from land. "Children, have ye any meat?" "They answered Him, No." He would make them confess how utterly empty they really were and how the night's fishing had gone for nothing.

He called to them again, "Cast the net on the right side of the ship, and ye shall find." I think that must have electrified Peter. He remembered when that same voice said, "Let down your nets for a draught," on the other occasion when he had toiled all the night, and had taken nothing. In obedience to the stranger's command, "They cast therefore, and now they were not able to draw it for the multitude of fishes."

"Therefore that disciple whom Jesus loved saith unto Peter, It is the Lord." John knew He was the only One who could call the treasure of the deep into their nets. He was the Creator of the fish that they had taken, in accordance with His Word.

"Now when Simon Peter heard that it was the Lord, he girt his fisher's coat unto him (for he was naked), and did cast himself into the sea." Nothing could hold him back now from the feet of Jesus, the Saviour whom he had denied. The other disciples came in the little ship after that, dragging the net with fishes.

"As soon as they were come to land they saw a fire of coals there, and fish laid thereon, and bread." They saw a fire of coals. I think there was something significant about that. Where had Peter denied his Lord? We read, "They made a fire of coals, and Peter stood by the fire." That fire of coals was the world's fire. Peter was in the wrong place. He put himself in the place of temptation. But this was the fire that the Lord had kindled. Think of it!

Think of the grace of Christ, the Son of God, cooking Peter's breakfast that morning! There was never anything that the Lord Jesus thought too humiliating for Him to do for those He loved. Jesus loved to serve. Do you love to serve? You who say you belong to Him. Do you love to serve, or do you like to be served? Do you love to obey, or to command? The flesh likes to be served. But the one who is walking in fellowship with the Lord Jesus Christ delights to obey and delights to serve.

So the Lord cooked Peter's breakfast. And He said, "Bring of the fish which ye have now caught." In addition to what He provided He would use what they had brought. Must it not have been a lovely sight? Just think of it, the fire of coals, the mist rising from the lake, and Jesus in the midst—and the disciples enjoying the fish that He Himself had prepared. What a picture!

Afterwards, when they had all enjoyed the repast that He made for them, they were wondering still.   You see Jesus must have looked different in resurrection to what He did before. He had been a Man of Sorrows and acquainted with grief, but now He was in that resurrection body that would never have a sign of pain or weariness again?

Could it be He? Were they making a mistake? But no one dared ask, for deep in their hearts they knew it was the Lord.

"Jesus then cometh, and taketh bread, and giveth them, and fish likewise." And they breakfasted with Him.   "This is now the third time that Jesus showed Himself to His disciples, after that He was risen from the dead.   So when they had dined, Jesus saith to Simon Peter, Simon, son of Jonas, lovest thou Me more than these?" You remember what Simon had said on the night of the betrayal, before they went out to the Garden.   "Master, though all men forsake You, yet will I not."   He was saying practically I love Him more than all the rest of them.   How did he feel now?   "Lovest thou Me more than these?"   I think He pointed to John and James and Thomas and the rest of them. And Peter answered, "Yea, Lord; Thou knowest that I love Thee.   He saith unto him, Feed My lambs."

There is something very interesting here. Greek scholars have often pointed out that there are two different words for "love" in this colloquy. One is used in 1 Cor. 13:1, and it is the strongest word for love that we have in the Bible. It is the word for a love that is absolutely unselfish and is used throughout the New Testament for God Himself; "God is love;" for the love of God for this world, and for our love to God and for the people of the Lord. It is used even for the love of that which people sometimes put in the place of God, such as for money, and the world. You can give these things the love that should go to God.

Then there is another word, and it is one that means affection such as exists between good friends. It is used for the love of one friend to another and for family affection. It suggests a lower quality of love than the first Word. When the Lord says to Peter, "Lovest thou Me more than these?" He used the word translated "love" in 1 Cor. 13. "Peter, have you an absolutely pure, unselfish love for Me, above what the others have?" That word challenged Peter and he could not rise to it. And so he uses the other word. He says, "Yea, Lord, Thou knowest I have affection for Thee." And the Lord says, "Very well. Peter, if you have affection for Me, care for My lambs." Then He said to him again the second

time, "Simon, son of Jonas, lovest thou Me?" And
again He uses the stronger word but Peter an-
swers with the weaker one. He says, "Lord,
Thou knowest that I have affection for Thee."
And Jesus says, "Very well, Peter, take care of
My flock." Then Jesus said to him the third time,
"Simon, son of Jonas, lovest thou Me?" He now
uses the lesser term; "Hast thou affection for
Me?" Peter was grieved that Jesus asked him for
the third time. How many times had Peter denied
Him? That is why the Lord asks him three times.
Peter broke right down and said, "Lord, Thou
knowest all things; Thou knowest that I love
Thee." ("Thou knowest that I have affection for
Thee.") As much as to say, "O Lord, I do not
deserve Thy confidence. Thou knowest all about
me. Thou knowest even in spite of my failure
and denial, I love Thee still. And Jesus said
"Feed My sheep."

So Peter was restored publicly to his special
work as an apostle.

But you remember Peter said to Him, "Lord,
I am ready to go with You to prison and death."
So the Lord Jesus said to him, "Verily, verily, I
say unto thee, When thou wast young, thou
girdedst thyself, and walkedst whither thou
wouldest: but when thou shalt be old, thou shalt
stretch forth thy hands, and another shall gird
thee, and carry thee whither thou wouldest not.

This spake He, signifying by what death he should glorify God."

You see what this really meant. "Peter, you said you were willing to go to prison and to death for Me, and you are going to do it. When you were young you went your own way, but when you are old you are going to be bound with chains and taken to prison and death for Me." And if we can trust early Church History this is just what happened about the year A.D. 69 or 70, for Peter was in prison for Christ's sake and he was taken out to death. They were going to nail him to a cross, and Peter said, "No, no! My Lord died like that. I am not worthy to die as He did." And he said, "Hang me on that cross head downward." Oh, yes; Peter loved Christ, and he really intended to be true to Him, but he forgot that the spirit is willing but the flesh is weak. But in after years he was given grace to do as he had promised.

When the Saviour had spoken this, He said, "Follow Me." And Peter took that literally, for the Lord began to walk along the lake and Peter followed. And that disciple which Jesus loved was also following, and Peter said, "And what shall this man do?" "Jesus saith to him, If I will that he tarry till I come, what is that to thee? Follow thou Me." As much as to say, "Peter, it is not your responsibility as to what My other dis-

ciples do. I will order the path of each one. You
are to die for Me, but if I choose that John live
till I come back again, what is that to thee? Follow thou Me." Most Christians will die. Some
will be living when He comes back again. The
disciples understood the difference.

"Then went this saying abroad among the
brethren, that that disciple should not die: yet
Jesus said not unto him, He shall not die; but,
If I will that he tarry till I come, what is that
to thee?" He says the same thing to each one of
us, "If I will that he tarry till I come, what is
that to thee?" We are to serve in the place in
which He has put us, and leave everyone else to
serve where He puts them. And if some of us
should be living when He does come, we will rejoice together when we stand in His presence.

With this John concludes his wonderful Gospel
which has been well called the greatest book in
the world. Speaking of himself, he says, "This
is the disciple which testifieth of these things,
and wrote these things: and we know that his testimony is true. And there are also many other
things which Jesus did, the which, if they should
be written every one, I suppose that even the
world itself could not contain the books that
should be written." John, guided by the Spirit
of God, selected just eight miracles and a number
of discourses of our Lord Jesus Christ and

grouped them together in this book.   These were
only a few of the things that Jesus said and did.
If everything He said and did were recorded, the
libraries of the world could not contain all the
books that would be written.   Only the books of
Eternity could tell all there is to be related of that
wondrous life of the Word who became flesh to
secure our redemption and make known the
Father's Names.